T0392258

The Dimensions of a Higher Intelligent Living Being

Part 1

Jeffery A. Smith

authorHOUSE®

AuthorHouse™
1663 Liberty Drive
Bloomington, IN 47403
www.authorhouse.com
Phone: 1 (800) 839-8640

Published by AuthorHouse   09/18/2015

ISBN: 978-1-5049-4836-4 (sc)
ISBN: 978-1-5049-4828-9 (e)

Library of Congress Control Number: 2015915085

Print information available on the last page.

*Any people depicted in stock imagery provided by Thinkstock are models,
and such images are being used for illustrative purposes only.
Certain stock imagery © Thinkstock.*

This book is printed on acid-free paper.

Contents

Introduction

I would like to talk about the dimensions of a higher intelligent living being because I think any dimension is the dimensions of a higher intelligent living being, and therefore, I think any dimension is in relation to a higher intelligent living being because I think any dimension is the dimensions of a higher intelligent living being. I would like to talk about how any dimension is the dimensions of a higher intelligent living being because I think any dimension is of a higher intelligent living being for any dimension to be the dimensions of a higher intelligent living being, and therefore, I think any dimension is in relation to a higher intelligent living being because I think any dimension is of a higher intelligent living being. I would like to talk about the dimensions of a higher intelligent living being because I think everything is created by a higher intelligent living being that I choose to call God for any dimension to be created by a higher intelligent living being that I choose to call God, and therefore, I would like to talk about how any dimension is the dimensions of a higher intelligent living being because I think everything is created by a higher intelligent living being that I choose to call God for any dimension to be the dimensions of a higher intelligent living being as I think everything is created by a higher intelligent living being that I choose to call God for any dimension to be of a higher intelligent living being. I think the dimensions of a higher intelligent living being supports creation because I think everything is created by a higher intelligent living being that I choose to call God for any dimension to be a creation of a higher intelligent living being, and therefore, I think the dimensions of a higher intelligent living being is about creation because I think everything is created by a higher intelligent living being that I choose to call God for any dimension to be a creation of a higher intelligent living being.

I would like to talk about the dimensions of a higher intelligent living being with if, than statements to be supporting how any dimension is the dimensions of a higher intelligent living being because I think if, than statements is very effective for me to be supporting what I think, and therefore, I am thinking with a progression of thought with if, than statements because I think if, than statements can support what I think. I would like to be thinking with a progression of thought with if, than statements to be supporting how any dimension is the dimensions of a higher intelligent living being because I think the words if and than are words to be supporting what I possibly think is true, without knowing with absolute certainty what is true, and therefore, I would like to be talking about what I think with if, than statements to be supporting what I think because I can be dictating what I think, without if, than statements to be supporting what I think, even though, I would like to talk about what I think with if, than statements to be supporting what I think because I do not think I can dictate what I think, if I do not know with absolute certainty what is true. I think the words if and than is a progression of thought of what I possibly think is true because I think the words if and than are words that can support what I possibly think is true, and therefore, I am thinking with a progression of thought with the words if and than because I think the words if and than are words that can support what I possibly think is true. I can be right or wrong about what I think because I do not think know with absolute certainty what is true, however, I can only speak for myself about what I think is true because I do not know with absolute certainty what is true, and therefore, I think someone can like or dislike what I think because I think someone can agree or disagree with what I think, even though, I think someone can take what someone likes, and leave the rest about what I think as I think someone can take this writing or leave it because I can be right or wrong about what I think. I can think with an honest or dishonest progression of thought about what I think because I can be right or wrong about what I think, and therefore, I am thinking with a progression of thought with what I think because I can be right or wrong about what I think.

I would like talk about what I think because I can talk about something to be supporting what I think, and therefore, I would like to be talking about what I think of something because I can talk about what I think of something to be supporting what I think of something. I would like to talk about the dimensions of a higher intelligent living being with what I think of something to be supporting how any dimension is the dimensions of a higher intelligent living being because I think what I think of something is very effective for me to be supporting what I think, and therefore, I am thinking with a progression of thought with what I think of something because I think what I think of something can support what I think. I would like to be thinking with a progression of thought with what I think of something to be supporting how any dimension is the dimensions of a higher intelligent living being because I think what I think of something can support what I possibly think is true, without knowing with absolute certainty what is true, and therefore, I would like to be talking about what I think with what I think of something to be supporting what I think, without dictating what I think because I do not know with absolute certainty what is true. I think what I think of something is a progression of thought of what I possibly think is true because I think what I think of something can support what I possibly think is true, and therefore, I am thinking with a progression of thought with what I think of something because I think what I think of something can support what I possibly think is true. I can be right or wrong about what I think of something because I do not think know with absolute certainty what is true, even though, I like to say I think because I can only speak for myself about what I think is true, however, I am speaking for myself about what I think is true because I can only speak for myself about what I think is true, and therefore, I think someone can like or dislike what I think of something because I think someone can agree or disagree with what I think of something, even though, I think someone can take what someone likes, and leave the rest about what I think of something because I can be right or wrong about what I think of something. I can think with an honest or dishonest progression of thought about what I think of something because I can be right or wrong about what I think of something, even though, I can talk about what I think because I can talk about what I think of something to be supporting what I think, and therefore, I am thinking with a progression of thought with what I think of something because I can be right or wrong about what I think of something.

I can think with a progression of thought because I can think with an honest or dishonest progression of thought about what I think, and what I think of something, even though, I would like to think with deducting reasoning about what I think is true as I would like to think with an honest progression of thought about what I think is true because I would like to be ruling out all possibilities of what I do not think is true, until I can come up with the best possible possibility of what I think is true, and therefore, I think the truth is the best possible possibility of what I think is true because I can rule out all possibilities of what I do not think is true, until I can come up with the best possible possibility of what I think is true. I can think about what I think is true because I can think with deducting reasoning about what I think is true as I can think with an honest progression of thought about what I think is true, and therefore, I think what I think is true can support how any dimension is the dimensions of a higher intelligent living being because I can talk about the dimensions of a higher intelligent living being with deducting reasoning about what I think is true as I can talk about the dimensions of a higher intelligent living being with an honest progression of thought about what I think is true. I think would like to be talking about what I think is true with one thought in relation to another thought because I think one thought is reaffirming or supporting another thought with what I think is true for one thought to be in relation to another thought with what I think is true, and therefore, I think one thought is in relation to another thought with what I think is true because I think one thought is reaffirming or supporting another thought with what I think is true for one thought to be in relation to another thought with what I think is true. I think one thought reaffirming or supporting another thought with what I think is true is a progression of thought of what I think is true because I think one thought reaffirming or supporting another thought can support what I think is true, and therefore, I am thinking with a progression of thought with what I think is true because I think one thought is reaffirming or supporting another thought with what I think is true. I would like to think of this writing as being a progression of thought because I think one thought is reaffirming or supporting another thought with what I think is true for this writing to be a progression of thought with what I think is true, even though, I can be right or wrong about what I think is true because I can be right or wrong about one thought reaffirming or supporting another thought with what I think is true, however, I can only speak for myself about what I think is true because I think one thought reaffirming or supporting another thought in this writing is what I think is true, and therefore, I think someone can like or dislike what I think is true because I think someone can agree or disagree with what I think is true, even though, I think someone can take what someone likes, and leave the rest about what I think is true as I think someone can take this writing or leave it because I can be right or wrong about one thought reaffirming or supporting another thought with what I think true. I can think with an honest or dishonest progression of thought about what I think is true because I can be right or wrong about one thought reaffirming or supporting another thought with what I think is true, and therefore, I am thinking with a progression of thought with what I think is true because I can be right or wrong about one thought reaffirming or supporting another thought with what I think is true.

I can think with a progression of thought because I can think with an honest or dishonest progression of thought about what I think is true, and therefore, I can think with an honest or dishonest progression of thought because I can be right or wrong about what I think, and what I think of something, and what I think is true, even though, I would like to think I am thinking with an honest progression of thought because I think one thought is reaffirming or supporting another thought with what I think is true for me to be thinking with a honest progression of thought. I would like to talk about what I think is true because I do not think I can think about what I think is true, without one thought reaffirming or supporting another thought with what I think is true, however, I think I can talk about what I think is true because I think one thought is reaffirming or supporting another thought with what I think is true, and therefore, I would like to think with deducting reasoning about what I think is true as I would like to think with an honest progression of thought about what I think is true because I think one thought is reaffirming or supporting another thought with what I think is true. I think this writing is a collection of my thoughts about what I think because I think one thought is reaffirming or supporting another thought with what I think is true, and therefore, I would like to think of this writing as being a progression of thought because I think this writing is a collection of my thoughts about what I think. I would like to give some examples of what I think of something because I think some examples of what I think of something can explain how I think something is what something in life, however, I am not going to be giving an example for everything I think because I think there would be too many examples of what I think, and therefore, I would like to be leaving what I think up to someone to be thinking about how someone can relate from someone's own experience about what I think because I am talking from my own experience about what I think, even though, I think someone can possibly relate to what I think because I think there is more than one thought or idea to be supporting what I think with one thought reaffirming or supporting another thought with what I think is true for someone to possibly relate to what I think. I mainly did this writing for me because I was thinking about what I think is true for me to be working on myself as I was working on this writing, even though, I would like to be sharing my thoughts with someone who is interested in reading this writing because I hope someone can understand, appreciate, and enjoy a lot the thoughts I have came up with for this writing for this writing to be good for someone as I think this writing has been good for me to be working on this writing, and therefore, I think this writing can be therapeutic, and help someone as I think this writing can be therapeutic, and help me because I think there is something someone can relate to with this writing for this writing to be good for someone as I think this writing has been good for me to be working on this writing for this writing to be good for me to be thinking about something in relation to this writing. I think one thought reaffirming or supporting another thought with what I think is true can support how any dimension is the dimensions of a higher intelligent living being because I can talk about the dimensions of a higher intelligent living being with deducting reasoning about what I think is true as I can talk about the dimensions of a higher intelligent living being with an honest progression of thought about what I think is true, and therefore, I would like talk about the dimensions of a higher intelligent living being with one thought reaffirming or supporting another thought with what I think is true because I think one thought reaffirming or supporting another thought with what I think is true can support how any dimension is the dimensions of a higher intelligent living being. I think each chapter is a theme because I think each chapter is about how dimensions are in life for any dimension to be the dimensions of a higher intelligent living being, and therefore, I think each chapter is a process because I think each chapter is a theme about how dimensions are in life for any dimension to be the dimensions of a higher intelligent living being.

I would like to mention I have included every dimension I will be writing about on the front cover of the book because I think each dimension on the front cover of the book is the dimensions of higher intelligent living being for any dimension to be the dimensions of a higher intelligent living being, and therefore, I think the dimensions of a higher intelligent living being is about how dimensions are in life because I think each dimension on the front cover of the book is the dimensions of a higher intelligent living being for any dimension to be the dimensions of a higher intelligent living being. I think the dimensions of a higher intelligent living being supports creation because I think each dimension on the front cover of the book is the dimensions of a higher intelligent living being for any dimension to be the dimensions of a higher intelligent living being, and therefore, I think the dimensions of a higher intelligent living being is about creation because I think each dimension on the front cover of the book is the dimensions of a higher intelligent living being for any dimension to be the dimensions of a higher intelligent living being. I think any dimension is how any dimension is in life because I think there are 35 dimensions that is the dimensions of a higher intelligent living being for any dimension to be overlapping, and co-existing along with each others dimensions, and therefore, I think the dimensions of a higher intelligent living being is about how dimensions are in life because I think there are 35 dimensions that is overlapping, and co-existing along with each others dimensions for any dimension to be the dimensions of a higher intelligent living being. I think the dimensions of a higher intelligent living being is about how dimensions are in life for any dimension to be the dimensions of a higher intelligent living being because I think there are 35 dimensions that is the dimensions of a higher intelligent living being for any dimension to be the dimensions of a higher intelligent living being, and therefore, I think this is a list of the 35 dimensions that is the dimensions of a higher intelligent living being for any dimension to be the dimensions of a higher intelligent living being: God - God's state of consciousness, God's will, God's mind, God's thoughts, God's being; someone – someone's state of consciousness, someone's will, someone's mind, someone's thoughts, someone's being; something – something's will, something's mind, something's thoughts, something's being; something that is opposite of something else; something that is opposite of itself; everything or life– God's thoughts or the dimension of thought, someone, something; Mass – the three dimensions of length, time, sound, color, temperature or heat, gravity, weight, energy, light or brightness; space or the universe – someone, something or mass; astral plain or limbo; heaven; hell.

Chapter 1

What dimensions are in life

I would like to talk about dimensions because I am interested in understanding how dimensions are in life, and therefore, I would like to talk about what dimensions are in life, before talking about how dimensions are in life because I do not think I can explain how dimensions are in life, before I can explain what dimensions are in life. I do not think I can explain how dimensions are in life, before I can explain what dimensions are in life because I do not think I can understand how dimensions are in life, before I can understand what dimensions are in life. I do not think I can understand how dimensions are in life, before I can understand what dimensions are in life because I think how dimensions are in life is a result of what dimensions are in life. I think how dimensions are in life is a result of what dimensions are in life because I think what dimensions are in life is how dimensions are able to be how dimensions are in life. I think what dimensions are in life is how dimensions are able to be how dimensions are in life because I think how dimensions are able to be what dimensions are in life is how dimensions are able to be how dimensions are in life, and therefore, I would like to talk about what dimensions are in life, before talking about how dimensions are in life because I think what dimensions are in life is how dimensions is able to be how dimensions are in life. If I think what dimensions are in life is how dimensions is able to be how dimensions are in life, than I would like to think about what dimensions are in life with deductive reasoning because I would like to think about what the best possible possibility there can possibly be to be supporting what dimensions are in life, and therefore, what are dimensions in life? I think dimensions is something that is of any dimensions state of reality that is overlapping, and co-existing along with other dimensions that is of any dimensions state of reality because I think dimensions is how dimensions is able to be what dimensions are in life, and therefore, I think dimensions are what dimensions are in life because I think dimensions is how dimensions is able to be what dimensions are in life. If I think dimensions is how dimensions is able to be what dimensions are in life, than I think any dimension is something that is of any dimensions state of reality that is overlapping, and co-existing along with other dimension that is of any dimensions state of reality because I think dimensions is how any dimension is able to be what any dimension is in life, and therefore, I think dimensions are what dimensions are in life because I think dimensions is how any dimension is able to be what any dimension is in life.

If I think dimensions is how any dimension is able to be what any dimension is in life, than how is any dimension able to be what any dimension is in life? I think any dimension able to be what any dimension is in life because I think any dimension is something. I think any dimension is something because I think any dimension is taking place in life as being something. I think any dimension is taking place in life as being something because I think any dimension is something that is taking place in life as being something. I think any dimension is something that is taking place in life as being something because I think any dimension is something, and therefore, I think the dimension of width can be an example of how I think any dimension is something because I think the dimension of width is any length that is going left to right within any body of mass. If I think the dimension of width is any length that is going left to right within any body of mass, than I think the dimension of width is something that is taking place in life as being something because I think the dimension of width is the only length that is going left to right within any body of mass, and therefore, I think the dimension of width is something because I think the dimension of width is something that is taking place in life as being something. If I think the dimension of width is something, than I think any dimension, such as the dimension of width is something because I think any dimension, such as the dimension of width is something that is taking place in life as being something.

If I think any dimension, such as the dimension of width is something, than I think any dimension can be anything because I think anything is something as I think any dimension is something. I think anything is something as I think any dimension is something because I think anything is something that is taking place in life as being something as I think any dimension is something that is taking place in life as being something, and therefore, I think the dimension of length can be an example of how any dimension can be anything because I think anything is something as I think the dimension of length is something. If I think anything is something as I think the dimension of length is something, than I think the dimension of length is anything as I think the dimension of length is something because I think the dimension of length is any length that is going upwards and downwards within any body of mass, and therefore, I think the dimension of length is anything as I think the dimension of length is something that is taking place in life as being something because I think the dimension of length is the only length that is going upwards and downwards within any body of mass. If I think the dimension of length is anything as I think the dimension of length is something that is taking place in life as being something, than I think the dimension of length is anything as I think the dimension of length is something because I think anything is something that is taking place in life as being something as I think the dimension of length is something that is taking place in life as being something, and therefore, I think any dimension, such as the dimension of length can be anything as I think any dimension, such as the dimension of length is something because I think anything is something that is taking place in life as being something as I think any dimension, such as the dimension of length is something that is taking place in life as being something.

If I think any dimension, such as the dimension of length can be anything as I think any dimension, such as the dimension of length is something, than I do not think someone can possibly be able to be knowing for themselves, as to how any dimension can possibly be able to be taking place in life as I think any dimension is something that is taking place in life as being something, but I think someone can observe, and try to understand for themselves, as to how any dimension is taking place in life as I think any dimension is something, and therefore, I think an example of how I do not think someone can possibly be able to be knowing for themselves, as to how any dimension can possibly be able to be taking place in life as I think any dimension is something that is taking place in life as being something, but I think someone can observe, and try to understand for themselves, as to how any dimension is taking place in life as I think any dimension is something can be the dimension of depth because I think the dimension of depth is taking place in life as I think the dimension of depth is something. I think the dimension of depth is taking place in life as I think the dimension of depth is something because I think the dimension of depth is any length in depth that is going backwards and forwards within any body of mass, and therefore, I think the dimension of depth is taking place in life as I think the dimension of depth is something that is taking place in life as being something because I think the dimension of depth is the only length that is going backwards and forwards within any body of mass. If I think the dimension of depth is taking place in life as I think the dimension of depth is something that is taking place in life as being something, than I do not think someone can possibly be able to be knowing for themselves, as to how the dimension of depth is able to be taking place in life as I think the dimension of depth is something that is taking place in life as being something because I do not think someone can possibly be able to be knowing for themselves, as to how the dimension of depth is able to be the only length that is going backwards and forwards within any body of mass, but I think someone can observe, and try to understand for themselves, as to how the dimension of depth is taking place in life as I think the dimension of depth is something because I think someone can observe, and try to understand for themselves, as to how the dimension of depth is any length that is going backwards and forwards within any body of mass, and therefore, I do not think someone can possibly be able to be knowing for themselves, as to how any dimension, such as the dimension of depth can possibly be able to be taking place in life as I think any dimension, such as the dimension of depth is something that is taking place in life as being something, but I think someone can observe, and try to understand for themselves, as to how any dimension, such as the dimension of depth is taking place in life as I think any dimension, such as the dimension of depth is something because I think someone can observe, and try to understand for themselves, as to how any dimension, such as the dimension of depth is in life. If I think someone can observe, and try to understand for themselves, as to how any dimension, such as the dimension of depth is in life, than I think the exact same thing can be said about anything that is able to be taking place in life as I think any dimension, such as the dimension of depth can be anything that is able to be taking place in life because I think anything is something that is taking place in life as being something as I think any dimension, such as the dimension of depth is something that is taking place in life as being something, and therefore, I think any dimension is able to be taking place in life as I think any dimension is something because I think any dimension can be anything as I think any dimension is something.

If I think any dimension can be anything as I think any dimension is something, than I think any dimension able to be what any dimension is in life because I think any dimension is something that is of any dimensions state of reality. I think any dimension is something that is of any dimensions state of reality because I think any dimension is something that is taking place within any dimensions state of reality, and therefore, how is any dimension able to be something that is taking place within any dimensions state of reality? I think any dimension is something that is able to be taking place within any dimensions state of reality because I think any dimension is taking place within any dimensions state of reality as I think any dimension is something, and therefore, how is any dimension able to be taking place within any dimensions state of reality as I think any dimension is something? I think any dimension is able to be taking place within any dimensions state of reality as I think any dimension is something because I think any dimension is of any dimensions state of reality as I think any dimension is something. I think any dimension is of any dimensions state of reality as I think any dimension is something because I think any dimension is something that is taking place within any dimensions state of reality, and therefore, I think any dimension is something that is of any dimensions state of reality because I think any dimension is of any dimensions state of reality as I think any dimension is something. If I think any dimension is of any dimensions state of reality as I think any dimension is something, than I think the dimension of width can be an example of how I think any dimension is something that is of any dimensions state of reality because I think the dimension of width is of the dimension of widths state of reality as I think the dimension of width is something. I think the dimension of width is of the dimension of widths state of reality as I think the dimension of width is something because I think the dimension of width is any length that is going left to right within any body of mass, and therefore, I think the dimension of width is something that is of the dimension widths state of reality because I think the dimension of width is something that is taking place within the dimension of widths state of reality. I think the dimension of width is something that is taking place within the dimension of widths state of reality because I think the dimension of width is taking place within the dimension of widths dimension as I think the dimension of width is something, and therefore, I think the dimension of width is able to be taking place within the dimension of widths state of reality as I think the dimension of width is something because I think the dimension of width is of dimensions of widths state of reality as I think the dimension of width is something. I think the dimension of width is of dimensions of widths state of reality as I think the dimension of width is something because I think the dimension of width is something that is taking place within the dimension widths state of reality, and therefore, I think the dimension of width is something that is of its own state of reality because I think the dimension of width is of the dimension of widths state of reality as I think the dimension of width is something. If I think the dimension of width is of the dimension of widths state of reality as I think the dimension of width is something, than I think any dimension is something that is of any dimensions state of reality as I think the dimension of width is something that is of the dimension of widths state of reality because I think any dimension is something that is of any dimensions state of reality as I think any dimension is something.

If I think any dimension is something that is of any dimensions state of reality as I think any dimension is something, than I think any dimension is a state of reality because I think any dimension is something that is of any dimensions state of reality, and therefore, I think any state of reality is a dimension because I think any state of reality is something that is of any dimensions state of reality. If I think any state of reality is a dimension, than I think any dimension is a dimension, and a state of reality as I think any state of reality is a dimension, and a state of reality because I think any dimension is something that is of any dimensions state of reality as I think any state of reality is something that is of any dimensions state of reality, and therefore, I think any dimension can be anything, and a dimension, and a state of reality as I think any state of reality can be anything, and a dimension, and a state of reality because I think any dimension is something that is of any dimensions state of reality as I think any state of reality is something that is of any dimensions state of reality. If I think any dimension can be anything, and a dimension, and a state of reality as I think any state of reality can be anything, and a dimension, and a state of reality, than I think any anything, such as the dimension of width is a dimension, and a state of reality as I think the dimension of width can be anything, and a dimension, and a state of reality because I think the dimension of width is something that is of the dimension of widths state of reality, and therefore, I think any state of reality is something as I think any dimension is something because I think any state of reality is something that is taking place in life as being something as I think any dimension is something that is taking place in life as being something. If I think any state of reality is something as I think any dimension is something, than I think any dimension, and any state of reality can be exactly the same something because I think any dimension, and any state of reality can be exactly the same something that is taking place in life as being something, even though, I think any dimension, and any state of reality can be something completely different because I think any dimension, and any state of reality can be something completely different that is taking place in life as being something, but I think any dimension, and any state of reality can be exactly the same something because I think any dimension can be exactly the same something that is of any dimensions state of reality as I think any state of reality can be exactly the same something that is of any dimensions state of reality.

If I think any dimension, and any state of reality can exactly the same something, than I think any dimension, and any state of reality can exactly the same anything because I think anything, any dimension, and any state of reality is something that can be exactly the same, even though, I think any dimension, and any state of reality can be anything completely different because I think anything, any dimension, and any state of reality is something that can be completely different, however, I think anything, any dimension, and any state of reality is something because I think anything, any dimension, and any state of reality is something that is taking place in life as being something. If I think anything, any dimension, and any state of reality is something, than I think anything, any dimension, and any state of reality can be exactly the same something because I think anything, any dimension, and any state of reality can be exactly the same something that is taking place in life as being something, even though, I think anything, any dimension, and any state of reality can be something completely different because I think anything, any dimension, and any state of reality can be something completely different that is taking place in life as being something, but I think anything, any dimension, and any state of reality can be exactly the same something because I think anything, any dimension, and any state of reality can be exactly the same something that is of any dimensions state of reality. If I think anything, any dimension, and any state of reality can be exactly the same something, than I think someone can think of something as being anything, any dimension, and any state of reality as I think someone can think of something as being whatever someone chooses to be thinking of what something is in life because I think something is what something is in life as I think something is whatever someone chooses to be thinking of what something is in life, and therefore, I think someone can think of anything, and any dimension, and any state of reality as being whatever someone chooses to be thinking of what anything is in life, and what any dimension is in life, and what any state of reality is in life as I think someone can think of something as being whatever someone chooses to be thinking of what something is in life because I think something is what something is in life as I think something is whatever someone chooses to be thinking of what something is in life. If I think something is what something is in life as I think something is whatever someone chooses to be thinking of what something is in life, than I think anything, and any dimension, and any state of reality doesn't necessarily have to be thought of by someone as being something as I think something doesn't necessarily have to be thought of by someone as being anything, and any dimension, and any state of reality because I think someone can think of anything, and any dimension, and any state of reality as being whatever someone chooses to be thinking of what anything is in life, and what any dimension is in life, and what any state of reality is in life as I think someone can think of something as being whatever someone chooses to be thinking of what something is in life. If I think someone can think of anything, and any dimension, and any state of reality as being whatever someone chooses to be thinking of what anything is in life, and what any dimension is in life, and what any state of reality is in life as I think someone can think of something as being whatever someone chooses to be thinking of what something is in life, than I think someone can think of anything, and any dimension, and any state of reality, and something as being whatever any person chooses to be thinking of what anything is in life, and what any dimension is in life, and what any state of realty is in life, and what something is in life with whatever language someone can be able to be communicating with themselves because I think there are several different languages someone can be able to be communicating with themselves for someone to be thinking of what anything is in life, and what any dimension is in life, and what any state of realty is in life, and what something is in life with whatever language someone can be able to be communicating with themselves, and therefore, I think someone can think of anything, and any dimension, and any state of reality, and something as being whatever someone chooses to be thinking of what anything is in life, and what any dimension is in life, and what any state of realty is in life, and what something is in life with whatever language someone can be able to be speaking because I think there are several different languages someone can be able to be communicating with themselves for someone to be able to be communicating more than one language for themselves.

If I think there are several different languages someone can be able to be communicating with themselves for someone to be able to be communicating more than one language for themselves, than I think someone can be able to be speaking, reading, writing, and drawing more than one language for themselves because I think there are several different languages someone can be able to be communicating with themselves for there are several different languages someone can be able to be speaking, reading, writing, and drawing for themselves, and therefore, I think there are several different languages someone can be able to be speaking, reading, writing, and drawing for themselves because I think any of the different languages someone can be able to be speaking, reading, writing, and drawing for themselves can be made up with any selection of different numbers, letters, symbols, and pictures that can be apart of making up any of the different languages, in which someone can be able to be speaking, reading, writing, and drawing for themselves, and I think there can be different combinations of any of the different numbers, letters, symbols, and pictures that can be apart of making up any of the different words, that can be apart of making up any of the different languages, in which someone can be able to be speaking, reading, writing, and drawing for themselves, and I think any of the different combinations of any of the different numbers, letters, symbols, and pictures that can be apart of making up any of the different words, that can be apart of making up any of the different languages, in which someone can be able to be speaking, reading, writing, and drawing for themselves can be representing what someone can think of what something is in life because I think someone can think of what something is in life as being whatever someone chooses to be thinking of what something is in life with any of the different languages someone can be able to be communicating with themselves, even though, I think any of the different combinations of any of the different numbers, letters, symbols, and pictures that can be apart of making up any of the different words, that can be apart of making up any of the different languages, in which someone can be able to be speaking, reading, writing, and drawing for themselves that can be representing something completely different, as to what someone can think of what something is in life because I think someone can think of what something is in life as being whatever someone chooses to be thinking of what something is in life with any of the different languages someone can be able to be communicating with themselves, however, I think there can be several different combinations of any of the different numbers, letters, symbols, and pictures that can be apart of making up several different words, that can be apart of making up any of the different languages, in which someone can be able to be speaking, reading, writing, and drawing for themselves that can be representing exactly the same something, as to what someone can think of what something is in life because I think someone can think of what something is in life as being whatever someone chooses to be thinking of what something is in life with any language someone can be able to be communicating with themselves. If I think someone can think of what something is in life as being whatever someone thinks of what something is in life with any language someone can be able to be communicating with themselves, than I think there can be more than one group of words, that can be apart of making up any sentence in any of the different languages, in which someone can be able to be speaking, reading, writing, and drawing for themselves that can be representing what someone can think of what something is in life because I think someone can think of what something is in life as being whatever someone chooses to be thinking of what something is in life with any language someone can be able to be communicating with themselves, and therefore, I think someone can be able to be speaking, reading, writing, and drawing more than one of the different languages with any of the different combinations of any of the different numbers, letters, symbols, and pictures that can be apart of making up any of the different words, that can be apart of making up any of the different languages, in which someone can be able to be speaking, reading, writing, and drawing for themselves that can be representing what someone can think of what something is in life because I think someone can think of what something is in life as being whatever someone chooses to be thinking of what something is in life with any of the different languages someone can be able to be communicating with themselves. If I think someone can think of what something is in life as being whatever someone chooses to be thinking of what something is in life with any of the different languages someone can be able to be communicating with themselves, than I think some of the different languages, in which someone can be able to be speaking, reading, writing, and drawing for themselves could have some of the exact same numbers, letters, symbols, and pictures that can be apart of making up some of the exact same words, that can be apart of making up some of the different languages, in which someone can be able to be speaking, reading, writing, and drawing for themselves that can be representing the exact same something, as to what someone can think of what something is in life because I think someone can think of what something is in life as being whatever someone chooses to be thinking of what something is in life with any of the different languages someone can be able to be communicating with themselves, however, I think some of the different languages, in which someone can be able to be speaking, reading, writing, and drawing for themselves could have some of the exact same numbers, letters, symbols, and pictures that can be apart of making up some of the exact same words, that can be apart of making up some of the different languages, in which someone can be able to be speaking, reading, writing, and drawing for themselves that can be representing something completely different, as to what someone can think of what something is in life because I think someone can think of what something is in life as being whatever someone chooses to be thinking of what something is in life with any of the different languages someone can be able to be communicating with themselves.

If I think someone can think of what something is in life as being whatever someone chooses to be thinking of what something is in life with any of the different languages someone can be able to be communicating with themselves, than I think any of the different numbers, letters, symbols, and pictures that can be apart of making up any of the different languages, in which someone can be able to be speaking, reading, writing, and drawing for themselves can either be alike or unalike each others numbers, letters, symbols, and pictures because I think some of the exact same numbers, letters, symbols, and pictures that can be apart of making up some of the different languages, in which someone can able to be speaking, reading, writing, and drawing for themselves can be representing exactly the same something as I think someone can think of some of the exact same numbers, letters, symbols, and pictures that can be apart of making up some of the different languages, in which someone can be able to be speaking, reading, writing, and drawing for themselves as being of the exact same numbers, letters, symbols, and pictures that can be alike each others numbers, letters, symbols, and pictures, and I think some of the exact same numbers, letters, symbols, and pictures that can be apart of making up some of the different languages, in which someone can be able to be speaking, reading, writing, and drawing for themselves can be representing something completely different as I think someone can think of some of the exact same numbers, letters, symbols, and pictures that can be apart of making up some of the different languages, in which someone can be able to be speaking, reading, writing, and drawing for themselves as being of completely different numbers, letters, symbols, and pictures that can be unalike each others numbers, letters, symbols, and pictures, and therefore, I think any of the different numbers, letters, symbols, and pictures that can be apart of making up any of the different languages, in which someone can able to be speaking, reading, writing, and drawing for themselves can be representing exactly the same something because I think someone can think of any of the different numbers, letters, symbols, and pictures that can be apart of making up any of the different languages, in which someone can able to be speaking, reading, writing, and drawing for themselves as being exactly the same kind of numbers, letters, symbols, and pictures that can be apart of making up any of the different languages, in which someone can be able to be speaking, reading, writing, and drawing for themselves, even though, I think any of the different numbers, letters, symbols, and pictures that can be apart of making up any of the different languages, in which someone can able to be speaking, reading, writing, and drawing for themselves can be representing exactly the same something with any of the different numbers, letters, symbols, and pictures not appearing to be the same as each others numbers, letters, symbols, and pictures as I think any of the different numbers, letters, symbols, and pictures that can be apart of making up any of the different languages, in which someone can able to be speaking, reading, writing, and drawing for themselves can be representing something completely different with any of the different numbers, letters, symbols, and pictures not appearing to be the same as each others numbers, letters, symbols, and pictures because I think someone can think of any of the different numbers, letters, symbols, and pictures that can be apart of making up any of the different languages, in which someone can able to be speaking, reading, writing, and drawing for themselves as being completely different kind of numbers, letters, symbols, and pictures that can be apart of making up any of the other different languages, in which someone can be able to be speaking, reading, writing, and drawing for themselves. If I think someone can think of any of the different numbers, letters, symbols, and pictures that can be apart of making up any of the different languages, in which someone can able to be speaking, reading, writing, and drawing for themselves as being completely different kind of numbers, letters, symbols, and pictures that can be apart of making up any of the other different languages, in which someone can be able to be speaking, reading, writing, and drawing for themselves, than I think someone can think of making up any new word for themselves with any of the different combinations of any of the different numbers, letters, symbols, and pictures that is already apart of making up any of the different languages, in which someone can be able to be speaking, reading, writing, and drawing for themselves that can be representing exactly the same something as any other word that is already apart of making up any of the different languages, in which someone can be able to be speaking, reading, writing, and drawing for themselves, and I think someone can think of making up any new word for themselves with any of the different combinations of any of the different numbers, letters, symbols, and pictures that is already apart of making up any of the different languages, in which someone can be able to be speaking, reading, writing, and drawing for themselves that can be representing something completely different because I think someone can think of what something is in life as being whatever someone chooses to be thinking of what something is in life with any language someone can possibly be able to be communicating with themselves, and therefore, I think someone can think of making up a new language with any selection of the same numbers, letters, symbols, and pictures that can be apart of making up any language that someone can be able to be speaking, reading, writing, and drawing for themselves, or I think someone can think of making up a new language with any new selection of different numbers, letters, symbols, and pictures that is not apart of making up any language that someone can be able to be speaking, reading, writing, and drawing for themselves, and I think any of the different combinations of any selection of the same or new numbers, letters, symbols, and pictures that someone can think of making up for themselves can be apart of making up any new selection of different words, that can be apart of making up any new language, in which someone can be able to be speaking, reading, writing, and drawing for themselves can be representing what someone can think of what something is in life because I think someone can think of what something is in life as being whatever someone chooses to be thinking of what something is in life with any language someone can possibly be able to be communicating with themselves.

If I think someone can think of what something is in life as being whatever someone chooses to be thinking of what something is in life with any language someone can possibly be able to be communicating with themselves, than I think there can possibly be other intelligent living beings that can possibly be from another planet that is taking place somewhere within the universe because I think if there is a lot of different living species that has been able to be living on this planet in which a lot of human beings like to think of it as being called the planet Earth, than I think all of the different species that has been able to be living on the planet Earth is a very good indication that there can possibly be other intelligent living beings, that can possibly be from another planet that is taking place somewhere within the universe because I do not think out of any of the planets that can possibly be able to be taking place around any of the stars, that can possibly be able to be taking place anywhere in the universe, that the planet Earth is the only planet that is able to be having any living species living on any planet in the universe, and therefore, I think someone can think all life on Earth could have come from the planet Earth because I think someone can think all life on Earth could have come from any of the chemicals, that can be coming from the water in the ocean mixing with any lava that can be coming up from the bottom of the ocean floor. I think someone can think all life on Earth could have come from any of the chemicals, that can be coming from the water in the ocean mixing with any lava that can be coming up from the bottom of the ocean floor because I think someone can think any of the chemicals, that can be coming from the water in the ocean mixing with any lava that can be coming up from the bottom of the ocean floor can be apart of making up any of the species body that has been able to be living on the planet Earth, even though, I think someone can think all life on Earth could have from somewhere in the universe because I think someone can think all life on Earth could have come from any amino acids, that could have come from any meteoroids that can be carrying any amino acids on them, that could have ended up landing somewhere on the planet Earth, after any meteoroids that can be carrying any amino acids on them came from somewhere in the universe. I think someone can think all life on Earth could have come from any amino acids, that could have come from any meteoroids that can be carrying any amino acids on them, that could have ended up landing somewhere on the planet Earth, after any meteoroids that can be carrying any amino acids on them came from somewhere in the universe because I think someone can think any amino acids, that could have come from any meteoroids that can be carrying any amino acids on them, that could have ended up landing somewhere on the planet Earth, after any meteoroids that can be carrying any amino acids on them came from somewhere in the universe can be apart of making up any of the species body, that consists of having any amino acids that has been able to be living on the planet Earth, even though, I do not know if all life on Earth came from the planet Earth as I do not know if all life on Earth came from somewhere in the universe because I think all life on Earth could have come from the planet Earth as I think all life on Earth could have come from somewhere in the universe, however, I think any meteoroids that can be carrying any amino acids on them suggests there could possibly be life on another planet that can be taking place somewhere within the universe because I think any amino acids, that could have come from any meteoroids that can be carrying any amino acids on them, that could have ended up landing somewhere on the planet Earth could have possibly of come from another planet that was taking place somewhere within the universe, and therefore, I think there could have been life on another planet that was taking place somewhere within the universe because I think any amino acids, that could have come from any meteoroids that can be carrying any amino acids on them, that could have ended up landing somewhere on the planet Earth could have possibly of been able to be apart of making up any other species body, that could consist of having any amino acids that could have possibly of been living on another planet that was taking place somewhere within the universe.

If I think there could have been life on another planet that was taking place somewhere within the universe, than I think there can possibly be life on another planet that can be taking place somewhere within the universe because I think amino acids can possibly be able to be apart of making up any other species body, that can consist of having any amino acids that can possibly be living on another planet that can be taking place somewhere within the universe, and therefore, I think there could have been life on another planet that was taking place somewhere within the universe as I think there can possibly be life on another planet that can be taking place somewhere within the universe because I think there are meteoroids that can be carrying amino acids on them, that can be landing somewhere on the planet Earth, after any meteoroids that can be carrying any amino acids on them can be coming from somewhere in the universe, even though, I think there can possibly be life on another planet that can be taking place somewhere within the universe because I think there is too much supporting evidence on Earth to be supporting the possibility of their being other intelligent living beings that could have or can possibly be coming to Earth from another planet that could have been or can be taking place somewhere within the universe. If I think there can possibly be life on another planet that can be taking place somewhere within the universe, than I think there can possibly be other intelligent living beings that can possibly be from another planet that is taking place somewhere within the universe because I think there can possibly be several intelligent living beings that can possibly be from several planets that is taking place somewhere within the universe, and therefore, I think someone can possibly be of any of the several intelligent living beings that can possibly be from several planets that is taking place somewhere within the universe because I think someone can possibly be of any of the several intelligent living beings that can possibly be from several planets that is taking place somewhere within the universe, that can possibly be thinking of the possibility of their being several intelligent living beings that can possibly be from several planets that is taking place somewhere within the universe. I think someone can possibly be of any of the several intelligent living beings that can possibly be from several planets that is taking place somewhere within the universe, that can possibly be thinking of the possibility of their being several intelligent living beings that can possibly be from several planets that is taking place somewhere within the universe because I think someone can possibly be thinking of the possibility of their being several intelligent living beings that can possibly be from several planets that is taking place somewhere within the universe as I think there can possibly be several intelligent living beings that can possibly be thinking of the possibility of their being several intelligent living beings that can possibly be from several planets that is taking place somewhere within the universe, and therefore, I think someone is a living being because I think someone is an intelligent living being as I think any intelligent living being is someone.

If I think someone is a living being, than I think someone can possibly think of making up a new language for themselves because I think there can possibly be other selections of different numbers, letters, symbols, and pictures that can possibly be apart of making up any different language that someone has not been able to be thinking of making up for themselves, and therefore, I think there can possibly be different combinations of any of the different numbers, letters, symbols, and pictures that can possibly be apart of making up any of the different words, that can possibly be apart of making up any different language, in which someone has not been able to be speaking, reading, writing, and drawing for themselves that can possibly be representing what someone can think of what something is in life because I think someone can think of what something is in life as being whatever someone chooses to be thinking of what something is in life with any language someone has not been be able to be communicating with themselves. If I think someone can think of what something is in life as being whatever someone chooses to be thinking of what something is in life with any language someone has not been be able to be communicating with themselves, than I think someone can think about what any of the different numbers, letters, symbols, and pictures there are in life in which someone can possibly be able to be speaking, reading, writing and drawing for themselves that can possibly be representing what someone can think of what something is in life because I think someone can think of what something is in life as being whatever someone chooses to be thinking of what something is in life with any language someone is able to be communicating with themselves, and therefore, I do not think there is any set number, letter, symbol, and picture in which someone can possibly be able to be speaking, reading, writing and drawing for themselves that can possibly be representing what someone can think of what something is in life because I think someone can think of what something is in life as being whatever someone chooses to be thinking of what something is in life with any language someone is able to be communicating with themselves. I think someone can think of what something is in life as being whatever someone chooses to be thinking of what something is in life with any language someone is able to be communicating with themselves because I think what something is in life is whatever something is in life as I think something is whatever something is in life, and therefore, I think any number, letter, symbol, and picture can possibly be of any other number, letter, symbol, and picture in which someone can possibly be able to be speaking, reading, writing and drawing for themselves that can possibly be representing what someone can think of what something is in life because I think something is whatever something is in life. If I think something is whatever something is in life, than I think any number, letter, symbol, and picture in which someone can possible be able to be speaking, reading, writing and drawing for themselves can be apart of making any language, in which someone can possibly be able to be speaking, reading, writing, and drawing for themselves that can possibly be representing what someone can think of what something is in life because I think any language someone can possibly be able to be speaking, reading, writing and drawing for themselves can consist of any number, letter, symbol, and picture that can be apart of making any language, in which someone can possibly be able to be speaking, reading, and writing and drawing for themselves that can possibly be representing what someone can think of what something is in life, and therefore, I do not think someone can possibly be able to be knowing for themselves, as to what all of the possible different combinations of any of different numbers, letters, symbols, and pictures there are in life that can possibly be apart of making up all of the different words, that can possibly be apart of making up all of the different languages, in which someone can possibly be able to be speaking, reading, writing, and drawing for themselves that can possibly be representing what someone can think of what something is in life because I do not think someone can possibly be able to be knowing for themselves, as to what every possibly language someone can possibly be able to be communicating with themselves, but I think someone can think about what any of the different combinations of the different numbers, letters, symbols, and pictures there are in life that can be apart of making up any of the different words, that can be apart of making up any of the different languages, in which someone can possibly be able to be speaking, reading, writing, and drawing for themselves that can possibly be representing what someone can think of what something is in life because I think someone can think of what something is in life as being whatever someone chooses to be thinking of what something is in life with any language someone is able to be communicating with themselves.

If I think someone can think of what something is in life as being whatever someone chooses to be thinking of what something is in life with any language someone is able to be communicating with themselves, than I think someone can think of what anything is in life, and what any dimension is in life, and what any state of reality is in life, and what something is in life with any of the different combinations of any of the different numbers, letters, symbols, and pictures that can be apart of making up all of the different words, that can possibly be apart of making up all of the different languages, in which someone can possibly be able to be speaking, reading, writing and drawing for themselves that can possibly be representing what someone can think of what something is in life because I think someone can think of what something is in life as being whatever someone chooses to be thinking of what something is in life with any language someone is able to be communicating with themselves, and therefore, I think someone can think of anything, and any dimension, and any state of reality, and something as being whatever someone chooses to be thinking of what anything is in life, and what any dimension is in life, and what any state of reality is in life, and what something is in life because I think someone can think of what something is in life as being whatever someone chooses to be thinking of what something is in life with any language someone is able to be communicating with themselves. If I think someone can think of what something is in life as being whatever someone chooses to be thinking of what something is in life with any language someone is able to be communicating with themselves, than I think someone can think of what someone is in life with any of the different combinations of any of the different numbers, letters, symbols, and pictures that can be apart of making up all of the different words, that can possibly be apart of making up all of the different languages, in which someone can possibly be able to be speaking, reading, writing and drawing for themselves that can possibly be representing what someone can think of what someone is in life because I think someone can think of what someone is in life as being whatever someone chooses to be thinking of what someone is in life with any language someone is able to be communicating with themselves. I think someone can think of what someone is in life as being whatever someone chooses to be thinking of what someone is in life with any language someone is able to be communicating with themselves because I think what someone is in life is whatever someone is in life as I think someone is whatever someone is in life, and therefore, I think someone can think of what someone is in life as being whatever someone chooses to be thinking of what someone is in life because I think someone can think of what someone is in life as being whatever someone chooses to be thinking of what someone is in life with any language someone is able to be communicating with themselves. If I think someone can think of what someone is in life as being whatever someone chooses to be thinking of what someone is in life with any language someone is able to be communicating with themselves, than I do not think someone can possibly be able to be knowing for themselves, as to what all of the possible different combinations of any of different numbers, letters, symbols, and pictures there are in life that can possibly be apart of making up all of the different words, that can possibly be apart of making up all of the different languages, in which someone can possibly be able to be speaking, reading, writing, and drawing for themselves that can possibly be representing what someone can think of what someone is in life because I do not think someone can possibly be able to be knowing for themselves, as to what every possibly language someone can possibly be able to be communicating with themselves, but I think someone can think about what any of the different combinations of the different numbers, letters, symbols, and pictures there are in life that can be apart of making up any of the different words, that can be apart of making up any of the different languages, in which someone can possibly be able to be speaking, reading, writing, and drawing for themselves that can possibly be representing what someone can think of what someone is in life because I think someone can think of what someone is in life as being whatever someone chooses to be thinking of what someone is in life with any language someone is able to be communicating with themselves.

If I think someone can think of what someone is in life as being whatever someone chooses to be thinking of what someone is in life with any language someone is able to be communicating with themselves, than I do not think someone necessarily has to think any dimension is something that is of any dimensions state of reality that is overlapping, and co-existing along with other dimension that is of any dimensions state of reality because I think if any dimension is any state of reality as I think any dimension, and any state of reality can be exactly the same something, than I think someone can think any dimension is something that is overlapping, and co-existing along with any other dimension that is something because I think any dimension is something as I think any dimension is something that is overlapping, and co-existing along with any other dimension that is something, and therefore, I think the closest I can possibly come to be defining what any dimension is in life is I think any dimension is something because I think if any dimension isn't something, than is there anything that isn't something? I do not think there is anything that isn't something because I do not think someone can think of anything that isn't something, and therefore, I think any dimension is something because I do not think there is anything that isn't something. If I think any dimension is something, than I think anything can be an example of something because I think anything is something as I think any dimension is something, and therefore, I think any dimension is something that is overlapping, and co-existing along with any other dimension that is something because I think any dimension is something. If I think any dimension is something that is overlapping, and co-existing along with any other dimension that is something, than I think something is overlapping, and co-existing along with something else because I think something is something else as I think something is taking place in life as being something, and therefore, I think something is something as I think something is taking place in life as being something because I think something is something that is something of itself. I think something is something that is something of itself because I think something is how something is able to be taking place in life as being something. I think something is how something is able to be taking place in life as being something because I think how something is able to be taking place in life as being something is something, and therefore, I think any dimension is something that is overlapping, and co-existing along with any other dimension that is something because I think any dimension is something as I think something is overlapping, and co-existing along with something. If I think any dimension is something that is overlapping, and co-existing along with any other dimension that is something, than I think any dimension is overlapping, and co-existing along with any other dimension because I think any dimension is something as I think something is overlapping, and co-existing along with something, and therefore, I think something is overlapping, and co-existing along with something else because I think something is something else as I think something is overlapping, and co-existing along with something. If I think something is overlapping, and co-existing along with something else, than I think someone can think of any dimension as being something as I think any dimension is something that is overlapping, and co-existing along with any other dimension that is something because I think any dimension is something as I think any dimension is something that is taking place in life as being something, and therefore, I think I can think any dimension is something that is overlapping, and co-existing along with any other dimension that is something with each of these different combinations of each of these different letters, that can be apart of making up each of these different words, that can be apart of making up the English language, in which I am able to be speaking, reading, and writing for myself that can be representing what I can think of what any dimension is in life because I think any dimension is something that is taking place in life as being something.

If I think any dimension is something that is taking place in life as being something, than I think any dimension is something as I think any dimension is something that is overlapping, and co-existing along with any other dimension that is something because I think any dimension is something as I think any dimension is something that is taking place in life as being something, and therefore, I think a dimension is something because I think a dimension is any dimension as I think any dimension is something. If I think a dimension is something, than I do not think there is any difference between any dimension, and something because I think any dimension is something that is taking place in life as being something as I think something is something that is taking place in life as being something, and therefore, I think any dimension is overlapping, and co-existing along with any other dimension as I think something is overlapping, and co-existing along with something else because I think any dimension is something as I think something is something else. If I think any dimension is something as I think something is something else, than I think any dimension that is taking place in life as being something is something that is taking place in life as being something as I think something that is taking place in life as being something is any dimension that is taking place in life as being something because I think any dimension is something as I think something is something. I think any dimension is something as I think something is something because I think any dimension is something as I think something is any dimension. I think any dimension is something as I think something is any dimension because I think any dimension is something that is taking place in life as being something as I think something is something that is taking place in life as being any dimension. I think any dimension is something that is taking place in life as being something as I think something is something that is taking place in life as being any dimension because I think any dimension is something that is taking place in life as being something as I think something is something that is taking place in life as being something. I think any dimension is something that is taking place in life as being something as I think something is something that is taking place in life as being something because I think any dimension is something as I think any dimension is something that is taking place in life as being something, and therefore, I think any dimension is something because I think any dimension is something that is taking place in life as being something.

If I think any dimension is something, than how is any dimension able to be something that is taking place in life as being something? I think if I can think any dimension is something that is overlapping, and co-existing along with any other dimension that is something with each of these different combinations of each of these different letters, that can be apart of making up each of these different words, that can be apart of making up the English language, in which I am able to be speaking, reading, and writing for myself that can be representing what I can think of what any dimension is in life, than I think someone can think of what any dimension is in life with any of the different combinations of any of the different letters, that can be apart of making up any of the different words, that can be apart of making up any language, in which someone can possibly be able to be speaking, reading, and writing for themselves that can possibly be representing what someone can think of what any dimension is in life because I think someone can think of what any dimension is in life as being whatever someone chooses to be thinking of what any dimension is in life with any language someone is able to be communicating with themselves, but I do not think someone thinking of what any dimension is in life with any of the different combinations of any of the different letters, that can be apart of making up any of the different words, that can be apart of making up any language, in which someone can possibly be able to be speaking, reading, and writing for themselves is what any dimension in life because I think any of the different combinations of any of the different letters, that can be apart of making up any of the different words, that can be apart of making up any language, in which someone can possibly be able to be speaking, reading, and writing for themselves are images, in which someone can make with any object, such as ink from a pen that can be apart of making up any of the different combinations of any of the different letters, that can be apart of making up any of the different words, that can be apart of making any language, in which someone can possibly be able to be speaking, reading, and writing for themselves can possibly be representing what someone can think of what something is in life, such as what someone can think of what any dimension is in life, and therefore, how is any dimension able to be something that is taking place in life as being something? I think how any dimension is something that is taking place in life as being something is how any dimension is able to be something that is taking place in life as being something, even though, I do not think someone can possibly be able to be knowing for themselves, as to how any dimension is able to be something that is taking place in life as being something because I think how any dimension is able to be something that is taking place in life as being something is intellectually beyond someone's intelligence, as to how any dimension is able to be something that is taking place in life as being something, but I think someone can try understand for themselves, as to how any dimension is something that is taking place in life as being something because I think how any dimension is something that is taking place in life as being something is how any dimension is able to be something that taking place in life as being something.

I think how any dimension is something that is taking place in life as being something is how any dimension is able to be something that taking place in life as being something because I think how any dimension is something that is taking place in life as being something is a result of how any dimension is able to be something that is taking place in life as being something. I think how any dimension is something that is taking place in life as being something is a result of how any dimension is able to be something that is taking place in life as being something because I think how any dimension is something that is taking place in life as being something is an indication of how any dimension is able to be something that is taking place in life as being something. I think how any dimension is something that is taking place in life as being something is an indication of how any dimension is able to be something that is taking place in life as being something because I do not know how any dimension is able to be something that is taking place in life as being something is able to be an indication of how any dimension is something that is taking place in life as being something. I do not know how any dimension is able to be something that is taking place in life as being something is able to be an indication of how any dimension is something that is taking place in life as being something because I do not know how any dimension is able to be something that is taking place in life as being something, but I think how any dimension is something that is taking place in life as being something is an indication of how any dimension is able to be something that is taking place in life as being something because I think someone can notice for themselves, as to how any dimension is something that is taking place in life as being something as I think how any dimension is something that is taking place in life as being something is an indication of how any dimension is able to be something that is taking place in life as being something. If I think how any dimension is something that is taking place in life as being something is an indication of how any dimension is able to be something that is taking place in life as being something, than I think someone can try to understand for themselves, as to how dimensions are in life is in relation to what dimensions are in life because I think what dimensions are in life is how any dimension is something that is taking place in life as being something, and I think how dimensions are in life is how any dimension is able to be something that is taking place in life as being something, and therefore, I think what dimensions are in life is a result of how dimensions are in life as I think what dimensions are in life is an indication of how dimensions are in life because I think how any dimension is able to be something that is taking place in life as being something is how any dimension is something that is taking place in life as being something, even though, I think someone can try to understand for themselves, as to what dimensions are in life because I think someone can notice for themselves, as to how any dimension is something that is taking place in life as being something as I think how any dimension is something that is taking place in life as being something is how dimensions are able to be what dimensions are in life.

Chapter 2

The possibility of a higher intelligent living being

I think I would like to talk about how dimensions are in life is in relation to what dimensions are in life by talking about the possibility of a higher intelligent living being, that can possibly have something to do with how dimensions are in life is in relation to what dimensions are in life because I think there can possibly be a higher intelligent living being that can somehow be responsible for how everything is able to be taking place in life, and therefore, I think someone can possibly be able to be understanding for themselves, as to whether or not if there can possibly be a higher intelligent living being that can somehow be responsible for how everything is able to be taking place in life is someone asking themselves how is everything able to be taking place in life because I think someone can think of the possibility of there being a higher intelligent living being that can somehow be responsible for how everything is able to be taking place in life, from someone asking themselves how is everything able to be taking place in life, and then I think someone can try to understand for themselves, as to how there can possibly be a higher intelligent living being that can somehow be responsible for how everything is able to be taking place in life because I think someone ask themselves how is everything able to be taking place in life for someone to be thinking of the possibility of there being a higher intelligent living being that can somehow be responsible for how everything is able to be taking place in life. If I think someone can try to understand for themselves, as to how there can possibly be a higher intelligent living being that can somehow be responsible for how everything is able to be taking place in life, than I think everything in the universe is how everything is able to be taking place in the universe because I think how everything is able to be taking place in the universe is everything in the universe, and therefore, I think the universe is everything in the universe as I think everything in the universe is the universe because I think the universe is everything that is taking place in the universe as I think everything in the universe is how everything is able to be taking place in the universe. If I think the universe is everything in the universe as I think everything in the universe is the universe, than I think someone can try to understand for themselves, as to how there can possibly be a higher intelligent living being that can somehow be responsible for everything in the universe as I think someone can try to understand for themselves, as to how there can possibly be a higher intelligent living being that can somehow be responsible for how everything is able to be taking place in the universe because I think everything in the universe is how everything is able to be taking place in the universe, and therefore, how can there possibly be a higher intelligent living being that can somehow be responsible for everything in the universe? I think there can possibly be a higher intelligent living being that can somehow be responsible for everything in the universe because I think everything in the universe is a collection of how any dimension is overlapping, and co-existing along with any other dimension that is apart of making up everything in the universe. I think everything in the universe is a collection of how any dimension is overlapping, and co-existing along with any other dimension that is apart of making up everything in the universe because I think how any dimension is overlapping, and co-existing along with any other dimension is how any dimension is apart of making up everything in the universe, and therefore, I think everything in the universe is a collection of how any dimension is able to be what any dimension is in life because I think how any dimension is overlapping, and co-existing along with any other dimension is how any dimension is able to be what any dimension is in life. If I think everything in the universe is a collection of how any dimension is able to be what any dimension is in life, than I think everything in the universe is a collection of how any dimension is apart of making up everything in the universe because I think how any dimension is overlapping, and co-existing along with any other dimension is how any dimension is apart of making up everything in the universe, and therefore, I think there can possibly be a higher intelligent living being that can somehow be responsible for everything in the universe because I think how everything in the universe is a collection of how any dimension is apart of making up everything in the universe is an indication that there can possibly be a higher intelligent living being that is somehow able to be responsible for everything in the universe.

If I think there can possibly be a higher intelligent living being that can somehow be responsible for everything in the universe, than I think how something is taking place in the universe is how something is taking place in life because I think how something is able to be taking place in the universe is how something is able to be taking place in life. I think how something is able to be taking place in the universe is how something is able to be taking place in life because I think how something is able to be taking place in the universe is apart of making up how something is able to be taking place in life, and therefore, I think how something is taking place in the universe is how everything is taking place in the universe because I think how something is able to be taking place in the universe is how everything is able to be taking place in the universe. I think how something is able to be taking place in the universe is how everything is able to be taking place in the universe because I think how something is able to be taking place in the universe is apart of making up how everything is able to be taking place in the universe, even though, I do not think someone can be able to be knowing for themselves, as to how everything is able to be taking place in the universe because I do not think someone can be able to be creating and re-creating how something, and how everything is taking place in the universe as I think how something, and how everything is taking place in the universe is how everything is able to be taking place in the universe, and therefore, I think everything in the universe is intellectually beyond someone's intelligence, as to how everything is able to be taking place in the universe because I do not think someone can be able to be knowing for themselves, as to how everything is able to be taking place in the universe, even though, I think someone can try to understand for themselves, as to how everything is taking place in the universe because I think how everything is able to be taking place in the universe is how everything is taking in the universe, however, I think everything in the universe is beyond someone because I think everything in the universe is intellectually beyond someone's intelligence, as to how everything is able to be taking place in the universe. If I think everything in the universe is beyond someone, than I think there has to be a higher intelligent being that is somehow able to be responsible for everything in the universe because I think everything in the universe is intellectually beyond someone's intelligence, as to how everything is able to be taking place in the universe, even though, I think someone can think someone doesn't need to be thinking of the possibility of there being a higher intelligent living being that can somehow be able to be responsible for everything in the universe because I think someone can think someone can eventually be able to be figuring everything out for themselves how something, and how everything is able to be taking place in the universe. I think someone can think someone can eventually be able to be figuring everything out for themselves how something, and how everything is able to be taking place in the universe because I think someone can think someone has science for someone to be able to prove and explain how something, and how everything is able to be taking place in the universe, but I do not think science can be able to prove and explain how something, and how everything is able to be taking place in the universe because I think science can only be able to prove and explain how something, and how everything is taking place in the universe, and therefore, I think there has to be a higher intelligent living being that is somehow able to be responsible for everything in the universe because I do not think someone can be able to be knowing for themselves, as to how everything is able to be taking place in the universe. If I think there has to be a higher intelligent living being that is somehow able to be responsible for everything in the universe, than I think someone can say if there is a higher intelligent living being, than prove there is a higher intelligent living being because I think someone can think someone can't prove or disprove, as to whether or not if there is a higher intelligent living being, and therefore, I think someone can think someone can't prove there is a higher intelligent living being because I think someone can think someone can't think of how there can possibly be any proof of how there possibly a higher intelligent living being, even though, I think someone can prove there is a higher intelligent living being because I think if someone can say if there is a higher intelligent living being, than prove there is a higher intelligent living being, than what can someone specifically use as an example of how there can possibly be a higher intelligent living being because I think something can be used as an example of how there can possibly be a higher intelligent living being. I think something can be used as an example of how there can possibly be a higher intelligent living being because I do not think someone can be able to be knowing for themselves, as to how something is able to be taking place in the universe, and therefore, I think something is intellectually beyond someone's intelligence, as to how something is able to be taking place in the universe because I do not think someone can be able to be knowing for themselves, as to how something is able to be taking place in the universe, even though, I think someone can try to understand for themselves, as to how something is taking place in the universe because I think how someone is able to be taking place in the universe is how something is taking in the universe. If I think how something is able to be taking place in the universe is how something is taking in the universe, than I think there can be lots of proof or supporting evidence to be supporting the possibility of there being a higher intelligent living being that can somehow be responsible for everything in the universe as I think someone can think of something as being proof or supporting evidence of how there can possibly be a higher intelligent living being that can somehow be responsible for everything in the universe because I do not think someone can be able to be knowing for themselves, as to how something is able to be taking place in the universe, and therefore, I think someone can prove there is a higher intelligent living being that is somehow able to be responsible for everything in the universe because I think everything in the universe is intellectually beyond someone's intelligence, as to how everything is able to be taking place in the universe, even though, I think someone can choose, as to whether or not if someone can think of how there can possibly be any proof of how there can possibly be a higher intelligent living being because I think someone can think someone can't prove or disprove, as to whether or not if there is a higher intelligent living being.

If I think someone can think someone can't prove or disprove, as to whether or not if there is a higher intelligent living being, than I think someone can think there is no higher intelligent living being that is somehow able to be responsible for everything in the universe because I think someone can think everything is just by chance with how everything is able to be taking place in the universe, even though, I think if everything is just by chance with how everything is able to be taking place in the universe, than I think that would suggest that everything in the universe is nothing because I think everything in the universe has come from nothing for everything in the universe to be nothing, but how can someone think everything in the universe has come from nothing, when everything in the universe is something? I do not think everything in the universe has come from nothing because I do not think everything in the universe is nothing for everything in the universe to come from nothing, and therefore, I think everything in the universe has come from something because I think everything in the universe is something for everything in the universe to come from something. If I think everything in the universe has come from something, than I do not think everything in the universe has come from nothing because I think everything in the universe is something for everything in the universe to come from something, and therefore, I do not think everything is just by chance with how everything is able to be taking place in the universe because I do not think everything in the universe has come from nothing, even though, I think nothing is nothing because I think nothing is the absence of something, however, I do not think everything in the universe has come from nothing because I do not think someone can truly be able to be knowing for themselves, as to just exactly what absolutely nothing is in life. I do not think someone can truly be able to be knowing for themselves, as to just exactly what absolutely nothing is in life because I do not think there is such a thing as there being absolutely nothing, and therefore, I do not think everything in the universe could have possibly of come from nothing because I do not think there is such a thing as there being absolutely nothing. I do not think there is such a thing as there being absolutely nothing because I do not think there is such a thing as there being an absolute absence of something, and therefore, I do not think someone can truly be able to be knowing for themselves, as to just exactly what absolutely nothing is in life because I do not think there is such a thing as there being an absolute absence of something. If I do not think someone can truly be able to be knowing for themselves, as to just exactly what absolutely nothing is in life, than I do not think someone can truly be able to be knowing for themselves, as to just exactly what an absolute absence of something is in life because I do not think there is such a thing as there being an absolute absence of something, and therefore, I do not think everything in the universe has come from nothing because I do not think there is such a thing as there being an absolute absence of something, even though, I do not think someone can truly be able to be knowing for themselves, as to just exactly what an absolute absence of something is in life as I do not think there is such a thing as there being an absolute absence of something because I think something is constantly something.

If I think something is constantly something, than I think the number 0 is a number that can be representing nothing because I think the number 0, and nothing can be representing the absence of something, from when something was taking place in its own time and place as being something, but I think the number 0, and nothing is something that is taking place as being something because I think the number 0, and nothing can be representing the absence of something, from when something was taking place in its own time and place as being something, and therefore, I do not think someone can possibly be able to be knowing for themselves, as to just exactly what an absolute absence of something is in life because I think the number 0, and nothing is something that is taking place in life as being something as I think the number 0, and nothing is something that can be representing the absence of something, from when something was taking place in its own time and place as being something. If I do not think someone can possibly be able to be knowing for themselves, as to just exactly what an absolute absence of something is in life, than I think the absence of something is something is taking place in life as being something because I think the absence of something, from when something was taking place in its own time and place as being something is taking place in life as being something as I think the absence of something is taking place in another time and place as being something, from when something was taking place in its own time and place as being something, and therefore, I do not think there is such a thing as there being absolutely nothing because I think something is taking place in another time and place, from something being taken away from something else that is taking place in someone else's own time and place as I think time, and space, and anything else is in between something that is being taken away from something else that is taking place in someone else's own time and place for there to be no such thing as there being absolutely nothing. If I do not think there is such a thing as there being absolutely nothing, than I think the absence of something is something that is constantly something because I think the absence of something is something that is taking place in life as being something as I think the absence of something is taking place in another time and place as being something, from when something was taking place in its own time and place as being something, and therefore, I do not think there is any possible way in how someone can possibly be able to be knowing for themselves, as to just exactly what an absolute absence of something is in life as I think what an absolute absence of something is in life is an absolute absence of something because I think the absence of something is something that is constantly something.

If I think the absence of something is something that is constantly something, than I think something is nothing as I think nothing is something because I think nothing is something that is constantly something as I think nothing is the absence of something, from when something was taking place in its own time and place in life as being something, and therefore, I think nothing came from something, before something came from nothing because I think there would have to be an absence of something, from when something was taking place in its own time and place in life for there to be nothing as I think nothing is the absence of something, from when something was taking place in its own time and place in life. If I think nothing came from something, before something came from nothing, than I think mathematically something would have to come before nothing because I think there would have to be something that is being subtracted or being taken away from something else that is equivalent or equal in value as something for there to be nothing, and therefore, I think an example of how I think there would have to be something that is being subtracted or being taken away from something else that is equivalent or equal in value as something for there to be nothing can be something such as 1-1=0 because I think the number 1 is being subtracted or being taken away from the number 1 that is equivalent or equal in value as the number 1 for there to be nothing. If I think the number 1 is being subtracted or being taken away from the number 1 that is equivalent or equal in value as the number 1 for there to be nothing, than I think mathematically something would have to come before nothing because I do not think someone can possibly be able to add nothing to nothing for there to be something, and therefore, I think an example of how I do not think someone can possibly be able to add nothing to nothing for there to be something can be something such as 0+0=1 because I do not think the number 0 can be added to the number 0 for there to be something greater than the number 0 or nothing. If I do not think the number 0 can be added to the number 0 for there to be something greater than the number 0 or nothing, than I do not think something can possibly have come from nothing because I think nothing came from something that is being subtracted or being taken away from something else that is equivalent or equal in value as something for there to be nothing, and therefore, I think nothing came from something, before something came from nothing because I do not think something can possibly have come from nothing as I think something would have to come before nothing. I do not think something can possibly have come from nothing as I think something would have to come before nothing because I think something is constantly something for nothing to be coming from something, and therefore, I think nothing came from something, before something came from nothing because I think something is constantly something for nothing to be coming from something.

If I think nothing came from something, before something came from nothing, than I think something is constantly something, regardless of how smart someone is in life, and I think something is constantly something, regardless if someone has any disability, such as someone being deaf or blind or not, and I think something is constantly something, regardless of how someone chooses to be thinking something with any of the different languages someone is able to be to be communicating with themselves, and I think something is constantly something, regardless if someone is in the exact same time and place as something or not because I think something is something for something to constantly be something, and therefore, I think something is constantly something because I think something is something for something to constantly be something. I think something is something for something to constantly be something because I do not think something can be something, without something constantly being something, and therefore, I think something is infinitely something because I think something is constantly something. If I think something is infinitely something, than I think something is in infinity because I think something is infinitely something, and therefore, I think something is infinite because I think something is infinity. I think something is infinity because I think something is in infinity, and therefore, I think something is something because I think something is constantly something. If I think something is constantly something, than I think something is constant because I think something is constantly something for something to be constant, and therefore, I think something is constantly something because I think something is infinite. If I think something is constantly something, than I think something is constantly something because I think something is forever taking place in life as being something as I think something is permanently taking place in life as being something, and therefore, I think something is always able to be taking place in life as being something as I think something is constantly something because I do not think something is permanently able to be destroyed.

If I do not think something is permanently able to be destroyed, than I think everything in the universe is something that is constantly something because I think everything in the universe is something that is able to be taking place in life as being something, and therefore, I think everything in the universe is something that is able to be taking place in life as being something as I think something is able to be taking place in life as being something because I think everything in the universe is something that is constantly something as I think something is constantly something. I think everything in the universe is something that is constantly something as I think something is constantly something because I think everything in the universe consists of something that is apart of making up everything in the universe. I think everything in the universe consists of something that is apart of making up everything in the universe because I think everything in the universe is a collection of any dimension that is apart of making up everything in the universe as I think everything in the universe is a collection of something that is apart of making up everything in the universe, and therefore, I think how any dimension is something is how something is able to be taking place in life as being something because I think any dimension is something as I think something is something. If I think how any dimension is something is how something is able to be taking place in life as being something, than I think any dimension is something as I think something is any dimension because I think any dimension is something as I think something is any dimension, and therefore, I think any dimension is something that is overlapping, and co-existing along with any other dimension that is something as I think something is any dimension that is overlapping, and co-existing along with something that is any other dimension because I think any dimension is something as I think something is any dimension. If I think any dimension is something as I think something is any dimension, than I think everything in the universe consists of something that is apart of making up everything in the universe as I think everything in the universe consists of any dimension that is apart of making up everything in the universe because I think any dimension is something that is apart of making up everything in the universe as I think something is any dimension that is apart of making up everything in the universe, and therefore, I think everything in the universe is something that is constantly something as I think something is constantly something because I think everything in the universe consists of something that is apart of making up everything in the universe. If I think everything in the universe is something that is constantly something as I think something is constantly something, than I think everything in the universe is constantly something as I think everything in the universe is something that is constantly something because I think everything in the universe is something as I think something is constantly something, and therefore, I think everything in the universe is infinitely something as I think something is infinitely something because I think everything in the universe is constantly something as I think something is constantly something. If I think everything in the universe is infinitely something as I think something is infinitely something, than I think everything in the universe is in infinity because I think everything in the universe is infinitely something, and therefore, I think everything in the universe is infinite because I think everything in the universe is infinity. I think everything in the universe is infinity because I think everything in the universe is in infinity, and therefore, I think everything in the universe is constantly something as I think something is constantly something because I think everything in the universe consists of something that is apart of making up everything in the universe. If I think everything in the universe is constantly something as I think something is constantly something, than I think everything in the universe is constant because I think something is apart of making up everything in the universe for everything in the universe to always able to be taking place in life as being something as I think everything in the universe is constantly something, and therefore, I think everything in the universe is constantly something because I think everything in the universe is infinite.

If I think everything in the universe is constantly something, than I think someone can think of everything in the universe as being the universe or space as I think someone can think of everything in the universe as being the dimension of the universe or space because I think the universe or space is everything in the universe as I think the dimension of the universe or space is everything in the universe, and therefore, I think the universe is something because I think the universe is everything in the universe. If I think the universe is something, than I think everything in the universe is a collection of how any dimension is apart of making up the universe because I think how any dimension is overlapping, and co-existing along with any other dimension is how any dimension is apart of making up the universe, and therefore, I think everything in the universe is apart of making up the universe because I think everything in the universe is a collection of how any dimension is apart of making up the universe. If I think everything in the universe is a collection of how any dimension is apart of making up the universe, than I think everything in the universe is a dimension as I think everything in the universe is something because I think everything in the universe is apart of making up the universe, and therefore, I think everything in the universe is overlapping, and co-existing along with everything in the universe because I think everything in the universe is apart of making up the universe. If I think everything in the universe is overlapping, and co-existing along with everything in the universe, than I think the universe is a dimension as I think the universe is something because I think everything in the universe is apart of making up the universe, and therefore, I think the universe is overlapping, and co-existing along with everything in the universe because I think everything in the universe is apart of making up the universe, even though, I do not know if someone can possibly be able to be knowing for themselves, as to how big the universe is in life because I do not know if someone can be able to be knowing for themselves everything in the universe, however, I think everything in the universe is taking place within the universe, without being the universe as I think everything in the universe is apart of the universe, without being the universe because I think everything in the universe is apart of making up the universe. If I think everything in the universe is taking place within the universe, without being the universe as I think everything in the universe is apart of the universe, without being the universe, than I think the universe is intellectually beyond someone's intelligence, as to how the universe is in life because I do not think someone can be able to be knowing for themselves, as to how everything is able to be taking place in the universe, even though, I think someone can try to understand for themselves, as to how the universe is in life because I think how everything is able to be taking place in the universe is how everything is taking in the universe, however, I think the universe is beyond someone because I think the universe is intellectually beyond someone's intelligence, as to how everything is able to be taking place in the universe. If I think the universe is beyond someone, than I think the universe is a collection of how any dimension is apart of making up the universe because I think how any dimension is overlapping, and co-existing along with any other dimension is how any dimension is apart of making up the universe, and therefore, I think everything in the universe is apart of making up the universe because I think the universe is a collection of how any dimension is apart of making up the universe. If I think the universe is a collection of how any dimension is apart of making up the universe, than I think the universe is everything in the universe as I think everything in the universe is the universe because I think everything in the universe is apart of making up the universe, and therefore, I think the universe is beyond everything in the universe because I think everything in the universe is apart of making up the universe as I think the universe is everything in universe. If I think the universe is beyond everything in the universe, than I think everything in the universe is multi-dimensional because I think everything in the universe is a collection of how any dimension is apart of making up the universe as I think everything in the universe is apart of making up the universe, and therefore, I think the universe is multi-dimensional because I think the universe is a collection of how any dimension is apart of making up the universe as I think everything in the universe is apart of making up the universe.

If I think the universe is multi-dimensional, than I think something is a dimension as I think something is something because I think everything in the universe is of something. I think everything in the universe is of something because I think something is apart of making up everything in the universe, and therefore, I think everything in the universe is of something as I think something is apart of making up everything in the universe because I think everything in the universe consists of something that is apart of making up everything in the universe. If I think everything in the universe consists of something that is apart of making up everything in the universe, than I think someone can think of something as being the dimension of something because I think something is apart of making up everything in the universe, and therefore, I think something is overlapping, and co-existing along with everything in the universe because I think something is apart of making up everything in the universe. If I think something is overlapping, and co-existing along with everything in the universe, than I think the universe is of something as I think something is apart of making up the universe because I think the universe consists of something that is apart of making up everything in the universe, and therefore, I think something is overlapping, and co-existing along with the universe because I think something is apart of making up everything in the universe. If I think something is overlapping, and co-existing along with the universe, than I think someone is a dimension as I think someone is something because I think everything in the universe is of someone. I think everything in the universe is of someone because I think someone is apart of making up everything in the universe, and therefore, I think everything in the universe is of someone as I think someone is apart of making up everything in the universe because I think everything in the universe consists of someone that is apart of making up everything in the universe. If I think everything in the universe consists of someone that is apart of making up everything in the universe, than I think someone can think of someone as being the dimension of someone because I think someone is apart of making up everything, and therefore, I think someone is overlapping, and co-existing along with everything in the universe because I think someone is apart of making up everything in the universe. If I think someone is overlapping, and co-existing along with everything in the universe, than I think the universe is of someone as I think someone is apart of making up the universe because I think the universe consists of someone that is apart of making up everything in the universe, and therefore, I think someone is overlapping, and co-existing along with the universe because I think someone is apart of making up everything in the universe.

If I think someone is overlapping, and co-existing along with the universe, than I think everything in the universe is something as I think everything in the universe consists of something that is apart of making up everything in the universe because I think everything in the universe somehow must have come from something as I think everything in the universe is something, and therefore, I think everything in the universe somehow must have come from something that is of a higher intelligence living being because I think everything in the universe is something that is somehow able to be beyond someone's intelligence, as to how everything is able to be taking place in the universe as being something. If I think everything in the universe somehow must have come from something that is of a higher intelligence living being, than I think everything in the universe somehow must have come from a higher intelligent living being that is both someone and something, that is somehow able to be responsible for everything in the universe because I think everything in the universe is intellectually beyond someone's intelligence, as to how everything is able to be taking place in the universe, and therefore, I think everything in the universe somehow must have come from a higher intelligent living being that is someone that is something of itself, that is somehow able to be responsible for everything in the universe because I think everything in the universe somehow must have come from a higher intelligent living being that is both someone and something, that is somehow able to be responsible for everything in the universe. If I think everything in the universe somehow must have come from a higher intelligent living being that is someone that is something of itself, that is somehow able to be responsible for everything in the universe, than I do not think everything in the universe is a creation of itself because I think if everything in the universe is intellectually beyond someone's intelligence, as to how everything is able to be taking place in the universe, than I think everything in the universe is intellectually beyond itself for everything in the universe not to be a creation of itself, and therefore, I do not think everything in the universe is a creation of itself because I think everything in the universe somehow must have come from a higher intelligent living being that is someone that is something of itself, that is somehow able to be responsible for everything in the universe. If I do not think everything in the universe is a creation of itself, than I think this higher intelligent living being has somehow created something to constantly be something as I think this higher intelligent living being has somehow created everything in the universe to constantly be something because I do not think this higher intelligent living being created something to permanently be destroyed as I do not think this higher intelligent living being created everything in the universe to permanently be destroyed, and therefore, I think this higher intelligent living being is someone that is something of itself, that is somehow able to be responsible for everything in the universe because I think this higher intelligent living being has somehow created something to constantly be something as I think this higher intelligent living being has somehow created everything in the universe to constantly be something. If I think this higher intelligent living being is someone that is something of itself, that is somehow able to be responsible for everything in the universe, than I think everything in the universe is how everything is able to be taking place in the universe because I think this higher intelligent living being is someone that is something of itself, that is somehow able to be responsible for everything in the universe as I think this higher intelligent living being is someone that is something of itself, that is somehow able to be responsible for how everything is able to be taking place in the universe.

If I think everything in the universe is how everything is able to be taking place in the universe, than I think this higher intelligent living being is someone that is something of itself, that can understand every possible way in how someone can possibly be communicating with any of the different combinations of any of the different numbers, letters, symbols, and pictures that can be apart of making up any of the different words, that can be apart of making up any of the different languages, in which someone can be able to be speaking, reading, writing, and drawing for themselves, along with any other form of communication, such as any form of sign language that can be representing what someone can think of what something is in life because I think someone can be communicating with themselves, someone else, something, and this higher intelligent living being in any possible way in how someone can possibly be communicating with themselves, someone else, something, and this higher intelligent living, and therefore, I think someone can say something to this higher intelligent living being with any of the different languages, in which someone can possibly be able to be speaking, reading, and writing for themselves that can possibly be representing what someone can think of what something is in life because I think this higher intelligent living being is someone that is something of itself, that can understand every possible way in how someone can possibly be communicating with themselves, and this higher intelligent living as I think someone can understand any possible way in how someone can possibly be communicating with themselves, and this higher intelligent living. If I think this higher intelligent living being is someone that is something of itself, that can understand every possible way in how someone can possibly be communicating with themselves, and this higher intelligent living as I think someone can understand any possible way in how someone can possibly be communicating with themselves, and this higher intelligent living, than I think someone can choose to be thinking of calling themselves, and someone else a name with any of the different combinations of any of the different numbers, letters, symbols, and pictures that can be apart of making up any of the different words, that can be apart of making up any of the different languages, in which someone can be able to be speaking, reading, writing, and drawing for themselves that can be representing a name that someone can choose to be thinking of calling themselves, and someone else because I think someone can understand any possible way in how someone can possibly be communicating with themselves, and someone else, and therefore, I think someone can choose to be thinking of calling this higher intelligent living a name with any of the different combinations of any of the different numbers, letters, symbols, and pictures that can be apart of making up any of the different words, that can be apart of making up any of the different languages, in which someone can possibly be able to be speaking, reading, writing, and drawing for themselves that can possibly be representing a name that someone can choose to be thinking of calling this higher intelligent living being because I think this higher intelligent living being is someone that is something of itself, that can understand every possible way in how someone can possibly be communicating with themselves, and this higher intelligent living as I think someone can understand any possible way in how someone can possibly be communicating with themselves, and this higher intelligent living. If I think this higher intelligent living being is someone that is something of itself, that can understand every possible way in how someone can possibly be communicating with themselves, and this higher intelligent living as I think someone can understand any possible way in how someone can possibly be communicating with themselves, and this higher intelligent living, than I think this higher intelligent living being can be someone's choice, as to what someone can choose to be thinking of calling this higher intelligent living beings name is in life because I think someone can choose to be thinking of calling this higher intelligent living a name with any of the different combinations of any of the different numbers, letters, symbols, and pictures that can be apart of making up any of the different words, that can be apart of making up any of the different languages, in which someone can possibly be able to be speaking, reading, writing, and drawing for themselves that can possibly be representing a name that someone can choose to be thinking of calling this higher intelligent living being, and therefore, I think there can be several different names that someone can choose to be thinking of calling this higher intelligent living being because I think someone can choose to be thinking of calling this higher intelligent living any name with any of the different combinations of any of the different numbers, letters, symbols, and pictures that can be apart of making up any of the different words, that can be apart of making up any of the different languages, in which someone can possibly be able to be speaking, reading, writing, and drawing for themselves that can possibly be representing any name that someone can choose to be thinking of calling this higher intelligent living being. If I think there can be several different names that someone can choose to be thinking of calling this higher intelligent living being, than I do not think there is any set name for someone because I do not think someone has come into life with someone's own name for someone to be able to be knowing with absolute certainty, as to just exactly what someone's own name is in life as I think someone can choose to be thinking of calling themselves, and someone else any name with any of the different combinations of any of the different numbers, letters, symbols, and pictures that can be apart of making up any of the different words, that can be apart of making up any of the different languages, in which someone can possibly be able to be speaking, reading, writing, and drawing for themselves that can possibly be representing any name that someone can choose to be thinking of calling themselves, and someone else, and therefore, I do not think there is any set name for this higher intelligent living being because I think someone can choose to be thinking of calling this higher intelligent living any name with any of the different combinations of any of the different numbers, letters, symbols, and pictures that can be apart of making up any of the different words, that can be apart of making up any of the different languages, in which someone can possibly be able to be speaking, reading, writing, and drawing for themselves that can possibly be representing any name that someone can choose to be thinking of calling this higher intelligent living being. If I do not think there is any set name for this higher intelligent living being, than I do not someone can truly be able to be knowing, as to just exactly what this higher intelligent living beings true name is in life because I do not think someone is this higher intelligent living being for someone to be able to be knowing with absolute certainty, as to just exactly what this higher intelligent living being thinks what this higher intelligent living beings name is in life, and therefore, I think this higher intelligent living being may or may not have a name for someone to be able to be knowing with absolute certainty, as to just exactly what this higher intelligent living being thinks what this higher intelligent living beings name is in life because I do not someone can truly be able to be knowing, as to just exactly what this higher intelligent living beings true name is in life, but I think someone can think of what this higher intelligent living beings name is in life because I think someone can choose to be thinking of calling this higher intelligent living a name with any of the different combinations of any of the different numbers, letters, symbols, and pictures that can be apart of making up any of the different words, that can be apart of making up any of the different languages, in which someone can possibly be able to be speaking, reading, writing, and drawing for themselves that can possibly be representing a name that someone can choose to be thinking of calling this higher intelligent living being.

If I think someone can think of what this higher intelligent living beings name is in life, than I think someone can choose to be calling this higher intelligent living being by the name God because I think the name God is a word that has been passed onto someone from someone else that has chosen to be calling this higher intelligent living being by the name God, and therefore, I think I would like to continue to be calling this higher intelligent living being by the name God because I have noticed from my experience that this higher intelligent living being does respond to the name God, whenever I choose to be saying something to this higher intelligent living being, otherwise, if I didn't get any response from this higher intelligent living being with the name God, whenever I choose to be saying something to this higher intelligent living being, than I wouldn't continue to be calling this higher intelligent living being by the name God, and I would think of another a name to be calling this higher intelligent living being with any of the different combinations of any of the different letters, that can be apart of making up a word, that can be apart of making up the English language, in which I am able to be speaking, reading, and writing for myself that can be representing a name that I can choose to be calling this higher intelligent living being, until this higher intelligent living being does respond to a name that I can choose to be calling this higher intelligent living being, whenever I choose to be saying something to this higher intelligent living being, however, I am going to continue to be calling this higher intelligent living being by the name God because I have noticed from my experience that this higher intelligent living being does respond to the name God, whenever I choose to be saying something to this higher intelligent living being. If I am going to continue to be calling this higher intelligent living being by the name God, than I think someone can choose to be thinking of calling this higher intelligent living a name with any of the different combinations of any of the different numbers, letters, symbols, and pictures that can be apart of making up any of the different words, that can be apart of making up any of the different languages, in which someone can possibly be able to be speaking, reading, writing, and drawing for themselves that can possibly be representing a name that someone can choose to be thinking of calling this higher intelligent living being because I do not think someone will choose to be calling this higher intelligent living being a name, if this higher intelligent living being doesn't respond to a name that someone can choose to be calling this higher intelligent living being, whenever someone chooses to be saying something to this higher intelligent living being, and therefore, I think someone can choose to be calling this higher intelligent living being a name that this higher intelligent living being is going to be responding to someone, whenever someone chooses to be saying something to this higher intelligent living being because I do not think someone will choose to be calling this higher intelligent living being a name, if this higher intelligent living being doesn't respond to a name that someone can choose to be calling this higher intelligent living being, whenever someone chooses to be saying something to this higher intelligent living being. If I think someone can choose to be calling this higher intelligent living being a name that this higher intelligent living being is going to be responding to someone, whenever someone chooses to be saying something to this higher intelligent living being, than I think someone can choose to be thinking of calling this higher intelligent living being by the name God with each of these different combinations of each of these letters, that can be apart of making up this word, that can be apart of making up any of the different languages, in which someone can possibly be able to be speaking, reading, and writing for themselves that can possibly be representing a name that someone can choose to be thinking of calling this higher intelligent living being because I think this higher intelligent living being can respond to the name God that someone can choose to calling this higher intelligent living being, whenever someone chooses to be saying something to this higher intelligent living being, and therefore, I think there can be a mutual agreement between this higher intelligent living being and someone, as to what someone can choose to be thinking of calling what this higher intelligent living beings name is in life because I think this higher intelligent living being can respond to a name that someone can choose to be thinking of calling this higher intelligent living being, whenever someone chooses to be saying something to this higher intelligent living being, even though, I think this higher intelligent living being can respond to the exact same name that someone can choose to be thinking of calling this higher intelligent living being, whenever someone chooses to be saying something to this higher intelligent living being because I think there can be a mutual agreement between this higher intelligent living being and someone, as to what someone can choose to be thinking of calling what this higher intelligent living beings name is in life. If I think there can be a mutual agreement between this higher intelligent living being and someone, as to what someone can choose to be thinking of calling what this higher intelligent living beings name is in life, than I think someone can think of what this higher intelligent living being is in life with any of the different combinations of any of the different letters, that can be apart of making up any of the different words, that can be apart of making up any of the different languages, in which someone can possibly be able to be speaking, reading, and writing for themselves that can possibly be representing what someone can think of what this higher intelligent living being is in life because I think this higher intelligent living can respond to someone that can be thinking of what this higher intelligent living being is in life, whenever someone chooses to be saying something to this higher intelligent living, and therefore, I think there can be a mutual agreement between this higher intelligent living being and someone, as to what someone can think of what this higher intelligent living being is in life because I think this higher intelligent living being can respond to someone that can be thinking of what this higher intelligent living being is in life, whenever someone chooses to be saying something to this higher intelligent living being, even though, I think someone can think of what this higher intelligent living being is in life as I think someone can choose to be calling this higher intelligent living being by the name God because I think this higher intelligent living being can respond to the name God that someone can choose to calling this higher intelligent living being, whenever someone chooses to be saying something to this higher intelligent living being.

If I think this higher intelligent living being can respond to the name God that someone can choose to calling this higher intelligent living being, whenever someone chooses to be saying something to this higher intelligent living being, than I think there can be a mutual agreement between this higher intelligent living being and someone, as to what someone can choose to be thinking of calling what this higher intelligent living beings name is in life because I think there can be so many different words someone can possibly be able to be thinking of making up with any of the different combinations of any of the different numbers, letters, symbols, and pictures that can be apart of making up any of the different words, that can be apart of making up any of the different languages, in which someone can possibly be able to be speaking, reading, writing, and drawing for themselves that can possibly be representing so many different things, as to what someone can choose to be thinking of what something is in life, even though, I think someone can choose to be thinking of making any word with any of the different combinations of any of the different numbers, letters, symbols, and pictures that can be apart of making up any of the different words, that can be apart of making up any of the different languages, in which someone can possibly be able to be speaking, reading, writing, and drawing for themselves that can specifically be representing what someone can choose to be thinking of what something is in life because I think any word can be very confusing for someone to be associating a word that can specifically be representing what someone can choose to be thinking of what something is in life, along with another word that can specifically be representing what someone can choose to be thinking of what something else is in life, and therefore, I think someone can think of making up a word with any of the different combinations of any of the different numbers, letters, symbols, and pictures that can be apart of making up any of the different words, that can be apart of making up any of the different languages, in which someone can possibly be able to be speaking, reading, writing, and drawing for themselves that can specifically be representing a name that someone can choose to be thinking of calling this higher intelligent living being because I think any word can be very confusing for someone to be associating a word that can specifically be representing what someone can choose to be thinking of what something is in life, along with a word that can specifically be representing a name that can choose to be thinking of calling this higher intelligent living being. If I think any word can be very confusing for someone to be associating a word that can specifically be representing what someone can choose to be thinking of what something is in life, along with another word that can specifically be representing what someone can choose to be thinking of what something else is in life, than I think an example of how I think someone can be thinking of making up a word with any of the different combinations of any of the different numbers, letters, symbols, and pictures that can be apart of making up any of the different words, that can be apart of making up any of the different languages, in which someone can possibly be able to be speaking, reading, writing, and drawing for themselves that can specifically be representing a name that someone can choose to be thinking of calling this higher intelligent living being can be the word chair in relation to the word God, that someone can choose to be thinking of calling this higher intelligent living because I do not think someone can choose to be thinking of making up the word chair with each of these different combinations of each of these different letters, that can be apart of making up this word, that can be apart of making up the English language, in which someone can be able to be speaking, reading, and writing for themselves, that can specifically be representing a name that someone can choose to be thinking of calling this higher intelligent living being. I do not think someone can choose to be thinking of making up the word chair with each of these different combinations of each of these different letters, that can be apart of making up this word, that can be apart of making up the English language, in which someone can be able to be speaking, reading, and writing for themselves, that can specifically be representing a name that someone can choose to be thinking of calling this higher intelligent living being because I think the word chair is a word that someone can choose to be thinking of making up with each of these different combinations of each of these different letters, that can be apart of making up this word, that can be apart of making up the English language, in which someone can be able to be speaking, reading, and writing for themselves that can specifically be representing any object that someone can be able to be making, and sitting on, and therefore, I think the word chair is not a word that someone can choose to be thinking of making up with each of these different combinations of each of these different letters, that can be apart of making up this word, that can be apart of making up the English language, in which someone can be able to be speaking, reading, and writing for themselves that can specifically be representing a name that someone can choose to be thinking of calling this higher intelligent living being because I think the word chair is a word that someone can choose to be thinking of making up with each of these different combinations of each of these different letters, that can be apart of making up this word, that can be apart of making up the English language, in which someone can be able to be speaking, reading, and writing for themselves that can specifically be representing any object that someone can be able to be making, and sitting on.

      If I think the word chair is a word that someone can choose to be thinking of making up with each of these different combinations of each of these different letters, that can be apart of making up this word, that can be apart of making up the English language, in which someone can be able to be speaking, reading, and writing for themselves that can specifically be representing any object that someone can be able to be making, and sitting on, than I think someone can think of making up a word with any of the different combinations of any of the different numbers, letters, symbols, and pictures that can be apart of making up any of the different words, that can be apart of making up any of the different languages, in which someone can possibly be able to be speaking, reading, writing, and drawing for themselves that can specifically be representing a name that someone can choose to be thinking of calling this higher intelligent living being because I think this higher intelligent living being can respond to a name that someone can choose to be thinking of calling this higher intelligent living being, whenever someone chooses to be saying something to this higher intelligent living being, and therefore, I think the word God can be a word that someone can choose to be thinking of making up with each of these different combinations of each of these different letters, that can be apart of making up this word, that can be apart of making up any of the different languages, in which someone can be able to be speaking, reading, and writing for themselves that can specifically be representing a name that someone can choose to be thinking of calling this higher intelligent living being because I think this higher intelligent living being can respond to the name God that someone can choose to calling this higher intelligent living being, whenever someone chooses to be saying something to this higher intelligent living being. I think this higher intelligent living being can respond to the name God that someone can choose to calling this higher intelligent living being, whenever someone chooses to be saying something to this higher intelligent living being because I think this higher intelligent living being can respond to a name that someone can choose to be thinking of calling this higher intelligent living being, whenever someone chooses to be saying something to this higher intelligent living being. I think this higher intelligent living being can respond to a name that someone can choose to be thinking of calling this higher intelligent living being, whenever someone chooses to be saying something to this higher intelligent living being because I think someone can choose to be thinking of calling this higher intelligent living a name with any of the different combinations of any of the different numbers, letters, symbols, and pictures that can be apart of making up any of the different words, that can be apart of making up any of the different languages, in which someone can possibly be able to be speaking, reading, writing, and drawing for themselves that can specifically be representing a name that someone can choose to be thinking of calling this higher intelligent living being, and therefore, I think there can be a mutual agreement between this higher intelligent living being and someone, as to what someone can choose to be thinking of calling what this higher intelligent living beings name is in life because I think someone can choose to be thinking of calling this higher intelligent living a name with any of the different combinations of any of the different numbers, letters, symbols, and pictures that can be apart of making up any of the different words, that can be apart of making up any of the different languages, in which someone can possibly be able to be speaking, reading, writing, and drawing for themselves that can specifically be representing a name that someone can choose to be thinking of calling this higher intelligent living being. If I think there can be a mutual agreement between this higher intelligent living being and someone, as to what someone can choose to be thinking of calling what this higher intelligent living beings name is in life, than I do not think this higher intelligent living being can only be someone's choice, as to what someone can choose to be thinking of calling what this higher intelligent living beings name is in life because I think this higher intelligent living being can be any group of intelligent living beings group consciousness, as to what any group of intelligent living beings can choose to be thinking of calling what any group of intelligent living beings thinks what this higher intelligent living beings name is in life, and therefore, I think there can be a mutual agreement between this higher intelligent living and any group of intelligent living beings, as to what any group of intelligent living beings can choose to be thinking of calling what this higher intelligent living beings name is in life because I think this higher intelligent living being can be any group of intelligent living beings group consciousness, as to what any group of intelligent living beings can choose to be thinking of calling what any group of intelligent living beings thinks what this higher intelligent living beings name is in life.

If I think there can be a mutual agreement between this higher intelligent living, and any group of intelligent living beings, as to what any group of intelligent living beings can choose to be thinking of calling what this higher intelligent living beings name is in life, than I think there can be a mutual agreement between someone and any group of intelligent living beings, as to what someone can choose to be thinking of what something is in life because I think someone can choose to be thinking of what something is in life with any of the different combinations of any of the different numbers, letters, symbols, and pictures that can be apart of making up any of the different words, that can be apart of making up any of the different languages, in which someone can possibly be able to be speaking, reading, writing, and drawing for themselves that can specifically be representing what someone can choose to be thinking of what something is in life, even though, I think someone can be right or wrong, as to what someone can choose to be thinking of what something is in life because I think someone can be right or wrong about what someone can choose to be thinking of what something is in life with any of the different combinations of any of the different numbers, letters, symbols, and pictures that can be apart of making up any of the different words, that can be apart of making up any of the different languages, in which someone can possibly be able to be speaking, reading, writing, and drawing for themselves that can specifically be representing what someone can choose to be thinking of what something is in life, and therefore, I think someone can question something, as to whether or not if someone thinks something is right or wrong because I think someone can be right or wrong about what someone thinks of something. I think someone can be right or wrong about what someone thinks of something because I think someone can be right or wrong about what someone can think of what something is in life, and therefore, I think there can be a mutual agreement between someone and any group of intelligent living beings, as to what someone can choose to be thinking of what something is in life because I think something can be any group of intelligent living beings group consciousness, as to what any group of intelligent living beings can choose to be thinking of what something is in life. If I think there can be a mutual agreement between someone, and any group of intelligent living beings, as to what someone can choose to be thinking of what something is in life, than I think there can be a mutual agreement between this higher intelligent living being and any group of intelligent living beings, as to what any group of intelligent living beings can choose to be thinking of what something is in life because I think this higher intelligent living being is someone that is something of itself, that can be able to understand what any group of intelligent living beings can choose to be thinking of what something is in life as I think any group of intelligent living beings can choose to be thinking of what something is in life with any of the different combinations of any of the different numbers, letters, symbols, and pictures that can be apart of making up any of the different words, that can be apart of making up any of the different languages, in which any group of intelligent living beings can possibly be able to be speaking, reading, writing, and drawing for themselves that can specifically be representing what any group of intelligent living beings can choose to be thinking of what something is in life, and therefore, I think this higher intelligent living being is somehow able to be responsible for any of the different combinations of any of the different numbers, letters, symbols, and pictures that can be apart of making up any of the different words, that can be apart of making up any of the different languages, in which someone can possibly be able to be speaking, reading, writing, and drawing for themselves that can specifically be representing what someone can choose to be thinking of what something is in life because I think this higher intelligent living being is someone that is something of itself, that is somehow able to be responsible for everything in the universe.

If I think this higher intelligent living being is someone that is something of itself, that is somehow able to be responsible for everything in the universe, than I do not think someone can possibly be able to be knowing for themselves, as to what the oldest or what the first language there is in life that someone has been able to be speaking, reading, writing, and drawing for themselves because I think any of the different languages someone is able to be communicating with themselves, someone else, and this higher intelligent living being consists any of the different combinations of any of the different numbers, letters, symbols, and pictures that can be apart of making up any of the different words, that can be apart of making up any of the different languages, in which someone can possibly be able to be speaking, reading, writing, and drawing for themselves that can specifically be representing what someone can choose to be thinking of what something is in life, but I think the shape of a I(line) and a O(circle) appear to be the most common shapes that can specifically be representing what someone can think of what any number, letter, symbol and picture there is in life that someone can possibly be able to be speaking, reading, writing and drawing for themselves that can specifically be representing what someone can choose to be thinking of what something is in life, and therefore, I think the shape of a I(line) is the most predominate or common shape of all shapes because I think the shape of a I(line) is apart of making up every shape. I think the shape of a I(line) is apart of making up every shape because I think the shape of a I(line) is a shape of every shape as I think the shape of a I(line) is a shape that is apart of making up every shape. I think the shape of a I(line) is a shape of every shape as I think the shape of a I(line) is a shape that is apart of making up every shape because I do not think every shape would be a shape, without the shape of a I(line) that is apart of making every shape, and therefore, I think the shape of a I(line) is the most common shape that can specifically be representing what someone can think of what any number, letter, symbol, and picture there is in life that someone can possibly be able to be speaking, reading, writing and drawing for themselves that can specifically be representing what someone can choose to be thinking of what something is in life because I think the shape of a I(line) is apart of making up every shape. If I think the shape of a I(line) is apart of making up every shape, than I do not think any number, letter, symbol, shape, and picture is any more or any less significantly important than any other number, letter, symbol, shape, and picture because I think every number, letter, symbol, shape and, picture consists of the shape of a I(line) that is apart of making up every number, letter, symbol, shape, and picture, and therefore, I think there can be a mutual agreement between this higher intelligent living being and someone, as to what someone can choose to be thinking of what something is in life because I think this higher intelligent living being is someone that is something of itself, that can be able to understand what someone can choose to be thinking of what something is in life as I think someone can choose to be thinking of what something is in life with any of the different combinations of any of the different numbers, letters, symbols, and pictures that can be apart of making up any of the different words, that can be apart of making up any of the different languages, in which someone can possibly be able to be speaking, reading, writing, and drawing for themselves that can specifically be representing what someone can choose to be thinking of what something is in life.

If I think there can be a mutual agreement between this higher intelligent living being and someone, as to what someone can choose to be thinking of what something is in life, than I think someone can choose to be thinking of calling this higher intelligent living a name with any of the different combinations of any of the different numbers, letters, symbols, and pictures that can be apart of making up any of the different words, that can be apart of making up any of the different languages, in which someone can possibly be able to be speaking, reading, writing, and drawing for themselves that can specifically be representing a name that someone can choose to be thinking of calling this higher intelligent living being because I think this higher intelligent living being is someone that is something of itself, that can specifically respond to a name that someone can choose to be thinking of calling this higher intelligent living being, whenever someone chooses to be saying something to this higher intelligent living being, and therefore, I think there can be a mutual agreement between this higher intelligent living being and someone, as to what someone can choose to be thinking of calling what this higher intelligent living beings name is in life as I think there can be a mutual agreement between this higher intelligent living being and any group of intelligent living beings, as to what any group of intelligent living beings can choose to be thinking of calling what this higher intelligent living beings name is in life because I think this higher intelligent living being is someone that is something of itself, that can specifically respond to a name that someone can choose to be thinking of calling this higher intelligent living being, whenever someone chooses to be saying something to this higher intelligent living being. If I think there can be a mutual agreement between this higher intelligent living being and someone, as to what someone can choose to be thinking of calling what this higher intelligent living beings name is in life as I think there can be a mutual agreement between this higher intelligent living being and any group of intelligent living beings, as to what any group of intelligent living beings can choose to be thinking of calling what this higher intelligent living beings name is in life, than I think this higher intelligent living being is someone that is something of itself, that can be able to understand what someone can choose to be thinking of what something is in life as I think this higher intelligent living being is someone that is something of itself, that can be able to understand what any group of intelligent living being can choose to be thinking of what something is in life because I think this higher intelligent living being is somehow able to be responsible for any of the different combinations of any of the different numbers, letters, symbols, and pictures that can be apart of making up any of the different words, that can be apart of making up any of the different languages, in which someone can possibly be able to be speaking, reading, writing, and drawing for themselves that can specifically be representing what someone can choose to be thinking of what something is in life, and therefore, I think there can be a mutual agreement between this higher intelligent living being and someone, as to what someone can choose to be thinking of what something is in life as I think there can be a mutual agreement between what this higher intelligent living being and any group of intelligent living beings, as to what any group of intelligent living beings can choose to be thinking of what something is in life because I think this higher intelligent living being is somehow able to be responsible for any of the different combinations of any of the different numbers, letters, symbols, and pictures that can be apart of making up any of the different words, that can be apart of making up any of the different languages, in which someone can possibly be able to be speaking, reading, writing, and drawing for themselves that can specifically be representing what someone can choose to be thinking of what something is in life. If I think there can be a mutual agreement between this higher intelligent living being and someone, as to what someone can choose to be thinking of what something is in life as I think there can be a mutual agreement between what this higher intelligent living being and any group of intelligent living beings, as to what any group of intelligent living beings can choose to be thinking of what something is in life, than I think there can be a mutual agreement between this higher intelligent living being and someone, as to what someone can choose to be thinking of what this higher intelligent living being is in life as I think there can be a mutual agreement between someone and any group of intelligent living beings, as to what someone can choose to be thinking of what this higher intelligent living being is in life because I think someone can choose to be thinking of what this higher intelligent living being is in life with any of the different combinations of any of the different numbers, letters, symbols, and pictures that can be apart of making up any of the different words, that can be apart of making up any of the different languages, in which someone can possibly be able to be speaking, reading, writing, and drawing for themselves that can specifically be representing what someone can choose to be thinking of what this higher intelligent living being is in life, and therefore, I think there can be a mutual agreement between this higher intelligent living being and any group of intelligent living beings, as to what any group of intelligent living beings can choose to be thinking of what this higher intelligent living being is in life because I think this higher intelligent living being can be any group of intelligent living beings group consciousness, as to what any group of intelligent living beings can choose to be thinking of what this higher intelligent living being is in life.

If I think there can be a mutual agreement between this higher intelligent living being and any group of intelligent living beings, as to what any group of intelligent living beings can choose to be thinking of what this higher intelligent living being is in life, than I think there can be several different words someone can choose to be thinking of calling this higher intelligent living being because I think someone can choose to be thinking of calling this higher intelligent living being any word with any of the different combinations of any of the different numbers, letters, symbols, and pictures that can be apart of making up any of the different words, that can be apart of making up any of the different languages, in which someone can possibly be able to be speaking, reading, writing, and drawing for themselves that can specifically be representing any word that someone can choose to be thinking of calling this higher intelligent living being, and therefore, I think there can be several different names someone can choose to be thinking of calling this higher intelligent living being because I think someone can choose to be thinking of calling this higher intelligent living being any name with any of the different combinations of any of the different numbers, letters, symbols, and pictures that can be apart of making up any of the different names, that can be apart of making up any of the different languages, in which someone can possibly be able to be speaking, reading, writing, and drawing for themselves that can specifically be representing any name that someone can choose to be thinking of calling this higher intelligent living being. If I think there can be several different names someone can choose to be thinking of calling this higher intelligent living being, than I think any word is any name as I think any name is any word, and I think a word is a name as I think a name is a word because I think someone can choose to be thinking of making any word, and any name with any of the different combinations of any of the different numbers, letters, symbols, and pictures that can be apart of making up any of the different words, that can be apart of making up any of the different languages, in which someone can possibly be able to be speaking, reading, writing, and drawing for themselves that can specifically be representing what someone can choose to be thinking of what something is in life, and therefore, I think any word can be the name of any word because I think someone

35

can choose to be thinking of making any word, and any name with any of the different combinations of any of the different numbers, letters, symbols, and pictures that can be apart of making up any of the different words, that can be apart of making up any of the different languages, in which someone can possibly be able to be speaking, reading, writing, and drawing for themselves that can specifically be representing what someone can choose to be thinking of what something is in life. If I think any word can be the name of any word, than I do not think there is any set word, and name for someone, and something, and this higher intelligent living being because I think someone can choose to be thinking of calling themselves, someone else, something, and this higher intelligent living being any word, and any name with any of the different combinations of any of the different numbers, letters, symbols, and pictures that can be apart of making up any of the different words, that can be apart of making up any of the different languages, in which someone can possibly be able to be speaking, reading, writing, and drawing for themselves that can possibly be representing any word, and any name that someone can choose to be thinking of calling themselves, someone else, something, and this higher intelligent living being, and therefore, I think someone can call themselves, someone else, something, and this higher intelligent living being any word, and any name because I do not think there is any set word, and name for someone, and something, and this higher intelligent living being for someone to be calling themselves, someone else, something, and God any word, and any name, even though, I think there can specifically be a word, and name for someone, something, and this higher intelligent living being because I think someone can choose to be thinking of calling themselves, someone else, something, and this higher intelligent living being any word, and any name with any of the different combinations of any of the different numbers, letters, symbols, and pictures that can be apart of making up any of the different words, that can be apart of making up any of the different languages, in which someone can possibly be able to be speaking, reading, writing, and drawing for themselves that can specifically be representing any word, and any name that someone can choose to be thinking of calling themselves, someone else, something, and this higher intelligent living being. If I think there can specifically be a word, and name for someone, something, and this higher intelligent living being, than I think someone can agree with someone else, as to what something is in life with any word, and any name that can specifically be representing what someone can choose to be thinking of what something is in life because I think someone can choose to be thinking of making any word, and any name with any of the different combinations of any of the different numbers, letters, symbols, and pictures that can be apart of making up any of the different words, that can be apart of making up any of the different languages, in which someone can possibly be able to be speaking, reading, writing, and drawing for themselves that can specifically be representing what someone can choose to be thinking of what something is in life, and therefore, I think there can be a mutual agreement between this higher intelligent living being and someone, as to what something is in life as I think there can be a mutual agreement between someone and any group of intelligent living beings, as to what someone can choose to be thinking of what something is in life because I think someone can choose to be thinking of making any word, and any name with any of the different combinations of any of the different numbers, letters, symbols, and pictures that can be apart of making up any of the different words, that can be apart of making up any of the different languages, in which someone can possibly be able to be speaking, reading, writing, and drawing for themselves that can specifically be representing what someone can choose to be thinking of what something is in life.

If I think there can be a mutual agreement between this higher intelligent living being and someone, as to what something is in life as I think there can be a mutual agreement between someone and any group of intelligent living beings, as to what someone can choose to be thinking of what something is in life, than I think there can be several different words, and names someone can choose to be thinking of calling this higher intelligent living being because I think someone can choose to be thinking of making any name, and any word with any of the different combinations of any of the different numbers, letters, symbols, and pictures that can be apart of making up any of the different words, that can be apart of making up any of the different languages, in which someone can possibly be able to be speaking, reading, writing, and drawing for themselves that can specifically be representing any name, and any word that someone can choose to be thinking of calling this higher intelligent living being, and therefore, I think there can be a mutual agreement between this higher intelligent living being and someone, as to what someone can choose to be thinking of what this higher intelligent living beings name is in life as I think there can be a mutual agreement between someone and any group of intelligent living beings, as to what someone can choose to be thinking of what this higher intelligent living beings name is in life because I think someone can choose to be thinking of making any name, and any word with any of the different combinations of any of the different numbers, letters, symbols, and pictures that can be apart of making up any of the different words, that can be apart of making up any of the different languages, in which someone can possibly be able to be speaking, reading, writing, and drawing for themselves that can specifically be representing any name, and any word that someone can choose to be thinking of calling this higher intelligent living being. If I think there can be a mutual agreement between this higher intelligent living being and someone, as to what someone can choose to be thinking of what this higher intelligent living beings name is in life as I think there can be a mutual agreement between someone and any group of intelligent living beings, as to what someone can choose to be thinking of what this higher intelligent living beings name is in life, than I think someone can choose to be thinking of calling this higher intelligent living any word, and any name with any of the different combinations of any of the different numbers, letters, symbols, and pictures that can be apart of making up any of the different words, that can be apart of making up any of the different languages, in which someone can possibly be able to be speaking, reading, writing, and drawing for themselves that can specifically be representing any word, and any name that someone can choose to be thinking of calling this higher intelligent living being because I think this higher intelligent living being is someone that is something of itself, that can specifically respond to any word, and any name that someone can choose to be thinking of calling this higher intelligent living being, whenever someone chooses to be saying something to this higher intelligent living being. I think this higher intelligent living being is someone that is something of itself, that can specifically respond to any word, and any name that someone can choose to be thinking of calling this higher intelligent living being, whenever someone chooses to be saying something to this higher intelligent living being because I think this higher intelligent living being is someone that is something of itself, that is somehow able to be responsible for everything in the universe, and therefore, I think there can be a mutual agreement between this higher intelligent living being and someone, as to what someone can choose to be thinking of calling what this higher intelligent living beings name is in life as I think there can be a mutual agreement between this higher intelligent living being and any group of intelligent living beings, as to what any group of intelligent living beings can choose to be thinking of calling what this higher intelligent living beings name is in life because I think this higher intelligent living being is someone that is something of itself, that can specifically respond to any word, and any name that someone can choose to be thinking of calling this higher intelligent living being, whenever someone chooses to be saying something to this higher intelligent living being.

If I think there can be a mutual agreement between this higher intelligent living being and someone, as to what someone can choose to be thinking of calling what this higher intelligent living beings name is in life as I think there can be a mutual agreement between this higher intelligent living being and any group of intelligent living beings, as to what any group of intelligent living beings can choose to be thinking of calling what this higher intelligent living beings name is in life, than I think someone can choose calling this higher intelligent living being God, Lord, supreme being, Allah, Goddess, the creator, and any other name someone can choose to be thinking of calling this higher intelligent living being because I think there can be several different names someone can choose to be thinking of calling this higher intelligent living being, and therefore, I think there can be a mutual agreement between this higher intelligent living being and someone, as to what someone can choose to be thinking of what this higher intelligent living beings name is in life as I think there can be a mutual agreement between someone and any group of intelligent living beings, as to what someone can choose to be thinking of what this higher intelligent living beings name is in life because I think there can be several different words, and names someone can choose to be thinking of calling this higher intelligent living being. If I think there can be a mutual agreement between this higher intelligent living being and someone, as to what someone can choose to be thinking of what this higher intelligent living beings name is in life as I think there can be a mutual agreement between someone and any group of intelligent living beings, as to what someone can choose to be thinking of what this higher intelligent living beings name is in life, than I think someone can think the word God is just a word for this higher intelligent living being because I think someone can think the word God is not a name for this higher intelligent living being, but I think the word God is a name for this higher intelligent living being because I think any word is any name, and therefore, I do not think the word God is just a word for this higher intelligent living being because I think the word God can be the name of this higher intelligent living being. If I do not think the word God is just a word for this higher intelligent living being, than I think the word God is a name for this higher intelligent living being because I think the word God can be the name of this higher intelligent living being, and therefore, I think someone can think of the word God as being the name of this higher living being because I think the word God can be the name of this higher intelligent living being.

If I think someone can think of the word God as being the name of this higher living being, than I think the word God can possibly be a bad word amongst any other group of intelligent living beings, that can possibly be from another planet that is taking place in the universe because I think any word can be a good or bad word from one group of intelligent living beings to the next group of intelligent living beings, that can possibly be from each of their own planet that is taking place in the universe, and therefore, I do not think any group of intelligent living beings, that can possibly be from any planet that is taking place in the universe can possibly be able to be knowing for themselves, as to what word can be a good or a bad word, that any group of intelligent livings can choose to be thinking of calling what any group of intelligent living beings thinks of what this higher intelligent living beings name is in life because I think any word can be a good or bad word from one group of intelligent living beings to the next group of intelligent living beings, that can possibly be from each of their own planet that is taking place in the universe. If I think any word can be a good or bad word from one group of intelligent living beings to the next group of intelligent living beings, that can possibly be from each of their own planet that is taking place in the universe, than I do not think someone can possibly be able to be knowing for themselves, as to what every possibly name there is in life for this higher intelligent living being because I think there can be several different names someone can choose to be thinking of calling this higher intelligent living being, but I think someone can choose to be thinking of calling this higher intelligent living being any name with any of the different combinations of any of the different numbers, letters, symbols, and pictures that can be apart of making up any of the different words, that can be apart of making up any of the different languages, in which someone can possibly be able to be speaking, reading, writing, and drawing for themselves that can specifically be representing any name that someone can choose to be thinking of calling this higher intelligent living being because I think this higher intelligent living being is someone that is something of itself, that can specifically respond to any name that someone can choose to be thinking of calling this higher intelligent living being, whenever someone chooses to be saying something to this higher intelligent living being. If I think this higher intelligent living being is someone that is something of itself, that can specifically respond to any name that someone can choose to be thinking of calling this higher intelligent living being, whenever someone chooses to be saying something to this higher intelligent living being, than I think I would like to be calling this higher intelligent living being God because I think this higher intelligent living being is someone that is something of itself, that can specifically respond to the name God that someone can choose to be thinking of calling this higher intelligent living being, whenever someone chooses to be saying something to this higher intelligent living being, and therefore, I think God is someone that is something of itself, that is somehow able to be responsible for everything in the universe because I think someone can call this higher intelligent living being God as I think this higher intelligent living being is someone that is something of itself, that is somehow able to be responsible for everything in the universe. If I think God is someone that is something of itself, that is somehow able to be responsible for everything in the universe, than I think this higher intelligent living being is someone that is something of itself, that can specifically respond to the name God that someone can choose to be thinking of calling this higher intelligent living being, whenever someone chooses to be saying something to this higher intelligent living being because I think someone can call this higher intelligent living being God as I think God is someone that is something of itself, that is somehow able to be responsible for everything in the universe, and therefore, I think God is someone that is something of itself, that is somehow able to be responsible for everything in the universe because I think there can possibly be a higher intelligent living being that can somehow be responsible for how everything is able to be taking place in life.

Chapter 3

God

I would like to talk about how dimensions are in life in relation to what dimensions are in life by talking about God, that can possibly have something to do with how dimensions are in life is in relation to what dimensions are in life because I think God is someone that is something of itself, that is somehow able to be responsible for everything in the universe, and therefore, I think God is somehow able to be responsible for everything in the universe because I think God is someone that is something of itself, that is somehow able to be responsible for everything in the universe. If I think God is somehow able to be responsible for everything in the universe, than I think God is intellectually beyond someone's intelligence, as to what God is in life because I do not think someone can be able to be knowing for themselves, as to how God is able to be responsible for everything in the universe, even though, I think someone can try to understand for themselves, as to what God is in life because I think how everything is taking place in the universe is how God can somehow be able to be responsible for everything in the universe, however, I think God is beyond someone because I think everything in the universe is intellectually beyond someone's intelligence, as to how God is able to be responsible for everything in the universe. If I think God is beyond someone, than I think God is somehow able to be responsible for everything in the universe because I think everything in the universe is intellectually beyond someone's intelligence, as to how everything is able to be taking place in the universe, and therefore, I think someone can think of God as being the dimension of God because I think God is somehow able to be responsible for everything in the universe.

If I think someone can think of God as being the dimension of God, than I think God is allowing for everything to be taking place in its own time and place in the universe because I do not think God is interfering with everything that can be taking place in its own time and place in the universe. I do not think God is interfering with everything that can be taking place in its own time and place in the universe because I think everything is taking place in its own time and place in the universe for God not to be interfering with everything that can be taking place in its own time and place in the universe, and therefore, I do not think God has a choice with everything that can be taking place in its own time and place in the universe because I do not think God is interfering with everything that can be taking place in its own time and place in the universe. If I do not think God has a choice with everything that can be taking place in its own time and place in the universe, than I think God is somehow able to be responsible for everything that can be taking place in its own time and place in the universe because I do not think God is interfering with everything that can be taking place in its own time and place in the universe as I think God is somehow able to be responsible for everything in the universe, and therefore, I think God is beyond everything in the universe because I do not think God is interfering with everything that can be taking place in its own time and place in the universe as I think God is somehow able to be responsible for everything in the universe. If I think God is beyond everything in the universe, than I do not think God is interfering with everything in the universe because I do not think God is interfering with everything that can be taking place in its own time and place in the universe for God not to be interfering with everything in the universe, and therefore, I think God is always good, and right because I do not think God is interfering with everything in the universe. If think God is always good, and right, than I think everything in the universe is taking place within God, without being God as I think everything in the universe is apart of God, without being God because I do not think God is interfering with everything in the universe, and therefore, I think God is overlapping, and co-existing along with everything in the universe because I do not think God is interfering with everything in the universe. If I think God is overlapping, and co-existing along with everything in the universe, than I think the universe is taking place within God, without being God as I think the universe is apart of God, without being God because I do not think God is interfering with everything in the universe, and therefore, I think God is overlapping, and co-existing along with the universe because I do not think God is interfering with everything in the universe.

If I think God is overlapping, and co-existing along with the universe, than I think everything is intellectually beyond someone's intelligence, as to how everything is able to be taking place in life because I do not think someone can be able to be knowing for themselves, as to how everything is able to be taking place in life, even though, I think someone can try to understand for themselves, as to how everything is taking place in life because I think how everything is able to be taking place in life is how everything is taking place in life, however, I think everything is beyond someone because I think everything is intellectually beyond someone's intelligence, as to how everything is able to be taking place in life. If I think everything is beyond someone, than I think God is somehow able to be responsible for everything because I think God is someone that is something of itself, that is somehow able to be responsible for everything, and therefore, I think God is an intelligent living being because I think God is someone that is something of itself, that is somehow able to be responsible for everything for God to be an intelligent living being. If I think God is an intelligent living being, than I think God is a living being because I think God is an intelligent living being for God to be a living being, and therefore, I think God is how God is able to be what God is in life because I think God is an intelligent living being for God to be how God is able to be what God is in life. If I think God is how God is able to be what God is in life, than I think God is somehow able to be responsible for everything because I think everything is intellectually beyond someone's intelligence, as to how everything is able to be taking place in life, and therefore, I think someone can think of God as being the dimension of God because I think God is somehow able to be responsible for everything. If I think someone can think of God as being the dimension of God, than I think everything is intellectually beyond someone's intelligence, as to how God is able to be responsible for everything because I do not think someone can be able to be knowing for themselves, as to how God is able to be responsible for everything, even though, I think someone can try to understand for themselves, as to how God is able to be responsible for everything because I think how everything is taking place in life is how God can somehow be able to be responsible for everything, however, I think God is beyond someone because I think everything is intellectually beyond someone's intelligence, as to how God is able to be responsible for everything. If I think God is beyond someone, than I think God is somehow able to be responsible for everything because I think how God is able to be what God is in life is how God is somehow able to be responsible for everything, even though, I do not think someone can be able to be knowing for themselves, as to how God is able to be what God is in life because I do not think someone can be able to be knowing for themselves, as to how God is able to be responsible for everything, however, I think someone can try to understand for themselves, as to how God is in life because I think how everything is taking place in the universe is how God can somehow be able to be responsible for everything in the universe. If I think someone can try to understand for themselves, as to how God is in life, than I think God is allowing for everything to be taking place in its own time and place because I do not think God is interfering with everything that can be taking place in its own time and place. I do not think God is interfering with everything that can be taking place in its own time and place because I think everything is taking place in its own time and place for God not to be interfering with everything that can be taking place in its own time and place, and therefore, I do not think God has a choice with everything that can be taking place in its own time and place because I do not think God is interfering with everything that can be taking place in its own time and place. If I do not think God has a choice with everything that can be taking place in its own time and place, than I think God is somehow able to be responsible for everything that can be taking place in its own time and place because I do not think God is interfering with everything that can be taking place in its own time and place as I think God is somehow able to be responsible for everything, and therefore, I think God is beyond everything because I do not think God is interfering with everything that can be taking place in its own time and place as I think God is somehow able to be responsible for everything. If I think God is beyond everything, than I think God is behind everything because I think God is beyond everything for God to be behind everything, even though, I do not think God is interfering with everything because I do not think God is interfering with everything that can be taking place in its own time and place for God not to be interfering with everything, and therefore, I think God is always good, and right because I do not think God is interfering with everything.

If think God is always good, and right, than I think everything is taking place within God, without being God as I think everything is apart of God, without being God because I do not think God is interfering with everything, and therefore, I think God is overlapping, and co-existing along with everything because I do not think God is interfering with everything, even though, I think God is somehow able to be taking place within God's own single dimension because I do not think someone, and something is able to be overlapping, and co-existing along with everything as I think God is overlapping, and co-existing along with everything. If I think God is somehow able to be taking place within God's own single dimension, than I think God is somehow able to be responsible for how dimensions are in life is in relation to what dimensions are in life because I think God is somehow able to be responsible for everything, and therefore, I think God is somehow able to be responsible for how any dimension is able to be what any dimension is in life because I think God is somehow able to be responsible for everything. If I think God is somehow able to be responsible for how any dimension is able to be what any dimension is in life, than I think God is somehow able to be responsible for how any dimension is apart of making up everything because I think God is somehow able to be responsible for everything, and therefore, I think everything is the dimensions of a higher intelligent living being as I think everything is the dimensions of God because I think God is a higher intelligent living being, that is somehow able to be responsible for everything.

If I think everything is the dimensions of a higher intelligent living being as I think everything is the dimensions of God, than I do not think someone can be able to be knowing for themselves, as to how God is able to be responsible for everything because I do not think someone can be able to be knowing for themselves, as to how many dimensions, and how many of each dimension there can possibly be able to be taking place in life as I think how many dimensions, and how many of each dimension there can possibly be able to be taking place in life is how God is able to be responsible for everything, and therefore, I think life is a mystery because I do not think someone knows everything as I do not think someone can be able to know for themselves, as to how God is able to be responsible for everything, but I think someone can try to understand for themselves, as to how someone, and something is taking place in life because I think how someone, and something is taking place in life is how many dimensions, and how many of each dimension there can possibly be able to be taking place in life. If I think someone can try to understand for themselves, as to how someone, and something is taking place in life, than I think God is somehow able to be responsible for how someone, and something is able to be taking place in life because I think God is somehow able to be responsible for everything, even though, I do not think someone can be able to be knowing for themselves, as to how God is able to be responsible for how someone, and something is able to be taking place in life because I do not think someone can be able to be knowing for themselves, as to how God is able to be responsible for everything, however, I think someone can try to understand for themselves, as to how God can possibly be responsible for how someone, and something is taking place in life because I think someone can try to understand for themselves, as to how someone, and something is taking place in life, even though, I think how God is able to be responsible for everything is God's way of saying everything is none of someone's business, as to how God is able to be responsible for everything because I think everything is only God's business, as to how God is able to be responsible for everything. If I think everything is only God's business, as to how God is able to be responsible for everything, than I do not think someone can be able to be knowing for themselves, as to how someone, and something is able to be taking place in life because I do not think someone can be able to be knowing for themselves, as to how God is able to be responsible for how someone, and something is in life, and therefore, I think someone, and something is intellectually beyond someone's intelligence, as to how someone, and something is able to be taking place in life because I do not think someone can be able to be knowing for themselves, as to how God is able to be responsible for how someone, and something is in life, even though, I think someone can try to understand for themselves, as to how someone, and something is taking place in life because I think someone can try to understand for themselves, as to how God can possibly be responsible for how someone, and something is taking place in life, however, I think someone, and something is beyond someone, and something because I think someone, and something is intellectually beyond someone's intelligence, as to how someone, and something is able to be taking place in life.

If I think someone, and something is beyond someone, and something, than I think everything is how everything is able to be taking place in life because I think everything is everything in life, and therefore, I think life is everything as I think everything is life because I think life is everything in life as I think everything in life is life. If I think life is everything as I think everything is life, than I think life is a dimension as I think everything is a dimension because I think life is something as I think everything is something. I think life is something as I think everything is something because I think life is everything as I think everything is life, and therefore, I think someone can think of everything as being the dimension of everything or the dimension of life or life as I think someone can think of life as being the dimension of life or the dimension of everything or everything because I think life is everything as I think everything is life. If I think life is everything as I think everything is life, than I think everything in the universe is of everything because I think everything in the universe is apart of making up everything. I think everything in the universe is apart of making up everything because I think everything in the universe is taking place in life, and therefore, I think everything in the universe is overlapping, and co-existing along with everything because I think everything in the universe is taking place in life. If I think everything in the universe is overlapping, and co-existing along with everything, than I think everything in the universe is taking place within life, without being life as I think everything in the universe is apart of life, without being life because I think everything in the universe is taking place in life, and therefore, I think the universe is of everything because I think the universe is apart of making up everything. I think the universe is apart of making up everything because I think the universe is taking place in life, and therefore, I think the universe is overlapping, and co-existing along with everything because I think the universe is taking place in life. If I think the universe is overlapping, and co-existing along with everything, than I think the universe is taking place within life, without being life as I think the universe is apart of life, without being life because I think the universe is taking place in life, and therefore, I think everything is of everything because I think everything is apart of making up everything. I think everything is apart of making up everything because I think everything is taking place in life, and therefore, I think everything is overlapping, and co-existing along with everything because I think everything is taking place in life. If I think everything is overlapping, and co-existing along with everything, than I think everything is taking place within life, without being life as I think everything is apart of life, without being life because I think everything is taking place in life, and therefore, I think someone can think of everything or life as being the dimension of reality or reality because I think life is reality as reality is life. If I think someone can think of everything or life as being the dimension of reality or reality, than I do not know if there is any other universe that is beyond this universe because I do not think someone can go beyond this universe, but I think there can possibly be more beyond this universe because I think there can possibly be more dimensions that can be apart of making up everything, and therefore, I think everything is beyond the universe because I think there can possibly be more dimensions that can be apart of making up everything.

If I think everything is beyond the universe, than I think everything is a dimension as I think everything is something because I think everything is apart of making up everything, and therefore, I think everything is overlapping, and co-existing along with everything because I think everything is apart of making up everything, even though, I do not know if someone can possibly be able to be knowing for themselves, as to how big everything is in life because I do not know if someone can be able to be knowing everything in life, but I think everything is taking place within everything, without being everything as I think everything is apart of everything, without being everything because I think everything is apart of making up everything, and therefore, I think everything is life as I think life is everything because I think everything is apart of making up everything as I think everything is apart of making up life. If I think everything is life as I think life is everything, than I think everything is a collection of how any dimension is overlapping, and co-existing along with any other dimension that is apart of making up everything because I think how any dimension is overlapping, and co-existing along with any other dimension is how any dimension is apart of making up everything, and therefore, I think everything is a collection of how any dimension is apart of making up everything because I think how any dimension is overlapping, and co-existing along with any other dimension is how any dimension is apart of making up everything. If I think everything is a collection of how any dimension is apart of making up everything, than I think everything is overlapping, and co-existing along with everything because I think everything is a collection of how any dimension is overlapping, and co-existing along with any other dimension that is apart of making up everything, and therefore, I think everything is apart of making up everything because I think everything is a collection of how any dimension is apart of making up everything. If I think everything is a collection of how any dimension is apart of making up everything, than I think everything is multi-dimensional because I think everything is a collection of how any dimension is apart of making up everything as I think everything is apart of making up everything, and therefore, I think everything is beyond everything as I think life is beyond everything because I think everything is apart of making up everything as I think everything is apart of making up life. If I think everything is beyond everything as I think life is beyond everything, than I think there can possibly be other dimensional plains, like the universe is a dimensional plain because I think everything is multi-dimensional for there to possibly be other dimensional plains, and therefore, I think everything is complex because I think everything is multi-dimensional for everything to be complex, however, I do not think everything is complicating because I think someone can think of how everything is in life for everything not to be complicating.

If I do not think everything is complicating, than I think something is a dimension as I think something is something because I think everything is of something. I think everything is of something because I think something is apart of making up everything, and therefore, I think everything is of something as I think something is apart of making up everything because I think everything consists of something that is apart of making up everything. If I think everything consists of something that is apart of making up everything, than I think someone can think of something as being the dimension of something because I think something is apart of making up everything, and therefore, I think something is overlapping, and co-existing along with everything because I think something is apart of making up everything. If I think something is overlapping, and co-existing along with everything, than I think everything is something that is constantly something because I think everything is something that is able to be taking place in life as being something, and therefore, I think everything is something that is able to be taking place in life as being something as I think something is able to be taking place in life as being something because I think everything is something that is constantly something as I think something is constantly something. I think everything is something that is constantly something as I think something is constantly something because I think everything consists of something that is apart of making up everything. I think everything consists of something that is apart of making up everything because I think everything is a collection of any dimension that is apart of making up everything as I think everything is a collection of something that is apart of making up everything, and therefore, I think everything consists of something that is apart of making up everything as I think everything consists of any dimension that is apart of making up everything because I think any dimension is something that is apart of making up everything as I think something is any dimension that is apart of making up everything. If I think everything consists of something that is apart of making up everything as I think everything consists of any dimension that is apart of making up everything, than I think everything is something that is constantly something as I think something is constantly something because I think everything consists of something that is apart of making up everything. If I think everything is something that is constantly something as I think something is constantly something, than I think everything is constantly something as I think everything is something that is constantly something because I think everything is something as I think something is constantly something, and therefore, I think everything is infinitely something as I think something is infinitely something because I think everything is constantly something as I think something is constantly something. If I think everything is infinitely something as I think something is infinitely something, than I think everything is in infinity because I think everything is infinitely something, and therefore, I think everything is infinite because I think everything is infinity. I think everything is infinity because I think everything is in infinity, and therefore, I think everything is constantly something as I think something is constantly something because I think everything consists of something that is apart of making up everything. If I think everything is constantly something as I think something is constantly something, than I think everything is constant because I think something is apart of making up everything for everything to always able to be taking place in life as being something as I think everything is constantly something, and therefore, I think everything is constantly something because I think everything is infinite. If I think everything is constantly something, than I think God is somehow able to be responsible for everything that is constantly something because I think God is somehow able to be responsible for everything for everything to be constantly something, and therefore, I think God is infinite because I think God is somehow able to be responsible for everything for everything to be constantly something. If I think God is infinite, than I think God is somehow able to be responsible for everything that is infinite because I think God is somehow able to be responsible for everything for everything to be infinite, and therefore, I think God is infinite because I think God is somehow able to be responsible for everything for everything to be infinite. If I think God is infinite, than I think God is somehow able to be responsible for something that is constantly something because I think God is somehow able to be responsible for everything for something to be constantly something, and therefore, I think God is infinite because I think God is somehow able to be responsible for something that is constantly something. If I think God is infinite, than I think God is somehow able to be responsible for something that is infinite because I think God is somehow able to be responsible for everything for something to be infinite, and therefore, I think God is infinite because I think God is somehow able to be responsible for something that is infinite.

If I think God is infinite, than I do not think everything is infinitely going to be taking place in life, before everything is going to be taking place in life because I do not think someone has ever experienced how everything is infinitely going to be taking place in life, before everything is going to be taking place in life, and therefore, how is everything infinite? I think everything is infinite because I think everything is infinitely going from one moment to the next moment. I think everything is infinitely going from one moment to the next moment because I do not think someone can live in the moment for someone not to be able to knowing for themselves, as to what a moment is in life. I do not think someone can live in the moment for someone not to be able to knowing for themselves, as to what a moment is in life because I do not think someone can live in a moment for someone not to be living in the moment. I do not think someone can live in a moment for someone not to be living in the moment because I do not think someone can stop everything for someone not to be living in a moment. I do not think someone can stop everything for someone not to be living in a moment because I think everything is infinitely going from one moment to the next moment for someone not to be living in a moment, and therefore, I do not think someone can possibly be able to be knowing for themselves, as to what the smallest among smallest fraction of a second is in life for someone not to be able to be knowing for themselves, as to how much time there is life that is going from one moment to the next moment because I do not think someone can stop everything for someone not to be able to measuring what the smallest among smallest fraction of a second is in life that is going from one moment to the next moment. If I do not think someone can possibly be able to be knowing for themselves, as to what the smallest among smallest fraction of a second is in life, than I do not think someone can possibly be able to be knowing for themselves, as to what the smallest among smallest fraction of a number is in life, and what the smallest among smallest number is in life, and what the biggest among biggest fraction of a number is in life, and what the biggest among biggest number is in life because I think everything is infinitely going from one moment to the next moment, and therefore, I think everything is infinite because I think everything is infinitely going from one moment to the next moment for everything to be infinite. If I think everything is infinite, than I think everything is constant because I think everything is constantly going from one moment to the next moment. I think everything is constantly going from one moment to the next moment because I think everything is infinitely going from one moment to the next moment for everything to constantly be going from one moment to the next moment, and therefore, I think everything is infinitely in motion as I think everything is constantly in motion because I think everything is infinitely going from one moment to the next moment as I think everything is constantly going from one moment to the next moment.

If I think everything is infinitely in motion as I think everything is constantly in motion, than I think God is somehow able to be responsible for everything that is infinitely in motion as I think God is somehow able to be responsible for everything that is constantly in motion because I think God is somehow able to be responsible for everything for God to somehow be able to be responsible for everything that is infinitely in motion as I think God is somehow able to be responsible for everything for God to somehow be able to be responsible for everything that is constantly in motion, and therefore, I think everything is infinitely in motion as I think everything is constantly in motion because I think God is somehow able to be responsible for everything that is infinitely in motion as I think God is somehow able to be responsible for everything that is constantly in motion. I think God is somehow able to be responsible for everything that is infinitely in motion as I think God is somehow able to be responsible for everything that is constantly in motion because I think everything is apart of God as I think God is somehow able to be responsible for everything, and therefore, I think God is infinitely in motion as I think God is constantly in motion because I think God is somehow able to be responsible for everything that is infinitely in motion as I think God is somehow able to be responsible for everything that is constantly in motion. If I think God is infinitely in motion as I think God is constantly in motion, than I think God is the greatest producer because I think God is somehow able to be responsible for everything that is infinitely in motion as I think God is somehow able to be responsible for everything for God to be the greatest producer, and therefore, I think everything is a motion picture because I think everything is constantly in motion for everything to be a motion picture. If I think everything is a motion picture, than I think God is somehow able to be responsible for everything that is a motion picture because I think God is somehow able to be responsible for everything that is constantly in motion for God to somehow be able to be responsible for everything that is a motion picture, and therefore, I think everything is a motion picture because I think God is somehow able to be responsible for everything that is constantly in motion for everything to be a motion picture. If I think everything is a motion picture, than I think everything is God's motion picture because I think God is somehow able to be responsible for everything that is constantly in motion for everything to be God's motion picture, and therefore, I think God is the greatest producer because I think everything is God's motion picture for God to be the greatest producer.

If I think God is the greatest producer, than I think God is constantly someone and something because I think God is someone that is something of itself, that is somehow able to be responsible for everything, and therefore, I think God is constantly something because I think God is constantly someone and something. If I think God is constantly something, than I think God is someone and something for God to constantly be someone and something because I do not think God can be someone, without God constantly being something, and therefore, I think God is infinitely someone and something because I think God is constantly someone and something. If I think God is infinitely someone and something, than I think God is in infinity because I think God is infinitely someone and something, and therefore, I think God is infinite because I think God is infinity. I think God is infinity because I think God is in infinity, and therefore, I think God is someone and something because I think God is constantly someone and something. If I think God is constantly someone and something, than I think God is constant because I think

God is constantly someone and something for God to be constant, and therefore, I think God is constantly something because I think God is infinite. If I think God is constantly something, than I do not think God is somehow able to be responsible for God that is constantly something because I think God is someone that is something of itself, that is somehow able to be responsible for everything for God to be constantly something, and therefore, I think God is infinite because I think God is someone that is something of itself, that is somehow able to be responsible for everything for God to be constantly something. If I think God is infinite, than I do not think God is somehow able to be responsible for God being infinite because I think God is someone that is something of itself, that is somehow able to be responsible for everything for God to be infinite, and therefore, I think God is infinite because I think God is someone that is something of itself, that is somehow able to be responsible for everything for God to be infinite.

If I think God is infinite, than I think everything is infinitely going from one moment to the next moment as I think everything is constantly going from one moment to the next moment because I think God is somehow able to be responsible for everything that is infinitely going from one moment to the next moment as I think God is somehow able to be responsible for everything that is constantly going from one moment to the next moment for everything to be infinite. I think God is somehow able to be responsible for everything that is infinitely going from one moment to the next moment as I think God is somehow able to be responsible for everything that is constantly going from one moment to the next moment for everything to be infinite because I think God is somehow able to be responsible for everything, and therefore, I think God is living in infinity as I think God is living from one moment to the next moment because I think God is somehow able to be responsible for everything that is infinitely going from one moment to the next moment. If I think God is living in infinity as I think God is living from one moment to the next moment, than I think God is infinite because I think God is living in infinity as I think God is living from one moment to the next moment, and therefore, I think God is living from one moment to the next moment because I think God is living in infinity as I think God is living from one moment to the next moment. If I think God is living from one moment to the next moment, than I think God is infinite because I think God is incalculable, as to what God is in life, and therefore, I think God is beyond everything because I think God is incalculable, as to what God is in life.

If I think God is beyond everything, than I do not think someone can be able to be knowing for themselves, as to how someone, and something is able to be taking place in life because I do not think someone can be able to be creating and re-creating how someone, and something is taking place in life as I think how someone, and something is taking place in life is how someone, and something is able to be taking place in life, and therefore, I think someone, and something is intellectually beyond someone's intelligence, as to how someone, and something is able to be taking place in life because I do not think someone can be able to be knowing for themselves, as to how someone, and something is able to be taking place in life, even though, I think someone can try to understand for themselves, as to how someone, and something is taking place in life because I think how someone, and something is able to be taking place in life is how someone, and something is taking place in life. If I think how someone, and something is able to be taking place in life is how someone, and something is taking place in life, than I think someone is a dimension as I think someone is something because I think everything is of someone. I think everything is of someone because I think someone is apart of making up everything, and therefore, I think everything is of someone as I think someone is apart of making up everything because I think everything consists of someone that is apart of making up everything. If I think everything consists of someone that is apart of making up everything, than I think someone can think of someone as being the dimension of someone because I think someone is apart of making up everything, and therefore, I think someone is overlapping, and co-existing along with everything because I think someone is apart of making up everything. If I think someone is overlapping, and co-existing along with everything, than I think everything is something that is able to be taking place in life as being something as I think someone is able to be taking place in life as being something because I think everything is constantly something as I think someone is constantly something. I think everything is constantly something as I think someone is constantly something because I think everything consists of someone that is apart of making up everything, and therefore, I think everything is something that is constantly something as I think someone is constantly something because I think everything consists of someone that is apart of making up everything. If I think everything is something that is constantly something as I think someone is constantly something, than I think someone is constantly something because I think someone is something for someone to constantly be something. I think someone is something for someone to constantly be something because I do not think someone can be someone, without someone constantly being something, and therefore, I think someone is infinitely something because I think someone is constantly something. If I think someone is infinitely something, than I think someone is in infinity because I think someone is infinitely something, and therefore, I think someone is infinite because I think someone is infinity. I think someone is infinity because I think someone is in infinity, and therefore, I think someone is something because I think someone is constantly something. If I think someone is constantly something, than I think someone is constant because I think someone is constantly something for someone to be constant, and therefore, I think someone is constantly something because I think someone is infinite. If I think someone is constantly something, than I think God is somehow able to be responsible for someone that is constantly something because I think God is somehow able to be responsible for everything for someone to be constantly something, and therefore, I think God is infinite because I think God is somehow able to be responsible for everything for someone to be constantly something. If I think God is infinite, than I think God is somehow able to be responsible for someone that is infinite as I think someone is infinite because I think God is somehow able to be responsible for everything for someone to be infinite, and therefore, I think God is infinite because I think God is somehow able to be responsible for everything for someone to be infinite.

If I think God is infinite, than I think someone is living from one moment to the next moment because I do not think someone can live in a moment for someone not to be living in the moment as I do not think someone can live in a moment for someone to be living from one moment to the next moment, and therefore, I think someone is living in infinity as I think someone is living from one moment to the next moment because I think everything is infinitely going from one moment to the next moment. If I think someone is living in infinity as I think someone is living from one moment to the next moment, than I think someone is living in infinity with every passing moment because I think someone is living in infinity as I think someone is living from one moment to the next moment, and therefore, I think someone is infinite because I think someone is living in infinity as I think someone is living from one moment to the next moment. If I think someone is infinite, than I think someone can think someone can think of nothing because I think someone can think of nothing as being nothing as I think someone can think of something as being nothing, but I think someone can think of something as I think someone can be think of nothing because I think nothing is something for someone to be thinking of something, and nothing, and therefore, I think someone is infinite as I think someone is living from one moment to the next moment because I do not think someone can not possibly be able to be thinking of absolutely nothing as I think someone is living from one moment to the next moment, even though, I do not think someone can possibly be able to be knowing for themselves what infinity is in life because I do not think someone can possibly be able to be knowing for themselves how everything is infinite, but I think someone can think of what infinity is in life because I think infinity is something that is incalculable, such as everything that is constantly going from one moment to the next moment. If I think someone can think of what infinity is in life, than I think someone is infinite because I think someone is incalculable, as to what someone is in life, and therefore, I think someone is beyond everything as I think someone is beyond something because I think someone is incalculable, as to what someone is in life. If I think someone is incalculable, as to what someone is in life, than I think something is infinite because I think something is incalculable, as to what something is in life, and therefore, I think something is beyond something because I think something is incalculable, as to what something is in life, even though, I think someone can calculate what something is in life because I think something consists of every possible mathematical number, and formula that is apart of making up something, however, I think something is infinite as I think something is incalculable, as to what something is in life because I do not think someone can possibly be able to be knowing for themselves, as to what every possible mathematical number, and formula that is apart of making up something. If I think something is infinite as I think something is incalculable, as to what something is in life, than I think everything is infinite because I think everything is incalculable, as to what everything is in life, and therefore, I think everything is beyond everything as I think everything is beyond someone because I think everything is incalculable, as to what everything is in life as I do not think someone can possibly be able to be knowing for themselves, as to what everything is in life.

If I think everything is beyond everything as I think everything is beyond someone, than I think everything is a creation of God because I think God is somehow able to be responsible for everything for everything to be a creation of God, and therefore, I think everything is a creation of how God is able to be what God is in life because I think God is somehow able to be responsible for everything for everything to be a creation of how God is able to be what God is in life. If I think everything is a creation of how God is able to be what God is in life, than I think everything is a creation of God as I think everything is God's creation because I think God is somehow able to be responsible for everything, and therefore, I think God is how God is able to be what God is in life because I think everything is a creation of God as I think God is somehow able to be responsible for everything. If I think God is how God is able to be what God is in life, than I think life is everything as I think everything is life because I think God is somehow able to be responsible for everything, and therefore, I think life is God as I think God is life because I think everything is a creation of God as I think God is somehow able to be responsible for everything. If I think life is God as I think God is life, than I think everything is life as I think life is everything because I think everything is apart of life, and therefore, I think life is in God as I think everything is in God because I think God is beyond everything as I think God is somehow able to be responsible for everything. If I think life is in God as I think everything is in God, than I think everything is how everything is able to be taking place in life as I think how everything is able to be taking place in life is everything because I think God is somehow able to be responsible for everything as I think God is somehow able to be responsible for how everything is able to be taking place in life, and therefore, I think God is somehow able to be responsible for everything as I think God is somehow able to be responsible for creating everything because I think God created everything for God to somehow be able to be responsible for everything as I think God created everything for God to somehow be able to be responsible for creating everything.

If I think God is somehow able to be responsible for everything as I think God is somehow able to be responsible for creating everything, than I think God is allowing for someone, and something to be taking place in its own time and place because I do not think God is interfering with someone, and something that can be taking place in its own time and place. I do not think God is interfering with someone, and something that can be taking place in its own time and place because I think someone, and something is taking place in its own time and place for God not to be interfering with someone, and something that can be taking place in its own time and place, and therefore, I do not think God has a choice with someone, and something that can be taking place in its own time and place because I do not think God is interfering with someone, and something that can be taking place in its own time and place. If I do not think God has a choice with someone, and something that can be taking place in its own time and place, than I think God is somehow able to be responsible for someone, and something that can be taking place in its own time and place because I do not think God is interfering with someone, and something that can be taking place in its own time and place as I think God is somehow able to be responsible for everything, and therefore, I think God is beyond someone, and something because I do not think God is interfering with someone, and something that can be taking place in its own time and place as I think God is somehow able to be responsible for everything. If I think God is beyond someone, and something, than I do not think God is interfering with someone, and something because I do not think God is interfering with someone, and something that can be taking place in its own time and place for God not to be interfering with someone, and something, and therefore, I think God is always good, and right because I do not think God is interfering with someone, and something.

If I think God is always good, and right, than I think God created everything as I think God created someone, and something because I think God is somehow able to be responsible for creating everything for God to be creating everything as I think God is somehow able to be responsible for creating everything for God to be creating someone, and something, and therefore, I think everything is of God as I think someone, and something is of God because I think God created everything for everything to be of God as I think God created everything for someone, and something to be of God. If I think everything is of God as I think someone, and something is of God, than I think someone is a dimension as I think something is a dimension because I think God created someone for someone to be a dimension as I think God created something for something to be a dimension, and therefore, I think everything is a dimension because I think God created everything for everything to be a dimension. If I think everything is a dimension, than I think everything is overlapping, and co-existing along with God as I think someone, and something is overlapping, and co-existing along with God because I think God created everything for everything to be overlapping, and co-existing along with God as I think God created someone, and something for someone, and something to be overlapping, and co-existing along with God, and therefore, I think God created everything to be overlapping, and co-existing along with God as I think God created someone, and something to be overlapping, and co-existing along with God because I think God created everything for everything to be overlapping, and co-existing along with God as I think God created someone, and something for someone, and something to be overlapping, and co-existing along with God. If I think God created everything to be overlapping, and co-existing along with God as I think God created someone, and something to be overlapping, and co-existing along with God, than I think everything is overlapping, and co-existing along

51

with everything as I think someone, and something is overlapping, and co-existing along with everything because I think God created everything for everything to be overlapping, and co-existing along with everything as I think God created someone, and something for someone, and something to be overlapping, and co-existing along with everything, and therefore, I think God created everything to be overlapping, and co-existing along with everything as I think God created someone, and something to be overlapping, and co-existing along with everything because I think God created everything for everything to be overlapping, and co-existing along with everything as I think God created someone, and something for someone, and something to be overlapping, and co-existing along with everything. If I think God created everything to be overlapping, and co-existing along with everything as I think God created someone, and something to be overlapping, and co-existing along with everything, than I think God created everything to be infinite as I think God created someone, and something to be infinite because I think God is infinite for God to be creating everything to be infinite as I think God is infinite for God to be creating someone, and something to be infinite, and therefore, I think everything is infinite as I think someone, and something is infinite because I think God created everything to be infinite as I think God created someone, and something to be infinite.

If I think everything is infinite as I think someone, and something is infinite, than I think God is experiencing everything because I think God created everything for God to be experiencing everything, and therefore, I think someone can experience God as I think someone can experience someone, and something because I think God created everything for someone to be experiencing God as I think God created everything for someone to be experiencing someone, and something. If I think someone can experience God as I think someone can experience someone, and something, than I think someone's experience with God is someone's own experience with God as I think someone's experience with someone, and something is someone's own experience with someone, and something because I think God created everything for someone to be experiencing God as I think God created everything for someone to be experiencing someone, and something, and therefore, I think someone's experience with God is someone's relationship with God because I think someone's experience with God is someone's own experience with God for someone's experience with God to be someone's own relationship with God. If I think someone's experience with God is someone's relationship with God, than I think God is everywhere because I think God is somehow able to be responsible for everything for God to be everywhere, and therefore, I think someone can have a relationship with God anywhere because I think God is everywhere for someone to have a relationship with God anywhere. I think God is everywhere for someone to have a relationship with God anywhere because I think God created everything for someone to have a relationship with God anywhere as I think God created everything for God to be everywhere, and therefore, I think God can be someone's God because I think God created someone for God to be someone's God as I think God created everything for God to be someone's God.

If I think God can be someone's God, than I think God is how God is able to be what God is in life because I think God created everything for God to be how God is able to be what God is in life, and therefore, I think everything is God's work as I think everything is of God's work because I think God created everything for everything to be God's work as I think God created everything for everything to be of God's work. If I think everything is God's work as I think everything is of God's work, than I think God works in mysterious ways because I think everything is of God's work as I think God created everything for God to be working in mysterious ways, and therefore, I think something that someone can possibly be working on in someone's life is God's work as I think something that someone can possibly be working on in someone's life is of God's work because I think everything is God's work as I think everything is of God's work. I think everything is God's work as I think everything is of God's work because I think everything is a creation of God for everything to be God's work as I think everything is a creation of God for everything to be of God's work. I think everything is a creation of God for everything to be God's work as I think everything is a creation of God for everything to be of God's work because I think everything is of God's work for everything to be God's work as I think God created everything for everything to be a creation of God, and therefore, I think everything is created by God because I think God created everything for everything to be created by God. If I think everything is created by God, than I think everything is a creation of God for everything to be God's work as I think everything is a creation of God for everything to be of God's work because I think everything is of God's work for everything to be God's work as I think everything is created by God for everything to be a creation of God, and therefore, I think everything is a creation of God as I think everything is God's creation because I think everything is created by God for everything to be a creation of God as I think everything is created by God for everything to be God's creation. If I think everything is a creation of God as I think everything is God's creation, than I think everything is of God's creation because I think everything is created by God for everything to be of God's creation, and therefore, I think everything is God's creation because I think everything is of God's creation as I think everything is a creation of God for everything to be God's creation.

If I think everything is God's creation, than I do not think a gift is just someone's God given ability to have something, and I do not think a gift is just someone's God given ability to be doing something, and I do not think a gift is just something that someone gets or gives because I think a gift is everything. I think a gift is everything because I think everything is a gift. I think everything is a gift because I think everything is God's gift. I think everything is God's gift because I think everything is of God's creation for everything to be God's gift, and therefore, I think something is someone's choice for someone to be thinking of something as being someone's gift because I think everything is God's gift. If I think something is someone's choice for someone to be thinking of something as being someone's gift, than I think someone can be grateful for something as I think someone can be thankful for something because I think someone being grateful for something is someone being thankful for something. I think someone being grateful for something is someone being thankful for something because I think someone's gratitude is someone's thankfulness, and therefore, I think someone can be grateful for everything as I think someone can be thankful for everything because I think everything is God's gift for someone to be grateful for everything as I think everything is God's gift for someone to be thankful for everything, even though, I think something is someone's choice for someone to be grateful or thankful for something because I think everything is God's gift for someone to be grateful or thankful for something, however, I think someone can be grateful or thankful of God because I think everything is God's gift as I think God created someone for someone to be grateful or thankful of God.

If I think someone can be grateful or thankful of God, than I think God is perfect because I think everything is created by God for God to be perfect, and therefore, I think everything is perfect because I think everything is created by God for everything to be perfect. If I think everything is perfect, than I do not think someone can possibly be able to be knowing for themselves something that is completely perfect or imperfect because I do not think someone has ever experienced something that is completely perfect or imperfect, but I think everything is perfect because I think God created everything for everything to be perfect, and therefore, I think God is responsible for creating everything because I think God created everything as I think everything is created by God for God to be responsible for creating everything. If I think God is responsible for creating everything, than I think God must have been alone, before God created everything because I think there was nothing, before God created everything, and therefore, I think God created everything for God as I think God created everything for someone because I think God created everything for God not to be alone as I think God created everything for someone not to be alone. If I think God created everything for God as I think God created everything for someone, than I do not think God always being alone is something that is good for God as I do not think someone always being alone is something that is good for someone because I think God created everything for God not to always be alone as I think God created everything for someone not to always be alone, and therefore, I do not think God created someone for someone to always be alone because I think God created everything for someone not to always be alone, even though, I do not think someone can always be alone because I think God created everything for someone not to always be alone with themselves, someone else, something, and God in someone's life.

If I do not think someone can always be alone, than I do not think everything came from nothing for everything to be starting out as being nothing because I think if everything came from nothing for everything to be starting out as being nothing, than I think everything would be nothing as I think everything would be an endless void of nothingness with everything being nothing because I think nothing is nothing for everything to be nothing, and therefore, I do not think everything came from nothing for everything to be starting out as being nothing because I do not think everything is nothing as I do not think everything is an endless void of nothingness with everything being nothing. If I do not think everything came from nothing for everything to be starting out as being nothing, than I do not think there is nothingness because I do not think there is absolutely nothing for there not to be nothingness. I do not think there is absolutely nothing for there not to be nothingness because I think everything, and nothing is something for there not to be nothingness, and therefore, I do not think everything could have come from nothing for everything to be coming from nothingness because I think everything, and nothing is created for everything not to be coming from nothingness. If I do not think everything could have come from nothing for everything to be coming from nothingness, than I think everything, and nothing is something for there not to be nothingness because I think everything, and nothing must have come from something for everything, and nothing to be something. I think everything, and nothing must have come from something for everything, and nothing to be something because I think everything, and nothing is of something for everything, and nothing to be something, and therefore, I think everything, and nothing must have come from God because I think everything, and nothing is of God for everything, and nothing to be something. I think everything, and nothing is of God for everything, and nothing to be something because I think everything, and nothing is something as I think God is something. I think everything, and nothing is something as I think God is something because I think God is something for everything, and nothing to be coming from something. I think God is something for everything, and nothing to be coming from something because I think everything, and nothing is of God as I think God is something, and therefore, I think everything, and nothing is of something for everything, and nothing to be something because I think everything, and nothing is of God for everything, and nothing to be something. If I think everything, and nothing is of something for everything, and nothing to be something, than I do not think there was nothing before God created everything because I think God came before God created everything, and therefore, I do not think there is absolutely nothing because I think everything, and nothing is of God as I think God is something. If I do not think there is absolutely nothing, than I think everything, and nothing somehow must have come from God being both someone, and something because I do not think everything could have come from nothing for everything to be coming from nothingness, and therefore, I think God is someone that is something of itself, that is somehow able to be responsible for everything because I do not think everything could have come from nothing for everything to be coming from nothingness.

If I do not think everything could have come from nothing for everything to be coming from nothingness, than I think God is someone that is something of itself, that is somehow able to be responsible for creating everything because I think God is someone that is something of itself, that is somehow able to be responsible for everything, and therefore, I think God is everywhere as I think God is everything because I think God is somehow able to be responsible for creating everything for God to be everywhere as I think God is somehow able to be responsible for creating everything for God to be everywhere. If I think God is everywhere as I think God is everything, than I think dimensions is creation as I think creation is dimensions because I think everything is of God's creation, and therefore, I think dimensions supports everything as being created because I think God created everything for dimensions to be supporting everything as being created. If I think dimensions supports everything as being created, than I think God owns everything because I think God created everything for God to be owning everything, but I do not think God is claiming ownership of everything because I do not think God is interfering with everything for God not to be claiming ownership of everything, and therefore, I do not think someone can be able to be claiming ownership of something as much someone thinks someone can own something because I think God created everything for someone not to be owning something. If I do not think someone can be able to be claiming ownership of something as much someone thinks someone can own something, than I do not think someone can label something that someone can think as being someone's own thought or idea because I think if someone can label something that someone can think as being someone's own thought or idea, than I think someone can be claming ownership of something that someone can think as being someone's own thought or idea, but I do not think someone can claim ownership of something that someone can think as being someone's own thought or idea because I do not think something is someone's originally thought or idea for someone not to be claiming ownership of something, and therefore, I do not think someone can label something that someone can think as being someone's own thought or idea because I do not think something is someone's originally thought or idea for someone not to be claiming ownership of something, even though, I think someone can think of what something is in life, and how something is in life, without labeling something as being someone's own thought or idea because I do not think something is someone's originally thought or idea for someone to be thinking of what something is in life, and how something is in life. If I think someone can think of what something is in life, and how something is in life, without labeling something as being someone's own thought or idea, than I do not like to be labeling someone with any word for me to thinking of someone as being completely different from myself because I think someone labeling someone else with any word for someone to be thinking of themselves as being completely different from someone else is separatism, and not unity with someone in relation to someone else, even though, I do not think someone is completely different from someone else because I think someone is fundamentally the same as someone else for someone not to be completely different from someone else, however, I think someone can be different from someone else because I think someone can think of doing something, that can be different from what someone else can think of doing something, and I think someone can think of something, that can be different from what someone else can think of something for someone to be different from someone else, and therefore, I think separation can be good for someone because I think someone else can do something wrong for someone to be unhappy or unable to be living with someone else, and I think someone can be unhappy or unable to be living where someone is in life for separation to be good for someone.

If I think separation can be good for someone, than I think someone that doesn't take God into consideration with themselves is someone's way of thinking someone doesn't care about God because I think someone that isn't taking God into consideration with everything is someone that isn't taking God into consideration with themselves as I think someone that isn't taking God into consideration with everything is someone that doesn't care about God, but I do not think someone can possibly be able to think of everything, without taking God into consideration with how God is somehow able to be responsible for creating everything because I think everything is intellectually beyond someone's intelligence, as to how everything is able to be taking place in life, and therefore, I do not think someone can base someone's thoughts around God because I do not think someone's thoughts is greater than God for someone not to be able to be basing someone's thoughts around God. I do not think someone's thoughts is greater than God for someone not to be able to be basing someone's thoughts around God because I do not think someone can think of enough thoughts of God for someone not to be able to be basing someone's thoughts around God, and therefore, I do not think someone is greater than God for someone not to be able to be basing someone's thoughts around God because I think God is greater than everything as I think God is somehow able to be responsible for creating everything. If I do not think someone is greater than God for someone not to be able to be basing someone's thoughts around God, than I do not think God is any group or any organization or any following or any religion of any kind for someone not to be able to be basing someone's thoughts of any group or any organization or any following or any religion of any kind on God because I think God is an intelligent living being for someone not to be basing someone's thoughts of any group or any organization or any following or any religion of any kind on God, and therefore, I do not think someone can base any group or any organization or any following or any religion of any kind on God because I think God is an intelligent living being for someone not to be basing any group or any organization or any following or any religion of any kind on God. I think God is an intelligent living being for someone not to be basing any group or any organization or any following or any religion of any kind on God because I think God is an intelligent living being for someone to be communicating to God in any possible way in how someone can communicate to God. I think God is an intelligent living being for someone to be communicating to God in any possible way in how someone can communicate to God because I think God created everything for someone to be communicating to God, and therefore, I think someone could try to be controlling someone else, from someone basing someone's thoughts of any group or any organization or any following or any religion of any kind on God, but I do not think someone can completely control someone else, from someone basing someone's thoughts of any group or any organization or any following or any religion of any kind on God because I do not think God is any group or any organization or any following or any religion of any kind for someone not to be able to be basing someone's thoughts of any group or any organization or any following or any religion of any kind on God.

If I do not think someone can completely control someone else, from someone basing someone's thoughts of any group or any organization or any following or any religion of any kind on God, than I do not think someone can base someone's thoughts around everything because I do not think someone's thoughts is greater than everything for someone not to be able to be basing someone's thoughts around everything. I do not think someone's thoughts is greater than everything for someone to be able to be basing someone's thoughts around everything because I do not think someone can think of enough thoughts of everything for someone not to be able to be basing someone's thoughts around everything, and therefore, I do not think someone is greater than everything for someone not to be able to be basing someone's thoughts around everything because I think everything is greater than someone for someone not to be able to be basing someone's thoughts around everything. If I do not think someone is greater than everything for someone not to be able to be basing someone's thoughts around everything, than I do not think everything is any group or any organization or any following or any religion of any kind because I think life is everything as I think everything is life, even though, I think someone can be apart of a group for someone to be thinking about what someone thinks of God, and life because I think someone can be in an organized or unorganized meeting with someone else for someone to be communicating with someone else about what someone thinks of God, and life as I think someone can be communicating with someone else about what someone thinks of God, and life for someone to be thinking about what someone thinks of God, and life, however, I think what someone thinks of God, and life is someone's own interpretation, as to what someone thinks of God, and life because I think God, and life is beyond someone with how God, and everything is in life, and therefore, I do not think someone is going to agree with what everyone thinks of God, and life because I think what someone thinks of God, and life is someone's own interpretation, as to what someone thinks of God, and life for everyone not to be agreeing with what everyone thinks of God, and life.

If I do not think someone is going to agree with what everyone thinks of God, and life, than I do not think everything is a creation of itself because I think if everything is intellectually beyond someone's intelligence, as to how everything is taking place in life, than I think everything is intellectually beyond itself for everything not to be a creation of itself, and therefore, I do not think everything is a creation of itself because I think everything is a creation of God for everything not to be a creation of itself. If I do not think everything is a creation of itself, than I think God is the creator of everything because I think God is somehow able to be responsible for creating everything as I think everything is intellectually beyond itself for everything not to be a creation of itself, and therefore, I think God is the greatest artist as I think God is the greatest producer because I think God is the creator of everything for God to be the greatest artist as I think God is the creator of everything for God to be the greatest producer. If I think God is the greatest artist as I think God is the greatest producer, than I think God is a creator of everything, not a destroyer of everything because I think God is somehow able to be creating everything to permanently be taking place in life. I think God is somehow able to be creating everything to permanently be taking place in life because I think God is somehow able to be responsible for creating everything, and therefore, I think God is the creator of everything as I think God is a higher intelligent living being because I think God is somehow able to be responsible for creating everything.

Chapter 4

God's will

I would like to talk about how dimensions are in life in relation to what dimensions are in life by talking about God's will, that can possibly have something to do with how dimensions are in life is in relation to what dimensions are in life because I think God is somehow able to be responsible for God having a will, and therefore, I think God is a choice because I think God has a choice. I think God has a choice because I think God is a choice for God to have a choice. I think God is a choice for God to have a choice because I think God has a choice of what God is doing. I think God has a choice of what God is doing because I think God has a choice, and therefore, I think God is in motion because I think God has a choice of what God is doing for God to be in motion. If I think God is in motion, than I think God has a choice because I think God has a will as I think God has a choice. I think God has a will as I think God has a choice because I think God has a will for God to have a choice. I think God has a will for God to have a choice because I do not think God would have a choice, if God doesn't have a will. I do not think God would have a choice, if God doesn't have a will because I do not think God would have a choice of what God is doing, if God doesn't have a will for God to have a choice of what God is doing, but I think God has a will for God to have a choice of what God is doing because I think God has a choice of what God is doing, and therefore, I think God has a will as I think God has a choice because I think God has a will for God to have a choice of what God is doing. I think God has a will for God to have a choice of what God is doing because I think God's will is God's choice. I think God's will is God's choice because I think God has a will as I think God has a choice. I think God has a will as I think God has a choice because I think God has a choice for God to have a will as I think God has a will for God to have a choice. I think God has a choice for God to have a will as I think God has a will for God to have a choice because I think God's will is God's choice as I think God's choice is God's will. I think God's will is God's choice as I think God's choice is God's will because I think God has a will as I think God has a choice, and therefore, I think God has a will for God to be having God's free will because I think God has God's free will with God having a choice of what God is doing. I think God has God's free will with God having a choice of what God is doing because I think God has a will. I think God has a will because I think God's will is what God does as I think what God does is God's will. I think God's will is what God does as I think what God does is God's will because I think God has a will for what God does, even though, I think someone can think of all kinds of different words for someone to be describing what someone thinks God's will is in life because I think God has will for someone to be thinking of all kinds of different words for someone to be describing what someone thinks God's will is in life, however, I think God has a will because I think God's will is what God is doing as I think God's will is what God does. If I think God has a will, than I think someone can think of all kinds of words for someone to be describing what someone thinks what God can do because I think God has will for someone to be thinking of all kinds of different words for someone to be describing what someone thinks what God can do, and therefore, I think everything God does is God's will as I think everything God does is God's choice because I think God's will is God's choice for God to be doing everything God does. If I think everything God does is God's will as I think everything God does is God's choice, than I think God will do something because I think God has will for God to be doing something, and therefore, I think God can do something with someone, and something because I think God has a will for God to be doing something with someone, and something. If I think God can do something with someone, and something, than I think what God thinks is what God does because I do not think God would think what God thinks, without God doing what God is doing with God's will, and therefore, I think God is in motion because I think God has a will for God to be in motion.

If I think God is in motion, than I think God's will is how God is doing what God is doing because think God's will is what God is doing, and therefore, I think God's will is taking place within God, without being God as I think God's will is apart of God, without being God because I think God's will is how God is doing what God is doing. If I think God's will is taking place within God, without being God as I think God's will is apart of God, without being God, than I do not think God's will is God because I think God's will is taking place within God, without being God as I think God's will is apart of God, without being God, and therefore, I do not think God is a choice of itself as I think God has a will for God to have a choice because I do not think God's will is God. If I do not think God is a choice of itself as I think God has a will for God to have a choice, than I think God's will is apart of God for God to have a will because I think God has a will for God to be doing what God is doing. I think God has a will for God to be doing what God is doing because I think God's will is God's choice. I think God's will is God's choice because I think God's will is apart of God for God to have a choice. I think God's will is apart of God for God to have a choice because I think God's choice is God's will. I think God's choice is God's will because I think God's choice is what God is doing as I think God's will is what God is doing. I think God's choice is what God is doing as I think God's will is what God is doing because I think what God is doing is God's choice as I think what God is doing is God's will. I think what God is doing is God's choice as I think what God is doing is God's will because I think God's choice is God's will as I think God's will is God's choice. I think God's choice is God's will as I think God's will is God's choice because I think God has a will as I think God has a choice. I think God has a will as I think God has a choice because I think God has God's free will. I think God has God's free will because I think God has a will for God to be having God's free will. I think God has a will for God to be having God's free will because I think God has God's free will with God having a choice of what God is doing. I think God has God's free will with God having a choice of what God is doing because I think God has a choice. I think God has a choice because I think God has will for God to be having a choice, and therefore, I think God has a will because I think God's will is how God is doing what God is doing. I think God's will is how God is doing what God is doing because I think what God is doing is how God is doing what God is doing. I think what God is doing is how God is doing what God is doing because I think God has a will. I think God has a will because I think God's will is what God is doing. I think God's will is what God is doing because I think what God is doing is how God is doing what God is doing. I think what God is doing is how God is doing what God is doing because I think God's will is a dimension. I think God's will is a dimension because I think God's will is something for God's will to be a dimension. I think God's will is something for God's will to be a dimension because I think God's will is what God is doing. I think God's will is what God is doing because I think God has a will as I think God's will is a dimension, and therefore, I think someone can think of God's will as being the dimension of God's will because I think the dimension of God's will is what God is doing.

If I think the dimension of God's will is what God is doing, than I think God's will is apart of God because I think God has a will for God to be doing what God is doing, but I do not think God's will is God because I think God's will is how God is doing what God is doing, and therefore, I think God's will comes from God because I think God's will is apart of God for God's will to be coming from God, but I do not think God's will is God because I think God's will is what God is doing. I think God's will is what God is doing because I think God's will is God having a choice of what God is doing. I think God's will is God having a choice of what God is doing because I do not think God would be able to be doing anything, without God having a will. I do not think God would be able to be doing anything, without God having a will because I think God not having a will is like God not being able to somehow be responsible for everything in the universe as I think God is somehow able to be responsible for everything in the universe, and therefore, I think God's will is how God is able to be a living being because I think God's will is God having a choice of what God is doing. If I think God's will is how God is able to be a living being, than I think God's will is somehow able to be responsible for everything in the universe because I think God's will is apart of God as I think God is somehow able to be responsible for everything in the universe, and therefore, I think God's will is God's free will as I think God's will is somehow able to be responsible for everything in the universe because I think God's will is allowing for everything to be taking place in its own time and place in the universe. I think God's will is allowing for everything to be taking place in its own time and place in the universe because I do not think God's will is interfering with everything that can be taking place in its own time and place in the universe. I do not think God's will is interfering with everything that can be taking place in its own time and place in the universe because I think everything is taking place in its own time and place in the universe for God's will not to be interfering with everything that can be taking place in its own time and place in the universe, and therefore, I do not think God's will has a choice with everything that can be taking place in its own time and place in the universe because I do not think God's will is interfering with everything that can be taking place in its own time and place in the universe. If I do not think God's will has a choice with everything that can be taking place in its own time and place in the universe, than I think God's will is somehow able to be responsible for everything that can be taking place in its own time and place in the universe because I do not think God's will is interfering with everything that can be taking place in its own time and place in the universe as I think God's will is somehow able to be responsible for everything in the universe, and therefore, I think God's will is beyond everything in the universe because I do not think God's will is interfering with everything that can be taking place in its own time and place in the universe as I think God's will is somehow able to be responsible for everything in the universe.

If I think God's will is beyond everything in the universe, than I do not think God's will is interfering with everything in the universe because I do not think God's will is interfering with everything that can be taking place in its own time and place in the universe for God's will not to be interfering with everything in the universe, and therefore, I think God's will is always good, and right because I do not think God's will is interfering with everything in the universe. If think God's will is always good, and right, than I think God is always good, and right with God's will because I do not think God's will is interfering with everything in the universe as I think God's will is apart of God, and therefore, I think God can do something that is always good, and right with God's will because I think God is always good, and right with God's will. If I think God can do something that is always good, and right with God's will, than I do not think someone can possibly be able to be doing God's will because I do not think someone is God for someone not to be having God's will as I do not think someone is God for someone not to be able to be doing God's will, and therefore, I do not think someone can do God's will because I do not think someone can always do something that is good, and right with everything someone can possibly be doing as I think God can do something that is always good, and right with God's will. If I do not think someone can do God's will, than I think someone can do like God's will because I think someone can do something that is good, and right like God can do something that is always good, and right with God's will, and therefore, I think someone can do God's will because I think someone can do something that is good, and right like God can do something that is always good, and right with God's will. If I think someone can do God's will, than I think someone is doing God's work as I think someone is doing God's will because I think someone can do God's will for someone to be doing God's work, and therefore, I think God is doing God's work as I think God is doing God's will because I think God can do God's will for God to be doing God's work. If I think God is doing God's work as I think God is doing God's will, than I think God's will is overlapping, and co-existing along with everything in the universe because I do not think God's will is interfering with everything in the universe as I think God's will is somehow able to be responsible for everything in the universe, and therefore, I think God's will is overlapping, and co-existing along with the universe because I do not think God's will is interfering with everything in the universe as I think God's will is somehow able to be responsible for everything in the universe. If I think God's will is overlapping, and co-existing along with the universe, than I think God created everything in the universe with God's will because I think God's will is apart of God as I think God is somehow able to be responsible for creating everything, and therefore, I think God's will is overlapping, and co-existing along with everything in the universe as I think God's will is overlapping, and co-existing along with the universe because I think God created everything in the universe with God's will for God's will to be overlapping, and co-existing along with everything in the universe as I think God created everything in the universe with God's will for God's will to be overlapping, and co-existing along with the universe.

If I think God's will is overlapping, and co-existing along with everything in the universe as I think God's will is overlapping, and co-existing along with the universe, than I think God's will is intellectually beyond someone's intelligence, as to what God's will is in life because I do not think someone can be able to be knowing for themselves, as to how God can be doing what God is doing, even though, I think someone can try to understand for themselves, as to what God's will in life because I think God's will is how God can be doing what God is doing, however, I think God's will is beyond someone because I think God's will is intellectually beyond someone's intelligence, as to what God's will is in life. If I think God's will is beyond someone, than I think God's will is somehow able to be responsible for everything because I think God's will is apart of God as I think God is somehow able to be responsible for creating everything, and therefore, I think God's will is in the exact same single dimension of God because I think God's will is apart of God as I think God is somehow able to be responsible for creating everything. If I think God's will is in the exact same single dimension of God, than I think everything is a creation of God as I think God's will is apart of God because I think God's will is apart of God as I think God is somehow able to be responsible for creating everything, and therefore, I think God's will is apart of how God is able to be what God is in life as I think everything is a creation of how God is able to be what God is in life because I think God's will is apart of God as I think God is somehow able to be responsible for creating everything. If I think God's will is apart of how God is able to be what God is in life as I think everything is a creation of how God is able to be what God is in life, than I think God's will is a creation of God as I think everything is a creation of God because I think God's will is apart of God as I think God is somehow able to be responsible for creating everything, and therefore, I think God's will is God's creation as I think everything is God's creation because I think God's will is apart of God as I think God is somehow able to be responsible for creating everything.

If I think God's will is God's creation as I think everything is God's creation, than I think God's will is allowing for everything to be taking place in its own time and place because I do not think God's will is interfering with everything that can be taking place in its own time and place. I do not think God's will is interfering with everything that can be taking place in its own time and place because I think everything is taking place in its own time and place for God's will not to be interfering with everything that can be taking place in its own time and place, and therefore, I do not think God's will has a choice with everything that can be taking place in its own time and place because I do not think God's will is interfering with everything that can be taking place in its own time and place. If I do not think God's will has a choice with everything that can be taking place in its own time and place, than I think God's will is somehow able to be responsible for everything that can be taking place in its own time and place because I do not think God's will is interfering with everything that can be taking place in its own time and place as I think God's will is somehow able to be responsible for everything, and therefore, I think God's will is beyond everything because I do not think God's will is interfering with everything that can be taking place in its own time and place as I think God's will is somehow able to be responsible for everything. If I think God's will is beyond everything, than I do not think God's will is interfering with everything because I do not think God's will is interfering with everything that can be taking place in its own time and place for God's will not to be interfering with everything, and therefore, I think God's will is always good, and right because I do not think God's will is interfering with everything. If think God's will is always good, and right, than I think God is always good, and right with God's will because I do not think God's will is interfering with everything as I think God's will is apart of God, and therefore, I think God's will is overlapping, and co-existing along with everything because I do not think God's will is interfering with everything as I think God's will is somehow able to be responsible for everything. If I think God's will is overlapping, and co-existing along with everything, than I think God created everything with God's will because I think God's will is apart of God as I think God is somehow able to be responsible for creating everything, and therefore, I think God's will is overlapping, and co-existing along with everything because I think God created everything with God's will for God's will to be overlapping, and co-existing along with everything. If I think God's will is overlapping, and co-existing along with everything, than I think God created something with God's will because I think God's will is apart of God as I think God is somehow able to be responsible for creating something, and therefore, I think God's will is overlapping, and co-existing along with something because I think God created something with God's will for God's will to be overlapping, and co-existing along with something. If I think God's will is overlapping, and co-existing along with something, than I think God created someone with God's will because I think God's will is apart of God as I think God is somehow able to be responsible for creating everything, and therefore, I think God's will is overlapping, and co-existing along with someone because I think God created someone with God's will for God's will to be overlapping, and co-existing along with someone. If I think God's will is overlapping, and co-existing along with someone, than I think God, someone, and something is a choice for God to be choosing to be doing something with God, someone, and something because I think God has a will for God to be choosing to be doing something with God, someone, and something, and therefore, I think God has a will because I think God can choose to be doing something with God, someone, and something for God to be having a will. If I think God has a will, than I think God is somehow able to be responsible for God having a will because I think God's will is apart of God as I think God is somehow able to be responsible for creating everything, and therefore, I think God has a will because I think God's will is apart of God as I think God is somehow able to be responsible for creating everything.

Chapter 5

God's state of consciousness

I would like to talk about how dimensions are in life in relation to what dimensions are in life by talking about God's state of consciousness, that can possibly have something to do with how dimensions are in life is in relation to what dimensions are in life because I think God is somehow able to be responsible for God having a state of consciousness, and therefore, I think God's state of consciousness is how God is able to be doing what God is doing because I think God's state of consciousness is what God is able to be doing. If I think God's state of consciousness is how God is able to be doing what God is doing, than I think God's state of consciousness is taking place within God, without being God as I think God's state of consciousness is apart of God, without being God because I think God's state of consciousness is how God is able to be doing what God is doing, and therefore, I do not think God's state of consciousness is God because I think God's state of consciousness is taking place within God, without being God as I think God's state of consciousness is apart of God, without being God. If I do not think God's state of consciousness is God, than I think God's state of consciousness is apart of God for God to have a state of consciousness because I think God has a state of consciousness for God to be able to be doing what God is doing, and therefore, I think God's state of consciousness is apart of God for God to have a state of consciousness because I think God has a state of consciousness for God to be able to be doing what God is doing. If I think God's state of consciousness is apart of God for God to have a state of consciousness, than I think God has a state of consciousness because I think God's state of consciousness is how God is able to be doing what God is doing, and therefore, I think God's state of consciousness is a dimension because I think God's state of consciousness is something for God's state of consciousness to be a dimension. I think God's state of consciousness is something for God's state of consciousness to be a dimension because I think God's state of consciousness is how God is able to be doing what God is doing, and therefore, I think someone can think of God's state of consciousness as being the dimension of God's state of consciousness because I think the dimension of God's state of consciousness is how God is able to be doing what God is doing.

If I think the dimension of God's state of consciousness is how God is able to be doing what God is doing, than I think God's state of consciousness is apart of God because I think God has a state of consciousness for God to be able to be doing what God is doing, but I do not think God's state of consciousness is God because I think God's state of consciousness is how God is able to be doing what God is doing, and therefore, I think God's state of consciousness comes from God because I think God's state of consciousness is apart of God for God's state of consciousness to be coming from God, but I do not think God's state of consciousness is God because I think God's state of consciousness is how God is able to be doing what God is doing. I think God's state of consciousness is how God is able to be doing what God is doing because I do not think God would be able to be doing anything, without God having a state of consciousness. I do not think God would be able to be doing anything, without God having a state of consciousness because I think God not having a state of consciousness is like God not being able to somehow be responsible for everything in the universe as I think God is somehow able to be responsible for everything in the universe, and therefore, I think God's state of consciousness is how God is able to be a living being because I think God's state of consciousness is how God is able to be doing what

God is doing. If I think God's state of consciousness is how God is able to be a living being, than I think God's state of consciousness is somehow able to be responsible for everything in the universe because I think God's state of consciousness is apart of God as I think God is somehow able to be responsible for everything in the universe, and therefore, I think God's state of consciousness is how God is able to be doing what God is doing as I think God's state of consciousness is somehow able to be responsible for everything in the universe because I think God's state of consciousness is allowing for everything to be taking place in its own time and place in the universe. I think God's state of consciousness is allowing for everything to be taking place in its own time and place in the universe because I do not think God's state of consciousness is interfering with everything that can be taking place in its own time and place in the universe. I do not think God's state of consciousness is interfering with everything that can be taking place in its own time and place in the universe because I think everything is taking place in its own time and place in the universe for God's state of consciousness not to be interfering with everything that can be taking place in its own time and place in the universe, and therefore, I do not think God's state of consciousness has a choice with everything that can be taking place in its own time and place in the universe because I do not think God's state of consciousness is interfering with everything that can be taking place in its own time and place in the universe. If I do not think God's state of consciousness has a choice with everything that can be taking place in its own time and place in the universe, than I think God's state of consciousness is somehow able to be responsible for everything that can be taking place in its own time and place in the universe because I do not think God's state of consciousness is interfering with everything that can be taking place in its own time and place in the universe as I think God's state of consciousness is somehow able to be responsible for everything in the universe, and therefore, I think God's state of consciousness is beyond everything in the universe because I do not think God's state of consciousness is interfering with everything that can be taking place in its own time and place in the universe as I think God's state of consciousness is somehow able to be responsible for everything in the universe.

If I think God's state of consciousness is beyond everything in the universe, than I do not think God's state of consciousness is interfering with everything in the universe because I do not think God's state of consciousness is interfering with everything that can be taking place in its own time and place in the universe for God's state of consciousness not to be interfering with everything in the universe, and therefore, I think God's state of consciousness is always good, and right because I do not think God's state of consciousness is interfering with everything in the universe. If think God's state of consciousness is always good, and right, than I think God is always good, and right with God's state of consciousness because I do not think God's state of consciousness is interfering with everything in the universe as I think God's state of consciousness is apart of God, and therefore, I think God can do something that is always good, and right with God's state of consciousness because I think God is always good, and right with God's state of consciousness. If I think God can do something that is always good, and right with God's state of consciousness, than I think God's state of consciousness is overlapping, and co-existing along with everything in the universe because I do not think God's state of consciousness is interfering with everything in the universe as I think God's state of consciousness is somehow able to be responsible for everything in the universe, and therefore, I think God's state of consciousness is overlapping, and co-existing along with the universe because I do not think God's state of consciousness is interfering with everything in the universe as I think God's state of consciousness is somehow able to be responsible for everything in the universe. If I think God's state of consciousness is overlapping, and co-existing along with the universe, than I think God created everything in the universe with God's state of consciousness because I think God's state of consciousness is apart of God as I think God is somehow able to be responsible for creating everything, and therefore, I think God's state of consciousness is overlapping, and co-existing along with everything in the universe as I think God's state of consciousness is overlapping, and co-existing along with the universe because I think God created everything in the universe with God's state of consciousness for God's state of consciousness to be overlapping, and co-existing along with everything in the universe as I think God created everything in the universe with God's state of consciousness for God's state of consciousness to be overlapping, and co-existing along with the universe.

If I think God's state of consciousness is overlapping, and co-existing along with everything in the universe as I think God's state of consciousness is overlapping, and co-existing along with the universe, than I think God's state of consciousness is intellectually beyond someone's intelligence, as to what God's state of consciousness is in life because I do not think someone can be able to be knowing for themselves, as to how God is able to be doing what God is doing, even though, I think someone can try to understand for themselves, as to what God's state of consciousness in life because I think God's state of consciousness is how God is able to be doing what God is doing, however, I think God's state of consciousness is beyond someone because I think God's state of consciousness is intellectually beyond someone's intelligence, as to what God's state of consciousness is in life. If I think God's state of consciousness is beyond someone, than I think God's state of consciousness is somehow able to be responsible for everything because I think God's state of consciousness is apart of God as I think God is somehow able to be responsible for creating everything, and therefore, I think God's state of consciousness is in the exact same single dimension of God because I think God's state of consciousness is apart of God as I think God is somehow able to be responsible for creating everything. If I think God's state of consciousness is in the exact same single dimension of God, than I think everything is a creation of God as I think God's state of consciousness is apart of God because I think God's state of consciousness is apart of God as I think God is somehow able to be responsible for creating everything, and therefore, I think God's state of consciousness is apart of how God is able to be what God is in life as I think everything is a creation of how God is able to be what God is in life because I think God's state of consciousness is apart of God as I think God is somehow able to be responsible for creating everything. If I think God's state of consciousness is apart of how God is able to be what God is in life as I think everything is a creation of how God is able to be what God is in life, than I think God's state of consciousness is a creation of God as I think everything is a creation of God because I think God's state of consciousness is apart of God as I think God is somehow able to be responsible for creating everything, and therefore, I think God's state of consciousness is God's creation as I think everything is God's creation because I think God's state of consciousness is apart of God as I think God is somehow able to be responsible for creating everything.

If I think God's state of consciousness is God's creation as I think everything is God's creation, than I think God's state of consciousness is allowing for everything to be taking place in its own time and place because I do not think God's state of consciousness is interfering with everything that can be taking place in its own time and place. I do not think God's state of consciousness is interfering with everything that can be taking place in its own time and place because I think everything is taking place in its own time and place for God's state of consciousness not to be interfering with everything that can be taking place in its own time and place, and therefore, I do not think God's state of consciousness has a choice with everything that can be taking place in its own time and place because I do not think God's state of consciousness is interfering with everything that can be taking place in its own time and place. If I do not think God's state of consciousness has a choice with everything that can be taking place in its own time and place, than I think God's state of consciousness is somehow able to be responsible for everything that can be taking place in its own time and place because I do not think God's state of consciousness is interfering with everything that can be taking place in its own time and place as I think God's state of consciousness is somehow able to be responsible for everything, and therefore, I think God's state of consciousness is beyond everything because I do not think God's state of consciousness is interfering with everything that can be taking place in its own time and place as I think God's state of consciousness is somehow able to be responsible for everything. If I think God's state of consciousness is beyond everything, than I do not think God's state of consciousness is interfering with everything because I do not think God's state of consciousness is interfering with everything that can be taking place in its own time and place for God's state of consciousness not to be interfering with everything, and therefore, I think God's state of consciousness is always good, and right because I do not think God's state of consciousness is interfering with everything. If think God's state of consciousness is always good, and right, than I think God is always good, and right with God's state of consciousness because I do not think God's state of consciousness is interfering with everything as I think God's state of consciousness is apart of God, and therefore, I think God's state of consciousness is overlapping, and co-existing along with everything because I do not think God's state of consciousness is interfering with everything as I think God's state of consciousness is somehow able to be responsible for everything. If I think God's state of consciousness is overlapping, and co-existing along with everything, than I think God created everything with God's state of consciousness because I think God's state of consciousness is apart of God as I think God is somehow able to be responsible for creating everything, and therefore, I think God's state of consciousness is overlapping, and co-existing along with everything because I think God created everything with God's state of consciousness for God's state of consciousness to be overlapping, and co-existing along with everything. If I think God's state of consciousness is overlapping, and co-existing along with everything, than I think God created something with God's state of consciousness because I think God's state of consciousness is apart of God as I think God is somehow able to be responsible for creating something, and therefore, I think God's state of consciousness is overlapping, and co-existing along with something because I think God created something with God's state of consciousness for God's state of consciousness to be overlapping, and co-existing along with something. If I think God's state of consciousness is overlapping, and co-existing along with something, than I think God created someone with God's state of consciousness because I think God's state of consciousness is apart of God as I think God is somehow able to be responsible for creating everything, and therefore, I think God's state of consciousness is overlapping, and co-existing along with someone because I think God created someone with God's state of consciousness for God's state of consciousness to be overlapping, and co-existing along with someone.

If I think God's state of consciousness is overlapping, and co-existing along with someone, than I think God has a state of consciousness as I think God has a will because I think God has a state of consciousness for God's will. I think God has a state of consciousness for God's will because I think God has a choice of God, someone, and something for God to be having a state of consciousness for God's will. I think God has a choice of God, someone, and something for God to be having a state of consciousness for God's will because I think God can choose to be doing something with God, someone, and something for God to be having a state of consciousness for God's will. I think God can choose to be doing something with God, someone, and something for God to be having a state of consciousness for God's will because I think God is aware of God choosing to be doing something with God, someone, and something for God to be having a state of consciousness for God's will. I think God is aware of God choosing to be doing something with God, someone, and something for God to be having a state of consciousness for God's will because I think God has a state of consciousness with God's will for God to be aware of God choosing to be doing something with God, someone, and something. I think God has a state of consciousness with God's will for God to be aware of God choosing to be doing something with God, someone, and something because I think God has a state of consciousness for God's will. I think God has a state of consciousness for God's will because I think God is aware of what God is doing for God to be having a state of consciousness with God's will. I think God is aware of what God is doing for God to be having a state of consciousness with God's will because I think God will do what God is doing from God being aware of what God is doing, and therefore, I think God has a state of consciousness with God's will because I think God has a state of consciousness as I think God has a will. I think God has a state of consciousness as I think God has a will because I think God has a state of consciousness for what God is doing with God's will, and therefore, I think God has a state of consciousness because I think God has a state of consciousness for what God is doing with God's will. If I think God has a state of consciousness, than I think God has a state of consciousness for God's will because I think God has a state of consciousness for what God is doing with God's will. I think God has a state of consciousness for what God is doing with God's will because I think God has a state of consciousness for God to be aware of what God is doing with God's will. I think God has a state of consciousness for God to be aware of what God is doing with God's will because I think God has a state of consciousness for God to be aware of what God is doing. I think God has a state of consciousness for God to be aware of what God is doing because I think God has a state of consciousness for what God is doing. I think God has a state of consciousness for what God is doing because I think God has a state of consciousness for God's will as I think God's will is what God is doing, and therefore, I think God's will is overlapping, and co-existing along with God's state of consciousness because I think God has state of consciousness for God to be aware of what God is doing with God's will.

If I think God's will is overlapping, and co-existing along with God's state of consciousness, than I think God's state of consciousness is God's awareness because I think how God is able to be doing what God is doing with God's state of consciousness is how God is able to be aware of what God is doing. I think how God is able to be doing what God is doing with God's state of consciousness is how God is able to be aware of what God is doing because I think God is consciously aware of what God is doing with God's state of consciousness, and therefore, I think God's state of consciousness is God's state of awareness because I think God's state of consciousness is how God is able to be doing what God is doing as I think God's state of awareness is how God is able to be doing what God is doing. If I think God's state of consciousness is God's state of awareness, than I think God's state of consciousness is God's sense of awareness as I think God's state of awareness is God's sense of awareness because I think God's state of consciousness is God's state of awareness as I think God's sense of awareness is how God is able to be doing what God is doing, and therefore, I think God is constantly aware of what God is doing as I think God is aware of what God is doing because I think God is aware of what God is doing with God's state of consciousness for God to constantly be aware of what God is doing. If I think God is constantly aware of what God is doing as I think God is aware of what God is doing, than I think God has a state of consciousness for God to be intelligent because I do not think God can be able to be thinking of anything, and I do not think God can be able to be doing anything, without God having a state of consciousness for God to be aware of what God is thinking, and doing as I think God is aware of what God is thinking, and doing with God having a state of consciousness for God to be intelligent, and therefore, I think God's state of consciousness is how God is able to be intelligent because I think God can be aware of what God is doing with God having a state of consciousness for God having a state of consciousness to be how God is able to be intelligent. If I think God's state of consciousness is how God is able to be intelligent, than I think God is somehow able to be responsible for God having a state of consciousness because I think God's state of consciousness is apart of God as I think God is somehow able to be responsible for creating everything, and therefore, I think God has a state of consciousness because I think God's state of consciousness is apart of God as I think God is somehow able to be responsible for creating everything.

Chapter 6

God's thoughts

I would like to talk about how dimensions are in life in relation to what dimensions are in life by talking about God's thoughts, that can possibly have something to do with how dimensions are in life is in relation to what dimensions are in life because I think everything is somehow able to be a creation of God as I think God is somehow able to be responsible for creating everything, and therefore, how can everything possibly be able to be a creation of God as I think God is somehow able to be responsible for creating everything? I do not think I will ever be able to be knowing for myself, as to how everything can possibly be able to be a creation of God as I think God is somehow able to be responsible for creating everything, but I think God is somehow able to be responsible for creating everything because I think God is somehow able to be knowing, as to how everything is able to be created in life, and therefore, I think everything is somehow able to be created with God's thoughts because I think God is somehow able to be knowing, as to how everything is able to be created in life. If I think everything is somehow able to be made with God's thoughts, than I think God created everything with God's thoughts because I think God is somehow able to be knowing, as to how everything is able to be created in life, and therefore, I think God has thoughts because I think God created everything with God's thoughts for God to be having thoughts. If I think God has thoughts, than I think everything is a collection of thoughts that is somehow able to be made from the creation of God's thoughts that is apart of making up everything because I think God created everything with God's thoughts, and therefore, I think each and every thought that is somehow able to be made from the creation of God's thoughts that is apart of making up everything is somehow able to be made from God because I think how God is able to be God is how God is able to be creating God's thoughts from God. If I think how God is able to be God is how God is able to be creating God's thoughts from God, than I think God created everything with God's thoughts because I think everything is created by God for God to be creating everything with God's thoughts, and therefore, I think God created everything because I think God created everything with God's thoughts for God to be creating everything.

If I think God created everything, than I think God created everything to be overlapping, and co-existing along with everything because I think God created everything with God's thoughts for God to be creating everything to be overlapping, and co-existing along with everything, even though, I think someone can ask themselves is God a thought for God to be creating everything with God's thoughts? I do not think God is a thought for God to be creating everything with God's thoughts because I do not think a thought can create any other thought for God to be creating everything with God's thoughts as I do not think a thought can create any other thought for God not to be a thought, and therefore, I do not think a thought can create any other thought because I think a thought alike any other thought for a thought not to be creating any other thought. If I do not think a thought can create any other thought, than I think a thought is created because I do not think a thought can create any other thought for a thought to be created, and therefore, I do not think God is a thought for God to be creating everything with God's thoughts because I think a thought is created for God to be creating everything with God's thoughts as I think a thought is created for God not to be a thought. If I do not think God is a thought for God to be creating everything with God's thoughts, than I think a thought is created from God because I do not think God is a thought for God to be creating everything with God's thoughts, and therefore, I think God is beyond all thoughts because I think God created everything with God's thoughts for God to be beyond all thoughts. If I think God is beyond all thoughts, than I think everything is somehow able to be made from the creation of God's thoughts that is apart of making up everything because I do not think God is a thought for God to be creating everything with God's thoughts, and therefore, I think God created everything with God's thoughts because I do not think God is a thought for God to be creating everything with God's thoughts. If I think God created everything with God's thoughts, than I think a thought is any thought because I think any thought is a thought, and therefore, I think any thought is how any thought is able to be a thought because I think how any thought is able to be a thought is any thought. If I think any thought is how any thought is able to be a thought, than I think any thought is how any thought is able to be a thought as I think how any thought is able to be a thought is any thought because I think God is somehow able to be responsible for any thought as I think God is somehow able to be responsible for how any thought is able to be a thought. I think God is somehow able to be responsible for any thought as I think God is somehow able to be responsible for how any thought is able to be a thought because I think God created everything with God's thoughts, and therefore, I do not think God can be able to be creating everything from God being a thought for everything to be a thought because I do not think God is a thought for God to be creating everything with God's thoughts. If I do not think God can be able to be creating everything from God being a thought for everything to be a thought, than I do not think God is a thought because I think a thought is created from God for God not to be a thought, and therefore, I do not think God is a creation of itself because I do not think God is a thought for God not to be a creation of itself. I do not think God is a thought for God not to be a creation of itself because I think if God is a thought for God to be a creation of itself, than I think God would be a creation of itself from God being a thought, but I do not think God is a creation of itself from God being a thought because I do not think God is a thought for God not to be a creation of itself from God being a thought, and therefore, I do not think God is a thought for God not to be a creation of itself because I think God created everything with God's thoughts for God to be beyond all thoughts. If I do not think God is a thought for God not to be a creation of itself, than I think God is someone that is something of itself, that is somehow able to be creating everything somehow with God's thoughts because I think God is someone that is something of itself, that is somehow able to be beyond everything as I think everything is a thought, and therefore, I think everything is God's thoughts because I think God created everything with God's thoughts for everything to be God's thoughts.

If I think everything is God's thoughts, than I think someone can think God is a thought as I think someone can think God is a figment of someone's imagination because I think someone can think God doesn't exist, but I do not think God is a thought as I do not think God is a figment of someone's imagination because I think everything is intellectually beyond someone's imagination, as to how everything is able to be taking place in life, and therefore, I do not think God is a thought that is a figment of someone's imagination because I think God is someone that is something of itself, that is somehow able to be responsible for everything, even though, I think someone can think God doesn't exist because I think someone can think life is an illusion or a dream or a fantasy, however, where did all of the thoughts come from that is apart of making up everything, and that is including all of the thoughts that someone can possibly be able to be thinking for someone to be thinking life is an illusion or a dream or a fantasy? I think all of the thoughts that is apart of making up everything somehow must have come from God as I think God is someone that is something of itself, that is somehow able to be responsible for everything because I think if all of the thoughts that is apart of making up everything didn't somehow come from God as I think God is someone that is something of itself, that is somehow able to be responsible for everything, than I think all of the thoughts that is apart of making up everything would be an illusion or a dream or a fantasy because I think all of the thoughts that is apart of making up everything has come from nothing, and therefore, I think all of the thoughts that is apart of making up everything would be nothing because I think all of the thoughts that is apart of making up everything has come from nothing, but I do not think all of the thoughts that is apart of making up everything is nothing because I think all of the thoughts that is apart of making up everything is constantly something. I think all of the thoughts that is apart of making up everything is constantly something because I think all of the thoughts that is apart of making up everything is something that is constantly something, and therefore, I think all of the thoughts that is apart of making up everything somehow must have come from something because I think all of the thoughts that is apart of making up everything is something. If I think all of the thoughts that is apart of making up everything somehow must have come from something, than I think all of the thoughts that is apart of making up everything somehow must have come from God because I think God is someone that is something of itself, that is somehow able to be responsible for everything, and therefore, I do not think all of the thoughts that is apart of making up everything is an illusion or a dream or a fantasy because I think all of the thoughts that is apart of making up everything is constantly something. If I do not think all of the thoughts that is apart of making up everything is an illusion or a dream or a fantasy, than I think everything is constantly something because I think all of the thoughts that is apart of making up everything is constantly something, and therefore, I do not think life is an illusion or a dream or a fantasy because I think everything is constantly something for life not to be an illusion or a dream or a fantasy. If I do not think life is an illusion or a dream or a fantasy, than I think someone can think life is an illusion or a dream or a fantasy because I think someone can think all of the thoughts that can be apart of making up everything could have somehow come from God's imagination for life to be an illusion or a dream or a fantasy. I think someone can think all of the thoughts that can be apart of making up everything could have somehow come from God's imagination for life to be an illusion or a dream or a fantasy because I think God created everything with God's thoughts for life to be an illusion or a dream or a fantasy, and therefore, I think God created everything with God's imagination because I think God created everything with God's thoughts for God to be creating everything with God's imagination, even though, I do not life is an illusion or a dream or a fantasy because I think everything is happening for a reason with how everything is in life. I think everything is happening for a reason with how everything is in life because I think all of the thoughts that is apart of making up everything is how everything is happening for a reason, and therefore, I think God created everything to be happening for a reason with how everything is in life because I think God is creating everything with God's thoughts for everything to be happening for a reason with how everything is in life.

If I think God created everything to be happening for a reason with how everything is in life, than I think any thought is God's choice with how any thought is able to be a thought as I think any thought is apart of making up everything because I do not think any thought is able to be having a choice with how any thought is able to be a thought as I think any thought is apart of making up everything, and therefore, I think any thought is God's choice with how any thought is able to be a thought because I think any thought is of God's thoughts with how any thought is able to be a thought. If I think any thought is God's choice with how any thought is able to be a thought, than I think how any thought is able to be a thought is a choice of itself with how any thought is able to be a thought as I think how any thought is able to be a thought is God's choice with how any thought is able to be a thought because I think any thought is a choice of itself with how any thought is able to be a thought as I think any thought is God's choice with how any thought is able to be a thought, and therefore, I think any thought is a choice of itself with how any thought is able to be a thought as I think any thought is apart of making up everything because I think any thought is God's choice with how any thought is able to be a thought as I think any thought is apart of making up everything. If I think any thought is a choice of itself with how any thought is able to be a thought as I think any thought is apart of making up everything, than I think any thought that someone can possibly be able to thinking about in someone's life is a choice of itself with how any thought is able to be a thought because I think any thought is a choice of itself with how any thought is able to be a thought as I think any thought is apart of making up everything, and therefore, I think any thought that someone can possibly be able to thinking about in someone's life is of God's thoughts as I think any thought that someone can possibly be able to thinking about in someone's life is a choice of itself with how any thought is able to be a thought because I do not think any thought is someone's choice with how any thought is able to be a thought as I do not think any thought that someone can possibly be able to thinking about in someone's life is someone's choice with how any thought is able to be a thought. If I think any thought that someone can possibly be able to thinking about in someone's life is of God's thoughts as I think any thought that someone can possibly be able to thinking about in someone's life is a choice of itself with how any thought is able to be a thought, than I think any thought is of God's thoughts with how any thought is able to be a thought as I think any thought is choice of itself with how any thought is able to be a thought because I think any thought is God's choice with how any thought is able to be a thought as I think any thought is apart of making up everything, and therefore, I think any thought is a choice of itself with how any thought is able to be a thought because I think any thought is of God's thoughts with how any thought is able to be a thought as I think any thought is God's choice with how any thought is able to be a thought. If I think any thought is a choice of itself with how any thought is able to be a thought, than I think any thought is a choice of itself with any thought that is apart of making up how everything is in life because I think any thought is of God's thoughts with any thought that is apart of making up how everything is in life as I think any thought is God's choice with any thought that is apart of making up how everything is in life, and therefore, I think any thought is a choice of itself with how any thought is able to be a thought as I think any thought is apart of making up how everything is in life because I think any thought is a choice of itself with any thought that is apart of making up how everything is in life.

If I think any thought is a choice of itself with any thought that is apart of making up how everything is in life, than I think any thought is constantly something as I think everything is constantly something because I think any thought is apart of making up everything as I think everything is any thought that is apart of making up everything, and therefore, I think any thought is how everything is constantly something because I think any thought is everything as I think any thought is apart of making up everything. If I think any thought is how everything is constantly something, than I think any thought is how everything is constantly something as I think God's thoughts is how everything is constantly something because I think any thought is apart of making up everything as I think any thought is of God's thoughts that is apart of making up everything, even though, I do not think someone can possibly be able to be knowing for themselves, as to how any thought is able to be a thought as I think any thought is apart of making up everything because I do not think someone can possibly be able to be knowing for themselves, as to how any thought is able to be of God's thoughts that is apart of making up everything, but I think any thought somehow must have come from God as I think everything somehow must have come from God because I think any thought is of God's thoughts that is apart of making up everything as I think God is someone that is something of itself, that is somehow able to be responsible for everything. If I think any thought somehow must have come from God as I think everything somehow must have come from God, than I think God is beyond any thought as I think God is beyond all thoughts because I do not think any thought is able to be having a choice with how any thought is able to be a thought as I think any thought is apart of making up everything, and therefore, I think any thought is of God's thoughts as I think any thought is apart of making up everything because I think any thought is God's choice with how any thought is able to be a thought as I think any thought is apart of making up everything. If I think any thought is of God's thoughts as I think any thought is apart of making up everything, than I think any thought is a choice of itself with how any thought is able to be a thought as I think any thought is apart of making up everything because I do not think any thought is able to be having a choice with how any thought is able to be a thought as I think any thought is apart of making up everything, and therefore, I think God is beyond any thought as I think God is beyond all thoughts because I think any thought is a choice of itself with how any thought is able to be a thought as I think any thought is apart of making up everything. If I think God is beyond any thought as I think God is beyond all thoughts, than I do not think God is interfering with any thought as I think any thought is apart of making up everything because I think any thought is a choice of itself with how any thought is able to be a thought as I think any thought is apart of making up everything, and therefore, I think God is beyond any thought as I think God is beyond all thoughts because I do not think God is interfering with any thought as I think any thought is apart of making up everything. If I think God is beyond any thought as I think God is beyond all thoughts, than I do not think God is interfering with God's thoughts as I do not think God is interfering with any thought because I think any thought is of God's thoughts as I think any thought is apart of making up everything, and therefore, I do not think God is interfering with any thought as I do not think God is interfering with everything because I do not God is interfering with any thought that can be taking place in its own time and place as I do not think God is interfering with everything that can be taking place in its own time and place. If I do not think God is interfering with any thought as I do not think God is interfering with everything, than I do not think God is interfering with any thought as I think any thought is apart of making up everything because I think any thought can be taking place in its own time and place as I think any thought is apart of making up everything that can be taking place in its own time and place, and therefore, I think any thought is somehow taking place within God, without being God as I think any thought is apart of God, without being God because I do not think God is interfering with any thought as I think any thought is apart of making up everything.

If I do not think God is interfering with any thought as I think any thought is apart of making up everything, than I think God is someone that is something of itself, that is somehow able to be beyond any thought as I think God is someone that is something of itself, that is somehow able to be beyond everything because I think God is someone that is something of itself, that is somehow able to be responsible for any thought as I think God is someone that is something of itself, that is somehow able to be responsible for everything. I think God is someone that is something of itself, that is somehow able to be responsible for any thought as I think God is someone that is something of itself, that is somehow able to be responsible everything because I think any thought is God's choice with how any thought is able to be a thought as I think everything is God's choice with how everything is able to be taking place in life. I think any thought is God's choice with how any thought is able to be a thought as I think everything is God's choice with how everything is able to be taking place in life because I think God is someone that is something of itself, that is somehow able to be responsible for any thought as I think any thought is apart of making up everything, and therefore, I think any thought is apart of making up everything because I think any thought is a thought as I think a thought is apart of making up everything for any thought to be apart of making up everything. If I think a thought is apart of making up everything for any thought to be apart of making up everything, than I think everything first came from a thought as I think everything is of a thought because I think everything is a thought as I think a thought is apart of making up everything, and therefore, I think God is someone that is something of itself, that is somehow able to be beyond any thought as I think God is someone that is something of itself, that is somehow able to be beyond everything because I think God is someone that is something of itself, that is somehow able to be responsible for any thought as I think any thought is apart of making up everything.

If I think God is someone that is something of itself, that is somehow able to be beyond any thought as I think God is someone that is something of itself, that is somehow able to be beyond everything, than I do not think God is created as I think God is someone that is something of itself, that is somehow able to be responsible for everything because I do not think God is someone that is something of itself, that is somehow able to be created from a thought as I think a thought is any thought that is apart of making up everything. I do not think God is someone that is something of itself, that is somehow able to be created from a thought as I think a thought is any thought that is apart of making up everything because I think God is someone that is something of itself, that is somehow able to be beyond any thought as I think any thought is apart of making up everything, and therefore, I do not think God is a creation of any other God that is someone that is something of itself because I do not think God is someone that is something of itself, that is somehow able to be created from a thought, that is of any other God that is someone that is something of itself as I do not think God is someone that is something of itself, that is somehow able to be created from a thought. If I do not think God is a creation of any other God that is someone that is something of itself, than I do not think God is a creation of itself because I do not think God is someone that is something of itself, that is somehow able to be created from a thought for God not to be a creation of itself, and therefore, I think God is someone that is something of itself, that is somehow able to be whatever God is in life, that is somehow able to be responsible for everything as I think God is how God is able to be what God is in life because I do not think God is someone that is something of itself, that is somehow able to be created from a thought as I think a thought is any thought that is apart of making up everything. If I do not think God is someone that is something of itself, that is somehow able to be created from a thought as I think a thought is any thought that is apart of making up everything, than I do not think God is created as I think God is someone that is something of itself, that is somehow able to be responsible for everything because I do not think God is someone that is something of itself, that is somehow able to be created from a thought as I think a thought is any thought that is apart of making up everything, and therefore, I do not think God is a creation of God's thoughts as I think God's thoughts is any thought that is apart of making up everything because I think God is creating everything with God's thoughts for everything to be taking place within God as I think God is someone that is something of itself, that is somehow able to be whatever God is life, that is somehow able to be responsible for everything. If I do not think God is a creation of God's thoughts as I think God's thoughts is any thought that is apart of making up everything, than I do not think God is taking place within anything as I do not think God is taking place within everything because I think God is creating everything with God's thoughts for everything to be taking place within God, and therefore,

I do not think God is living anywhere because I do not think God is taking place within everything for God not to living anywhere. If I do not think God is living anywhere, than I think God is somehow able to be living beyond everything because I think God is beyond everything as I think God is somehow able to be responsible for creating everything, and therefore, I think everything is living or residing within God because I think God created everything with God's thoughts that is apart of making up everything for everything to be living or residing within God. If I think everything is living or residing within God, than I think God is somehow able to be responsible for creating everything because I think God created everything with God's thoughts for God to somehow be able to be responsible for creating everything, and therefore, I think God's thoughts is somehow taking place within God, without being God as I think God's thoughts is apart of God, without being God because I think God created everything with God's thoughts that is apart of making up everything for everything to be living or residing within God. If I think God's thoughts is somehow taking place within God, without being God as I think God's thoughts is apart of God, without being God, than I do not think God is interfering with God's thoughts as I think God's thoughts is apart of making up everything because I think God's thoughts can be taking place in its own time and place as I think God's thoughts is apart of making up everything that can be taking place in its own time and place, and therefore, I think God's thoughts is somehow taking place within God, without being God as I think God's thoughts is apart of God, without being God because I do not think God is interfering with God's thoughts as I think God's thoughts is apart of making up everything.

If I do not think God is interfering with God's thoughts as I think God's thoughts is apart of making up everything, than I do not think God needs to be having any trial and error with God's thoughts for God to be able to be creating everything with God's thoughts because I think God is always good, and right as I think God is somehow able to be creating everything with God's thoughts, and therefore, I do not think God needs to question anything that God created with God's thoughts because I do not think God needs to be having any trial and error with God's thoughts for God to be able to be creating everything with God's thoughts. If I do not think God needs to question anything that God created with God's thoughts, than I do not think God makes any mistakes because I think God is always good, and right as I think God is somehow able to be creating everything with God's thoughts, and therefore, I do not think everything all comes down to what the very first thought is in life that is apart of making up everything as I think everything all comes down to God that is somehow able to be responsible for everything because I think God is someone that is something of itself, that is somehow able to be whatever God is life, that is somehow able to be responsible for everything. If I think God is someone that is something of itself, that is somehow able to be whatever God is life, that is somehow able to be responsible for everything, than I think God is in life as I think everything is in life because I think God is someone that is something of itself, that is somehow able to be whatever God is in life, that is somehow able to be responsible for everything. I think God is someone that is something of itself, that is somehow able to be whatever God is in life, that is somehow able to be responsible for everything because I think God is someone that is something of itself, that is somehow able to be beyond any thought as I think any thought is apart of making up everything, and therefore, I think God is whatever God is in life as I think God is someone that is something of itself, that is somehow able to be whatever God is in life because I think God is whatever God is in life as I think God is someone that is something of itself. If I think God is whatever God is in life as I think God is someone that is something of itself, than I think God is in life as I think God is whatever God is in life because I think God is whatever God is in life as I think God is someone that is something of itself, that is somehow able to be whatever God is in life, and therefore, I think God is nothing as I think God is someone that something of itself because I think God is in life as I think God is whatever God is in life. If I think God is nothing as I think God is someone that something of itself, than I think God is something as I think God is nothing because I think God is in life as I think God is whatever God is in life, and therefore, I think everything is created from something as I think everything is created from nothing because I think everything is created by God as I think God is something, and nothing. If I think everything is created from something as I think everything is created from nothing, than I think someone can think of God as being itself because I think the word it in the word itself is implying that God is something as I think the word self in the word itself is implying that God is someone. I think the word it in the word itself is implying that God is something as I think the word self in the word itself is implying that God is someone because I think God is someone that is something for someone to be thinking of God as being itself as I think God is someone that is something of itself, even though, I think God is something as I think God is someone because I think the words some and one in the word someone is something for God to be something as I think God is someone, however, I think God is someone because I think God is an intelligent living being for God to be someone, and therefore, I think God is someone that is something of itself because I think God is someone and something for God to be someone that is something of itself. If I think God is someone that is something of itself, than I think God is intelligent because I think God created everything for God to be intelligent, and therefore, I think God being intelligent strongly indicates that God is someone because I think God created everything from God being intelligent for God to be someone.

If I think God being intelligent strongly indicates that God is someone, than I do not think God is created as I do not think God is a creation of itself because I think God is something as I think God is whatever God is in life. I think God is something as I think God is whatever God is in life because I think God is something of itself as I think God is whatever God is in life. I think God is something of itself as I think God is whatever God is in life because I do not think God is of something of itself as I think God is something of itself. I do not think God is of something of itself as I think God is something of itself because I do not think God is a creation of itself for God to be of something of itself. I do not think God is a creation of itself for God to be of something of itself because I do not think God is created for God not to be a creation of itself. I do not think God is created for God not to be a creation of itself because I think God is something as I think God is whatever God is in life. I think God is something as I think God is whatever God is in life because I do not think God is of something as I think God is something. I do not think God is of something as I think God is something because I think something is of God as I think God is something. I think something is of God as I think God is something because I think God is something as I think God is whatever God is in life, and therefore, I do not think God is created as I do not think God is a creation of itself because I think God is someone as I think God is something. I think God is someone as I think God is something because I think God is someone as I think God is whatever God is in life. I think God is someone as I think God is whatever God is in life because I think God is someone of itself as I think God is whatever God is in life. I think God is someone of itself as I think God is whatever God is in life because I do not think God is of someone of itself as I think God is someone of itself. I do not think God is of someone of itself as I think God is someone of itself because I do not think God is a creation of itself for God to be of someone of itself. I do not think God is a creation of itself for God to be of someone of itself because I do not think God is created for God not to be a creation of itself. I do not think God is created for God not to be a creation of itself because I think God is someone as I think God is whatever

God is in life, and therefore, I think God is someone as I think God is something because I think God is in life as I think God is whatever God is in life. I think God is in life as I think God is whatever God is in life because I think God is somehow able to be someone that is something of itself as I think God is someone that is something of itself, that is somehow able to be whatever God is in life. I think God is somehow able to be someone that is something of itself as I think God is someone that is something of itself, that is somehow able to be whatever God is in life because I think God is someone as I think God is whatever God is in life. I think God is someone as I think God is whatever God is in life because I do not think God is of someone as I think God is something. I do not think God is of someone as I think God is something because I think someone is of God as I think God is something. I think someone is of God as I think God is something because I think God is someone as I think God is whatever God is in life.

If I think someone is of God as I think God is something, than I do not think something can represent God because I do not think God is something for something to be representing God. I do not think God is something for something to be representing God because I do not think God is of something for something to be representing God. I do not think God is of something for something to be representing God because I think something is of God as I think God is somehow able to be responsible for something. I think something is of God as I think God is somehow able to be responsible for something because I think everything is something as I think God is somehow able to be responsible for everything. I think everything is something as I think God is somehow able to be responsible for everything because I think something is apart of making up everything as I think God is somehow able to be responsible for everything, and therefore, I think something is of God as I think God is somehow able to be responsible for everything because I think God is whatever God is in life as I think God is somehow able to be responsible for everything. If I think something is of God as I think God is somehow able to be responsible for everything, than I do not think something can represent God because I think God is whatever God is in life as I think God is somehow able to be responsible for everything, and therefore, I do not think God is something for something to be representing God because I think God is whatever God is in life as I think God is somehow able to be responsible for everything. If I do not think God is something for something to be representing God, than I do not think God is someone or something for someone to idolizing or worshipping God because I do not think God is of someone or something for someone to be idolizing or worshipping God. I do not think God is of someone or something for someone to be idolizing or worshipping God because I think God is someone that is always there for someone as I think God is everywhere with someone, and therefore, I do not think God is someone or something for someone to be kneeling down to God because I do not think God is of someone or something for someone to be kneeling down to God, even though, I think someone can kneel down to God because I think someone can acknowledge to themselves and God, as to how important God is to someone from someone kneeling down to God, but I do not think someone has to be acknowledging to themselves and God, as to how important God is to someone from kneeling down to God because I do not think someone kneeling down to God is a prerequisite or a requirement for someone to be acknowledging to themselves and God, as to how important God is to someone. I do not think someone kneeling down to God is a prerequisite or a requirement for someone to be acknowledging to themselves and God, as to how important God is to someone because I think God is always important to everyone, without someone having to be kneeling down to God. I think God is always important to everyone, without someone having to be kneeling down to God because I do not think someone has to be kneeling down to God for God to be important to someone, and therefore, I think someone can very simply be thankful to God with someone acknowledging to themselves and God, as to how important God is to someone because I think God is someone that is always there for someone as I think God is everywhere with someone for God to always be important to everyone, however, I do not think someone has to be summiting themselves to God from someone kneeling down to God because I think someone can live by God's example from someone trying to be good like God.

If I do not think someone has to be summiting themselves to God from someone kneeling down to God, than I think all history is God's history because I think God created everything for all history to be God's history, and therefore, I think the history of life is God's history because I think all history is God's history for the history of life to be God's history. If I think the history of life is God's history, than I do not think God has a history as I think God is someone that is something of itself, that is somehow able to be responsible for how everything is able to be taking place in life because I do not think God is created for God not to be having a history, and therefore, I do not think God has an age, as to how young, and how old God can possibly be in life because I do not think God is created for God not to be having an age, as to how young, and how old God can possibly be in life. If I do not think God has an age in life, as to how young, and how old God can possibly be in life, than I think someone can question, as to where God has come from, even though, I do not think someone can question, as to where God has come from because I do think God is created for someone not to question, as to where God has come from, and therefore, I do not think God has a beginning and an end because I do not think God is created for God not to be having a beginning and an end. If I do not think God has a beginning and an end, than I do not think God has an age because I do not think God is created for God to have an age, and therefore, I think someone can think of God as being a being or as being a spirit or as being an entity, however, I do not know if God is a spirit or an entity as I think God is a being because I think God is someone that is something of itself, that is somehow able to be whatever God is in life, that is somehow able to be responsible for everything for God to be a being. If I do not know if God is a spirit or an entity as I think God is a being, than I do not think someone can possibly be able to have any conception, as to what God is in life because I do not think someone can possibly be able to know what God is in life for someone to be able to have any conception, as to what God is in life, and therefore, I think God is beyond someone's imagination, as to what someone thinks God is in life because I do not think someone can possibly be able to conceive, as to what God is in life for someone not to be able to have any conception, as to what someone thinks God is in life. I do not think someone can possibly be able to conceive, as to what God is in life for someone not to be able to have any conception, as to what someone thinks God is in life because I do not think God is created for someone not to be able to have any conception, as to what God is in life. I do not think God is created for someone not to be able to have any conception, as to what God is in life because I think God is in life as I think God is whatever God is in life for God to be what God is in life, and therefore, I think everything is created from God not being created because if I think everything is created from God being created, than I think God would be created from everything being created, but I do not think God is created from everything being created because I do not think God is created for God not to be created from everything being created, and therefore, I think everything would have to be created from God not being created for everything to be created because I do not think God is created for everything to be created by God. If I think everything would have to be created from God not being created for everything to be created, than I do not think someone can think of God as being a creature or a species because I do not think God is created for God not to be a creature or a species as I think God is whatever God is that is somehow able to be responsible for everything, and therefore, I think God is infinite because I do not think God is created as I think God is whatever God is in life for God to be infinite.

If I think God is infinite, than I think any thought is a dimension that is overlapping, and co-existing along with God because I think any thought is something that is completely different from God that is something. I think any thought is something that is completely different from God that is something because I think any thought is God's choice with how any thought is able to be a thought as I think any thought is somehow able to be created within God, without being God, and therefore, I think any thought is taking place within God, without being God as I think any thought is apart of God, without being God because I think any thought is of God's thoughts, without being God as I think any thought is God's choice with how any thought is able to be a thought, and therefore, I think any thought is overlapping, and co-existing along with God because I think any thought is taking place within God, without being God as I think any thought is apart of God, without being God. If I think any thought is overlapping, and co-existing along with God, than I think someone can think of any thought as being the dimension of thought as I think someone can think of how any thought is able to be a thought as being the dimension of thought because I think any thought is how any thought is able to be a thought. I think any thought is how any thought is able to be a thought of itself because I think the dimension of thought is any thought as I think any thought is apart of making up everything, and therefore, I think the dimension of thought is the dimension of God's thoughts because I think the dimension of thought is any thought that is apart of making up everything as I think the dimension of God's thoughts is any thought that is apart of making up everything. If I think the dimension of thought is the dimension of God's thoughts, than I think God's thoughts is infinity as I think God's thoughts is incalculable because I do not think someone can possibly be able to be knowing for themselves, as to what God's thoughts are in life as I think God's thoughts is apart of making up everything, and therefore, I think what someone thinks of something is subjective, as to what someone thinks something is in life, and not objective, as to what someone thinks something is in life because I do not think someone can possibly be able to be knowing for themselves, as to what any thought is in life that is apart of making up everything as I think what any thought is in life that is apart of making up everything is God's thoughts that is apart of making up everything.

If I think what someone thinks of something is subjective, as to what someone thinks something is in life, and not objective, as to what someone thinks something is in life, than I think the dimension of God's thoughts is overlapping, and co-existing along with God as I think the dimension of thought is overlapping, and co-existing along with God because I think the dimension of thought is the dimension of God's thoughts as I think God's thoughts is God's choice with what God's thoughts are in life. I think the dimension of thought is the dimension of God's thoughts as I think God's thoughts is God's choice with what God's thoughts are in life because I think God's thoughts is any thought as I think any thought is God's choice with how any thought is able to be a thought of itself, and therefore, I think God's thoughts is taking place within God, without being God as I think God's thoughts is apart of God, without being God because I think God's thoughts is any thought as I think any thought is God's choice with how any thought is able to be a thought of itself. If I think God's thoughts is taking place within God, without being God as I think God's thoughts is apart of God, without being God, than I think God's thoughts is overlapping, and co-existing along with God because I think God's thoughts is any thought as I think any thought is God's choice with how any thought is able to be a thought of itself, and therefore, I think

God's state of consciousness is overlapping, and co-existing along with God's thoughts because I think God thinks of God's thoughts with God's state of consciousness. I think God thinks of God's thoughts with God's state of consciousness because I think God's state of consciousness is how God is able to be doing what God is doing as I think God's state of consciousness is how God is able to be thinking of God's thoughts, and therefore, I think God's will is overlapping, and co-existing along with God's thoughts because I think God thinks of God's thoughts with God's will. I think God thinks of God's thoughts with God's will because I think God's will is how God is doing what God is doing as I think God's will is how God is thinking of God's thoughts, and therefore, I think how God is doing what God is doing with God's will is how God is thinking what God is thinking with God's thoughts because I think God's will is somehow able to be responsible for any thought as I think God's will is somehow able to be responsible for everything. If I think how God is doing what God is doing with God's will is how God is thinking what God is thinking with God's thoughts, than I think how God is able to be doing what God is doing with God's state of consciousness is how God is able to be thinking what God is thinking with God's thoughts because I think God's state of consciousness is somehow able to be responsible for any thought as I think God's state of consciousness is somehow able to be responsible for everything, and therefore, I think how God is able to be God is how God is able to be thinking what God is able to be thinking with God's thoughts because I think God is somehow able to be responsible for any thought as I think God is somehow able to be responsible for everything. If I think how God is able to be God is how God is able to be thinking what God is able to be thinking with God's thoughts, than I think God, and God's state of consciousness, and God's will thinks of God's thoughts because I think God thinks of God's thoughts with God, and God's state of consciousness, and God's will as I think God, and God's state of consciousness, and God's will is somehow able to be responsible for everything.

If I think God, and God's state of consciousness, and God's will thinks of God's thoughts, than I think God is someone that is something of itself, that is somehow able to be beyond God's thoughts as I think God is someone that is something of itself, that is somehow able to be beyond any thought because I think God's thoughts is God's choice with what God's thoughts are in life as I think any thought is God's choice with how any thought is able to be a thought, and therefore, I think God is someone that is something of itself, that is somehow able to be beyond any thought as I think God is someone that is something of itself, that is somehow able to be responsible for any thought because I think any thought is God's choice with how any thought is able to be a thought as I think any thought is apart of making up everything. If I think God is someone that is something of itself, that is somehow able to be beyond any thought as I think God is someone that is something of itself, that is somehow able to be responsible for any thought, than I do not think someone can possibly be able to be knowing for themselves, as to how God is able to be someone that is something of itself, that is somehow able to be beyond any thought as I think God is someone that is something of itself, that is somehow able to be responsible for any thought, and I do not think someone can possibly be able to be knowing for themselves, as to how any thought is able to God's choice with how any thought is able to be a thought as I think any thought is apart of making up everything, but I think God is someone that is something of itself, that is somehow able to be beyond any thought as I think God is someone that is something of itself, that is somehow able to be responsible for any thought because I think any thought is God's choice with how any thought is able to be a thought as I think any thought is apart of making up everything.

If I think any thought is God's choice with how any thought is able to be a thought as I think any thought is apart of making up everything, than I think someone can just imagine, as to how much thought has gone into everything as I think any thought that is apart of making up everything is how much thought that has gone into everything because I do not think someone can possibly be able to be knowing for themselves, as to how much thought that is apart of making up everything, however, I think God knows, as to how much thought that is apart of making up everything because I think any thought that is apart of making up everything is God's choice with how any thought is able to be a thought that is apart of making up everything, and therefore, I do not think someone can possibly be able to be knowing for themselves, as to how much there is in life, and how old everything is in life because I do not think someone can possibly be able to be knowing for themselves, as to how much thought that is apart of making up everything, however, I think God knows, as to how much there is in life, and how old everything is in life because I think any thought that is apart of making up everything is God's choice with how any thought is able to be a thought that is apart of making up everything. If I think God knows, as to how much there is in life, and how old everything is in life, than I do not think someone can possibly be able to be knowing for themselves, as to how much thought has gone into everything because I think how much thought that has gone into everything is God's choice with how much thought there has gone into everything, however, I think God knows, as to how much thought has gone into everything because I think any thought that is apart of making up everything is God's choice with how any thought is able to be a thought that is apart of making up everything, and therefore, I do not think someone can possibly be able to be knowing for themselves, as to how much more thought there can possibly be able to be going into everything because I think how much more thought that can possibly be going into everything is God's choice with how much more thought that can possibly be going into everything, however, I think God knows, as to how much more thought there can possibly be able to be going into everything because I think any thought that is apart of making up everything is God's choice with how any thought is able to be a thought that is apart of making up everything. If I think God knows, as to how much more thought there can possibly be able to be going into everything, than I think God knows as to what the very first thought is that is apart of making up everything, and I think God knows as to what the very last thought is that is apart of making up everything for everything to be able to be going around in full circle, and that is if there is a last thought that is apart of making up everything for everything to be able to be going around in full circle because I think any thought that is apart of making up everything is God's choice with how any thought is able to be a thought that is apart of making up everything, even though, I do not think there is a last thought that is apart of making up everything for everything to be able to be going around in full circle because I think if there is a last thought that is apart of making up everything for everything to be able to be going around in full circle, than I think God will stop thinking with any thought that is apart of making up everything because I think any thought that is apart of making up everything is God's choice with any thought that is apart of making up everything, and therefore, I think everything will come to an end because I think God will stop thinking with any thought that is apart of making up everything, but I do not think everything will come to an end because I do not think God will stop thinking with any thought that is apart of making up everything. If I do not think everything will come to an end, than I do not think someone can possibly be able to be knowing for themselves, as to what the very first thought is in life, and what the very last thought is in life that is apart of making up everything for someone not to be able to be knowing for themselves, if there is a last thought that is apart of making up everything for everything to be able to be going around in full circle because I do not think God will stop thinking with any thought that is apart of making up everything, and therefore, I do not think there is a last thought that is apart of making up everything for everything to be able to be going around in full circle because I do not think God will stop thinking with any thought that is apart of making up everything as I think any thought that is apart of making up everything is God's choice with any thought that is apart of making up everything.

If I do not think there is a last thought that is apart of making up everything for everything to be able to be going around in full circle, than I think God knows everything with how everything is able to be taking place in life because I think any thought that is apart of making up everything is God's choice with how any thought is able to be a thought that is apart of making up everything, and therefore, I think God is all knowing with everything because I think any thought that is apart of making up everything is God's choice with how any thought is able to be a thought that is apart of making up everything. If I think God is all knowing with everything, than I think God's attention span is so vast, and so great with everything because I think God is constantly aware of everything as I think God knows everything with how everything is able to be taking place in life, and therefore, I think God is constantly aware of what someone is doing because I think God is constantly aware of everything as I think God knows everything with how everything is able to be taking place in life. If I think God is constantly aware of what someone is doing, than I think someone is constantly aware of what someone is doing as I think God is constantly aware of what someone is doing because I think someone can be aware of what someone is doing as I think God is constantly aware of everything, and therefore, I think someone is constantly aware of what someone is thinking of doing as I think someone is constantly aware of what someone is doing because I think someone can be aware of what someone is thinking about in someone's life as I think someone can be aware of what someone is doing. I think someone can be aware of what someone is thinking about in someone's life as I think someone can be aware of what someone is doing because I think what someone is doing is what someone is thinking of doing. I think what someone is doing is what someone is thinking of doing because I do not think someone can be doing something, without someone thinking of doing something, and therefore, I think someone is constantly aware of what someone is thinking of doing as I think God is constantly aware of what someone is thinking of doing because I think someone is constantly aware of what someone is doing as I think God is constantly aware of what someone is doing. If I think someone is constantly aware of what someone is thinking of doing as I think God is constantly aware of what someone is thinking of doing, than I do not think someone can keep any secrets from themselves as I do not think someone can keep any secrets from God because I think someone is constantly aware of what someone is thinking of doing as I think God is constantly aware of what someone is thinking of doing, and therefore, I think God knows everything with how everything is able to be taking place in life because I think God is constantly aware of everything, but I do not think God knows everything that is going to be taking place in life, before everything is going to be taking place in life because I think if God knows everything that is going to be taking place in life, before everything is going to be taking place in life, than I think God created everything to be like a television show for God's amusement for God to be watching, but I do not think God created everything to be like a television show for God's amusement for God to be watching because I do not think God knows everything that is going to be taking place in life, before everything is going to be taking place in life.

I do not think God knows everything that is going to be taking place in life, before everything is going to be taking place in life because I think the only way I think God can possibly be able to be knowing everything that is going to be taking place in life, before everything is going to be taking place in life is if God knows what the last thought is in life, but I do not think God knows what the last thought is in life because I do not think God will stop thinking with any thought that is apart of making up everything as I think any thought that is apart of making up everything is God's choice with any thought that is apart of making up everything, and therefore, I do not think God knows everything that is going to be taking place in life, before everything is going to be taking place in life because if I think God knows everything that is going to be taking place in life, before everything is going to be taking place in life, than I think God would be controlling, managing, and manipulating everything for everything to be taking place in life, before everything is going to be taking place in life, but I do not think God is controlling, managing, and manipulating everything for everything to be taking place in life, before everything is going to be taking place because I do not think God is interfering with everything for everything not to be taking place in life, before everything is going to be taking place in life, and therefore, I do not think God knows everything that is going to be taking place in life, before everything is going to be taking place in life because I do not think God is interfering with everything as I think any thought that is apart of making up everything is God's choice with any thought that is apart of making up everything. I do not think God is interfering with everything as I think any thought that is apart of making up everything is God's choice with any thought that is apart of making up everything because I think God is all knowing with everything as I think God knows everything with how everything is able to be taking place in life, and therefore, I do not think someone is doing God's will with someone trying to control themselves, someone else, and something because I do not think God is controlling everything for someone not to be doing God's will with someone trying to control themselves, someone else, and something.

If I do not think someone is doing God's will with someone trying to control themselves, someone else, and something, than I do not someone can live without someone asking something because I think someone is always thinking about something for someone to be asking something, and therefore, I think someone can always learn something because I think someone can always be thinking about something for someone to always be learning something as I think someone can always ask something for someone to always be learning something. If I think someone can always learn something, than I think someone can always learn something new from what someone thinks of something because I do not think someone can possibly be able to be learning enough, as to what someone thinks of something as I think what someone thinks of something is how someone can be able to learning something, and therefore, I think life is a school or classroom as I think everything is a school or classroom because I think someone can learn something from what someone thinks of something as I think something is apart of making up everything. If I think life is a school or classroom as I think everything is a school or classroom, than I think everything is God's school of life because I think life is a school for someone to be learning from something as I think something is apart of making up everything, and therefore, I think someone of any age can be learning something from what someone thinks of something because I do not think someone can learn enough, as to what someone thinks of something. If I think someone of any age can be learning something from what someone thinks of something, than I do not think someone can graduate from someone learning something because I think life is a school for someone to be learning from something as I think something is apart of making up everything, and therefore, I think someone can think of themselves as being a student because I think life is a school for someone to be thinking of themselves as being a student. If I think someone can think of themselves as being a student, than I think someone can think of themselves as being a student of life because I think someone is a student in life for someone to be a student of life, and therefore, I think someone can be a teacher as I think someone can be a student because I think someone can teach something to someone for someone to be a teacher as I think someone can learn something from someone, and something for someone to be a student, even though, I think someone has to be teachable for someone to be learning something because I think someone has to be teachable for someone to be student. I think someone has to be teachable for someone to be student because I think someone has to be willing to be learning something for someone to be a student, and therefore, I think God is the greatest teacher because I think someone can learn something from everything that God has created for God to be the greatest teacher. If I think God is the greatest teacher, than I think someone can be a student and a teacher because I think someone can ask and answer questions for someone to be a student and a teacher, and therefore, I think God created someone to be a student and a teacher because I think God created everything with God's thoughts for God to be creating someone to be asking and answering questions as I think God created someone to be asking and answering questions for God to be creating someone to be a student and a teacher. If I think God created someone to be a student and a teacher, than I do not think someone can graduate from God's school of life because I think someone can always ask and answer questions as I think someone can learn something from everything that God has created for someone not to be graduating from God's school of life, and therefore, I think God is never tired of teaching because I think someone can always learn something from everything that God has created for God to be never be tired of teaching, even though, I think someone can think God is testing someone because I think someone can think God can be good or bad for someone to be thinking God is testing someone, however, I do not think God is good or bad for God to be testing someone because I think God is always good, and right for God not to be interfering with everything as I do not think God is interfering with everything for God not to be testing someone.

If I do not think God is good or bad for God to be testing someone, than I think someone can be learning a lesson because I think someone can learn from something for someone to be learning a lesson. I think someone can learn from something for someone to be learning a lesson because I think someone can think about what someone thinks of something for someone to be learning a lesson. I think someone can think about what someone thinks of something for someone to be learning a lesson because I think someone can learn a lesson from something. I think someone can learn a lesson from something because I think someone can think about what something is in life for someone to be learning a lesson from something. I think someone can think about what something is in life for someone to be learning a lesson from something because I think someone's lesson is a lesson in life. I think someone's lesson is a lesson in life because I think someone can learn from something for someone's lesson to be a lesson in life. I think someone can learn from something for someone's lesson to be a lesson in life because I think someone can learn from something for something to be someone's lesson in life. I think someone can learn from something for something to be someone's lesson in life because I think everything is a lesson in life as I think something is a lesson in life. I think everything is a lesson in life as I think something is a lesson in life because I think everything is of something for everything to be a lesson in life. I think everything is of something for everything to be a lesson in life because I think someone can learn from something for everything to be a lesson in life. I think someone can learn from something for everything to be a lesson in life because I think someone can learn from everything that is something for everything to be someone's lesson in life.

If I think someone can learn from something for everything to be a lesson in life, than I do not think someone knows everything because I do not think someone knows what everything is in life. I do not think someone knows what everything is in life because I do not think someone knows how everything is in life. I do not think someone knows how everything is in life because I think how everything is in life is what everything is in life, and therefore, I think God knows everything because I think God knows what everything is in life. If I think God knows everything, than I think someone can only think about what something is in life because I do not think someone knows what something is in life as I do not think someone knows what everything is in life, and therefore, I don't know what I don't know because I do not know what something is in life. If I don't know what I don't know, than I think God knows what something is in life because I think God knows everything for God to know what something is in life. I think God knows everything for God to know what something is in life because I think God knows what everything is in life. I think God knows what everything is in life because I think God knows how everything is in life, and therefore, I think God knows everything because I think God created everything with God's thoughts for God to know how everything is in life. If I think God knows everything, than I do not think everything is obvious, as much as someone would like to think everything is obvious because I think everything is unobvious for everything not to be obvious. I think everything is unobvious for everything not to be obvious because I do not think someone knows what everything is in life for everything to be unobvious as I do not think someone knows what everything is in life for everything not to be obvious, and therefore, I do not think someone knows anything because I do not think someone knows what everything is in life for someone not to be knowing anything. I do not think someone knows what everything is in life for someone not to be knowing anything because I do not think someone knows how everything is able to be what everything is in life for someone not to be knowing anything. I do not think someone knows how everything is able to be what everything is in life for someone not to be knowing anything because I do not think someone knows what God's thoughts are in life that is apart of making up everything for someone not to be knowing how everything is able to be what everything is in life as I do not think someone knows what God's thoughts are in life that is apart of making up everything for someone not to be knowing anything, and therefore, I do not think someone knows anything because I do not think someone knows what God's thoughts are in life as I think God's thoughts is apart of making up everything for someone not to be knowing anything, however, I think someone can think someone knows something because I think someone can think about how someone or something is in life for someone to be understanding how someone or something is in life as I think someone can understand how someone or something is in life for someone to be thinking someone knows something.

If I think someone can think someone knows something, than I think any thought is overlapping, and co-existing along with everything because I think any thought is apart of making up everything, and therefore, I think the dimension of thought is overlapping, and co-existing along with the dimension of life because I think the dimension of thought is any thought as I think any thought is apart of making up everything. If I think the dimension of thought is overlapping, and co-existing along with the dimension of life, than I think everything is of a thought because I think everything is a thought. I think everything is a thought because I think a thought is how any thought is able to be a thought that is apart of making up everything as I think a thought is any thought that is apart of making up everything, and therefore, I think there is a multi-dimensional of thought that is apart of making up everything because I think everything is a thought as I think a thought is any thought that is apart of making up everything. If I think there is a multi-dimensional of thought that is apart of making up everything, than I think there is a multi-dimensional dimension of thought that is apart of making up everything as I think there is a multi-dimensional dimension of God's thoughts that is apart of making up everything because I think any thought is apart of making up everything as I think God's thoughts is apart of making up everything, and therefore, I think the dimension of thought is overlapping, and co-existing along with the universe as I think the dimension of thought is overlapping, and co-existing along with the dimension of life because I think any thought is apart of making up everything in the universe as I think any thought is apart of making up everything. If I think the dimension of thought is overlapping, and co-existing along with the universe as I think the dimension of thought is overlapping, and co-existing along with the dimension of life, than I think there is a multi-dimensional dimension of thought that is apart of making up everything in the universe as I think there is a multi-dimensional dimension of thought that is apart of making up everything because I think any thought is apart of making up everything in the universe as I think any thought is apart of making up everything.

If I think there is a multi-dimensional dimension of thought that is apart of making up everything in the universe as I think there is a multi-dimensional dimension of thought that is apart of making up everything, than I think any thought is how any thought is able to be what a thought is in life because I think any thought is what a thought is in life, and therefore, what is a thought? I think a thought is an idea of what a thought is in life because I think an idea is a thought of what a thought is in life. I think an idea is a thought of what a thought is in life because I think an idea is a thought of what an idea is in life, and therefore, I think an idea is a thought as I think a thought is an idea because I think an idea is a thought of what an idea is in life as I think a thought is an idea of what an idea is in life. If I think an idea is a thought as I think a thought is an idea, than I think a thought is an idea as I think an idea is a thought because I think an idea is a thought of what a thought is in life as I think a thought is an idea of what a thought is in life, and therefore, I think a thought is a thought of what a thought is in life as I think a thought is an idea of what a thought is in life because I think how an idea is able to be a thought is how a thought is able to be an idea. If I think a thought is a thought of what a thought is in life as I think a thought is an idea of what a thought is in life, than I think how an idea is able to be a thought of what a thought is in life is how a thought is able to be an idea of what a thought is in life because I think how an idea is able to be a thought is how an idea is able to be a thought of what a thought is in life as I think how a thought is able to be an idea is how a thought is able to be an idea of what a thought is in life, and therefore, I think an idea is a thought as I think a thought is an idea because I think an idea is a thought of what a thought is in life as I think a thought is an idea of what a thought is in life, even though, I think a thought is something that is a thought as I think an idea is something that is a thought because I think a thought is an idea as I think a thought is something that is a thought.

If I think a thought is something that is a thought as I think an idea is something that is a thought, than I think a thought is a thought as I think a thought is something because I think a thought is something that is a thought. I think a thought is something that is a thought because I think a thought is something that is a thought of what something is in life as I think something is what something is in life. I think a thought is something that is a thought of what something is in life as I think something is what something is in life because I think a thought is something that is a thought of how something is in life as I think something is how something is in life, and therefore, I think something is a thought because I think something is a thought of how something is in life. If I think something is a thought, than I think a thought is something as I think something is a thought because I think something is of a thought. I think something is of a thought because I think a thought is something that is a thought as I think something is something that is a thought, and therefore, I think a thought is something as I think something is a thought because I think a thought is something that is a thought as I think something is something that is a thought. If I think a thought is something as I think something is a thought, than I think something is a thought as I think something is something because I think a thought is something as I think something is a thought, and therefore, I think a thought is something that is a thought of how something is in life as I think something is how something is in life because I think how something is in life is how a thought is in life. If I think a thought is something that is a thought of how something is in life as I think something is how something is in life, than I think something is a thought as I think a thought is something because I think a thought is something that is a thought of how something is in life, and therefore, I think the color blue can be an example of how I think a thought is something that is a thought of how something is in life because I think how the color blue is something is how I think a thought is something that is a thought of how something is in life. I think how the color blue is something is how I think a thought is something that is a thought of how something is in life because I think the color blue is something that is a thought. I think the color blue is something that is a thought because I think the color blue is something that is a thought of how the color blue is something. I think the color blue is something that is a thought of how the color blue is something because I think a thought is something that is a thought of how the color blue is something, and therefore, I think a thought is something that is a thought of how something is in life because I think a thought is something that is a thought of how the color blue is something.

If I think a thought is something that is a thought of how something is in life, than I do not think someone can possibly be able to be knowing for themselves, as to how the color blue is able to be something because I think the color blue is something that is intellectually beyond someone's intelligence, as to how the color blue is able to be something, however, I think God knows how the color blue is able to be something because I think God created everything with God's thoughts for God to be knowing how something, such as the color blue is able to be something, and therefore, I think the color blue is something that is a thought of how the color blue is something as I think the color blue is something that is God's thoughts of how the color blue is something because I think God created everything with God's thoughts for the color blue to be something that is a thought as I think God created everything with God's thoughts for the color blue to be something that is God's thoughts. If I think the color blue is something that is a thought of how the color blue is something as I think the color blue is something that is God's thoughts of how the color blue is something, than I think a thought is something that is a thought of how something is in life as I think a thought is something that is God's thoughts of how something is in life because I think God created everything with God's thoughts for a thought to be something that is a thought as I think God created everything with God's thoughts for a thought to be something that is God's thoughts, and therefore, I think a thought is something that is a thought of how something is in life because I think a thought is something. I think a thought is something because I think a thought is how something is in life as I think a thought is apart of making up how something is in life. I think a thought is how something is in life as I think a thought is apart of making up how something is in life because I think a thought is something that is a thought of how something is in life, and therefore, I think a thought is apart of making up how something is in life because I think a thought is something that is apart making up of how something is in life as I think a thought is something that is a thought of how something is in life. If I think a thought is apart of making up how something is in life, than I think a thought is apart of something as I think a thought is apart of how something is in life because I think a thought is apart of making up something as I think a thought is apart of making up how something is in life, and therefore, I think something is how something is in life as I think how something is in life is something because I think a thought is apart of making up something as I think a thought is apart of making up how something is in life. If I think something is how something is in life as I think how something is in life is something, than I think a thought is apart of making up something because I think a thought is something that is apart of making up something, and therefore, I think a thought must have come before something as I think something must have come from a thought because I think a thought is apart of making up something. If I think a thought must have come before something as I think something must have come from a thought, than I think something is taking place within a thought, without being a thought as I think something is apart of a thought, without being a thought because I think a thought is apart making up something, and therefore, I think something is a thought as I think something is of a thought because I think a thought is apart of making up something.

If I think something is a thought as I think something is of a thought, than I think a thought is a dimension that is overlapping, and co-existing along with something that is a dimension because I think a thought is something that is overlapping, and co-existing along with something. I think a thought is something that is overlapping, and co-existing along with something because I think a thought is something as I think a thought is something that is apart of making up something, and therefore, I think a thought is something as I think something is a thought because I think a thought is something that is apart of making up something for something to be something. If I think a thought is something as I think something is a thought, than I think a thought is something as I think something is something because I think a thought is something that is apart of making up something for something to be something, and therefore, I think a thought is overlapping, and co-existing along with something because I think a thought is something that is apart of making up something for something to be something. If I think a thought is overlapping, and co-existing along with something, than I think a thought is the dimension of thought because I think the dimension of thought is of a thought. I think the dimension of thought is of a thought because I think a thought is something that is apart of making up something, and therefore, I think the dimension of thought is overlapping, and co-existing along with something because I think the dimension of thought is of a thought as I think a thought is something that is apart of making up something.

If I think the dimension of thought is overlapping, and co-existing along with something, than I think a thought is of God's thought or idea because I think a thought is of God's choice with how a thought is able to be a thought as I think how any thought is able to be a thought is of God's choice with how any thought is able to be a thought, and therefore, I think a thought is any thought as I think any thought is a thought because I think a thought is how any thought is able to be a thought as I think any thought is how any thought is able to be a thought. If I think a thought is any thought as I think any thought is a thought, than I think any thought is of a thought because I think any thought is a thought as I think a thought is apart of making up something, and therefore, I think a thought is God's thought or idea as I think any thought is God's thought or idea because I think a thought is of God's thoughts that is apart of making up something as I think any thought is of God's thoughts that is apart of making up something. If I think a thought is God's thought or idea as I think any thought is God's thought or idea, than I think something is of God's thought or idea as I think something is of a thought because I think a thought is of God's thoughts that is apart of making up something as I think a thought is something that is apart of making up something, and therefore, I think someone can think of a thought as being the dimension of God's thoughts as I think someone can think of a thought as being the dimension of thought because I think a thought is of God's thoughts as I think a thought is something that is apart of making up something. If I think someone can think of a thought as being the dimension of God's thoughts as I think someone can think of a thought as being the dimension of thought, than I think the dimension of God's thoughts is overlapping, and co-existing along with something as I think the dimension of thought is overlapping, and co-existing along with something because I think the dimension of thought is of God's thoughts that is apart of making up something as I think the dimension of thought is of a thought that is apart of making up something. I think the dimension of thought is of God's thoughts that is apart of making up something as I think the dimension of thought is of a thought that is apart of making up something because I think a thought is the dimension of God's thoughts as I think a thought is the dimension of thought. I think a thought is the dimension of God's thoughts as I think a thought is the dimension of thought because I think a thought is of God's thoughts as I think a thought is something that is apart of making up something.

If I think a thought is the dimension of God's thoughts as I think a thought is the dimension of thought, than I think any thought is overlapping, and co-existing along with everything as I think a thought is overlapping, and co-existing along with something because I think any thought is something that is apart of making up everything as I think a thought is something that is apart of making up something, and therefore, I think the dimension of thought is overlapping, and co-existing along with everything as I think the dimension of thought is overlapping, and co-existing along with something because I think the dimension of thought is of any thought as I think the dimension of thought is of a thought. I think the dimension of thought is of any thought as I think the dimension of thought is of a thought because I think any thought is the dimension of thought as I think a thought is the dimension of thought, and therefore, I think the dimension of God's thoughts is overlapping, and co-existing along with everything as I think the dimension of God's thoughts is overlapping, and co-existing along with something because I think any thought is of God's thoughts as I think a thought is of God's thoughts. I think any thought is of God's thoughts as I think a thought is of God's thoughts because I think God's thoughts is any thought as I think God's thoughts a thought. I think God's thoughts is any thought as I think God's thoughts a thought because I think any thought is something that is apart of making everything as I think a thought is something that is apart of making up something.

If I think God's thoughts is any thought as I think God's thoughts a thought, than I think a thought is something that is apart of making up something because I think a thought is something that is a thought as I think a thought is something that is the instructions of something, and therefore, how is a thought able to be something that is the instructions of something? I think a thought able to be something that is the instructions of something because I think something is of the instructions of how something is in life as I think a thought is something that is the instructions of how something is in life. I think something is of the instructions of how something is in life as I think a thought is something that is the instructions of how something is in life because I think a thought is something that is an instruction of how something is in life, and therefore, I think a thought is something that is a thought as I think a thought is something that is an instruction because I think a thought is an instruction of how a thought is able to be what a thought is in life as I think a thought is a thought of how a thought is able to be what a thought is in life. If I think a thought is something that is a thought as I think a thought is something that is an instruction, than I think a thought is something that is a thought as I think a thought is something that is an instruction of something because I think a thought is something that is an instruction of how something is in life as I think a thought is something that is a thought of how something is in life, and therefore, I do not think someone can possibly be able to be knowing for themselves, as to what a thought is in life because I do not think someone can possibly be able to be knowing for themselves, as to what the very essence of what a thought is in life as I think the very essence of what a thought is in life is the very essence of how a thought is able to be what a thought is in life. I do not think someone can possibly be able to be knowing for themselves, as to what the very essence of what a thought is in life as I think the very essence of what a thought is in life is the very essence of how a thought is able to be what a thought is in life because I do not think someone can possibly be able to be knowing for themselves, as to how a thought is able to be something that is a thought of how something is in life as I think how a thought is able to be something that is a thought of how something is in life is the very essence of what a thought is in life, and therefore, I do not think someone can ever be able to be knowing for themselves, as to how a thought is able to be a thought as I think how a thought is able to be something that is a thought of how something is in life is the very essence of how a thought is able to be a thought because I do not think someone can possibly be able to be knowing for themselves, as to what a thought is in life. If I do not think someone can possibly be able to be knowing for themselves, as to what a thought is in life, than I think a thought is God's instruction because I think God created everything with God's thoughts for a thought to be God's instruction. I think God created everything with God's thoughts for a thought to be God's instruction because I think any thought is an instruction as I think a thought is God's instruction with how any thought is able to be a thought, and therefore, I think a thought is God's instruction of something as I think a thought is God's instruction of everything because I think God created everything with God's thoughts for a thought to be God's instruction of something as I think God created everything with God's thoughts for a thought to be God's instruction of everything.

If I think a thought is God's instruction of something as I think a thought is God's instruction of everything, than I think God is somehow able to be responsible for how a thought is able to be what a thought is in life because I think a thought is something that is beyond someone's intelligence, as to how a thought is able to be something that is a thought of how something is in life as I think how a thought is able to be something that is a thought of how something is in life is how a thought is able to be what a thought is in life, and therefore, I think God created a thought to be what a thought is in life because I think God created everything with God's thoughts for God to be creating a thought to be what a thought is in life. If I think God created a thought to be what a thought is in life, than I think what a thought is in life is how a thought is able to be what a thought is in life because I think how a thought is able to be something that is a thought of how something is in life is what a thought is in life, even though, I think how a though is able to be something that is a thought of how something is in life is God's choice with how a thought is able to be something that is a thought of how something is in life because I think a thought is God's choice with how a thought is able to be a thought as I think a thought is apart of making up something. If I think a thought is God's choice with how a thought is able to be a thought as I think a thought is apart of making up something, than I think any thought is God's choice with how any thought is able to be a thought as I think any thought is apart of making up everything because I think a thought is God's choice with how a thought is able to be a thought that is apart of making up something as I think any thought is God's choice with how any thought is able to be a thought that is apart of making up everything, and therefore, I think any thought is something that is the instructions of everything as I think a thought is something that is the instructions of something because I think any thought is something that is an instruction of how everything is in life as I think a thought is something that is an instruction of how something is in life. If I think any thought is something that is the instructions of everything as I think a thought is something that is the instructions of something, than I think any thought is something that is a thought of how everything is in life as I think any thought is something that is an instruction of how everything is in life because I think any thought is something that is an instruction of how everything is in life as I think a thought is something that is an instruction of how something is in life, and therefore, I do not think someone can possibly be able to be knowing for themselves, as to what the very essence of what a thought is in life as I think the very essence of what a thought is in life is the very essence of how a thought is able to be what a thought is in life because I do not think someone can possibly be able to be knowing for themselves, as to how any thought is able to be something that is a thought of how everything is in life as I think how a thought is able to be something that is a thought of how everything is in life is the very essence of what a thought is in life. If I do not think someone can possibly be able to be knowing for themselves, as to how any thought is able to be something that is a thought of how everything is in life as I think how a thought is able to be something that is a thought of how everything is in life is the very essence of what a thought is in life, than I do not think someone can ever be able to be knowing for themselves, as to how much thought is apart of making up everything because I do not think someone can ever be able to be knowing for themselves, as to how any thought is able to be a thought that is apart of making up everything as I think how any thought is able to be a thought that is apart of making up everything is how much thought is apart of making up everything, and therefore, I do not think someone can ever be able to be knowing for themselves, as to how much of everything is able to be taking place in life because I do not think someone can ever be able to be knowing for themselves, as to how any thought is able to be a thought that is apart of making up everything as I think how any thought is able to be a thought that is apart of making up everything is how much of everything is able to be taking place in life.

If I do not think someone can ever be able to be knowing for themselves, as to how much of everything is able to be taking place in life, than I think a thought is any thought as I think any thought is a thought because I think a thought is apart of making up something as I think any thought is apart of making up something, and therefore, I think any thought is apart of making up something as I think any thought is apart of making up everything because I think any thought is how any thought is able to be a thought that is apart of making up something as I think any thought is how any thought is able to be a thought that is apart of making up everything. If I think any thought is how any thought is able to be a thought that is apart of making up something as I think any thought is how any thought is able to be a thought that is apart of making up everything, than I think any thought is apart of making up something as I think any thought is apart of making up everything because I think something is an image or a reflection of any thought that is apart of making up something as I think everything is an image or a reflection of any thought that is apart of making up everything, and therefore, I think God is somehow able to be responsible for how something is able to be an image or a reflection of any thought that is apart of making up something as I think God is somehow able to be responsible for how everything is able to be an image or a reflection of any thought that is apart of making up everything because I think something is intellectually beyond someone's intelligence, as to how something is able to be an image or a reflection of any thought that is apart of making up something as I think everything is intellectually beyond someone's intelligence, as to how everything is able to be an image or a reflection of any thought that is apart of making up everything. If I think God is somehow able to be responsible for how something is able to be an image or a reflection of any thought that is apart of making up something as I think God is somehow able to be responsible for how everything is able to be an image or a reflection of any thought that is apart of making up everything, than I think

God created something to be an image or a reflection of any thought that is apart of making up something as I think God created everything to be an image or a reflection of any thought that is apart of making up everything because I think God created everything with God's thoughts for something to be an image or a reflection of any thought that is apart of making up something as I think God created everything with God's thoughts for everything to be an image or a reflection of any thought that is apart of making up everything, and therefore, I think an example of how I think something is an image or a reflection of any thought that is apart of making up something can be something that can appear to be taking place on any computer monitor because I think something that can appear to be taking place on any computer monitor is an image or a reflection of any thought that can be apart of making up something that can appear to be taking place on any computer monitor, in which someone can be programming the thoughts of something to appear to be taking place on any computer monitor as I think someone can be programming the thoughts of something to appear to be taking place on any computer monitor from someone entering or typing the thoughts of something on any computer for something to appear to be taking place on any computer monitor, and therefore, I think something is an image or a reflection of any thought that is apart of making up something as I think everything is an image or a reflection of any thought that is apart of making up everything because I think any thought is apart of making up something as I think any thought is apart of making up everything.

If I think something is an image or a reflection of any thought that is apart of making up something as I think everything is an image or a reflection of any thought that is apart of making up everything, than I think something is a picture of any thought that is apart of making up the picture of something as I think everything is a picture of any thought that is apart of making up the picture of everything because I think something is an image or a reflection of any thought that is apart of making up something as I think everything is an image or a reflection of any thought that is apart of making up everything, and therefore, I think something is a picture as I think God is somehow able to be responsible for the picture of something because I think something is a picture of any thought that is apart of making up the picture of something as I think God created everything with God's thoughts for God's thoughts to be apart of making up the picture of something. If I think something is a picture of itself as I think God is somehow able to be responsible for the picture of something, than I think something is a picture as I think something is a picture of God's thoughts because I think something is a picture of any thought that is apart of making up the picture of something as I think any thought is of God's thoughts that is apart of making up something, and therefore, I think everything is a picture as I think God is somehow able to be responsible for the picture of everything because I think everything is a picture of any thought that is apart of making up the picture of everything as I think God created everything with God's thoughts for God's thoughts to be apart of making up the picture of everything. If I think everything is a picture as I think God is somehow able to be responsible for the picture of everything, than I think everything is a picture as I think everything is a picture of God's thoughts because I think everything is a picture God's thoughts that is apart of making up the picture of everything as I think God's thoughts is apart of making up everything, and therefore, I think any thought is something as I think any thought is everything because I think something is any thought as I think everything is any thought. I think something is any thought as I think everything is any thought because I think any thought is apart of making up something for something to be any thought as I think any thought is apart of making up everything for everything to be any thought. I think any thought is apart of making up something for something to be any thought as I think any thought is apart of making up everything for everything to be any thought because I think something is of any thought that is apart of making up something as I think everything is of any thought that is apart of making up everything, but I do not think any thought is of something that is apart of making up something as I do not think any thought is of everything that is apart of making up everything because I think something is of any thought that is apart of making up something as I think everything is of any thought that is apart of making up everything.

If I think something is of any thought that is apart of making up something as I think everything is of any thought that is apart of making up everything, than I think any thought is God's instructions because I think God created everything with God's thoughts for any thought to be God's instructions. I think God created everything with God's thoughts for any thought to be God's instructions because I think any thought is an instruction as I think any thought is God's instruction with how any thought is able to be a thought, and therefore, I think any thought is God's instructions of something as I think any thought is God's instructions of everything because I think God created everything with God's thoughts for any thought to be God's instructions of something as I think God created everything with God's thoughts for any thought to be God's instructions of everything. If I think any thought is God's instructions of something as I think any thought is God's instructions of everything, than I think God's thoughts is God's instructions because I think God created everything with God's thoughts for God's thoughts to be God's instructions, and therefore, I think a thought is something as I think any thought is something because I think something is a thought as I think something is any thought. I think something is a thought as I think something is any thought because I think a thought is apart of making up something as I think any thought is apart of making up something. I think a thought is apart of making up something as I think any thought is apart of making up something because I think something is of a thought that is apart of making up something as I think something is of any thought that is apart of making up something. I think something is of a thought that is apart of making up something as I think something is of any thought that is apart of making up something because I think a thought is the instructions of something as I think any thought is the instructions of something. I think a thought is the instructions of something as I think any thought is the instructions of something because I do not think any thought is something that is physically able to be appearing to be taking place in life as being something as I think something is physically able to be appearing to be taking place in life as being something. I do not think any thought is something that is physically able to be appearing to be taking place in life as being something as I think something is physically able to be appearing to be taking place in life as being something because I do not think something can physically be able to be appearing to be taking place in life as being something, without something being able to be having any instructions from any thought that is apart of making up something for something to physically be able to be appearing to be taking place in life as being something, however, I think something that is physically able to be appearing to be taking place in life as being something is of any thought that is apart of making up something because I think any thought is something that is the instructions of something for something to physically be able to be appearing to be taking place in life as being something, and therefore, I think something is of any thought that is apart of making up something because I think any thought is the instructions of something.

If I think something is of any thought that is apart of making up something, than I think the dimension of thought is of an unknown dimension as I think the dimension of thought is of any thought that is apart of making up something because I do not think any thought is something that is physically able to be appearing to be taking place in life as being something as I think something is physically able to be appearing to be taking place in life as being something, and therefore, I think any thought is apart of making up something because I think any thought is something that is a thought as I think any thought is something that is the instructions of something. If I think any thought is apart of making up something, than I do not think the dimension of thought is something that is physically able to be appearing to be taking place in life as being something as I think something is physically able to be appearing to be taking place in life as being something because I think the dimension of thought is of an unknown dimension as I think the dimension of thought is of any thought that is apart of making up something, and therefore, I think the dimension of God's thoughts is of an unknown dimension as I think the dimension of thought is of an unknown dimension because I think the dimension of God's thoughts is the dimension of thought as I think the dimension of thought is of any thought that is apart of making up something. If I think the dimension of God's thoughts is of an unknown dimension as I think the dimension of thought is of an unknown dimension, than I think God's thoughts is of an unknown dimension as I think the dimension of thought is of an unknown dimension because I think God's thoughts is the dimension of thought as I think the dimension of thought is any thought that is apart of making up something, and therefore, I think the dimension of thought is apart of making up something because I think the dimension of thought is something that is a thought as I think the dimension of thought is something that is the instructions of something.

If I think the dimension of thought is apart of making up something, than I think a thought is any thought as I think something is any thought because I think any thought is a thought as I think any thought is apart of making up something, and therefore, I think a dimension is a thought as I think a thought is a dimension because I think a dimension is of a thought as I think a thought is apart of making up a dimension. If I think a dimension is a thought as I think a thought is a dimension, than I think a dimension is any thought as I think any thought is a dimension because I think a dimension is of any thought as I think any thought is apart of making up a dimension, and therefore, I think a thought is a dimension as I think a thought is any dimension because I think a thought is apart of making up a dimension as I think a thought is apart of making any dimension. If I think a thought is a dimension as I think a thought is any dimension, than I think any dimension is a thought as I think a thought is any dimension because I think any dimension is of a thought as I think a thought is apart of making up any dimension, and therefore, I think any thought is a dimension as I think any thought is any dimension because I think any thought is apart of making up a dimension as I think any thought is apart of making up any dimension. If I think any thought is a dimension as I think any thought is any dimension, than I think any dimension is any thought as I think any thought is any dimension because I think any dimension is of any thought as I think any thought is apart of making up any dimension. If I think any dimension is any thought as I think any thought is any dimension, than I think a dimension is something as I think something is a dimension because I think a dimension is of something as I think something is apart of making up a dimension, and therefore, I think a dimension is something as I think any dimension is something because I think something is apart of making up a dimension as I think something is apart of making up any dimension. If I think a dimension is something as I think any dimension is something, than I think any dimension is something as I think something is any dimension because I think any dimension is of something as I think something is apart of making up any dimension, and therefore, I think a dimension is something as I think a dimension is a thought because I think something is apart of making up a dimension as I think a thought is apart of making up a dimension. If I think a dimension is something as I think a dimension is a thought, than I think any dimension is something as I think any dimension is any thought because I think something is apart of making any dimension as I think any thought is apart of making up any dimension.

If I think any dimension is something as I think any dimension is any thought, than I think something is overlapping, and co-existing along with something else because I think something is a dimension that is overlapping, and co-existing along with something else that is a dimension. I think something is a dimension that is overlapping, and co-existing along with something else that is a dimension because I think something is any dimension as I think something is apart of making up any dimension, and therefore, I think someone can think of something as being the dimension of something because I think the dimension of something is something as I think any dimension is something. I think the dimension something is something as I think any dimension is something because I think the dimension of something is of something as I think any dimension is of something. I think the dimension of something is of something as I think any dimension is of something because I think something is apart of making up the dimension of something as I think something is apart of making up any dimension, and therefore, I think the dimension of something is overlapping, and co-existing along with any other dimension of something because I think the dimension of something is something as I think something is apart of making up the dimension of something. If I think the dimension of something is overlapping, and co-existing along with any other dimension of something, than I think a dimension of something is overlapping, and co-existing along with any other dimension of something because I think something is a dimension of something as I think something is the dimension of something, and therefore, I think the dimension of something is overlapping, and co-existing along with the dimension of something as I think the dimension of something is overlapping, and co-existing along with any other dimension of something because I think the dimension of something is something as I think any other dimension of something is something. If I think the dimension of something is overlapping, and co-existing along with the dimension of something as I think the dimension of something is overlapping, and co-existing along with any other dimension of something, than I think the dimension of God's thoughts is overlapping, and co-existing along with any other dimension of God's thoughts as I think the dimension of something is overlapping, and co-existing along with any other dimension of something because I think the dimension of God's thoughts is something as I think the dimension of something is something.

If I think the dimension of God's thoughts is overlapping, and co-existing along with any other dimension of God's thoughts as I think the dimension of something is overlapping, and co-existing along with any other dimension of something, than I think any dimension is overlapping, and co-existing along with any dimension as I think something is overlapping, and co-existing along with something because I think any dimension is something as I think something is something, and therefore, I think any dimension is overlapping, and co-existing along with any dimension as I think any dimension is overlapping, and co-existing along with any other dimension because I think any dimension is any dimension as I think any dimension can be any other dimension. If I think any dimension is overlapping, and co-existing along with any dimension as I think any dimension is overlapping, and co-existing along with any other dimension, than I do not think there is a set number for any dimension because I think any dimension is equally important as any other dimension as I think any dimension is something that is overlapping, and co-existing along with any other dimension that is something, and therefore, I do not think someone can possibly be able to be numbering for themselves, as to how many different dimensions there are in

life because I do not think someone can possible be able to be knowing for themselves, as to how many different dimensions there are in life. If I do not think someone can possibly be able to be numbering for themselves, as to how many different dimensions there are in life, than I think any dimension is overlapping, and co-existing along with something as I think something is overlapping, and co-existing along with any dimension because I think any dimension is something as I think something is any dimension, and therefore, I think any dimension is overlapping, and co-existing along with any dimension as I think any thought is overlapping, and co-existing along with any thought because I think any dimension is any thought as I think any thought is any thought. If I think any dimension is overlapping, and co-existing along with any dimension as I think any thought is overlapping, and co-existing along with any thought, than I think any dimension is overlapping, and co-existing along with any thought as I think any thought is overlapping, and co-existing along with any dimension because I think any dimension is any thought as I think any thought is any dimension, and therefore, I think any thought is overlapping, and co-existing along with any thought as I think something is overlapping, and co-existing along with something because I think any thought is something as I think something is something.
If I think any thought is overlapping, and co-existing along with any thought as I think something is overlapping, and co-existing along with something, than I think any thought is overlapping, and co-existing along with something as I think something is overlapping, and co-existing along with any thought because I think any thought is something as I think something is any thought, and therefore, I think any thought is apart of making up any dimension as I think any thought is apart of making up something because I think something is any dimension as I think something is of any thought. If I think any thought is apart of making up any dimension as I think any thought is apart of making up something, than I think a thought is a dimension as I think any thought is a dimension because I think a dimension is a thought as I think a dimension is any thought, and therefore, I think a thought is a dimension that is overlapping, and co-existing along with something that is a dimension because I think a dimension is a thought as I think a dimension is something. If I think a thought is a dimension that is overlapping, and co-existing along with something that is a dimension, than I think the dimension of thought is overlapping, and co-existing along with the dimension of something because I think the dimension of thought is any thought as I think any thought is apart of making up something, and therefore, I think the dimension of God's thoughts is overlapping, and co-existing along with the dimension of something as I think the dimension of thought is overlapping, and co-existing along with the dimension of something because I think the dimension of God's thoughts is any thought as I think any thought is apart of making up something.

If I think the dimension of God's thoughts is overlapping, and co-existing along with the dimension of something as I think the dimension of thought is overlapping, and co-existing along with the dimension of something, than I think any thought is constantly something as I think something is constantly something because I think something is of any thought as I think any thought is apart of making up something, and therefore, I think a thought is constantly something as I think any thought is constantly something because I think a thought is any thought as I think any thought is apart of making up something. If I think a thought is constantly something as I think any thought is constantly something, than I think a thought is how something is able to be constantly something because I think a thought is apart of making up something as I think a thought is apart of making up how something is able to be constantly something, and therefore, I think any thought is how something is able to be constantly something because I think any thought is apart of making up something as I think any thought is apart of making up how something is able to be constantly something. If I think any thought is how something is able to be constantly something, than I think any thought is how something is able to be constantly something as I think God's thoughts is how something is able to be constantly something because I think any thought is of God's thoughts as I think God's thoughts is apart of making up how something is able to be constantly something, and therefore, I think God's thoughts is apart of making up how something is able to be constantly something because I think God's thoughts is apart of making up something as I think something is constantly something. If I think God's thoughts is apart of making up how something is able to be constantly something, than I do not think someone can possibly be able to be knowing for themselves, as to how something is able to be constantly something because I do not think someone can possibly be able to be knowing for themselves, as to how something is able to be something as I think something is how something is able to be something, but I think someone can think about what something is in life with any language that someone can possibly be able to be communicating with themselves because I think what something is in life is how something is in life. If I think what something is in life is how something is in life, than I do not think someone can possibly be able to be knowing for themselves, as to how any thought is able to be constantly something because I do not think someone can possibly be able to be knowing for themselves, as to how any thought is able to be something as I think any thought is how any thought is able to be something, but I think any thought is something because I think something is of any thought as I think any thought is apart of making up something.

If I think any thought is something, than I think a thought is overlapping, and co-existing along with any thought because I think a thought is any thought for a thought to be a dimension that is overlapping, and co-existing along with any thought that is a dimension. I think a thought is any thought for a thought to be a dimension that is overlapping, and co-existing along with any thought that is a dimension because I think any thought is something as I think any thought is apart of making up something, and therefore, I think someone can think of a thought as being the dimension of thought because I think the dimension of thought is a thought as I think a thought is any thought. If I think someone can think of a thought as being the dimension of thought, than I think the dimension of thought is of a thought because I think the dimension of thought is a thought as I think a thought is apart of making up something, and therefore, I think the dimension of thought is of any thought because I think the dimension of thought is any thought as I think any thought is apart of making up something. If I think the dimension of thought is of any thought, than I think something is of the dimension of thought as I think something is of a thought because I think the dimension of thought is apart of making up something as I think a thought is apart of making up something, and therefore, I think something is of the dimension of thought as I think something is of any thought because I think the dimension of thought is apart of making up something as I think any thought is apart of making up something. If I think something is of the dimension of thought as I think something is of any thought, than I think the dimension of thought is overlapping, and co-existing along with any other dimension of thought because I think the dimension of thought is something as I think the dimension of thought is apart of making up something, and therefore, I think a dimension of thought is overlapping, and co-existing along with any other dimension of thought because I think a thought is a dimension of thought as I think a thought is the dimension of thought. If I think a dimension of thought is overlapping, and co-existing along with any other dimension of thought, than I think the dimension of God's thoughts is overlapping, and co-existing along with any other dimension of God's thoughts as I think a dimension of thought is overlapping, and co-existing along with any other dimension of thought because I think the dimension of God's thoughts is a thought as I think the dimension of God's thoughts is the dimension of thought.

If I think the dimension of God's thoughts is overlapping, and co-existing along with any other dimension of God's thoughts as I think a dimension of thought is overlapping, and co-existing along with any other dimension of thought, than I think the dimension of thought is overlapping, and co-existing along with the dimension of thought as I think the dimension of thought is overlapping, and co-existing along with any other dimension of thought because I think the dimension of thought is any thought as I think any other dimension of thought is any thought, and therefore, I think the dimension of God's thoughts is overlapping, and co-existing along with any other dimension of God's thoughts as I think the dimension of thought is overlapping, and co-existing along with any other dimension of thought because I think the dimension of God's thoughts is the dimension of thought as I think the dimension of thought is the dimension of God's thoughts. If I think the dimension of God's thoughts is overlapping, and co-existing along with any other dimension of God's thoughts as I think the dimension of thought is overlapping, and co-existing along with any other dimension of thought, than I think the dimension of God's thoughts is overlapping, and co-existing along the dimension of God's thoughts as I think the dimension of thought is overlapping, and co-existing along with the dimension of thought because I think the dimension of God's thoughts is any thought as I think the dimension of thought is any thought, and therefore, I think the dimension of thought is overlapping, and co-existing along with the dimension of thought as I think the dimension of thought is overlapping, and co-existing along with the dimension of something because I think the dimension of thought is any thought as I think any thought is apart of making up something. If I think the dimension of thought is overlapping, and co-existing along with the dimension of thought as I think the dimension of thought is overlapping, and co-existing along with the dimension of something, than I think the dimension of God's thoughts is overlapping, and co-existing along with the dimension of God's thoughts as I think the dimension of God's thoughts is overlapping, and co-existing along with the dimension of something because I think the dimension of God's thoughts is any thought as I think any thought is apart of making up something, and therefore, I think the dimension of God's thoughts is overlapping, and co-existing along with the dimension of God's thoughts as I think the dimension of something is overlapping, and co-existing along with the dimension of something because I think the dimension of God's thoughts is something as I think the dimension of something is something. If I think the dimension of God's thoughts is overlapping, and co-existing along with the dimension of God's thoughts as I think the dimension of something is overlapping, and co-existing along with the dimension of something, than I think the dimension of thought is overlapping, and co-existing along with the dimension of thought as I think the dimension of something is overlapping, and co-existing along with the dimension of something because I think the dimension of thought is something as I think the dimension of something is something.

I think the dimension of thought is something as I think the dimension of something is something because I think the dimension of thought is any thought as I think the dimension of something is of any thought. I think the dimension of thought is any thought as I think the dimension of something is of any thought because I think the dimension of thought is any thought as I think any thought is apart of making up the dimension of something. I think the dimension of thought is any thought as I think any thought is apart of making up the dimension of something because I think the dimension of something is something as I think any thought is apart of making up something. I think the dimension of something is something as I think any thought is apart of making up something because I think the dimension of something is of the dimension of thought as I think the dimension of thought is any thought. I think the dimension of something is of the dimension of the dimension of thought as I think the dimension of thought is any thought because I think the dimension of thought is apart of making up the dimension of something as I think the dimension of thought is any thought. I think the dimension of thought is apart of making up the dimension of something as I think the dimension of thought is any thought because I think the dimension of something is of any thought as I think any thought is apart of making up something. I think the dimension of something is of any thought as I think any thought is apart of making up something because I think the dimension of something is of the dimension of thought as I think the dimension of thought is apart of making up the dimension of something. I think the dimension of something is of the dimension of thought as I think the dimension of thought is apart of making up the dimension of something because I think the dimension of thought is any thought as I think any thought is apart of making up something, and therefore, I think there is a multi-dimensional dimension of thought with the dimension of thought because I think the dimension of thought is multi-dimensional. I think the dimension of thought is multi-dimensional because I think the dimension of thought is any thought as I think any thought is apart of making up something, and therefore, I think there is a multi-dimensional dimension of thought with the dimension of God's thoughts because I think the dimension of God's thoughts is multi-dimensional. I think the dimension of God's thoughts is multi-dimensional because I think the dimension of God's thoughts is any thought as I think any thought is apart of making up something, and therefore, I think there is a multi-dimensional dimension of thought with the dimension of something because I think the dimension of something is multi-dimensional. I think the dimension of something is multi-dimensional because I think the dimension of something is of the dimension of thought as I think the dimension of thought is apart of making up the dimension of something, and therefore, I think the dimension of thought is multi-dimensional as I think the dimension of something is multi-dimensional because I think the dimension of thought, and the dimension of something is of any thought as I think any thought is apart of making up something.

If I think the dimension of thought is multi-dimensional as I think the dimension of something is multi-dimensional, than I think the dimension of thought is overlapping, and co-existing along with the dimension of life because I think the dimension of life is of the dimension of thought as I think the dimension of thought is apart of making up the dimension of life. I think the dimension of life is of the dimension of thought as I think the dimension of thought is apart of making up the dimension of life because I think the dimension of life is everything as I think the dimension of thought is any thought that is apart making up of everything, and therefore, I think the dimension of life is of the dimension of thought as I think the dimension of thought is apart of making up the dimension of life because I think everything is of any thought as I think any thought is apart making up of everything. If I think the dimension of life is of the dimension of thought as I think the dimension of thought is apart of making up the dimension of life, than I think everything consists of any thought as I think any thought is apart of making up something, and I think everything consists of something that is apart of making up everything as I think any thought is apart of making up something that is apart of making up everything, and therefore, I think everything consists of any thought, and something that is apart of making up everything because I think any thought is apart of making up something that is apart of making up everything as I think any thought, and something are both something that is apart of making up everything. If I think everything consists of any thought, and something that is apart of making up everything, than I think any thought is apart of making up something as I think any thought is apart of making up everything because I think any thought is apart of making up something that is apart of making up everything, and therefore, I think everything is something because I think everything consists of any thought, and something that is apart of making up everything. If I think everything is something, than I think everything is inter-related because I think everything consists of any thought, and something as I think any thought is apart of making something that is apart of making up everything, and therefore, I think everything is in synchronicity because I think everything inter-related for everything to be in synchronicity. I think everything inter-related for everything to be in synchronicity because I think everything is related to God for everything to be in synchronicity as I think everything is related to God for everything to be inter-related, and therefore, I think everything is in synchronicity with God because I think everything is related to God for everything to be in synchronicity with God. I think everything is related to God for everything to be in synchronicity with God because I think everything is created by God for everything to be in synchronicity as I think everything is created by God for everything to be related to God. I think everything is created by God for everything to be in synchronicity as I think everything is created by God for everything to be related to God because I think God created everything for everything to be in synchronicity, even though, I think everything can appear as though the dimension of life is of one singular dimension as I think the dimension of life is everything, but I do not think the dimension of life is of one singular dimension as I think the dimension of life is everything because I think everything consists of any thought, and something that is apart of making up everything, and therefore, I think the dimension of thought, and the dimension of something is overlapping, and co-existing with the dimension of life because I think any thought is apart of making up something that is apart of making up everything.

If I think the dimension of thought, and the dimension of something is overlapping, and co-existing with the dimension of life, than how is something able to be something as I think how something is able to be something is how something is able to be what something is in life? I do not think someone can possibly be able to be knowing for themselves, as to how something is able to be something because I do not think someone can possibly be able to be knowing for themselves, as to what the very essence of how something is able to be something as I think what the very essence of how something is able to be something is the very essence of how something is able to be what something is in life. I do not think someone can possibly be able to be knowing for themselves, as to what the very essence of how something is able to be something as I think what the very essence of how something is able to be something is the very essence of how something is able to be what something is in life because I do not think someone can possibly be able to be knowing for themselves, as to how something is able to be something as I think how something is able to be something is the very essence of how something is able to be what something is in life, and therefore, I think God is somehow able to be responsible for how something is able to be something because I think something is intellectually beyond someone's intelligence, as to how something is able to be something as I think how something is able to be something is the very essence of how something is able to be what something is in life. If I think God is somehow able to be responsible for how something is able to be something, than I think how something is able to be something is God's choice with how something is able to be something as I think how something is able to be something is of any thought that is apart of making up something because I think God is somehow able to be responsible for how something is able to be something, and therefore, I think everything all comes down to what the first thought is in life that is apart of making up something as I think what the first thought is in life that is apart of making up something is God's choice with what the first thought is in life that is apart of making up something because I think how the first thought is able to be what the first thought is in life that is apart of making up something is any thought that is apart of making up everything as I think any thought that is apart of making up everything is God's choice with how any thought is able to be a thought that is apart of making up everything.

If I think everything all comes down to what the first thought is in life that is apart of making up something, than I do not think someone can possibly be able to be knowing for themselves, as to how any thought is able to be a thought that is apart of making up everything is able to be God's choice with any thought that is apart of making up everything because I do not think someone can possibly be able to be knowing for themselves, as to how God is able to be having a choice with how God is somehow able to be responsible for any thought that is apart of making up everything. I do not think someone can possibly be able to be knowing for themselves, as to how God is able to be having a choice with how God is somehow able to be responsible for any thought that is apart of making up everything because I do not think someone can possibly be able to be knowing for themselves, as to how God is able to be having a choice, but I think how God is able to be having a choice is God's will because I think how God is doing what God is doing is God's will as I think how God is doing what God is doing is how God is able to be having a choice. If I think how God is able to be having a choice is God's will, than I think how God is doing what God is doing is God's will as I think how God is doing what God is doing is God's choice because I think what God's choice is in life is God's will, and therefore, I think the dimension of God's will is God's choice because I think what God's choice is in life is God's will. If I think the dimension of God's will is God's choice, than I think God's choice is God's will because I think how God is able to be having a choice is God's will as I think what God's choice is in life is God's will, even though, I do not think someone can possibly be able to be knowing for themselves, as to how God is able to be having a choice because I do not think someone can possibly be able to be knowing for themselves, as to how God is doing what God is doing in life as I think how God is doing what God is doing is how God is able to be having a choice, and therefore, I think how God is able to be having a choice is how God is somehow able to be responsible for any thought that is apart of making up everything because I think any thought that is apart of making up everything is God's choice with any thought that is apart of making up everything.

If I think how God is able to be having a choice is how God is somehow able to be responsible for any thought that is apart of making up everything, than I think how God is able to be having a choice consists of God being able to be having one kind of choice with how God is somehow able to be responsible for any thought that is apart of making up everything because I think God's choice is always a good, and always a right kind of choice with how God is somehow able to be responsible for any thought that is apart of making up everything, and therefore, I do not think God has a bad or a wrong kind of choice with how God is somehow able to be responsible for any thought that is apart of making up everything because I do not think God's choice is ever a bad or ever a wrong kind of choice with how God is somehow able to be responsible for any thought that is apart of making up everything. I do not think God's choice is ever a bad or ever a wrong kind of choice with how God is somehow able to be responsible for any thought that is apart of making up everything because I think God created everything with God's thoughts for God to be knowing how any thought is able to be a thought that is apart of making up everything, and therefore, I think God's choice is always good, and right with how God is somehow able to be responsible for any thought that is apart of making up everything because I think God created everything with God's thoughts for God to be knowing how any thought is able to be a thought that is apart of making up everything.

If I think God's choice is always good, and right with how God is somehow able to be responsible for any thought that is apart of making up everything, than I think God's will is always good, and right as I think God's choice is always good, and right because I think God's will is God's choice as I think God's choice is always good, and right with how God is somehow able to be responsible for any thought that is apart of making up everything, and therefore, I think God's will can be thought of as being of God's free will because I think God's free will is God's will as I think God's will is God's choice. If I think God's will can be thought of as being of God's free will, than I think God's free will, and God's will, and God's choice is always good, and right with how God is somehow able to be responsible for any thought that is apart of making up everything because I think God created everything with God's thoughts for God to be knowing how any thought is able to be a thought that is apart of making up everything, and therefore, I think any thought that is apart of making up everything is God's choice with any thought that is apart of making up everything because I think God created everything with God's thoughts for God to be knowing how any thought is able to be a thought that is apart of making up everything.

If I think God created everything with God's thoughts for God to be knowing how any thought is able to be a thought that is apart of making up everything, than I think any thought is apart of making something as I think any thought is apart of making up everything because I think any thought is apart of making up something that is apart of making up everything, and therefore, I think the sound of any note that someone can be able to be playing on any guitar can be an example of how any thought is apart of making up something because I think the sound of any note that someone can be able to be playing on any guitar is a thought that is any thought as I think any thought is apart of making up something. I think the sound of any note that someone can be able to be playing on any guitar is a thought that is any thought as I think any thought is apart of making up something because I think any note of any sound that someone can be able to be playing on any guitar is something as I think any note of any sound that someone can be able to be playing on any guitar is an image or a reflection of how the sound of any note that someone can be able to be playing on any guitar is able to be a thought. I think any note of any sound that someone can be able to be playing on any guitar is something as I think any note of any sound that someone can be able to be playing on any guitar is an image or a reflection of how the sound of any note that someone can be able to be playing on any guitar is able to be a thought because I think any note of any sound that someone can be able to be playing on any guitar is how something is in life as I think how something is in life is of any thought, and therefore, I think the sound of any note that someone can be able to be playing on any guitar is apart of making up any note of any sound that someone can be able to be playing on any guitar because I think any thought is apart of making up something as I think any thought is apart of making up how something is in life. I think any thought is apart of making up something as I think any thought is apart of making up how something is in life because I think something is how something is in life as I think any thought is apart of making up something, and therefore, I think any thought is apart of making up something because I think the sound of any note that someone can be able to be playing on any guitar is apart of making up any note of any sound that someone can be able to be playing on any guitar. If I think any thought is apart of making up something, than I think the sound of any note that someone can be able to be playing of any guitar, and any note of any sound that someone can be able to be playing on any guitar is apart of making up everything as I think any thought, and something is apart of making up everything because I think everything consists of the sound of any note that someone can be able to be playing on any guitar, and any note of any sound that someone can be able to be playing on any guitar that is apart of making up everything as I think everything consists of any thought, and something that is apart of making up everything, and therefore, I think any thought is apart of making up something that is apart of making up everything because I think the sound of any note that someone can be able to be playing on any guitar is apart of making up any note of any sound that someone can be able to be playing on any guitar that is apart of making up everything.

If I think any thought is apart of making up something that is apart of making up everything, than I think God is somehow able to be responsible for creating any sound of any note, and any note of any sound, and any different combination of any sound of any note, and any different combination of any note of any sound that someone can possibly be able to be playing on any guitar as I think any sound of any note, and any note of any sound is apart of making up any different combination of any sound of any note, and any different combination of any note of any sound that is able to be coming from any object because I think God is somehow able to be responsible for creating any sound that is able to be coming from any object, that someone can be able to be playing any different arrangement of sounds that is able to be coming from any object. I think God is somehow able to be responsible for creating any sound that is able to be coming from any object, that someone can be able to be playing any different arrangement of sounds that is able to be coming from any object because I do not think someone is able to be creating any sound that is able to be coming from any object as I think God is somehow able to be responsible for creating any sound that is able to be coming from any object, and therefore, I think someone can be able to be making sounds that is able to be coming from any object that someone can be playing, and I think someone can be able to be making their own sound of music from someone playing with any object for someone to be making any different arrangement of sounds that is able to be coming from any object, but I do not think any sound of music that someone can possibly be able to be making is completely someone's own music as I do not think any sound of music that someone is able to be making is someone's race of music because I think any sound of music that someone can possibly be able to making is God's music. I think any sound of music that someone can possibly be able to making is God's music because I think God created every possible sound of music that is able to be coming from any sound that is able to be coming from any object, before someone has ever been able to be playing any sound of music from someone playing with any object for someone to be making any different arrangement of sounds that is able to be coming from any object, and therefore, I think every possible sound of music that someone can possibly be able to making is God's music because I think God created every possible sound of music that is able to be coming from any sound that is able to be coming from any object for someone to be discovering and enjoying. If I think every possible sound of music that someone can possibly be able to making is God's music, than I think God created all sound for God to be creating all music because I think God created everything with God's thoughts for God to be creating all music as I think God created everything with God's thoughts for God to be creating all sound, and therefore, I think all music is God's music because I think God created all music for all music to be God's music.

If I think all music is God's music, than I do not think someone is able to be creating any music because I do not think someone is able to be creating the sound of any sound that is able to be coming from any object for someone not to be able to be creating any music, and therefore, I think someone is only be able to be making music with any sound that is able to be coming from any object because I do not think someone is able to be creating any music. If I think someone is only be able to be making music with any sound that is able to be coming from any object, than I do not think someone can possibly be able to be knowing for themselves, as to what creation is in life because I do not think someone can create something for someone not to be able to be knowing for themselves, as to what creation is in life. I do not think someone can create something for someone not to be able to be knowing for themselves, as to what creation is in life because I do not think someone can create any thought for someone not to be able to be creating something. I do not think someone can create any thought for someone not to be able to be creating something because I do not think someone can create any thought that is apart of making up something, and therefore, I do not think someone can create something as I think someone can be experiencing something because I think something is created by God as I think something is a creation of God's thoughts that is apart of making up something.

If I do not think someone can create something as I think someone can be experiencing something, than I think someone can only be able to be imitating something that someone can possibly experience as I think something has come before someone for someone to come along, and to be imitating something that someone can possibly experience because I do not think someone can create something from something's very existence as I think God can create something from something's very existence, even though, I think someone can think someone is creating something as I think someone is imitating something, however, I do not think someone is actually creating something as I think someone is imitating something because I do not think someone is able to creating something as I think God is able to be creating something. If I do not think someone is able to creating something as I think God is able to be creating something, than I think someone can think someone is creating something as I think someone is making something because I think someone is making something as I think someone is imitating something, but I do not think someone is actually creating something as I think someone is making something because I do not think someone is able to creating something as I think someone is making something, however, I think something that isn't wrong is someone's preference, as to whether or not if someone is going to be liking something that isn't wrong as I think someone's music is someone's preference, as to whether or not if someone is going to be liking the sound of someone's music because I think something that isn't wrong is of God's creation as I think all music is God's music, and therefore, I think God is the greatest musician because I think God created all music for God to be the greatest musician. I think God created all music for God to be the greatest musician because I think God is the creator of all music as I think God created all music for all music to be God's music, even though, I do not think there is such a thing as there being good or bad music because I think God is the creator of all music as I think God created all music for all music to be God's music, and therefore, I think all sound is God's music because I think God created everything with God's thoughts for God to be creating all sound as I think God created all sound for all sound to be God's music.

If I think all sound is God's music, than I think God is the greatest artist because I think God created everything for God to be the greatest artist. I think God created everything for God to be the greatest artist because I think everything is of God's work of art for God to be the greatest artist. I think everything is of God's work of art for God to be the greatest artist because I think God is the creator of everything for everything to be of God's work of art. I think God is the creator of everything for everything to be of God's work of art because I think God created everything for everything to be beautiful, and therefore, I think everything is beautiful because I think God created everything for everything to be beautiful. If I think everything is beautiful, than I think everything is someone's preference, as to what someone thinks is beautiful or not because I think everything is of God's work of art for everything to be beautiful, and therefore, I think God is the greatest artist because I think everything is of God's work of art for everything to be beautiful. If I think God is the greatest artist, than I think God created something for someone to be imitating something as I think God created something for someone to be an artist because I think someone can be imitating something for someone to be an artist, and therefore, I think everything is of God's creation for someone to be an artist with everything because I think God created everything with God's thoughts for someone to be an artist with everything, even though, I think God is the greatest artist because I think God created everything with God's thoughts for God to be the greatest artist.

If I think God is the greatest artist, than I think someone can think someone can figure out what thoughts are in life because I think someone can think thoughts are only able to be taking place within parts of someone's brain as I think someone can think thoughts are images that is being made from parts of someone's brain, and chemicals that is taking place within parts of a someone's brain, but I do not think someone's thoughts explain how everything is able to be a thought because I think how everything is in life is how everything is able to be a thought. I think how everything is in life is how everything is able to be a thought because I think someone is able to be having someone's thoughts from something that someone can experience that is a thought, and therefore, I do not think thoughts are just images that is being made from parts of someone's brain as I think someone can think thoughts are only able to be taking place within parts of someone's brain because I do not think someone's thoughts explain how everything is able to be a thought. I do not think someone's thoughts explain how everything is able to be a thought because I think someone's thoughts is a reflection of how everything is able to be a thought. I think someone's thoughts is a reflection of how everything is able to be a thought because I think someone's thoughts is identical to how everything is in life, and therefore, I think everything is a thought because I think someone is able to be having someone's thoughts from something that someone can experience that is a thought. If I think everything is a thought, than I think everything is a picture of how everything is able to be a thought because I think someone's thoughts are images that is somehow able to be identical to something that is a picture of how something is able to be a thought, even though, I think someone can think someone can figure out, as to just exactly what thoughts are in life by trying to figure out, as to just exactly someone's thoughts are in life from someone connecting probes of a mechanical device onto someone's head, or from someone to be getting someone else to be placing someone's head into a machine that is a mechanical device that is designed by someone to try to be detecting, as to what someone's thoughts are in life from what someone is thinking about in someone's head, but I do not think someone can be able to figure out, as to just exactly what thoughts are in life by trying to figure out, as to just exactly what someone's thoughts are in life from someone connecting probes of a mechanical device onto someone's head, or from someone to be getting someone else to be placing someone's head into a machine that is a mechanical device that is designed by someone to try to be detecting, as to what someone's thoughts are in life from what someone is thinking about in someone's head because I think someone will only be able to figure out is how thoughts are in life, and not what thoughts are in life. I think someone will only be able to figure out is how thoughts are in life, and not what thoughts are in life because I think someone will only be able to figure out is how someone's thoughts are in life, and not what someone's thoughts are in life. I think someone will only be able to figure out is how someone's thoughts are in life, and not what someone's thoughts are in life because I do not think there is any mechanical device that someone can be able to design or build that is going to be able to be indicating or detecting in any sort of way, as to just exactly what any mechanical devices thoughts are in life that is apart of making up how any mechanical device is able to be what any mechanical device is in life as I think everything is made up of thoughts that is apart of making up everything as being something. I do not think there is any mechanical device that someone can be able to design or build that is going to be able to be indicating or detecting in any sort of way, as to just exactly what any mechanical devices thoughts are in life that is apart of making up how any mechanical device is able to be what any mechanical device is in life as I think everything is made up of thoughts that is apart of making up everything as being something because I think what someone's thoughts are in life is identical to what something's thoughts are in life as I think something, such as any mechanical device that someone can be making to try to be detecting, as to what someone's thoughts are in life from what someone is thinking about in someone's head is something that is of what something's thoughts are in life, and therefore, I do not think someone can possibly be able to be knowing for themselves, as to what the very essence of what someone's thoughts are in life because I do not think someone can possibly be able to be knowing for themselves, as to what the very essence of what something's thoughts are in life that is of how something is in life as I think what someone's thoughts are in life is identical to what something's thoughts are in life that is apart of making up how something is in life.

If I do not think someone can possibly be able to be knowing for themselves, as to what the very essence of what someone's thoughts are in life, than I do not think someone can possibly be able to be knowing for themselves, as to how any thought is able to be a thought as I think how any thought is able to be a thought is what someone's thoughts are in life because I do not think any thought is someone's choice with how any thought is able to be a thought as I think how any thought is able to be a thought is what someone's thoughts are in life, and therefore, I do not think someone can possibly be able to be knowing for themselves, as to how any thought is able to be a thought as I think how any thought is able to be a thought is what something's thoughts are in life because I do not think any thought is someone's choice with how any thought is able to be a thought as I think how any thought is able to be a thought is what something's thoughts are in life that is apart of making up how something is in life. If I do not think someone can possibly be able to be knowing for themselves, as to how any thought is able to be a thought as I think how any thought is able to be a thought is what something's thoughts are in life, than I think any thought is God's choice with how any thought is able to be a thought because I think how any thought is able to be a thought is what someone's thoughts are in life, and how any thought is able to be a thought is what something's thoughts are in life that is apart of making up how something is in life, and therefore, I do not think any thought is something's choice with how any thought is able to be a thought as I think how any thought is able to be a thought is what something's thoughts are in life that is apart of making up how something is in life because I think what something's thoughts are in life that is apart of making up how something is in life is of how any thought is able to be thought of itself as I think any thought is God's choice with how any thought is able to be a thought, however, I think someone can try to understand for themselves, as to how something's thoughts are in life because I think how something is in life is how something's thoughts are in life. If I think someone can try to understand for themselves, as to how something's thoughts are in life, than I do not think any thought is someone's choice with how any thought is able to be a thought as I think how any thought is able to be a thought is what someone's thoughts are in life because I think what someone's thoughts are in life is of how any thought is able to be a thought as I think any thought is God's choice with how any thought is able to be a thought, however, I think someone can try to understand for themselves, as to how someone's thoughts are in life from how something is in relation to what someone's thoughts are in life because I think what someone is thinking about in someone's life is what someone's thoughts are in life, and therefore, I think someone can try to understand for themselves, as to how thoughts are in life because I think someone can try to understand for themselves, as to how something's thoughts are in life as I think someone can try to understand for themselves, as to how someone's thoughts are in life from how something is in relation to what someone's thoughts are in life for someone to be trying to understand for themselves, as to how thoughts are in life.

If I think someone can try to understand for themselves, as to how thoughts are in life, than I think how thoughts are in life is how thoughts are able to be what thoughts are in life because I think how any thought is able to be a thought is how thoughts are able to be what thoughts are in life, and therefore, I think how thoughts are in life is how thoughts are able to be what thoughts are in life as I think how thoughts are in life is how any thought is able to be a thought because I think how any thought is able to be a thought is how thoughts are able to be what thoughts are in life. If I think how any thought is able to be a thought is how thoughts are able to be what thoughts are in life, than I think how any thought is a thought is how thoughts are in life because I think how any thought is a thought is how any thought is able to be a thought as I think how thoughts are in life is how any thought is able to be a thought, and therefore, I think how any thought is a thought is how any thought is able to be a thought as I think how any thought is a thought is how thoughts are in life because I think how thoughts are in life is how any thought is able to be a thought. If I think how thoughts are in life is how any thought is able to be a thought, than I think God is somehow able to be responsible for any thought because I think any thought is God's choice with how any thought is able to be a thought as I think how any thought is a thought is how any thought is able to be a thought, and therefore, I think God is somehow able to be responsible for how any thought is able to be a thought because I think any thought is God's choice with how any thought is able to be a thought as I think how any thought is a thought is how any thought is able to be a thought.

If I think God is somehow able to be responsible for how any thought is able to be a thought, than how is God somehow able to be responsible for any thought? I think God is somehow be able to be responsible for any thought because I think God is somehow able to be creating any thought somehow within God, and therefore, how is God somehow able to be creating any thought somehow within God? I think God is somehow able to be creating any thought somehow within God because I think God is somehow able to be creating any thought somehow with God's state of consciousness, along with God's will as I think God's state of consciousness, and God's will is apart of God, and therefore, I think any thought is of God because I think God is somehow able to be creating any thought somehow with God's state of consciousness, along with God's will as I think God's state of consciousness, and God's will is apart of God. If I think any thought is of God, than I think any thought is somehow able to be taking place within God, without being God as I think any thought is apart of God, without being God because I think God is somehow able to be creating any thought somehow with God's state of consciousness, along with God's will as I think God's state of consciousness, and God's will is apart of God, and therefore, I think God is somehow able to be creating any thought somehow within God because I think any thought is somehow able to be taking place within God, without being God as I think any thought is apart of God, without being God.

If I think God is somehow able to be creating any thought somehow within God, than I think God is somehow able to be creating someone somehow within God as I think God is somehow able to be creating God's thoughts somehow within God because I think God created everything with God's thoughts for God to be creating someone, and therefore, I think everything consists of God's thoughts, someone, and something that is apart of making up everything because I think God created everything with God's thoughts for God's thoughts, someone, and something to be apart of making up everything.

If I think everything consists of God's thoughts, someone, and something that is apart of making up everything, than how is God somehow able to be creating someone somehow within God? I think God is somehow able to be creating someone somehow within God because I think God is somehow able to be creating someone somehow with God's state of consciousness, along with God's will as I think God's state of consciousness, and God's will is apart of God, and therefore, I think someone is of God because I think God is somehow able to be creating someone somehow with God's state of consciousness, along with God's will as I think God's state of consciousness, and God's will is apart of God. If I think someone is of God, than I think someone is somehow able to be taking place within God, without being God as I think someone is apart of God, without being God because I think God is somehow able to be creating someone somehow with God's state of consciousness, along with God's will as I think God's state of consciousness, and God's will is apart of God, and therefore, I think God is somehow able to be creating someone somehow within God because I think someone is somehow able to be taking place within God, without being God as I think someone is apart of God, without being God.

If I think God is somehow able to be creating someone somehow within God, than I think God is somehow able to be creating something somehow within God as I think God is somehow able to be creating any thought somehow within God because I think something is of any thought as I think any thought is apart of making up something, and therefore, how is God somehow able to be creating something somehow within God? I think God is somehow able to be creating something somehow within God because I think God is somehow able to be creating something somehow with God's state of consciousness, along with God's will as I think God's state of consciousness, and God's will is apart of God, even though, I do not think God is somehow able to be creating something somehow with God's state of consciousness, along with God's will exactly the same as I think God is somehow able to be creating any thought somehow within God because I think something is an image or a reflection of any thought that is apart of making up something as I think any thought is the instructions of something, and therefore, I think something is of God because I think God is somehow able to be creating something somehow with God's state of consciousness, along with God's will as I think God's state of consciousness, and God's will is apart of God. If I think something is of God, than I think something is somehow able to be taking place within God, without being God as I think something is apart of God, without being God because I think God is somehow able to be creating something somehow with God's state of consciousness, along with God's will as I think God's state of consciousness, and God's will is apart of God, and therefore, I think God is somehow able to be creating something somehow within God because I think something is somehow able to be taking place within God, without being God as I think something is apart of God, without being God.

If I think God is somehow able to be creating something somehow within God, than I think God is somehow able to be creating everything somehow within God as I think God is somehow able to be creating any thought, and something somehow within God because I think everything consists of any thought, someone, and something that is apart of making up everything, and therefore, how is God somehow able to be creating everything somehow within God? I think God is somehow able to be creating everything somehow within God because I think God is somehow able to be creating everything somehow with God's state of consciousness, along with God's will as I think God's state of consciousness, and God's will is apart of God, and therefore, I think everything is of God because I think God is somehow able to be creating everything somehow with God's state of consciousness, along with God's will as I think God's state of consciousness, and God's will is apart of God. If I think everything is of God, than I think everything is somehow able to be taking place within God, without being God as I think everything is apart of God, without being God because I think God is somehow able to be creating everything somehow with God's state of consciousness, along with God's will as I think God's state of consciousness, and God's will is apart of God, and therefore, I think God is somehow able to be creating everything somehow within God because I think everything is somehow able to be taking place within God, without being God as I think everything is apart of God, without being God.

If I think God is somehow able to be creating everything somehow within God, than I think God is somehow able to be creating God's thoughts somehow within God as I think God is somehow able to be creating everything somehow within God because I think God created everything with God's thoughts for God's thoughts to be apart of making up everything, and therefore, how is God somehow able to be creating God's thoughts somehow within God? I think God is somehow able to be creating God's thoughts somehow within God because I think God is somehow able to be creating God's thoughts somehow with God's state of consciousness, along with God's will as I think God's state of consciousness, and God's will is apart of God, and therefore, I think God's thoughts is of God because I think God is somehow able to be creating God's thoughts somehow with God's state of consciousness, along with God's will as I think God's state of consciousness, and God's will is apart of God. If I think God's thoughts is of God, than I think God's thoughts is somehow able to be taking place within God, without being God as I think God's thoughts is apart of God, without being God because I think God is somehow able to be creating God's thoughts somehow with God's state of consciousness, along with God's will as I think God's state of consciousness, and God's will is apart of God, and therefore, I think God is somehow able to be creating God's thoughts because I think God's thoughts is somehow able to be taking place within God, without being God as I think God's thoughts is apart of God, without being God. If I think God is somehow able to be creating God's thoughts, than I think God is somehow able to be responsible for creating everything because I think God created everything with God's thoughts for God to be creating everything, and therefore, I think God has thoughts because I think God is somehow able to be knowing, as to how everything is able to be created in life for God to be creating everything with God's thoughts.

Chapter 7

God's mind

I would like to talk about how dimensions are in life in relation to what dimensions are in life by talking about God's mind, that can possibly have something to do with how dimensions are in life is in relation to what dimensions are in life because I think God is somehow creating everything with God's mind as I think God is somehow able to be responsible for creating everything. I think God is somehow creating everything with God's mind as I think God is somehow able to be responsible for creating everything because I think everything is somehow being stored within God, without being God as I think God is somehow able to be creating everything to somehow be able to be taking place within God, without being God. I think everything is somehow being stored within God, without being God as I think God is somehow able to be creating everything to somehow be able to be taking place within God, without being God because I think everything is taking place within the entire area of how everything is able to be taking place in life as I think God is somehow able to be creating everything to somehow be able to be taking place within God, without being God, and therefore, I think God is somehow able to be storing everything to somehow be able to be taking place within God, without being God as I think God is somehow able to be creating everything to somehow be able to be taking place within God, without being God because I think God is somehow able to be creating everything to somehow be able to be taking place within the entire area of everything as I think God is somehow able to be creating everything to somehow be able to be taking place within God, without being God. I think God is somehow able to be creating everything to somehow be able to be taking place within the entire area of everything as I think God is somehow able to be creating everything to somehow be able to be taking place within God, without being God because I do not think everything is intellectually beyond God with how everything is in life as I think God is somehow able to be creating everything to somehow be able to be taking place within God, without being God. I do not think everything is intellectually beyond God with how everything is in life as I think God is somehow able to be creating everything to somehow be able to be taking place within God, without being God because I do not think everything is someone that is something of itself, that is somehow able to be knowing, as to how everything is in life. I do not think everything is someone that is something of itself, that is somehow able to be knowing, as to how everything is in life because I think everything is something that isn't able to be knowing, as to how everything is in life. I think everything is something that isn't able to be knowing, as to how everything is in life because I think if everything is intellectually beyond someone's intelligence in life, as to how everything is able to be taking place in life, than I think everything must be the work of God as I think God is someone that is something of itself, that is somehow able to be knowing, as to how everything is able to be taking place in life, and therefore, I do not think everything is intellectually beyond God with how everything is in life as I think God is somehow able to be creating everything to somehow be taking place within God, without being God because I do not think everything is intellectually able to be beyond God with how everything is in life as I think God is somehow able to be creating everything to somehow be taking place within God, without being God. I do not think everything is intellectually able to be beyond God with how everything is in life as I think God is somehow able to be creating everything to somehow be taking place within God, without being God because I do not think everything is intellectually beyond itself for everything not to be able to be intellectually beyond God with how everything is in life as I think God is somehow able to be creating everything to somehow be taking place within God, without being God.

If I do not think everything is intellectually able to be beyond God with how everything is in life as I think God is somehow able to be creating everything to somehow be taking place within God, without being God, than I do not think everything is physically beyond God as I think God is somehow able to be creating everything to somehow be taking place within God, without being God because if I do not think everything is intellectually able to be beyond God with how everything is in life as I think God is somehow able to be creating everything to somehow be taking place within God, without being God, than I do not think everything is physically able to be beyond God with how everything is in life as I think God is somehow able to be creating everything to somehow be taking place within God, without being God, and therefore, I do not think everything is intellectually and physically beyond God as I think God is somehow able to be creating everything to somehow be taking place within God, without being God because I do not think everything is intellectually and physically able to be beyond God as I think God is somehow able to be creating everything to somehow be taking place within God, without being God. If I do not think everything is intellectually and physically able to be beyond God as I think God is somehow able to be creating everything to somehow be taking place within God, without being God, than I think everything must somehow be able to be taking place within God, without being God as I think God is somehow able to be creating everything to somehow be taking place within God, without being God because I do not think everything is intellectually and physically beyond God as I think God is somehow able to be creating everything to somehow be taking place within God, without being God, and therefore, I think God is somehow able to be creating everything to somehow be able to be taking place within a storage area of God as I think God is somehow able to be creating everything to somehow be able to be taking place within God, without being God because I do not think everything is intellectually and physically beyond God as I think God is somehow able to be creating everything to somehow be taking place within God, without being God. If I think God is somehow able to be creating everything to somehow be able to be taking place within a storage area of God as I think God is somehow able to be creating everything to somehow be able to be taking place within God, without being God, than I think God is somehow able to be creating everything to be taking place within the entire area of how everything is able to be taking place in life for God to somehow be creating everything to be taking place within a storage area of God as I think God is somehow able to be creating everything to somehow be taking place within God, without being God because I do not think everything that is taking place within the entire area of how everything is able to be taking place in life is intellectually and physically able to be beyond God as I think God is somehow able to be creating everything to somehow be taking place within God, without being God. I do not think everything that is taking place within the entire area of how everything is able to be taking place in life is intellectually and physically able to be beyond God as I think God is somehow able to be creating everything to somehow be taking place within God, without being God because I do not think everything is intellectually and physically able to be beyond God as I think God is somehow able to be creating everything to somehow be taking place within God, without being God, and therefore, I think God is somehow able to be creating everything to be taking place within the entire area of how everything is able to be taking place in life for God to somehow be creating everything to be taking place within a storage area of God as I think God is somehow able to be creating everything to somehow be taking place within God, without being God because I think God is somehow able to be creating everything to be taking place within the entire area of how everything is able to be taking place in life to somehow be taking place within a storage area of God as I think God is somehow able to be creating everything to somehow be taking place within God, without being God. If I think God is somehow able to be creating everything to be taking place within the entire area of how everything is able to be taking place in life for God to somehow be creating everything to be taking place within a storage area of God as I think God is somehow able to be creating everything to somehow be taking place within God, without being God, than I think God is somehow able to be creating everything to somehow be able to be taking place within a storage area of God as I think God is somehow able to be creating everything to somehow be able to be taking place within God, without being God because I think God is somehow able to be creating everything to be taking place within the entire area of how everything is able to be taking place in life as I think God is somehow able to be creating everything to somehow be taking place within God, without being God, and therefore, I do not God is interfering with everything that can be taking place in its own time and place as I think God is somehow able to be creating everything to somehow be taking place within God, without being God because I think God is somehow able to be creating everything to somehow be able to be taking place within a storage area of God as I think God is somehow able to be creating everything to somehow be able to be taking place within God, without being God.

If I do not God is interfering with everything that can be taking place in its own time and place as I think God is somehow able to be creating everything to somehow be taking place within God, without being God, than I think everything that is taking place within the entire area of everything is the storage area of God as I think everything is the storage area of God because I think everything that is taking place within the entire area of everything is everything as I think God is somehow able to be creating everything to somehow be able to be taking place within a storage area of God, and therefore, I think there is a storage area of God because I think God is somehow able to be creating everything to somehow be able to be taking place within a storage area of God. If I think there is a storage area of God, than I think God is somehow able to be creating everything to somehow be able to be taking place within this storage area of God because I think God is somehow able to be creating everything to somehow be able to be taking place within a storage area of God, and therefore, I think how God is somehow able to be creating everything to somehow be able to be taking place within this storage area of God is how God is somehow able to be creating everything to somehow be able to be taking place within God, without being God because I think God is somehow able to be creating everything to somehow be able to be taking place within this storage area of God for God to somehow be able to be creating everything to somehow be able to be taking place within God, without being God. If I think how God is somehow able to be creating everything to somehow be able to be taking place within this storage area of God is how God is somehow able to be creating everything to somehow be able to be taking place within God, without being God, than I think everything is somehow able to be taking place within the storage area of God because I think God is somehow able to be creating everything to somehow be able to be taking place within the storage area of God, and therefore, I think the storage area of God is for everything as I think the storage area of God is for God because I think everything is somehow able to be taking place within the storage area of God as I think God is somehow able to be creating everything to somehow be able to be taking place within the storage area of God, even though, I do not think someone can possibly be able to be knowing for themselves, as to what the storage area of God is in life because I do not think someone can possibly be able to be knowing for themselves, as to how God is somehow able to be creating everything to somehow be able to be taking place within the storage area of God, but I think God is somehow able to be having a storage area of God because I think everything is somehow be able to be taking place within the storage area of God as I think God is somehow able to be creating everything to somehow be able to be taking place within the storage area of God. If I think God is somehow able to be having a storage area of God, than I think everything is somehow able to be taking place within God, without being God because I think God is somehow able to be creating everything to somehow be able to be taking place within the storage area of God, and therefore, I think everything is somehow able to be taking place within the storage area of God, without being God because I think everything is somehow able to be taking place within God, without being God. I think everything is somehow able to be taking place within God, without being God because I think God is somehow able to be creating everything to somehow be able to be taking place within God, without being God. I think God is somehow able to be creating everything to somehow be able to be taking place within God, without being God because I think God is somehow able to be creating everything to somehow be able to be taking place within the storage area of God, and therefore, I think God is somehow able to be creating everything to somehow be able to be taking place within the storage area of God somehow with God's state of consciousness, along with God's will as I think God's state of consciousness, and God's will is apart of God, without being God because I think God is somehow able to be creating everything to somehow be able to be taking place within God, without being God.

If I think God is somehow able to be creating everything to somehow be able to be taking place within the storage area of God somehow with God's state of consciousness, along with God's will, than I think the storage area of God is something because I think God is somehow able to be creating everything to somehow be able to be taking place within the storage area of God, and therefore, I think the storage area of God is something that is overlapping, and co-existing along with everything that is something because I think God is somehow able to be creating everything to somehow be able to be taking place within the storage area of God. If I think the storage area of God is something that is overlapping, and co-existing along with everything that is something, than I think the storage area of God is something that is overlapping, and co-existing along with everything that is something because I think God is somehow able to be creating everything to somehow be able to be taking place within the storage area of God, and therefore, I think the storage area of God is a dimension that is overlapping, and co-existing along with everything that is a dimension because I think God is somehow able to be creating everything to somehow be able to be taking place within the storage area of God. If I think the storage area of God is a dimension that is overlapping, and co-existing along with everything that is a dimension, than I think someone can think of the storage area of God as being the dimension of God's mind or God's mind because I think God's mind is the dimension of God's mind as I think God's mind is the storage area of God, and therefore, I think God has a mind because I think God's mind is the storage area of God. If I think God has a mind, than I think God's mind is overlapping, and co-existing along with the dimension of life as I think the dimension of life is everything because I think God is somehow able to be creating everything to somehow be able to be taking place within God's mind as I think God is somehow able to be creating everything to somehow be able to be taking place within the storage area of God, and therefore, I think everything is God's mind as I think everything is the storage area of God because I think God is somehow able to be creating everything to somehow be able to be taking place within God's mind as I think God is somehow able to be creating everything to somehow be able to be taking place within the storage area of God.

If I think everything is God's mind as I think everything is the storage area of God, than I think God's mind is the storage area of God as I think the storage area of God is God's mind because I think God's mind is the entire area of everything as I think the storage area of God is the entire area of everything, and therefore, I think God's mind is a singular dimension as I think God is taking place within God's own singular dimension because I think God's mind is the entire area of everything as I think God is somehow able to be creating everything to somehow be able to be taking place within God's mind. If I think God's mind is a singular dimension as I think God is taking place within God's own singular dimension, than I think God is somehow able to be creating everything to somehow be able to be taking place within God's mind somehow with God's state of consciousness, along with God's will as I think God is somehow able to be creating everything to somehow be able to be taking place within the storage area of God somehow with God's state of consciousness, along with God's will because I think God's mind is the storage area of God, and therefore, I think the dimension of God's mind is overlapping, and co-existing along with God's will, and God's state of consciousness because I think God is somehow able to be creating everything to somehow be able to be taking place within God's mind somehow with God's state of consciousness, along with God's will. If I think the dimension of God's mind is overlapping, and co-existing along with God's will, and God's state of consciousness, than I think God's mind is overlapping, and co-existing along with God because I think God's mind is a storage area of God. I think God's mind is a storage area of God because I think God's mind is somehow able to be taking place within God, without being God as I think God's mind is apart of God, without being God. I think God's mind is somehow able to be taking place within God, without being God as I think God's mind is apart of God, without being God because I think God is somehow creating everything to be taking place within God, without being God as I think God is somehow creating everything to somehow be apart of God, without being God. I think God is somehow creating everything to be taking place within God, without being God as I think God is somehow creating everything to somehow be apart of God, without being God because I think God is somehow creating everything to be taking place within God's mind, without being God's mind as I think God is somehow creating everything to somehow be apart of God's mind, without being God's mind. I think God is somehow creating everything to be taking place within God's mind, without being God's mind as I think God is somehow creating everything to somehow be apart of God's mind, without being God's mind because I think God's mind is a storage area of God, and therefore, I think God's mind is a creation of God as I think God's mind is God's creation because I think God's mind is the entire area of everything as I think God is somehow able to be creating everything to somehow be able to be taking place within God's mind.

If I think God's mind is a creation of God as I think God's mind is God's creation, than I think God is somehow able to be creating everything to somehow be able to be taking place within God's mind as I think God is somehow able to be creating everything to somehow be able to be taking place within the storage area of God because I think God's mind is a storage area of God as I think God's mind is the storage area of God, and therefore, I think God's mind is like any hard drive that can be apart of any computer because I think God's mind is a storage area of God that is apart of God, without being God as I think any hard drive is a storage area of any computer that can be apart of any computer, without being any computer. I think God's mind is a storage area of God that is apart of God, without being God as I think any hard drive is a storage area of any computer that can be apart of any computer, without being any computer because I think God is somehow able to be creating everything to somehow be able to be taking place within God's mind as I think everything that can be saved on any computer can be saved on any hard drive that can be apart of any computer, even though, I do not think God's mind is exactly alike any hard drive that can be apart of any computer because I do not think someone can possibly be able to be knowing for themselves, as to how God is somehow able to be creating everything to somehow be able to be taking place within God's mind for someone not to be able to be knowing for themselves, as to what God's mind is in life as I think someone can make any hard drive that can be apart of any computer for someone to be understanding for themselves, as to what any hard drive is in life that can apart of any computer, and therefore, I do not think someone can make God's mind as I think someone can make any hard drive that can be apart of any computer because I think God is somehow able to be creating everything to somehow be able to be taking place within God's mind for God's mind to be a storage area of God, however, I think someone can understand what God's mind is in life because I think someone can understand everything is God's mind. If I think someone can understand what God's mind is in life, than I think God is somehow able to be creating any thought to somehow be able to be taking place within God's mind as I think God is somehow able to creating something to somehow be able to be taking place within God's mind because I think something is of any thought as I think any thought is apart of making up something, and therefore, I think God is somehow able to be creating any thought to somehow be able to be taking place within God's mind as I think God is somehow able to creating everything to somehow be able to be taking place within God's mind because I think everything is of any thought as I think any thought is apart of making up something that is apart of making up everything.

If I think everything is of any thought as I think any thought is apart of making up something that is apart of making up everything, than I think God is somehow able to be creating God's thoughts to somehow be able to be taking place within God's mind as I think God is somehow able to be creating any thought to somehow be able to be taking place within God's mind because I think any thought is of God's thoughts as I think God's thoughts is any thought. I think any thought is of God's thoughts as I think God's thoughts is apart of making up any thought because I think any thought is God's thoughts as I think any thought is of God's thoughts. I think any thought is God's thoughts as I think any thought is of God's thoughts because I think any thought is God's thoughts as I think God's thoughts is any thought. I think any thought is God's thoughts as I think God's thoughts is any thought because I think any thought is of God's thoughts as I think God's thoughts is apart of making up any thought. I think any thought is of God's thoughts as I think God's thoughts is apart of making up any thought because I think any thought is of God's thoughts that is apart of making up any thought as I think God is somehow creating God's thoughts to somehow be able to be taking place within God's mind. I think any thought is of God's thoughts that is apart of making up any thought as I think God is somehow creating God's thoughts to somehow be able to be taking place within God's mind because I think God's thoughts is taking place within God's mind, without being God's mind as I think God's thoughts is apart of God's mind, without being God's mind. I think God's thoughts is taking place within God's mind, without being God's mind as I think God's thoughts is apart of God's mind, without being God's mind because I think God is somehow able to be creating any thought to somehow be able to be taking place within God's mind as I think God is somehow able to be creating God's thoughts to somehow be able to be taking place within God's mind. I think God is somehow able to be creating any thought to somehow be able to be taking place within God's mind as I think God is somehow able to be creating God's thoughts to somehow be able to be taking place within God's mind because I think any thought is God's thoughts as I think God's thoughts is any thought, and therefore, I think God's thoughts is overlapping, and co-existing along with God's mind because I think

God's thoughts is any thought as I think God is somehow able to be creating any thought to somehow be able to be taking place within God's mind. I think God's thoughts is any thought as I think God is somehow able to be creating any thought to somehow be able to be taking place within God's mind because I think any thought is taking place within God's mind, without being God's mind as I think any thought is apart of God's mind, without being God's mind. I think any thought is taking place within God's mind, without being God's mind as I think any thought is apart of God's mind, without being God's mind because I think God is somehow able to be creating God's thoughts to somehow be able to be taking place within God's mind as I think God is somehow able to be creating any thought to somehow be able to be taking place within God's mind. I think God is somehow able to be creating God's thoughts to somehow be able to be taking place within God's mind as I think God is somehow able to be creating any thought to somehow be able to be taking place within God's mind because I think any thought is of God's thoughts as I think God's thoughts is apart of making up any thought, and therefore, I think the dimension of thought is overlapping, and co-existing along with God's mind because I think the dimension of thought is God's thoughts as I think God is somehow able to be creating God's thoughts to somehow be able to be taking place within God's mind.

If I think the dimension of thought is overlapping, and co-existing along with God's mind, than I think God is somehow able to be creating God's thoughts to somehow be able to be taking place within God's mind as I think God is somehow able to be creating everything to somehow be able to be taking place within God's mind because I think everything is of God's thoughts as I think God's thoughts is apart of making up something that apart of making up everything. I think God's thoughts is apart of making everything as I think God's thoughts is apart of making up something that apart of making up everything because I think everything is of God's thoughts as I think God's thoughts is apart of making up everything, and therefore, I think something is of God's thoughts as I think everything is of God's thoughts because I think God's thoughts is apart of making something as I think God's thoughts is apart of making up everything. If I think something is of God's thoughts as I think everything is of God's thoughts, than I think something is everything as I think everything is something because I think something is of God's thoughts as I think everything is of God's thoughts, and therefore, I think everything is God's thoughts as I think God's thoughts is everything because I think everything is of God's thoughts as I think God's thoughts is apart of making up everything. I think everything is of God's thoughts as I think God's thoughts is apart of making up everything because I think everything is a creation of God as I think everything is God's creation, even though, I do not think everything is of itself for everything to be a creation of itself because if I think everything is intellectually beyond someone's intelligence, as to how everything is able to be taking place in life, than I think everything is intellectually beyond itself for everything not to be a creation of itself, and therefore, I do not think everything is of itself for everything to be a creation of itself because I think everything is of God for everything to be a creation of itself. I think everything is of God for everything to be a creation of itself because I think everything is a creation of God as I think God is somehow able to be responsible for everything, and therefore, I think everything is a creation of God as I think everything is God's creation because I think everything is God's creation as I think everything is of God's thoughts. I think everything is God's creation as I think everything is of God's thoughts because I think everything is a creation of God's thoughts as I think God's thoughts is apart of making up everything.

I think everything is a creation of God's thoughts as I think God's thoughts is apart of making up everything because I think everything is of God's thoughts that is apart of making up everything as I think

God is somehow creating God's thoughts to somehow be able to be taking place within God's mind. I think everything is of God's thoughts that is apart of making up everything as I think God is somehow creating God's thoughts to somehow be able to be taking place within God's mind because I think God's thoughts is taking place within God's mind, without being God's mind as I think God's thoughts is apart of God's mind, without being God's mind. I think God's thoughts is taking place within God's mind, without being God's mind as I think God's thoughts is apart of God's mind, without being God's mind because I think God is somehow able to be creating any thought to somehow be able to be taking place within God's mind as I think God is somehow able to be creating God's thoughts to somehow be able to be taking place within God's mind. I think God is somehow able to be creating any thought to somehow be able to be taking place within God's mind as I think God is somehow able to be creating God's thoughts to somehow be able to be taking place within God's mind because I think any thought is God's thoughts as I think God's thoughts is any thought, and therefore, I think everything is taking place within God's mind, without being God's mind as I think everything is apart of God's mind, without being God's mind because I think God is somehow able to be creating God's thoughts to somehow be able to be taking place, within God's mind as I think God is somehow able to be creating everything to somehow be able to be taking place within God's mind. I think God is somehow able to be creating God's thoughts to somehow be able to be taking place within God's mind as I think God is somehow able to be creating everything to somehow be able to be taking place within God's mind because I think everything is of God's thoughts as I think God's thoughts is apart of making up everything, and therefore, I think God is able to be thinking for God with God's thoughts as I think God's thoughts is somehow able to be taking place within God's mind because I think God is somehow able to be creating God's thoughts to somehow be able to be taking place within God's mind as I think God is somehow able to be creating everything to somehow be able to be taking place within God's mind.

If I think God is able to be thinking for God with God's thoughts as I think God's thoughts is somehow able to be taking place within God's mind, than I think everything is overlapping, and co-existing along with God's mind as I think the dimension of life is overlapping, and co-existing along with God's mind because I think everything is the dimension of life as I think God is somehow able to be creating everything to somehow be able to be taking place within God's mind, and therefore, I think God is somehow able to be creating a picture of everything to somehow be able to be taking place within God's mind as I think God is somehow creating everything to somehow be able to be taking place within God's mind because I think God is somehow able to be creating a picture of everything with God's thoughts as I think God is somehow creating everything to somehow be able to be taking place within God's mind. I think God is somehow able to be creating a picture of everything with God's thoughts as I think God is somehow creating everything to somehow be able to be taking place within God's mind because I think everything is a picture of God's thoughts as I think God is somehow able to be creating everything to somehow be able to be taking place within God's mind. I think everything is a picture of God's thoughts as I think God is somehow able to be creating everything to somehow be able to be taking place within God's mind because I think God is somehow able to be creating a picture of everything with God's thoughts as I think God is somehow able to be creating a picture of everything to somehow be able to be taking place within God's mind. I think God is somehow able to be creating a picture of everything with God's thoughts as I think God is somehow able to be creating a picture of everything to somehow be able to be taking place within God's mind because I think God is somehow creating a picture of everything with God's thoughts that is apart of making up the picture of everything as I think

God is somehow able to creating everything to somehow be able to be taking place within God's mind. I think God is somehow creating a picture of everything with God's thoughts that is apart of making up the picture of everything as I think God is somehow able to creating everything to somehow be able to be taking place within God's mind because I think God is somehow able to be creating God's thoughts that is apart of making up the picture of everything as I think God is somehow able to creating everything to somehow be able to be taking place within God's mind. I think God is somehow able to be creating God's thoughts that is apart of making up the picture of everything as I think God is somehow able to creating everything to somehow be able to be taking place within God's mind because I think God is somehow able to be creating God's thoughts to somehow be able to be taking place within God's mind as I think God is somehow able to be creating everything to somehow be able to be taking place within God's mind.

If I think God is somehow able to be creating God's thoughts that is apart of making up the picture of everything as I think God is somehow able to creating everything to somehow be able to be taking place within God's mind, than I think everything is an intelligent design as I think everything is God's intelligent design because I think everything is God's intelligent design for everything to be an intelligent design. I think everything is God's intelligent design for everything to be an intelligent design because I think God is somehow able to be creating a picture of everything with God's thoughts for everything to be God's intelligent design as I think God is somehow able to be creating a picture of everything to somehow be able to be taking place within God's mind for everything to be God's intelligent design, and therefore, I think everything is God's creation or God's design because I think God created everything with God's thoughts for everything to be God's creation or God's design as I think everything is created by God for everything to be God's creation or God's design. If I think everything is God's creation or God's design, than I think God is the greatest architect or designer because I think everything is God's creation or design for God to be the greatest architect or designer, even though, I do not think God has a house because if I think God has a house, than I think everything would be God's house because I think God would have created everything for everything to be God's house, but I do not think God created everything for everything to be God's house because I do not think God is residing within everything for everything to be God's house. I do not think God is residing within everything for everything to be God's house because I do not think God is taking place within everything for everything to be God's house. I do not think God is taking place within everything for everything to be God's house because I think everything is taking place within God for everything not to be God's house. I think everything is taking place within God for everything not to be God's house because I think God created everything for God to be beyond everything as I think God is beyond everything for everything not to be God's house, and therefore, I do not think God has a house because I do not think God is residing within everything for God not to be having a house, even though, I think someone can think God created everything for everything to be God's house because I think everything is God's design for someone to be thinking of everything as being God's house, but I do not think everything is God's house because I think everything is of God's creation for everything to be God's design as I think everything is of God for everything to be of God's creation, and not God's house for God not to be residing within everything. I think everything is of God's creation for everything to be God's design as I think everything is of God for everything to be of God's creation, and not God's house for God not to be residing within everything because I think God is somehow able to be creating a picture of everything to somehow be able to be taking place within God's mind for everything to be God's intelligent design, and therefore, I think someone is taking place in a miniscule portion of the entire picture of everything as I think God is somehow able to be creating a picture of everything to somehow be able to be taking place within God's mind because I do not think someone can possibly be able to imagine for themselves, as to how big everything is in life. I do not think someone can possibly be able to imagine for themselves, as to how big everything is in life because I think someone is living in a miniscule portion of the entire picture of everything for someone not to be able to be imagining with themselves, as to how big everything is in life, and therefore, I do not know if someone will ever be able to experience everything because I do not think someone can possibly be able to knowing for themselves, as to how big everything is in life for someone to be able to be experiencing everything as I think God created everything for God know how big everything is in life.

If I do not know if someone will ever be able to experience everything, than I think God is somehow able to be creating God's thoughts to somehow be able to be taking place within God's mind as I think God is somehow able to be creating something to somehow be able to be taking place within God's mind because I think something is of God's thoughts as I think God's thoughts is apart of making up something. I think something is of God's thoughts as I think God's thoughts is apart of making up something because I think something is God's thoughts as I think something is of God's thoughts. I think something is God's thoughts as I think something is of God's thoughts because I think something is God's thoughts as I think God's thoughts is something. I think something is God's thoughts as I think God's thoughts is something because I think something is of God's thoughts as I think God's thoughts is apart of making up something. I think something is of God's thoughts as I think God's thoughts is apart of making up something because I think something is of God's thoughts that is apart of making up something as I think God is somehow creating God's thoughts to somehow be able to be taking place within God's mind. I think something is of God's thoughts that is apart of making up something as I think God is somehow creating God's thoughts to somehow be able to be taking place within God's mind because I think God's thoughts is taking place within God's mind, without being God's mind as I think God's thoughts is apart of God's mind, without being God's mind. I think God's thoughts is taking place within God's mind, without being God's mind as I think God's thoughts is apart of God's mind, without being God's mind because I think God is somehow able to be creating something to somehow be able to be taking place within God's mind as I think God is somehow able to be creating God's thoughts to somehow be able to be taking place within God's mind. I think God is somehow able to be creating something to somehow be able to be taking place within God's mind as I think God is somehow able to be creating God's thoughts to somehow be able to be taking place within God's mind because I think something is God's thoughts as I think God's thoughts is any thought, and therefore, I think something is taking place within God's mind, without being God's mind as I think something is apart of God's mind, without being God's mind because I think God is somehow able to be creating God's thoughts to somehow be able to be taking place within God's mind as I think God is somehow able to be creating something to somehow be able to be taking place within God's mind. I think God is somehow able to be creating God's thoughts to somehow be able to be taking place within God's mind as I think God is somehow able to be creating something to somehow be able to be taking place within God's mind because I think something is of God's thoughts as I think God's thoughts is apart of making up something, and therefore, I think the dimension of something is overlapping, and co-existing along with God's mind because I think the dimension of something is something as I think God is somehow able to be creating something to somehow be able to be taking place within God's mind.

If I think the dimension of something is overlapping, and co-existing along with the dimension of God's mind, than I think God is somehow able to be creating a picture of something to somehow be able to be taking place within God's mind as I think God is somehow creating something to somehow be able to be taking place within God's mind because I think God is somehow able to be creating a picture of something with God's thoughts as I think God is somehow creating something to somehow be able to be taking place within God's mind. I think God is somehow able to be creating a picture of something with God's thoughts as I think God is somehow creating something to somehow be able to be taking place within God's mind because I think something is a picture of God's thoughts as I think God is somehow able to be creating something to somehow be able to be taking place within God's mind. I think something is a picture of God's thoughts as I think God is somehow able to be creating something to somehow be able to be taking place within God's mind because I think God is somehow able to be creating a picture of something with God's thoughts as I think God is somehow able to be creating a picture of something to somehow be able to be taking place within God's mind. I think God is somehow able to be creating a picture of something with God's thoughts as I think God is somehow able to be creating a picture of something to somehow be able to be taking place within God's mind because I think God is somehow creating a picture of something with God's thoughts that is apart of making up the picture of something as I think God is somehow able to creating something to somehow be able to be taking place within God's mind. I think God is somehow creating a picture of something with God's thoughts that is apart of making up the picture of something as I think God is somehow able to creating something to somehow be able to be taking place within God's mind because I think God is somehow able to be creating God's thoughts that is apart of making up the picture of something as I think God is somehow able to creating something to somehow be able to be taking place within God's mind. I think God is somehow able to be creating God's thoughts that is apart of making up the picture of something as I think God is somehow able to creating something to somehow be able to be taking place within God's mind because I think God is somehow able to be creating God's thoughts to somehow be able to be taking place within God's mind as I think God is somehow able to be creating something to somehow be able to be taking place within God's mind.

If I think God is somehow able to be creating God's thoughts that is apart of making up the picture of something as I think God is somehow able to creating something to somehow be able to be taking place within God's mind, than I do not think any thought is a creation of itself because if I think everything is intellectually beyond someone's intelligence, as to how everything is able to be taking place in life, than I think any thought is intellectually beyond itself for any thought not to be a creation of itself, and therefore, I do not think any thought is a creation of itself because I think any thought is a creation of God as I think God is somehow able to be responsible for creating everything. If I do not think any thought is a creation of itself, than I think any thought is a creation of God as I think any thought is God's creation because I think any thought is God's creation as I think any thought is of God's thoughts. I think any thought is God's creation as I think any thought is of God's thoughts because I think God's thoughts is any thought as I think any thought is apart of making up something. I think God's thoughts is any thought as I think any thought is apart of making up something because I think any thought is of God's thoughts that is apart of making up something as I think God is somehow creating any thought to somehow be able to be taking place within God's mind. I think any thought is of God's thoughts that is apart of making up something as I think God is somehow creating any thought to somehow be able to be taking place within God's mind because I think any thought is something as I think God is somehow able to be creating something to somehow be able to be taking place within God's mind, and therefore, I think any thought is taking place within God's mind, without being God's mind as I think any thought is apart of God's mind, without being God's mind because I think God is somehow able to be creating any thought to somehow be able to be taking place within God's mind as I think God is somehow able to be creating something to somehow be able to be taking place within God's mind. I think God is somehow able to be creating any thought to somehow be able to be taking place within God's mind as I think God is somehow able to be creating something to somehow be able to be taking place within God's mind because I think something is of any thought as I think any thought is apart of making up something, and therefore, I think God is somehow able to be responsible for any thought because I think God is somehow able to be responsible for how any thought is able to be any thought. If I think God is somehow able to be responsible for any thought, than I think God is somehow able to be responsible for any thought as I think God is somehow able to be responsible for how any thought is able to be any thought because I think any thought is of God as I think God is somehow able to be apart of making up any thought, and therefore, I think any thought is God as I think God is any thought because I think God is somehow able to be creating any thought to somehow be able to be taking place within God's mind as I think God is somehow able to be creating something to somehow be able to be taking place within God's mind.

If I think any thought is God as I think God is any thought, than I do not think God's thoughts is a creation of itself because if I think everything is intellectually beyond someone's intelligence, as to how everything is able to be taking place, than I think God's thoughts is intellectually beyond itself for God's thoughts not to be a creation of itself, and therefore, I do not think God's thoughts is a creation of itself because I think God's thoughts is a creation of God as I think God is somehow able to be responsible for creating everything. If I do not think God's thoughts is a creation of itself, than I think God's thoughts is a creation of God as I think God's thoughts is God's creation because I think God's thoughts is a creation of any thought as I think God's thoughts is a creation of God. I think God's thoughts is a creation of any thought as I think God's thoughts is a creation of God because I think any thought is of God's thoughts as I think God's thoughts is of God's creation. I think any thought is of God's thoughts as I think God's thoughts is of God's creation because I think God's thoughts is any thought as I think God's thoughts is God's creation. I think God's thoughts is any thought as I think God's thoughts is God's creation because I think God's thoughts is a creation of any thought as I think God's thoughts is apart of making up something. I think God's thoughts is a creation of any thought as I think God's thoughts is apart of making up something because I think God's thoughts is any thought that is apart of making up something as I think God is somehow creating God's thoughts to somehow be able to be taking place within God's mind. I think God's thoughts is any thought that is apart of making up something as I think God is somehow creating God's thoughts to somehow be able to be taking place within God's mind because I think God's thoughts is something as I think God is somehow able to be creating something to somehow be able to be taking place within God's mind, and therefore, I think God's thoughts is taking place within God's mind, without being God's mind as I think God's thoughts is apart of God's mind, without being God's mind because I think God is somehow able to be creating God's thoughts to somehow be able to be taking place within God's mind as I think God is somehow able to be creating something to somehow be able to be taking place within God's mind. I think God is somehow able to be creating God's thoughts to somehow be able to be taking place within God's mind as I think God is somehow able to be creating something to somehow be able to be taking place within God's mind because I think God's thoughts is any thought as I think any thought is apart of making up something, and therefore, I think God is somehow able to be responsible for

God's thoughts because I think God is somehow able to be responsible for how God's thoughts is able to be God's thoughts. If I think God is somehow able to be responsible for God's thoughts, than I think God is somehow able to be responsible for God's thoughts as I think God is somehow able to be responsible for how God's thoughts is able to be God's thoughts because I think God's thoughts is of God as I think God is somehow able to be apart of making up God's thoughts, and therefore, I think God's thoughts is God as I think God is God's thoughts because I think God is somehow able to be responsible for God's thoughts as I think God is somehow able to be responsible for how God's thoughts is able to be God's thoughts.

If I think God's thoughts is God as I think God is God's thoughts, than I think everything is a creation of God as I think everything is God's creation because I think everything is a creation of God's thoughts as I think everything is a creation of God. I think everything is a creation of God's thoughts as I think everything is a creation of God because I think everything is of God's thoughts as I think everything is of God's creation. I think everything is of God's thoughts as I think everything is of God's creation because I think everything is God's thoughts as I think everything is God's creation. I think everything is God's thoughts as I think everything is God's creation because I think everything is a creation of God's thoughts as I think God's thoughts is apart of making up everything. I think everything is a creation of God's thoughts as I think God's thoughts is apart of making up everything because I think everything is of God's thoughts that is apart of making up everything as I think God is somehow creating God's thoughts to somehow be able to be taking place within God's mind. I think everything is of God's thoughts that is apart of making up everything as I think God is somehow creating everything to somehow be able to be taking place within God's mind because I think everything is God's thoughts as I think God is somehow able to be creating God's thoughts to somehow be able to be taking place within God's mind, and therefore, I think everything is taking place within God's mind, without being God's mind as I think everything is apart of God's mind, without being God's mind because I think God is somehow able to be creating God's thoughts to somehow be able to be taking place within God's mind as I think God is somehow able to be creating everything to somehow be able to be taking place within God's mind. I think God is somehow able to be creating God's thoughts to somehow be able to be taking place within God's mind as I think God is somehow able to be creating everything to somehow be able to be taking place within God's mind because I think everything is of God's thoughts as I think God's thoughts is apart of making up everything, and therefore, I think God is somehow able to be responsible for everything because I think God is somehow able to be responsible for how everything is able to be everything. If I think God is somehow able to be responsible for everything, than I think God is somehow able to be responsible for everything as I think God is somehow able to be responsible for how everything is able to be everything because I think everything is of God for God to somehow be able to be responsible for everything, and therefore, I think everything is of God's doing because I think everything is of God as I think God is somehow able to be responsible for everything. If I think everything is of God's doing, than I think everything has everything to do with everything because I think everything is of everything for everything to be having everything to be doing with everything, even though, I think God has everything to do with everything because I think everything is of God for God to be having everything to be doing with everything, and therefore, I think everything is God as I think God is everything because I think everything is of God's thoughts as I think God is somehow able to be creating God's thoughts to somehow be able to be taking place within God's mind.

If I think everything is God as I think God is everything, than I do not think something is a creation of itself because if I think everything is intellectually beyond someone's intelligence, as to how everything is able to be taking place, than I think something is intellectually beyond itself for something not to be a creation, and therefore, I do not think something is a creation of itself because I think something is of God for something not to be a creation of itself. I think something is of God for something not to be a creation of itself because I think something is a creation of God as I think God is somehow able to be responsible for everything, and therefore, I think something is a creation of God as I think something is God's creation because I think something is a creation of God's thoughts as I think something is a creation of God. I think something is a creation of God's thoughts as I think something is a creation of God because I think something is of God's thoughts as I think something is of God's creation. I think something is of God's thoughts as I think something is of God's creation because I think something is God's thoughts as I think something is God's creation. I think something is God's thoughts as I think something is God's creation because I think something is a creation of God's thoughts as I think God's thoughts is apart of making up something. I think something is a creation of God's thoughts as I think God's thoughts is apart of making up something because I think something is of God's thoughts that is apart of making up something as I think God is somehow creating God's thoughts to somehow be able to be taking place within God's mind. I think something is of God's thoughts that is apart of making up something as I think God is somehow creating God's thoughts to somehow be able to be taking place within God's mind because I think something is God's thoughts as I think God is somehow able to be creating something to somehow be able to be taking place within God's mind, and therefore, I think something is taking place within God's mind, without being God's mind as I think something is apart of God's mind, without being God's mind because I think God is somehow able to be creating God's thoughts to somehow be able to be taking place within God's mind as I think God is somehow able to be creating something to somehow be able to be taking place within God's mind. I think God is somehow able to be creating God's thoughts to somehow be able to be taking place within God's mind as I think God is somehow able to be creating something to somehow be able to be taking place within God's mind because I think something is of God's thoughts as I think God's thoughts is apart of making up something, and therefore, I think God is somehow able to be responsible for something because I think God is somehow able to be responsible for how something is able to be something. If I think God is somehow able to be responsible for something, than I think God is somehow able to be responsible for something as I think God is somehow able to be responsible for how something is able to be something because I think something is of God for God to somehow able to be responsible for something, and therefore, I think something is God as I think God is something because I think something is of God's thoughts as I think God is somehow able to be creating God's thoughts to somehow be able to be taking place within God's mind.

If I think something is God as I think God is something, than I think someone is a thought because I think someone is of a thought. I think someone is of a thought because I think someone is of a thought as I think a thought is apart of making up someone, and therefore, I think someone is a thought as I think a thought is someone because I think someone is of a thought as I think a thought is apart of making up someone. If I think someone is a thought as I think a thought is someone, than I think someone is any thought as I think someone is a thought because I think a thought is any thought as I think someone is a thought, and therefore, I think someone is any thought as I think any thought is someone because I think someone is of any thought as I think any thought is apart of making up someone. If I think someone is any thought as I think any thought is someone, than I think someone is of the dimension of thought as I think someone is of any thought because I think the dimension of thought is any thought as I think any thought is apart of making up someone, and therefore, I think the dimension of thought is apart of making up someone as I think any thought is apart of making up someone because I think someone is of the dimension of thought as I think someone is of any thought. If I think the dimension of thought is apart of making up someone as I think any thought is apart of making up someone, than I think someone is of the dimension of thought because I think the dimension of thought is apart of making up someone, and therefore, I think someone is the dimension of thought as I think the dimension of thought is someone because I think someone is of the dimension of thought as I think the dimension of thought is apart of making up someone. If I think someone is the dimension of thought as I think the dimension of thought is someone, than I think someone is of God's thoughts as I think someone is of any thought because I think God's thoughts is any thought as I think any thought is apart of making up someone, and therefore, I think God's thoughts is apart of making up someone as I think any thought is apart of making up someone because I think someone is of God's thoughts as I think someone is of any thought. If I think God's thoughts is apart of making up someone as I think any thought is apart of making up someone, than I think someone is of God's thoughts because I think God's thoughts is apart of making up someone, and therefore, I think someone is God's thoughts as I think God's thoughts is someone because I think someone is of God's thoughts as I think God's thoughts is apart of making up someone.

If I think someone is God's thoughts as I think God's thoughts is someone, than I think someone can think of someone as being of the dimension of someone because I think the dimension of someone is someone, and therefore, I think the dimension of thought is overlapping, and co-existing along with the dimension of thought as I think the dimension of thought is overlapping, and co-existing along with the dimension of someone because I think the dimension of thought is any thought as I think any thought is apart of making up someone. If I think the dimension of thought is overlapping, and co-existing along with the dimension of thought as I think the dimension of thought is overlapping, and co-existing along with the dimension of someone, than I think the dimension of God's thoughts is overlapping, and co-existing along with the dimension of God's thoughts as I think the dimension of God's thoughts is overlapping, and co-existing along with the dimension of someone because I think the dimension of God's thoughts is any thought as I think any thought is apart of making up someone, and therefore, I think the dimension of God's thoughts is overlapping, and co-existing along with the dimension of God's thoughts as I think the dimension of someone is overlapping, and co-existing along with the dimension of someone because I think the dimension of God's thoughts is someone as I think the dimension of someone is someone. If I think the dimension of God's thoughts is overlapping, and co-existing along with the dimension of God's thoughts as I think the dimension of someone is overlapping, and co-existing along with the dimension of someone, than I think the dimension of thought is overlapping, and co-existing along with the dimension of thought as I think the dimension of something is overlapping, and co-existing along with the dimension of someone because I think the dimension of thought is someone as I think the dimension of someone is someone. If I think the dimension of thought is overlapping, and co-existing along with the dimension of thought as I think the dimension of someone is overlapping, and co-existing along with the dimension of someone, than I think there is a multi-dimensional dimension of thought with the dimension of thought because I think the dimension of thought is multi-dimensional. I think the dimension of thought is multi-dimensional because I think the dimension of thought is any thought as I think any thought is apart of making up someone, and therefore, I think there is a multi-dimensional dimension of thought with the dimension of God's thoughts because I think the dimension of God's thoughts is multi-dimensional. I think the dimension of God's thoughts is multi-dimensional because I think the dimension of God's thoughts is any thought as I think any thought is apart of making up someone, and therefore, I think there is a multi-dimensional dimension of thought with the dimension of someone because I think the dimension of someone is multi-dimensional. I think the dimension of someone is multi-dimensional because I think the dimension of someone is of the dimension of thought as I think the dimension of thought is apart of making up the dimension of someone, and therefore, I think the dimension of thought is multi-dimensional as I think the dimension of someone is multi-dimensional because I think the dimension of thought, and the dimension of someone is of any thought as I think any thought is apart of making up someone.

If I think the dimension of thought is multi-dimensional as I think the dimension of someone is multi-dimensional, than I think someone is something because I think someone is of something. I think someone is of something because I think something is apart of making up someone, and therefore, I think someone is something as I think something is someone because I think someone is of something as I think something is apart of making up someone, even though, I do not think someone can possibly be able to knowing for themselves, as to how someone is able to be of something because I do not think someone can possibly be able to be knowing for themselves, as to how something is able to be apart of making up someone, but I think someone is somehow able to be of something because I think something is somehow able to be apart of making up someone. If I think someone is somehow able to be of something, than I think someone is something as I think something is something because I think someone is something as I think something is something of itself. I think someone is something as I think something is something of itself because I think someone is something of themselves as I think something is something of itself. I think someone is something of themselves as I think something is something of itself because I think someone is of something of itself for someone to be someone that is something of themselves as I think something is of something of itself for something to be something that is something of itself. I think someone is of something of itself for someone to be someone that is something of themselves as I think something is of something of itself for something to be something that is something of itself because I think someone is someone that is something of themselves as I think something is something that is something of itself. I think someone is someone that is something of themselves as I think something is something that is something of itself because I think someone is something as I think something is something of itself, even though, I think I need to be distinguishing the difference between someone and something as I think someone is someone that is something of themselves, and I think something is something that is something of itself because I think someone and something are both something. If I think someone and something are both something, than I think someone can think of someone as being of the dimension of someone because I think the dimension of someone is someone as I think someone is something, and therefore, I think someone is overlapping, and co-existing along with something because I think someone is of something as I think something is apart of making up someone. If I think someone is overlapping, and co-existing along with something, than I think someone is something as I think something is someone because I think someone is of something as I think something is apart of making up someone, but I do not think something is of someone because I do not think someone is apart of making up something. I do not think someone is apart of making up something because I think someone is someone that is something of itself as I think something is something that is something of itself, and therefore, I think someone is something as I think something is someone because I think someone is someone that is something of themselves as I think someone is something that is something of itself. I think someone is someone that is something of themselves as I think someone is something that is something of itself because I think someone is of something as I think something is apart of making up someone. I think someone is of something as I think something is apart of making up someone because I think someone is something as I think something is someone.

If I think someone is of something as I think something is apart of making up someone, than I think everything is something as I think something is something because I think everything is of something as I think something is apart of making up everything. I think everything is of something as I think something is apart of making up everything because I think everything is something that is something of itself as I think something is something that is something of itself. I think everything is something that is something of itself as I think something is something that is something of itself because I think everything is something as I think something is something, and therefore, I think everything is something because I do think there is any difference between everything, and something for everything to be one in the same as something as I think everything is exactly the same as something for everything to be something. I do think there is any difference between everything, and something for everything to be one in the same as something as I think everything is exactly the same as something for everything to be something because I think something is apart of making up everything for everything to be something as I think something is apart of making up everything for everything is exactly the same as something. If I do think there is any difference between everything, and something for everything to be one in the same as something as I think everything is exactly the same as something for everything to be something, than I think an example of how I think everything is exactly the same as something for everything to be something can be a quarter because I think someone can think of one side a quarter as being heads, and I think someone can think of the other side of a quarter as being tails, even though, I do not think there is any difference between heads, and tales being on either side of the quarter for heads, and tales to be exactly the same as the quarter because I think the quarter is apart of making up the heads and tales on the same quarter for heads, and tales to be exactly the same as the quarter, and therefore, I think heads, and tales is exactly the same as the quarter for heads, and tales to be something as I think heads, and tales is exactly the same as the quarter for a quarter to be something because I think everything is the same as something for everything to be something. If I think everything is the same as something for everything to be something, than I think the dimension of life is overlapping, and co-existing along with something as I think the dimension of life is everything because I think everything is of something as I think something is apart of making up everything, and therefore, I think something has everything to do with everything because I think everything is something for something to be having everything to be doing with everything. If I think everything is something for something to be having everything to be doing with everything, than I think the dimension of something is multi-dimensional because I think the dimension of something is something as I think something is apart of making everything, and therefore, I think something is multi-dimensional because I think everything is of something as I think something is apart of making up everything.

If I think something is multi-dimensional, than I think everything is something as I think someone is something because I think everything is of someone as I think someone is apart of making up everything. I think everything is of someone as I think someone is apart of making up everything because I think everything is something that is something of itself as I think someone is someone that is something of themselves. I think everything is something that is something of itself as I think someone is someone that is something of themselves because I think everything is something as I think someone is something. If I think everything is something that is something of itself as I think someone is someone that is something of themselves, than I think the dimension of life is overlapping, and co-existing along with someone as I think the dimension of life is everything because I think everything is of someone as I think someone is apart of making up everything, and therefore, I think someone has everything to do with everything because I think everything is of someone for someone to be having everything to be doing with everything. If I think someone has everything to do with everything, than I think the dimension of someone is multi-dimensional because I think the dimension of someone is someone as I think someone is apart of making everything, and therefore, I think someone is multi-dimensional because I think everything is of someone as I think someone is apart of making up everything.

If I think someone is multi-dimensional, than I think someone is overlapping, and co-existing along with the dimension of thought as I think the dimension of thought is any thought because I think someone is of any thought as I think any thought is apart of making up someone, and therefore, I think someone is any thought as I think someone is something because I think any thought is apart of making up someone as I think any thought is apart of making up something. If I think someone is any thought as I think someone is something, than I think any thought is someone as I think someone is any thought because I think someone is of any thought as I think any thought is apart of making up someone. I think someone is of any thought as I think any thought is apart of making up someone because I think any thought is something as I think someone is something, and therefore, I think any thought is something as I think something is something of itself because I think any thought is any thought that is something of itself as I think something is something that is something of itself. I think any thought is any thought that is something of itself as I think something is something that is something of itself because I think any thought is something as I think any thought is apart of making up something. If I think any thought is any thought that is something of itself as I think something is something that is something of itself, than I think any thought is any thought that is something of itself as I think someone is someone that is something of themselves because I think any thought is something as I think any thought is apart of making up someone, and therefore, I think the dimension of someone is overlapping, and co-existing along with the dimension of thought as I think the dimension of thought is any thought because I think someone is of any thought as I think any thought is apart of making up someone.

If I think the dimension of someone is overlapping, and co-existing along with the dimension of thought as I think the dimension of thought is any thought, than I think something is any thought as I think any thought is something because I think something is of any thought as I think any thought is apart of making up something, but I do not think any thought is of something because I do not think something is apart of making up any thought. I do not think something is apart of making up any thought because I think something is something that is something of itself as I think any thought is any thought that is something of itself, and therefore, I think something is any thought as I think any thought is something because I think something is something that is something of itself as I think something is any thought that is something of itself. I think something is something that is something of itself as I think something is any thought that is something of itself because I think something is of any thought as I think any thought is apart of making up something. I think something is of any thought as I think any thought is apart of making up something because I think something is any thought as I think any thought is something. If I think something is of any thought as I think any thought is apart of making up something, than I think someone is any thought as I think any thought is someone because I think someone is of any thought as I think any thought is apart of making up someone, but I do not think any thought is of someone because I do not think someone is apart of making up any thought. I do not think someone is apart of making up any thought because I think someone is someone that is something of themselves as I think any thought is any thought that is something of itself, and therefore, I think someone is any thought as I think any thought is someone because I think someone is someone that is something of themselves as I think someone is any thought that is something of itself. I think someone is someone that is something of themselves as I think someone is any thought that is something of itself because I think someone is of any thought as I think any thought is apart of making up someone. I think someone is of any thought as I think any thought is apart of making up someone because I think someone is any thought as I think any thought is someone.

If I think someone is of any thought as I think any thought is apart of making up someone, than I think someone is God's thoughts as I think someone is something because I think God's thoughts is apart of making up something as I think God's thoughts is apart of making up someone, and therefore, I think God's thoughts is someone as I think someone is God's thoughts because I think someone is of God's thoughts as I think God's thoughts is apart of making up someone. If I think God's thoughts is someone as I think someone is God's thoughts, than I think God's thoughts is something as I think something is something of itself because I think God's thoughts is any thought that is something of itself as I think something is something that is something of itself. I think God's thoughts is any thought that is something of itself as I think something is something that is something of itself because I think God's thoughts is something as I think God's thoughts is apart of making up something. If I think God's thoughts is any thought that is something of itself as I think something is something that is something of itself, than I think God's thoughts is any thought that is something of itself as I think someone is someone that is something of themselves because I think God's thoughts is something as I think God's thoughts is apart of making up someone, and therefore, I think someone is overlapping, and co-existing along with God's thoughts as I think God's thoughts is any thought because I think someone is of God's thoughts as I think God's thoughts is apart of making up someone.

If I think someone is overlapping, and co-existing along with God's thoughts as I think God's thoughts is any thought, than I think something is God's thoughts as I think God's thoughts is something because I think something is of God's thoughts as I think God's thoughts is apart of making up something, but I do not think God's thoughts is of something because I do not think something is apart of making up God's thoughts. I do not think something is apart of making up God's thoughts because I think something is something that is something of itself as I think God's thoughts is any thought that is something of itself, and therefore, I think something is God's thoughts as I think God's thoughts is something because I think something is something that is something of itself as I think something is any thought that is something of itself. I think something is something that is something of itself as I think something is any thought that is something of itself because I think something is of God's thoughts as I think God's thoughts is apart of making up something. I think something is of God's thoughts as I think God's thoughts is apart of making up something because I think something is God's thoughts as I think God's thoughts is something, even though, I do not think someone can possibly be able to knowing for themselves, as to how something is able to be of God's thoughts because I do not think someone can possibly be able to be knowing for themselves, as to how God's thoughts is able to be apart of making up something, but I think something is somehow able to be of God's thoughts because I think God's thoughts is somehow able to be apart of making up something. If I think something is somehow able to be of God's thoughts, than I think someone is God's thoughts as I think God's thoughts is someone because I think someone is of God's thoughts as I think God's thoughts is apart of making of someone, but I do not think God's thoughts is of someone because I do not think someone is apart of making up God's thoughts. I do not think someone is apart of making up God's thoughts because I think someone is someone that is something of themselves as I think God's thoughts is any thought that is something of itself, and therefore, I think someone is God's thoughts as I think God's thoughts is someone because I think someone is someone that is something of themselves as I think someone is any thought that is something of itself. I think someone is someone that is something of themselves as I think someone is any thought that is something of itself because I think someone is of God's thoughts as I think God's thoughts is apart of making up someone. I think someone is of God's thoughts as I think God's thoughts is apart of making up someone because I think someone is God's thoughts as I think God's thoughts is someone, even though, I do not think someone can possibly be able to knowing for themselves, as to how someone is able to be of God's thoughts because I do not think someone can possibly be able to be knowing for themselves, as to how God's thoughts is able to be apart of making up someone, but I think someone is somehow able to be of God's thoughts because I think God's thoughts is somehow able to be apart of making up someone.

If I think someone is somehow able to be of God's thoughts, than I think the dimension of someone is the dimension of God's thoughts because I think the dimension of someone is of the dimension of God's thoughts. I think the dimension of someone is of the dimension of God's thoughts because I think the dimension of God's thoughts is any thought as I think God's thoughts is apart of making up someone, and therefore, I think the dimension of someone is the dimension of thought because I think the dimension of someone is of the dimension of thought. I think the dimension of someone is of the dimension of thought because I think the dimension of thought is any thought as I think any thought is apart of making up someone, and therefore, I think the dimension of someone is the dimension of something because I think the dimension of someone is of the dimension of something. I think the dimension of someone is of the dimension of something because I think the dimension of something is something as I think something is apart of making up someone, and therefore, I think the dimension of something is the dimension of God's thoughts because I think the dimension of something is of the dimension of God's thoughts. I think the dimension of something is of the dimension of God's thoughts because I think the dimension of God's thoughts is any thought as I think God's thoughts is apart of making up something, and therefore, I think the dimension of something is the dimension of thought because I think the dimension of something is of the dimension of thought. I think the dimension of something is of the dimension of thought because I think the dimension of thought is any thought as I think any thought is apart of making up something.

If I think the dimension of something is of the dimension of thought, than I think someone is of something as I think everything is of something because I think something is apart of making up someone as I think something is apart of making up everything, and therefore, I think everything is of someone as I think everything is of something because I think someone is apart of making up everything as I think something is apart of making up everything. I think someone is apart of making up everything as I think something is apart of making up everything because I think everything consists of someone, and something that is apart of making of everything, and therefore, I think someone is apart of making up everything because I think everything is of someone as I think someone is apart of making up everything. If I think someone is apart of making up everything, than I think everything is of any thought as I think everything is of someone because I think any thought is apart of making up everything as I think someone is apart of making up everything, and therefore, I think any thought, someone, and something is equivalent to everything because I think everything consists of any thought, someone, and something that is apart of making up everything. If I think any thought, someone, and something is equivalent to everything, than I think someone is of God's thoughts as I think everything is of God's thoughts because I think God's thoughts is apart of making up someone as I think God's thoughts is apart of making up everything, and therefore, I think everything consists of God's thoughts, someone, and something that is apart of making up everything as I think everything consists of any thought, someone, and something that is apart of making up everything because I think God's thoughts is any thought as I think everything consists of any thought, someone, and something that is apart of making up everything. If I think everything consists of God's thoughts, someone, and something that is apart of making up everything as I think everything consists of any thought, someone, and something that is apart of making up everything, than I think God's thoughts, someone, and something is equivalent to everything because I think everything consists of God's thoughts, someone, and something that is apart of making up everything, and therefore, I think everything is everything because I think everything is equivalent to everything. If I think everything is everything, than I think everything is everything as I think everything is equivalent to everything because I think everything is of everything as I think everything is apart of making up everything, and therefore, I think everything is one because I think everything is everything as I think everything is equivalent to everything. If I think everything is one, than I think everything is one with God as I think everything is one because I think God created everything to be one with God as I think God created everything to be one. I think God created everything to be one with God as I think God created everything to be one because I think God is one as I think everything is one. I think God is one as I think everything is one because I think God is one as I think everything is one with God, and therefore, I think God created someone to be one with God as I think God created someone to be one with everything because I think God created everything to be one with God as I think God created someone to be one with God. If I think God created someone to be one with God as I think God created someone to be one with everything, than I think someone can be one with everything as I think someone can one with God because I think God created someone to be one with everything as I think God created someone to be one with God.

If I think someone can be one with everything as I think someone can one with God, than I think everything is everything because I think everything is of God's thoughts, someone, and something that is apart of making up everything as I think God's thoughts, someone, and something is apart of making up everything for everything to be everything, but I do not think God's thoughts, someone, and something is of everything because I do not think everything is apart of making up God's thoughts, someone, and something, and therefore, I think everything is of God's thoughts, someone, and something that is apart of making up everything because I do not think everything is apart of making up God's thoughts, someone, and something. If I think everything is of God's thoughts, someone, and something that is apart of making up everything, than I think everything is something as I think everything is something that is something of itself because I think everything consists of everything that is apart of making up everything as I think everything consists of God's thoughts, someone, and something that is apart of making up everything, and therefore, I think everything is everything because I think everything is apart of making up everything as I think God's thoughts, someone, and something is apart of making up everything. If I think everything is everything, than I think God's thoughts is the instructions of something as I think any thought is the instructions of something because I think something is of God's thoughts as I think God's thoughts is the instructions of something, and therefore, I think any thought is the instructions of someone as I think any thought is the instructions of something because I think someone is of any thought as I think any thought is the instructions of something. If I think any thought is the instructions of someone as I think any thought is the instructions of something, than I think God's thoughts is the instructions of someone as I think any thought is the instructions of someone because I think someone is of God's thoughts as I think God's thoughts is the instructions of someone, and therefore, I think any thought is the instructions of everything as I think any thought is the instructions of something because I think everything is of any thought as I think any thought is the instructions of everything. If I think any thought is the instructions of everything as I think any thought is the instructions of something, than I think God's thoughts is the instructions of everything as I think any thought is the instructions of everything because I think everything is of God's thoughts as I think God's thoughts is the instructions of everything, and therefore, I think God is programming everything as I think God is creating everything with God's thoughts because I think everything is the instructions of God's thoughts as I think God's thoughts apart of making up everything.

If I think God is programming everything as I think God is creating everything with God's thoughts, than I think a thought is a choice as I think a thought is a choice of itself because I think a thought is any thought as I think any thought is a choice of itself, and therefore, I think a thought is a choice as I think any thought is a choice because I think a thought is a choice of itself as I think any thought is a choice of itself. If I think a thought is a choice as I think any thought is a choice, than I think a thought is God's choice as I think any thought is God's choice because I think a thought is of God's choice with how a thought is able to be a thought of itself as I think any thought is of God's choice with how any thought is able to be a thought of itself, and therefore, I think an idea is a choice as I think a thought is a choice because I think an idea is a thought as I think a thought is a choice of itself. If I think an idea is a thought as I think a thought is a choice of itself, than I think an idea is a choice as I think a thought is a choice because I think an idea is a choice of itself as I think a thought is a choice of itself, and therefore, I think an idea is God's choice as I think a thought is God's choice because I think an idea is of God's choice with how an idea is able to be an idea of itself as I think a thought is of God's choice with how a thought is able to be a thought of itself. If I think an idea is God's choice as I think a thought is God's choice, than I think an idea is any thought as I think an idea is a thought because I think an idea is a thought as I think a thought is any thought, and therefore, I think an idea is a choice as I think any thought is a choice because I think an idea is any thought as I think any thought is a choice of itself. If I think an idea is any thought as I think any thought is a choice of itself, than I think an idea is a choice as I think any thought is a choice because I think an idea is choice of itself as I think any thought is a choice of itself, and therefore, I think God's thoughts is a choice as I think any thought is a choice because I think God's thoughts is any thought as I think any thought is a choice of itself. If I think God's thoughts is any thought as I think any thought is a choice of itself, than I think God's thoughts is a choice as I think any thought is a choice because I think God's thoughts is a choice of itself as I think any thought is a choice of itself, and therefore, I think God's thoughts is God's choice as I think any thought is God's choice because I think God's thoughts is of God's choice with how God's thoughts is able to be a thought of itself as I think any thought is of God's choice with how any thought is able to be a thought of itself. If I think God's thoughts is God's choice as I think any thought is God's choice, than I think someone is a choice as I think God's thoughts is a choice because I think someone is of God's thoughts as I think God's thoughts is a choice of itself, and therefore, I think someone is a choice as I think God's thoughts is a choice because I think someone is a choice of itself as I think God's thoughts is a choice of itself. If I think someone is a choice as I think God's thoughts is a choice, than I think someone is God's choice as I think God's thoughts is God's choice because I think someone is of God's choice with how someone is able to be a thought of itself as I think God's thoughts is of God's choice with how God's thoughts is able to be a thought of itself, and therefore, I think something is a choice as I think God's thoughts is a choice because I think something is of God's thoughts as I think God's thoughts is a choice of itself. If I think something is of God's thoughts as I think God's thoughts is a choice of itself, than I think something is a choice as I think God's thoughts is a choice because I think something is a choice of itself as I think God's thoughts is a choice of itself, and therefore, I think something is God's choice as I think God's thoughts is God's choice because I think something is of God's choice with how something is able to be a thought of itself as I think God's thoughts is of God's choice with how God's thoughts is able to be a thought of itself. If I think something is God's choice as I think God's thoughts is God's choice, than I think everything is a choice as I think God's thoughts is a choice because I think everything is of God's thoughts as I think God's thoughts is a choice of itself, and therefore, I think everything is a choice as I think God's thoughts is a choice because I think everything is a choice of itself as I think God's thoughts is a choice of itself. If I think everything is a choice as I think God's thoughts is a choice, than I think everything is God's choice as I think God's thoughts is God's choice because I think everything is of God's choice with how everything is able to be a thought of itself as I think God's thoughts is of God's choice with how God's thoughts is able to be a thought of itself.

If I think everything is God's choice as I think God's thoughts is God's choice, than I think the dimension of life is the dimension of thought because I think the dimension of life is of the dimension of thought. I think the dimension of life is of the dimension of thought because I think the dimension of thought is any thought as I think any thought is apart of making up everything, and therefore, I think the dimension of life is the dimension of God's thoughts as I think the dimension of life is the dimension of thought because I think the dimension of God's thoughts is any thought as I think the dimension of thought is any thought. If I think the dimension of life is the dimension of God's thoughts as I think the dimension of life is the dimension of thought, than I think the dimension of life is the dimension of God's thoughts because I think the dimension of life is of the dimension of God's thoughts. I think the dimension of life is of the dimension of God's thoughts because I think the dimension of God's thoughts is any thought as I think any thought is apart of making up everything, and therefore, I think the dimension of life is the dimension of someone because I think the dimension of life is of the dimension of someone. I think the dimension of life is of the dimension of someone because I think the dimension of someone is someone as I think someone is apart of making up everything, and therefore, I think the dimension of life is the dimension of something because I think the dimension of life is of the dimension of something. I think the dimension of life is of the dimension of something because I think the dimension of something is something as I think something is apart of making up everything, and therefore, I think the dimension of life is equivalent to the dimension of thought, the dimension of someone, and the dimension of something because I think the dimension of life consists of the dimension of thought, the dimension of someone, and the dimension of something that is apart of making up the dimension of life. If I think the dimension of life is equivalent to the dimension of thought, the dimension of someone, and the dimension of something, than I think the dimension of life is overlapping, and co-existing along with every dimension because I think every dimension is the dimension of life, and therefore, I think every dimension is overlapping, and co-existing along with every dimension as I think everything is overlapping, and co-existing along with everything because I think every dimension is everything as I think everything consists of every dimension that is apart of making up everything. I think every dimension is everything as I think everything consists of every dimension that is apart of making up everything because I think every dimension is the dimension of life as I think everything is the dimension of life, and therefore, I think the dimension of life is the dimension of life because I think the dimension of life is equivalent to the dimension of life. If I think the dimension of life is the dimension of life, than I think the dimension of life is the dimension of life as I think the dimension of life is equivalent to the dimension of life because I think the dimension of life is of the dimension of life as I think the dimension of life is apart of making up the dimension of life.

If I think the dimension of life is the dimension of life as I think the dimension of life is equivalent to the dimension of life, than I think the dimension of life is the dimension of life as I think the dimension of life is the dimension of God's mind because I think the dimension of life is equivalent to the dimension of life as I think the dimension of life is equivalent to the dimension of God's mind. I think the dimension of life is equivalent to the dimension of life as I think the dimension of life is equivalent to the dimension of God's mind because I think the dimension of life is everything as I think the dimension of God's mind is the entire area of everything, even though, I do not think someone can possibly be able to be knowing for themselves, as to how many dimensions of thought there is in life because I think every dimension of thought is incalculable, as to how many dimensions of thought there is in life, but I think everything is of any thought as I think any thought is apart of making up everything because I think God is somehow creating any thought to somehow be able to be taking place within God's mind. If I think everything is of any thought as I think any thought is apart of making up everything, than I do not think someone can possibly be able to be knowing for themselves, as to how many dimensions of God's thoughts there is in life because I think every dimension of God's thoughts is incalculable, as to how many dimensions of God's thoughts there is in life, but I think everything is of God's thoughts as I think God's thoughts is apart of making up everything because I think God is somehow creating God's thoughts to somehow be able to be taking place within God's mind. If I think everything is of God's thoughts as I think God's thoughts is apart of making up everything, than I do not think someone can possibly be able to be knowing for themselves, as to how many dimensions of something there is in life because I think every dimension of something is incalculable, as to how many dimensions of something there is in life, but I think everything is of something as I think something is apart of making up everything because I think God is somehow creating something to somehow be able to be taking place within God's mind. If I think everything is of something as I think something is apart of making up everything, than I do not think someone can possibly be able to be knowing for themselves, as to how many dimensions of someone there is in life because I think every dimension of someone is incalculable, as to how many dimensions of someone there is in life, but I think everything is of someone as I think someone is apart of making up everything because I think God is somehow able to be creating someone to somehow be able to be taking place within God's mind.

If I think everything is of someone as I think someone is apart of making up everything, than I do not think someone is a creation of themselves because if I think everything is intellectually beyond someone's intelligence, as to how everything is able to be taking place in life, than I think someone is intellectually beyond themselves for someone not to be a creation of themselves, and therefore, I do not think someone is a creation of themselves because I think someone is of God for someone not to be a creation of themselves. I think someone is of God for someone not to be a creation of themselves because I think someone is a creation of God as I think God is somehow able to be responsible for everything, and therefore, I think someone is a creation of God as I think someone is God's creation because I think someone is a creation of God's thoughts as I think someone is a creation of God. I think someone is a creation of God's thoughts as I think someone is a creation of God because I think someone is of God's thoughts as I think someone is of God's creation. I think someone is of God's thoughts as I think someone is of God's creation because I think someone is God's thoughts as I think someone is God's creation. I think someone is God's thoughts as I think someone is God's creation because I think someone is a creation of God's thoughts as I think God's thoughts is apart of making up someone. I think someone is a creation of God's thoughts as I think God's thoughts is apart of making up someone because I think someone is of God's thoughts that is apart of making up someone as I think God is somehow creating God's thoughts to somehow be able to be taking place within God's mind. I think someone is of God's thoughts that is apart of making up someone as I think God is somehow creating God's thoughts to somehow be able to be taking place within God's mind because I think someone is God's thoughts as I think God is somehow able to be creating someone to somehow be able to be taking place within God's mind, and therefore, I think someone is taking place within God's mind, without being God's mind as I think someone is apart of God's mind, without being God's mind because I think God is somehow able to be creating God's thoughts to somehow be able to be taking place within God's mind as I think God is somehow able to be creating someone to somehow be able to be taking place within God's mind. I think God is somehow able to be creating God's thoughts to somehow be able to be taking place within God's mind as I think God is somehow able to be creating someone to somehow be able to be taking place within God's mind because I think someone is of God's thoughts as I think God's thoughts is apart of making up someone, and therefore, I think God is somehow able to be responsible for someone because I think God is somehow able to be responsible for how someone is able to be someone. If I think God is somehow able to be responsible for someone, than I think God is somehow able to be responsible for someone as I think God is somehow able to be responsible for how someone is able to be someone because I think someone is of God for God to somehow able to be responsible for someone, and therefore, I think someone is God as I think God is someone because I think someone is of God's thoughts as I think God is somehow able to be creating God's thoughts to somehow be able to be taking place within God's mind.

If I think someone is God as I think God is someone, than I think God is somehow able to be creating a thought to somehow be taking place within God's mind as I think God is somehow able to be creating God's thoughts to somehow be able to be taking place within God's mind because I think a thought is any thought as I think any thought is God's thoughts, and therefore, I think God first created something as I think God created a thought because I think a thought is something as I think something is a thought. If I think God first created something as I think God created a thought, than I think God first created a thought as I think God first created something because I think God first created something as I think God created a thought, and therefore, I think God first created God's mind as I think God first created something because I think God's mind is something as I think something is apart of making up God's mind. I think God's mind is something as I think something is apart of making up God's mind because I think God's mind is the entire area of everything as I think everything consists of something that is apart of making up everything, and therefore, I think God's mind consists of any thought, someone, and something that is apart of making up the entire area of God's mind as I think God's mind is the entire area of everything because I think everything consists of any thought, someone, and something that is apart of making up everything as I think everything is the entire area of God's mind. If I think everything consists of any thought, someone, and something that is apart of making up everything as I think everything is the entire area of God's mind, than I think God's mind consists of any thought, someone, and something that is apart of making up God's mind as I think God's mind consists of any thought, someone, and something that is apart of making up the entire area of God's mind because I think God's mind is everything as I think God's mind is the entire area of everything, and therefore, I think God's mind is of any thought, someone, and something as I think any thought, someone, and something is apart of making up God's mind because I think God's mind consists of any thought, someone, and something that is apart of making up God's mind. If I think God's mind is of any thought, someone, and something as I think any thought, someone, and something is apart of making up God's mind, than I think God's mind is the entire area of everything as I think everything is the entire area of God's mind because I think God's mind is everything as I think everything is God's mind. I think God's mind is everything as I think everything is God's mind because I think God's mind consists of any thought, someone, and something that is apart of making up God's mind as I think everything consists of any thought, someone, and something that is apart of making up everything, and therefore, I think God's mind is of God's thoughts, someone, and something as I think God's thoughts, someone, and something is apart of making up God's mind because I think God's thoughts is any thought as I think God's mind consists of any thought, someone, and something that is apart of making up God's mind. If I think God's mind is of God's thoughts, someone, and something as I think God's thoughts, someone, and something is apart of making up God's mind, than I think everything is a mind because I think everything that is apart of making up everything is a mind. I think everything that is apart of making up everything is a mind because I think everything is a mind as I think everything is God's mind. I think everything is a mind as I think everything is God's mind because I think God's mind is everything for everything to be a mind as I think God's mind is everything for everything to be God's mind. I think God's mind is everything for everything to be a mind as I think God's mind is everything for everything to be God's mind because I think God's mind is of everything as I think everything is apart of making up God's mind.

I think God's mind is of everything as I think everything is apart of making up God's mind because I think God's mind is everything as I think everything is God's mind. I think God's mind is everything as I think everything is God's mind because I think God's mind is God's mind as I think God's mind is equivalent to God's mind. I think God's mind is God's mind as I think God's mind is equivalent to God's mind because I think God's mind is of God's mind as I think God's mind is apart of making up God's mind, even though, I think God's mind is everything because I think everything is apart of making up the entire area of everything for everything to be apart of making up God's mind as I think everything is apart of making up God's mind for everything to be God's mind, and therefore, I think everything is overlapping, and co-existing along with God's mind because I think everything is apart of making up God's mind for everything to be overlapping, and co-existing along with God's mind. If I think everything is overlapping, and co-existing along with God's mind, than I think God's thoughts is everything because I think God's thoughts is apart of making up everything for God's thoughts to be everything, and therefore, I think God's thoughts is overlapping, and co-existing along with everything because I think God's thoughts is apart of making up everything for God's thoughts to be overlapping, and co-existing with everything. If I think God's thoughts is overlapping, and co-existing along with everything, than I think God's mind is God's thoughts because I think God's thoughts is apart of making up everything for God's thoughts to be apart of making up God's mind as I think God's thoughts is apart of making up God's mind for God's mind to be God's thoughts, and therefore, I think God's thoughts is overlapping, and co-existing along with God's mind because I think God's thoughts is apart of making up God's mind for God's thoughts to be overlapping, and co-existing along with God's mind.

If I think God's thoughts is overlapping, and co-existing along with God's mind, than I think the dimension of God's mind is the dimension of thought because I think the dimension of God's mind is of the dimension of thought. I think the dimension of God's mind is of the dimension of thought because I think the dimension of thought is any thought as I think any thought is apart of making up God's mind, and therefore, I think the dimension of God's mind is the dimension of God's thoughts as I think the dimension of God's mind is the dimension of thought because I think the dimension of God's thoughts is any thought as I think the dimension of thought is any thought. If I think the dimension of God's thoughts is any thought as I think the dimension of thought is any thought, than I think the dimension of God's mind is the dimension of God's thoughts because I think the dimension of God's mind is of the dimension of God's thoughts. I think the dimension of God's mind is of the dimension of God's thoughts because I think the dimension of God's thoughts is any thought as I think any thought is apart of making up God's mind, and therefore, I think the dimension of God's mind is the dimension of something because I think the dimension of God's mind is of the dimension of something. I think the dimension of God's mind is of the dimension of something because I think the dimension of something is something as I think something is apart of making up God's mind, and therefore, I think the dimension of God's mind is the dimension of someone because I think the dimension of God's mind is of the dimension of someone. I think the dimension of God's mind is of the dimension of someone because I think the dimension of someone is someone as I think someone is apart of making up God's mind, and therefore, I think the dimension of God's mind is equivalent to the dimension of thought, the dimension of something, and the dimension of someone because I think the dimension of life consists of the dimension of thought, the dimension of something, and the dimension of someone that is apart of making up the dimension of God's mind. If I think the dimension of God's mind is equivalent to the dimension of thought, the dimension of something, and the dimension of someone, than I think the dimension of God's mind is the dimension of God's mind as I think the dimension of life is the dimension of life because I think the dimension of God's mind is equivalent to the dimension of God's mind as I think the dimension of life is equivalent to the dimension of life, and therefore, I think the dimension of God's mind is the dimension of life as I think the dimension of life is the dimension of God's mind because I think the dimension of God's mind is of the dimension of life as I think the dimension of life is apart of making up the dimension of God's mind. If I think the dimension of God's mind is the dimension of life as I think the dimension of life is the dimension of God's mind, than I think the dimension of God's mind is the dimension of God's mind as I think the dimension of God's mind is equivalent to the dimension of God's mind because I think the dimension of God's mind is of the dimension of God's mind as I think the dimension of God's mind is apart of making up the dimension of God's mind.

If I think the dimension of God's mind is the dimension of God's mind as I think the dimension of God's mind is equivalent to the dimension of God's mind, than I think the dimension of God's mind is God's mind as I think God's mind is everything because I think God's mind is the dimension of God's mind as I think everything is God's mind, and therefore, I think God is somehow creating everything to somehow be able to be taking place within God's mind as I think everything is God's mind because I think God is somehow creating everything as I think God is somehow creating God's mind. I think God is somehow creating everything as I think God is somehow creating God's mind because I think everything is God's mind as I think God's mind is everything, and therefore, I think life is God's mind as I think life is everything because I think God's mind is life as I think everything is life. If I think life is God's mind as I think life is everything, than I think God's mind is God as I think everything is God because I think God is life as I think life is God, and therefore, I think everything is God's mind as I think God's mind is everything because I think God is somehow able to be creating everything somehow with God's state of consciousness, along with God's will as I think God is somehow able to be creating God's mind somehow with God's state of consciousness, along with God's will. If I think everything is God's mind as I think God's mind is everything, than I think God's mind is God as I think God is God's mind because I think God is somehow creating everything as I think God is somehow creating God's mind. I think God is somehow creating everything as I think God is somehow creating God's mind because I think God is somehow creating everything to somehow be able to be taking place within God's mind as I think everything is God's mind.

If I think God is somehow creating everything as I think God is somehow creating God's mind, than I do not think someone can possibly be able to be knowing for themselves, as to just exactly how small God's mind has started out as being in life, and I do not think someone can possibly be able to be knowing for themselves, as to just exactly how big God's mind can possibly be in life because I do not think someone can possibly be able to be knowing for themselves, as to just exactly what the very first thought is in life that God created to somehow be able to be taking place within God's mind, and I do not think someone can possibly be able to be knowing for themselves, as to just exactly how many more thoughts God can possibly be able to be creating to somehow be able to be taking place within God's mind as I think God is somehow able to be creating any thought that is of God's thoughts to somehow be able to be taking place within God's mind, however, I think God's mind can continue to be getting bigger and bigger, and more and more vast within the entire area of God's mind because I think God can continue to be creating more and more thoughts of any thought that is of God's thoughts to somehow be able to be taking place within God's mind. If I think God's mind can continue to be getting bigger and bigger, and more and more vast within the entire area of God's mind, than I think God's mind is unlimited in size, as to how big God's mind can possibly be in life as I think God's mind can go on, and on forever in size because I think God can continue to be creating more, and more thoughts of any thought that is of God's thoughts to somehow be able to be taking place within God's mind, and therefore, I think God's mind is incalculable, as to how big God's mind can possibly be in life because I think God's mind is unlimited in size, as to how big God's mind can possibly be in life. If I think God's mind is incalculable, as to how big God's mind can possibly be in life, than I think God's mind is constantly able to be something because I think God's mind is the entire area of everything, and therefore, I think God's mind is infinite because I think God's mind is in infinity. I think God's mind is in infinity because I think God's mind is constantly able to be something, and therefore, I think God's mind is infinity because I think God's mind is in infinity. If I think God's mind is infinity, than I think God's mind is infinity as I think God's mind is incalculable because I do not think someone can possibly be able to be knowing for themselves, as to just exactly how big God's mind can possibly be in life as I think God's mind is incalculable, as to how big God's mind can possibly be in life. I do not think someone can possibly be able to be knowing for themselves, as to just exactly how big God's mind can possibly be in life as I think God's mind is incalculable, as to how big God's mind can possibly be in life because I think God is somehow able to be creating God's thoughts to somehow be able to be taking place within God's mind as I think God is somehow able to be creating everything to somehow be able to be taking place within God's mind, and therefore, I think God's mind is infinity as I think God's mind is incalculable because I think God is somehow able to be creating God's thoughts to somehow be able to be taking place within God's mind as I think God is somehow able to be creating everything to somehow be able to be taking place within God's mind. If I think God's mind is infinity as I think God's mind is incalculable, than I think God's mind is infinite because I think God is infinite for God to infinitely somehow be able to be creating God's thoughts to somehow be able to be taking place within God's mind as I think God is infinitely somehow able to be creating God's thoughts to somehow be able to be taking place within God's mind for God's mind to be infinite, and therefore, I think God's mind is infinity as I think God's mind is incalculable because I think God is infinitely somehow able to be creating God's thoughts to somehow be able to be taking place within God's mind from God being infinite as I think God is infinitely somehow able to be creating everything to somehow be able to be taking place within God's mind from God being infinite.

If I think God's mind is infinity as I think God's mind is incalculable, than I think God's mind is God's thoughts as I think God's mind is everything because I think God's mind is everything as I think God's thoughts is everything. I think God's mind is everything as I think God's thoughts is everything because I think God's mind is the entire area of everything as I think God's thoughts is the entire area of everything. I think God's mind is the entire area of everything as I think God's thoughts is the entire area of everything because I think God's thoughts is apart of making up the entire area of everything as I think God's thoughts is apart of making up everything. I think God's thoughts is apart of making up the entire area of everything as I think God's thoughts is apart of making up everything because I think everything is the entire area of everything as I think God's mind is the entire area of everything. I think everything is the entire area of everything as I think God's mind is the entire area of everything because I think God's thoughts is everything as I think God's mind is everything. I think God's thoughts is everything as I think God's mind is everything because I think God's thoughts is God's mind as I think God's mind is God's thoughts. I think God's thoughts is God's mind as I think God's mind is God's thoughts because I think God's mind is the entire area of God's thoughts that is apart of making up everything. I think God's mind is the entire area of God's thoughts that is apart of making up everything because I think God's mind is a storage area of God's thoughts for God's mind to be a storage area of everything. I think God's mind is a storage area of God's thoughts for God's mind to be a storage area of everything because I think God has a mind. I think God has a mind because I think God's mind is the entire area of God's thoughts that is apart of making up everything.

I think God's mind is the entire area of God's thoughts that is apart of making up everything because I think God's mind is the entire area of God's thoughts that is apart of making up God's mind as I think everything is the entire area of God's thoughts that is apart of making up everything. I think God's mind is the entire area of God's thoughts that is apart of making up God's mind as I think everything is the entire area of God's thoughts that is apart of making up everything because I think God's mind is God's thoughts as I think everything is God's thoughts. I think God's mind is God's thoughts as I think everything is God's thoughts because I think God's thoughts is something that is apart of making up God's mind for God's mind to be God's thoughts as I think God's thoughts is something that is apart of making everything for everything to be God's thoughts. I think God's thoughts is something that is apart of making up God's mind for God's mind to be God's thoughts as I think God's thoughts is something that is apart of making everything for everything to be God's thoughts because I think something is of God's thoughts for God's thoughts to be apart of making up God's mind as I think something is of God's thoughts for God's thoughts to be apart of making up everything. I think something is of God's thoughts for God's thoughts to be apart of making up God's mind as I think something is of God's thoughts for God's thoughts to be apart of making up everything because I think God's thoughts is something as I think something is of God's thoughts for God's thoughts to be something, and therefore, I think God's thoughts is like something because I think God's thoughts is the same as something as I think God's thoughts is something, but I do not think God's thoughts is alike something as I think God's thoughts is something because I think something is of God's thoughts for God's thoughts to be something, and therefore, I think God's thoughts is something as I think something is God's thoughts because I think something is of God's thoughts for God's thoughts to be something as I think something is of God's thoughts for something to be God's thoughts. I think something is of God's thoughts for God's thoughts to be something as I think something is of God's thoughts for something to be God's thoughts because I think something is of God's thoughts for something to be something as I think something is of God's thoughts for God's thoughts to be something. I think something is of God's thoughts for something to be something as I think something is of God's thoughts for God's thoughts to be something because I think God's thoughts is something. I think God's thoughts is something because I think God's thoughts is something in God's mind for God's thoughts to be something. I think God's thoughts is something in God's mind for God's thoughts to be something because I think God's thoughts is God's thoughts of something in God's mind for God's thoughts to be something in God's mind. I think God's thoughts is God's thoughts of something in God's mind for God's thoughts to be something in God's mind because I think something is of God's thoughts for God's thoughts to be of something in God's mind.

If I think God's thoughts is God's thoughts of something in God's mind for God's thoughts to be something in God's mind, than I think God's mind is unlimited in size with God's thoughts of something because I think God's thoughts of something is unlimited in God's mind. I think God's thoughts of something is unlimited in God's mind because I think God's thoughts of something is limitless in God's mind. I think God's thoughts of something is limitless in God's mind because I do not think there is any limit of God's thoughts of something in God's mind for God's thoughts of something to be unlimited in God's mind. I do not think there is any limit of God's thoughts of something in God's mind for God's thoughts of something to be unlimited in God's mind because I do not think God can think enough about something in God's mind. I do not think God can think enough about something in God's mind because I do not think God can not think of something for God not to be able to be thinking enough about something in God's mind, and therefore, I do not think God can think enough about something in God's mind because I think God's thoughts of something is unlimited in God's mind. I think God's thoughts of something is unlimited in God's mind because I think God's thoughts of something is infinite in God's mind for God's thoughts of something to be unlimited in God's mind. I think God's thoughts of something is infinite in God's mind for God's thoughts of something to be unlimited in God's mind because I think God's thoughts of something is created by God being infinite for God's thoughts of something to be infinite in God's mind, and therefore, I think God's thoughts of something is unlimited in God's mind because I think God's thoughts of something is created by God being infinite for God's thoughts of something to be unlimited in God's mind. If I think God's thoughts of something is unlimited in God's mind, than I think something is of God's thoughts is in God's mind as I think God's thoughts is something in God's mind because I think something is of God's thoughts for God's thoughts to be something in God's mind. I think something is of God's thoughts for God's thoughts to be something in God's mind because I think God's thoughts is something in God's mind as I think God's thoughts is in God's mind. I think God's thoughts is something in God's mind as I think God's thoughts is in God's mind because I think God's thoughts is something for God's thoughts to be in God's mind. I think God's thoughts is something for God's thoughts to be in God's mind because I think God's thoughts is something in God's mind. I think God's thoughts is something in God's mind because I think God's thoughts is in God's mind for God's thoughts to be something in God's mind. I think God's thoughts is in God's mind for God's thoughts to be something in God's mind because I think God has thoughts as I think God's thoughts is in God's mind, and therefore, I think someone can think of God's thoughts of something as being God's thoughts because I think something is of God's thoughts for someone to be thinking of God's thoughts of something as being God's thoughts.

If I think someone can think of God's thoughts of something as being God's thoughts, than I think God's mind is unlimited in size with God's thoughts because I think God's thoughts is unlimited in God's mind. I think God's thoughts is unlimited in God's mind because I think God's thoughts is limitless in God's mind. I think God's thoughts is limitless in God's mind because I do not think there is any limit of God's thoughts in God's mind for God's thoughts to be unlimited in God's mind. I do not think there is any limit of God's thoughts in God's mind for God's thoughts to be unlimited in God's mind because I think God can think of everything in God's mind that God can experience in life. I think God can think of everything in God's mind that God can experience in life because I think God can think of everything in God's mind for God to be experiencing in life. I think God can think of everything in God's mind for God to be experiencing in life because I think God is experiencing everything with God's thoughts in God's mind. I think God is experiencing everything with God's thoughts in God's mind because I think everything is of God's thoughts for God to be thinking of everything in God's mind that God can experience in life, and therefore, I think God can think of everything that is something in God's mind because I think God can think of the thoughts of everything in God's mind that God can experience in life. I think God can think of the thoughts of everything in God's mind that God can experience in life because I think God can think of something's thoughts of everything in God's mind that God can experience in life. I think God can think of something's thoughts of everything in God's mind that God can experience in life because I think everything is of something for God to be thinking of something's thoughts of everything in God's mind that God can experience in life. I think everything is of something for God to be thinking of something's thoughts of everything in God's mind that God can experience in life because I think God can think of everything that is something in God's mind. I think God can think of everything that is something in God's mind because I do not think God can think enough about God's thoughts in God's mind. I do not think God can think enough about God's thoughts in God's mind because I do not think God can not think of God's thoughts for God not to be thinking enough about God's thoughts in God's mind, and therefore, I do not think God can think enough about God's thoughts in God's mind because I think God's thoughts is unlimited in God's mind. I think God's thoughts is unlimited in God's mind because I think God's thoughts is infinite in God's mind for God's thoughts to be unlimited in God's mind. I think God's thoughts is infinite in God's mind for God's thoughts to be unlimited in God's mind because I think God's thoughts is created by God being infinite for God's thoughts to be infinite in God's mind, and therefore, I think God's thoughts is unlimited in God's mind because I think God's thoughts is created by God being infinite for God's thoughts to be infinite in God's mind.

If I think God's thoughts is unlimited in God's mind, than I think God's thoughts is infinite in God's mind for God's thoughts to be unlimited in God's mind because I think God's thoughts is infinite. I think God's thoughts is infinite because I think God's thoughts is of God for God's thoughts to be infinite. I think God's thoughts is of God for God's thoughts to be infinite because I think God's thoughts is of God being infinite for God's thoughts to be infinite. I think God's thoughts is of God being infinite for God's thoughts to be infinite because I think God's thoughts is created by God being infinite for God's thoughts to be infinite. I think God's thoughts is created by God being infinite for God's thoughts to be infinite because I think God's thoughts is infinite. I think God's thoughts is infinite because I think God's thoughts is constant for God's thoughts to be infinite. I think God's thoughts is constant for God's thoughts to be infinite because I think God is constantly thinking of something for God's thoughts to be infinite. I think God is constantly thinking of something for God's thoughts to be infinite because I think God is constantly thinking of something in God's mind for God's thoughts to be infinite. I think God is constantly thinking of something in God's mind for God's thoughts to be infinite because I think God is constantly thinking of God's thoughts of something in God's mind for God's thoughts to be infinite. I think God is constantly thinking of God's thoughts of something in God's mind for God's thoughts to be infinite because I think God is constantly thinking of something's thoughts in God's mind for God's thoughts to be infinite. I think God is constantly thinking of something's thoughts in God's mind for God's thoughts to be infinite because I think God's thoughts of something is constantly taking place within God's mind for God's thoughts to be infinite. I think God's thoughts of something is constantly taking place within God's mind for God's thoughts to be infinite because I think something is of God's thoughts as I think God's thoughts is constantly taking place within God's mind for God's thoughts to be infinite. I think something is of God's thoughts as I think God's thoughts is constantly taking place within God's mind for God's thoughts to be infinite because I think God is infinitely thinking of something's thoughts in God's mind for God's thoughts to be infinite, and therefore, I think God is infinitely thinking of something's thoughts in God's mind for God's thoughts to be infinite because I think God's thoughts of something is infinitely taking place within God's mind for God's thoughts to be infinite. I think God's thoughts of something is infinitely taking place within God's mind for God's thoughts to be infinite because I think something is of God's thoughts as I think God's thoughts is infinitely taking place within God's mind for God's thoughts to be infinite. I think something is of God's thoughts as I think God's thoughts is infinitely taking place within God's mind for God's thoughts to be infinite because I think God's thoughts is infinite.

I think God's thoughts is infinite because I think God thinks for God's thoughts to be infinite. I think God thinks for God's thoughts to be infinite because I think God thinks of God's thoughts for God's thoughts to be infinite. I think God thinks of God's thoughts for God's thoughts to be infinite because I think God's thinks. I think God thinks because I think God thinks of God's thoughts for God to think, and therefore, I think God's thoughts of something is God's choice for God's thoughts to be of something because I think something is of God's thoughts for God's thoughts to be God's choice of something. I think something is of God's thoughts for God's thoughts to be God's choice of something because I think God's thoughts of something is God's choice of something. I think God's thoughts of something is God's choice of something because I think God's thoughts of something in God's mind is God's choice of something in God's mind. I think God's thoughts of something in God's mind is God's choice of something in God's mind because I think every thought in God's mind is God's choice of something in God's mind. I think every thought in God's mind is God's choice of something in God's mind because I think every thought in God's mind is God's choice for every thought in God's mind to be of something in God's mind. I think every thought in God's mind is God's choice for every thought in God's mind to be of something in God's mind because I think everything God can think of in life is God's choice. I think everything God can think of in life is God's choice because I think God always has a choice for God to be thinking of something. I think God always has a choice for God to be thinking of something because I think something is of God's thoughts for something to be God's choice. If I think God always has a choice for God to be thinking of something, than I do not think God can think of God because I do not think God is of God's thoughts for God to be thinking God, however, I think God can think of someone, and something as I think God can think of God's thoughts because I think someone, and something is of God's thoughts for God to be thinking of someone, and something, and therefore, I think God can think of God's thoughts of someone, and something because I think someone, and something is of God's thoughts for God to be thinking of God's thoughts of someone, and something in God's mind with God's state of consciousness, along with God's will that is apart of God. If I think God can think of God's thoughts of someone, and something, than I think God can think of someone, and something because I think someone, and something is of God's thoughts for God to be thinking of someone, and something in God's mind with God's state of consciousness, along with God's will that is apart of God. If I think God can think of someone, and something, than I think God can choose to be thinking of someone, and something as I think God can think of someone, and something because I think God can choosing to be thinking of someone, and something with God's will as I think God can think of someone, and something with God's state of consciousness, along with God's will, and God's thoughts, and God's mind that is apart of God, and therefore, I think God's state of consciousness, God's will, God's thoughts, and God's mind is apart of God because I think God can think of someone, and something with God's state of consciousness, along with God's will, and God's thoughts, and God's mind that is apart of God.

If I think God's state of consciousness, God's will, God's thoughts, and God's mind is apart of God, than I think God can think of what God thinks of someone, and something because I think God can think of what God thinks of someone, and something in God's mind with God's state of consciousness, along with God's will that is apart of God, and therefore, I think God can think of someone, and something in God's mind because I think God is mentally able to be thinking of someone, and something in God's mind. I think God is mentally able to be thinking of someone, and something in God's mind because I think God can think of God's thoughts of someone, and something in God's mind as I think God's mind is apart of God. I think God can think of God's thoughts of someone, and something in God's mind as I think God's mind is apart of God because I think God can think of God's thoughts of someone, and something in God's mind as I think God's mind is apart of God, and therefore, I think God can think of God's thoughts of someone, and something because I do not think God would be able to thinking of someone, and something in God's mind, without someone, and something being of God's thoughts for God to be thinking of someone, and something in God's mind, even though, I think God can think of someone, and something because I think someone, and something is of God's thoughts for God to be thinking of someone, and something. If I think God can think of someone, and something, than I do not think God has a subconscious because I do not think God is randomly choosing to be thinking of God's thoughts of someone, and something in God's mind with God's state of consciousness, along with God's will that is apart of God for God not to be having a subconscious, even though, I think someone can think God has a subconscious because I think God is allowing everything that is of God's thoughts to be randomly be taking place in it's own time and place for someone to be thinking God has a subconscious, however, I do not think God has a subconscious because I do not think God is randomly choosing everything that is of God's thoughts to be randomly be taking place in it's own time and place for God not to be having a subconscious. If do not think God has a subconscious, than I think someone can think God has a conscious because I think someone can think God is always good, and right about what God thinks of someone, and something in God's mind with God's state of consciousness, along with God's will that is apart of God for someone to be thinking God has a conscious, however, I do not think God has a conscious because I think God is perfect for God to be aware of everything with God's state of consciousness as I think God is perfect for God not to be having a conscious, and therefore, I do not think God has a conscious, and a subconscious because I think God is perfect for God to be aware of everything with God's state of consciousness as I think God is perfect for God not to be having a conscious, and a subconscious.

If I do not think God has a conscious, and a subconscious, than I do not think God dreams because I do not think God is at rest for God not to be dreaming, and therefore, I do not think God is at rest because I do not think God rests for God to be at rest. If I do not think God rests for God to be at rest, than I do not think God is at rest as I do not think God rests because I think God is infinite for God not to be at rest as I think God is infinite for God not to rest. I think God is infinite for God not to be at rest as I think God is infinite for God not to rest because I think God has no beginning and no end for God not to be at rest as I think God has not beginning and no end for God not to rest, and therefore, I think God is infinite because I do not think God has a history as I think God has no beginning and no end for God to be infinite. I do not think God has a history as I think God has no beginning and no end for God to be infinite because I do not think God is created as I think God is whatever God is for God to be infinite, and therefore, I think God always has been, and I think God always is, and I think God always will be because I think God has no beginning and no end for God to always be infinite. If I think God always has been, and I think God always is, and I think God always will be, than I do not think God dreams because I do not think God rests for God not to be dreaming, and therefore, I do not think God has dreams, and fantasy's because I do not think God is randomly choosing to be thinking of God's thoughts of someone, and something in God's mind with God's state of consciousness, along with God's will that is apart of God for God not to be having dreams, and fantasy's, however, I think God can think of someone, and something for God to be consciously be thinking of someone, and something because I think God is always good, and right for God to be thinking of someone, and something with God's state of consciousness, along with God's will, and God's thoughts, and God's mind that is apart of God.

If I think God can think of someone, and something for God to be consciously be thinking of someone, and something, than I think something is of God's thoughts for something to be God's choice because I think God's thoughts is something as I think God's thoughts is God's choice for God to be creating God's thoughts to be taking place within God's mind. I think God's thoughts is something as I think God's thoughts is God's choice for God to be creating God's thoughts to be taking place within God's mind because I think God is somehow creating God's thoughts to permanently be taking place within God's mind as I think God is somehow able to be creating God's thoughts to somehow be able to be taking place within

God's mind. I think God is somehow creating God's thoughts to permanently be taking place within God's mind as I think God is somehow able to be creating God's thoughts to somehow be able to be taking place within God's mind because I think God is somehow creating God's thoughts to be taking place within the entire area of God's mind as I think God is somehow able to be creating God's thoughts to somehow be able to be taking place within God's mind. I think God is somehow creating God's thoughts to be taking place within the entire area of God's mind as I think God is somehow able to be creating God's thoughts to somehow be able to be taking place within God's mind because I think God's mind is the entire area of everything as I think God is somehow creating God's thoughts to be taking place within the entire area of God's mind, and therefore, I think God's mind is the entire area of God's thoughts as I think God's mind is the entire area of everything because I think everything is of God's thoughts as I think God's thoughts is apart of making up everything. If I think God's mind is the entire area of God's thoughts as I think God's mind is the entire area of everything, than I think God is somehow creating everything to permanently be taking place within God's mind as I think God is somehow creating God's thoughts to permanently be taking place within God's mind because I think everything is of God's thoughts as I think God is somehow able to be creating everything to somehow be able to be taking place within God's mind, and therefore, I think God is somehow creating everything to permanently be taking place within God's mind as I think God is somehow able to be creating everything to somehow be able to be taking place within God's mind because I think God is somehow creating everything to be taking place within the entire area of God's mind as I think God is somehow able to be creating everything to somehow be able to be taking place within God's mind. I think God is somehow creating everything to be taking place within the entire area of God's mind as I think God is somehow able to be creating everything to somehow be able to be taking place within God's mind because I think God's mind is the entire area of everything as I think God is somehow creating everything to be taking place within the entire area of God's mind, and therefore, I think God is somehow saving or preserving everything as I think God is somehow creating everything to somehow be able to be taking place within God's mind because I think God is somehow creating everything to be taking place within the entire area of everything as I think God is somehow able to be creating everything to somehow be able to be taking place within God's mind, even though, I think do not think God is creating everything to be a waste as I think God is somehow able to be creating everything to somehow be able to be taking place within God's mind because I think God is somehow able to be saving or preserving everything as I think God is somehow able to be creating everything to somehow be able to be taking place within God's mind.

If I think do not think God is creating everything to be a waste as I think God is somehow able to be creating everything to somehow be able to be taking place within God's mind, than I think God is somehow creating something to permanently be taking place within God's mind as I think God is somehow creating everything to permanently be taking place within God's mind because I think everything is of something as I think something is apart of making up everything to somehow be able to be taking place within the entire area of God's mind, and therefore, I think God is somehow creating something to permanently be taking place within God's mind as I think God is somehow able to be creating something to somehow be able to be taking place within God's mind because I think God is somehow creating something to be taking place within the entire area of God's mind as I think God is somehow able to be creating something to somehow be able to be taking place within God's mind. I think God is somehow creating something to be taking place within the entire area of God's mind as I think God is somehow able to be creating something to somehow be able to be taking place within God's mind because I think God's mind is the entire area of everything as I think God is somehow creating something to be taking place within the entire area of God's mind, and therefore, I think God is somehow saving or preserving something as I think God is somehow creating something to somehow be able to be taking place within God's mind because I think God is somehow creating something to be taking place within the entire area of everything as I think God is somehow able to be creating something to somehow be able to be taking place within God's mind, even though, I think do not think God is creating something to be a waste as I think God is somehow able to be creating something to somehow be able to be taking place within God's mind because I think God is somehow able to be saving or preserving something as I think God is somehow able to be creating something to somehow be able to be taking place within God's mind. If I think do not think God is creating something to be a waste as I think God is somehow able to be creating something to somehow be able to be taking place within God's mind, than I think God is somehow creating someone to permanently be taking place within God's mind as I think God is somehow creating something to permanently be taking place within God's mind because I think someone is something of themselves as I think something is apart of making up someone to somehow be able to be taking place within God's mind, and therefore, I think God is somehow creating someone to permanently be taking place within God's mind as I think God is somehow able to be creating someone to somehow be able to be taking place within God's mind because I think God is somehow creating someone to be taking place within the entire area of God's mind as I think God is somehow able to be creating someone to somehow be able to be taking place within God's mind. I think God is somehow creating someone to be taking place within the entire area of God's mind as I think God is somehow able to be creating someone to somehow be able to be taking place within God's mind because I think God's mind is the entire area of everything as I think God is somehow creating someone to be taking place within the entire area of God's mind, and therefore, I think God is somehow saving or preserving someone as I think God is somehow creating someone to somehow be able to be taking place within God's mind because I think God is somehow creating someone to be taking place within the entire area of everything as I think God is somehow able to be creating someone to somehow be able to be taking place within God's mind, even though, I think do not think God is creating someone to be a waste as I think God is somehow able to be creating someone to somehow be able to be taking place within God's mind because I think God is somehow able to be saving or preserving someone as I think God is somehow able to be creating someone to somehow be able to be taking place within God's mind. If I think do not think God is creating someone to be a waste as I think God is somehow able to be creating someone to somehow be able to be taking place within God's mind, than I think someone is living someone's life as I think someone is living someone's life in God's mind because I think someone is living as I think God is somehow able to be creating everything to somehow be able to be taking place within God's mind, and therefore, I think someone is living as I think someone is living in God's mind because I think everything is taking place within God's mind as I think God is somehow able to be creating everything to somehow be able to be taking place within God's mind. If I think someone is living as I think someone is living in God's mind, than I think someone is living in God's mind as I think someone is living somewhere because I think God is somehow creating someone to be able to be taking place somewhere within God's mind as I think God is somehow creating everything to somehow be able to be taking place within God's mind.

If I think someone is living in God's mind as I think someone is living somewhere, than I do not think someone is any more or any less significantly important than someone else because I think God created everyone equally in God's mind, regardless of what someone's status or situation is in life, and therefore, I think God created everyone equally in God's mind, regardless of what someone thinks of themselves, or what someone's situation is in life because I think God created someone as being equally significantly important as someone else in God's mind. If I think God created someone as being equally significantly important as someone else in God's mind, than I think God created something as being equally significantly important as something else in God's mind because who's to say that a rock is worth more than a stick, when God created something equally as something else in God's mind, and therefore, I do not think something is any more or any less significantly important than something else because I think God created something as being equally significantly important as something else in God's mind. If I do not think something is any more or any less significantly important than something else, than I do not think someone is any more or any less significantly important than something as I do not think something is any more or any less significantly important than someone because I think God created someone as being equally significantly important as something in God's mind, and therefore, I think everything all balances out as being equally significantly important with everything because I think God created everything as being equally significantly important in God's mind. I think God created everything as being equally significantly important in God's mind because who's to say that someone is worth more than someone else, and who's to say that something is worth more than something else, when everything is created equally in God's mind, and therefore, I think everything is created equally in God's mind because I think God created everything equally in God's mind, regardless of what everything is in life. I think God created everything equally in God's mind, regardless of what everything is in life because I think God created everything as being equally significantly important in God's mind, and therefore, I think everyone is equal because I think God created everyone equally in God's mind as I think God created everything equally in God's mind. If I think everyone in life is equal, than I think someone can think about what the greatest gift is in life because I think someone can think God can do something with someone, and something for someone to be thinking about what the greatest gift is in life, even though, I do not think there is a greatest gift because I think God created everything equally in God's mind for God to be able to be doing something with everything as I think everything is God's gift for there not to be a greatest gift.

If I do not think there is a greatest gift, than I think God created someone to be more significantly important to God, more so than I think God created something to be more significantly important to God because I do not think God created something to be able to be communicating to God in any possibly way as I think God created someone to be able to be communicating to God in any possible way in how someone can possibly be able to be communicating to God, and therefore, I do not think God created someone to be completely alone because I think God created someone to be able to be communicating to themselves, someone else, something, and God in any possible way in how someone can possibly be able to be communicating to themselves, someone else, something, and God. If I do not think God created someone to be completely alone, than I think someone is speaking God's words whenever someone is saying something to themselves, someone else, something, and God because I think God created someone to be able to be communicating to themselves, someone else, something, and God in any possible way in how someone can possibly be able to be communicating to themselves, someone else, something, and God, and therefore, I do not think someone is completely alone as I think someone can be alone because I think someone is amongst everything that God has created for someone to be with God as I think someone is amongst everything that God has created for someone not to be completely alone. If I do not think someone is completely alone as I think someone can be alone, than I think someone is with

God everywhere someone goes because I think someone is amongst everything that God has created for someone to be with God everywhere someone goes. I think someone is amongst everything that God has created for someone to be with God everywhere someone goes because I think God is somehow creating someone to be with God as I think God is somehow creating someone to somehow be able to be taking place within God's mind. I think God is somehow creating someone to be with God as I think God is somehow creating someone to somehow be able to be taking place within God's mind because I think God is somehow creating someone to somehow be able to be taking place within God's mind as I think God is somehow creating everything to somehow be able to be taking place within God's mind. I think God is somehow creating someone to somehow be able to be taking place within God's mind as I think God is somehow creating everything to somehow be able to be taking place within God's mind because I think everything is of someone as I think someone is apart of making up everything, and therefore, I think God is somehow creating everything to be with God as I think God is somehow creating someone to be with God because I think everything is of someone as I think God is somehow creating everything to somehow be able to be taking place within God's mind. If I think God is somehow creating everything to be with God as I think God is somehow creating someone to be with God, than I think God is somehow creating everything to be with God because I think God is somehow creating everything with God's mind as I think God is somehow able to be responsible for everything, and therefore, I think God is somehow creating everything to somehow be able to be taking place within God's mind because I think God is somehow creating everything with God's mind as I think God is somehow able to be responsible for everything.

Chapter 8

God's being

I would like to talk about how dimensions are in life in relation to what dimensions are in life by talking about God's being, that can possibly have something to do with how dimensions are in life is in relation to what dimensions are in life because I think God's being is of the dimension of God for God to be God's being. I think God's being is of the dimension of God for God to be God's being because I think God's being is how God is able to be a living being, and therefore, I think God's being is how God is able to be what God is in life because I think God's being is how God is able to be doing what God is able to be doing. If I think God's being is how God is able to be what God is in life, than I think God's being is how God is able to be a living being because I think God's being is how God is able to be what God is in life as I think God's being is the very existence of what God is in life, and therefore, I think God's being is how God is able to be a higher intelligent living being because I think God's being is how God is able to be doing what God is able to be doing as I think God's intelligence is how God is able to be doing what God is able to be doing. If I think God's being is how God is able to be a higher intelligent living being, than I think God's intelligence is entirely all based on how much God is able to be doing what God is able to be doing with God's being because I do not think what God is able to be thinking of with God's thoughts is how God is able to be intelligent. I do not think what God is able to be thinking of with God's thoughts is how God is able to be intelligent because I think how God is able to be doing what God is able to be doing with God's being is how God is able to be intelligent. I think how God is able to be doing what God is able to be doing with God's being is how God is able to be intelligent because I think God's being is how God is able to be doing what God is able to be doing as I think God's intelligence is how God is able to be doing what God is able to be doing, even though, I think what God is able to be thinking of with God's thoughts is God's signs of intelligence of how God is able to be intelligent because I think what God is able to be thinking of with God's thoughts is how God is intelligent, but I do not think what God is able to be thinking of with God's thoughts is how God is able to be intelligent because I think how God is able to be doing what God is able to be doing with God's being is how God is able to be intelligent. If I do not think what God is able to be thinking of with God's thoughts is how God is able to be intelligent, than I think God's intelligence is God's signs of intelligence because I think God's signs of intelligence is what God is able to be thinking of with God's thoughts, but I do not think God's signs of intelligence is God's intelligence because I think God's intelligence is how God is able to be doing what God is able to be doing as I think how God is able to be doing what God is able to be doing with God's being is how God is able to be intelligent, and therefore, I think someone can think of God's being as being the dimension of God's being because I think God's being is how God is able to be doing what God is doing. If I think someone can think of God's being as being the dimension of God, than I think God is how God is able to be doing what God is doing because I think God's being is how God is able to be doing what God is doing, and therefore, I think someone can think of God as being the dimension of God as I think someone can think of God as being the dimension of God's being or God's being because I think God is how God is able to be doing what God is doing as I think God's being is how God is able to be doing what God is doing.

148

If I think someone can think of God as being the dimension of God as I think someone can think of God as being the dimension of God's being or God's being, than I think God's state of consciousness is apart of God's being for God's being to be able to have a sense of awareness because I think God has a state of consciousness for God's being to be able to be aware of what God is doing with God's will, along with God's thoughts that is somehow able to be taking place within God's mind as I think God's state of consciousness, along with God's will, and God's thoughts, and God's mind is apart of God's being. I think God has a state of consciousness for God's being to be able to be aware of what God is doing with God's will, along with God's thoughts that is somehow able to be taking place within God's mind as I think God's state of consciousness, along with God's will, and God's thoughts, and God's mind is apart of God's being because I do not think God can be able to be aware of what God is doing with God's will, along with God's thoughts that is somehow able to be taking place within God's mind, without God having a state of consciousness for God to be able to be doing what God is doing with God's will, along with God's thoughts that is somehow able to be taking place within God's mind, and therefore, I think God's state of consciousness is apart of God's being because I think God has a state of consciousness for God to be able to be aware of what God is doing with God's will, along with God's thoughts that is somehow able to be taking place within God's mind that is apart of God's being. If I think God's state of consciousness is apart of God's being, than I think God has a state of consciousness for God to be having a sense of awareness because I think God is able to be aware of what God is doing with God's state of consciousness as I think God's state of consciousness is apart of God's being, and therefore, I think God has a state of consciousness for God to be aware of what God is doing as I think God has a state of consciousness for God to be aware of everything because I think God has a state of consciousness for God to be aware of what God is doing as I think God has a state of consciousness for God to be aware of everything. I think God has a state of consciousness for God to be aware of what God is doing as I think God has a state of consciousness for God to be aware of everything because I think God is constantly aware of what God is doing as I think God is constantly aware of everything. I think God is constantly aware of what God is doing as I think God is constantly aware of everything because I think God's state of consciousness is apart of God's being as I think God is somehow able to be responsible for creating everything, and therefore, I think God's state of consciousness, God's will, God's thoughts, and God's mind is apart of God's being because I think God is somehow able to be responsible for creating everything with God's state of consciousness, God's will, God's thoughts, and God's mind that is apart of God's being.

If I think God's state of consciousness, God's will, God's thoughts, and God's mind is apart of God's being, than I think God's state of consciousness is apart of God's being because I think God has a state of consciousness for God to be aware of what God is doing, but I do not think God's state of consciousness is God's being because I think God's state of consciousness is how God is able to be aware of what God is doing, and I think God's being is how God is able to be what God is in life. I think God's state of consciousness is how God is able to be aware of what God is doing, and I think God's being is how God is able to be what God is in life because I think God's state of consciousness is how God is able to be aware of what God is doing with God's being. I think God's state of consciousness is how God is able to be aware of what God is doing with God's being because I do not think God would be aware of anything, without God having a state of consciousness. I do not think God would be aware of anything, without God having a state of consciousness because I think God not having a state of consciousness is like God not being aware of what God created as I think God is somehow able to be responsible for creating everything, and therefore, I think God's state of consciousness is how God is able to be a living being because I think God's state of consciousness is how God is able to be aware of what God is doing. If I think God's state of consciousness is how God is able to be a living being, than I think God has a state of consciousness for God's will because I do think God can be aware of what God is doing with God's will, without God having a state of consciousness for God's will, even though, I think God can be aware of what God is doing with God's will because I think God has a state of consciousness for God to be aware of what God is doing with God's will, and therefore, I think God has a state of consciousness for God's will because I think God has a state of consciousness for what God is doing with God's will. If I think God has a state of consciousness for God's will, than I think God's will comes from God's being because I think God's will is apart of God's being for God's will to be coming from God's being, but I do not think God's will is God's being because I think God's will is what God is doing, and I think God's being is how God is able to be what God is in life. I think God's will is what God is doing, and I think God's being is how God is able to be what God is in life because I think God's will is God having a choice of what God is doing with God's being. I think God's will is God having a choice of what God is doing with God's being because I do not think God would be able to be doing anything, without God having a will. I do not think God would be able to be doing anything, without God having a will because I think God not having a will is like God not being able to be creating everything as I think God is somehow able to be responsible for creating everything, and therefore, I think God's will is how God is able to be a living being because I think God's will is what God is doing.

If I think God's will is how God is able to be a living being, than I think God is a higher intelligent living being that is someone that is something of itself, that is somehow able to be responsible for everything because I think everything somehow must have come from God as being a higher intelligent living being that is both someone and something, that is somehow able to be responsible for everything as I think everything somehow must have come from both someone and something that is of God as being a higher intelligent living being, that is somehow able to be responsible for everything, and therefore, I think God is someone that is something of itself because I think God is an intelligent living being that is someone that is something of itself. I think God is an intelligent living being that is someone that is something of itself because I think how God is able to be an intelligent living being from God's being is how God is able to be someone that is something of itself. I think how God is able to be an intelligent living being from God's being is how God is able to be someone that is something of itself because I think God's being is an intelligent living being, that is somehow able to be whatever God's being in life as I think God is someone that is something of itself, and therefore, how is God able to be an intelligent living being that is someone that is something of itself? I think God is able to be an intelligent living being that is someone that is something of itself because I think God can think for God with God's thoughts that is apart of making up everything, somehow from God's being for God to be able to be an intelligent living being that is someone that is something of itself. I think God can think for God with God's thoughts that is apart of making up everything, somehow from God's being for God to be able to be an intelligent living being that is someone that is something of itself because I do not think something is an intelligent living being that is something that is something of itself. I do not think something is an intelligent living being that is something that is something of itself because I do not think something can think for itself for something to be an intelligent living being that is something that is something of itself. I do not think something can think for itself for something to be an intelligent living being that is something that is something of itself because I think something can only be able to be respond to whatever the thoughts are in life that is apart of making up something, and therefore, I do not think something is an intelligent living being that is something that is something of itself because I think something can only be able to be respond to whatever the thoughts are in life that is apart of making up something. If I do not think something is an intelligent living being that is something that is something of itself, than I think God is able to be an intelligent living being that is someone that is something of itself because I do not think something can think for itself for something to be an intelligent living being that is something that is something of itself as I think God can think for God for God to be able to be an intelligent living being that is someone that is something of itself.

If I think God is able to be an intelligent living being that is someone that is something of itself, than I do not think I can just think of God as being something because I think if I just think of God as being something, than I think God is something that is something of itself, but I do not think God is something that is something of itself because I think a rock is something that is something of itself. I think a rock is something that is something of itself because I think a rock is dead weight for a rock to be something that is something of itself. I think a rock is dead weight for a rock to be something that is something of itself because I do not think a rock is an intelligent living being for a rock to be something that is something of itself. I do not think a rock is an intelligent living being for a rock to be something that is something of itself because I do not think a rock can think for itself for a rock not to be an intelligent living being. I do not think a rock can think for itself for a rock not to be an intelligent living being because I think a rock can only be able to respond to whatever the thoughts are in life that is apart of making up how a rock is able to be a rock for a rock to be something that is something of itself, but I think God is an intelligent living being because I think God can think for God with what God's thoughts are in life that is apart of making up everything, somehow from God's being for God to be an intelligent living being. If I think God is an intelligent living being, than I do not think God is something that is something of itself because I think God can think for itself with what God's thoughts are in life that is apart of making up everything, somehow from God's being for God to be an intelligent living being, and therefore, I do not think I can just think of God as being something because I do not think God is something that is something of itself. If I do not think I can just think of God as being something, than I think God is someone that is something of itself because I think God can think for God with what God's thoughts are in life that is apart of making up everything, somehow from God's being for God to be an intelligent living being that is someone that is something of itself, even though, I think God is something because I think something is proof that God is something. I think something is proof that God is something because I think something is created by God being something for something to be something, otherwise, I do not think something would exist, if something isn't created by God being something, but I think something does exist because I think something is created by God being something for something to be something, and therefore, I think something is of the same likeness as God because I think something is something as I think God is something.

If I think something is of the same likeness as God, than I do not think I can just think of God as being someone because I think God is someone as I think God is something. I think God is someone as I think God is something because I think God would have to be someone for God to be able to be something. I think God would have to be someone for God to be able to be something because I think God is an intelligent living being for God to be someone that is something of itself, and therefore, I think how God is able to be someone is how God is able to be something because I do not think God can be able to be someone, without God being something for God to be someone that is something of itself. I do not think God can be able to be someone, without God being something for God to be someone that is something of itself because I do not think God can think for God with what God's thoughts are in life that is apart of making up everything, somehow from God's being for God to be an intelligent living being, if I do not think God is someone that is something of itself, but I think God is someone that is something of itself because I think God can think for God with what God's thoughts are in life that is apart of making up everything, somehow from God's being for God to be someone that is something of itself. If I think God is someone that is something of itself, than I think God is someone as I think God is something because I think God can think for God with what God's thoughts are in life that is apart of making up everything, somehow from God's being for God to be an intelligent living being, and therefore, I do not think I can just think of God as being someone because I think God is someone that is something of itself. I think God is someone that is something of itself because I think God is someone as I think God is something, and therefore, I think someone can think of God as being someone or something as I think God is someone that is something of itself because I think God is someone that is something of itself, that is somehow able to be responsible for everything. If I think someone can think of God as being someone or something as I think God is someone that is something of itself, than I think God is God's self as I think God is itself because I think God is someone that is something of God's self that is somehow able to be responsible for everything as I think God is someone that is something of itself, that is somehow able to be responsible for everything, even though, I think God is someone because I think everyone is proof that God is someone. I think everyone is proof that God is someone because I think everyone is created by God being someone for everyone to be someone, otherwise, I do not think someone would exist, if someone isn't created by God being someone, but I think someone does exist because I think someone is created by God being someone for everyone to be someone, and therefore, I think everyone is of the same likeness as God because I think everyone is someone as I think God is someone. If I think everyone is of the same likeness as God, than I think God is someone as I think God is something because I think God created someone for God to be someone as I think God created something for God to be something, and therefore, I think God created someone, and something as I think someone, and something is apart of making up everything for God to somehow be responsible for creating everything because I think God is someone, and something for God to be creating someone, and something as I think God is someone, and something for God to be someone that is something of itself, that is somehow able to be responsible for creating everything. If I think God created someone, and something as I think someone, and something is apart of making up everything for God to somehow be responsible for creating everything, than I think God created everything to be of the same likeness of God because I think God created someone, and something that is apart of making up everything with God being someone, and something for God to be creating everything to be of the same likeness of God, and therefore, I think everything is of the same likeness as God because I think God created everything to be of the same likeness of God for everything to be of the same likeness as God. If I think everything is of the same likeness of God, than I think there are a lot of similarities and a lot of differences between God and everything because I think God created everything with God being someone that is something of itself for there to be a lot of similarities and a lot of differences between God and everything, and therefore, I think God created everything for there to be a lot of similarities and a lot of differences between God and everything because I think God created everything with God being someone, and something for everything to consists of someone, and something that is apart of making up everything.

If I think God created everything for there to be a lot of similarities and a lot of differences between God and everything, than I think God is a higher intelligent living being that is someone that is something of itself, that is somehow able to be responsible for everything as I think God is someone that is something of itself, that is somehow able to be responsible for everything because I think God is someone that is something of itself that is a higher intelligent living being, that is somehow able to be knowing, as to how everything is able to be taking place in life, somehow from God's being as I think God is someone that is something of itself that is a higher intelligent living being, that is somehow able to be knowing, as to how everything is able to be taking place in life with God's thoughts that is apart of God's being, and therefore, I think it can be very difficult for someone to be able to be understanding, and accepting for themselves, as to how God can possibly be able to be a higher intelligent living being that is someone that is something of itself, that is somehow able to be responsible for everything, when I think it is physically impossible for someone to be able to be noticing for themselves, as to how God is able to be a higher intelligent living being that is someone that is something of itself, that is somehow able to be responsible for everything because I do not think God is physically appearing to be taking place in life as being someone that is something of itself as I think God is someone that is something of itself, that is somehow able to be responsible for everything. I do not think God is physically appearing to be taking place in life as being someone that is something of itself as I think God is someone that is something of itself, that is somehow able to be responsible for everything because I think God is of an unknown dimension as I think God is someone that is something of itself, that is somehow able to be whatever God is in life, and therefore, I think God is God's being because I think God's being is someone that is something of itself, that is somehow able to be responsible for everything for God to be someone that is something of itself, that is somehow able to be responsible for everything. If I think God is God's being, than I think God is whatever God is in life because I think God's being is whatever God's being is in life for God to be whatever God in life, and therefore, I think God is God's being because I think God's being is whatever God's being is in life for God to be God's being. If I think God is God's being, than I do not think God's being is physically appearing to be taking place in life as being someone that is something of itself as I think God's being is someone that is something of itself, that is somehow able to be responsible for everything because I think God's being is of an unknown dimension as I think God's being is someone that is something of itself, that is somehow able to be whatever God's being is in life, and therefore, I think God's will, and God's state of consciousness, and God's thoughts, and God's mind is of an unknown dimension as I think God's will, and God's state of consciousness, and God's thoughts, and God's mind is apart of God's being because I think God's will, and God's state of consciousness, and God's thoughts, and God's mind is somehow able to be whatever God's will is in life, and whatever God's state of consciousness is in life, and whatever God's thoughts are in life, and whatever God's mind is in life as I think God's will, and God's state of consciousness, and God's thoughts, and God's mind is apart of God's being that is someone that is something of itself, that is somehow able to be whatever God's being is in life.

If I think God's will, and God's state of consciousness, and God's thoughts, and God's mind is of an unknown dimension, than I think how everything is able to be taking place in life as being something of itself is how everything is physically able to be appearing to be taking place in life as being something of itself as I think how everything is able to be taking place in life as being something of itself is of an unknown dimension because I think how everything is able to be taking place in life as being something of itself is somehow able to be whatever everything is in life as I think how everything is able to be taking place in life as being something of itself is apart of God's being that is someone that is something of itself, that is somehow able to be whatever God's is in life. I think how everything is able to be taking place in life as being something of itself is somehow able to be whatever everything is in life as I think how everything is able to be taking place in life as being something of itself is apart of God's being that is someone that is something of itself, that is somehow able to be whatever God's is in life because I do not think someone can possibly be able to be knowing for themselves, as to how everything is able to be taking place in life as being something of itself. I do not think someone can possibly be able to be knowing for themselves, as to how everything is able to be taking place in life as being something of itself because I do not think someone can possibly be able to be knowing for themselves, as to how everything is able to be taking place in life as being a thought as I think how everything is able to be taking place in life as being something of itself is how everything is able to be taking place in life as being a thought. I do not think someone can possibly be able to be knowing for themselves, as to how everything is able to be taking place in life as being a thought as I think how everything is able to be taking place in life as being something of itself is how everything is able to be taking place in life as being a thought because I think the only way in how someone can possibly be able to be knowing for themselves, as to how everything is able to be taking place in life as being a thought is if someone is God, or if someone is greater than God for someone to be able to be knowing for themselves, as to how everything is able to be taking place in life as being a thought as I think how everything is able to be taking place in life as being a thought is of God's thoughts, but I do not think someone can possibly ever be God, and I do not think someone can possibly ever be greater than God for someone to be able to be knowing for themselves, as to how everything is able to be taking place in life as being a thought because I do not think someone can possibly be able to be knowing for themselves, as to how everything is able to be taking place in life as being something of itself as I think how everything is able to be taking place in life as being something of itself is how everything is able to be taking place in life as being a thought, and therefore, I think how everything is able to be taking place in life as being something of itself is how everything is able to be taking place in life as being a thought as I think how everything is able to be taking place in life as being something of itself is how everything is physically able to be appearing to be taking place in life as being something of itself because I think how everything is able to be taking place in life as being something of itself is somehow able to be whatever everything is in life, even though, I do not think how everything is able to be taking place in life as being something of itself is of how everything is physically able to be appearing to be taking place in life as being something of itself because I think how everything is able to be taking place in life as being something of itself is somehow able to be whatever everything is in life as I think how everything is able to be taking place in life as being something of itself is apart of God's being that is someone that is something of itself, that is somehow able to be whatever God's being is in life. If I do not think how everything is able to be taking place in life as being something of itself is of how everything is physically able to be appearing to be taking place in life as being something of itself, than I think everything is of an unknown dimension as I think everything consists of someone, and something that is apart of making up everything because I think everything is somehow able to be whatever everything is in life as I think everything is apart of God's being that is someone that is something of itself, that is somehow able to be whatever God's being is in life, and therefore, I think someone, and something is of an unknown dimension as I think someone, and something is apart of God's being because I think someone, and something is somehow able to be whatever someone, and something is in life as I think someone, and something is apart of God's being that is someone that is something of itself, that is somehow able to be whatever God's being is in life. If I think someone, and something is of an unknown dimension as I think someone, and something is apart of God's being, than I think God is someone that is something of itself, that is somehow able to be way beyond how everything is physically able to be appearing to be taking place in life as being something of itself as I think God is someone that is something of itself, that is somehow able to be responsible for everything because I do not think God is physically appearing to be taking place in life as being something of itself as I think God is someone that is something of itself, that is somehow able to be responsible for everything, and therefore, I think God is of a Zen quantum physics because I think God is beyond everything for God to be beyond all physics, even though, I think God is present as I do not think God is present because I do not think God is physically appearing to be taking place in life as being something of itself as I think God is someone that is something of itself, that is somehow able to be responsible for everything.

If I think God is present as I do not think God is present, than I do not think I can think of God as being something, before I can think of God as being someone because if I do think of God as being something, before I think of God as being someone, than that would mean that God would not exist at all because I do not think God is physically appearing to be taking place in life as being something of itself for someone not to be able to be knowing for themselves, as to how God is able to be something of itself. I do not think God is physically appearing to be taking place in life as being something of itself for someone not to be able to be knowing for themselves, as to how God is able to be something of itself because I think God's being is whatever God's being is in life, and therefore, I do not think I can think of God as being something, before I can think of God as being someone because I do not think God is physically appearing to be taking place in life as being something of itself for someone not to be able to be knowing for themselves, as to how God is able to be something of itself. If I do not think I can think of God as being something, before I can think of God as being someone, than I think I can think of God as being someone, before I can think of God as being something because I think I can think of God as being someone that is of a higher intelligent living being, that is somehow able to be responsible for everything, before I can think of God as being something, and therefore, I think someone can think of God as being someone as I think someone can think of God as being something because I think someone can think of God as being someone that is of a higher intelligent living being, that is somehow able to be responsible for everything as I think God is someone that is something of itself, that is somehow able to be whatever God is in life. I think someone can think of God as being someone that is of a higher intelligent living being, that is somehow able to be responsible for everything as I think God is someone that is something of itself, that is somehow able to be whatever God is in life because I think God is someone that is of a higher intelligent living being, that is somehow able to be responsible for everything as I think God is someone that is something of itself, that is somehow able to be whatever God is in life, and therefore, I think I can think of God as being someone, before I can think of God as being something because I think God is someone that is of a higher intelligent living being, that is somehow able to be responsible for everything as I think God is someone that is something of itself, that is somehow able to be whatever God is in life. If I think I can think of God as being someone, before I can think of God as being something, than I think God is someone that is of a higher intelligent living being, that is somehow able to be responsible for everything as I think God is whatever God is in life because I do not think I can of God as being whatever God is in life as I think God is someone that is of a higher intelligent living being, that is somehow able to be responsible for everything. I do not think I can of God as being whatever God is in life as I think God is someone that is of a higher intelligent living being, that is somehow able to be responsible for everything because if I do think of God as being whatever God is in life as I think God is someone that is of a higher intelligent living being, that is somehow able to be responsible for everything, than I do not think I can think of God as being someone that is of a higher intelligent living being, that is somehow able to be responsible for everything as I think God is whatever God is in life, but

I can think of God as being someone that is of a higher intelligent living being, that is somehow able to be responsible for everything as I think God is whatever God is in life because I do not think I can think of God as being whatever God is in life as I think God is someone that is of a higher intelligent living being, that is somehow able to be responsible for everything. I do not think I can think of God as being whatever God is in life as I think God is someone that is of a higher intelligent living being of itself, that is somehow able to be responsible for everything because I do not think I can think of God as being something, before I can think of God as being someone, and therefore, I think I can think of God as being someone, before I can think of God as being something because I think God is someone that is of a higher intelligent living being, that is somehow able to be responsible for everything as I think God is whatever God is in life. If I think I can think of God as being someone, before I can think of God as being something, than I think God is a higher intelligent living being, that is somehow able to be responsible for everything because I think God is someone that is something of itself, that is somehow able to be responsible for everything. I think God is someone that is something of itself, that is somehow able to be responsible for everything because I think God is someone that is of a higher intelligent living being, that is somehow able to be responsible for everything as I think God is someone that is something of itself, that is somehow able to be whatever God is in life, and therefore, I think God is somehow able to be responsible for everything because I think God is someone that is of a higher intelligent living being, that is somehow able to be responsible for everything as I think God is someone that is something of itself, that is somehow able to be whatever God is in life.

If I think God is somehow able to be responsible for everything, than I think God is someone that is something of itself, that is somehow able to be responsible for everything because I think God is someone that is something of itself, that is somehow able to be respond to any word whenever someone chooses to be thinking of saying something to God. I think God is someone that is something of itself, that is somehow able to be respond to any word whenever someone chooses to be thinking of saying something to God because I do not think something, such as a rock can possibly be able to respond to any word whenever someone can choose to be thinking of saying something to a rock, but I think God is someone that is something of itself because I think God can respond to any word whenever someone can choose to be thinking of saying something to God, and therefore, I think God is someone that is something of itself, that is somehow able to be responsible for everything because I think God is someone that is something of itself, that is somehow able to be respond to any word whenever someone can choose to be thinking of saying something to God. If I think God is someone that is something of itself, that is somehow able to be responsible for everything, than I think God is someone that is something of itself, that is somehow able to be responsible for everything because I think God is someone that is something of itself, that is somehow able to be responsible for every possible way in how someone can possibly be communicating, and therefore, I think God is someone that is something of itself, that is somehow able to be responsible for everything as I think God is somehow able to be responsible for everything because I think how God is able to be someone that is something of itself, that is somehow able to be responsible for everything is how God is able to be responsible for everything. I think how God is able to be someone that is something of itself, that is somehow able to be responsible for everything is how God is able to be responsible for everything because I think God's being is how God is someone that is something of itself as I think God is someone that is something of itself, that is somehow able to be responsible for everything. I think God's being is how God is someone that is something of itself as I think God is someone that is something of itself, that is somehow able to be responsible for everything because I think God's being is of the dimension of God for God to be God's being.

Chapter 9

How everything is in relation to God

I would like to talk about how dimensions are in life in relation to what dimensions are in life by talking about how everything is in relation to God, that can possibly have something to do with how dimensions are in life is in relation to what dimensions are in life because I think how God is somehow able to be responsible for creating everything is how everything is in relation, and therefore, how is everything in relation to God? I think everything is in relation to God because I think God is somehow able to be responsible for creating everything for everything to be in relation to God, and therefore, I think God is somehow able to be responsible for how everything is in life because I think God is somehow able to be responsible for creating everything for God to somehow be able to be responsible for how everything is in life. If I think God is somehow able to be responsible for how everything is in life, than I think everything is in relation to God because I think God is somehow able to be responsible for how everything is in life for everything to be in relation to God, and therefore, I think God is responsible for everything that is good, and everything that is bad because I think God is somehow able to be responsible for creating everything for God to be responsible for everything that is good, and everything that is bad, even though, I do not think God is only responsible for everything that is good because I think God is responsible for everything that is good, and everything that is bad. I think God is responsible for everything that is good, and everything that is bad because I think God is always good, and right as I think God is somehow able to be responsible for creating everything. I think God is always good, and right as I think God is somehow able to be responsible for creating everything because I think God is always good, and right with how God is somehow able to be responsible for creating everything as I think how God is able to be someone that is something of itself, that is somehow able to be responsible for creating everything is how God is somehow able to be responsible for creating everything, and therefore, I think everything is in relation to God because I think God is responsible for everything that is good, and everything that is bad for everything to be in relation to God, even though, I think someone can think about what God's characteristics are in life as I think God's characteristics are good because I think God is always good, and right as I think God is somehow able to be responsible for creating everything. If I think someone can think about what God's characteristics are in life as I think God's characteristics are good, than I think God is good as I think God represents everything that is good because I think God is always good, and right with how God is somehow able to be responsible for creating everything, and therefore, I think God represents the truth because I think God is good as I think God represents everything that is good.

If I think God represents the truth, than I think someone is speaking God's words as I think someone can be communicating in every possible way in how someone can possibly be able to be speaking because I think God is somehow able to be responsible for every possible way in how someone can possibly be communicating as I think God is somehow able to be responsible for creating everything, and therefore, I think someone is speaking someone's words as I think someone is speaking God's words because I think someone's words is God's words as I think God is somehow able to be responsible for every possible way in how someone can possibly be communicating. I think someone's words is God's words as I think God is somehow able to be responsible for every possible way in how someone can possibly be communicating because I think every possible way in how someone is able to be communicating is God's language as I think God is somehow able to be responsible for every possible way in how someone can possibly be communicating. I think every possible way in how someone is able to be communicating is God's language as I think God is somehow able to be responsible for every possible way in how someone can possibly be communicating because I think every possible way in how someone is able to be communicating is of God's thoughts as I think God's thoughts is apart of making up every possible way how someone is able to be communicating. I think every possible way in how someone is able to be communicating is of God's thoughts as I think God's thoughts is apart of making up every possible way how someone is able to be communicating because I think everything is of God's thoughts as I think God's thoughts is apart of making up everything, and therefore, I think every possible way in how someone is able to be communicating is someone's language as I think every possible way in how someone is able to be communicating is God's language because I think every possible way in how someone is able to be communicating is God's language as I think God is somehow able to be responsible for every possible way in how someone can possibly be communicating. I think every possible way in how someone is able to be communicating is God's language as I think God is somehow able to be responsible for every possible way in how someone can possibly be communicating because I think every possible way in how someone can be communicating is of God's creation for every possible way in how someone can be communicating to be God's language. I think every possible way in how someone can be communicating is of God's creation for every possible way in how someone can be communicating to be God's language because I think God is the creator of everything for every possible way in how someone can be communicating to be God's language, and therefore, I think everyone is a messenger of God because I think any possible way in how everyone can be communicating is God's language for everyone to be a messenger of God. If I think everyone is a messenger of God, than I think God can understand any possible way in how someone can possibly be able to be communicating because I think God is somehow able to be responsible for every possible way in how someone can possibly be communicating as I think God is somehow able to be responsible for creating everything, and therefore, I think God is the greatest linguist because I think God can understand every possible way in how someone can possibly be able to be communicating. If I think God is the greatest linguist, than I think God can understand any possible way in how someone can possibly be able to be communicating because I think every possible way in how someone is able to be communicating is God's language, and therefore, I think everything is in relation to God because I think every possible way in how someone is able to be communicating is God's language for everything to be in relation to God.

If I think every possible way in how someone is able to be communicating is God's language for everything to be in relation to God, than I do not think something has a name because I do not think someone knows what something's name is in life for something not to have a name. I do not think someone knows what something's name is in life for something not to have a name because I think something is created, without something having a name. I think something is created, without something having a name because I think something is nameless. I think something is nameless because I do not think something has a name for something to be nameless. I do not think something has a name for something to be nameless because I do not think someone knows, as to what God's thoughts are in life that is apart of making up something for someone not to be able to be knowing for themselves, as to what something's name is in life, and therefore, I think something's name is an adopted name, that someone can choose to be giving something a name with any language that someone can possibly be able to be speaking, reading, and writing for something to be having a name because I think someone can give something a name for someone to be identifying what something is in life. If I think someone can give something a name for someone to be identifying what something is in life, than I do not think someone has a name because I do not think someone knows what someone's name is in life for someone not to have a name. I do not think someone knows what someone's name is in life for someone not to have a name because I think someone is created, without someone having a name. I think someone is created, without someone having a name because I think someone is nameless, when someone begins to be coming into life with someone's life. I think someone is nameless, when someone begins to be coming into life with someone's life because I do not think someone has a name, when someone begins to be coming into life with someone's life for someone to be nameless. I do not think someone has a name, when someone begins to be coming into life with someone's life for someone to be nameless because I do not think someone knows, as to what God's thoughts are in life that is apart of making up someone for someone not to be able to be knowing for themselves, as to what someone's name is in life, and therefore, I think someone's name is an adopted name, that someone can choose to be giving someone else, and themselves a name with any language that someone can possibly be able to be speaking, reading, and writing for someone to be having a name because I think someone can give someone else, and themselves a name for someone to be identifying who someone is in life. If I think someone can give someone else, and themselves a name for someone to be identifying who someone is in life, than I think everything is nameless because I think everything consists of someone, and something that is nameless as I think everything consists of someone, and something that is apart of making up everything, and therefore, I do not think God has a name because I do not think someone knows what God's name is in life for God not to be having a name. I do not think someone knows what God's name is in life for God not to be having a name because I do not think God is created for God not to be having a name. I do not think God is created for God not to be having a name because I think God is nameless. I think God is nameless because I do not think God has a name for God to be nameless, and therefore, I think God's name is an adopted name, that someone can choose to be giving God a name with any language that someone can possibly be able to be speaking, reading, and writing for God to be having a name because I think someone can give God a name for someone to be identifying who God is in life. If I think someone can give God a name for someone to be identifying who God is in life, than I think everything is nameless because I do not think God is created for God to be nameless as I think God is nameless for God to be creating everything to be nameless, and therefore, I think everything is in relation to God because I think everything is nameless for everything to be in relation to God. If I think everything is nameless for everything to be in relation to God, than I do not think everything has a label because I think everything is nameless for everything not to be having a label, even though, I think everything can have a label because I think someone can give something a name for everything to be having a label, however, I think there is an infinite amount of names for everything because I think everything is created by God being infinite as I think everything is nameless for there to be an infinite amount of names for everything, and therefore, I think everything is in relation to God because I think everything is created by God being infinite for there to be an infinite amount of names for everything as I think there is an infinite amount of names for everything for everything to be in relation to God.

If I think there is an infinite amount of names for everything for everything to be in relation to God, than I think someone can thank God for something that is of God's creation as I think someone can thank God for everything that is of God's creation because I think everything is of something as I think God is somehow able to be responsible for creating everything, and therefore, I think someone can thank

God for providing someone with something that is of God's creation because I do not think someone would be alive, without God providing someone with something that is of God's creation. I do not think someone would be alive, without God providing someone with something that is of God's creation because I think all life that is someone is being sustained by God. I think all life that is someone is being sustained by God because I think God sustaining someone's life with God providing someone with something for someone to be sustaining someone's life. I think God sustaining someone's life with God providing someone with something for someone to be sustaining someone's life because I think God is sustaining someone's life with God providing someone with something that is a food and beverage for someone to be eating and drinking. I think God is sustaining someone's life with God providing someone with something that is a food and beverage for someone to be eating and drinking because I think something that is a food and beverage is something that is of God's creation for someone to be eating and drinking, and therefore, I think someone can thank God for providing someone with something to be eating and drinking as I think someone can thank God for providing someone with something that is of God's creation because I do not think someone would be alive, without God providing someone with something to be eating and drinking as I do not think someone would be alive, without God providing someone with something that is of God's creation. I do not think someone would be alive, without God providing someone with something to be eating and drinking as I do not think someone would be alive, without God providing someone with something that is of God's creation because I think someone can eat and drink something for someone to be staying alive as I think someone can eat and drink something that is of God's creation for someone to be staying alive, and therefore, I think someone can thank God for something as I think someone can thank God for providing something for someone because I think God is the creator of everything for God to be the provider of everything. If I think someone can thank God for something as I think someone can thank God for providing something for someone, than I think God is the provider of everything because I think God created everything for God to be providing someone with something that someone can be eating, and drinking, wearing, and making as shelter, and therefore, I think everything is in relation to God because I think God is the provider of everything for everything to be in relation to God.

If I think God is the provider of everything for everything to be in relation to God, than I think everything is happening for a reason with how everything is taking place in life because I think God is somehow able to be responsible for how everything is able to be happening for a reason with how everything is able to be taking place in life. I think God is somehow able to be responsible for how everything is able to be happening for a reason with how everything is able to be taking place in life because I think God is somehow able to be responsible for creating everything, and therefore, I think everything is happening for a reason because I think God is somehow able to be responsible for how everything is able to be happening for a reason for everything to be happening for a reason. I think God is somehow able to be responsible for how everything is able to be happening for a reason for everything to be happening for a reason because I think God created everything for everything to be happening for a reason as I think God created everything for God to somehow be able to be responsible for how everything is able to be happening for a reason. I think God created everything for everything to be happening for a reason as I think God created everything for God to somehow be able to be responsible for how everything is able to be happening for a reason because I think God created everything for God to be creating everything to be happening for a reason, and therefore, I think God created everything to be happening for a reason because I think God created everything for God to be creating everything to be happening for a reason. If I think God created everything to be happening for a reason, than I think everything is happening for a reason because I think God created everything to be happening for a reason for everything to be happening for a reason, and therefore, I think an example of how I think God created everything to be happening for a reason can be how God is somehow able to be knowing every possible reason, as to how the planet Earth is able to be going around the sun because I think God created everything with God's thoughts for God to be responsible for every possible thought that is involved with how the planet Earth is able to be going around the sun. I think God created everything with God's thoughts for God to be responsible for every possible thought that is involved with how the planet Earth is able to be going around the sun because I think God created everything with God's thoughts for God to be responsible for every possible thought that is involved with everything as I think every possible thought that is involved with everything is how everything is able to be happening for a reason, and therefore, I think God created everything to be happening for a reason because I think God created everything with God's thoughts for God to be responsible for every possible thought that is involved with everything as I think every possible thought that is involved with everything is how everything is able to be happening for a reason. I think God created everything with God's thoughts for God to be responsible for every possible thought that is involved with everything as I think every possible thought that is involved with everything is how everything is able to be happening for a reason because I think God is always good, and right with how God is somehow able to be responsible for creating everything. I think God is always good, and right with how God is somehow able to be responsible for creating everything because I think God created everything for God to always be good, and right with how God is somehow able to be responsible for creating everything, and therefore, I think everything is happening for a reason because I think God is always good, and right with how God is somehow able to be responsible for creating everything for everything to be happening for a reason. If I think everything is happening for a reason, than I think everything is in relation to God because I think God created everything to be happening for a reason for everything to be in relation to God, and therefore, I think God is somehow able to be responsible for creating everything because I think God created everything with God's thoughts for God to somehow be able to be responsible for everything. I think God created everything with God's thoughts for God to somehow be able to be responsible for everything because I think God's thoughts is apart of making up everything for God to somehow be able to be responsible for everything as I think God's thoughts is apart of making up everything for God to be creating everything with God's thoughts, and therefore, I think everything is in relation to God because I think God created everything with God's thoughts for everything to be in relation to God. If I think God created everything with God's thoughts for everything to be in relation to God, than I think God is responsible for every possible thought that is involved with everything because I think God's thoughts is apart of making up everything for God to be responsible for every possible thought that is involved with everything, and therefore, I think everything is in relation to God because I think God is responsible for every possible thought that is involved with everything for everything to be in relation to God. If I think God is responsible for every possible thought that is involved with everything for everything to be in relation to God, than I think everything is happening for a reason because I think God created everything with God's thoughts for everything to be happening for a reason, and therefore, I think everything is in relation to God because I think everything is happening for a reason with God creating everything with God's thoughts for everything to be in relation to God. If I think everything is happening for a reason with God creating everything with God's thoughts for everything to be in relation to God, than I think God created everything to be happening for a reason because I think God created everything with God's thoughts for God to be creating everything to be happening for a reason, and therefore, I think everything is in relation to God because I think God created everything with God's thoughts for God to be creating everything to be happening for a reason with God's thoughts as I think God created everything to be happening for a reason with God's thoughts for a reason for everything to be in relation to God.

If I think God created everything to be happening for a reason with God's thoughts for a reason for everything to be in relation to God, than I think everything is God's plan because I think God created everything to be happening for a reason for everything to be God's plan, but I do not think everything is God's plan because I do not think God is interfering with everything as I think God is somehow able to be responsible for creating everything, and therefore, I think everything is God's plan because I think God is somehow able to be responsible for creating everything as I think God created everything for everything to be God's plan, even though, I do not think everything is God's plan because I do not think God is responsible for how everything is in life. I do not think God is responsible for how everything is in life because I do not think God is interfering with everything as I think everything can be taking place in its own time and place, and therefore, I do not think God has a plan for everything as I do not think God has a plan for someone because I do not think God is interfering with everything for God not to be responsible for how everything is in life as I do not think God is interfering with everything for God not to be responsible for how someone is in life, even though, I think God can have a plan for someone because I think God can help someone with something as I think God can help someone to be doing something for God to be having a plan for someone. I think God can help someone with something as I think God can help someone to be doing something for God to be having a plan for someone because I think God can help someone to be doing what is best for someone, and therefore, I think God has a plan for someone because I think God can help someone to be doing what is best for someone for God to be having a plan for someone. I think God can help someone to be doing what is best for someone for God to be having a plan for someone because I think someone can ask God to be helping someone to be doing what is best for someone for God to be having a plan for someone, and therefore, I think someone can think about what God's plan is for someone because I think someone can ask God to be helping someone to be doing what is best for someone for someone to be thinking about what God's plan is for someone. If I think someone can think about what God's plan is for someone, than I think God can help someone to be thinking about what God's plan is for someone because I think someone can ask God to be helping someone to be doing what is best for someone for God to be helping someone to be thinking about what God's plan is for someone, and therefore, I think someone can think about what God's plan is for someone because I think God can help someone to be thinking about what God's plan is for someone for someone to be thinking about what God's plan is for someone. If I think someone can think about what God's plan is for someone, than I think God can help someone to be thinking about what is best for someone because I think someone can ask God to be helping someone to be doing what is best for someone for God to be helping someone to be thinking about what is best for someone, and therefore, I think God can help someone to be thinking about what God's plan is for someone because I think God can help someone to be thinking about what is best for someone for God to be helping someone to be thinking about what God's plan is for someone. If I think God can help someone to be thinking about what God's plan is for someone, than I think God has a plan for everyone because I think God has a plan for someone for God to be having a plan for everyone, and therefore, I think everything is in relation to God because I think God has a plan for everyone for everything to be in relation to God.

If I think God has a plan for everyone for everything to be in relation to God, than I do not think everything is pre-destined to happen because I think everything can be taking place in its own time and place for everything not to be pre-destined to happen. I think everything can be taking place in its own time and place for everything not to be pre-destined to happen because I do not think God is interfering with everything for everything not to be pre-destined to happen as I do not think God is interfering with everything for everything to be taking place in its own time and place. I do not think God is interfering with everything for everything not to be pre-destined to happen as I do not think God is interfering with everything for everything to be taking place in its own time and place because I do not think God is interfering with everything as I think everything can be taking place in its own time and place, and therefore, I think everything is in relation to God because I do not think God is interfering with everything as I think everything can be taking place in its own time and place for everything to be in relation to God. If I do not think God is interfering with everything as I think everything can be taking place in its own time and place for everything to be in relation to God, than I think God is somehow able to be responsible for how everything is able to be happening for a reason because I do not think God is interfering with everything as I think God is somehow able to be responsible for creating everything, and therefore, I think everything is in relation to God because I do not think God is interfering with everything as I think God is somehow able to be responsible for creating everything for everything to be in relation to God. If do not think God is interfering with everything as I think God is somehow able to be responsible for creating everything for everything to be in relation to God, than I do not think God is responsible for making the impossible possible because I do not think God is interfering with everything as I think everything can be taking place in its own time and place, however, I think God is somehow able to be responsible for making the impossible possible with how God is somehow able to be responsible for creating everything because I think God is making the impossible possible by making everything possible, and therefore, I think everything is a miracle as I think everything is God's miracle because I think everything is happening for a reason for everything to be a miracle as I think God created everything for everything to be God's miracle, but I do not think everything is God's miracle with how everything is taking place in life because I do not think God is interfering with everything as I think everything can be taking place in its own time and place. If I do not think everything is God's miracle with how everything is taking place in life, than I think someone doing something good for themselves, and someone else is a miracle as I think God doing something good for someone is a miracle because I think everything is happening for a reason for someone to be doing something good for themselves, and someone else to be a miracle as I think God created everything to be happening for a reason for God to be doing something good for someone to be a miracle, and therefore, I think everything is in relation to God because I think someone doing something good for themselves, and someone else is a miracle as I think God doing something good for someone is a miracle for everything to be in relation to God.

If I think someone doing something good for themselves, and someone else is a miracle as I think God doing something good for someone is a miracle for everything to be in relation to God, than I think everything is happening for a reason because I think everything is randomly taking place in its own time and place for everything to be happening for a reason, and therefore, I think someone can try to understand for themselves, as to how everything is happening for a reason because I think everything is randomly taking place in its own time and place for everything to be happening for a reason. I think everything is randomly taking place in its own time and place for everything to be happening for a reason because I do not think someone, something, and God is interfering with everything for everything to be happening for a reason, and therefore, I think everything is in relation to God because I do not think someone, something, and God is interfering with everything for everything to be in relation to God. If I do not think someone, something, and God is interfering with everything for everything to be in relation to God, than I think everything is randomly happening for a reason as I think everything is random because I think everything is randomly taking place in its own time and place for everything to be happening for a reason, and therefore, I think someone can try to predict for themselves, as to what someone thinks is going to happen because I think someone can think about how everything is randomly taking place in its own time and place for someone to be predicting for themselves, as to what someone thinks is going to happen. I think someone can think about how everything is randomly taking place in its own time and place for someone to be predicting for themselves, as to what someone thinks is going to happen because I think how everything is randomly taking place in its own time and place is how everything is happening for a reason, and therefore, I think everything is randomly taking place in its own time and place for everything to be happening for a reason because I do not think God is interfering with everything as I think everything is randomly taking place in its own time and place. I do not think God is interfering with everything as I think everything is randomly taking place in its own time and place because I do not think God is interfering with everything as I think God is somehow able to be responsible for creating everything, and therefore, I think everything is randomly taking place in its own time and place for everything to be happening for a reason because I do not think God is interfering with everything for everything to be happening for a reason. I do not think God is interfering with everything for everything to be happening for a reason because I do not think God is interfering with everything as I think everything is randomly taking place in its own time and place, and therefore, I think everything is in relation to God because I do not think God is interfering with everything as I think everything is randomly taking place in its own time and place for everything to be in relation to God. If I do not think God is interfering with everything as I think everything is randomly taking place in its own time and place for everything to be in relation to God, than I think God is somehow able to be responsible for how everything is randomly taking place in its own time and place because I do not think God is interfering with everything as I think God is somehow able to be responsible for creating everything, and therefore, I think everything is in relation to God because I think God is somehow able to be responsible for how everything is randomly taking place in its own time and place for everything to be in relation to God. If I think God is somehow able to be responsible for how everything is randomly taking place in its own time and place for everything to be in relation to God, than I think God is somehow able to be responsible for how everything is able to be happening for a reason because I do not think God is interfering with everything as I think God is somehow able to be responsible for creating everything, and therefore, I think God is always good, and right with how God is somehow able to be responsible for creating everything because I do not think God is interfering with everything as I think God is somehow able to be responsible for creating everything. If I think God is always good, and right with how God is somehow able to be responsible for creating everything, than I think everything is randomly taking place in its own time and place because I think God created everything with God's thoughts for everything to randomly be taking place in its own time and place, and therefore, I think everything is in relation to God because I think everything is randomly taking place in its own time and place with God creating everything with God's thoughts for everything to be in relation to God. If I think everything is randomly taking place in its own time and place with God creating everything with God's thoughts for everything to be in relation to God, than I think God created everything to randomly be taking place in its own time and place because I think God created everything with God's thoughts for God to be creating everything to randomly be taking place in its own time and place, and therefore, I think everything is relation to God because I think God created everything with God's thoughts for God to be creating everything to randomly be taking place in its own time and place with God's thoughts as I think God created everything to randomly be taking place in its own time and place with God's thoughts for everything to be in relation to God.

If I think God created everything to randomly be taking place in its own time and place with God's thoughts for everything to be in relation to God, than I do not think everything is just by coincidence that everything is created because I do not think everything is just by chance that everything is created for everything not to be just by coincidence that everything is created, and therefore, I do not think everything is just by chance that everything is created because I think everything is happening for a reason for everything not to be just by chance that everything is created, even though, I think everything is happening by chance because I think everything is randomly taking place in its own time and place for everything to be happening by chance, however, I do not think everything is happening just by chance because I think everything is happening for a reason for everything not to be happening just by chance. If I do not think everything is happening just by chance, than I think everything is happening for a reason because I think God created everything to randomly be taking place in its own time and place with God's thoughts for everything to be happening a reason, and therefore, I think everything is in relation to God because I think God created everything to randomly be taking place in its own time and place with God's thoughts for God to be creating everything to be happening a reason as I think God created everything to be happening for a reason for everything to be in relation to God, even though, I think everything is happening for a reason, regardless if someone is aware of what the reason is for something or not because I think someone might not be able to be aware of what the reason is for something that is happening as I think everything is somehow able to be happening for a reason. If I think everything is happening for a reason, than I think everything is a risk because I think everything can be a good or bad risk for someone to be taking a good or bad risk as I think someone can take a good or bad risk for everything to be a risk, and therefore, I think everything can be a good or a bad risk because I think someone can do something for the right or wrong reasons for everything to be a good or a bad risk. I think someone can do something for the right or wrong reasons for everything to be a good or a bad risk because I do not think there is any guarantees for everything to be a good or bad risk, and therefore, I do not think there is any guarantees because I think everything is random for there to be no guarantees. I think everything is random for there to be no guarantees because I thing everything is random with how everything is in life. I thing everything is random with how everything is in life because I think God is somehow able to be responsible for how everything is random in life. I think God is somehow able to be responsible for how everything is random in life because I think God created everything to randomly be taking place in its own time and place with God's thoughts for God to somehow be able to be responsible for how everything is random in life, and therefore, I think everything is in relation to God because I think God created everything to randomly be taking place in its own time and place with God's thoughts for there to be no guarantees as I do not think there is any guarantees for everything to be in relation to God.

If I do not think there is any guarantees for everything to be in relation to God, than I think God is somehow able to be responsible for every possible way in how everything is able to be taking place in life because I think God created everything with God's thoughts for God to somehow be able to be responsible for every possible way in how everything is able to be taking place in life, and therefore, I think everything is in relation to God because I think God is somehow able to be responsible for every possible way in how everything is able to be taking place in life for everything to be in relation to God. If I think God is somehow able to be responsible for every possible way in how everything is able to be taking place in life for everything to be in relation to God, than I think an example of how I think God is somehow able to be responsible for every possible way in how everything is able to be taking place in life can be how God is somehow able to be responsible for how every part is able to be apart of making up a car, before someone was ever able to be making up a car with any of the parts that is apart of making up a car because I think God knew how every part is able to be apart of making up a car, before someone was ever able to be making up a car with any of the parts that is apart of making up a car. I think God knew how every part is able to be apart of making up a car, before someone was ever able to be making up a car with any of the parts that is apart of making up a car because I think God knows every thought that has gone into every part that is apart of making up a car, before someone was ever able to be making up a car with any of the parts that is apart of making up a car. I think God knows every thought that has gone into every part that is apart of making up a car, before someone was ever able to be making up a car with any of the parts that is apart of making up a car because I think God is responsible for every thought that has gone into every part that is apart of making up a car as I think every thought that has gone into every part that is apart of making up a car is of God's thoughts that is apart of making up every part that is apart of making up a car, and therefore, I think God is somehow able to be responsible for every possible way in how everything is able to be taking place in life as I think God is somehow able to be responsible every thought that is apart of making up how everything is able to be taking place in life because I think God created everything with God's thoughts for God to somehow be able to be responsible for every possible way in how everything is able to be taking place in life. If I think God created everything with God's thoughts for God to somehow be able to be responsible for every possible way in how everything is able to be taking place in life, than I think there are human beings who likes to think of themselves as being inventors with how any human being is able to be understanding, and making something for themselves, and I think human beings are discoverers with how any human being is able to be understanding, and making something for themselves because I do not think any human being is completely able to be creating something as much as God is able to be creating something with any thought that is apart of making up something as I think God created everything with God's thoughts that is apart of making up how everything is able to be taking place in life, and therefore, I think God is the greatest inventor because I think God created everything with God's thoughts that is apart of making up how everything is able to be taking place in life for God to be the greatest inventor. If I think God is the greatest inventor, than I think God knows how everything is potentially able to be taking place in life with every thought that is apart of making up everything because I think God created everything with God's thoughts that is apart of making up how everything is able to be taking place in life for God to be knowing how everything is potentially able to be taking place in life with every thought that is apart of making up everything, and therefore, I think everything is in relation to God because I think God knows how everything is potentially able to be taking place in life with every thought that is apart of making up everything for everything to be in relation to God.

If I think God knows how everything is potentially able to be taking place in life with every thought that is apart of making up everything for everything to be in relation to God, than I think God can be working on creating more thoughts, that can be apart of making up something because I think God created everything with God's thoughts for God to be creating any thought, that can be apart of making up something, and therefore, I think everything is in relation to God because I think God can be working on creating more thoughts, that can be apart of making up something for everything to be in relation to God. If I think God can be working on creating more thoughts, that can be apart of making up something for everything to be in relation to God, than I think an example of I think God can be working on creating more thoughts, that can be apart of making up something can be how God can be working on creating more thoughts that can apart of making up any irrational number because I do not think someone can possibly be able to be knowing for themselves, as to what the very last number in thought there is in life, that can apart of making up any irrational number as I think any irrational number can be going on and on forever with any additional thought of any additional number, that can be apart of making up any irrational number, and therefore, I think God can be working on creating more thoughts, that can be apart of making up something because I think God created something with God's thoughts for God to be working on creating more thoughts, that can be apart of making up something. If I think God can be working on creating more thoughts, that can be apart of making up something, than I think God is infinitely creating because I think God can be working on creating more thoughts, that can be apart of making up something, and therefore, I do not know if there is nothing new with how God is somehow able to be responsible for creating everything because I think God can be working on creating something new with God's thoughts. I think God can be working on creating something new with God's thoughts because I do not think someone can possibly be able to be knowing for themselves everything that is able to be taking place in life, and therefore, I do not know if there is nothing new with how God is somehow able to be responsible for creating everything because I think if there is nothing new with how God is able to be responsibly for creating everything, than I think everything would come to a halt because I do not think God would be working on creating something new with God's thoughts for everything to be coming to a halt, but I do not think everything is coming to a halt because I think God can be working on creating something new with God's thoughts for everything not to be coming to a halt, and therefore, I think everything is in relation to God because I think God can be working on creating something new with God's thoughts for everything to be in relation to God. If I think God can be working on creating something new with God's thoughts for everything to be in relation to God, than I think God is somehow able to be responsible for how everything is in life because I think God created everything with God's thoughts for God to somehow be able to be responsible for how everything is in life, and therefore, I think everything is in relation to God because I think God is somehow able to be responsible for how everything is in life for everything to be in relation to God. If I think God is somehow able to be responsible for how everything is in life for everything to be in relation to God, than I think God is somehow able to be responsible for creating everything because I think God created everything with God's thoughts for God to somehow be able to be responsible for creating everything, and therefore, I think everything is in relation to God because I think God is somehow able to be responsible for creating everything for everything to be in relation to God. If I think God is somehow able to be responsible for creating everything for everything to be in relation to God, than I think God is in relation to everything for everything to be in relation to God because I think God is somehow able to be responsible for how everything is in life as I think God is somehow able to be responsible for creating everything for everything to be in relation to God, and therefore, I think everything is in relation to God because I think God is in relation to everything for everything to be in relation to God. If I think God is in relation to everything for everything to be in relation to God, than I think God created everything for everything to be in relation to God because I think God created everything with God's thoughts for everything to be in relation to God, and therefore, I think everything is in relation to God because I think God created everything for everything to be in relation to God.

Chapter 10

How any dimension is able to be overlapping, and co-existing along with any other dimension

I would like to talk about how dimensions are in life in relation to what dimensions are in life by talking about how any dimension is able to be overlapping, and co-existing along with any other dimension, that could have something to do with how dimensions are in relation to what dimensions are in life because I think any dimension is overlapping, and co-existing along with any other dimension, and therefore, how is any dimension able to be overlapping, and co-existing along with any other dimension? I think any dimension is able to be overlapping, and co-existing along with any other dimension because I think any dimension is either alike or unalike any other dimension for any dimension to be able to be overlapping, and co-existing along with any other dimension, and therefore, I think any dimension is like any other dimension as I think any dimension is overlapping, and co-existing along with any other dimension because I think any dimension is alike any other dimension as I think any dimension is overlapping, and co-existing along with any other dimension. If I think any dimension is alike any other dimension as I think any dimension is overlapping, and co-existing along with any other dimension, than I think the dimension of width can be an example of how I think any dimension is alike any other dimension as I think any dimension is overlapping, and co-existing along with any other dimension because I think the dimension of width is alike any other dimension of width as I think the dimension of width is overlapping, and co-existing along with any other dimension. I think the dimension of width is alike any other dimension of width as I think the dimension of width is overlapping, and co-existing along with any other dimension because I think the dimension of width is any length in width of the dimension of width as I think the dimension of width is any length that is going left to right within any body of mass, and therefore, I think any dimension is alike any other dimension as I think any dimension is overlapping, and co-existing along with any other dimension because I think the dimension of width is alike any other dimension in width as I think the dimension of width is overlapping, and co-existing along with any other dimension.

If I think the dimension of width is alike any other dimension in width as I think the dimension of width is overlapping, and co-existing along with any other dimension, than I think any dimension is alike any other dimension as I think any dimension is overlapping, and co-existing along with any other dimension because I think any dimension is alike any other dimension as I think any dimension is overlapping, and co-existing along with the same dimension, and therefore, I think the dimension of length can be an example of how any dimension is alike any other dimension as I think any dimension is overlapping, and co-existing along with the same dimension because I think the dimension of length is alike any other dimension in length as I think the dimension of length is overlapping, and co-existing along with the same dimension. I think the dimension of length is alike any other dimension in length as I think the dimension of length is overlapping, and co-existing along with the same dimension because I think the dimension of length is any length in length of the dimension of length as I think the dimension of length is any length that is going upwards and downwards within any body of mass, and therefore, I think any dimension is alike any other dimension as I think any dimension is overlapping, and co-existing along with the same dimension because I think the dimension of length is alike any other dimension in length as

I think the dimension of length is overlapping, and co-existing along with the same dimension. I think the dimension of length is alike any other dimension in length as I think the dimension of length is overlapping, and co-existing along with the same dimension because I think each dimension in length is alike each others dimensions in length as I think the dimension of length is overlapping, and co-existing along with any other dimension in length, and therefore, how can the dimension of length be overlapping, and co-existing along with any other dimension in length as I think the dimension of length is overlapping, and co-existing along with the same dimension? I think the dimension of length can be overlapping, and co-existing along with any other dimension in length as I think the dimension of length is overlapping, and co-existing along with the same dimension because I think if one length of the dimension of length, that is taking place on one side of an object comes in contact with another length of the dimension of length, that is taking place on one side of another object, than I think each length of the dimension in length is coming in contact with each others length, while each dimension of length is taking place on each of their own completely separate object, and therefore, I think each length of the dimension in length is overlapping, and co-existing along with each others length because I think each length of the dimension in length is coming in contact with each others length, while each dimension of length taking place on each of their own completely separate object, even though, I do not think each length of the dimension of length can be completely apart of each others length as I think each length of the dimension in length is coming in contact with each others length, while each dimension of length taking place on each of their own completely separate object because I think each length of the dimension of length can be separated from each others lengths as I think each length of the dimension of length is taking place on each of their own completely separate object, that can be separated from each other, however, I think each length of the dimension of length can be overlapping, and co-existing along with each others length because I think each length of the dimension in length can come in contact with each others length, while each dimension of length taking place on each of their own completely separate object. If I think each length of the dimension of length can be overlapping, and co-existing along with each others length, than I think the dimension of length is alike any other dimension in length as I think the dimension of length is overlapping, and co-existing along with the same dimension because I think each length of the dimension in length can come in contact with each others length, while each dimension of length taking place on each of their own completely separate object, and therefore, I think any dimension is alike any other dimension as I think any dimension is overlapping, and co-existing along with the same dimension because I think the dimension of length is alike any other dimension in length as I think the dimension of length is overlapping, and co-existing along with the same dimension.

If I think any dimension is alike any other dimension as I think any dimension is overlapping, and co-existing along with the same dimension, than I think any dimension is like any other dimension as I think any dimension is overlapping, and co-existing along with any other dimension because I think any dimension is unalike any other dimension as I think any dimension is overlapping, and co-existing along with any other dimension, and therefore, I think the dimension of depth can be an example how I think any dimension is unalike any other dimension as I think any dimension is overlapping, and co-existing along with any other dimension because I think the dimension of depth is unalike any other dimension as I think the dimension of depth is overlapping, and co-existing along with any other dimension. I think the dimension of depth is unalike any other dimension as I think the dimension of depth is overlapping, and co-existing along with any other dimension because I think the dimension of depth is any length in depth of the dimension of depth as I think the dimension of depth is any length that is going backwards and forwards within any body of mass, and therefore, I think any dimension is unalike any other dimension as I think any dimension is overlapping, and co-existing along with any other dimension because I think the dimension of depth is unalike any other dimension as I think the dimension of depth is overlapping, and co-existing along with any other dimension. If I think any dimension is unalike any other dimension as I think any dimension is overlapping, and co-existing along with any other dimension, than I think any dimension is like any other dimension as I think any dimension is overlapping, and co-existing along with any other dimension because I think any dimension is either alike or unalike any other dimension as I think any dimension is overlapping, and co-existing along with any other dimension, and therefore, I think any dimension is able to be overlapping, and co-existing along with any other dimension because I think any dimension is either alike or unalike any other dimension as I think any dimension is overlapping, and co-existing along with any other dimension.

If I think any dimension is either alike or unalike any other dimension as I think any dimension is overlapping, and co-existing along with any other dimension, than I think the three dimensions of length is the dimensions of length, width, and depth because I think the dimensions of length, width, and depth is any length in length, width, and depth that is able to be taking place within body of mass, and therefore, I think the three dimensions of length is alike the three dimensions of lengths length because I think the three dimensions of length can be any length in length, width, and depth that is able to be taking place within body of mass, even though, I do not think any length of the three dimensions of lengths length necessarily has to be exactly the same length for any the three dimension of lengths to be alike any of the three dimensions of lengths length because I think the three dimensions of length can be any length in length, width, and depth that is able to be taking place within any body of mass, however, I think there can be more than one length of the three dimensions of length that is able to be taking place within body of mass because I think the three dimensions of length can be any length in length, width, and depth that is able to be taking place within body of mass. If I think there can be more than one length of the three dimensions of length that is able to be taking place within body of mass, than I do not think someone can possibly be able to knowing for themselves, as to just exactly how many lengths of the three dimensions of length is able taking place within any body of mass because I think the three dimensions of length can be any length in length, width, and depth that is able to be taking place within body of mass, and therefore, I do not think someone can possibly be able to be knowing for themselves, as to just exactly how many lengths of the three dimensions of length there are in life because I think the three dimensions of length can be of any length in length, width, and depth that is able to be taking place within body of mass, but I think the three dimensions of length is alike the three dimension in lengths length, regardless of how often the three dimensions of length is able to be alike the three dimensions of lengths length because I think the three dimensions of length can be any length in length, width, and depth that is able to be taking place within body of mass for the three dimensions of length to be alike the three dimension in lengths length. If I think the three dimensions of length is alike the three dimension in lengths length, than I think the three dimensions of length is alike the three dimensions of length because I think the three dimensions of length is alike the three dimensions of lengths length for the three dimensions of length to be alike the three dimensions of length, and therefore, I think the three dimensions of length is alike the three dimensions of lengths length as I think the three dimensions of length is alike the three dimensions of length because I think the three dimensions of length can be any length in length, width, and depth that is able to be taking place within body of mass for the three dimensions of length to be alike the three dimensions of lengths length as I think the three dimensions of length can be any length in length, width, and depth that is able to be taking place within body of mass for the three dimensions of length to be alike the three dimensions of length.

If I think the three dimensions of length is alike the three dimensions of lengths length as I think the three dimensions of length is alike the three dimensions of length, than I think the three dimensions of length is similar with how the three dimensions of length is able to be taking place within any within body of mass because I think the three dimensions of length can be any length in length, width, and depth that is able to be taking place within body of mass, but I think the three dimensions of length is unalike the three dimensions of length because I think the three dimensions of length are completely different dimensions with how the three dimensions of length are in life. I think the three dimensions of length are completely different dimensions with how the three dimensions of length are in life because I think the dimension of length is any length that is going upwards and downwards within any body of mass, and I think the dimension of width is any length that is going left to right within any body of mass, and I think the dimension of depth is any length that is going backwards and forwards within any body of mass, and therefore, I think any length of the three dimensions of length are completely different dimensions in lengths because I think the three dimensions of length are completely different dimensions with how the three dimensions of length are in life. If I think the three dimensions of length are completely different dimensions with how the three dimensions of length are in life, than I think the three dimensions of length is unalike the three dimensions of length because I think the three dimensions of length is unalike the three dimensions of lengths length for the three dimensions of length to be unalike the three dimensions of length, and therefore, I think the three dimensions of length is unalike the three dimensions of lengths length as I think the three dimensions of length is unalike the three dimensions of length because I think any length of the three dimensions of length are completely different dimensions in lengths for the three dimensions of length to be unalike the three dimensions of lengths length as I think any length of the three dimensions of length are completely different dimensions in lengths for the three dimensions of length to be unalike the three dimensions of length.

If I think the three dimensions of length is unalike the three dimensions of lengths length as I think the three dimensions of length is unalike the three dimensions of length, than how is any dimension able to be overlapping, and co-existing along with any other dimension as I think any dimension is unalike any other dimension? I think any dimension is able to be overlapping, and co-existing along with any other dimension as I think any dimension is unalike any other dimension because I think the dimension of width is able to be overlapping, and co-existing along with the dimension of length as I think the dimension of width is unalike the dimension of length. I think the dimension of width is able to be overlapping, and co-existing along with the dimension of length as I think the dimension of width is unalike the dimension of length because I think the dimension of width is overlapping, and co-existing along with the dimension of length as I think any length of the dimension of width, and any length of the dimension of length is taking place within body of mass. I think the dimension of width is overlapping, and co-existing along with the dimension of length as I think any length of the dimension of width, and any length of the dimension of length is taking place within body of mass because I think the dimension of width is overlapping, and co-existing along with the dimension of length as I think the dimension of width is unalike the dimension of length, and therefore, I think the dimension of width is able to be overlapping, and co-existing along with the dimension of length as I think the dimension of width is unalike the dimension of length because I think the dimension of width is overlapping, and co-existing along with the dimension of length as I think the dimension of width is unalike the dimension of length. If I think the dimension of width is able to be overlapping, and co-existing along with the dimension of length as I think the dimension of width is unalike the dimension of length, than I think any dimension is overlapping, and co-existing along with any other dimension as I think any dimension is unalike any other dimension because I think the dimension of width is overlapping, and co-existing along with the dimension of length as I think the dimension of width is unalike the dimension of length, and therefore, I think any dimension is able to be overlapping, and co-existing along with any other dimension as I think any dimension is unalike any other dimension because I think any dimension is overlapping, and co-existing along with any other dimension as I think any dimension is unalike any other dimension.

If I think any dimension is able to be overlapping, and co-existing along with any other dimension as I think any dimension is unalike any other dimension, than I do not think someone can possibly be able to be knowing for themselves, as to just exactly how many dimensions there are in life that is overlapping, and co-existing along with any other dimension because I do not think someone can possibly be able to be knowing for themselves, as to just exactly how many dimensions there are in life that is unalike any other dimension, but I think any dimension is overlapping, and co-existing along with any other dimension, regardless of how often any dimension is able to be unalike any other dimension because I think any dimension is unalike any other dimension for any dimension to be overlapping, and co-existing along with any other dimension. If I think any dimension is unalike any other dimension for any dimension to be overlapping, and co-existing along with any other dimension, than I think any dimension is able to be overlapping, and co-existing along with any other dimension as I think any dimension is alike any other dimension because I think any dimension is overlapping, and co-existing along with any other dimension as I think any dimension is alike any other dimension, even though, I do not think someone can possibly be able to be knowing for themselves, as to just exactly how many dimensions there are in life as I think any dimension is overlapping, and co-existing along with any other dimension because I do not think someone can possibly be able to be knowing for themselves, as to just exactly how many dimensions there are in life that is alike any other dimension, but I think any dimension is overlapping, and co-existing along with any other dimension, regardless of how often any dimension is able to be alike any other dimension because I think any dimension is alike any other dimension for any dimension to be overlapping, and co-existing along with any other dimension. If I think any dimension is alike any other dimension for any dimension to be overlapping, and co-existing along with any other dimension, than I think any dimension is able to be overlapping, and co-existing along with any other dimension as I think any dimension is overlapping, and co-existing along with any other dimension because I think any dimension is either alike or unalike any other dimension as I think any dimension is overlapping, and co-existing along with any other dimension, and therefore, I think any dimension can be very interesting and thought provoking for someone to be thinking about how any dimension is either alike or unalike any other dimension as I think any dimension is overlapping, and co-existing along with any other dimension because I think any dimension is either be alike or unalike any other dimension for any dimension to be overlapping, and co-existing along with any other dimension.

If I think any dimension is either be alike or unalike any other dimension for any dimension to be overlapping, and co-existing along with any other dimension, than how is any dimension able to be alike any other dimension as I think any dimension is alike any other dimension? I think any dimension is able to be alike any other dimension as I think any dimension is alike any other dimension because I think any dimension is a copy of any other dimension as I think any dimension is alike any other dimension, and therefore, I think someone can be wondering to themselves, as to how any dimension is able to be a copy of any other dimension as I think any dimension is alike any other dimension? I think any dimension is able to be a copy of any other dimension as I think any dimension is alike any other dimension because I think any dimension is a copy of any dimensions own blue print as I think any dimension is alike any other dimension, and therefore, I think someone can be wondering to themselves, as to how any dimension is able to be a copy of any dimensions own blue print as I think any dimension is alike any other dimension? I think any dimension is able to be a copy of any dimensions own blue print as I think any dimension is alike any other dimension because I think any dimension is a copy of any dimensions original copy as I think any dimension is alike any other dimension, even though, I do not think someone can possibly be able to be knowing for themselves, as to how any dimension is able to be a copy of any dimensions original copy as I think any dimension is alike any other dimension because I do not think someone can possibly be able to be knowing for themselves, as to how any dimension is able to be alike or a copy of any other dimension as I think any dimension is alike any other dimension, but I think any dimension is able to be alike any other dimension as I think any dimension is alike any other dimension because I think any dimension is alike any other dimension with how any dimension is able to be alike any other dimension. I think any dimension is alike any other dimension with how any dimension is able to be alike any other dimension because I think any dimension is a copy of any other dimension as I think any dimension is alike any other dimension, and therefore, I think the dimension of width can be an example of how I think any dimension is a copy of any other dimension as I think any dimension is alike any other dimension because I think the dimension of width is a copy of any other dimension of width as I think the dimension of width is alike any other dimension of width. I think the dimension of width is a copy of any other dimension of width as I think the dimension of width is alike any other dimension of width because I think the dimension of width physically appears to be alike any other dimension of width as I think the dimension of width is alike any other dimension of width. I think the dimension of width physically appears to be alike any other dimension of width as I think the dimension of width is alike any other dimension of width because I think the dimension of width physically appears to be identical with any other dimension of width as I think the dimension width is alike any other dimension of width. I think the dimension of width physically appears to be identical with any other dimension of width as I think the dimension width is alike any other dimension of width because I think the dimension of width is identical to any other dimension of width as I think the dimension of width is alike any other dimension of width. I think the dimension of width is identical to any other dimension of width as I think the dimension of width is alike any other dimension of width because I think the dimension of width is a copy of any other dimension of width as I think the dimension of width is alike any other dimension of width. I think the dimension of width is a copy of any other dimension of width as I think the dimension of width is alike any other dimension of width because I think any dimension is a copy of any other dimension as I think any dimension is alike any other dimension. I think any dimension is a copy of any other dimension as I think any dimension is alike any other dimension because I think any dimension is a copy of any dimensions original copy as I think any dimension is alike any other dimension.

If I think any dimension is a copy of any other dimension as I think any dimension is alike any other dimension, than I think any dimension is able to be alike any other dimension as I think any dimension is alike any other dimension because I think any dimension is alike any other dimension with how any dimension is able to be alike any other dimension. I think any dimension is alike any other dimension with how any dimension is able to be alike any other dimension because I think any dimension is a copy of any dimensions original copy as I think any dimension is alike any other dimension, and therefore, I do not think someone can possibly be able to be knowing for themselves, as to how many dimensions there are in life that is able to be alike any other dimension as I think any dimension is alike any other dimension because I do not think someone can possibly be able to be knowing for themselves, as to how many copies of any dimension there are in life as I think any dimension is a copy of any other dimension. I do not think someone can possibly be able to be knowing for themselves, as to how many copies of any dimension there are in life as I think any dimension is a copy of any other dimension because I do not think someone can possibly be able to be knowing for themselves, as to what any dimensions original copy is in life as I think any dimension is a copy of any dimensions original copy, but I think any dimension is alike any other dimension, regardless of how many copies of any dimension there are in life because I think any dimension is a copy of any dimensions original copy as I think any dimension is alike any other dimension. If I think any dimension is a copy of any dimensions original copy as I think any dimension is alike any other dimension, than I think any dimension is a copy of any other dimension as I think any dimension is alike any other dimension because I think God is somehow able to be responsible for creating how any dimension is able to be a copy of any dimensions original copy as I think any dimension is alike any other dimension. I think God is somehow able to be responsible for creating how any dimension is able to be a copy of any dimensions original copy as I think any dimension is alike any other dimension because I do not think someone can possibly be able to be knowing for themselves, as to how any dimension is able to be a copy of any dimensions original copy as I think any dimension is alike any other dimension, but I think someone can understand for themselves, as to how any dimension is a copy of any dimensions original copy as I think any dimension is alike any other dimension because I think someone can understand for themselves, as to how any dimension is a copy of any other dimension as I think any dimension is alike any other dimension.

If I think someone can understand for themselves, as to how any dimension is a copy of any other dimension as I think any dimension is alike any other dimension, than how is any dimension able to be unlike any other dimension as I think any dimension is unlike any other dimension? I think any dimension is able to be unlike any other dimension as I think any dimension is unlike any other dimension because I think any dimension that is unalike any other dimension is alike any dimension that is alike that dimension. I think any dimension that is unalike any other dimension is alike any dimension that is alike that dimension because I think any dimension that is alike any dimension is a copy any dimension as I think any dimension is unalike any other dimension, and therefore, I think any dimension is able to be unlike any other dimension as I think any dimension is unlike any other dimension because I think any dimension is a copy of any dimension as I think any dimension is unlike any other dimension, even though, I think someone can be wondering to themselves, as to how any dimension is able to be a copy of any dimension as I think any dimension is unlike any other dimension? I think any dimension is able to be a copy of any dimension as I think any dimension is unlike any other dimension because I think any dimension is a copy of any dimensions own blue print as I think any dimension is unlike any other dimension, and therefore, I think someone can be wondering to themselves, as to how any dimension is able to be a copy of any dimensions own blue print as I think any dimension is unlike any other dimension? I think any dimension is able to be a copy of any dimensions own blue print as I think any dimension is unlike any other dimension because I think any dimension is a copy of any dimensions original copy as I think any dimension is unlike any other dimension, even though, I do not think someone can possibly be able to be knowing for themselves, as to how any dimension is able to be a copy of any dimensions original copy as I think any dimension is unlike any other dimension because I do not think someone can possibly be able to be knowing for themselves, as to how any dimension is able to be a copy of any dimension as I think any dimension is unalike any other dimension, but I think any dimension is able to be unlike any other dimension as I think any dimension is unlike any other dimension because I think any dimension is unlike any other dimension with how any dimension is able to be unlike any other dimension. I think any dimension is unlike any other dimension with how any dimension is able to be unlike any other dimension because I think any dimension is a copy of any dimension as I think any dimension is unlike any other dimension, and therefore, I think the dimension of width can be an example of how I think any dimension is a copy of any dimension as I think any dimension is unlike any other dimension because I think the dimension of width is a copy of any length of the dimension of width as I think the dimension of width is unlike any length of the dimension of length. I think the dimension of width is a copy of any length of the dimension of width as I think the dimension of width is unlike any length of the dimension of length because I think the dimension of width physically appears to be alike any length of the dimension of width as I think the dimension of width is unlike any length of the dimension of length. I think the dimension of width physically appears to be alike any length of the dimension of width as I think the dimension of width is unlike any length of the dimension of length because I think the dimension of width physically appears to be identical with any length of the dimension of width as I think the dimension width is unlike any length of the dimension of length. I think the dimension of width physically appears to be identical with any length of the dimension of width as I think the dimension width is unlike any length of the dimension of length because I think the dimension of width is identical to any length of the dimension of width as I think the dimension of width is unlike any length of the dimension of length. I think the dimension of width is identical to any length of the dimension of width as I think the dimension of width is unlike any length of the dimension of length because I think the dimension of width is a copy of any length of the dimension of width as I think the dimension of width is unalike any length of the dimension of length. I think the dimension of width is a copy of any length of the dimension of width as I think the dimension of width is unalike any length of the dimension of length because I think any dimension is a copy of any dimension as I think any dimension is unlike any other dimension. I think any dimension is a copy of any dimension as I think any dimension is unlike any other dimension because I think any dimension is a copy of any dimensions original copy as I think any dimension is unlike any other dimension.

I think any dimension is a copy of any dimensions original copy as I think any dimension is unlike any other dimension because I think any dimension is a copy of any other dimension as I think any dimension is alike any other dimension, and therefore, I think any dimension is able to be alike or unlike any other dimension because I think any dimension is a copy of any other dimension for any dimension to alike or unlike any other dimension. I think any dimension is a copy of any other dimension for any dimension to alike or unlike any other dimension because I think any dimension is alike any other dimension for any dimension to be alike or unlike any other dimension. I think any dimension is alike any other dimension for any dimension to be alike or unlike any other dimension because I think any dimension is alike or unalike any other dimension for any dimension to be overlapping, and co-existing along with any other dimension. I think any dimension is alike or unalike any other dimension for any dimension to be overlapping, and co-existing along with any other dimension because I think any dimension is alike or unalike any other dimension for any dimension to be alike any other dimension. I think any dimension is alike or unalike any other dimension for any dimension to be alike any other dimension because I think every dimension is alike or unalike every other dimension for every dimension to be alike every other dimension, and therefore, I think every dimension is countless because I think there is a countless amount of dimensions for every dimension to be countless. If I think every dimension is countless, than I think there is an infinite amount of dimensions as I think every dimension is infinite because I think every dimension is created by God being infinite for there to be an infinite amount of dimensions as I think every dimension is created by God being infinite for every dimension to be infinite, and therefore, I do not think someone can be able to knowing for themselves, as to just exactly how many dimensions there are in life that is alike and unalike any other dimension because I think there is a countless amount of dimensions for someone not to be knowing for themselves, as to just exactly how many dimensions there are in life that is alike and unalike any other dimension, even though, I think God knows how many dimensions there are in life that is alike and unalike any other dimension because I think every dimension is created by God for God to be able to be knowing how many dimensions there are in life that is alike and unalike any other dimension.

．

If I think God knows how many dimensions there are in life that is alike and unalike any other dimension, than I think God created any dimension to be alike or unalike any other dimension because I think God created everything with God's thoughts for God to be creating any dimension to be alike or unalike any other dimension, and therefore, I think any dimension is able to be alike or unlike any other dimension because I think God created any dimension to be alike or unalike any other dimension with God's thoughts for any dimension to be able to be alike or unlike any other dimension. If I think any dimension is able to be alike or unlike any other dimension, than I think any dimension is a copy of any other dimension for any dimension to alike or unlike any other dimension because I think God created everything with God's thoughts for any dimension to be alike or unlike any other dimension as I think God created everything with God's thoughts for any dimension to be a copy of any other dimension, and therefore, I think any dimension is a copy of God's thoughts for any dimension to be alike or unalike any other dimension because I think God created everything with God's thoughts for any dimension to be alike or unlike any other dimension as I think God created everything with God's thoughts for any dimension to be a copy of God's thoughts. If I think any dimension is a copy of God's thoughts for any dimension to be alike or unalike any other dimension, than I think any dimension is alike or unalike any other dimension for any dimension to be overlapping, and co-existing along with any other dimension because I think God created everything with God's thoughts for any dimension to be overlapping, and co-existing along with any other dimension as I think God created everything with God's thoughts for any dimension to be alike or unlike any other dimension, and therefore, I think any dimension is able to be overlapping, and co-existing along with any other dimension because I think God created everything with God's thoughts for any dimension to be able to be overlapping, and co-existing along with any other dimension. If I think any dimension is able to be overlapping, and co-existing along with any other dimension, than I think God created any dimension to be overlapping, and co-existing along with any other dimension because I think God created everything with God's thoughts for God to be creating any dimension to be overlapping, and co-existing along with any other dimension, and therefore, I think any dimension is able to be overlapping, and co-existing along with any other dimension because I think God created any dimension to be overlapping, and co-existing along with any other dimension for any dimension to be overlapping, and co-existing along with any other dimension.

If I think any dimension is able to be overlapping, and co-existing along with any other dimension, than I think any dimension can have a name because I think the name of any dimension is someone calling any dimension any name that someone chooses to be calling any dimension for any dimension to have a name, and therefore, I think any dimension has a name because I think someone can choose to be calling any dimension a name for any dimension to be having a name. If I think any dimension has a name, than I think any dimension is overlapping, and co-existing along with any other dimension as I think any dimension can have a name because I think someone can name any dimension that is overlapping, and co-existing along with any other dimension, and therefore, I think any dimension has a name because I think someone can name any dimension as I think any dimension is overlapping, and co-existing along with any other dimension. If I think any dimension has a name, than I think any dimension can have a meaning because I think the meaning of any dimension is someone thinking about how any dimension is in life for any dimension to be having a meaning, and therefore, I think any dimension has a meaning because I think someone can think about how any dimension is in life for any dimension to be having a meaning. If I think any dimension has a meaning, than I think any dimension is overlapping, and co-existing along with any other dimension as I think any dimension can have a meaning because I think someone can think about how any dimension is in life that is overlapping, and co-existing along with any other dimension, and therefore, I think any dimension has a meaning because I think someone can think about how any dimension is in life as I think any dimension is overlapping, and co-existing along with any other dimension. If I think any dimension has a meaning, than I think any dimension can have a purpose because I think the purpose of any dimension is how any dimension is in life for any dimension to be having a purpose, and therefore, I think any dimension has a purpose because I think any dimensions purpose is how any dimension is in life for any dimension to be having a purpose. If I think any dimension has a purpose, than I think any dimension is overlapping, and co-existing along with any other dimension as I think any dimension can have a purpose because I think the purpose of any dimension is how any dimension is in life for any dimension to be overlapping, and co-existing along with any other dimension, and therefore, I think any dimension has a purpose because I think the purpose of any dimension is how any dimension is in life as I think any dimension is overlapping, and co-existing along with any other dimension. If I think any dimension has a purpose, than I think someone can think about what any dimensions purpose is in life because I think someone can think about how any dimension is in life for someone to be thinking about what any dimensions purpose is in life, and therefore, I think any dimension has a purpose because I think someone can think about what any dimensions purpose is in life for any dimension to be having a purpose, even though, I think any dimension can have a meaning, and a purpose because I think any dimensions meaning, and purpose is how any dimension is in life for any dimension to be having a meaning, and a purpose. If I think any dimension can have a meaning, and a purpose, than I think any dimension can have a purpose because I think the purpose of any dimension is how any dimension is able to be what any dimension is in life, and therefore, I think an example of how I think the purpose of any dimension is how any dimension is able to be what any dimension is in life can be the dimension of width because I think the purpose of the dimension of width is how the dimension of width is able to be what the dimension of width is in life. I think the purpose of the dimension of width is how the dimension of width is able to be what the dimension of width is in life because I think the dimension of width is the only length that is going right to left within any body of mass, and therefore, I think any dimension has a purpose because I think the purpose of any dimension is how any dimension is able to be what any dimension is in life. If I think any dimension has a purpose, than I think any dimension is overlapping, and co-existing along with any other dimension as I think any dimension can have a name, meaning, and purpose because I think any dimension can have a name, meaning, and purpose for any dimension to be alike or unalike any other dimension, and therefore, I think any dimension has a name, meaning, and purpose because I think any dimension is alike or unalike any other dimension for any dimension to be overlapping, and co-existing along with any other dimension.

Chapter 11

The embodiment of God

I would like to talk about how dimensions are in life in relation to what dimensions are in life by talking about the embodiment of God, that can possibly have something to do with how dimensions are in life is in relation to what dimensions are in life because I think the embodiment of God is of the dimension of God as I think God is the dimension of God for the embodiment of God to be God, and therefore, I think God's state of consciousness, and God's will, and God's thoughts, and God's mind, and God's being are characteristics or features that is apart of making up the embodiment of God as I think the embodiment of God is apart of God because I think God is how God is able to be what God is in life as I think the embodiment of God is apart of how God is able to be what God is in life. I think God is how God is able to be what God is in life as I think the embodiment of God is apart of how God is able to be what God is in life because I think God is what God is in life as I think the embodiment of God is apart of what God is in life. I think God is what God is in life as I think the embodiment of God is apart of what God is in life because I think God is the embodiment of God as I think the embodiment of God is apart of God, and therefore, I think God's state of consciousness, and God's will, and God's thoughts, and God's mind, and God's being are all completely different characteristics or features of God because I think God's state of consciousness is what God is able to be doing, and I think God's will is what God is doing, and I think God's mind is a storage area of God's thoughts, and I think God's being is what God is in life, even though, I think God's state of consciousness, and God's will, and God's thoughts, and God's mind, and God's being are all completely different characteristics or features of God that is apart of making up the embodiment of God because I think God consists of God having God's state of consciousness, and God's will, and God's thoughts, and God's mind, and God's being that is apart of making up the embodiment of God. I think God consists of God having God's state of consciousness, and God's will, and God's thoughts, and God's mind, and God's being that is apart of making up the embodiment of God because I think the embodiment of God is apart of God. I think the embodiment of God is apart of God because I think God's state of consciousness, and God's will, and God's thoughts, and God's mind is taking place within God's being, without being God's being for God's state of consciousness, and God's will, and God's thoughts, and God's mind is apart of God's being, without being God's being. I think God's state of consciousness, and God's will, and God's thoughts, and God's mind is taking place within God's being, without being God's being for God's state of consciousness, and God's will, and God's thoughts, and God's mind is apart of God's being, without being God's being because I think God's state of consciousness, and God's will, and God's thoughts, and God's mind, and God's being is apart of making up the embodiment of God. I think God's state of consciousness, and God's will, and God's thoughts, and God's mind, and God's being is apart of making up the embodiment of God because I think the embodiment of God is apart of God. I think the embodiment of God is apart of God because I think the embodiment of God is God's state of consciousness, and God's will, and God's thoughts, and God's mind, and God's being for the embodiment of God to be apart of God, and therefore, I think the embodiment of God is overlapping, and co-existing along with the dimension of God because I think the embodiment of God is apart of God. I think the embodiment of God is apart of God because I think the embodiment of God is God.

I think the embodiment of God is God because I think the embodiment of God consists of God's state of consciousness, and God's will, and God's thoughts, and God's mind, and God's being that is apart God. I think the embodiment of God consists of God's state of consciousness, and God's will, and God's thoughts, and God's mind, and God's being that is apart God because I think the embodiment of God is God as I think God is the embodiment of God. I think the embodiment of God is God as I think God is the embodiment of God because I think the embodiment of God is what God is in life, and therefore, I think God is multi-dimensional because I think God's state of consciousness, and God's will, and God's thoughts, and God's mind, and God's being is apart of making up the embodiment of God for God to be multi-dimensional. If I think God is multi-dimensional, than I think God created the embodiment of God with God's being because I think God's state of consciousness, and God's will is apart of God's being as I think God created God's thoughts, and God's mind to be apart of God's being for God to be creating the embodiment of God with God's being, and therefore, I think God created the embodiment of God because I think God created the embodiment of God with God's being for God to be creating the embodiment of God. If I think God created the embodiment of God, than I think God created the embodiment of God to be multi-dimensional because I think God created the embodiment of God with God's being for God to be creating the embodiment of God to be multi-dimensional, and therefore, I think the embodiment of God is of the dimensions of a higher intelligent living being because I think God created the embodiment of God to be multi-dimensional for the embodiment of God to be of the dimensions of a higher intelligent living being, even though, I think God's state of consciousness, and God's will, and God's thoughts, and God's mind, and God's being is overlapping, and co-existing along with God's state of consciousness, and God's will, and God's thoughts, and God's mind, and God's being because I think God's state of consciousness, and God's will, and God's thoughts, and God's mind, and God's being is apart of making up the embodiment of God.

If I think God's state of consciousness, and God's will, and God's thoughts, and God's mind, and God's being is apart of making up the embodiment of God, than I think the embodiment of God is how God is able to be someone as I think the embodiment of God is how God is able to be a living being because I think the embodiment of God consists of God having a state of consciousness, and God having a will, and God having thoughts, and God having a mind that is apart of God's being for the embodiment of God to be how God is able to be someone as I think the embodiment of God consists of God having a state of consciousness, and God having a will, and God having thoughts, and God having a mind that is apart of God's being for the embodiment of God to be how God is able to be living being, and therefore, I think God is the embodiment of God for God to be a living being because I think God consists of God having a state of consciousness, and God having a will, and God having thoughts, and God having a mind that is apart of God's being for God to be a living being as I think the embodiment of God consists of God having a state of consciousness, and God having a will, and God having thoughts, and God having a mind that is apart of God's being for God to be a living being. If I think God is the embodiment of God for God to be a living being, than I think the embodiment of God is what God is in life because I think God is the embodiment of God for the embodiment of God to be what God is in life, and therefore, I think the embodiment of God is a dimension that is overlapping, and co-existing along with any dimension that is apart of making up the embodiment of God as I think any dimension that is apart of making up the embodiment of God are all of the completely different characteristics or features of God that is apart of making up the embodiment of God because I think all of the completely different characteristics or features of God that is apart of making up the embodiment of God are all completely different parts or aspects of God as I think the embodiment of

God is how God is able to be a living being with all of the completely different characteristics or features of God that is apart of making up the embodiment of God. If I think the embodiment of God is a dimension that is overlapping, and co-existing along with any dimension that is apart of making up the embodiment of God, than I think God's being is a dimension that is overlapping, and co-existing along with the embodiment of God because I think the embodiment of God is somehow able to be taking place within God's being, without being God's being as I think the embodiment of God is apart of God's being, without being God's being. I think the embodiment of God is somehow able to be taking place within God's being, without being God's being as I think the embodiment of God is apart of God's being, without being God's being because I think God's being is God as I think God is someone that is something of itself, that is somehow able to be whatever God is in life, and therefore, I think God's being is the very existence of what God is in life because I think God's being is someone that is something of itself, that is somehow able to be whatever God is in life.

If I think God's being is the very existence of what God is in life, than I think God's being is how God is able to be doing what God is able to be doing because I think how God is able to be doing what God is able to be doing with God's being is how God is able to be doing what God is able to be doing. I think how God is able to be doing what God is able to be doing with God's being is how God is able to be doing what God is able to be doing because I think God is able to be doing what God is able to be doing with God's being for God to be able to be doing what God is able to be doing, and therefore, I think God's being is someone that is something of itself, that is somehow able to be doing what God's being is able to be doing because I think how God is able to be doing what God is able to be doing with God's being is how God's being is able to be someone, and something. I think how God is able to be doing what God is able to be doing with God's being is how God's being is able to be someone, and something because I do not think God's being can possibly be able to be doing what God's being is able to be doing, without God being someone that is something of itself, that is somehow able to be doing what God's being is able to be doing, and therefore, I think God's being is someone that is something of itself as I think God's being is how God is able to be doing what God is able to be doing because I think God's being is someone that is something of itself, that is somehow able to be doing what God's being is able to be doing. If I think God's being is someone that is something of itself, that is somehow able to be doing what God's being is able to be doing, than I think God is someone that is something of itself, that is somehow able to be doing what God is able to be doing because I think God's being is someone that is something of itself, that is somehow able to be doing what God's being is able to be doing for God to be someone that is something of itself, that is somehow able to be doing what God is able to be doing, and therefore, I think God is someone that is something of itself, that is somehow able to be responsible for everything because I think God's being is someone that is something of itself, that is somehow able to be responsible for everything for God to be someone that is something of itself, that is somehow able to be responsible for everything. If I think God is someone that is something of itself, that is somehow able to be responsible for everything, than I think God's being is someone that is something of itself, that is somehow able to be responsible for everything because I think how God's being is someone that is something of itself, that is somehow able to be doing what God's being is able to be doing is how God's being is someone that is something of itself, that is somehow able to be responsible for everything, and therefore, I think God is someone that is something of itself, that is somehow able to be responsible for everything because I think how God's being is someone that is something of itself, that is somehow able to be doing what God's being is able to be doing is how God is someone that is something of itself, that is somehow able to be responsible for everything. If I think God is someone that is something of itself, that is somehow able to be responsible for everything, than I think God's being is the being of the embodiment of God because I think God's being is someone that is something of itself, that is somehow able to be whatever God is in life for God's being to be the being of the embodiment of God, and therefore, I think the embodiment of God is apart of how God is able to be a living being because I think the embodiment of God is apart of God's being as I think God's being is someone that is something of itself, that is somehow able to be whatever God is in life.

If I think the embodiment of God is apart of how God is able to be a living being, than I think God's being is a dimension, that is somehow able to be creating the embodiment of God with any dimension that is apart of making up the embodiment of God as I think the embodiment of God is apart of how God is able to be a living being because I think any dimension that is apart of making up the embodiment of God is somehow able to be taking place within God's being, without being God's being as I think any dimension that is apart of making up the embodiment of God is somehow able to be apart of God's being, without being God's being. I think any dimension that is apart of making up the embodiment of God is somehow able to be taking place within God's being, without being God's being as I think any dimension that is apart of making up the embodiment of God is somehow able to be apart of God's being, without being God's being because I think the embodiment of God is somehow created by God's being for the embodiment of God to be apart of God's being, even though, I do not think God's being is created from the embodiment of God because I think the embodiment of God is apart of God's being, without being God's being, and therefore, I think the embodiment of God is constantly able to be something because I think God's being is someone that is something of itself, that is somehow able to be creating the embodiment of God to constantly be able to be something. If I think the embodiment of God is constantly able to be something, than I think the embodiment of God is infinite because I think the embodiment of God is in infinity. I think the embodiment of God is in infinity because I think the embodiment of God is constantly able to be something, and therefore, I think the embodiment of God is infinity because I think the embodiment of God is in infinity, even though, I think the embodiment of God is infinity as I think the embodiment of God is infinitely incalculable because I do not think someone can possibly be able to be knowing for themselves, as to what the embodiment of God is in life as I think the embodiment of God is apart of God's being, however, I think God is constantly able to be someone that is something of itself as I think God's being is constantly able to be someone that is something of itself because I think God's being is somehow able to be creating the embodiment of God to constantly be able to be something. If I think God is constantly able to be someone that is something of itself as I think God's being is constantly able to be someone that is something of itself, than I think God is in infinity as I think God's being is in infinity because I think God is constantly able to be someone that is something of itself as I think God's being is constantly able to be someone that is something of itself, and therefore, I think God is infinite as I think the God's being is infinite because I think God is infinity as I think God's being is infinity. I think God is infinity as I think God's being is infinity because I think God is in infinity as I think God's being is in infinity, and therefore, I think the embodiment of God is infinite as I think the embodiment of God is apart of God because I think the embodiment is created by God being infinite for the embodiment of God to be infinite. If I think the embodiment of God is infinite as I think the embodiment of God is apart of God, than I think God is immortal as I think God is infinite because I think God is infinite for God to be immortal. I think God is infinite for God to be immortal because I think God is infinitely immortal. I think God is infinitely immortal because I think God is infinite for God to be infinitely immortal.

If I think God is infinitely immortal, than I think God's state of consciousness, and God's will, and God's mind, and God's thoughts is somehow able to be taking place within God's being, without being God's being is in life as I think God's state of consciousness, and God's will, and God's mind, and God's thoughts is apart of God's being, without being God's being because I think God's state of consciousness, and God's will, and God's thoughts, and God's mind is somehow created by God's being for God's state of consciousness, and God's will, and God's thoughts, and God's mind to be apart of God's being. I think God's state of consciousness, and God's will, and God's thoughts, and God's mind is somehow created by God's being for God's state of consciousness, and God's will, and God's thoughts, and God's mind to be apart of God's being because I think God's state of consciousness, and God's will, and God's thoughts, and God's mind is any dimension that is apart of making up the embodiment of God, that is somehow able to be taking place within God's being, without being God's being as I think any dimension that is apart of making up the embodiment of God is somehow able to be apart of God's being, without being God's being. I think God's state of consciousness, and God's will, and God's thoughts, and God's mind is any dimension that is apart of making up the embodiment of God, that is somehow able to be taking place within God's being, without being God's being as I think any dimension that is apart of making up the embodiment of God is somehow able to be apart of God's being, without being God's being because I think God's being is the being of the embodiment of God as I think the embodiment of God is apart of how God is able to be a living being, even though, I do not think someone can possibly be able to be knowing for themselves, as to how God's being is able to be someone that is something of itself, that is somehow able to be whatever God's being as I think how God's being is able to be someone that is something of itself, that is somehow able to be whatever God's being is how God's being is able to be the being of the embodiment of God, and I do not think someone can possibly be able to be knowing for themselves, as to how God's being is able to be a dimension of itself, that is somehow able to be creating the embodiment of God with any dimension that is apart of making up the embodiment of God, but I think God's being is somehow able to be someone that is something of itself, that is somehow able to be whatever God's being, and I think God's being is a dimension, that is somehow able to be creating the embodiment of God with any dimension that is apart of making up the embodiment of God because I think God's being is the being of the embodiment of God as I think the embodiment of God is apart of how God is able to be a living being, and therefore, I think God's being is how God able to be a living being as I think the embodiment of God is apart of how God is able to be a living being because I think God's being is how God is able to be what God is in life as I think the embodiment of God is apart of how God is able to be what God is in life. If I think God's being is how God able to be a living being as I think the embodiment of God is apart of how God is able to be a living being, than I think someone can think of God's being, and the embodiment of God as being God because I think God is God's being, and the embodiment of God as I think God is how God is able to be what God is in life, and therefore, I think God's being, and the embodiment of God supports God as being a living being as I think God is a higher intelligent living being, that is someone that is something of itself, that is somehow able to be responsible for everything because I think God is God's being, and the embodiment of God as I think the embodiment of God is apart of how God is able to be a living being.

If I think God's being, and the embodiment of God supports God as being a living being, than I think God's being is how God is doing what God is doing with God's will, and I think God's being is how God is able to be doing what God is doing with God's state of consciousness because I think how God is able to be doing what God is able to be doing with God's being is how God is doing what God is doing with

God's will, and I think how God is able to be doing what God is able to be doing with God's being is how God is able to be doing what God is doing with God's state of consciousness, and therefore, I think God's being is how God is able to be making any choices with God's will because I think how God is able to be doing what God is able to be doing with God's being is how God is able to be making any choices with God's will. I think how God is able to be doing what God is able to be doing with God's being is how God is able to be making any choices with God's will because I think what God is doing is what God's being is doing. I think what God is doing is what God's being is doing because I think God is doing what God's being is doing. I think God is doing what God's being is doing because I think God's being is how God is able to be doing what God is able to be doing as I think God's state of consciousness, and God's will, and God's thoughts, and God's mind is apart of God's being. I think God's being is how God is able to be doing what God is able to be doing as I think God's state of consciousness, and God's will, and God's thoughts, and God's mind is apart of God's being because I think God is doing what God is doing with God's state of consciousness, along with God's will, and God's thoughts, and God's mind that is apart of God's being. I think God is doing what God is doing with God's state of consciousness, along with God's will, and God's thoughts, and God's mind that is apart of God's being because I think God is doing what God's being is doing as I think God's state of consciousness, and God's will, and God's thoughts, and God's mind is apart of God's being. I think God is doing what God's being is doing as I think God's state of consciousness, and God's will, and God's thoughts, and God's mind is apart of God's being because I think God's being is ultimately what makes God able to be making any choices as I think God's state of consciousness, and God's will, and God's thoughts, and God's mind is apart of God's being. I think God's being is ultimately what makes God able to be making any choices as I think God's state of consciousness, and God's will, and God's thoughts, and God's mind is apart of God's being because I think the embodiment of God consists of God having a state of consciousness, and God having a will, and God having thoughts, and God having a mind that is apart of God's being for God's being to ultimately be able to be making any choices, and therefore, I think God's state of consciousness, and God's will, and God's thoughts, and God's mind, and God's being is apart of making up the embodiment of God because I think the embodiment of God is of the dimension of God as I think God is the dimension of God for the embodiment of God to be God.

Chapter 12

The embodiment of someone

I would like to talk about how dimensions are in life in relation to what dimensions are in life by talking about the embodiment of someone, that can possibly have something to do with how dimensions are in life is in relation to what dimensions are in life because I think the embodiment of someone is of the dimension of someone as I think someone is the dimension of someone for the embodiment of someone to be someone, and therefore, I think someone is a choice because I think someone has a choice. I think someone has a choice because I think someone is a choice for someone to have a choice. I think someone is a choice for someone to have a choice because I think someone is a choice of themselves for someone to have a choice. I think someone is a choice of themselves for someone to have a choice because I think someone is a choice of themselves of what someone is doing, and therefore, I think an example of how I think someone is a choice of themselves of what someone is doing can be someone dropping a glass cup because I think someone can drop a glass cup for someone to be a choice of themselves of what someone is doing. I think someone can drop a glass cup for someone to be a choice of themselves of what someone is doing because I do not think someone can drop a glass cup if someone is not a choice of themselves of what someone is doing, but I think someone can drop a glass cup because I think someone is a choice of themselves of what someone is doing for someone to be dropping a glass cup, and therefore, I think someone is a choice of themselves of what someone is doing because I think someone is a choice of themselves for someone to have a choice. I think someone is a choice of themselves for someone to have a choice because I think someone has a choice, and therefore, I think someone is in motion because I think someone is a choice for someone to be in motion as I think someone is a choice of themselves of what someone is doing for someone to be in motion.

If I think someone is in motion, than I think someone has a choice because I think someone has a will as I think someone has a choice. I think someone has a will as I think someone has a choice because I think someone has a will for someone to have a choice. I think someone has a will for someone to have a choice because I do not think someone would have a choice, if someone doesn't have a will. I do not think someone would have a choice, if someone doesn't have a will because I do not think someone would have a choice of what someone is doing, if someone doesn't have a will for someone to have a choice of what someone is doing, but I think someone has a will for someone to have a choice of what someone is doing because I think someone has a choice of what someone is doing, and therefore, I think someone has a will as I think someone has a choice because I think someone has a will for someone to have a choice of what someone is doing. If I think someone has a will for someone to have a choice of what someone is doing, than I think someone has a will as I think someone has a choice because I think someone is a choice of themselves of what someone is doing for someone to have a will as I think someone is a choice of themselves of what someone is doing for someone to have a choice. I think someone is a choice of themselves of what someone is doing for someone to have a will as I think someone is a choice of themselves of what someone is doing for someone to have a choice because I think someone has a will for someone to have a choice. I think someone has a will for someone to have a choice because I do not think someone would have a choice, if someone doesn't have a will. I do not think someone would have a choice, if someone doesn't have a will because I do not think someone would be a choice of themselves of what someone is doing, if someone doesn't have a will for someone to be a choice of themselves of what someone is doing, but I think someone has a will for someone to be a choice of themselves of what someone is doing because I think someone is a choice of themselves of what someone is doing, and therefore, I think someone has a will as I think someone has a choice because I think someone has a will for someone to be a choice of themselves of what someone is doing. I think someone has a will for someone to be a choice of themselves of what someone is doing because I think someone's will is someone's choice. I think someone's will is someone's choice because I think someone has a will as I think someone has a choice. I think someone has a will as I think someone has a choice because I think someone is a choice of themselves for someone to have a will as I think someone is a choice of themselves for someone to have a choice. I think someone is a choice of themselves for someone to have a will as I think someone is a choice of themselves for someone to have a choice because I think someone is a choice as I think someone has a choice. I think someone is a choice as I think someone has a choice because I think someone is a choice as I think someone has a will. I think someone is a choice as I think someone has a will because I think someone has a will as I think someone has a choice, and therefore, I think someone has a will because if I think someone can drop glass cup, than I do not think someone can drop a glass cup just because a glass cup will drop from someone dropping a glass cup, but I think someone can drop a glass cup because I think someone has a will for someone to be dropping a glass cup. I think someone has a will for someone to be dropping a glass cup because I think someone will drop a glass cup for someone to be dropping a glass cup as I think someone will drop a glass cup for someone to have a will, and therefore, I think someone's will is what someone does as I think what someone does is someone's will because I think someone has a will for what someone does. If I think someone has a will for what someone does, than I think someone can think of all kinds of different words for someone to be describing what someone thinks someone's will is in life because I think someone has will for someone to be thinking of all kinds of different words for someone to be describing what someone thinks someone's will is in life, and therefore, I think someone has a will because I think someone's will is what someone is doing as I think someone's will is what someone does. If I think someone has a will, than I think someone can think of all kinds of words for someone to be describing what someone thinks what someone can do in life because I think someone has will for someone to be thinking of all kinds of different words for someone to be describing what someone thinks what someone can do in life, and therefore, I think everything someone does is someone's will as I think everything someone does is someone's choice because I think someone's will is someone's choice for someone to be doing everything someone does. If I think everything someone does is someone's will as I think everything someone does is someone's choice, than I think someone will do something because I think someone has will for someone to be doing something, and therefore, I think someone can do something with themselves, someone else, something, and God because I think someone has a will for someone to be doing something with themselves, someone else, something, and God. If I think someone can do something with themselves, someone else, something, and God, than I think what someone does is what someone thinks because I do not think someone can do what someone thinks, without someone doing what someone is doing with someone's will for someone to be doing what someone thinks, and therefore, I think someone is in motion because I think someone has a will for someone to be in motion.

If I think someone is in motion, than I think someone's will is like God's will because I think someone's will is how someone is doing what someone is doing as I think God's will is how God is doing what God is doing. I think someone's will is how someone is doing what someone is doing as I think God's will is how God is doing what God is doing because I think someone's will is what someone is doing as I think God's will is what God is doing, and therefore, I think someone's will is like God's will because I think someone is created by God for someone to have a will. I think someone is created by God for someone to have a will because I think God created someone to have a will for someone to be doing what someone is doing. I think God created someone to have a will for someone to be doing what someone is doing because I think someone's will is someone's choice. I think someone's will is someone's choice because I think someone's choice is God's choice for someone to have a choice. I think someone's choice is God's choice for someone to have a choice because I think someone is created by God for someone to have a choice. I think someone is created by God for someone to have a choice because I think someone's choice is someone's will. I think someone's choice is someone's will because I think someone's choice is what someone is doing as I think someone's will is what someone is doing. I think someone's choice is what someone is doing as I think someone's will is what someone is doing because I think what someone is doing is someone's choice as I think what someone is doing is someone's will. I think what someone is doing is someone's choice as I think what someone is doing is someone's will because I think someone's choice is someone's will as I think someone's will is someone's choice. I think someone's choice is someone's will as I think someone's will is someone's choice because I think someone has a will as I think someone has a choice, and therefore, I think someone's will is God's choice for someone to have a will because I think someone has a will for someone to be doing what someone is doing. If I think someone's will is God's choice for someone to have a will, than I think someone has someone's free will because I think someone has a will for someone to be having someone's free will. I think someone has a will for someone to be having someone's free will because I think someone has someone's free will with someone having a choice of what someone is doing. I think someone has someone's free will with someone having a choice of what someone is doing because I think someone has a choice. I think someone has a choice because I think someone has a will for someone to be having a choice, and therefore, I think someone has a will because I think someone's will is how someone is doing what someone is doing. I think someone's will is how someone is doing what someone is doing because I think what someone is doing is how someone is doing what someone is doing. I think what someone is doing is how someone is doing what someone is doing because I think someone has a will. I think someone has a will because I think someone's will is what someone is doing, and therefore, I think someone has a will as I think God has a will because I think someone's will is what someone is doing as I think God's will is what God is doing. If I think someone has a will as I think God has a will, than I think someone's will is what someone is doing because I think what someone is doing is how someone is doing what someone is doing. I think what someone is doing is how someone is doing what something is doing because I think someone's will is a dimension. I think someone's will is a dimension because I think someone's will is something for someone's will to be a dimension. I think someone's will is something for someone's will to be a dimension because I think someone's will is what someone is doing. I think someone's will is what someone is doing because I think someone has a will as I think someone's will is a dimension, and therefore, I think someone can think of someone's will as being the dimension of someone's will because I think someone's will is what someone is doing. If I think someone can think of someone's will as being the dimension of someone's will, than I think someone, something, and God is a choice for someone to be choosing to be doing something with themselves, someone else, something, and God because I think someone has a will for someone to be choosing to be doing something with themselves, someone else, something, and God, and therefore, I think someone has a will because I think someone can choose to be doing something with themselves, someone else, something, and God for someone to be having a will.

If I think someone has a will, than I think someone has a state of consciousness as I think someone has a will because I think someone has a state of consciousness for someone's will. I think someone has a state of consciousness for someone's will because I think someone has a choice of themselves, someone else, something, and God for someone to be having a state of consciousness for someone's will. I think someone has a choice of themselves, someone else, something, and God for someone to be having a state of consciousness for someone's will because I think someone can choose to be doing something with themselves, someone else, something, and God for someone to be having a state of consciousness for someone's will. I think someone can choose to be doing something with themselves, someone else, something, and God for someone to be having a state of consciousness for someone's will because I think someone is consciously aware of someone choosing to be doing something with themselves, someone else, something, and God for someone to be having a state of consciousness for someone's will. I think someone is consciously aware of someone choosing to be doing something with themselves, someone else, something, and God for someone to be having a state of consciousness for someone's will because I think someone has a state of consciousness with someone's will for someone to be consciously aware of someone choosing to be doing something with themselves, someone else, something, and God. I think someone has a state of consciousness with someone's will for someone to be consciously aware of someone choosing to be doing something with themselves, someone else, something, and God because I think someone has a state of consciousness for someone's will. I think someone has a state of consciousness for someone's will because I think someone can be consciously aware of what someone is doing for someone to be having a state of consciousness with someone's will. I think someone can be consciously aware of what someone is doing for someone to be having a state of consciousness with someone's will because I think someone will do what someone is doing from someone being aware of what someone is doing, and therefore, I think someone has a state of consciousness with someone's will because I think someone has a state of consciousness as I think someone has a will. I think someone has a state of consciousness as I think someone has a will because I think someone has a state of consciousness for what someone is doing with someone's will, and therefore, I think someone has a state of consciousness because I think someone has a state of consciousness for what someone is doing with someone's will.

If I think someone has a state of consciousness, than I think someone's state of consciousness is like God's state of consciousness because I think someone's state of consciousness is how someone is able to be doing what someone is doing as I think God's state of consciousness is how God is able to be doing what God is doing. I think someone's state of consciousness is how someone is able to be doing what someone is doing as I think God's state of consciousness is how God is able to be doing what God is doing because I think someone's state of consciousness is what someone is able to be doing as I think God's state of consciousness is what God is able to be doing, and therefore, I think someone's state of consciousness is like God's state of consciousness because I think someone is created by God for someone to have a state of consciousness. I think someone is created by God for someone to have a state of consciousness because I think God created someone to have a state of consciousness for someone to be able to be doing what someone is doing. I think God created someone to have a state of consciousness for someone to be able to be doing what someone is doing because I think someone's state of consciousness is God's choice for someone to have a state of consciousness. I think someone's state of consciousness is God's choice for someone to have a state of consciousness because I think someone has a state of consciousness for someone to be able to be doing what someone is doing. If I think someone's state of consciousness is God's choice for someone to have a state of consciousness, than I think someone has a state of consciousness because I think someone's state of consciousness is how someone is able to be doing what someone is doing. I think someone's state of consciousness is how someone is able to be doing what someone is doing because I think what someone is able to be doing is how someone is able to be doing what someone is doing. I think what someone is able to be doing is how someone is able to be doing what someone is doing because I think someone has a state of consciousness for someone to be able to be doing what someone is doing, and therefore, I think someone has a state of consciousness as I think God has a state of consciousness because I think someone's state of consciousness is how someone is able to be doing what someone is doing as I think God's state of consciousness is how God is able to be doing what God is doing in life. If I think someone has a state of consciousness as I think God has a state of consciousness, than I think someone's state of consciousness is what someone is able to be doing because I think what someone is able to be doing is how someone is able to be doing what someone is doing. I think what someone is able to be doing is how someone is able to be doing what someone is doing because I think someone's state of consciousness is a dimension. I think someone's state of consciousness is a dimension because I think someone's state of consciousness is something for someone's state of consciousness to be a dimension. I think someone's state of consciousness is something for someone's state of consciousness to be a dimension because I think someone's state of consciousness is how someone is able to be doing what someone is doing. I think someone's state of consciousness is how someone is able to be doing what someone is doing because I think someone has a state of consciousness as I think someone's state of consciousness is a dimension, and therefore, I think someone can think of someone's state of consciousness as being the dimension of someone's state of consciousness because I think someone's state of consciousness is how someone is able to be doing what someone is doing.

If I think someone can think of someone's state of consciousness as being the dimension of someone's state of consciousness, than I think someone's state of consciousness is someone's awareness because I think how someone is able to be doing what someone is doing with someone's state of consciousness is how someone is able to be aware of what someone is doing. I think how someone is able to be doing what someone is doing with someone's state of consciousness is how someone is able to be aware of what someone is doing because I think someone is consciously aware of what someone is doing as I think someone is consciously aware of what someone is doing with someone's state of consciousness, and therefore, I think someone's state of consciousness is someone's state of awareness because I think someone's state of consciousness is how someone is able to be doing what someone is doing as I think someone's state of awareness is how someone is able to be doing what someone is doing. If I think someone's state of consciousness is someone's state of awareness, than I think someone's state of consciousness is someone's sense of awareness as I think someone's state of awareness is someone's sense of awareness because I think someone's state of consciousness is someone's state of awareness as I think someone's sense of awareness is how someone is able to be doing what someone is doing, and therefore, I think someone is constantly aware of what someone is doing as I think someone is consciously aware of what someone is doing because I think someone is consciously aware of what someone is doing as I think someone is consciously aware of what someone is doing with someone's state of consciousness. If I think someone is constantly aware of what someone is doing as I think someone is consciously aware of what someone is doing, than I think someone has a state of consciousness for someone to be intelligent because I do not think someone can be able to be thinking of anything, and I do not think someone can be able to be doing anything, without someone having a state of consciousness for someone to be aware of what someone is thinking, and doing as I think someone is aware of what someone is thinking, and doing with someone having a state of consciousness for someone to be intelligent, and therefore, I do not think someone's brain is how someone is able to be intelligent as I think someone's state of consciousness is how someone is able to be intelligent because I think someone can be aware of what someone is doing with someone having a state of consciousness for someone having a state of consciousness to be how someone is able to be intelligent. If I do not think someone's brain is how someone is able to be intelligent, than I do not think someone is stupid or dumb because I think someone has a state of consciousness for someone to be intelligent, and therefore, I do not think someone is any more or any less intelligent than someone else because I think someone has a state of consciousness for someone to be aware someone is intelligent.

If I do not think someone is any more or any less intelligent than someone else, than I think someone has a state of consciousness for someone's will because I think someone has a state of consciousness for what someone is doing with someone's will. I think someone has a state of consciousness for what someone is doing with someone's will because I think someone has a state of consciousness for someone to be aware of what someone is doing with someone's will. I think someone has a state of consciousness for someone to be aware of what someone is doing with someone's will because I think someone has a state of consciousness for someone to be aware of what someone is doing. I think someone has a state of consciousness for someone to be aware of what someone is doing because I think someone has a state of consciousness for what someone is doing. I think someone has a state of consciousness for what someone is doing because I think someone has a state of consciousness for someone's will as I think someone's will is what someone is doing, and therefore, I think someone's will is overlapping, and co-existing along with someone's state of consciousness because I think someone has state of consciousness for someone to be aware of what someone is doing with someone's will.

If I think the dimension of someone's will is overlapping, and co-existing along with the dimension of someone's state of consciousness, than I think someone is someone's being because I think someone's being is someone. I think someone's being is someone because I think someone's being is how someone is able to be what someone is in life. I think someone's being is how someone is able to be what someone is in life because I think someone's being is the very existence of what someone is in life. I think someone's being is the very existence of what someone is in life because I think the being of what someone is in life is the very existence of what someone is in life. I think very being of what someone is in life is the very existence of what someone is in life because I think someone's being is how someone is able to be what someone is in life as I think someone's being is the very existence of what someone is in life. I think someone's being is how someone is able to be what something is in life as I think someone's being is the very existence of what someone is in life because I think someone's being is what someone is in life, and therefore, I think someone is a being as I think God is a being because I think someone is of God's being for someone to be a being. I think someone is of God's being for someone to be a being because I think someone's being is the very existence of what someone is in life as I think God's being is the very existence of what God is in life. I think someone's being is the very existence of what someone is in life as I think God's being is the very existence of what God is in life because I think someone is of the very existence of what God is in life for someone to be of the very existence of what someone is in life, and therefore, I think someone's being is a dimension because I think someone's being is something for someone's being to be a dimension. I think someone's being is something for someone's being to be a dimension because

I think someone's being is how someone is able to be what someone is in life. I think someone's being is how someone is able to be what someone is in life because I think someone's being is someone as I think someone's being is what someone is in life, and therefore, I think someone can think of someone's being as being the dimension of someone's being because I think someone's being is what someone is in life. I think someone's being is what someone is in life because I think someone is someone's being. I think someone is someone's being because I think God created someone's being for someone to be what someone is in life, and therefore, I think someone can think of the dimension of someone's being as being the dimension of someone because I think someone is someone's being as I think someone is what someone's being is in life. If I think someone can think of the dimension of someone's being as being the dimension of someone, than I think someone's being is whatever someone's being is in life because I think someone's being is what someone's being is in life as I think what someone's being is in life is whatever someone's being is in life.

If I think someone's being is whatever someone's being is in life, than I think someone can think of someone as being a spirit or a soul as I think someone can think of someone's being as being a spirit or a soul because I think someone is someone's being as I think someone can think of someone as being a spirit or a soul. I think someone is someone's being as I think someone can think of someone as being a spirit or a soul because I think someone may have experienced someone being in the form of a ghost for someone to be thinking of someone as being a spirit or soul, even though, I have never experienced someone being in the form of a ghost for me to be thinking of someone as being a spirit or soul, and therefore, I do not think I can think of someone as being a spirit or a soul because I do not know what someone is in life for me to be thinking of someone as being a spirit or a soul, however, I think someone is something as I think someone is someone that is something of themselves because I think someone is of God's thoughts that is something for someone to be someone that is something of themselves, but I do not know what someone is in life because I think someone is of God's thoughts for someone to be someone that is something of themselves, however, I think someone can think of someone as being someone's being because I think someone is someone's being as I think someone's being is whatever someone's being is in life. If I think someone can think of someone as being someone's being, than I do not think someone is someone as much as someone thinks someone is someone because I think someone is something as I think someone is someone. I think someone is something as I think someone is someone because I think if the word someone gets broken down into two separate words some and one, than I think the word some in the word someone is something because I think the word some is something that is opposite to any other words, such as a lot that is something, and I think the word one in the word someone is something because I think the word one is a number that is something. If I think the word some in the word someone is something, than I think someone is something because I think the words some and one in the word someone is something, even though, I think someone can think of the word someone as being someone because I think someone is someone for someone to be thinking of the word someone as being someone, and therefore, I think someone is something as I think someone is someone because I think the words some and one in the word someone is something for someone to be something as I think someone is someone for someone to be thinking of the word someone as being someone. If I think someone is something as I think someone is someone, than I think someone is someone because I think someone is an intelligent living being for someone to be someone, and therefore, I think someone is someone that is something of themselves because I think someone is someone, and something for someone to be someone that is something of themselves. If I think someone is someone that is something of themselves, than I think someone is constantly taking place in life as being something of themselves as I think someone is constantly taking place in life as being someone of themselves because I think someone is constantly taking place in life as being someone that is something of themselves for someone to constantly be taking place in life as being something of themselves as I think someone is constantly taking place in life as being someone that is something of themselves for someone to constantly be taking place in life as being someone of themselves, and therefore, I think someone is someone as I think someone is something because I think someone is something of themselves for someone to be someone as I think someone is something of themselves for someone to be something. If I think someone is someone as I think someone is something, than I think someone is something of themselves that is constantly able to be taking place in life as being someone that is something of themselves as I think something is something of itself that is constantly able to be taking place in life as being something that is something of itself because I think someone is somehow created by God for someone to constantly be taking place in life as being someone that is something of themselves as I think something is somehow created by God for something to constantly be taking place in life as being something that is something of itself, and therefore, I think someone is interesting, as to how deep and complex someone is in life with how someone is in life because I think someone is something for someone to be someone that is something of themselves. If I think someone is interesting, as to how deep and complex someone is in life with how someone is in life, than I think something is interesting, as to how deep and complex something is in life with how something is in life because I think something is something as I think someone is something.

If I think something is interesting, as to how deep and complex something is in life with how something is in life, than I think someone is something because I think someone is someone that is something of themselves as I think someone is of someone that is something of itself. I think someone is someone that is something of themselves as I think someone is of someone that is something of itself because I think someone is of someone that is something of itself for someone to be someone that is something of themselves. I think someone is of someone that is something of itself for someone to be someone that is something of themselves because I think someone is of God being someone that is something of itself for someone to be someone that is something of themselves. I think someone is of God being someone that is something of itself for someone to be someone that is something of themselves because I think someone is of God as I think God is someone that is something of itself. I think someone is of God as I think God is someone that is something of itself because I think God is God's being as I think someone is of God's being for someone to be someone that is something of themselves. I think God is God's being as I think someone is of God's being for someone to be someone that is something of themselves because I think someone is of God's being as I think God's being is someone that is something of itself. I think someone is of God's being as I think God's being is someone that is something of itself because I think someone is of God's being for someone to be someone's being. I think someone is of God's being for someone to be someone's being because I think someone is someone's being as I think someone's being is someone that is something of themselves. I think someone is someone's being as I think someone's being is someone that is something of themselves because I think someone's being is someone that is something of themselves as I think someone is someone that is something of themselves, and therefore, I think someone is a being because I think someone is created by God being a being for someone to be a being. I think someone is created by God being a being for someone to be a being because I think someone is created by God being an intelligent living being for someone to be an intelligent living being. I think someone is created by God being an intelligent living being for someone to be an intelligent living being because I think someone is an intelligent living being for someone to be a being.

If I think someone is created by God being an intelligent living being for someone to be an intelligent living being, than I think someone's state of consciousness is apart of someone's being, but I do not think someone's state of consciousness is someone's being because I think someone's state of consciousness is how someone is able to be doing what someone is doing, and I think someone's being is what someone is in life. I think someone's state of consciousness is how someone is able to be doing what someone is doing, and I think someone's being is what someone is in life because I think someone's state of consciousness is how someone is able to be aware of what someone is doing. I think someone's state of consciousness is how someone is able to be aware of what someone is doing because I do not think someone would be aware of anything, without someone having a state of consciousness. I do not think someone would be aware of anything, without someone having a state of consciousness because I think someone not having a state of consciousness is like someone not being able to see what someone is doing, while someone is trying to drive a car, and therefore, I think someone's state of consciousness is how someone is able to be a living being because I think someone's state of consciousness is how someone is able to be aware of what someone is doing. If I think someone's state of consciousness is how someone is able to be a living being, than I think someone has a state of consciousness for someone's being because I do think someone can be consciously aware of what someone is doing, without someone having a state of consciousness for someone's being, even though, I think someone has a state of consciousness for someone's being because I think someone has a state of consciousness for what someone is doing with someone's being. I think someone has a state of consciousness for what someone is doing with someone's being because I think someone has a state of consciousness for someone to be aware of what someone is doing. I think someone has a state of consciousness for someone to be aware of what someone is doing because I think someone's state of consciousness is how someone is able to be aware of what someone is doing. I think someone's state of consciousness is how someone is able to be aware of what someone is doing because I think someone has a state of consciousness for someone to be aware of what someone is doing, and therefore, I think someone's state of consciousness is overlapping, and co-existing along with someone's being because I think someone's state of consciousness is how someone is able to be aware of what someone is doing. If I think someone's state of consciousness is overlapping, and co-existing along with someone's being, than I think someone's state of consciousness is someone's eyes or window to everything because I think someone can aware of everything with someone's state of consciousness for someone's state of consciousness to be someone's eyes or window to everything, and therefore, I think someone's state of consciousness is someone's eyes or window to God because I think someone can aware of everything that God has created with someone's state of consciousness for someone's state of consciousness to be someone's eyes or window to God.

If I think someone's state of consciousness is someone's eyes or window to God, than I think someone's will comes from someone's being, but I do not think someone's will is someone's being because I think someone's will is what someone is doing, and I think someone's being is what someone is in life. I think someone's will is what someone is doing, and I think someone's being is what someone is in life because I think someone's will is someone having a choice of what someone is doing. I think someone's will is someone having a choice of what someone is doing because I do not think someone would be able to be doing anything, without someone having a will. I do not think someone would be able to be doing anything, without someone having a will because I think someone not having a will is like someone not being able to move, while someone is trying to drive a car, and therefore, I think someone's will is how someone is able to be a living being because I think someone's will is someone having a choice of what someone is doing. If I think someone's will is how someone is able to be a living being, than I think someone has a will for someone's being because I do not think someone would be able to be doing anything, without someone having a will, and even though, I think someone has a will for someone's being because I think someone has a will for what someone is doing with someone's being. I think someone has a will for what someone is doing with someone's being because I think someone has a will for someone to be having a choice of what someone is doing. I think someone has a will for someone to be having a choice of what someone is doing because I think someone's will is someone having a choice of what someone is doing. I think someone's will is someone having a choice of what someone is doing because I think someone has a will for someone to be having a choice of what someone is doing, and therefore, I think someone's will is overlapping, and co-existing along with someone's being because I think someone's will is someone having a choice of what someone is doing.

If I think someone's will is overlapping, and co-existing along with someone's being, than I think someone has thoughts because I think someone is of the thoughts of someone for someone to have thoughts. I think someone is of the thoughts of someone for someone to have thoughts because I think someone is the thoughts of someone. I think someone is the thoughts of someone because I think someone is someone's thoughts of themselves as I think someone's thoughts of themselves is the thoughts of someone. I think someone is someone's thoughts of themselves as I think someone's thoughts of themselves is the thoughts of someone because I think someone is the thoughts of someone as I think the thoughts of someone is someone's thoughts of themselves. I think someone is the thoughts of someone as I think the thoughts of someone is someone's thoughts of themselves because I think someone is the thoughts of someone as I think someone is someone's thoughts of themselves. I think someone is the thoughts of someone as I think someone is someone's thoughts of themselves because I think someone is of the thoughts of someone for someone to be the thoughts of someone. I think someone is of the thoughts of someone for someone to be the thoughts of someone because I think the thoughts of someone is apart of making up someone for someone to be the thoughts of someone. I think the thoughts of someone is apart of making up someone for someone to be the thoughts of someone because I think someone is of the thoughts of someone for someone to be someone of themselves. I think someone is of the thoughts of someone for someone to be someone of themselves because I think the thoughts of someone is apart of making up someone for someone to be someone of themselves. I think the thoughts of someone is apart of making up someone for someone to be someone of themselves because I think someone is the thoughts of someone for someone to be someone of themselves.

I think someone is the thoughts of someone for someone to be someone of themselves because I think the thoughts of someone is of God's thoughts for someone to be someone of themselves. I think the thoughts of someone is of God's thoughts for someone to be someone of themselves because I think someone is of the thoughts of someone as I think God's thoughts is the thoughts of someone. I think someone is of the thoughts of someone as I think God's thoughts is the thoughts of someone because I think someone is of God's thoughts as I think the thoughts of someone is of God's thoughts. I think someone is of God's thoughts as I think the thoughts of someone is of God's thoughts because I think God's thoughts is the thoughts of someone as I think someone is of God's thoughts. I think God's thoughts is the thoughts of someone as I think someone is of God's thoughts because I think someone is God's thoughts. I think someone is God's thoughts because I think someone has thoughts. I think someone has thoughts because I think God's thoughts is apart of making up someone for someone to have thoughts, and therefore, I think someone has thoughts as I think God has thoughts because I think God's thoughts is apart of making up someone for someone to have thoughts as I think God's thoughts is apart of making up someone for God to have thoughts. I think God's thoughts is apart of making up someone for someone to have thoughts as I think God's thoughts is apart of making up someone for God to have thoughts because I think someone is God's thoughts. I think someone is God's thoughts because I think someone is of God's thoughts for someone to be God's thoughts. I think someone is of God's thoughts for someone to be God's thoughts because I think God's thoughts is apart of making up someone for someone to be God's thoughts. I think God's thoughts is apart of making up someone for someone to be God's thoughts because I think someone is of God's thoughts for someone to be someone of themselves. I think someone is of God's thoughts for someone to be someone of themselves because I think God's thoughts is apart of making up someone for someone to be someone of themselves. I think God's thoughts is apart of making up someone for someone to be someone of themselves because I think someone is God's thoughts for someone to be someone of themselves.

If I think God's thoughts is apart of making up someone for someone to be someone of themselves, than I think someone will do what someone does because I think someone will do what someone does with someone's will for someone to do what someone does. I think someone will do what someone does with someone's will for someone to do what someone does because I think someone will do what someone does with someone's thoughts of themselves for someone to do what someone does with someone's will as I think someone will do what someone does with the thoughts of someone for someone to do what someone does with someone's will. I think someone will do what someone does with someone's thoughts of themselves for someone to do what someone does with someone's will as I think someone will do what someone does with the thoughts of someone for someone to do what someone does with someone's will because I think someone's thoughts of themselves is the thoughts of someone as I think someone will do what someone does with someone's thoughts of themselves for someone to do what someone does with someone's will. I think someone's thoughts of themselves is the thoughts of someone as I think someone will do what someone does with someone's thoughts of themselves for someone to do what someone does with someone's will because I think someone's thoughts of themselves is the thoughts of someone for someone to do what someone does with someone's will. I think someone's thoughts of themselves is the thoughts of someone for someone to do what someone does with someone's will because I think someone is of the thoughts of themselves for someone to do what someone does with someone's will. I think someone is of the thoughts of themselves for someone to do what someone does with someone's will because I think someone's thoughts of themselves is of God's thoughts for someone to do what someone does with someone's will. I think someone's thoughts of themselves is of God's thoughts for someone to do what someone does with someone's will because I think someone will do what someone does with God's thoughts for someone to do what someone does with someone's will. I think someone will do what someone does with God's thoughts for someone to do what someone does with someone's will because I think someone is of God's thoughts for someone to do what someone does with someone's will.

If I think someone will do what someone does with God's thoughts for someone to do what someone does with someone's will, than I think someone is God's thoughts for someone to be someone of themselves because I think someone is the being of God's thoughts as I think someone's being is the being of God's thoughts. I think someone is the being of God's thoughts as I think someone's being is the being of God's thoughts because I think someone is someone's being as I think someone is of God's thoughts for someone to be the being of God's thoughts. I think someone is someone's being as I think someone is of God's thoughts for someone to be the being of God's thoughts because I think someone is of God's thoughts for someone to be whatever someone is in life. I think someone is of God's thoughts for someone to be whatever someone is in life because I think God's thoughts is whatever God's thoughts are in life that is apart of making up someone for someone to be whatever someone is in life. I think God's thoughts is whatever God's thoughts are in life that is apart of making up someone for someone to be whatever someone is in life because I think someone is God's thoughts for someone to be someone of themselves. I think someone is God's thoughts for someone to be someone of themselves because I think someone is of God's thoughts with how someone is able to be what someone is in life, and therefore, I think someone is of God's thoughts with what someone is in life as I think someone is of God's thoughts with how someone is able to be what someone is in life because I think what someone is in life is how someone is able to be what someone is in life. If I think what someone is in life is how someone is able to be what someone is in life, than I think someone is of God's thoughts with how someone is able to be what someone is in life because I think God's thoughts is apart of making up how someone is able to be what someone is in life. I think God's thoughts is apart of making up how someone is able to be what someone is in life because I think someone is God's thoughts with how someone is able to be what someone is in life, even though, I think someone's being is God's thoughts as I think someone is God's thoughts because I think someone is someone's being as I think someone is of God's thoughts with how someone is able to be what someone is in life, and therefore, I think someone's being is overlapping, and co-existing along with the dimension of God's thoughts because I think God's thoughts is apart of making up how someone is able to be what someone is in life as I think someone's being is how someone is able to be what someone is in life.

If I think someone's being is overlapping, and co-existing along with the dimension of God's thoughts, than I think someone's will is God's thoughts as I think someone is God's thoughts because I think someone's will is of God's thoughts with what someone is doing as I think someone is of God's thoughts with how someone is able to be what someone is in life. I think someone's will is of God's thoughts with what someone is doing as I think someone is of God's thoughts with how someone is able to be what someone is in life because I think God's thoughts is apart of making up someone's will for someone to be doing what someone is doing as I think God's thoughts is apart of making up someone for someone to be someone of themselves. I think God's thoughts is apart of making up someone's will for someone to be doing what someone is doing as I think God's thoughts is apart of making up someone for someone to be someone of themselves because I think someone's will is God's thoughts with what someone is doing as I think someone is God's thoughts with how someone is able to be what someone is in life, and therefore, I think someone's will is overlapping, and co-existing along with God's thoughts because I think God's thoughts is apart of making up someone's will for someone to be doing what someone is doing. If I think someone's will is overlapping, and co-existing along with God's thoughts, than I think someone's state of consciousness is God's thoughts as I think someone is God's thoughts because I think someone's state of consciousness is of God's thoughts with what someone is able to be doing as I think someone is of God's thoughts with how someone is able to be what someone is in life. I think someone's state of consciousness is of God's thoughts with what someone is able to be doing as I think someone is of God's thoughts with how someone is able to be what someone is in life because I think God's thoughts is apart of making up someone's state of consciousness for someone to be doing what someone is able to be doing as I think God's thoughts is apart of making up someone for someone to be someone of themselves. I think God's thoughts is apart of making up someone's state of consciousness for someone to be doing what someone is able to be doing as I think God's thoughts is apart of making up someone for someone to be someone of themselves because I think someone's state of consciousness is God's thoughts with what someone is able to be doing as I think someone is God's thoughts with how someone is able to be what someone is in life, and therefore, I think someone's state of consciousness is overlapping, and co-existing along with God's thoughts because I think God's thoughts is apart of making up someone's state of consciousness for someone to be doing what someone is able to be doing. If I think someone's state of consciousness is overlapping, and co-existing along with God's thoughts, than I think someone will do what someone does with someone's will because I think someone will do what someone does with someone's being for someone to do what someone does with someone's will. I think someone will do what someone does with someone's being for someone to do what someone does with someone's will because I think someone's being is what someone does with someone's will. I think someone's being is what someone does with someone's will because I think what someone is in life is what someone does as I think what someone is in life is what someone does with someone's will. I think what someone is in life is what someone does as I think what someone is in life is what someone does with someone's will because I think someone's being is of God's thoughts for someone to be doing what someone does with someone's will. I think someone's being is of God's thoughts for someone to be doing what someone does with someone's will because I think someone is of God's thoughts for someone to be what someone is in life as I think someone is of God's thoughts for someone to be doing what someone is doing with someone's will.

If I think someone's being is of God's thoughts for someone to be doing what someone does with someone's will, than I think someone has a mind because I think someone's mind is a storage area of someone. I think someone's mind is a storage area of someone because I think someone's mind is a storage area of someone's thoughts for someone's mind to be a storage area of someone. I think someone's mind is a storage area of someone's thoughts for someone's mind to be a storage area of someone because I think someone is a storage area of God's thoughts as I think someone's mind is a storage area of someone's thoughts. I think someone is a storage area of God's thoughts as I think someone's mind is a storage area of someone's thoughts because I think someone's mind is a storage area of God's thoughts for someone's mind to be a storage area of someone. I think someone's mind is a storage area of God's thoughts for someone's mind to be a storage area of someone because I think someone has a mind. I think someone has a mind because I think someone's mind is the entire area of God's thoughts that is apart of making up someone, and therefore, I think someone has a mind as I think God has a mind because I think someone's mind is the entire area of God's thoughts that is apart of making up someone as I think God's mind is the entire area of God's thoughts that is apart of making up everything. If I think someone has a mind as I think God has a mind, than I think someone's mind is like God's mind because I think someone's mind is a storage area of God's thoughts as I think God's mind is a storage area of God's thoughts, but I do not think someone's mind alike God's mind because I think someone's mind is the entire area of God's thoughts that is apart of making up someone as I think God's mind is the entire area of God's thoughts that is apart of making up everything, and therefore, I think someone's mind is unalike God's mind because I think someone is of God's thoughts as I think someone's mind is a storage area of God's thoughts that is apart of making up someone. I think someone is of God's thoughts as I think someone's mind is a storage area of God's thoughts that is apart of making up someone because I think someone's mind is the entire area of God's thoughts that is apart of making up someone. I think someone's mind is the entire area of God's thoughts that is apart of making up someone because I think someone's mind is all of God's thoughts that is apart of making up someone. I think someone's mind is all of God's thoughts that is apart of making up someone because I think someone's mind is all of God's thoughts that is apart of making up how someone is able to be what someone is in life with someone's being, and I think someone's mind is all of God's thoughts that is apart of making up how someone is able to be doing what someone is doing with someone's state of consciousness, and I think someone's mind is all of God's thoughts that is apart of making up how someone is doing what someone is doing with someone's will, and therefore, I think someone's mind is God's thoughts as I think someone's mind is someone's thoughts because I think someone's thoughts is God's thoughts as I think someone's mind is of God's thoughts that is apart of making up someone's mind. If I think someone's mind is God's thoughts as I think someone's mind is someone's thoughts, than I think someone's mind is unlimited in size because I think God can still be adding more of God's thoughts into someone's mind, that can be apart of making up how someone is able to be what someone is in life with someone's being, and I think God can still be adding more of God's thoughts into someone's mind, that can be apart of making up how someone is able to be doing what someone is doing with someone's state of consciousness, and I think God can still be adding more of God's thoughts into someone's mind, that can be apart of making up how someone is doing what someone is doing with someone's will, and therefore, I think someone's mind is unlimited because I do not think there is any limit with someone's thoughts of someone's mind for someone's mind to be unlimited. I do not think there is any limit with someone's thoughts of someone's mind for someone's mind to be unlimited because I think someone's mind is infinite for someone's mind to be unlimited. I think someone's mind is infinite for someone's mind to be unlimited because I think someone is created by God being infinite for someone's mind to be infinite, and therefore, I think someone's mind is unlimited because I think someone's mind is infinite for someone's mind to be unlimited. If I think someone's mind is unlimited, than I do not think someone can learn enough because I think someone's mind is infinite for someone not to be learning enough, and therefore, I do not God can teach enough because I think God's mind is infinite for God to be infinitely be creating something in God's mind as I think God can infinitely be creating something in God's mind for God not to be teaching enough. If I do not God can teach enough, than I think someone's mind is someone's thoughts because I think someone's thoughts is apart of making up someone's mind for someone's mind to be someone's thoughts, and therefore, I think someone's thoughts is overlapping, and co-existing along with someone's mind because I think someone's thoughts is apart of making up someone's mind for someone's thoughts to be overlapping, and co-existing along with someone's mind.

If I think someone's thoughts is overlapping, and co-existing along with someone's mind, than I think someone is a mind because I think someone's mind is someone. I think someone's mind is someone because I think someone is someone's mind. I think someone is someone's mind because I think someone is a mind. I think someone is a mind because I think someone is of God's thoughts for someone to be a mind. I think someone is of God's thoughts for someone to be a mind because I think God's thoughts is apart of making up someone for someone to be a mind. I think God's thoughts is apart of making up someone for someone to be a mind because I think someone's mind is the entire area of God's thoughts that is apart of making up someone, and therefore, I think someone is a mind as I think everything is a mind because I think God's mind is of someone for someone to be a mind as I think God's mind is of everything for everything to be a mind. I think God's mind is of someone for someone to be a mind as I think God's mind is of everything for everything to be a mind because I think someone is apart of making up God's mind for someone to be a mind as I think everything is apart of making up God's mind for everything to be a mind. I think someone is apart of making up God's mind for someone to be a mind as I think everything is apart of making up God's mind for everything to be a mind because I think someone's mind is someone that is apart of making up God's mind as I think everything's mind is everything that is apart of making up God's mind. I think someone's mind is someone that is apart of making up God's mind as I think everything's mind is everything that is apart of making up God's mind because I think someone is a mind as I think everything is a mind. I think someone is a mind as I think everything is a mind because I think someone is of God's thoughts for someone to be a mind as I think everything is of God's thoughts for everything to be a mind. I think someone is of God's thoughts for someone to be a mind as I think everything is of God's thoughts for everything to be a mind because I think God's thoughts is apart of making up someone for someone to be a mind as I think God's thoughts is apart of making up everything for everything to be a mind. I think God's thoughts is apart of making up someone for someone to be a mind as I think God's thoughts is apart of making up everything for everything to be a mind because I think someone's mind is the entire area of God's thoughts that is apart of making up someone as I think everything's mind is the entire area of God's thoughts that is apart of making up everything, and therefore, I think someone can think of someone's mind as being the dimension of someone's mind because I think someone's mind is a storage area of God's thoughts that is apart of making up someone. If I think someone can think of someone's mind as being the dimension of someone's mind, than I think someone's mind is overlapping, and co-existing along with God's mind because I think someone is apart of God's mind for someone to be a mind, and therefore, I think someone's mind is overlapping, and co-existing along with God's thoughts because I think someone's mind is all of God's thoughts that is apart of making up someone. I think someone's mind is all of God's thoughts that is apart of making up someone because I think someone is a mind as I think someone is God's thoughts. I think someone is a mind as I think someone is God's thoughts because I think someone's mind is someone as I think God's thoughts is someone. I think someone's mind is someone as I think God's thoughts is someone because I think someone is someone's mind as I think someone is God's thoughts. I think someone is someone's mind as I think someone is God's thoughts because I think someone's mind is someone as I think someone's mind is God's thoughts. I think someone's mind is someone as I think someone's mind is God's thoughts because I think someone is someone's mind as I think God's thoughts is someone's mind. I think someone is someone's mind as I think God's thoughts is someone's mind because I think someone's mind is the entire area of God's thoughts that is apart of making up someone. I think someone's mind is the entire area of God's thoughts that is apart of making up someone because I think someone is someone's mind as I think someone's mind is God's thoughts. I think someone is someone's mind as I think someone's mind is God's thoughts because I think someone is a mind as I think someone has a mind, and therefore, I think someone has a mind because I think someone is a mind for someone to have a mind.

If I think someone has a mind, than I think God created someone's state of consciousness to be apart of someone's being for someone's being to be able to have a sense of awareness because I think God created someone's state of consciousness for someone's being to be able to be aware of what someone is doing with someone's will, along with someone's thoughts that is somehow able to be taking place within someone's mind as I think someone's state of consciousness, along with someone's will, and someone's thoughts, and someone's mind is apart of someone's being. I think God created someone's state of consciousness for someone's being to be able to be aware of what someone is doing with someone's will, along with someone's thoughts that is somehow able to be taking place within someone's mind as I think someone's state of consciousness, along with someone's will, and someone's thoughts, and someone's mind is apart of someone's being because I do not think someone can be able to be aware of what someone is doing with someone's will, along with someone's thoughts that is somehow able to be taking place within someone's mind, without someone having a state of consciousness for someone to be able to be doing what someone is doing with someone's will, along with someone's thoughts that is somehow able to be taking place within someone's mind as I think someone's state of consciousness is apart of someone's being, even though, I do not think someone is able to be aware of what someone's being is in life with someone's state of consciousness as I think someone's state of consciousness is apart of someone's being, but I think God created someone's state of consciousness to have a sense of awareness with someone's state of consciousness because I think someone is able to be aware of what someone is doing with someone's state of consciousness as I think someone's state of consciousness is apart of someone's being, and therefore, I think someone has a state of consciousness for someone to be aware of what someone is doing as I think someone has a state of consciousness for someone to be aware of everything that someone can experience in someone's life because I think God created someone's state of consciousness for someone to be aware of what someone is doing as I think God created someone's state of consciousness for someone to be aware of everything someone can experience in someone's life. I think God created someone's state of consciousness for someone to be aware of what someone is doing as I think God created someone's state of consciousness for someone to be aware of everything someone can experience in someone's life because I think someone is consciously aware of what someone is doing as I think someone is consciously aware of everything someone can experience in someone's life. I think someone is consciously aware of what someone is doing as I think someone is consciously aware of everything someone can experience in someone's life because I think someone's state of consciousness is apart of someone's being as I think someone is consciously aware of everything someone can possibly be able to be experiencing in someone's life, and therefore, I think someone's state of consciousness, someone's will, someone's thoughts, and someone's mind is apart of someone's being because I think God is somehow able to be responsible for creating everything for God to be creating someone's state of consciousness, someone's will, someone's thoughts, and someone's mind to be apart of someone's being.

If I think someone's state of consciousness, someone's will, someone's thoughts, and someone's mind is apart of someone's being, than I think someone's state of consciousness, and someone's will, and someone's thoughts, and someone's mind, and someone's being are characteristics or features that is apart of making up the embodiment of someone as I think the embodiment of someone is apart of making up someone because I think someone is how someone is able to be what someone is in life as I think the embodiment of someone is apart of how someone is able to be what someone is in life. I think someone is how someone is able to be what someone is in life as I think the embodiment of someone is apart of how someone is able to be what someone is in life because I think someone is what someone is in life as I think the embodiment of someone is apart of making up what someone is in life. I think someone is what someone is in life as I think the embodiment of someone is apart of making up what someone is in life because I think someone is the embodiment of someone as I think the embodiment of someone is apart of making up someone, and therefore, I think someone's state of consciousness, and someone's will, and someone's thoughts, and someone's mind, and someone's being are all completely different characteristics or features of someone because I think someone's state of consciousness is what someone is able to be doing, and I think someone's will is what someone is doing, and I think someone's mind is a storage area of someone's thoughts, and I think someone's being is what someone is in life, even though, I think someone's state of consciousness, and someone's will, and someone's thoughts, and someone's mind, and someone's being are all completely different characteristics or features of someone that is apart of making up the embodiment of someone because I think someone consists of someone's state of consciousness, and someone's will, and someone's thoughts, and someone's mind, and someone's being that is apart of making up the embodiment of someone. I think someone consists of someone's state of consciousness, and someone's will, and someone's thoughts, and someone's mind, and someone's being that is apart of making up the embodiment of someone because I think the embodiment of someone is apart of making up someone, and therefore, I think someone is apart of making up everything because I think everything consists of someone as I think someone consists of someone having a state of consciousness, and someone having a will, and someone having thoughts, and someone having a mind, and someone's being that is apart of making up someone. I think everything consists of someone as I think someone consists of someone having a state of consciousness, and someone having a will, and someone having thoughts, and someone having a mind, and someone's being that is apart of making up someone because I think someone's state of consciousness, and someone's will, and someone's thoughts, and someone's mind, and someone's being are characteristics of someone that is apart of making up the embodiment of someone. I think someone's state of consciousness, and someone's will, and someone's thoughts, and someone's mind, and someone's being are characteristics of someone that is apart of making up the embodiment of someone because I think someone consists of someone's state of consciousness, and someone's will, and someone's thoughts, and someone's mind, and someone's being that is apart of making up the embodiment of someone. I think someone consists of someone's state of consciousness, and someone's will, and someone's thoughts, and someone's mind, and someone's being that is apart of making up the embodiment of someone because I think the embodiment of someone is apart of making up someone for the embodiment of someone to be apart of someone. I think the embodiment of someone is apart of making up someone for the embodiment of someone to be apart of someone because I think someone's state of consciousness, and someone's will, and someone's thoughts, and someone's mind is taking place within someone's being, without being someone's being as I think someone's state of consciousness, and someone's will, and someone's thoughts, and someone's mind is apart of someone's being, without being someone's being. I think someone's state of consciousness, and someone's will, and someone's thoughts, and someone's mind is taking place within someone's being without being someone's being as I think someone's state of consciousness, and someone's will, and someone's thoughts, and someone's mind is apart of someone's being without being someone's being because I think someone's state of consciousness, and someone's will, and someone's thoughts, and someone's mind, and someone's being is apart of making up the embodiment of someone. I think someone's state of consciousness, and someone's will, and someone's thoughts, and someone's mind, and someone's being is apart of making up the embodiment of someone because I think the embodiment of someone is apart of making up someone. I think the embodiment of someone is apart of making up someone because I think the embodiment of someone is someone's state of consciousness, and someone's will, and someone's thoughts, and someone's mind, and someone's being that is apart of making up someone. If I think the embodiment of someone is apart of making up someone, than I think everyone is exactly the same because I think everyone has a state of consciousness, and a will, and thoughts, and a mind, and a being for everyone to be exactly the same, and therefore, I think the embodiment of someone is overlapping, and co-existing along with the dimension of someone because I think the embodiment of someone is apart of making up someone. I think the embodiment of someone is apart of making up someone because I think the embodiment of someone is someone.

I think the embodiment of someone is someone because I think the embodiment of someone consists of someone's state of consciousness, and someone's will, and someone's thoughts, and someone's mind, and someone's being that is apart of making up someone. I think the embodiment of someone consists of someone's state of consciousness, and someone's will, and someone's thoughts, and someone's mind, and someone's being that is apart of making up someone because I think the embodiment of someone is someone as I think someone is the embodiment of someone. I think the embodiment of someone is someone as I think someone is the embodiment of someone because I think the embodiment of someone is what someone is in life, and therefore, I think someone is multi-dimensional because I think someone's state of consciousness, and someone's will, and someone's thoughts, and someone's mind, and someone's being is apart of making up the embodiment of someone for someone to be multi-dimensional. If I think someone is multi-dimensional, than I think God created the embodiment of someone with God's thoughts because I think someone is of God's thoughts for God to be creating the embodiment of someone with God's thoughts, and therefore, I think God created the embodiment of someone because I think God created the embodiment of someone with God's thoughts for God to be creating the embodiment of someone. If I think God created the embodiment of someone, than I think God created someone to be multi-dimensional because I think God created the embodiment of someone with God's thoughts for God to be creating someone to be multi-dimensional, and therefore, I think someone is of the dimensions of a higher intelligent living being because I think God created someone to be multi-dimensional for someone to be of the dimensions of a higher intelligent living being, even though, I think someone's state of consciousness, and someone's will, and someone's thoughts, and someone's mind, and someone's being is overlapping, and co-existing along with someone's state of consciousness, and someone's will, and someone's thoughts, and someone's mind, and someone's being because I think someone's state of consciousness, and someone's will, and someone's thoughts, and someone's mind, and someone's being is apart of making up the embodiment of someone. If I think someone's state of consciousness, and someone's will, and someone's thoughts, and someone's mind, and someone's being is apart of making up the embodiment of someone, than I think the embodiment of someone is infinite as I think the embodiment of someone is apart of making up someone because I think someone is created by God being infinite for the embodiment of someone to be infinite, and therefore, I think someone is infinite as I think someone consists of someone's state of consciousness, and something's will, and something's thoughts, and something's mind, and someone's being that is apart of making up the embodiment of someone because I think someone is created by God being infinite for someone to be infinite. If I think someone is created by God being infinite for someone to be infinite, than I think someone is immortal as I think someone is infinite because I think someone is infinite for someone to be immortal. I think someone is infinite for someone to be immortal because I think someone is infinitely immortal, even though, I think someone is mortal for someone to die, however, I think someone is infinitely immortal because I think someone is created by God being infinite for someone to be infinitely immortal.

If I think someone is infinitely immortal, than I think the embodiment of someone is how someone is able to be someone as I think the embodiment of someone is how someone is able to be alive because I think the embodiment of someone consists of someone having a state of consciousness, and someone having a will, and someone having thoughts, and someone having a mind that is apart of someone's being for the embodiment of someone to be how someone is able to be someone as I think the embodiment of someone consists of someone having a state of consciousness, and someone having a will, and someone having thoughts, and someone having a mind that is apart of someone's being for the embodiment of someone to be how someone is able to be alive, and therefore, I think someone is the embodiment of someone for someone to be alive because I think someone consists of someone having a state of consciousness, and someone having a will, and someone having thoughts, and someone having a mind that is apart of someone's being for someone to be alive as I think the embodiment of someone consists of someone having a state of consciousness, and someone having a will, and someone having thoughts, and someone having a mind that is apart of someone's being for someone to be alive. If I think someone is the embodiment of someone for someone to be alive, than I think someone is created by God for someone to be alive as I think the embodiment of someone is created by God for someone to be alive because I think someone is the embodiment of someone for someone to be alive as I think someone is God's choice for someone to alive, and therefore, I think someone is created by God for someone to be alive because I think someone is God's choice for someone to alive. If I think someone is created by God for someone to be alive, than I think someone's life is created by God for someone to be alive because I think someone's life is God's choice for someone to be alive. I think someone's life is God's choice for someone to be alive because I do not think someone's life is someone's choice for someone to be alive. I do not think someone's life is someone's choice for someone to be alive because I do not think someone can created themselves for someone's life not to be someone's choice for someone to be alive, and therefore, I think someone's life is created by God for someone to be alive because I do not think someone can created themselves for someone's life not to be someone's choice for someone to be alive. If I think someone's life is created by God for someone to be alive, than I think the embodiment of someone is what someone is in life because I think the embodiment of someone is created by God for the embodiment of someone to be what someone is in life. I think the embodiment of someone is created by God for the embodiment of someone to be what someone is in life because I think the embodiment of someone is God's choice for the embodiment of someone to be what someone is in life, and therefore, I think the embodiment of someone is what someone is in life because I think someone is the embodiment of someone for the embodiment of someone to be what someone is in life.

If I think the embodiment of someone is what someone is in life, than I think someone's being is how someone is doing what someone is doing with someone's will, and I think someone's being is how someone is able to be doing what someone is doing with someone's state of consciousness because I think how someone is able to be doing what someone is able to be doing with someone's being is how someone is doing what someone is doing with someone's will, and I think how someone is able to be doing what someone is able to be doing with someone's being is how someone is able to be doing what someone is doing with someone's state of consciousness, and therefore, I think someone's being is how someone is able to be making any choices with someone's will because I think how someone is able to be doing what someone is able to be doing with someone's being is how someone is able to be making any choices with someone's will. I think how someone is able to be doing what someone is able to be doing with someone's being is how someone is able to be making any choices with someone's will because I think what someone is doing is what someone's being is doing. I think what someone is doing is what someone's being is doing because I think someone is doing what someone's being is doing. I think someone is doing what someone's being is doing because I think someone's being is how someone is able to be doing what someone is able to be doing as I think someone's state of consciousness, and someone's will, and someone's thoughts, and someone's mind is apart of someone's being. I think someone's being is how someone is able to be doing what someone is able to be doing as I think someone's state of consciousness, and someone's will, and someone's thoughts, and someone's mind is apart of someone's being because I think someone is doing what someone is doing with someone's state of consciousness, along with someone's will, and someone's thoughts, and someone's mind that is apart of someone's being. I think someone is doing what someone is doing with someone's state of consciousness, along with someone's will, and someone's thoughts, and someone's mind that is apart of someone's being because I think someone is doing what someone's being is doing as I think someone's state of consciousness, and someone's will, and someone's thoughts, and someone's mind is apart of someone's being. I think someone is doing what someone's being is doing as I think someone's state of consciousness, and someone's will, and someone's thoughts, and someone's mind is apart of someone's being because I think someone's being is ultimately what makes someone able to be making any choices as I think someone's state of consciousness, and someone's will, and someone's thoughts, and someone's mind is apart of someone's being. I think someone's being is ultimately what makes someone able to be making any choices as I think someone's state of consciousness, and someone's will, and someone's thoughts, and someone's mind is apart of someone's being because I think the embodiment of someone consists of someone having a state of consciousness, and someone having a will, and someone having thoughts, and someone having a mind that is apart of someone's being for someone's being to ultimately be able to be making any choices, and therefore, I think someone's being is the thoughts of someone as I think someone's being is God's thoughts because I think the thoughts of someone is God's thought as I think someone is of God's thoughts that is apart of making up someone. If I think someone's being is the thoughts of someone as I think someone's being is God's thoughts, than I think someone does what the thoughts of someone is in life as I think someone does what God's thoughts are in life because I think someone is of the thoughts of someone that is apart of making up someone for someone to be doing what the thoughts of someone is in life as I think someone is of God's thoughts that is apart of making up someone for someone to be doing what God's thoughts are in life, and therefore, I think God is somehow able to be responsible for how someone is able to be doing what someone is able to be doing because I think God created how someone is in life with God's thoughts for God to somehow be able to be responsible for how someone is able to be doing what someone is able to be doing.

If I think God is somehow able to be responsible for how someone is able to be doing what someone is able to be doing, than I think God is responsible for what someone is able to be doing because I think God created how someone is in life with God's thoughts for someone to be able to be doing what someone is able to be doing as I think God created someone with God's thoughts for someone to be doing what someone is doing with how someone is in life, but is God responsible for what someone is doing? I think God is somehow able to be responsible for how someone is able to be doing what someone is able to be doing because I do not think someone can possibly be able to be knowing for themselves, as to how someone is in life for someone to be able to be doing what someone is able to be doing as I think God created someone with God's thoughts for God to be able to be knowing, as to how someone is in life for God to be responsible for how someone is able to be doing what someone is able to be doing, however, I do not think God is responsible for what someone is doing because I think God created someone to be having someone's free will for God not to be responsible for what someone is doing, and therefore, I think someone is responsible for what someone is doing because I think God created someone with God's thoughts for someone to be having a choice of right or wrong with someone's free will as I think someone has a choice of right or wrong with someone's free will for someone to be responsible for what someone is doing. I think God created someone with God's thoughts for someone to be having a choice of right or wrong with someone's free will as I think someone has a choice of right or wrong with someone's free will for someone to be responsible for what someone is doing because I think God created someone with God's thoughts for someone to be able to be choosing to be doing something that is right or wrong with someone having a choice of right or wrong as I think someone can choose to be doing something that is right or wrong with someone having a choice of right or wrong for someone to be responsible for what someone is doing, and therefore, I do not think God is responsible for what someone is doing because I think what someone is doing is someone's own choice, as to what someone is doing for God not to be responsible for what someone is doing. If I do not think God is responsible for what someone is doing, than I think God can be responsible for what someone is doing because I think God can help someone to be doing something for God to be responsible for what someone is doing as I think God created someone to be having a will for someone to be able to be doing what someone is doing, however, I do not think God is completely responsible for what someone is doing because I think someone can choose to be doing something with God or not for someone to be responsible for what someone is doing, and therefore, I think someone is responsible for what someone is doing because I think what someone chooses to be doing is someone's choice for someone to be responsible for what someone is doing.

If I think someone is responsible for what someone is doing, than I think someone's being is how someone is able to be intelligent because I think someone's being is how someone is able to be doing what someone is able to be doing as I think someone's intelligence is how someone is able to be doing what someone is able to be doing, and therefore, I do not think what someone is able to be thinking with someone's thoughts, and I do not think how much someone is able to be remembering or thinking with someone's thoughts is how someone is able to be intelligent because I think how someone is able to be doing what someone is able to be doing with someone's being is how someone is able to be intelligent. If I think how someone is able to be doing what someone is able to be doing with someone's being is how someone is able to be intelligent, than I think what someone is able to be thinking with someone's thoughts, and how much someone is able to be remembering or thinking with someone's thoughts is someone's signs of intelligence of how someone is able to be intelligent because I think what someone is able to be thinking with someone's thoughts, and how much someone is able to be remembering or thinking with someone's thoughts is how someone is intelligent, but I do not think what someone is able to be thinking with someone's thoughts, and how much someone is able to be remembering or thinking with someone's thoughts is how someone is able to be intelligent because I think how someone is able to be doing what someone is able to be doing with someone's being is how someone is able to be intelligent. If I think how someone is able to be doing what someone is able to be doing with someone's being is how someone is able to be intelligent, than I think someone's intelligence is someone's signs of intelligence because I think someone's signs of intelligence is what someone is able to be thinking with someone's thoughts, and how much someone is able to be remembering or thinking with someone's thoughts, but I do not think someone's signs of intelligence is someone's intelligence because I think someone's intelligence is how someone is able to be doing what someone is able to be doing as I think how someone is able to be doing what someone is able to be doing with someone's being is how someone is able to be intelligent.

If I do not think someone's signs of intelligence is someone's intelligence, than I think someone is of the likeness of God because I think someone is created by God for someone to be of the likeness of God, even though, I do not think someone is alike God because I do not think God is created for someone not to be alike God, however, I think someone is like God because I think someone has a state of consciousness, and a will, and thoughts, and a mind, and a being that is apart making up the embodiment of someone as I think God has state of consciousness, and a will, and thoughts, and a mind, and a being that is apart of making up the embodiment of God, but I do not think someone is alike God because I do not think someone's state of consciousness, and someone's will, and someone's thoughts, and someone's mind, and someone's being that is apart of making up the embodiment of someone is alike God's state of consciousness, and God's will, and God's thoughts, and God's mind, and God's being that is apart of making up the embodiment of God. I do not think someone's state of consciousness, and someone's will, and someone's thoughts, and someone's mind, and someone's being that is apart of making up the embodiment of someone is alike God's state of consciousness, and God's will, and God's thoughts, and God's mind, and God's being that is apart of making up the embodiment of God because I think God's state of consciousness, and God's will, and God's thoughts, and God's mind, and God's being that is apart of making up the embodiment of God is beyond someone's state of consciousness, and someone's will, and someone's thoughts, and someone's mind, and someone's being that is apart of making up the embodiment of someone. I think God's state of consciousness, and God's will, and God's thoughts, and God's mind, and God's being that is apart of making up the embodiment of God is beyond someone's state of consciousness, and someone's will, and someone's thoughts, and someone's mind, and someone's being that is apart of making up the embodiment of someone because I think someone's state of consciousness, and someone's will, and someone's thoughts, and someone's mind, and someone's being that is apart of making up the embodiment of someone is of God's state of consciousness, and God's will, and God's thoughts, and God's mind, and God's being that is apart of making up the embodiment of God for God's state of consciousness, and God's will, and God's thoughts, and God's mind, and God's being that is apart of making up the embodiment of God to be beyond someone's state of consciousness, and someone's will, and someone's thoughts, and someone's mind, and someone's being that is apart of making up the embodiment of someone. I think someone's state of consciousness, and someone's will, and someone's thoughts, and someone's mind, and someone's being that is apart of making up the embodiment of someone is of God's state of consciousness, and God's will, and God's thoughts, and God's mind, and God's being that is apart of making up the embodiment of God for God's state of consciousness, and God's will, and God's thoughts, and God's mind, and God's being that is apart of making up the embodiment of God to be beyond someone's state of consciousness, and someone's will, and someone's thoughts, and someone's mind, and someone's being that is apart of making up the embodiment of someone because I think God's state of consciousness, and God's will, and God's thoughts, and God's mind, and God's being that is apart of making up the embodiment of God is apart of making up someone's state of consciousness, and someone's will, and someone's thoughts, and someone's mind, and someone's mind that is apart of making up the embodiment of someone for God's state of consciousness, and God's will, and God's thoughts, and God's mind, and God's being that is apart of making up the embodiment of God to be beyond someone's state of consciousness, and someone's will, and someone's thoughts, and someone's mind, and someone's being that is apart of making up the embodiment of someone.

I think God's state of consciousness, and God's will, and God's thoughts, and God's mind, and God's being that is apart of making up the embodiment of God is apart of making up someone's state of consciousness, and someone's will, and someone's thoughts, and someone's mind, and someone's mind that is apart of making up the embodiment of someone for God's state of consciousness, and God's will, and God's thoughts, and God's mind, and God's being that is apart of making up the embodiment of God to be beyond someone's state of consciousness, and someone's will, and someone's thoughts, and someone's mind, and someone's being that is apart of making up the embodiment of someone because I think the embodiment of God is apart of making up the embodiment of someone. I think the embodiment of God is apart of making up the embodiment of someone because I think the embodiment of someone is of the embodiment of God. I think the embodiment of someone is of the embodiment of God because I think the embodiment of God is apart of making up someone that is the embodiment of someone. I think the embodiment of God is apart of making up someone that is the embodiment of someone because I think the embodiment of someone is of God's creation for God to be creating someone to be apart of the embodiment of God. I think the embodiment of someone is of God's creation for God to be creating someone to be apart of the embodiment of God because I think someone is apart of the embodiment of God as I think the embodiment of God is apart of God. I think someone is apart of the embodiment of God as I think the embodiment of God is apart of God because I think someone is of God for God to be creating someone to be apart of the embodiment of God. I think someone is of God for God to be creating someone to be apart of the embodiment of God because I think someone is apart of the embodiment of God as I think someone is of God. I think someone is apart of the embodiment of God as I think someone is of God because I think someone is apart of the embodiment of God for God to be creating someone to be apart of God. I think someone is apart of the embodiment of God for God to be creating someone to be apart of God because I think someone is of the embodiment of God as I think the embodiment of someone is of God. I think someone is of the embodiment of God as I think the embodiment of someone is of God because I think someone is of the embodiment of God for someone to be of God. I think someone is of the embodiment of God for someone to be of God because I think someone is of God as I think the embodiment of God is apart of God. I think someone is of God as I think the embodiment of God is apart of God because I think the embodiment of someone is of God for someone to be of God. I think the embodiment of someone is of God for someone to be of God because I think the embodiment of God is apart of God for God to be creating someone to be apart of God. I think the embodiment of God is apart of God for God to be creating someone to be apart of God because I think someone is of the embodiment of God for God to be creating someone to be apart of God. I think someone is of the embodiment of God for God to be creating someone to be apart of God because I think someone is of the embodiment of God as I think someone is of God. I think someone is of the embodiment of God as I think someone is of God because I think someone is of God for someone to be of the embodiment of God. I think someone is of God for someone to be of the embodiment of God because I think someone is of God for someone to be apart of the embodiment of God. I think someone is of God for someone to be apart of the embodiment of God because I think someone is apart of the embodiment of God as I think someone is apart of God. I think someone is apart of the embodiment of God as I think someone is apart of God because I think someone is of God's creation for God to be creating someone to be apart of God.

If I think someone is apart of the embodiment of God as I think someone is apart of God, than I think someone is overlapping, and co-existing along with God because I think someone is of the embodiment of God for God to be creating someone to be apart of God. I think someone is of the embodiment of God for God to be creating someone to be apart of God because I think the embodiment of someone is overlapping, and co-existing along with the embodiment of God. I think the embodiment of someone is overlapping, and co-existing along with the embodiment of God because I think someone is the embodiment of someone that is overlapping, and co-existing along with the embodiment of God that is apart of God. I think someone is the embodiment of someone that is overlapping, and co-existing along with the embodiment of God that is apart of God because I think someone is overlapping, and co-existing along with the embodiment of God. I think someone is overlapping, and co-existing along with the embodiment of God because I think someone is of God's creation for God to be creating someone to be apart of the embodiment of God. I think someone is of God's creation for God to be creating someone to be apart of the embodiment of God because I think someone is of the embodiment of God for someone to be of God. I think someone is of the embodiment of God for someone to be of God because I think someone is of God's creation for God to be creating someone to be apart of God. I think someone is of God's creation for God to be creating someone to be apart of God because I think someone is the embodiment of someone that is of the embodiment of God for someone to be apart of God. I think someone is the embodiment of someone that is of the embodiment of God for someone to be apart of God because I think the embodiment of someone is of God for the embodiment of someone to be of the embodiment of God. I think the embodiment of someone is of God for the embodiment of someone to be of the embodiment of God because I think the embodiment of someone is of God for the embodiment of someone to be apart of God. I think the embodiment of someone is of God for the embodiment of someone to be apart of God because I think the embodiment of someone is someone as I think someone is of God for someone to be apart of God. I think the embodiment of someone is someone as I think someone is of God for someone to be apart of God because I think the embodiment of someone is what someone is in life as I think someone is of God's creation for someone to be what someone is in life. I think the embodiment of someone is what someone is in life as I think someone is of God's creation for someone to be what someone is in life because I think the embodiment of someone is of the dimension of someone as I think someone is the dimension of someone for the embodiment of someone to be someone.

Chapter 13

The embodiment of something

I would like to talk about how dimensions are in life in relation to what dimensions are in life by talking about the embodiment of something, that can possibly have something to do with how dimensions are in life is in relation to what dimensions are in life because I think the embodiment of something is of the dimension of something as I think something is the dimension of something for the embodiment of something to be something, and therefore, I think something is a choice because I think something has a choice. I think something has a choice because I think something is a choice for something to have a choice. I think something is a choice for something to have a choice because I think something is a choice of itself for something to have a choice. I think something is a choice of itself for something to have a choice because I think something is a choice of itself of what something is doing, and therefore, I think an example of how I think something is a choice of itself of what something is doing can be a glass cup because I think a glass cup can break if someone drops a glass cup on a hard surface, like a cement side walk for a glass cup to be a choice of itself of what something is doing. I think a glass cup can break if someone drops a glass cup on a hard surface, like a cement side walk for a glass cup to be a choice of itself of what something is doing because I do not think a glass cup can break from someone dropping a glass cup on a hard surface, like a cement side walk if a glass cup is not a choice of itself of what something is doing, but I think a glass cup can break from someone dropping a glass cup on a hard surface, like a cement side walk because I think a glass cup is a choice of itself of what a glass cup is doing for a glass cup to break from someone dropping a glass cup on a hard surface, like a cement side walk, and therefore, I think something is a choice of itself of what something is doing because I think something is a choice of itself for something to have a choice. I think something is a choice of itself for something to have a choice because I think something has a choice, and therefore, I think something is in motion because I think something is a choice for something to be in motion as I think something is a choice of itself of what something is doing for something to be in motion.

If I think something is in motion, than I think something has a choice because I think something has a will as I think something has a choice. I think something has a will as I think something has a choice because I think something is a choice of itself of what something is doing for something to have a will as I think something is a choice of itself of what something is doing for something to have a choice. I think something is a choice of itself of what something is doing for something to have a will as I think something is a choice of itself of what something is doing for something to have a choice because I think something has a will for something to have a choice. I think something has a will for something to have a choice because I do not think something would have a choice, if something doesn't have a will. I do not think something would have a choice, if something doesn't have a will because I do not think something would be a choice of itself of what something is doing, if something doesn't have a will for something to be a choice of itself of what something is doing, but I think something has a will for something to be a choice of itself of what something is doing because I think something is a choice of itself of what something is doing, and therefore, I think something has a will as I think something has a choice because I think something has a will for something to be a choice of itself of what something is doing. I think something has a will for something to be a choice of itself of what something is doing because I think something's will is something's choice.

I think something's will is something's choice because I think something has a will as I think something has a choice. I think something has a will as I think something has a choice because I think something is a choice of itself for something to have a will as I think something is a choice of itself for something to have a choice. I think something is a choice of itself for something to have a will as I think something is a choice of itself for something to have a choice because I think something is a choice as I think something has a choice. I think something is a choice as I think something has a choice because I think something is a choice as I think something has a will. I think something is a choice as I think something has a will because I think something has a will as I think something has a choice. If I think something is a choice as I think something has a will, than I think something has a will because I think if someone drops something, like a glass cup, than I think something, like a glass cup will drop, not because someone drops something, like a glass cup, but I think something, like a glass cup will drop because I think something, like a glass cup has a will for something, like a glass cup to be dropping, and therefore, I think something will drop because I think something has a will for something to drop. If I think something has a will for something to drop, than I think something's will is how something is able to be having a gravitational pull, and any other force that is able to be coming from something because I think something has a will for something to be having a gravitational pull, and any other force that is able to be coming from something. I think something has a will for something to be having a gravitational pull, and any other force that is able to be coming from something because I think something's will is what something does as I think what something does is something's will. I think something's will is what something does as I think what something does is something's will because I think something has a will for what something does, and therefore, I think someone can think of all kinds of words for someone to be describing what someone thinks something's will is in life because I think something has will for someone to be thinking of all kinds of different words for someone to be describing what someone thinks something's will is in life. If I think someone can think of all kinds of words for someone to be describing what someone thinks something's will is in life, than I think something has a will because I think something's will is what something is doing as I think something's will is what something does, and therefore, I think someone can think of all kinds of words for someone to be describing what someone thinks what something can do because I think something has will for someone to be thinking of all kinds of different words for someone to be describing what someone thinks what something can do. If I think someone can think of all kinds of words for someone to be describing what someone thinks what something can do, than I think technology comes from something's will because I think technology is something's will. I think technology is something's will because I think technology is what something is doing as I think something's will is what something is doing, and therefore, I think someone is experiencing technology because I think someone is experiencing something's will for someone to be experiencing technology. I think someone is experiencing something's will for someone to be experiencing technology because I think someone is experiencing what something is doing for someone to be experiencing technology as I think something's will is what something is doing. If I think someone is experiencing something's will for someone to be experiencing technology, than I think something will do something because I think something has will for something to be doing something, and therefore, I think something can do something with itself, something, someone, and God because I think something has a will for something to be doing something with the itself, something, someone, and God. If I think something can do something with itself, something, someone, and God, than I think everything something does is something's will as I think everything something does is something's choice because I think something's will is something's choice for something to be doing everything that something does, and therefore, I think something is in motion because I think something has a will for something to be in motion.

If I think something is in motion, than I think something's will is like God's will because I think something's will is how something is doing what something is doing as I think God's will is how God is doing what God is doing. I think something's will is how something is doing what something is doing as I think God's will is how God is doing what God is doing because I think something's will is what something is doing as I think God's will is what God is doing, and therefore, I think something's will is like God's will because I think something is created by God for something to have a will. I think something is created by God for something to have a will because I think God created something to have a will for something to be doing what something is doing. I think God created something to have a will for something to be doing what something is doing because I think something's will is something's choice. I think something's will is something's choice because I think something's choice is God's choice for something to have a choice. I think something's choice is God's choice for something to have a choice because I think something is created by God for something to have a choice. I think something is created by God for something to have a choice because I think something's choice is something's will. I think something's choice is something's will because I think something's choice is what something is doing as I think something's will is what something is doing. I think something's choice is what something is doing as I think something's will is what something is doing because I think what something is doing is something's choice as I think what something is doing is something's will. I think what something is doing is something's choice as I think what something is doing is something's will because I think something's choice is something's will as I think something's will is something's choice. I think something's choice is something's will as I think something's will is something's choice because I think something has a will as I think something has a choice. I think something has a will as I think something has a choice because I think something has something's free will. I think something has something's free will because I think something has a will for something to be having something's free will. I think something has a will for something to be having something's free will because I think something has something's free will with something being a choice of itself of what something is doing. I think something has something's free will with something being a choice of itself of what something is doing because I think something has a choice. I think something has a choice because I think something has will for something to be having a choice.

If I think something has a choice, than I do not think something has a state of consciousness as I think something has a will because I do not think something has a state of consciousness for something's will. I do not think something has a state of consciousness for something's will because I do not think something has a choice of something, someone, and God for something not to be having a state of consciousness for something's will. I do not think something has a choice of someone, something, and God for something not to be having a state of consciousness for something's will because I do not think something can choose to be doing something with someone, something, and God for something not to be having a state of consciousness for something's will. I do not think something can choose to be doing something with someone, something, and God for something not to be having a state of consciousness for something's will because I do not think something is consciously aware of something choosing to be doing something with someone, something, and God for something not to be having a state of consciousness for something's will. I do not think something is consciously aware of something choosing to be doing something with someone, something, and God for something not to be having a state of consciousness for something's will because I do not think something has a state of consciousness with something's will for something to be consciously aware of something choosing to be doing something with someone, something, and God. I do not think something has a state of consciousness with something's will for something to be consciously aware of something choosing to be doing something with someone, something, and God because I do not think something has a state of consciousness for something's will, even though, I think someone can think something has a state of consciousness with something's will for something to be consciously aware of what something is doing because I think something is a choice of itself of what something is doing for something to be having a will, but I do not think something has a state of consciousness with something's will for something to be consciously aware of what something is doing because I do not think something has to be consciously aware of what something is doing for something not to be having a state of consciousness with something's will. I do not think something has to be consciously aware of what something is doing for something not to be having a state of consciousness with something's will because I think something will do what something is doing, regardless if something is aware of what something is doing or not, and therefore, I do not think something has a state of consciousness with something's will because I do not think something has a state of consciousness as I think something has a will. I do not think something has a state of consciousness as I think something has a will because I do not think something has a state of consciousness for what something is doing with something's will, and therefore, I do not think something has a state of consciousness because I do not think something has a state of consciousness for what something is doing with something's will.

If I do not think something has a state of consciousness, than I think something has a will because I think something's will is how something is doing what something is doing. I think something's will is how something is doing what something is doing because I think what something is doing is how something is doing what something is doing. I think what something is doing is how something is doing what something is doing because I think something has a will. I think something has a will because I think something's will is what something is doing, and therefore, I think something has a will as I think God has a will because I think something's will is what something is doing as I think God's will is what God is doing. If I think something has a will as I think God has a will, than I think something's will is what something is doing because I think what something is doing is how something is doing what something is doing. I think what something is doing is how something is doing what something is doing because I think something's will is a dimension. I think something's will is a dimension because I think something's will is something for something's will to be a dimension. I think something's will is something for something's will to be a dimension because I think something's will is what something is doing. I think something's will is what something is doing because I think something has a will as I think something's will is a dimension, and therefore, I think someone can think of something's will as being the dimension of something's will because I think the dimension of something's will is what something is doing. If I think someone can think of something's will as being the dimension of something's will, than I think something is a choice for something to be doing something with itself, something else, someone, and God because I think something has a will for something to be doing something with itself, something else, someone, and God, and therefore, I think something has a will because I think something can do something with itself, something else, someone, and God for something to be having a will.

If I think something has a will, than I think something is something's being because I think something's being is something. I think something's being is something because I think something's being is how something is able to be what something is in life. I think something's being is how something is able to be what something is in life because I think something's being is the very existence of what something is in life. I think something's being is the very existence of what something is in life because I think the being of what something is in life is the very existence of what something is in life. I think the being of what something is in life is the very existence of what something is in life because I think something's being is how something is able to be what something is in life as I think something's being is the very existence of what something is in life. I think something's being is how something is able to be what something is in life as I think something's being is the very existence of what something is in life because I think something's being is what something is in life, and therefore, I think something is a being as I think God is a being because I think something is of God's being for something to be a being. I think something is of God's being for something to be a being because I think something's being is the very existence of what something is in life as I think God's being is the very existence of what God is in life. I think something's being is the very existence of what something is in life as I think God's being is the very existence of what God is in life because I think something is of the very existence of what God is in life for something to be of the very existence of what something is in life, and therefore, I think something's being is a dimension because I think something's being is something for something's being to be a dimension. I think something's being is something for something's being to be a dimension because I think something's being is how something is able to be what something is in life. I think something's being is how something is able to be what something is in life because I think something's being is something as I think something's being is what something is in life, and therefore, I think someone can think of something's being as being the dimension of something's being because I think the dimension of something's being is what something is in life. I think the dimension of something's being is what something is in life because I think something is something's being. I think something is something's being because I think God created something's being for something to be what something is in life, and therefore, I think someone can think of the dimension of something's being as being the dimension of something because I think something is something's being as I think something is what something's being is in life.

If I think someone can think of the dimension of something's being as being the dimension of something, than I think something's will comes from something's being, but I do not think something's will is something's being because I think something's will is what something is doing, and I think something's being is what something is in life. I think something's will is what something is doing, and I think something's being is what something is in life because I think something's will is something having a choice of what something is doing. I think something's will is something having a choice of what something is doing because I do not think something would be able to be doing anything, without something having a will. I do not think something would be able to be doing anything, without something having a will because I think something not having a will is like something not being able to move, and therefore, I think something's will is how something is able to be something because I think something's will is something having a choice of what something is doing. If I think something's will is how something is able to be something, than I think something has a will for something's being because I do not think something would be able to be doing anything, without something having a will, even though, I think something has a will for something's being because I think something has a will for what something is doing with something's being. I think something has a will for what something is doing with something's being because I think something has a will for something to be having a choice of what something is doing. I think something has a will for something to be having a choice of what something is doing because I think something's will is something having a choice of what something is doing. I think something's will is something having a choice of what something is doing because I think something has a will for something to be having a choice of what something is doing, and therefore, I think something's will is overlapping, and co-existing along with of something's being because I think something's will is something having a choice of what something is doing.

If I think something's will is overlapping, and co-existing along with something's being, than I think something has thoughts because I think something is of the thoughts of something for something to have thoughts. I think something is of the thoughts of something for something to have thoughts because I think something is the thoughts of something. I think something is the thoughts of something because I think something is something's thoughts of itself as I think something's thoughts of itself is the thoughts of something. I think something is something's thoughts of itself as I think something's thoughts of itself is the thoughts of something because I think something is the thoughts of something as I think the thoughts of something is something's thoughts of itself. I think something is the thoughts of something as I think the thoughts of something is something's thoughts of itself because I think something is the thoughts of something as I think something is something's thoughts of itself. I think something is the thoughts of something as I think something is something's thoughts of itself because I think something is of the thoughts of something for something to be the thoughts of something. I think something is of the thoughts of something for something to be the thoughts of something because I think the thoughts of something is apart of making up something for something to be the thoughts of something. I think the thoughts of something is apart of making up something for something to be the thoughts of something because I think something is of the thoughts of something for something to be something of itself. I think something is of the thoughts of something for something to be something of itself because I think the thoughts of something is apart of making up something for something to be something of itself. I think the thoughts of something is apart of making up something for something to be something of itself because I think something is the thoughts of something for something to be something of itself.

I think something is the thoughts of something for something to be something of itself because I think the thoughts of something is of God's thoughts for something to be something of itself. I think the thoughts of something is of God's thoughts for something to be something of itself because I think something is of the thoughts of something as I think God's thoughts is the thoughts of something. I think something is of the thoughts of something as I think God's thoughts is the thoughts of something because I think something is of God's thoughts as I think the thoughts of something is of God's thoughts. I think something is of God's thoughts as I think the thoughts of something is of God's thoughts because I think God's thoughts is the thoughts of something as I think something is of God's thoughts. I think God's thoughts is the thoughts of something as I think something is of God's thoughts because I think something is God's thoughts. I think something is God's thoughts because I think something has thoughts. I think something has thoughts because I think God's thoughts is apart of making up something for something to have thoughts, and therefore, I think something has thoughts as I think God has thoughts because I think God's thoughts is apart of making up something for something to have thoughts as I think God's thoughts is apart of making up something for God to have thoughts. I think God's thoughts is apart of making up something for something to have thoughts as I think God's thoughts is apart of making up something for God to have thoughts because I think something is God's thoughts. I think something is God's thoughts because I think something is of God's thoughts for something to be God's thoughts. I think something is of God's thoughts for something to be God's thoughts because I think God's thoughts is apart of making up something for something to be God's thoughts. I think God's thoughts is apart of making up something for something to be God's thoughts because I think something is of God's thoughts for something to be something of itself. I think something is of God's thoughts for something to be something of itself because I think God's thoughts is apart of making up something for something to be something of itself. I think God's thoughts is apart of making up something for something to be something of itself because I think something is God's thoughts for something to be something of itself.

If I think God's thoughts is apart of making up something for something to be something of itself, than I think something will do what something does because I think something will do what something does with something's will for something to do what something does. I think something will do what something does with something's will for something to do what something does because I think something will do what something does with something's thoughts of itself for something to do what something does with something's will as I think something will do what something does with the thoughts of something for something to do what something does with something's will. I think something will do what something does with something's thoughts of itself for something to do what something does with something's will as I think something will do what something does with the thoughts of something for something to do what something does with something's will because I think something's thoughts of itself is the thoughts of something as I think something will do what something does with something's thoughts of itself for something to do what something does with something's will. I think something's thoughts of itself is the thoughts of something as I think something will do what something does with something's thoughts of itself for something to do what something does with something's will because I think something's thoughts of itself is the thoughts of something for something to do what something does with something's will. I think something's thoughts of itself is the thoughts of something for something to do what something does with something's will because I think something is of the thoughts of itself for something to do what something does with something's will. I think something is of the thoughts of itself for something to do what something does with something's will because I think something's thoughts of itself is of God's thoughts for something to do what something does with something's will. I think something's thoughts of itself is of God's thoughts for something to do what something does with something's will because I think something will do what something does with God's thoughts for something to do what something does with something's will. I think something will do what something does with God's thoughts for something to do what something does with something's will because I think something is of God's thoughts for something to do what something does with something's will.

If I think something will do what something does with God's thoughts for something to do what something does with something's will, than I think something is God's thoughts for something to be something of itself because I think something is the being of God's thoughts as I think something's being is the being of God's thoughts. I think something is the being of God's thoughts as I think something's being is the being of God's thoughts because I think something is something's being as I think something is of God's thoughts for something to be the being of God's thoughts. I think something is something's being as I think something is of God's thoughts for something to be the being of God's thoughts because I think something is of God's thoughts for something to be whatever something is in life. I think something is of God's thoughts for something to be whatever something is in life because I think God's thoughts is whatever God's thoughts are in life that is apart of making up something for something to be whatever something is in life. I think God's thoughts is whatever God's thoughts are in life that is apart of making up something for something to be whatever something is in life because I think something is God's thoughts for something to be something of itself. I think something is God's thoughts for something to be something of itself because I think something is of God's thoughts with how something is able to be what something is in life, and therefore, I think something is of God's thoughts with what something is in life as I think something is of God's thoughts with how something is able to be what something is in life because I think what something is in life is how something is able to be what something is in life. If I think what something is in life is how something is able to be what something is in life, than I think something is of God's thoughts with how something is able to be what something is in life because I think God's thoughts is apart of making up how something is able to be what something is in life. I think God's thoughts is apart of making up how something is able to be what something is in life because I think something is God's thoughts with how something is able to be what something is in life. If I think God's thoughts is apart of making up how something is able to be what something is in life, than I think something's being is God's thoughts as I think something is God's thoughts because I think something is something's being as I think something is of God's thoughts with how something is able to be what something is in life, and therefore, I think something's being is overlapping, and co-existing along with God's thoughts because I think God's thoughts is apart of making up how something is able to be what something is in life as I think something's being is how something is able to be what something is in life.

If I think something's being is overlapping, and co-existing along with God's thoughts, than I think something's will is God's thoughts as I think something is God's thoughts because I think something's will is of God's thoughts with what something is doing as I think something is of God's thoughts with how something is able to be what something is in life. I think something's will is of God's thoughts with what something is doing as I think something is of God's thoughts with how something is able to be what something is in life because I think God's thoughts is apart of making up something's will for something to be doing what something is doing as I think God's thoughts is apart of making up something for something to be something of itself. I think God's thoughts is apart of making up something's will for something to be doing what something is doing as I think God's thoughts is apart of making up something for something to be something of itself because I think something's will is God's thoughts with what something is doing as I think something is God's thoughts with how something is able to be what something is in life, and therefore, I think something's will is overlapping, and co-existing along with God's thoughts because I think God's thoughts is apart of making up something's will for something to be doing what something is doing. If I think something's will is overlapping, and co-existing along with God's thoughts, than I think something will do what something does with something's will because I think something will do what something does with something's being for something to do what something does with something's will. I think something will do what something does with something's being for something to do what something does with something's will because I think something's being is what something does with something's will. I think something's being is what something does with something's will because I think what something is in life is what something does as I think what something is in life is what something does with something's will. I think what something is in life is what something does as I think what something is in life is what something does with something's will because I think something's being is of God's thoughts for something to be doing what something does with something's will. I think something's being is of God's thoughts for something to be doing what something does with something's will because I think something is of God's thoughts for something to be what something is in life as I think something is of God's thoughts for something to be doing what something is doing with something's will.

If I think something's being is of God's thoughts for something to be doing what something does with something's will, than I think something has a mind because I think something's mind is a storage area of something. I think something's mind is a storage area of something because I think something's mind is a storage area of something's thoughts for something's mind to be a storage area of something. I think something's mind is a storage area of something's thoughts for something's mind to be a storage area of something because I think something is a storage area of God's thoughts as I think something's mind is a storage area of something's thoughts. I think something is a storage area of God's thoughts as I think something's mind is a storage area of something's thoughts because I think something's mind is a storage area of God's thoughts for something's mind to be a storage area of something. I think something's mind is a storage area of God's thoughts for something's mind to be a storage area of something because I think something has a mind. I think something has a mind because I think something's mind is the entire area of God's thoughts that is apart of making up something, and therefore, I think something has a mind as I think God has a mind because I think something's mind is the entire area of God's thoughts that is apart of making up something as I think God's mind is the entire area of God's thoughts that is apart of making up everything. If I think something has a mind as I think God has a mind, than I think something's mind is like God's mind because I think something's mind is a storage area of God's thoughts as I think God's mind is a storage area of God's thoughts, but I do not think something's mind alike God's mind because I think something's mind is the entire area of God's thoughts that is apart of making up something as I think God's mind is the entire area of God's thoughts that is apart of making up everything, and therefore, I think something's mind is unalike God's mind because I think something is of God's thoughts as I think something's mind is a storage area of God's thoughts that is apart of making up something. I think something is of God's thoughts as I think something's mind is a storage area of God's thoughts that is apart of making up something because I think something's mind is the entire area of God's thoughts that is apart of making up something. I think something's mind is the entire area of God's thoughts that is apart of making up something because I think something's mind is all of God's thoughts that is apart of making up something. I think something's mind is all of God's thoughts that is apart of making up something because I think something's mind is all of God's thoughts that is apart of making up how something is able to be what something is in life with something's being, and I think something's mind is all of God's thoughts that is apart of making up how something is doing what something is doing with something's will, and therefore, I think something's mind is God's thoughts as I think something's mind is something's thoughts because I think something's thoughts is God's thoughts as I think something's mind is of God's thoughts that is apart of making up something's mind. If I think something's mind is God's thoughts as I think something's mind is something's thoughts, than I think something's mind is unlimited in size because I think God can still be adding more of God's thoughts into something's mind, that can be apart of making up how something is able to be what something is in life with something's being, and I think God can still be adding more of God's thoughts into something's mind, that can be apart of making up how something is doing what something is doing with something's will, and therefore, I think something's mind is unlimited because I do not think there is any limit with something's thoughts of something's mind for something's mind to be unlimited. I do not think there is any limit with something's thoughts of something's mind for something's mind to be unlimited because I think something's mind is infinite for something's mind to be unlimited. I think something's mind is infinite for something's mind to be unlimited because I think something is created by God being infinite for something's mind to be infinite, and therefore, I think something's mind is unlimited because I think something's mind is infinite for something's mind to be unlimited. If I think something's mind is unlimited, than I think something's mind is something's thoughts because I think something's thoughts is apart of making up something's mind for something's mind to be something's thoughts, and therefore, I think something's thoughts is overlapping, and co-existing along with something's mind because I think something's thoughts is apart of making up something's mind for something's thoughts to be overlapping, and co-existing along with something's mind.

If I think something's thoughts is overlapping, and co-existing along with something's mind, than I think something is a mind because I think something's mind is something. I think something's mind is something because I think something is something's mind. I think something is something's mind because I think something is a mind. I think something is a mind because I think something is of God's thoughts for something to be a mind. I think something is of God's thoughts for something to be a mind because I think God's thoughts is apart of making up something for something to be a mind. I think God's thoughts is apart of making up something for something to be a mind because I think something's mind is the entire area of God's thoughts that is apart of making up something, and therefore, I think something is a mind as I think everything is a mind because I think God's mind is of something for something to be a mind as I think God's mind is of everything for everything to be a mind. I think God's mind is of something for something to be a mind as I think God's mind is of everything for everything to be a mind because I think something is apart of making up God's mind for something to be a mind as I think everything is apart of making up God's mind for everything to be a mind. I think something is apart of making up God's mind for something to be a mind as I think everything is apart of making up God's mind for everything to be a mind because I think something's mind is something that is apart of making up God's mind as I think everything's mind is everything that is apart of making up God's mind. I think something's mind is something that is apart of making up God's mind as I think everything's mind is everything that is apart of making up God's mind because I think something is a mind as I think everything is a mind. I think something is a mind as I think everything is a mind because I think something is of God's thoughts for something to be a mind as I think everything is of God's thoughts for everything to be a mind. I think something is of God's thoughts for something to be a mind as I think everything is of God's thoughts for everything to be a mind because I think God's thoughts is apart of making up something for something to be a mind as I think God's thoughts is apart of making up everything for everything to be a mind. I think God's thoughts is apart of making up something for something to be a mind as I think God's thoughts is apart of making up everything for everything to be a mind because I think something's mind is the entire area of God's thoughts that is apart of making up something as I think everything's mind is the entire area of God's thoughts that is apart of making up everything, and therefore, I think someone can think of something's mind as being the dimension of something's mind because I think the dimension of something's mind is a storage area of God's thoughts that is apart of making up something. If I think someone can think of something's mind as being the dimension of something's mind, than I think of something's mind is overlapping, and co-existing along with God's mind because I think something is apart of God's mind for something to be a mind, and therefore, I think something's mind is overlapping, and co-existing along with God's thoughts because I think something's mind is all of God's thoughts that is apart of making up something. I think something's mind is all of God's thoughts that is apart of making up something because I think something is a mind as I think something is God's thoughts. I think something is a mind as I think something is God's thoughts because I think something's mind is something as I think God's thoughts is something. I think something's mind is something as I think God's thoughts is something because I think something is something's mind as I think something is God's thoughts. I think something is something's mind as I think something is God's thoughts because I think something's mind is something as I think something's mind is God's thoughts. I think something's mind is something as I think something's mind is God's thoughts because I think something is something's mind as I think God's thoughts is something's mind. I think something is something's mind as I think God's thoughts is something's mind because I think something's mind is the entire area of God's thoughts that is apart of making up something. I think something's mind is the entire area of God's thoughts that is apart of making up something because I think something is something's mind as I think something's mind is God's thoughts. I think something is something's mind as I think something's mind is God's thoughts because I think something is a mind as I think something has a mind, and therefore, I think something has a mind because I think something is a mind for something to have a mind.

If I think something has a mind, than I think something's will, and something's thoughts, and something's mind, and something's being are characteristics or features that is apart of making up the embodiment of something as I think the embodiment of something is apart of making up something because I think something is how something is able to be what something is in life as I think the embodiment of something is apart of how something is able to be what something is in life. I think something is how something is able to be what something is in life as I think the embodiment of something is apart of how something is able to be what something is in life because I think something is what something is in life as I think the embodiment of something is apart of making up what something is in life. I think something is what something is in life as I think the embodiment of something is apart of making up what something is in life because I think something is the embodiment of something as I think the embodiment of something is apart of making up something, and therefore, I think something's will, and something's thoughts, and something's mind, and something's being are all completely different characteristics or features of something because I think someone's will is what something is doing, and I think something's mind is a storage area of something's thoughts, and I think something's being is what something is in life, even though, I think something's will, and something's thoughts, and something's mind, and something's being are all completely different characteristics or features of something that is apart of making up the embodiment of something because I think something consists of something's will, and something's thoughts, and something's mind, and something's being that is apart of making up the embodiment of something. I think something consists of something's will, and something's thoughts, and something's mind, and something's being that is apart of making up the embodiment of something because I think the embodiment of something is apart of making up something, and therefore, I think something is apart of making up everything because I think everything consists of something as I think something consists of something having a will, and something having thoughts, and something having a mind, and something's being that is apart of making up something. I think everything consists of something as I think something consists of something having a will, and something having thoughts, and something having a mind, and something's being that is apart of making up something because I think something's will, and something's thoughts, and something's mind, and something's being are characteristics of something that is apart of making up the embodiment of something. I think something's will, and something's thoughts, and something's mind, and something's being are characteristics of something that is apart of making up the embodiment of something because I think someone consists of something's will, and something's thoughts, and something's mind, and something's being that is apart of making up the embodiment of something. I think someone consists of something's will, and something's thoughts, and something's mind, and something's being that is apart of making up the embodiment of something because I think the embodiment of something is apart of making up something for the embodiment of something to be apart of something. I think the embodiment of something is apart of making up something for the embodiment of something to be apart of something because I think something's will, and something's thoughts, and something's mind is taking place within something's being, without being something's being as I think something's will, and something's thoughts, and something's mind is apart of something's being, without being something's being. I think something's will, and something's thoughts, and something's mind is taking place within something's being, without being something's being as I think something's will, and something's thoughts, and something's mind is apart of something's being, without being something's being because I think something's will, and something's thoughts, and something's mind, and something's being is apart of making up the embodiment of something. I think something's will, and something's thoughts, and something's mind, and something's being is apart of making up the embodiment of something because I think the embodiment of something is apart of making up something. I think the embodiment of something is apart of making up something because I think the embodiment of something is something's will, and something's thoughts, and something's mind, and something's being that is apart of making up something. If I think the embodiment of something is apart of making up something, than I think something is exactly the same as something else because I think something has a will, and thoughts, and a mind, and a being for something to be exactly the same as something else, and therefore, I think the embodiment of something is overlapping, and co-existing along with something because I think the embodiment of something is apart of making up something. I think the embodiment of something is apart of making up something because I think the embodiment of something is something.

I think the embodiment of something is something because I think the embodiment of something consists of something's will, and something's thoughts, and something's mind, and something's being that is apart of making up something. I think the embodiment of something consists of something's will, and something's thoughts, and something's mind, and something's being that is apart of making up something because I think the embodiment of something is something as I think something is the embodiment of something. I think the embodiment of something is something as I think something is the embodiment of something because I think the embodiment of something is what something is in life, and therefore, I think something is multi-dimensional because I think something's will, and something's thoughts, and something's mind, and something's being is apart of making up the embodiment of something for something to be multi-dimensional. If I think something is multi-dimensional, than I think God created the embodiment of something with God's thoughts because I think something is of God's thoughts for God to be creating the embodiment of something with God's thoughts, and therefore, I think God created the embodiment of something because I think God created the embodiment of something with God's thoughts for God to be creating the embodiment of something. If I think God created the embodiment of something, than I think God created something to be multi-dimensional because I think God created the embodiment of something with God's thoughts for God to be creating something to be multi-dimensional, however,

I think something's will, and something's thoughts, and something's mind, and something's being is overlapping, and co-existing along with something's will, and something's thoughts, and something's mind, and something's being because I think something's will, and something's thoughts, and something's mind, and something's being is apart of making up the embodiment of something, and therefore, I think something is of the dimensions of a higher intelligent living being because I think God created something to be multi-dimensional for something to be of the dimensions of a higher intelligent living being. If I think something is of the dimensions of a higher intelligent living being, than I think the embodiment of something is infinite as I think the embodiment of something is apart of making up something because I think something is created by God being infinite for the embodiment of something to be infinite, and therefore, I think something is infinite as I think something consists of something's will, and something's thoughts, and something's mind, and something's being that is apart of making up the embodiment of something because I think something is created by God being infinite for something to be infinite. If I think something is created by God being infinite for something to be infinite, than I think something is immortal as I think something is infinite because I think something is infinite for something to be immortal. I think something is infinite for something to be immortal because I think something is infinitely immortal. I think something is infinitely immortal because I think something is created by God being infinite for something to be infinitely immortal.

If I think something is infinitely immortal, than I think something's being is how something is doing what something is doing with something's will because I think how something is able to be doing what something is able to be doing with something's being is how something is doing what something is doing with something's will, and therefore, I think something's being is how something is able to be making any choices with something's will because I think how something is able to be doing what something is able to be doing with something's being is how something is able to be making any choices with something's will. I think how something is able to be doing what something is able to be doing with something's being is how something is able to be making any choices with something's will because I think what something is doing is what something's being is doing. I think what something is doing is what something's being is doing because I think something is doing what something's being is doing. I think something is doing what something's being is doing because I think something's being is how something is able to be doing what something is able to be doing as I think something's will, and something's thoughts, and something's mind is apart of something's being. I think something's being is how something is able to be doing what something is able to be doing as I think something's will, and something's thoughts, and something's mind is apart of something's being because I think something is doing what something's being is doing with something's will, and something's thoughts, and something's mind that is apart of something's being. I think something is doing what something's being is doing with something's will, and something's thoughts, and something's mind that is apart of something's being because I think something is doing what something's being is doing as I think something's will, and something's thoughts, and something's mind is apart of something's being. I think something is doing what something's being is doing as I think something's will, and something's thoughts, and something's mind is apart of something's being because I think something's being is ultimately what makes something able to be making any choices as I think something's will, and something's thoughts, and something's mind is apart of something's being. I think something's being is ultimately what makes something able to be making any choices as I think something's will, and something's thoughts, and something's mind is apart of something's being because I think the embodiment of something consists of something having a will, and something having thoughts, and something having a mind that is apart of something's being for something's being to ultimately be able to be making any choices, and therefore, I think something's being is the thoughts of something as I think something's being is God's thoughts because I think the thoughts of something is God's thought as I think something is of God's thoughts that is apart of making up something. If I think something's being is the thoughts of something as I think something's being is God's thoughts, than I think something does what the thoughts of something is in life as I think something does what God's thoughts are in life because I think something is of the thoughts of something that is apart of making up something for something to be doing what the thoughts of something is in life as I think something is of God's thoughts that is apart of making up something for something to be doing what God's thoughts are in life, and therefore, I think God is somehow able to be responsible for how something is able to be doing what something is able to be doing because I think God created how something is in life with God's thoughts for God to somehow be able to be responsible for how something is able to be doing what something is able to be doing.

If I think God is somehow able to be responsible for how something is able to be doing what something is able to be doing, than I think God is responsible for what something is able to be doing because I think God created how something is in life with God's thoughts for something to be able to be doing what someone is able to be doing as I think God created something with God's thoughts for something to be doing what something is doing with how something is in life, but is God responsible for what something is doing? I think God is somehow able to be responsible for how something is able to be doing what something is able to be doing because I think God created something with God's thoughts for God to be able to be knowing, as to how something is in life for God to be responsible for how something is able to be doing what something is able to be doing, however, I do not think God is responsible for what something is doing because I do not think God is interfering with everything for God not to be responsible for what something is doing, and therefore, I think something is doing what something is doing because I think God created something with God's thoughts for something to be a choice with something's free will as I think something is a choice with something's free will for something to be doing what something is doing. I think God created something with God's thoughts for something to be a choice with something's free will as I think something is a choice with something's free will for something to be doing what something is doing because I think God created something with God's thoughts for something to be a choice of itself of what something is doing as I think something is a choice of itself of what something is doing for something to be doing what something is doing, and therefore, I do not think God is responsible for what something is doing because I think something is a choice of itself, as to what something is doing for God not to be responsible for what something is doing. If I do not think God is responsible for what something is doing, than I think God can be responsible for what something is doing because I think God can help someone to be doing something with something for God to be responsible for what something is doing as I think God created something to be having a will for something to be doing what something is doing, however, I do not think God is completely responsible for what something is doing because I think something is a choice of itself for something to be doing what someone is doing, and therefore, I think something is doing what something is doing because I think something is a choice of itself for something to be doing what someone is doing.

If I think something is doing what something is doing, than I think something is of the likeness of God because I think something is created by God for something to be of the likeness of God, even though, I do not think something is alike God because I do not think God is created for something not to be alike

God, however, I think something is like God because I think something has a will, and thoughts, and a mind, and a being that is apart making up the embodiment of something as I think God has a will, and thoughts, and a mind, and a being that is apart of making up the embodiment of God, but I do not think something is alike God because I do not think something has a state of consciousness as I think God has a state of consciousness, and therefore, I do not think something's will, and something's thoughts, and something's mind, and something's being that is apart of making up the embodiment of something is alike God's state of consciousness, and God's will, and God's thoughts, and God's mind, and God's being that is apart of making up the embodiment of God because I think God's state of consciousness, and God's will, and God's thoughts, and God's mind, and God's being that is apart of making up the embodiment of God is beyond something's will, and something's thoughts, and something's mind, and something's being that is apart of making up the embodiment of something. I think God's state of consciousness, and God's will, and God's thoughts, and God's mind, and God's being that is apart of making up the embodiment of God is beyond something's will, and something's thoughts, and something's mind, and something's being that is apart of making up the embodiment of something because I think something's will, and something's thoughts, and something's mind, and something's being that is apart of making up the embodiment of something is of God's state of consciousness, and God's will, and God's thoughts, and God's mind, and God's being that is apart of making up the embodiment of God for God's state of consciousness, and God's will, and God's thoughts, and God's mind, and God's being that is apart of making up the embodiment of God to be beyond something's will, and something's thoughts, and something's mind, and something's being that is apart of making up the embodiment of something. I think something's will, and something's thoughts, and something's mind, and something's being that is apart of making up the embodiment of something is of God's state of consciousness, and God's will, and God's thoughts, and God's mind, and God's being that is apart of making up the embodiment of God for God's state of consciousness, and God's will, and God's thoughts, and God's mind, and God's being that is apart of making up the embodiment of God to be beyond something's will, and something's thoughts, and something's mind, and something's being that is apart of making up the embodiment of something because I think God's state of consciousness, and God's will, and God's thoughts, and God's mind, and God's that is apart of making up the embodiment of God is apart of making up something's will, and something's thoughts, and something's mind, and something's being that is apart of making up the embodiment of something for God's state of consciousness, and God's will, and God's thoughts, and God's mind, and God's being that is apart of making up the embodiment of God to be beyond something's will, and something's thoughts, and something's mind, and something's being that is apart of making up the embodiment of something.

I think God's state of consciousness, and God's will, and God's thoughts, and God's mind, and God's that is apart of making up the embodiment of God is apart of making up something's will, and something's thoughts, and something's mind, and something's being that is apart of making up the embodiment of something for God's state of consciousness, and God's will, and God's thoughts, and God's mind, and God's being that is apart of making up the embodiment of God to be beyond something's will, and something's thoughts, and something's mind, and something's being that is apart of making up the embodiment of something because I think the embodiment of God is apart of making up the embodiment of something. I think the embodiment of God is apart of making up the embodiment of something because I think the embodiment of something is of the embodiment of God. I think the embodiment of something is of the embodiment of God because I think the embodiment of God is apart of making up something that is the embodiment of something. I think the embodiment of God is apart of making up something that is the embodiment of something because I think the embodiment of something is of God's creation for God to be creating something to be apart of the embodiment of God. I think the embodiment of something is of God's creation for God to be creating something to be apart of the embodiment of God because I think something is apart of the embodiment of God as I think the embodiment of God is apart of God. I think something is apart of the embodiment of God as I think the embodiment of God is apart of God because I think something is of God for God to be creating something to be apart of the embodiment of God. I think something is of God for God to be creating something to be apart of the embodiment of God because I think something is apart of the embodiment of God as I think something is of God. I think something is apart of the embodiment of God as I think something is of God because I think something is apart of the embodiment of God for God to be creating something to be apart of God. I think something is apart of the embodiment of God for God to be creating something to be apart of God because I think something is of the embodiment of God as I think the embodiment of something is of God. I think something is of the embodiment of God as I think the embodiment of something is of God because I think something is of the embodiment of God for something to be of God. I think something is of the embodiment of God for something to be of God because I think something is of God as I think the embodiment of God is apart of God. I think something is of God as I think the embodiment of God is apart of God because I think the embodiment of something is of God for something to be of God. I think the embodiment of something is of God for something to be of God because I think the embodiment of God is apart of God for God to be creating something to be apart of God. I think the embodiment of God is apart of God for God to be creating something to be apart of God because I think something is of the embodiment of God for God to be creating something to be apart of God. I think something is of the embodiment of God for God to be creating something to be apart of God because I think something is of the embodiment of God as I think something is of God. I think something is of the embodiment of God as I think something is of God because I think something is of God for something to be of the embodiment of God. I think something is of God for something to be of the embodiment of God because I think something is of God for something to be apart of the embodiment of God. I think something is of God for something to be apart of the embodiment of God because I think something is apart of the embodiment of God as I think something is apart of God. I think something is apart of the embodiment of God as I think something is apart of God because I think something is of God's creation for God to be creating something to be apart of God.

If I think something is apart of the embodiment of God as I think something is apart of God, than I think something is overlapping, and co-existing along with God because I think something is of the embodiment of God for God to be creating something to be apart of God. I think something is of the embodiment of God for God to be creating something to be apart of God because I think the embodiment of something is overlapping, and co-existing along with the embodiment of God. I think the embodiment of something is overlapping, and co-existing along with the embodiment of God because I think something is the embodiment of something that is overlapping, and co-existing along with the embodiment of God that is apart of God. I think something is the embodiment of something that is overlapping, and co-existing along with the embodiment of God that is apart of God because I think something is overlapping, and co-existing along with the embodiment of God. I think something is overlapping, and co-existing along with the embodiment of God because I think something is of God's creation for God to be creating something to be apart of the embodiment of God. I think something is of

God's creation for God to be creating something to be apart of the embodiment of God because I think something is of the embodiment of God for something to be of God. I think something is of the embodiment of God for something to be of God because I think something is of God's creation for God to be creating something to be apart of God. I think something is of God's creation for God to be creating something to be apart of God because I think something is the embodiment of something that is of the embodiment of God for something to be apart of God. I think something is the embodiment of something that is of the embodiment of God for something to be apart of God because I think the embodiment of something is of God for the embodiment of something to be of the embodiment of God. I think the embodiment of something is of God for the embodiment of something to be of the embodiment of God because I think the embodiment of something is of God for the embodiment of something to be apart of God. I think the embodiment of something is of God for the embodiment of something to be apart of God because I think the embodiment of something is something as I think something is of God for something to be apart of God. I think the embodiment of something is something as I think something is of God for something to be apart of God because I think the embodiment of something is what something is in life as I think something is of God's creation for something to be what something is in life. I think the embodiment of something is what something is in life as I think something is of God's creation for something to be what something is in life because I think the embodiment of something is of the dimension of something as I think something is the dimension of something for the embodiment of something to be something.

Chapter 14

The embodiment of everything

    I would like to talk about how dimensions are in life in relation to what dimensions are in life by talking about the embodiment of everything, that can possibly have something to do with how dimensions are in life is in relation to what dimensions are in life because I think the embodiment of everything is of the dimension of life as I think everything is the dimension of life for the embodiment of everything to be everything, and therefore, I think everything is a choice because I think everything has a choice. I think everything has a choice because I think everything is a choice for everything to have a choice. I think everything is a choice for everything to have a choice because I think everything is a choice of itself for everything to have a choice. I think everything is a choice of itself for everything to have a choice because I think everything is a choice of itself of what everything is doing. I think everything is a choice of itself of what everything is doing because I think everything has a choice. If I think everything is a choice of itself of what everything is doing, than I think everything is in motion because I think everything is a choice for everything to be in motion as I think everything is a choice of itself of what everything is doing for everything to be in motion, and therefore, I think everything has a choice because I think everything consists of someone, and something that has a choice for everything to be having a choice.

    If I think everything has a choice, than I think everything has a will as I think everything has a choice because I think everything is a choice of itself of what everything is doing for everything to have a will as I think everything is a choice of itself of what everything is doing for everything to have a choice. I think everything is a choice of itself of what everything is doing for everything to have a will as I think everything is a choice of itself of what everything is doing for everything to have a choice because I think everything has a will for everything to have a choice. I think everything has a will for everything to have a choice because I do not think everything would have a choice, if everything doesn't have a will. I do not think everything would have a choice, if everything doesn't have a will because I do not think everything would be a choice of itself of what everything is doing, if everything doesn't have a will for everything to be a choice of itself of what everything is doing, but I think everything has a will for everything to be a choice of itself of what everything is doing because I think everything is a choice of itself of what everything is doing, and therefore, I think everything has a will as I think everything has a choice because I think everything has a will for everything to be a choice of itself of what everything is doing. I think everything has a will for everything to be a choice of itself of what everything is doing because I think everything's will is everything's choice. I think everything's will is everything's choice because I think everything has a will as I think everything has a choice. I think everything has a will as I think everything has a choice because I think everything is a choice of itself for everything to have a will as I think everything is a choice of itself for everything to have a choice. I think everything is a choice of itself for everything to have a will as I think everything is a choice of itself for everything to have a choice because I think everything is a choice as I think everything has a choice. I think everything is a choice as I think everything has a choice because I think everything is a choice as I think everything has a will. I think everything is a choice as I think everything has a will because I think everything has a will as I think everything has a choice, and therefore, I think everything has a will because I think everything is constantly in motion for everything to have a will. I think everything is constantly in motion for everything to have a will because I think everything is a choice of itself of what everything is doing for everything to have a will. I think everything is a choice of itself of what everything is doing for everything to have a will because I think everything has a will. I think everything has a will because I think everything consists of someone, and something that has a will for everything to be having a will, and therefore, I think everything's will is what everything does as I think what everything does is everything's will because I think everything has a will for what everything does. If I think everything has a will for what everything does, than I do not think something is motionless because I think everything is affecting everything for everything to be in motion as I think everything is in motion for something not to be motionless, and therefore, I think everything is constantly in motion because I think everything has a will for everything to be constantly in motion. If I think everything is constantly in motion, than I think someone can think of all kinds of different words for someone to be describing what someone thinks everything's will is in life because I think everything has will for someone to be thinking of all kinds of different words for someone to be describing what someone thinks everything's will is in life, and therefore, I think everything has a will because I think everything's will is what everything is doing as I think everything's will is what everything does. If I think everything has a will, than I think someone can think of all kinds of words for someone to be describing what someone thinks what everything can do because I think everything has will for someone to be thinking of all kinds of different words for someone to be describing what someone thinks what everything can do, and therefore, I think everything that everything does is everything's will as I think everything that everything does is everything's choice because I think everything's will is everything's choice for everything to be doing everything that everything does.

If I think everything that everything does is everything's will as I think everything that everything does is everything's choice, than I think everything's will is God's thoughts because I think God's thoughts has a will as I think everything has a will. I think God's thoughts has a will as I think everything has a will because I think everything is of God's thoughts for God's thoughts to be having a will as I think everything is of God's thoughts for everything to be having a will. I think everything is of God's thoughts for God's thoughts to be having a will as I think everything is of God's thoughts for everything to be having a will because I think God's thoughts is apart of making up everything for God's thoughts to be having a will as I think God's thoughts is apart of making up everything for everything to be having a will. I think God's thoughts is apart of making up everything for God's thoughts to be having a will as I think God's thoughts is apart of making up everything for everything to be having a will because I think God's thoughts has a will for God's thoughts to be having a will as I think God's thoughts has a will for everything to be having a will. I think God's thoughts has a will for God's thoughts to be having a will as I think God's thoughts has a will for everything to be having a will because I think everything has a will for God's thoughts to be having a will as I think everything has a will for everything to be having a will. I think everything has a will for God's thoughts to be having a will as I think everything has a will for everything to be having a will because I think God's thoughts has a will as I think everything has a will. I think God's thoughts has a will as I think everything has a will because I think God's thoughts has a choice for God's thoughts to be having a will as I think God's thoughts has a choice for everything to be having a will. I think God's thoughts has a choice for God's thoughts to be having a will as I think God's thoughts has a choice for everything to be having a will because I think God's thoughts has a choice for God's thoughts to be having a will as I think everything has a choice for everything to be having a will. I think God's thoughts has a choice for God's thoughts to be having a will as I think everything has a choice for everything to be having a will because I think God's thoughts has a choice as I think everything has a will. I think God's thoughts has a choice as I think everything has a will because I think God's thoughts has a will for God's thoughts to be having a choice as I think God's thoughts has a will for everything to be having a choice. I think God's thoughts has a will for God's thoughts to be having a choice as I think God's thoughts has a will for everything to be having a choice because I think everything has a will for God's thoughts to be having a choice as I think everything has a will for everything to be having a choice. I think everything has a will for God's thoughts to be having a choice as I think everything has a will for everything to be having a choice because I think God's thoughts has a choice as I think everything has a choice.

I think God's thoughts has a choice as I think everything has a choice because I think God's thoughts has a choice for God's thoughts to be having a choice as I think God's thoughts has a choice for everything to be having a choice. I think God's thoughts has a choice for God's thoughts to be having a choice as I think God's thoughts has a choice for everything to be having a choice because I think everything has a choice for God's thoughts to be having a choice as I think everything has a choice for everything to be having a choice. I think everything has a choice for God's thoughts to be having a choice as I think everything has a choice for everything to be having a choice because I think God's thoughts is apart of making up everything for everything to be having a choice. I think God's thoughts is apart of making up everything for everything to be having a choice because I think God's thoughts is a choice of itself for God's thoughts to be having a choice as I think everything is a choice of itself for everything to be having a choice. I think God's thoughts is a choice of itself for God's thoughts to be having a choice as I think everything is a choice of itself for everything to be having a choice because I think everything is a choice of itself for God's thoughts to be having a choice as I think everything is a choice of itself for everything to be having a choice. I think everything is a choice of itself for God's thoughts to be having a choice as I think everything is a choice of itself for everything to be having a choice because I think God's thoughts is apart of making up everything for everything to be a choice of itself. I think God's thoughts is apart of making up everything for everything to be a choice of itself because I think God's thoughts is a choice for God's thoughts to be a choice of itself as I think everything is a choice for everything to be a choice of itself. I think God's thoughts is a choice for God's thoughts to be a choice of itself as I think everything is a choice for everything to be a choice of itself because I think everything is a choice for God's thoughts to be a choice of itself as I think everything is a choice for everything to be a choice of itself. I think everything is a choice for God's thoughts to be a choice of itself as I think everything is a choice for everything to be a choice of itself because I think God's thoughts is apart of making up everything for everything to be a choice.

I think God's thoughts is apart of making up everything for everything to be a choice because I think God's thoughts is a choice as I think everything is a choice. I think God's thoughts is a choice as I think everything is a choice because I think God's thoughts has a choice as I think everything has a choice. I think God's thoughts has a choice as I think everything has a choice because I think God's thoughts is a choice for God's thoughts to be having a choice as I think everything is a choice for everything to be having a choice. I think God's thoughts is a choice for God's thoughts to be having a choice as I think everything is a choice for everything to be having a choice because I think God's thoughts is a choice of itself for God's thoughts to be having a choice as I think everything is a choice of itself for everything to be having a choice. I think God's thoughts is a choice of itself for God's thoughts to be having a choice as I think everything is a choice of itself for everything to be having a choice because I think God's thoughts is apart of making up everything for everything to be having a choice. I think God's thoughts is apart of making up everything for everything to be having a choice because I think everything consists of God's thoughts, and someone, and something that has a choice for everything to be having a choice. I think everything consists of God's thoughts, and someone, and something that has a choice for everything to be having a choice because I think God's thoughts is apart of making up everything that has a choice as I think God's thoughts is apart of making up everything. I think God's thoughts is apart of making up everything that has a choice as I think God's thoughts is apart of making up everything because I think God's thoughts has a choice as I think God's thoughts is apart of making up everything that has a choice. I think God's thoughts has a choice as I think God's thoughts is apart of making up everything that has a choice because I think God's thoughts has a choice as I think everything has a choice. I think God's thoughts has a choice as I think everything has a choice because I think God's thoughts is created by God for God's thoughts to have a choice as I think everything is created by God for everything to have a choice. I think God's thoughts is created by God for God's thoughts to have a choice as I think everything is created by God for everything to have a choice because I think God's thoughts is apart of making up everything as I think everything has a choice of what everything is doing. I think God's thoughts is apart of making up everything as I think everything has a choice of what everything is doing because I think everything is a choice of itself of what everything is doing. I think everything is a choice of itself of what everything is doing because I think everything has a will for everything to be a choice of itself of what everything is doing as I think everything has a choice for everything to be a choice of itself of what everything is doing. I think everything has a will for everything to be a choice of itself of what everything is doing as I think everything has a choice for everything to be a choice of itself of what everything is doing because I think everything has a will as I think everything has a choice. I think everything has a will as I think everything has a choice because I think everything's will is everything's choice for everything to be having a will, and therefore, I think everything in motion because I think everything has a will for everything to be in motion. If I think everything has a will for everything to be in motion, than I think God created everything to be having a will because I think God's thoughts is apart of making up everything for God to be creating everything to be having a will with God's thoughts, and therefore, I think God created everything to be in motion because I think God created everything to be having a will with God's thoughts for everything to be in motion. If I think God created everything to be in motion, than I think God created someone, and something to be having a will as I think God created everything to be having a will because I think God's thoughts is apart of making up someone, and something for God to be creating someone, and something to be having a will with God's thoughts as I think God's thoughts is apart of making up everything for God to be creating everything to be having a will with God's thoughts, and therefore, I think God created someone, and something to be in motion as I think God created everything to be in motion because I think God created someone, and something to be having a will with God's thoughts for someone, and something to be in motion as I think God created everything to be having a will with God's thoughts for everything to be in motion. If I think God created everything to be in motion, than I think God created God's thoughts to be in motion as I think God created everything to be in motion because I think God created everything to be having a will with God's thoughts for God's thoughts to be in motion as I think God created everything to be having a will with God's thoughts for everything to be in motion, and therefore, I think God's thoughts is in motion as I think everything is in motion because I think God created everything to be having a will with God's thoughts for God's thoughts to be in motion as I think God created everything to be having a will with God's thoughts for everything to be in motion.

If I think God's thoughts is in motion as I think everything is in motion, than I think everything's will is like God's will because I think everything's will is how everything is doing what everything is doing as I think God's will is how God is doing what God is doing. I think everything's will is how everything is doing what everything is doing as I think God's will is how God is doing what God is doing because I think everything's will is what everything is doing as I think God's will is what God is doing, and therefore, I think everything's will is like God's will because I think everything is created by God for everything to have a will. I think everything is created by God for everything to have a will because I think God created everything to have a will for everything to be doing what everything is doing. I think God created everything to have a will for everything to be doing what everything is doing because I think everything's will is everything's choice. I think everything's will is everything's choice because I think everything's choice is God's choice for everything to have a choice. I think everything's choice is God's choice for everything to have a choice because I think everything is created by God for everything to have a choice. I think everything is created by God for everything to have a choice because I think everything's choice is everything's will. I think everything's choice is everything's will because I think everything's choice is what everything is doing as I think everything's will is what everything is doing. I think everything's choice is what everything is doing as I think everything's will is what everything is doing because I think everything's choice is everything's will as I think everything's will is everything's choice. I think everything's choice is everything's will as I think everything's will is everything's choice because I think everything has a will as I think everything has a choice. I think everything has a will as I think everything has a choice because I think everything has everything's free will. I think everything has everything's free will because I think everything has a will for everything to be having everything's free will. I think everything has a will for everything to be having everything's free will because I think everything has everything's free will with everything being a choice of itself of what everything is doing. I think everything has everything's free will with everything being a choice of itself of what everything is doing because I think everything has a choice, however, I do not think everything has a state of consciousness as I think everything has a will because I do not think everything has a state of consciousness for everything's will. I do not think everything has a state of consciousness for everything's will because I think everything consists of something that doesn't have a state of consciousness for everything not to be having a state of consciousness, and therefore, I do not think God's thoughts has a state of consciousness as I do not think everything has a state of consciousness because I think God's thoughts is apart of making up something that doesn't have a state of consciousness for God's thoughts not to be having a state of consciousness as I think everything is of something that doesn't have a state of consciousness for everything not to be having a state of consciousness.

If I do not think God's thoughts has a state of consciousness as I do not think everything has a state of consciousness, than I think God's thoughts can have a state of consciousness because I think God created someone with God's thoughts for God to be creating someone to be having a state of consciousness with God's thoughts as I think God created someone to be having a state of consciousness with God's thoughts for God's thought to be having a state of consciousness, and therefore, I think God's thoughts is overlapping, and co-existing along with someone's state of consciousness because I think God created someone to be having a state of consciousness with God's thoughts for God's thought to be overlapping, and co-existing along with someone's state of consciousness. If I think God's thoughts is overlapping, and co-existing along with someone's state of consciousness, than I think something can have a state of consciousness because

I think God created someone to be having a state of consciousness with God's thoughts as I think God's thoughts is something for something to be having a state of consciousness, and therefore, I think something is overlapping, and co-existing along with God's thoughts as I think something is overlapping, and co-existing along with someone's state of consciousness because I think God created someone to be having a state of consciousness with God's thoughts for something to be overlapping, and co-existing along with God's thoughts as I think God created someone to be having a state of consciousness with God's thoughts for something to be overlapping, and co-existing along with someone's state of consciousness, even though, I do not think something has a state of consciousness because I think God's thoughts is apart of making up something that doesn't have a state of consciousness for something not to be having a state of consciousness.

If I do not think something has a state of consciousness, than I think God has a will, and a state of consciousness because I think God could have possibly created God's will, and God's state of consciousness with God's thoughts for God to be having a will, and a state of consciousness, even though, I do not know if God created God's will, and God's state of consciousness with God's thoughts for God to be having a will, and a state of consciousness because I think God's will, and God's state of consciousness could possibly not have been created as I do not think God is created for God to be having a will, and a state of consciousness, and therefore, I think God's will, and God's state of consciousness could possibly not have been created by God for God's will, and God's state of consciousness to be apart of God because I think God's will, and God's state of consciousness could possibly not have been created as I do not think God is created for God's will, and God's state of consciousness to be apart of God. If I think God's will, and God's state of consciousness could possibly not have been created by God for God's will, and God's state of consciousness to be apart of God, than I do not think God's state of consciousness, and God's will is created because I do not think God created God's state of consciousness, and God's will with God's thoughts for God's state of consciousness, and God's will not to be created, and therefore, I do not think God created God's state of consciousness, and God's will because I do not think God created God's state of consciousness, and God's will with God's thoughts for God's state of consciousness, and God's will not to be created. If I do not think God created God's state of consciousness, and God's will, than I think God's state of consciousness, and God's will is something as I think God's state of consciousness, and God's will is nothing because I think God's state of consciousness, and God's will is apart of God for God's state of consciousness, and God's will to be something as I do not think God's state of consciousness, and God's will is created for God's state of consciousness, and God's will to be nothing, and therefore, I think God's state of consciousness, God's will, and God is in the exact same single dimension of God because I do not think God, God's state of consciousness, and God's will is created as I think God's state of consciousness, and God's will is apart of God for God's state of consciousness, and God's will to be in the exact same single dimension of God. If I think God's state of consciousness, God's will, and God is in the exact same single dimension of God, than I think everything is a thought because I think God created everything with God's thoughts for everything to be a thought, and therefore, I think God created God's thoughts for God to be creating everything with God's thoughts as I think God created God's thoughts for God to be creating everything to be a thought because I think God created God's thoughts with God's state of consciousness, and God's will, without God, God's state of consciousness, and God's will being created for God to be creating everything with God's thoughts as I think God created God's thoughts with God's state of consciousness, and God's will, without God, God's state of consciousness, and God's will being created for God to be creating everything to be a thought, even though, I do not think someone can possibly be able to be knowing for themselves, as to how God created God's thoughts for God to be creating everything to be a thought because I think God created God's thoughts with God's state of consciousness, and God's will, without God, God's state of consciousness, and God's will being created for God to be creating everything to be a thought. If I do not think someone can possibly be able to be knowing for themselves, as to how God created God's thoughts for God to be creating everything to be a thought, than I think everything is a thought, except God, God's state of consciousness, and God's will because I think God created everything with God's thoughts, without God, God's state of consciousness, and God's will being created for everything to be a thought, and therefore, I think everything is created, except God, God's state of consciousness, and God's will because I think God created everything with God's thoughts, without God, God's state of consciousness, and God's will being created for everything to be created.

If I think everything is created, except God, God's state of consciousness, and God's will, than I think everything has a will because I think everything's will is how everything is doing what everything is doing. I think everything's will is how everything is doing what everything is doing because I think what everything is doing is how everything is doing what everything is doing. I think what everything is doing is how everything is doing what everything is doing because I think everything has a will. I think everything has a will because I think everything's will is what everything is doing, and therefore, I think everything has a will as I think God has a will because I think everything's will is what everything is doing as I think God's will is what God is doing. If I think everything has a will as I think God has a will, than I think everything's will is what everything is doing because I think what everything is doing is how everything is doing what everything is doing. I think what everything is doing is how everything is doing what everything is doing because I think everything's will is a dimension. I think everything's will is a dimension because I think everything's will is something for everything's will to be a dimension. I think everything's will is something for everything's will to be a dimension because I think everything's will is what everything is doing. I think everything's will is what everything is doing because I think everything has a will as I think everything's will is a dimension, and therefore, I think someone can think of everything's will as being the dimension of everything's will because I think the dimension of everything's will is what everything is doing. If I think someone can think of everything's will as being the dimension of everything's will, than I think someone can think of the dimension of everything's will as being the dimension of life's will or as being life's will because I think the dimension of life's will is life's will as I think life's will is everything that has a will. I think the dimension of life's will is life's will as I think life's will is everything that has a will because I think life's will is everything's will as I think everything has a will, and therefore, I think life has a will because I think life's will is everything's will as I think everything has a will. If I think life has a will, than I think everything is a choice for everything to be doing something with someone, something, and God because I think everything has a will for everything to be doing something with someone, something, and God, and therefore, I think everything has a will because I think everything can do something with someone, something, and God for everything to be having a will.

If I think everything has a will, than I think everything is everything's being because I think everything's being is everything. I think everything's being is everything because I think everything's being is how everything is able to be what everything is in life. I think everything's being is how everything is able to be what everything is in life because I think everything's being is the very existence of what everything is in life. I think everything's being is the very existence of what everything is in life because

I think the being of what everything is in life is the very existence of what everything is in life. I think the being of what everything is in life is the very existence of what everything is in life because I think everything's being is how everything is able to be what everything is in life as I think everything's being is the very existence of what everything is in life. I think everything's being is how everything is able to be what everything is in life as I think everything's being is the very existence of what everything is in life because I think everything's being is what everything is in life, and therefore, I think everything is a being as I think God is a being because I think everything is of God's being for everything to be a being. I think everything is of God's being for everything to be a being because I think everything's being is the very existence of what everything is in life as I think God's being is the very existence of what God is in life. I think everything's being is the very existence of what everything is in life as I think God's being is the very existence of what God is in life because I think everything is of the very existence of what God is in life for everything to be of the very existence of what everything is in life, and therefore, I think everything's being is a dimension because I think everything's being is something for everything's being to be a dimension. I think everything's being is something for everything's being to be a dimension because I think everything's being is how everything is able to be what everything is in life. I think everything's being is how everything is able to be what everything is in life because I think everything's being is everything as I think everything's being is what everything is in life, and therefore, I think someone can think of everything's being as being the dimension of everything's being because I think the dimension of everything's being is what everything is in life. If I think someone can think of everything's being as being the dimension of everything's being, than I think the dimension of everything's being is what everything is in life because I think everything is everything's being. I think everything is everything's being because I think God created everything's being for everything to be what everything is in life, and therefore, I think someone can think of the dimension of everything's being as being the dimension of everything because I think everything is everything's being as I think everything is what everything's being is in life. If I think someone can think of the dimension of everything's being as being the dimension of everything, than I think someone can think of the dimension of everything as being the dimension of life because I think life is everything, and therefore, I think everything's being is whatever everything's being is in life because I think everything's being is what everything's being is in life as I think what everything's being is in life is whatever everything's being is in life. I think everything's being is what everything's being is in life as I think what everything's being is in life is whatever everything's being is in life because I think everything is of God's thoughts for everything's being to be whatever everything's being is in life. I think everything is of God's thoughts for everything's being to be whatever everything's being is in life because I think everything's being is the being of God's thoughts as I think the being of God's thoughts is the being of everything.

If I think everything is of God's thoughts for everything's being to be whatever everything's being is in life, than I think everything's will comes from everything's being, but I do not think everything's will is everything's being because I think everything's will is what everything is doing in life, and I think everything's being is what everything is in life. I think everything's will is what everything is doing in life, and I think everything's being is what everything is in life because I think everything's will is everything having a choice of what everything is doing in life. I think everything's will is everything having a choice of what everything is doing in life because I do not think everything would be able to be doing anything without everything having a will. I do not think everything would be able to be doing anything without everything having a will because I think everything not having a will is like everything not being able to move, even though, I think everything is able to move because I think everything has a will for everything to be able to move, and therefore, I think everything has a will because I think everything's will is everything having a choice of what everything is doing. If I think everything has a will, than I think everything has a will for everything's being because I do not think everything would be able to be doing anything without everything having a will, and therefore, I think everything has a will for everything's being because I think everything has a will for what everything is doing with everything's being. I think everything has a will for what everything is doing with everything's being because I think everything has a will for everything to be having a choice of what everything is doing in life. I think everything has a will for everything to be having a choice of what everything is doing in life because I think everything's will is everything having a choice of what everything is doing in life, and therefore, I think everything's will is overlapping, and co-existing along with everything because I think everything's will is everything having a choice of what everything is doing in life. If I think everything's will is overlapping, and co-existing along with everything, than I think everything's will is overlapping, and co-existing along with God's thoughts because I think God's thoughts is apart of making up everything that has a choice.

If I think everything's will is overlapping, and co-existing along with God's thoughts, than I think everything has thoughts because I think everything is of the thoughts of everything for everything to have thoughts. I think everything is of the thoughts of everything for everything to have thoughts because I think everything is the thoughts of everything. I think everything is the thoughts of everything because I think everything is everything's thoughts as I think everything's thoughts is the thoughts of everything. I think everything is the thoughts of everything because I think everything is everything's thoughts as I think everything's thoughts is the thoughts of everything because I think everything is the thoughts of everything as I think the thoughts of everything is everything's thoughts. I think everything is the thoughts of everything as I think the thoughts of everything is everything's thoughts because I think everything is the thoughts of everything as I think everything is everything's thoughts. I think everything is the thoughts of everything as I think everything is everything's thoughts because I think everything is of the thoughts of everything for everything to be the thoughts of everything. I think everything is of the thoughts of everything for everything to be the thoughts of everything because I think the thoughts of everything is apart of making up everything for everything to be the thoughts of everything. I think the thoughts of everything is apart of making up everything for everything to be the thoughts of everything because I think everything is of the thoughts of everything for everything to be everything. I think everything is of the thoughts of everything for everything to be everything because I think the thoughts of everything is apart of making up everything for everything to be everything. I think the thoughts of everything is apart of making up everything for everything to be everything because I think everything is the thoughts of everything for everything to be everything.

I think everything is the thoughts of everything for everything to be everything because I think the thoughts of everything is of God's thoughts for everything to be everything. I think the thoughts of everything is of God's thoughts for everything to be everything because I think everything is of the thoughts of everything as I think God's thoughts is the thoughts of everything. I think everything is of the thoughts of everything as I think God's thoughts is the thoughts of everything because I think everything is of God's thoughts as I think the thoughts of everything is of God's thoughts. I think everything is of God's thoughts as I think the thoughts of everything is of God's thoughts because I think God's thoughts is the thoughts of everything as I think everything is of God's thoughts. I think God's thoughts is the thoughts of everything as I think everything is of God's thoughts because I think everything is God's thoughts. I think everything is God's thoughts because I think everything has thoughts. I think everything has thoughts because I think God's thoughts is apart of making up everything for everything to have thoughts, and therefore, I think everything has thoughts as I think God has thoughts because I think God's thoughts is apart of making up everything for everything to have thoughts as I think God's thoughts is apart of making up everything for God to have thoughts. I think God's thoughts is apart of making up everything for everything to have thoughts as I think God's thoughts is apart of making up everything for God to have thoughts because I think everything is God's thoughts. I think everything is God's thoughts because I think everything is of God's thoughts for everything to be God's thoughts. I think everything is of God's thoughts for everything to be God's thoughts because I think God's thoughts is apart of making up everything for everything to be God's thoughts. I think God's thoughts is apart of making up everything for everything to be God's thoughts because I think everything is of God's thoughts for everything to be everything. I think everything is of God's thoughts for everything to be everything because I think God's thoughts is apart of making up everything for everything to be everything. I think God's thoughts is apart of making up everything for everything to be everything because I think everything is God's thoughts for everything to be everything.

If I think God's thoughts is apart of making up everything for everything to be everything, than I think everything will do what everything does because I think everything will do what everything does with everything's will for everything to do what everything does. I think everything will do what everything does with everything's will for everything to do what everything does because I think everything will do what everything does with everything's thoughts for everything to do what everything does with everything's will as I think everything will do what everything does with the thoughts of everything for everything to do what everything does with everything's will. I think everything will do what everything does with everything's thoughts for everything to do what everything does with everything's will as I think everything will do what everything does with the thoughts of everything for everything to do what everything does with everything's will because I think everything's thoughts is the thoughts of everything as I think everything will do what everything does with everything's thoughts for everything to do what everything does with everything's will. I think everything's thoughts is the thoughts of everything as I think everything will do what everything does with everything's thoughts for everything to do what everything does with everything's will because I think everything's thoughts is the thoughts of everything for everything to do what everything does with everything's will. I think everything's thoughts is the thoughts of everything for everything to do what everything does with everything's will because I think everything is of the thoughts of everything for everything to do what everything does with everything's will. I think everything is of the thoughts of everything for everything to do what everything does with everything's will because I think everything's thoughts is of God's thoughts for everything to do what everything does with everything's will. I think everything's thoughts is of God's thoughts for everything to do what everything does with everything's will because I think everything will do what everything does with God's thoughts for everything to do what everything does with everything's will. I think everything will do what everything does with God's thoughts for everything to do what everything does with everything's will because I think everything is of God's thoughts for everything to do what everything does with everything's will.

If I think everything will do what everything does with God's thoughts for everything to do what everything does with everything's will, than I think everything is God's thoughts for everything to be everything because I think everything is the being of God's thoughts as I think everything's being is the being of God's thoughts. I think everything is the being of God's thoughts as I think everything's being is the being of God's thoughts because I think everything is everything's being as I think everything is of God's thoughts for everything to be the being of God's thoughts. I think everything is everything's being as I think everything is of God's thoughts for everything to be the being of God's thoughts because I think everything is of God's thoughts for everything to be whatever everything is in life. I think everything is of God's thoughts for everything to be whatever everything is in life because I think God's thoughts is whatever God's thoughts are in life that is apart of making up everything for everything to be whatever everything is in life. I think God's thoughts is whatever God's thoughts are in life that is apart of making up everything for everything to be whatever everything is in life because I think everything is God's thoughts for everything to be everything. I think everything is God's thoughts for everything to be everything because I think everything is of God's thoughts with how everything is able to be what everything is in life, and therefore, I think everything is of God's thoughts with what everything is in life as I think everything is of God's thoughts with how everything is able to be what everything is in life because I think what everything is in life is how everything is able to be what everything is in life. If I think what everything is in life is how everything is able to be what everything is in life, than I think everything is of God's thoughts with how everything is able to be what everything is in life because I think God's thoughts is apart of making up how everything is able to be what everything is in life. I think God's thoughts is apart of making up how everything is able to be what everything is in life because I think everything is God's thoughts with how everything is able to be what everything is in life, and therefore, I think everything's being is God's thoughts as I think everything is God's thoughts because I think everything is everything's being as I think everything is of God's thoughts with how everything is able to be what everything is in life. If I think everything's being is God's thoughts as I think everything is God's thoughts, than I think everything's being is overlapping, and co-existing along with God's thoughts because I think God's thoughts is apart of making up how everything is able to be what everything is in life as I think everything's being is how everything is able to be what everything is in life.

If I think everything's being is overlapping, and co-existing along with God's thoughts, than I think everything's will is God's thoughts as I think everything is God's thoughts because I think everything's will is of God's thoughts with what everything is doing as I think everything is of God's thoughts with how everything is able to be what everything is in life. I think everything's will is of God's thoughts with what everything is doing as I think everything is of God's thoughts with how everything is able to be what everything is in life because I think God's thoughts is apart of making up everything's will for everything to be doing what everything is doing as I think God's thoughts is apart of making up everything for everything to be what everything is in life. I think God's thoughts is apart of making up everything's will for everything to be doing what everything is doing as I think God's thoughts is apart of making up everything for everything to be what everything is in life because I think everything's will is God's thoughts with what everything is doing as I think everything is God's thoughts with how everything is able to be what everything is in life, and therefore, I think everything's will is overlapping, and co-existing along with God's thoughts because I think God's thoughts is apart of making up everything's will for everything to be doing what everything is doing. If I think everything's will is overlapping, and co-existing along with God's thoughts, than I think everything will do what everything does with everything's will because I think everything will do what everything does with everything's being for everything to do what everything does with everything's will. I think everything will do what everything does with everything's being for everything to do what everything does with everything's will because I think everything's being is what everything does with everything's will. I think everything's being is what everything does with everything's will because I think what everything is in life is what everything does as I think what everything is in life is what everything does with everything's will. I think what everything is in life is what everything does as I think what everything is in life is what everything does with everything's will because I think everything's being is of God's thoughts for everything to be doing what everything does with everything's will. I think everything's being is of God's thoughts for everything to be doing what everything does with everything's will because I think everything is of God's thoughts for everything to be what everything is in life as I think everything is of God's thoughts for everything to be doing what everything is doing with everything's will, and therefore, I think God is the greatest programmer because I think everything is of God's thoughts for everything to be doing what everything is doing in life.

If I think God is the greatest programmer, than I think everything has a mind because I think everything's mind is a storage area of everything. I think everything's mind is a storage area of everything because I think everything's mind is a storage area of everything's thoughts for everything's mind to be a storage area of everything. I think everything's mind is a storage area of everything's thoughts for everything's mind to be a storage area of everything because I think everything is a storage area of God's thoughts as I think everything's mind is a storage area of everything's thoughts. I think everything is a storage area of God's thoughts as I think everything's mind is a storage area of everything's thoughts because I think everything's mind is a storage area of God's thoughts for everything's mind to be a storage area of everything. I think everything's mind is a storage area of God's thoughts for everything's mind to be a storage area of everything because I think everything has a mind. I think everything has a mind because I think everything's mind is the entire area of God's thoughts that is apart of making up everything, and therefore, I think everything has a mind as I think God has a mind because I think everything's mind is the entire area of God's thoughts that is apart of making up everything as I think God's mind is the entire area of God's thoughts that is apart of making up everything. If I think everything has a mind as I think God has a mind, than I think everything's mind is like God's mind because I think everything's mind is a storage area of God's thoughts as I think God's mind is a storage area of God's thoughts, and therefore, I think everything's mind alike God's mind because I think everything's mind is the entire area of God's thoughts that is apart of making up everything as I think God's mind is the entire area of God's thoughts that is apart of making up everything. I think everything's mind is the entire area of God's thoughts that is apart of making up everything as I think God's mind is the entire area of God's thoughts that is apart of making up everything because I think everything's mind is God's mind. I think everything's mind is God's mind because I think everything's mind is a storage area of God's thoughts that is apart of making up everything as I think God's mind is a storage area of God's thoughts that is apart of making up everything. I think everything's mind is a storage area of God's thoughts that is apart of making up everything as I think God's mind is a storage area of God's thoughts that is apart of making up everything because I think God's mind is everything as I think everything's mind is the entire area of God's thoughts that is apart of making up everything. I think God's mind is everything as I think everything's mind is the entire area of God's thoughts that is apart of making up everything because I think everything's mind is all of God's thoughts that is apart of making up everything. I think everything's mind is all of God's thoughts that is apart of making up everything because I think everything's mind is all of God's thoughts that is apart of making up how everything is able to be what everything is in life with everything's being as I think everything's mind is all of God's thoughts that is apart of making up how everything is able to be doing what everything is doing with everything's will, and therefore, I think everything's mind is God's thoughts as I think everything's mind is everything's thoughts because I think everything's thoughts is God's thoughts as I think everything's mind is of God's thoughts that is apart of making up everything's mind. If I think everything's mind is God's thoughts as I think everything's mind is everything's thoughts, than I think everything's mind is unlimited in size because I think God can still be adding more of God's thoughts into everything's mind, that can be apart of making up how everything is able to be what everything is in life with everything's being, and I think God can still be adding more of God's thoughts into everything's mind, that can be apart of making up how everything is doing what everything is doing with everything's will, and therefore, I think everything's mind is unlimited because I do not think there is any limit with everything's thoughts of everything's mind for everything's mind to be unlimited. I do not think there is any limit with everything's thoughts of everything's mind for everything's mind to be unlimited because I think everything's mind is infinite for everything's mind to be unlimited. I think everything's mind is infinite for everything's mind to be unlimited because I think everything is created by God being infinite for everything's mind to be infinite, and therefore, I think everything's mind is unlimited because I think everything's mind is infinite for everything's mind to be unlimited. If I think everything's mind is unlimited, than I think everything's mind is everything's thoughts because I think everything's thoughts is apart of making up everything's mind for everything's mind to be everything's thoughts, and therefore, I think everything's thoughts is overlapping, and co-existing along with everything's mind because I think everything's thoughts is apart of making up everything's mind for everything's thoughts to be overlapping, and co-existing along with everything's mind.

If I think everything's thoughts is overlapping, and co-existing along with everything's mind, than I think everything is a mind because I think everything's mind is everything. I think everything's mind is everything because I think everything is everything's mind. I think everything is everything's mind because I think everything is a mind. I think everything is a mind because I think everything is of God's thoughts for everything to be a mind. I think everything is of God's thoughts for everything to be a mind because I think God's thoughts is apart of making up everything for everything to be a mind. I think God's thoughts is apart of making up everything for everything to be a mind because I think everything's mind is the entire area of God's thoughts that is apart of making up everything, and therefore, I think everything is a mind as I think everything is God's mind because I think God's mind is of everything for everything to be a mind as I think God's mind is of everything for God's mind to be a mind. I think God's mind is of everything for everything to be a mind as I think God's mind is of everything for God's mind to be a mind because I think everything is apart of making up God's mind for everything to be a mind as I think everything is apart of making up God's mind for God's mind to be a mind. I think everything is apart of making up God's mind for everything to be a mind as I think everything is apart of making up God's mind for God's mind to be a mind because I think everything's mind is everything that is apart of making up everything's mind as I think God's mind is everything that is apart of making up God's mind. I think everything's mind is everything that is apart of making up everything's mind as I think God's mind is everything that is apart of making up God's mind because I think everything is a mind as I think God's mind is everything, and therefore, I think

God's mind is everything as I think everything is a mind because I think everything is of God's thoughts for everything to be God's mind as I think everything is of God's thoughts for everything to be a mind. I think everything is of God's thoughts for everything to be God's mind as I think everything is of God's thoughts for everything to be a mind because I think God's thoughts is apart of making up everything for everything to be God's mind as I think God's thoughts is apart of making up everything for everything to be a mind. I think God's thoughts is apart of making up everything for everything to be God's mind as I think God's thoughts is apart of making up everything for everything to be a mind because I think God's mind is the entire area of God's thoughts that is apart of making up everything as I think everything's mind is the entire area of God's thoughts that is apart of making up everything, and therefore, I think someone can think of everything's mind as being the dimension of everything's mind because I think the dimension of everything's mind is a storage area of God's thoughts that is apart of making up everything. If I think someone can think of everything's mind as being the dimension of everything's mind, than I think everything's mind is overlapping, and co-existing along with God's mind because I think everything is apart of making up God's mind for everything to be a mind, and therefore, I think everything's mind is overlapping, and co-existing along with God's thoughts because I think everything's mind is all of God's thoughts that is apart of making up everything. I think everything's mind is all of God's thoughts that is apart of making up everything because I think everything is a mind as I think everything is God's thoughts. I think everything is a mind as I think everything is God's thoughts because I think everything's mind is everything as I think God's thoughts is everything. I think everything's mind is everything as I think God's thoughts is everything because I think everything is everything's mind as I think everything is God's thoughts. I think everything is everything's mind as I think everything is God's thoughts because I think everything's mind is everything as I think everything's mind is God's thoughts. I think everything's mind is everything as I think everything's mind is God's thoughts because I think everything is everything's mind as I think God's thoughts is everything's mind. I think everything is everything's mind as I think God's thoughts is everything's mind because I think everything's mind is the entire area of God's thoughts that is apart of making up everything. I think everything's mind is the entire area of God's thoughts that is apart of making up everything because I think everything is everything's mind as I think everything's mind is God's thoughts. I think everything is everything's mind as I think everything's mind is God's thoughts because I think everything is a mind as I think everything has a mind, and therefore, I think everything has a mind because I think everything is a mind for everything to have a mind. If I think everything has a mind, than I think everything is taking place within God's mind because I think God's mind is everything for everything to be taking place within God's mind, and therefore, I think someone is taking place, and living in God's mind because I think God's mind is everything for someone to be taking place, and living in God's mind.

If I think someone is taking place, and living in God's mind, than I think everything's will, and everything's thoughts, and everything's mind, and everything's being are characteristics or features that is apart of making up the embodiment of everything as I think the embodiment of everything is apart of making up everything because I think everything is how everything is able to be what everything is in life as I think the embodiment of everything is apart of how everything is able to be what everything is in life. I think everything is how everything is able to be what everything is in life as I think the embodiment of everything is apart of how everything is able to be what everything is in life because I think everything is what everything is in life as I think the embodiment of everything is apart of making up what everything is in life. I think everything is what everything is in life as I think the embodiment of everything is apart of making up what everything is in life because I think everything is the embodiment of everything as I think the embodiment of everything is apart of making up everything, and therefore, I think everything's will, and everything's thoughts, and everything's mind, and everything's being are all completely different characteristics or features of everything because I think everything's will is what everything is doing, and I think everything's mind is a storage area of everything's thoughts, and I think everything's being is what everything's is in life, even though, I think everything's will, and everything's thoughts, and everything's mind, and everything's being are all completely different characteristics or features of everything that is apart of making up the embodiment of everything because I think everything consists of everything's will, and everything's thoughts, and everything's mind, and everything's being that is apart of making up the embodiment of everything. I think everything consists of everything's will, and everything's thoughts, and everything's mind, and everything's being that is apart of making up the embodiment of everything because I think the embodiment of everything is apart of making up everything, and therefore, I think everything is apart of making up everything because I think everything consists of everything as I think everything consists of everything having a will, and everything having thoughts, and everything having a mind, and everything's being that is apart of making up everything. I think everything consists of everything as I think everything consists of everything having a will, and everything having thoughts, and everything having a mind, and everything's being that is apart of making up everything because I think everything's will, and everything's thoughts, and everything's mind, and everything's being are characteristics of everything that is apart of making up the embodiment of everything. I think everything's will, and everything's thoughts, and everything's mind, and everything's being are characteristics of everything that is apart of making up the embodiment of everything because I think everything consists of everything's will, and everything's thoughts, and everything's mind, and everything's being that is apart of making up the embodiment of everything. I think everything consists of everything's will, and everything's thoughts, and everything's mind, and everything's being that is apart of making up the embodiment of everything because I think everything's will, and everything's thoughts, and everything's mind is taking place within everything's being, without being everything's being as I think everything's will, and everything's thoughts, and everything's mind is apart of everything's being, without being everything's being. I think everything's will, and everything's thoughts, and everything's mind is taking place within everything's being, without being everything's being as I think everything's will, and everything's thoughts, and everything's mind is apart of everything's being, without being everything's being in because I think everything's will, and everything's thoughts, and everything's mind, and everything's being is apart of making up the embodiment of everything. I think everything's will, and everything's thoughts, and everything's mind, and everything's being is apart of making up the embodiment of everything because I think the embodiment of everything is apart of making up everything. I think the embodiment of everything is apart of making up everything because I think the embodiment of everything is everything's will, and everything's thoughts, and everything's mind, and everything's being that is apart of making up everything, and therefore, I think the embodiment of everything is overlapping, and co-existing along with the dimension of everything because I think the embodiment of everything is apart of making up everything. I think the embodiment of everything is apart of making up everything because I think the embodiment of everything is everything.

I think the embodiment of everything is everything because I think the embodiment of everything consists of everything's will, and everything's thoughts, and everything's mind, and everything's being that is apart of making up everything. I think the embodiment of everything consists of everything's will, and everything's thoughts, and everything's mind, and everything's being that is apart of making up everything because I think everything is the embodiment of everything. I think everything is the embodiment of everything because I think the embodiment of everything is everything as I think everything is the embodiment of everything. I think the embodiment of everything is everything as I think everything is the embodiment of everything because I think the embodiment of everything is what everything is in life, and therefore, I think everything is multi-dimensional because I think everything's will, and everything's thoughts, and everything's mind, and everything's being is apart of making up the embodiment of everything for everything to be multi-dimensional. If I think everything is multi-dimensional, than I think God created the embodiment of everything with God's thoughts because I think everything is of God's thoughts for God to be creating the embodiment of everything with God's thoughts, and therefore, I think God created the embodiment of everything because I think God created the embodiment of everything with God's thoughts for God to be creating the embodiment of everything. If I think God created the embodiment of everything, than I think God created everything to be multi-dimensional because I think God created the embodiment of everything with God's thoughts for God to be creating everything to be multi-dimensional, and therefore, I think everything is of the dimensions of a higher intelligent living being because I think God created everything to be multi-dimensional for everything to be of the dimensions of a higher intelligent living being, even though, I think the embodiment of everything is infinite as I think the embodiment of everything is apart of making up everything because I think everything is created by God being infinite for the embodiment of everything to be infinite. If I think the embodiment of everything is infinite as I think the embodiment of everything is apart of making up everything, than I think everything is infinite as I think everything consists of everything's will, and everything's thoughts, and everything's mind that is apart of making up the embodiment of everything because I think everything is created by God being infinite for everything to be infinite, and therefore, I think everything is immortal as I think everything is infinite because I think everything is infinite for everything to be immortal. I think everything is infinite for everything to be immortal because I think everything is infinitely immortal. I think everything is infinitely immortal because I think everything is created by God being infinite for everything to be infinitely immortal.

If I think everything is infinitely immortal, than I think everything's being is how everything is doing what everything is doing with everything's will because I think how everything is able to be doing what everything is able to be doing with everything's being is how everything is doing what everything is doing with everything's will, and therefore, I think everything's being is how everything is able to be making any choices with everything's will because I think how everything is able to be doing what everything is able to be doing with everything's being is how everything is able to be making any choices with everything's will. I think how everything is able to be doing what everything is able to be doing with everything's being is how everything is able to be making any choices with everything's will because I think what everything is doing is what everything's being is doing. I think what everything is doing is what everything's being is doing because I think everything is doing what everything's being is doing. I think everything is doing what everything's being is doing because I think everything's being is how everything is able to be doing what everything is able to be doing as I think everything's will, and everything's thoughts, and everything's mind is apart of everything's being. I think everything's being is how everything is able to be doing what everything is able to be doing as I think everything's will, and everything's thoughts, and everything's mind is apart of everything's being because I think everything is doing what everything is doing with everything's will, and everything's thoughts, and everything's mind that is apart of everything's being. I think everything is doing what everything is doing with everything's will, and everything's thoughts, and everything's mind that is apart of everything's being because I think everything is doing what everything's being is doing as I think everything's will, and everything's thoughts, and everything's mind is apart of everything's being. I think everything is doing what everything's being is doing as I think everything's will, and everything's thoughts, and everything's mind is apart of everything's being because I think everything's being is ultimately what makes everything able to be making any choices as I think everything's will, and everything's thoughts, and everything's mind is apart of everything's being. I think everything's being is ultimately what makes everything able to be making any choices as I think everything's will, and everything's thoughts, and everything's mind is apart of everything's being because I think everything's will, and everything's thoughts, and everything's mind is apart of making up the embodiment of everything as I think the embodiment of everything is apart of making up everything's being, and therefore, I think everything's being is the thoughts of everything as I think everything's being is God's thoughts because I think the thoughts of everything is God's thought as I think everything is of God's thoughts that is apart of making up everything. If I think everything's being is the thoughts of everything as I think everything's being is God's thoughts, than I think everything does what the thoughts of everything is in life as I think everything does what God's thoughts are in life because I think everything is of the thoughts of everything that is apart of making up everything for everything to be doing what the thoughts of everything is in life as I think everything is of God's thoughts that is apart of making up everything for everything to be doing what God's thoughts are in life, and therefore, I think God is somehow able to be responsible for how everything is able to be doing what everything is able to be doing because I think God created how everything is in life with God's thoughts for God to somehow be able to be responsible for how everything is able to be doing what everything is able to be doing.

If I think God is somehow able to be responsible for how everything is able to be doing what everything is able to be doing, than I think God is responsible for what everything is able to be doing because I think God created how everything is in life with God's thoughts for everything to be able to be doing what everything is able to be doing as I think God created everything with God's thoughts for everything to be doing what everything is doing, but is God responsible for what everything is doing in life? I think God is somehow able to be responsible for how everything is able to be doing what everything is able to be doing because I think God created everything with God's thoughts for God to be able to be knowing, as to how everything is in life for God to be responsible for how everything is able to be doing what everything is able to be doing, however, I do not think God is responsible for what everything is doing because I do not think God is interfering with everything for God not to be responsible for what everything is doing, and therefore, I think everything is doing what everything is doing because I think God created everything with God's thoughts for everything to be a choice with everything's free will as I think everything is a choice with everything's free will for everything to be doing what everything is doing. I think God created everything with God's thoughts for everything to be a choice with everything's free will as I think everything is a choice with everything's free will for everything to be doing what everything is doing because I think God created everything with God's thoughts for everything to be a choice of itself of what everything is doing as I think everything is a choice of itself of what everything is doing for everything to be doing what everything is doing, and therefore, I do not think God is responsible for what everything is doing because I think everything is a choice of itself, as to what everything is doing for God not to be responsible for what everything is doing as I think God created everything to be having a will for everything to be able to be doing what everything is doing. If I do not think God is responsible for what everything is doing, than I think everything is doing what everything is doing because I think everything is a choice of itself for everything to be doing what everything is doing.

If I think everything is doing what everything is doing, than I think everything is of the likeness of God because I think everything is created by God for everything to be of the likeness of God, even though, I do not think everything is alike God because I do not think God is created for everything not to be alike God, however, I think everything is like God because I think everything has a will, and thoughts, and a mind, and a being that is apart making up the embodiment of everything as I think God has a will, and thoughts, and a mind, and a being that is apart of making up the embodiment of God, but I do not think everything is alike God because I do not think everything has a state of consciousness as I think God has a state of consciousness, and therefore, I do not think everything's will, and everything's thoughts, and everything's mind, and everything's being that is apart of making up the embodiment of everything is alike God's state of consciousness, and God's will, and God's thoughts, and God's mind, and God's being that is apart of making up the embodiment of God because I think God's state of consciousness, and God's will, and God's thoughts, and God's mind, and God's being that is apart of making up the embodiment of God is beyond everything's will, and everything's thoughts, and everything's mind, and everything's being that is apart of making up the embodiment of everything. I think God's state of consciousness, and God's will, and God's thoughts, and God's mind, and God's being that is apart of making up the embodiment of God is beyond everything's will, and everything's thoughts, and everything's mind, and everything's being that is apart of making up the embodiment of everything because I think everything's will, and everything's thoughts, and everything's mind, and everything's being that is apart of making up the embodiment of everything is of God's state of consciousness, and God's will, and God's thoughts, and God's mind, and God's being that is apart of making up the embodiment of God for God's state of consciousness, and God's will, and God's thoughts, and God's mind, and God's being that is apart of making up the embodiment of God to be beyond everything's will, and everything's thoughts, and everything's mind, and everything's being that is apart of making up the embodiment of everything. I think everything's will, and everything's thoughts, and everything's mind, and everything's being that is apart of making up the embodiment of everything is of God's state of consciousness, and God's will, and God's thoughts, and God's mind, and God's being that is apart of making up the embodiment of God for God's state of consciousness, and God's will, and God's thoughts, and God's mind, and God's being that is apart of making up the embodiment of God to be beyond everything's will, and everything's thoughts, and everything's mind, and everything's being that is apart of making up the embodiment of everything because I think God's state of consciousness, and God's will, and God's thoughts, and God's mind, and God's being that is apart of making up the embodiment of God is apart of making up everything's will, and everything's thoughts, and everything's mind, and everything's being that is apart of making up the embodiment of everything for God's state of consciousness, and God's will, and God's thoughts, and God's mind, and God's being that is apart of making up the embodiment of God to be beyond everything's will, and everything's thoughts, and everything's mind, and everything's being that is apart of making up the embodiment of everything.

I think God's state of consciousness, and God's will, and God's thoughts, and God's mind, and God's being that is apart of making up the embodiment of God is apart of making up everything's will, and everything's thoughts, and everything's mind, and everything's being that is apart of making up the embodiment of everything for God's state of consciousness, and God's will, and God's thoughts, and God's mind, and God's being that is apart of making up the embodiment of God to be beyond everything's will, and everything's thoughts, and everything's mind, and everything's being that is apart of making up the embodiment of everything because I think the embodiment of God is apart of making up the embodiment of everything. I think the embodiment of God is apart of making up the embodiment of everything because I think the embodiment of God is apart of making up the embodiment of everything. I think the embodiment of God is apart of making up the embodiment of everything because I think the embodiment of everything is of the embodiment of God. I think the embodiment of everything is of the embodiment of God because I think the embodiment of God is apart of making up everything that is the embodiment of everything. I think the embodiment of God is apart of making up everything that is the embodiment of everything because I think the embodiment of everything is of God's creation for God to be creating everything to be apart of the embodiment of God. I think the embodiment of everything is of God's creation for God to be creating everything to be apart of the embodiment of God because I think everything is apart of the embodiment of God as I think the embodiment of God is apart of God. I think everything is apart of the embodiment of God as I think the embodiment of God is apart of God because I think everything is of God for God to be creating everything to be apart of the embodiment of God. I think everything is of God for God to be creating everything to be apart of the embodiment of God because I think everything is apart of the embodiment of God as I think everything is of God. I think everything is apart of the embodiment of God as I think everything is of God because I think everything is apart of the embodiment of God for God to be creating everything to be apart of God. I think everything is apart of the embodiment of God for God to be creating everything to be apart of God because I think everything is of the embodiment of God as I think the embodiment of everything is of God. I think everything is of the embodiment of God as I think the embodiment of everything is of God because I think everything is of the embodiment of God for everything to be of God. I think everything is of the embodiment of God for everything to be of God because I think everything is of God as I think the embodiment of God is apart of God. I think everything is of God as I think the embodiment of God is apart of God because I think the embodiment of everything is of God for everything to be of God. I think the embodiment of everything is of God for everything to be of God because I think the embodiment of God is apart of God for God to be creating everything to be apart of God. I think the embodiment of God is apart of God for God to be creating everything to be apart of God because I think everything is of the embodiment of God for God to be creating everything to be apart of God. I think everything is of the embodiment of God for God to be creating everything to be apart of God because I think everything is of the embodiment of God as I think everything is of God. I think everything is of the embodiment of God as I think everything is of God because I think everything is of God for everything to be of the embodiment of God. I think everything is of God for everything to be of the embodiment of God because I think everything is of God for everything to be apart of the embodiment of God. I think everything is of God for everything to be apart of the embodiment of God because I think everything is apart of the embodiment of God as I think everything is apart of God. I think everything is apart of the embodiment of God as I think everything is apart of God because I think everything is of God's creation for God to be creating everything to be apart of God.

If I think everything is apart of the embodiment of God as I think everything is apart of God, than I think everything is overlapping, and co-existing along with God because I think everything is of the embodiment of God for God to be creating everything to be apart of God. I think everything is of the embodiment of God for God to be creating everything to be apart of God because I think the embodiment of everything is overlapping, and co-existing along with the embodiment of God. I think the embodiment of everything is overlapping, and co-existing along with the embodiment of God because I think everything is the embodiment of everything that is overlapping, and co-existing along with the embodiment of God that is apart of God. I think everything is the embodiment of everything that is overlapping, and co-existing along with the embodiment of God that is apart of God because I think everything is overlapping, and co-existing along with the embodiment of God. I think everything is overlapping, and co-existing along with the embodiment of God because I think everything is of God's creation for God to be creating everything to be apart of the embodiment of God, and therefore, I think the embodiment of everything consists of the embodiment of something, and the embodiment of someone that is apart of making up the embodiment of everything because I think the embodiment of everything is everything, and I think the embodiment of something is something, and I think the embodiment of someone is someone as I think everything consists of something, and someone that is apart of making up everything. If I think the embodiment of everything consists of the embodiment of something, and the embodiment of someone that is apart of making up the embodiment of everything, than I think the embodiment of everything is overlapping, and co-existing along with the embodiment of something, and the embodiment of someone because I think the embodiment of everything consists of the embodiment of something, and the embodiment of someone that is apart of making up the embodiment of everything as I think the embodiment of everything is everything that consists of something, and someone that is apart of making up everything, and therefore, I think the embodiment of something is overlapping, and co-existing along with the embodiment of someone because I think the embodiment of something is something, and I think the embodiment of someone is someone that is apart of making up the embodiment of everything as I think the embodiment of everything is everything that consists of something, and someone that is apart of making up everything.

If I think the embodiment of something is overlapping, and co-existing along with the embodiment of someone, than I think everything is of God's creation for God to be creating everything to be apart of the embodiment of God because I think everything is of the embodiment of God for everything to be of God. I think everything is of the embodiment of God for everything to be of God because I think everything is of God's creation for God to be creating everything to be apart of God. I think everything is of God's creation for God to be creating everything to be apart of God because I think everything is the embodiment of everything that is of the embodiment of God for everything to be apart of God. I think everything is the embodiment of everything that is of the embodiment of God for everything to be apart of God because I think the embodiment of everything is of God for the embodiment of everything to be of the embodiment of God. I think the embodiment of everything is of God for the embodiment of everything to be of the embodiment of God because I think the embodiment of everything is of God for the embodiment of everything to be apart of God. I think the embodiment of everything is of God for the embodiment of everything to be apart of God because I think the embodiment of everything is everything as I think everything is of God for everything to be apart of God. I think the embodiment of everything is everything as I think everything is of God for everything to be apart of God because I think the embodiment of everything is what everything is in life as I think everything is of God's creation for everything to be what everything is in life. I think the embodiment of everything is what everything is in life as I think everything is of God's creation for everything to be what everything is in life because I think the embodiment of everything is of the dimension of life as I think everything is the dimension of life for the embodiment of everything to be everything.

Chapter 15

God has a choice of right or wrong

I would like to talk about how dimensions are in life in relation to what dimensions are in life by talking about God having a choice of right or wrong, that can possibly have something to do with how dimensions are in life is in relation to what dimensions are in life because I think God's choice of right or wrong is of the dimension of God's will for God to be having a choice of right or wrong, and therefore, I think God has a choice because I think God is always good, and right for God to be having a choice. I think God is always good, and right for God to be having a choice because I think God's being is ultimately what makes God's will able to be making any choices that is always good, and right with God's will as I think God's will is apart of God's being. I think God's being is ultimately what makes God's will able to be making any choices that is always good, and right with God's will as I think God's will is apart of God's being because I think God's being is ultimately what makes God able to be making any choices that is always good, and right as I think God's will is apart of God's being, and therefore, I think God has a sense of always being good, and right with God's will as I think God has a sense of always being good, and right with God's being because I think God's sense of always being good, and right comes from God's being for God's will to be able to be having a sense of always being good, and right with God's will. I think God's sense of always being good, and right comes from God's being for God's will to be able to be having a sense of always being good, and right with God's will because I think God's being is ultimately what makes God's will able to be making any choices that is always good, and right with God's will as I think God's will is apart of God's being, and therefore, I think God has a sense of always being good, and right as I think God has a sense of always being good, and right with God's being because I think God is God's being as I think God's being has a sense of always being good, and right. If I think God has a sense of always being good, and right as I think God has a sense of always being good, and right with God's being, than I think God has a sense of always being good, and right because I think God has a choice that is always good, and right, and therefore, I think God constantly has a choice that is always good, and right because I think God is constantly good, and right for God to constantly be having a choice that is always good, and right. If I think God constantly has a choice that is always good, and right, than I think God constantly has a sense of always being good, and right because I think God constantly has a choice that is always good, and right, and therefore, I think God has a sense of always being good, and right because I think God's sense of always being good, and right is God having a choice that is always good, and right. If I think God has a sense of always being good, and right, than I think God's sense of always being good, and right comes from God's being because I think God is always good, and right for God's sense of always being good, and right to come from God's being, but I do not think God created God's being to have a sense of always being good, and right because I do not think God's being is created by God for God's being to have a sense of always being good, and right. I do not think God's being is created by God for God's being to have a sense of always being good, and right because I think God is God's being as I do not think God is created for God's being to be created by God, and therefore, I think God's sense of always being good, and right comes from God's being because I think God's being has a sense of always being good, and right. I think God's being has a sense of always being good, and right because I think God's being has a choice that is always good, and right. I think God's being has a choice that is always good, and right because I think God's being is always good, and right for God's being to be having a choice that is always good, and right, and therefore, I think God has a choice that is always good, and right as I think God's being has a choice that is always good, and right because I think God is God's being as I think God is always good, and right for God to be having a choice that is always good, and right. If I think God has a choice that is always good, and right as I think God's being has a choice that is always good, and right, than I think God has a sense of always being good, and right because I think God has a choice that is always good, and right for God to be having a sense of always being good, and right, and therefore, I think God has a sense of always being good, and right as I think God's being has sense of always being good, and right because I think God is God's being as I think God has a sense of always being good, and right.

If I think God has a sense of always being good, and right as I think God's being has sense of always being good, and right, than I think God has a choice of right or wrong because I think God created right or wrong for God to have a choice of right or wrong. I think God created right or wrong for God to have a choice of right or wrong because I think God is always good, and right for God to be having a choice of right or wrong as I think God is always good, and right for God to be creating right or wrong, and therefore, I think God created right or wrong for God to be choosing right or wrong because I think God has a choice of right or wrong for God to be choosing right or wrong. If I think God created right or wrong for God to be choosing right or wrong, than I think God has a choice of right or wrong for God to be right because I think God is always good, and right with God having a choice of right and wrong for God to be right. I think God is always good, and right with God having a choice of right and wrong for God to be right because I think God is always good, and right for God to be having a choice of right and wrong, and therefore, I think God's being has a sense of right or wrong because I think God has a choice of right or wrong for God's being to be having a sense of right or wrong. If I think God's being has a sense of right or wrong, than I think God is always good, and right as I think God has a choice of right and wrong because I think God created right or wrong with God's sense of always being good, and right for God to be having a choice of right or wrong. I think God created right or wrong with God's sense of always being good, and right for God to be having a choice of right or wrong because I think God created right or wrong for God's sense of always being good, and right to be having a sense of right or wrong from God having a choice of right or wrong. I think God created right or wrong for God's sense of always being good, and right to be having a sense of right or wrong from God having a choice of right or wrong because I think God created God's sense of always being good, and right to be having a choice of right or wrong for God to be choosing right or wrong. I think God created God's sense of always being good, and right to be having a choice of right or wrong for God to be choosing right or wrong because I think God's sense of always being good, and right is God's choice as I think God created God's choice to be having a choice of right or wrong for God to be choosing right or wrong. I think God's sense of always being good, and right is God's choice as I think God created God's choice to be having a choice of right or wrong for God to be choosing right or wrong because I think God is always good, and right with God having a choice of right or wrong. If I think God is always good, and right with God having a choice of right or wrong, than I think God has two kinds of choices because I think God has a choice of right and wrong for God to be having two kinds of choices. I think God has a choice of right and wrong for God to be having two kinds of choices because I think God has a choice of right or wrong for God to be right. I think God has a choice of right or wrong for God to be right because I think God is constantly right. I think God is constantly right because I think God is always good, and right, and therefore, I think God has a choice of right and wrong because I think God has a sense of right or wrong from God choosing right or wrong. I think God has a sense of right or wrong from God choosing right or wrong because I think God's sense of right and wrong is a choice of right or wrong for God to be choosing right or wrong. I think God's sense of right and wrong is a choice of right or wrong for God to be choosing right or wrong because I think God's sense of right and wrong is God's choice of right or wrong as I think God has a choice of right or wrong for God to be choosing right or wrong. I think God's sense of right and wrong is God's choice of right or wrong as I think God has a choice of right or wrong for God to be choosing right or wrong because I think God is always good, and right with God having a choice of right or wrong.

I think God is always good, and right with God having a choice of right or wrong because I think God created right or wrong for God's being to be having a sense of right or wrong from God choosing right or wrong. I think God created right or wrong for God's being to be having a sense of right or wrong from God choosing right or wrong because I think God has a choice of right or wrong. I think God has a choice of right or wrong because I think God is always good, and right with God to be having a choice of right or wrong. I think God is always good, and right with God to be having a choice of right or wrong because I think God can choose something that is right or wrong, even though, I do not think something is right or wrong as I think someone thinks something is right or wrong because I think God can choose something that is right or wrong for God's being to have a sense of right or wrong as I think God's being is always good, and right with God's being having a sense of always being good, and right, and therefore, I think something is right or wrong because I think God can choose something that is right or wrong. I think God can choose something that is right or wrong because I think God has a choice of right or wrong for God to be choosing something that is right or wrong. I think God has a choice of right or wrong for God to be choosing something that is right or wrong because I think God can choose something that is right or wrong with God having a choice of right or wrong. I think God can choose something that is right or wrong with God having a choice of right or wrong because I think God has a choice of right or wrong for God's choices to be of God choosing something that is right or wrong. I think God has a choice of right or wrong for God's choices to be of God choosing something that is right or wrong because I think God can choose something that is right or wrong for God's choices to be of God choosing something that is right or wrong. I think God can choose something that is right or wrong for God's choices to be of God choosing something that is right or wrong because I think God has a choice of right or wrong for God to be choosing something that is right or wrong.

If I think God can choose something that is right or wrong for God's choices to be of God choosing something that is right or wrong, than I think God can choose something that is right or wrong with God having a choice of right or wrong because I think God can choose something that is right or wrong from someone choosing something that is right or wrong. I think God can choose something that is right or wrong from someone choosing something that is right or wrong because I think God can choose if someone is right or wrong about something from someone choosing something that is right or wrong. I think God can choose if someone is right or wrong about something from someone choosing something that is right or wrong because I think God created someone to be choosing something that is right or wrong for God to be choosing if someone is right or wrong about something. I think God created someone to be choosing something that is right or wrong for God to be choosing if someone is right or wrong about something because I think God has a choice of right or wrong for God to be choosing if someone is right or wrong about something. I think God has a choice of right or wrong for God to be choosing if someone is right or wrong about something because I think God can choose if someone is right or wrong about something from

God having a choice of right or wrong. I think God can choose if someone is right or wrong about something from God having a choice of right or wrong because I think God can choose if someone is right or wrong about something for God's being to have a sense of right or wrong as I think God's being is always good, and right with God's being having a sense of always being good, and right. I think God can choose if someone is right or wrong about something for God's being to have a sense of right or wrong as I think God's being is always good, and right with God's being having a sense of always being good, and right because I think God created someone to be right or wrong for God to be choosing if someone is right or wrong. I think God created someone to be right or wrong for God to be choosing if someone is right or wrong because I think God has a choice of right or wrong for God to be choosing if someone is right or wrong. I think God has a choice of right or wrong for God to be choosing if someone is right or wrong because I think God can choose if someone is right or wrong from God having a choice of right or wrong. I think God can choose if someone is right or wrong from God having a choice of right or wrong because I think God can choose if someone is right or wrong for God's being to have a sense of right or wrong as I think God's being is always good, and right with God's being having a sense of always being good, and right.

I think God can choose if someone is right or wrong for God's being to have a sense of right or wrong as I think God's being is always good, and right with God's being having a sense of always being good, and right because I think God is always good, and right as I think God has a choice of right or wrong. I think God is always good, and right as I think God has a choice of right or wrong because I think God is always good, and right with God having a choice of right or wrong. I think God is always good, and right with God having a choice of right or wrong because I think God is always good, and right with what God is in life. I think God is always good, and right with what God is in life because I think God's being is somehow always able to good, and right as I think God's state of consciousness, and God's will, and God's thoughts, and God's mind is apart of God's being. I think God's being is somehow always able to good, and right as I think God's state of consciousness, and God's will, and God's thoughts, and God's mind is apart of God's being because I think God's being is ultimately what makes God able to be making any choices that is always good, and right as I think God's state of consciousness, and God's will, and God's thoughts, and God's mind is apart of God's being, and therefore, I think God's will is apart of God's being for God's will to have a sense of always being good, and right with God's being because I do not think God can choosing something that is always good, and right, without God having a will for God to be choosing something that is always good, and right with God's will as I think God's will is apart of God's being. If I think God's will is apart of God's being for God's will to have a sense of always being good, and right with God's being, than I think God's will has a sense of always being good, and right because I think God can choose something that is always good, and right with God's will as I think God's will is apart of God's being, and therefore, I think God has a sense of consciousness for God to have a sense of always being good, and right because I do not think God can be consciously aware of God always being good, and right, without God having a sense of consciousness for God to have a sense of always being good, and right.

If I think God has a sense of consciousness for God to have a sense of always being good, and right, than I think God can think of something as being right or wrong because I think God can choose something that is right or wrong with God's thoughts for God to be thinking of something as being right or wrong. I think God can choose something that is right or wrong with God's thoughts for God to be thinking of something as being right or wrong because I think something is of God's thoughts for God to be choosing something that is right or wrong with God's thoughts. I think something is of God's thoughts for God to be choosing something that is right or wrong with God's thoughts because I think God can think of something as being right or wrong. I think God can think of something as being right or wrong because I think God can think of God's thoughts of something as being right or wrong for God to be thinking of something as being right or wrong. I think God can think of God's thoughts of something as being right or wrong for God to be thinking of something as being right or wrong because I think something is of God's thoughts for God to be thinking of God's thoughts of something as being right or wrong. I think something is of God's thoughts for God to be thinking of God's thoughts of something as being right or wrong because I think God's thoughts of something that can be right or wrong. I think God's thoughts of something that can be right or wrong because I think God has a choice of right or wrong for God to be choosing to be thinking of God's thoughts of something as being right or wrong. I think God has a choice of right or wrong for God to be choosing to be thinking of God's thoughts of something as being right or wrong because I think God is always good, and right for God to be thinking of God's thoughts of something as being right or wrong. I think God is always good, and right for God to be thinking of God's thoughts of something as being right or wrong because I think God can think of God's thoughts of something as being right or wrong for God thinking of something.

I think God can think of God's thoughts of something as being right or wrong for God thinking of something because I think God can think of something as being right or wrong. I think God can think of something as being right or wrong because I think God can choose something that is right or wrong with God's thoughts for God to be thinking of something as being right or wrong. I think God can choose something that is right or wrong with God's thoughts for God to be thinking of something as being right or wrong because I think God has a choice of right or wrong for God to be thinking of something as being right or wrong. I think God has a choice of right or wrong for God to be thinking of something as being right or wrong because I think God can choose to be thinking of something as being right or wrong with God's thoughts from God having a choice of right or wrong. I think God can choose to be thinking of something as being right or wrong with God's thoughts from God having a choice of right or wrong because I think God can choose to be thinking of something as being right or wrong with God having a sense of right or wrong as I think God is always good, and right with God having a sense of right or wrong. I think God can choose to be thinking of something as being right or wrong with God having a sense of right or wrong as I think God is always good, and right with God having a sense of right or wrong because I think God can think of something as being right or wrong with God always being good, and right for God to always be good, and right about what God thinks of something. If I think God can choose to be thinking of something as being right or wrong with God having a sense of right or wrong as I think God is always good, and right with God having a sense of right or wrong, than I think God can think of something as being right or wrong because I think God can choose to be thinking of something as being right or wrong with God's sense of right and wrong as I think God can choose to be thinking of something as being right or wrong with God's state of consciousness, and God's will, and God's thoughts, and God's mind that is apart of God's being, and therefore, I think God can choose to be thinking of something as being right or wrong with God's being because I think God can choose to be thinking of something as being right or wrong with God's state of consciousness, and God's will, and God's thoughts, and God's mind that is apart of God's being, however, I do not think something is right or wrong because I think God can choose something with God having a choice of right or wrong for something not to be right or wrong, however, I think God can choose yes or no with something because I think God has a choice of right or wrong for God to be choosing yes or no with something.

If I think God can choose yes or no with something, than I think God can think of God's thoughts as being right or wrong because I think God can choose something that is right or wrong with God's thoughts for God to be thinking of God's thoughts as being right or wrong. If I think God can think of God's thoughts as being right or wrong, than I think God can think of God's thoughts as being right or wrong as I think God can think of something as being right or wrong because I think God's thoughts is of God for God to be thinking of God's thoughts as being right or wrong as I think something is of God for God to be thinking of something as being right or wrong, and therefore, I think God can think of God's thoughts as being right or wrong because I think God has a choice of right or wrong for God to be thinking of God's thoughts as being right or wrong. I think God has a choice of right or wrong for God to be thinking of God's thoughts as being right or wrong because I think God can choose to be thinking of something as being right or wrong with God's thoughts from God having a choice of right or wrong. I think God can choose to be thinking of something as being right or wrong with God's thoughts from God having a choice of right or wrong because I think God can choose to be thinking of God's thoughts as being right or wrong with God having a sense of right or wrong as I think God is always good, and right with God having a sense of right or wrong. I think God can choose to be thinking of God's thoughts as being right or wrong with God having a sense of right or wrong as I think God is always good, and right with God having a sense of right or wrong because I think God can think of God's thoughts as being right or wrong with God always being good, and right for God to always be good, and right about what God thinks of God's thoughts. If I think God can choose to be thinking of God's thoughts as being right or wrong with God having a sense of right or wrong as I think God is always good, and right with God having a sense of right or wrong, than I think God can think of God's thoughts as being right or wrong because I think God can choose to be thinking of God's thoughts of something as being right or wrong with God's sense of right and wrong as I think God can choose to be thinking of God's thoughts of something as being right or wrong with God's state of consciousness, and God's will, and God's thoughts, and God's mind that is apart of God's being, and therefore, I think God can choose to be thinking of God's thoughts as being right or wrong with God's being because I think God can choose to be thinking of God's thoughts of something as being right or wrong with God's state of consciousness, and God's will, and God's thoughts, and God's mind that is apart of God's being, even though, I do not think God's thoughts is right or wrong because I think God can choose God's thoughts of something with God having a choice of right or wrong for God's thoughts not to be right or wrong, however, I think God can choose yes or no with God's thoughts because I think God has a choice of right or wrong for God to be choosing yes or no with God's thoughts.

If I think God can choose yes or no with God's thoughts, than I think God can think of someone as being right or wrong as I think God can think of something as being right or wrong because I think someone is of God's thoughts for God to be thinking of someone as being right or wrong as I think something is of God's thoughts for God to be thinking of something as being right or wrong, and therefore, I think God can think of someone as being right or wrong about something as I think God can think of someone as being right or wrong because I think God can choose someone that is right or wrong about something with God's thoughts for God to be thinking of someone as being right or wrong about something as I think God can choose someone that is right or wrong with God's thoughts for God to be thinking of someone as being right or wrong. If I think God can think of someone as being right or wrong about something as I think God can think of someone as being right or wrong, than I think God can think of someone as being right or wrong about something because I think God created someone to be choosing something that is right or wrong for God to be thinking of someone as being right or wrong about something. I think God created someone to be choosing something that is right or wrong for God to be thinking of someone as being right or wrong about something because I think God has a choice of right or wrong for God to be thinking of someone as being right or wrong about something. I think God has a choice of right or wrong for God to be thinking of someone as being right or wrong about something because I think God can choose to be thinking of someone as being right or wrong about something with God's thoughts from God having a choice of right or wrong. I think God can choose to be thinking of someone as being right or wrong about something with God's thoughts from God having a choice of right or wrong because I think God can choose to be thinking of someone as being right or wrong about something with God having a sense of right or wrong as I think God is always good, and right with God having a sense of right or wrong. I think God can choose to be thinking of someone as being right or wrong about something with God having a sense of right or wrong as I think God is always good, and right with God having a sense of right or wrong because I think God can think of someone as being right or wrong about something with God always being good, and right for God to always be good, and right about what God thinks of someone. If I think God can choose to be thinking of someone as being right or wrong about something with God having a sense of right or wrong as I think God is always good, and right with God having a sense of right or wrong, than I think God can think of someone as being right or wrong about something because I think God can choose to be thinking of someone as being right or wrong about something with God's sense of right and wrong as I think God can choose to be thinking of someone as being right or wrong about something with God's state of consciousness, and God's will, and God's thoughts, and God's mind that is apart of God's being, and therefore, I think God can choose to be thinking of someone as being right or wrong about something with God's being because I think God can choose to be thinking of someone as being right or wrong about something with God's state of consciousness, and God's will, and God's thoughts, and God's mind that is apart of God's being, however, I think God can choose yes or no with someone about something because I think God has a choice of right or wrong for God to be choosing yes or no with someone about something.

If I think God can choose yes or no with someone about something, than I think God has a choice of right or wrong because I think God has God's free will for God to be having a choice of right or wrong. I think God has God's free will for God to be having a choice of right or wrong because I think God's free will is God's choice as I think God's choice is God having a choice of right or wrong. I think God's free will is God's choice as I think God's choice is God having a choice of right or wrong because I think God's choice is God's free will. I think God's choice is God's free will because I think God's free will is God's will as I think God's choice is God's will. I think God's free will is God's will as I think God's choice is God's will because I think God's will is God's free will as I think God's will is God's choice. I think God's will is God's free will as I think God's will is God's choice because I think God has a choice with God's free will as I think God has a choice with God's will. I think God has a choice with God's free will as I think God has a choice with God's will because I think God has a choice of right or wrong with God's free will as I think God has a choice of right or wrong with God's will. I think God has a choice of right or wrong with God's free will as I think God has a choice of right or wrong with God's will because I think God has a choice of right or wrong.

I think God has a choice of right or wrong because I think God has a choice of right or wrong with God's free will for God to be right. I think God has a choice of right or wrong with God's free will for God to be right because I think God's free will is God's choice as I think God is always good, and right with God having a choice of right or wrong. I think God's free will is God's choice as I think God is always good, and right with God having a choice of right or wrong because I think God has a choice of right or wrong, and therefore, I think God has a choice of someone, and something that is right or wrong as I think God has a choice of right or wrong because I think God has a choice of right or wrong for God to be choosing someone, and something that is right or wrong. I think God has a choice of right or wrong for God to be choosing someone, and something that is right or wrong because I think God can choose someone, and something that is right or wrong for God to be right about someone, and something. I think God can choose someone, and something that is right or wrong for God to be right about someone, and something because I think God is always good, and right with God having a choice of right or wrong as I think God is always good, and right with God choosing someone, and something that is right or wrong. I think God is always good, and right with God having a choice of right or wrong as I think God is always good, and right with God choosing someone, and something that is right or wrong because I think God can choose someone, and something that is right or wrong with God having a choice of right or wrong. I think God can choose someone, and something that is right or wrong with God having a choice of right or wrong because I think God has a choice of someone, and something that is right or wrong with God's free will as I think God has a choice of right or wrong with God's free will. I think God has a choice of someone, and something that is right or wrong with God's free will as I think God has a choice of right or wrong with God's free will because I think God has a choice of right or wrong with God's free will for God to be choosing someone, and something that is right or wrong. I think God has a choice of right or wrong with God's free will for God to be choosing someone, and something that is right or wrong because I think God can choose someone, and something that is right or wrong with God's free will for God to be right about someone, and something. I think God can choose someone, and something that is right or wrong with God's free will for God to be right about someone, and something because I think God is always good, and right with God having a choice of right or wrong with God's free will as I think God is always good, and right with God choosing someone, and something that is right or wrong with God's free will. I think God is always good, and right with God having a choice of right or wrong with God's free will as I think God is always good, and right with God choosing someone, and something that is right or wrong with God's free will because I think God can choose someone, and something that is right or wrong with God's free will having a choice of right or wrong. I think God can choose someone, and something that is right or wrong with God's free will having a choice of right or wrong because I think God can choose someone, and something that is right or wrong with God's free will as I think God has a choice of right or wrong with God's free will, and therefore, I think someone can learn a lot from God's free will because I think someone can learn a lot from God choosing someone, and something that is right or wrong with God's free will. I think someone can learn a lot from God choosing someone, and something that is right or wrong with God's free will because I think someone can choose to be living by God's example or not. I think someone can choose to be living by God's example or not because I think God is always good, and right with God choosing someone, and something that is right or wrong with God's free will for someone to be choosing to be living by God's example or not, and therefore, I think God is always good, and right with God choosing someone, and something that is right or wrong with God's free will because I think God has a choice of someone, and something that is right or wrong with God's free will for God to be right about someone, and something as

I think God has a choice of someone, and something that is right or wrong for God to be right. I think God has a choice of someone, and something that is right or wrong with God's free will for God to be right about someone, and something as I think God has a choice of someone, and something that is right or wrong for God to be right because I think God is always good, and right with God having a choice of right or wrong with God's free will as I think God is always good, and right with God having a choice of right or wrong.

I think God is always good, and right with God having a choice of right or wrong with God's free will as I think God is always good, and right with God having a choice of right or wrong because I think God has a choice of right or wrong for God to always be good, and right. I think God has a choice of right or wrong for God to always be good, and right because I think God is always good, and right with God having a choice of right or wrong. I think God is always good, and right with God having a choice of right or wrong because I think God is always good, and right as I think God has a choice of right or wrong, and therefore, I think God has a choice of right or wrong for God to always be good, and right because I think God is always good, and right with God having a choice of something. I think God is always good, and right with God having a choice of something because I think God is always good, and right with God having a choice of something that is right or wrong. I think God is always good, and right with God having a choice of something that is right or wrong because I think God can choose of something that is right or wrong. I think God can choose of something that is right or wrong because I think God has a choice of right or wrong for God to be choosing something that is right or wrong. I think God has a choice of right or wrong for God to be choosing something that is right or wrong because I think God can choose something that is good, and right with God having a choice of something that is right or wrong. I think God can choose something that is good, and right with God having a choice of something that is right or wrong because I think God is always good, and right for God to be choosing something that is right or wrong. I think God is always good, and right for God to be choosing something that is right or wrong because I think God is always good, and right with God having a choice of something that is right or wrong. I think God is always good, and right with God having a choice of something that is right or wrong because I think God is always good, and right for God to be doing something that is always good, and right as I think God can choose something that is right or wrong. I think God is always good, and right for God to be doing something that is always good, and right as I think God can choose something that is right or wrong because I think God can choose to be doing something that is always good, and right as I think God can choose something that is right or wrong. I think God can choose to be doing something that is always good, and right as I think God can choose something that is right or wrong because I think God is always good, and right for God's choices to be of God choosing to be doing something that is always good, and right as I think God is always good, and right with God having a choice of right or wrong for God's choices to be of God choosing to be something that is right or wrong. I think God is always good, and right for God's choices to be of God choosing to be doing something that is always good, and right as I think God is always good, and right with God having a choice of right or wrong for God's choices to be of God choosing to be something that is right or wrong because I think God can choose to be doing something that is always good, and right for God's choices to be of God choosing to be doing something that is always good, and right as I think God can choose something that is right or wrong for God's choices to be of God choosing something that is right or wrong. I think God can choose to be doing something that is always good, and right for God's choices to be of God choosing to be doing something that is always good, and right as I think God can choose something that is right or wrong for God's choices to be of God choosing something that is right or wrong because I think God can choose to be doing something that is always good, and right for God to be choosing something that is right or wrong. I think God can choose to be doing something that is always good, and right for God to be choosing something that is right or wrong because I think God can do something that is always good, and right, and therefore, I think God can be doing something that is always good, and right with someone, and something from God doing something that is always good, and right because I think God can be doing something that is always good, and right as I think God can be doing something that is always good, and right with someone, and something. I think God can be doing something that is always good, and right as I think God can be doing something that is always good, and right with someone, and something because I think God is always good, and right for God to be doing something that is always good, and right as I think God is always good, and right for God to be doing something that is always good, and right with someone, and something. I think God is always good, and right for God to be doing something that is always good, and right as I think God is always good, and right for God to be doing something that is always good, and right with someone, and something because I think God is always good, and right for God to be doing something that is always good, and right as I think someone, and something is of God for God to be doing something that is always good, and right with someone, and something. If I think God is always good, and right for God to be doing something that is always good, and right as I think God is always good, and right for God to be doing something that is always good, and right with someone, and something, than I think God has a state of consciousness, along with God having a choice of right or wrong with God's will because I think God can choosing to be doing something that is good, and right with someone, and something with God always being good, and right with God having a choice of right or wrong with God's will for God to be aware of God choosing to be doing something that is good, and right with someone, and something, and therefore, I think God can choose to be doing something that is good, and right with someone, and something for God to be aware of God doing something that is good, and right with someone, and something because I think God is always good, and right with God having a choice of right or wrong with God's will for God to be aware of God choosing to be doing something that is right or wrong with someone, and something. If I think God can choose to be doing something that is good, and right with someone, and something for God to be aware of God doing something that is good, and right with someone, and something, than I think God's free will is God is always being good, and right with God having a choice of right or wrong for God to be choosing to be doing something that is always good, and right with someone, and something because I think God is always good, and right with God having a choice of right or wrong with God's will for God to be choosing to be doing something that is always good, and right with someone, and something, and therefore, I think God is always good, and right with God's free will because I think God is always good, and right with God having a choice of right or wrong for God to always be good, and right with God's free will.

If I think God is always good, and right with God's free will, than I think God can have goals because I think God can choose to be creating someone, and something for God to be having goals, and therefore, I think God has goals because I think God's choices is God's goals. I think God's choices is God's goals because I think God's choices is of God choosing to be doing something that is always good, and right as I think God can choose to be doing something that is always good, and right for God to be having goals. I think God's choices is of God choosing to be doing something that is always good, and right as I think God can choose to be doing something that is always good, and right for God to be having goals because I think God is always good, and right for God's choices to be of God choosing to be doing something that is always good, and right as I think God can choose to be doing something that is always good, and right for God's choices to be God's goals. I think God is always good, and right for God's choices to be of God choosing to be doing something that is always good, and right as I think God can choose to be doing something that is always good, and right for God's choices to be God's goals because I think God can choose to be doing something that is always good, and right for God to be having goals. I think God can choose to be doing something that is always good, and right for God to be having goals because I think God is always good, and right for God's goals to be of God choosing to be doing something that is always good, and right as I think God's goals is of God choosing to be doing something that is always good, and right for God to be having goals, even though, I do not think God has hope because I think God is always good, and right with God being aware of everything for God not to be having hope, however, I think God is hope because I think someone can have hope in God for God to be hope. If I think God is hope, than I think God can have dreams because I think God can have goals for God to be having dreams, and therefore, I think God's dreams can be God's goals because I think God's dreams can be God thinking of doing something that is good, and right for God's dreams to be God's goals. If I think God's dreams can be God's goals, than I think God's goals is God's dreams as I think God's dreams is God's goals because I think God's dreams is God thinking of doing something that is good, and right as I think God's goals is God thinking of doing something that is good, and right, and therefore, I think God's goals is God having dreams for God to be having goals because I do not think God can have goals, without God having dreams for God to be having goals, but I think God has dreams for God to be having goals because I think God's goals is God's dreams for God to be having goals. If I think God has dreams for God to be having goals, than I think God's purpose is God's goals because I think what God's goals are in life is what God's purpose is in life for God's purpose to be God's goals, and therefore, I think God's goal is God's purpose for God to be having a purpose because I do not think God can have a purpose, without God having a goal for God to be having a purpose. If I think God's goal is God's purpose for God to be having a purpose, than I think God's goal is God's purpose because I think God's purpose is what God's goal is in life of what God chooses to be doing for God's goal to be God's purpose. If I think God's goal is God's purpose, than I think God has a dream because I think everything is created by God for God to be having a dream, and therefore, I think everything is God's dream or vision because I think God created everything for everything to be God's dream or vision. If I think everything is God's dream or vision, than I think God created everything from God's imagination because I think God created everything with God's thoughts for God to be creating everything from God's imagination, and therefore, I think life is a dream as I think everything is a dream because I think life is God's dream for life to be a dream as I think God created everything with God's thoughts for everything to be a dream. I think life is God's dream for life to be a dream as I think God created everything with God's thoughts for everything to be a dream because I think God created everything with God's thoughts for life to be God's dream as I think God created everything with God's thoughts for everything to be God's dream, and therefore, I think everything is God's dream because I think God created everything with God's thoughts for everything to be God's dream, however, I do not think life is a dream with God dreaming about everything for life to be a dream because I think God created everything with God's thoughts for life to be God's dream or vision with how everything is created by God, and therefore, I think God can have dreams because I think God can be creating more in life with God's thoughts for God to be having dreams. If I think God can have dreams, than I think everything is living within God's dream because I think God created everything with God's thoughts for everything to be living within God's dream as I think God created everything with God's thoughts for everything to be God's dream, and therefore, I think life is God's dream because I think God is always good, and right with how God created everything. I think God is always good, and right with how God created everything because I think God is always good, and right for God to be doing something that is always good, and right.

I think God is always good, and right for God to be doing something that is always good, and right because I think God is always right. I think God is always right because I think God is always good, and right for God to always be right. I think God is always good, and right for God to always be right because I think God is always right about something. I think God is always right about something because I think God is always right about what God thinks. I think God is always right about what God thinks because I think God is always right about what God thinks of something. I think God is always right about what God thinks of something because I think God is always good, and right for God to always be right about what God thinks of something. I think God is always good, and right for God to always be right about what God thinks of something because I think God is always right about something that God can be thinking of in life. I think God is always right about something that God can be thinking of in life because I think God is always good, and right for God to be thinking of something. I think God is always good, and right for God to be thinking of something because I think God can choose to be thinking of something that is always good, and right with God's thoughts. I think God can choose to be thinking of something that is always good, and right with God's thoughts because I think something is of God's thoughts for God to be choosing to be thinking of something that is always good, and right with God's thoughts. I think something is of God's thoughts for God to be choosing to be thinking of something that is always good, and right with God's thoughts because I think God can choose to be thinking of something that is always good, and right with God's thoughts as I think God can choose something that is always good, and right with God's thoughts. I think God can choose to be thinking of something that is always good, and right with God's thoughts as I think God can choose something that is always good, and right with God's thoughts because I think God is always good, and right for God to be choosing to be thinking of something that is always good, and right with God's thoughts as I think God is always good, and right for God to be choosing something that is always good, and right with God's thoughts. I think God is always good, and right for God to be choosing to be thinking of something that is always good, and right with God's thoughts as I think God is always good, and right for God to be choosing something that is always good, and right with God's thoughts because I think God can think of something that is always good, and right with God's thoughts. I think God can think of something that is always good, and right with God's thoughts because I think God is always good, and right for God to be thinking of something that is always good, and right with God thoughts. I think God is always good, and right for God to be thinking of something that is always good, and right with God thoughts because I think God can choose something that is always good, and right with God's thoughts. I think God can choose something that is always good, and right with God's thoughts because I think God is always good, and right for God to be choosing something that is always good, and right with God's thoughts. I think God is always good, and right for God to be choosing something that is always good, and right with God's thoughts because I think God can choose to be thinking of something that is always good, and right with God's thoughts.

I think God can choose to be thinking of something that is always good, and right with God's thoughts because I do not think God's thoughts is right or wrong. I do not think God's thoughts is right or wrong because I do not think God's thoughts has a sense of right or wrong as I think God has a sense of right or wrong. I do not think God's thoughts has a sense of right or wrong as I think God has a sense of right or wrong because I do not think God's thoughts can choose something that is right or wrong for

God's thoughts to be able to be having a sense of right or wrong as I think God can choose something that is right or wrong for God to be having a sense of right or wrong. I do not think God's thoughts can choose something that is right or wrong for God's thoughts to be able to be having a sense of right or wrong as I think God can choose something that is right or wrong for God to be having a sense of right or wrong because I think God can choose something that is right or wrong with God's thoughts as I think God's thoughts of something is in God's mind that is apart of God's being. I think God can choose something that is right or wrong with God's thoughts as I think God's thoughts of something is in God's mind that is apart of God's being because I think God has a choice of right or wrong for God to be choosing something that is right or wrong with God's thoughts. If I think God can choose something that is right or wrong with God's thoughts as I think God's thoughts of something is in God's mind that is apart of God's being, than I think God can think of something as being right or wrong because I think God can choose something that is right or wrong with God's thoughts for God to be thinking of something as being right or wrong as I think God has a sense of right or wrong for God to be thinking of something as being right or wrong, and therefore, I think someone can think of God's thoughts as being right or wrong because I think God can choose something that is right or wrong with God's thoughts for someone to be thinking of God's thoughts as being right or wrong, but I do not think God's thoughts is right or wrong because I think God can choose something that is right or wrong with God's thoughts for God's thoughts not to be right or wrong. I think God can choose something that is right or wrong with God's thoughts for God's thoughts not to be right or wrong because I think God has a choice of right or wrong for God to be choosing something that is right or wrong with God's thoughts. I think God has a choice of right or wrong for God to be choosing something that is right or wrong with God's thoughts because I think God is always good, and right with God having a choice of something that is right or wrong with God's thoughts. I think God is always good, and right with God having a choice of something that is right or wrong with God's thoughts because I think God is always good, and right for God to be choosing something that is right or wrong with God's thoughts.

I think God is always good, and right for God to be choosing something that is right or wrong with God's thoughts because I think God is always good, and right with God having a choice of right or wrong. I think God is always good, and right with God having a choice of right or wrong because I think God has a choice of right or wrong for God to be having a choice of something that is right or wrong. I think God has a choice of right or wrong for God to be having a choice of something that is right or wrong because I think God is always good, and right with God having a choice of something that is right or wrong, but I do not think something is right or wrong because I think God can choose something that is always good, and right with God having a choice of right or wrong. I think God can choose something that is always good, and right with God having a choice of right or wrong because I think God is constantly able to be choosing something that is always good, and right. I think God is constantly able to be choosing something that is always good, and right because I think God is always good, and right for God to be choosing something that is always good, and right. I think God is always good, and right for God to be choosing something that is always good, and right because I do not think God can be wrong. I do not think God can be wrong because I do not think God can choose something that is wrong for God to be wrong. I do not think God can choose something that is wrong for God to be wrong because I think God can choose something that is always good, and right. I think God can choose something that is always good, and right because I think God has a sense of always being good, and right as I think God being instinctively has a sense of always being good, and right. I think God has a sense of always being good, and right as I think God instinctively has a sense of always being good, and right because I think God has a sense of always being good, and right for God to instinctively have a sense of always being good, and right, and therefore, I think God instinctively has a sense of always being good, and right as I think God's being instinctively has a sense of always being good, and right because I think God is God's being as I think God instinctively has a sense of always being good, and right. If I think God instinctively has a sense of always being good, and right as I think God's being instinctively has a sense of always being good, and right, than I think God has a sense of always being good, and right for God to instinctively have a sense of always being good, and right because I think God can choose something that is always good, and right for God to instinctively be having a sense of always being good, and right as I think God can choose something that is always good, and right for God to be having a sense of always being good, and right. I think God can choose something that is always good, and right for God to instinctively be having a sense of always being good, and right as I think God can choose something that is always good, and right for God to be having a sense of always being good, and right because I think God can choose something that is always good, and right with God's choice always being good, and right for God to be having a sense of always being good, and right as I think God's choice is always good, and right for God to instinctively be having a sense of always being good, and right. I think God can choose something that is always good, and right with God's choice always being good, and right for God to be having a sense of always being good, and right as I think God's choice is always good, and right for God to instinctively be having a sense of always being good, and right because I think God instinctively having a sense of always being good, and right is God having a sense of always being good, and right as I think God has a sense of always being good, and right with God's choice always being good, and right for God to be choosing something that is always good, and right, and therefore, I think God can choose something that is always good, and right with God's choice always being good, and right as I think God can choose something that is always good, and right with God having a sense of always being good, and right because I think God's choice that is always good, and right is God's sense of always being good, and right as I think God's choice is always good, right for God to be always be good, and right with God choosing something that is always good, and right. I think God's choice that is always good, and right is God's sense of always being good, and right as I think God's choice is always good, right for God to be always be good, and right with God choosing something that is always good, and right because I think God is always good, and right for God to be choosing something that is always good, and right, and therefore, I do not think God created God's sense of always being good, and right for God to be having a sense of always being good, and right because I think God's sense of always being good, and right is of God always being good, and right for God not to be creating God to be having a sense of always being good, and right.

If I do not think God created God's sense of always being good, and right for God to be having a sense of always being good, and right, than I think God has a sense of always being good, and right for God to be choosing someone, and something because I think someone, and something can be God's choice for God to be choosing someone, and something as I think God is always good, and right with God choosing someone, and something. I think someone, and something can be God's choice for God to be choosing someone, and something as I think God is always good, and right with God choosing someone, and something because I think God can choose someone, and something with God's choice always being good, and right for God to always be good, and right with God choosing someone, and something, and therefore, I think God can choose someone, and something with God's choice always being good, and right as I think God can choose someone, and something with God having a sense of always being good, and right because I think God's choice that is always good, and right is God's sense of always being good, and right as I think God's choice is always good, and right for God to be always be good, and right with God choosing someone, and something. I think God's choice that is always good, and right is God's sense of always being good, and right as I think God's choice is always good, and right for God to be always be good, and right with God choosing someone, and something because I think God is always good, and right with God choosing someone, and something, however, I do not think God can choose God because I do not think God is created for God to be choosing God., and therefore, I think God can have common sense because I think God has sense of right or wrong with God having a choice of right or wrong for God to sense someone doing something that is right or wrong with themselves, someone else, something, and God as I think God can sense someone doing something that is right or wrong with themselves, someone else, something, and God for God to be having common sense, even though, I do not think God can choose not to be having common sense because I think God is always good, and right with God having a choice of right or wrong for God to always be good, and right with God having a sense of someone doing something that is right or wrong with themselves, someone else, something, and God.

If I do not think God can choose not to be having common sense, than I think God can choose someone, and something with God having a sense of right or wrong because I think someone, and something is of God's thoughts for God to be choosing someone, and something as I think someone, and something is of God's thoughts for God to be choosing to be thinking of someone, and something as being right or wrong. I think someone, and something is of God's thoughts for God to be choosing someone, and something as I think someone, and something is of God's thoughts for God to be choosing to be thinking of someone, and something as being right or wrong because I think God can choose to be thinking of someone, and something with God having a sense of right or wrong. I think God can choose to be thinking of someone, and something with God having a sense of right or wrong because I think someone, and something is of God thoughts for God to be choosing to be thinking of someone, and something as being right or wrong. I think someone, and something is of God thoughts for God to be choosing to be thinking of someone, and something as being right or wrong because I think God has a choice of right or wrong for God to be choosing to be thinking of someone, and something as being right or wrong, and therefore, I think God can think of someone, and something as being right or wrong because I think God has a sense of right or wrong for God to be thinking of someone, and something as being right or wrong. If I think God can think of someone, and something as being right or wrong, than I think God can think of someone, and something with God having a choice of right or wrong as I think God can think of someone, and something with God having a sense of right or wrong because I think God's choice of right or wrong is God's sense of right or wrong as I think God has a choice of right or wrong for God to be thinking of someone, and something as being right or wrong. I think God's choice of right or wrong is God's sense of right or wrong as I think God has a choice of right or wrong for God to be thinking of someone, and something as being right or wrong because I think God is always good, and right with God having a choice of right or wrong for God to be thinking of someone, and something as being right or wrong, however, I do not think God can think of God as being right or wrong because I do not think God is created as I think God is always good, and right for God not to be thinking of God as being right or wrong.

If I do not think God can think of God as being right or wrong, than I think God can choose to be doing something with God, someone, and something because I think God can choosing to be thinking about doing something with God, someone, and something for God to be choosing to be doing something with God, someone, and something, and therefore, I think God has a sense of always being good, and right for God to be choosing to be doing something with God, someone, and something because I think someone, and something can be God's choice for God to be choosing to be doing something with God, someone, and something as I think God is always good, and right with God choosing to be doing God, something with someone, and something. I think someone, and something can be God's choice for God to be choosing to be doing something with God, someone, and something as I think God is always good, and right with God choosing to be doing something with God, someone, and something because I think God can choose to be doing something with God, someone, and something with God's choice that is always good, and right for God to always be good, and right with God choosing to be doing something with God, someone, and something, and therefore, I think God has a sense of always being good, and right for God to always be good, and right with God choosing to be doing something with God, someone, and something because I think God can choose to be doing something that is always good, and right with God, someone, and something with God having a sense of always being good, and right. I think God can choose to be doing something that is always good, and right with God, someone, and something with God having a sense of always being good, and right because I think God has a sense of always being good, and right for God to be choosing to be doing something that is always good, and right with God, someone, and something, and therefore, I think God can choose to be doing something with God, someone, and something with God's choice that is always good, and right as I think God can choose to be doing something with God, someone, and something with God having a sense of always being good, and right because I think God's choice that is always good, and right is God's sense of always being good, and right as I think God has a sense of always being good, and right for God to always be good, and right with God choosing to be doing something with God, someone, and something. I think God's choice that is always good, and right is God's sense of always being good, and right as I think God has a sense of always being good, and right for God to always be good, and right with God choosing to be doing something with God, someone, and something because I think God is always good, and right with God choosing to be doing something with God, someone, and something, however, I do not think God can choose God for God to be doing something with God because I do not think God is created for God to be choosing God as I think God can do something with everything for God to be doing something with God. If I do not think God can choose God for God to be doing something with God, than I do not think God has any wants or needs because I think God is always good, and right for God not to be having any wants or needs, and therefore, I do not think God wants or needs to be doing something with God, someone, and something because I think God is always good, and right for God to be doing something with God, someone, and something as I think God is always good, and right for God not to be wanting or needing to be doing something with God, someone, and something.

If I do not think God wants or needs to be doing something with God, someone, and something, than I think God has rights because I think God is always right about something for God to be having rights, and therefore, I think God can pass judgment onto someone because I think God can think of someone as being right or wrong about something with God having a choice of right or wrong for God to be passing judgment onto someone. I think God can think of someone as being right or wrong about something with God having a choice of right or wrong for God to be passing judgment onto someone because I think God always good, and right about what God thinks of someone for God to be passing true judgment onto someone. I think God always good, and right about what God thinks of someone for God to be passing true judgment onto someone because I think God has a true judgment of someone for God to be passing true judgment onto someone. I think God has a true judgment of someone for God to be passing true judgment onto someone because I think God has the right to be passing judgment onto someone. I think God has the right to be passing judgment onto someone because I think God has the ability to be passing judgment onto someone. I think God has the ability to be passing judgment onto someone because I think God has a choice of right or wrong for God to be having the ability, and the right to be passing judgment onto someone, and therefore, I think God is a judge with God passing judgment onto someone because I think God has a choice of right or wrong for God to be having the ability, and the right to be passing judgment onto someone, even though, I do not think is God judgmental towards someone with God passing false judgment onto someone because I think God is always good, and right for God to be passing true judgment onto someone, however, I think God can pass judgment onto someone, without God passing false judgment onto someone because I think God has the right to be passing judgment onto someone.

I think God has the right to be passing judgment onto someone because I think God has a choice of right or wrong for God to be thinking of someone as being good or bad as I think God can think of someone as being good or bad for God passing an honest judgment onto someone. I think God has a choice of right or wrong for God to be thinking of someone as being good or bad as I think God can think of someone as being good or bad for God passing an honest judgment onto someone because I think God can have an honest judgment of someone, as to whether or not if God thinks someone has done something right or wrong for God to be thinking of someone as being good or bad, and therefore, I think God can have a good judgment of someone because I think God is right about what God thinks of someone for God to be having a good judgment of someone. If I think God can have a good judgment of someone, than I do not think God can have a bad judgment of someone because I think God is always good, and right for God not to be wrong about what God thinks of someone as I do not think God is wrong about what God thinks of someone for God not to be having a bad judgment of someone, and therefore, I think God can have good judgment because I think someone can choose to be good or bad from someone choosing to be good with God. If I think God can have good judgment, than I think God instantly passes judgment onto someone because I think God instinctively passes judgment onto someone for God to be instantly passing judgment onto someone. I think God instinctively passes judgment onto someone for God to be instantly passing judgment onto someone because I think God instinctively has a sense of always being good, and right for God to instinctively be passing judgment onto someone.

If I think God instinctively passes judgment onto someone for God to be instantly passing judgment onto someone, than I think God can think of something as always being good, and right because I think God can choose something that is always good, and right. I think God can choose something that is always good, and right because I think God can choose something that is always good, and right with God's thoughts. I think God can choose something that is always good, and right with God's thoughts because I think something is of God's thoughts for God to be thinking of something that is always good, and right with God's thoughts. I think something is of God's thoughts for God to be thinking of something that is always good, and right with God's thoughts because I think God can think of something that is always good, and right with God's thoughts. I think God can think of something that is always good, and right with God's thoughts because I think God is always good, and right for God to be thinking of something that is always good, and right with God's thoughts. I think God is always good, and right for God to be thinking of something that is always good, and right with God's thoughts because I think God can choose to be thinking of something as being always good, and right. I think God can choose to be thinking of something as being always good, and right because I think God can choose something that is always good, and right with God's thoughts for God to be thinking of something as always being good, and right. I think God can choose something that is always good, and right with God's thoughts for God to be thinking of something as always being good, and right because I think something is of God's thoughts for God to be thinking of something as always good, and right. I think something is of God's thoughts for God to be thinking of something as always good, and right because I think God can think of something as always being good, and right. I think God can think of something as always being good, and right because I think God is always good, and right for God to be thinking of something as always being good, and right. I think God is always good, and right for God to be thinking of something as always being good, and right because I think God can think of something as always being good, and right with God's sense of always being good, and right as I think God can think of something as always being good, and right with God's state of consciousness, along with God's will, and God's thoughts, and God's mind that is apart of God's being. I think God can think of something as always being good, and right with God's sense of always being good, and right as I think God can think of something as always being good, and right with God's state of consciousness, along with God's will, and God's thoughts, and God's mind that is apart of God's being because I think God has a choice, and therefore, I think God always has a choice because I think God is always good, and right with God having a choice as I think God is always good, and right with God having a choice of right or wrong. I think God is always good, and right with God having a choice as I think God is always good, and right with God having a choice of right or wrong because I think God has a choice of right or wrong for God to be having a choice, and therefore, I think God has a choice of right or wrong because I think God's choice of right or wrong is of the dimension of God's will for God to be having a choice of right or wrong.

Chapter 16

Someone has a choice of right or wrong

I would like to talk about how dimensions are in life in relation to what dimensions are in life by talking about someone having a choice of right or wrong, that can possibly have something to do with how dimensions are in life is in relation to what dimensions are in life because I think someone's choice of right or wrong is of the dimension of someone's will for someone to be having a choice of right or wrong, and therefore, I think someone has a choice of right or wrong for someone to be having a choice of right and wrong because I think God created right or wrong for someone to have a choice of right or wrong. I think God created right or wrong for someone to have a choice of right or wrong because I think God created someone to have a choice of right or wrong. I think God created someone to have a choice of right or wrong because I think God has a choice of right or wrong for God to be creating someone to be having a choice of right or wrong. I think God has a choice of right or wrong for God to be creating someone to be having a choice of right or wrong because I think God created someone to be having a choice of right or wrong from God having a choice of right or wrong for God to be creating someone to be having a choice of right or wrong. I think God created someone to be having a choice of right or wrong from God having a choice of right or wrong for God to be creating someone to be having a choice of right or wrong because I think God created someone to be choosing to be right or wrong for someone to be right or wrong. I think God created someone to be choosing to be right or wrong for someone to be right or wrong because I think God created someone to be having a choice of right or wrong for someone to be right or wrong as I think God created someone to be having a choice of right or wrong for someone to be choosing to be right or wrong, and therefore, I think God created someone's being to be having a sense of right or wrong because I think God created someone to be having a choice of right or wrong for God to be creating someone's being to be having a sense of right or wrong. If I think God created someone's being to be having a sense of right or wrong, than I think God created someone to be choosing something that is right or wrong because I think God created someone to be having a choice of right or wrong for someone to be choosing something that is right or wrong, and therefore, I think God created someone to be right or wrong because I think God created someone to be having a choice of right or wrong for God to be creating someone to be right or wrong. I think God created someone to be having a choice of right or wrong for God to be creating someone to be right or wrong because I think someone is right or wrong. I think someone is right or wrong because I think someone has a sense of right or wrong for someone to be right or wrong. I think someone has a sense of right or wrong for something to be right or wrong because I think someone has a choice of right or wrong for someone to be right or wrong as I think someone has a choice of right or wrong for someone to be having a sense of right or wrong, and therefore, I think someone can choose something that is right or wrong for someone to be right or wrong because I think someone has a choice of right or wrong for someone to be right or wrong as I think someone has a choice of right or wrong for someone to be choosing something that is right or wrong. If I think someone can choose something that is right or wrong for someone to be right or wrong, than I think someone has two kinds of choices because I think someone has a choice of right and wrong for someone to be having two kinds of choices. I think someone has a choice of right and wrong for someone to be having two kinds of choices because I think someone has a choice of right or wrong for someone to be right or wrong. I think someone has a choice of right or wrong for someone to

264

be right or wrong because I think someone is right or wrong. I think someone is right or wrong because I think someone is constantly right or wrong. I think someone is constantly right or wrong because I think someone is always right or wrong. I think someone is always right or wrong because I think someone is right or wrong for someone to always be right or wrong, and therefore, I think someone has a choice of right or wrong because I think God created someone's being to be having a sense of right or wrong from God creating someone to be choosing right or wrong. I think God created someone's being to be having a sense of right or wrong from God creating someone to be choosing right or wrong because I think God created someone's sense of right and wrong to be a choice of right or wrong for someone to be choosing right or wrong. I think God created someone's sense of right and wrong to be a choice of right or wrong for someone to be choosing right or wrong because I think someone's sense of right and wrong is someone's choice of right or wrong as I think God created someone to be having a choice of right or wrong for someone to be choosing right or wrong. I think someone's sense of right and wrong is someone's choice of right or wrong as I think God created someone to be having a choice of right or wrong for someone to be choosing right or wrong because I think someone can be right or wrong with someone having a choice of right or wrong.

I think someone can be right or wrong with someone having a choice of right or wrong because I think someone can choose something that is right or wrong for someone to be right or wrong. I think someone can choose something that is right or wrong for someone to be right or wrong because I think God created someone's being to be choosing something that is right or wrong for someone's being to have a sense of right or wrong. I think God created someone's being to be choosing something that is right or wrong for someone's being to have a sense of right or wrong because I think God created someone to be having a choice of right or wrong for someone's being to be having a sense of right or wrong as I think God created someone to be having a choice of right or wrong for someone to be choosing something that is right or wrong, even though, I do not think something is right or wrong as I think someone thinks something is right or wrong because I think God created someone's being to be choosing something that is right or wrong for someone's being to have a sense of right or wrong, however, I think something can be right or wrong because I think someone can choose something that is right or wrong with someone having a choice of right or wrong for something to be right or wrong, and therefore, I think someone can choose something that is right or wrong because I think God created someone's being to be having a sense of right or wrong from God creating someone to be choosing something that is right or wrong. I think God created someone's being to be having a sense of right or wrong from God creating someone to be choosing something that is right or wrong because I think God created someone to be right or wrong about something from someone choosing something that is right or wrong. I think God created someone to be right or wrong about something from someone choosing something that is right or wrong because I think God created someone to be learning from someone choosing something that is right or wrong. I think God created someone to be learning from someone choosing something that is right or wrong because I think God created someone to be learning from something that is right or wrong. I think God created someone to be learning from something that is right or wrong because I think someone can learn from themselves, someone else, something, and God about something that is right or wrong. I think someone can learn from themselves, someone else, something, and God about something that is right or wrong because I think someone can think of something as being right or wrong with someone having a choice of right or wrong for someone to learn from themselves, someone else, something, and God about something that is right or wrong, and therefore, I think someone can learn from something that is right or wrong because I think someone can think of something as being right or wrong for someone to learn from something that is right or wrong.

If I think someone can learn from something that is right or wrong, than I think someone can be right or wrong because I think someone can be right or wrong about something for someone to be right or wrong, and therefore, I think someone can be right or wrong about something because I think someone has a choice of right or wrong for someone to be right or wrong about something, even though, I choose not to be saying for myself, as to how exactly I think someone can be right or wrong because I choose not to be saying for myself, as to how exactly I think someone can be right or wrong about something for me not to be saying for myself, as to how exactly I think someone can be right or wrong. I choose not to be saying for myself, as to how exactly I think someone can be right or wrong about something for me not to be saying for myself, as to how exactly I think someone can be right or wrong because I choose not to be saying for myself, as to what exactly I think is right or wrong for me not to be saying for myself, as to how exactly I think someone can be right or wrong. I choose not to be saying for myself, as to what exactly I think is right or wrong for me not to be saying for myself, as to how exactly I think someone can be right or wrong because I choose not to be taking someone's side for me not to be on someone's side about how exactly I think someone can be right or wrong. I choose not to be taking someone's side for me not to be on someone's side about how exactly I think someone can be right or wrong because I choose not to be taking someone's side for me not to be on someone's side about what exactly I think is right or wrong. I choose not to be taking someone's side for me not to be on someone's side about what exactly I think is right or wrong because I would like to be talking about what I think is true, without being on someone's side about what I think is right or wrong. I would like to be talking about what I think is true, without being on someone's side about what I think is right or wrong because I would like to be talking about what I think is true, without being on someone's side about how I think someone can be right or wrong. I would like to be talking about what I think is true, without being on someone's side about how I think someone can be right or wrong because I do not have all of the answers for me to be on someone's side about how I think someone can be right or wrong. I do not have all of the answers for me to be on someone's side about how I think someone can be right or wrong because I do not know every possible way, as to how someone can possibly be right or wrong for me to be on someone's side about how I think someone can be right or wrong, even though, I think someone can be right or wrong because I think someone can be right or wrong about something for someone to be right or wrong.

I think someone can be right or wrong about something for someone to be right or wrong because I think someone can think of something as being right or wrong for someone to be right or wrong about something. I think someone can think of something as being right or wrong for someone to be right or wrong about something because I think someone can choose something that is right or wrong with someone's thoughts for someone to be thinking of something as being right or wrong. I think someone can choose something that is right or wrong with someone's thoughts for someone to be thinking of something as being right or wrong because I think someone's thoughts is of something for someone to be choosing something that is right or wrong with someone's thoughts. I think someone's thoughts is of something for someone to be choosing something that is right or wrong with someone's thoughts because I think someone can think of something as being right or wrong. I think someone can think of something as being right or wrong because I think someone can think of someone's thoughts of something as being right or wrong for someone to be thinking of something as being right or wrong. I think someone can think of someone's thoughts of something as being right or wrong for someone to be thinking of something as being right or wrong because I think someone's thoughts is of something for someone to be thinking of someone's thoughts of something as being right or wrong. I think someone's thoughts is of something for someone to be thinking of someone's thoughts of something as being right or wrong because I think someone's thoughts of something can be right or wrong. I think someone's thoughts of something can be right or wrong because I think someone has a choice of right or wrong for someone to be choosing to be thinking of someone's thoughts of something as being right or wrong. I think someone has a choice of right or wrong for someone to be choosing to be thinking of someone's thoughts of something as being right or wrong because I think someone can be right or wrong for someone to be thinking of someone's thoughts of something as being right or wrong. I think someone can be right or wrong for someone to be thinking of someone's thoughts of something as being right or wrong because I think someone can think of someone's thoughts of something as being right or wrong for someone thinking of something. I think someone can think of someone's thoughts of something as being right or wrong for someone thinking of something because I think someone can think of something as being right or wrong. I think someone can think of something as being right or wrong because I think someone can choose something that is right or wrong with someone's thoughts for someone to be thinking of something as being right or wrong. I think someone can choose something that is right or wrong with someone's thoughts for someone to be thinking of something as being right or wrong because I think someone has a choice of right or wrong for someone to be thinking of something as being right or wrong. I think someone has a choice of right or wrong for someone to be thinking of something as being right or wrong because I think someone can choose to be thinking of something as being right or wrong with someone's thoughts from someone having a choice of right or wrong. I think someone can choose to be thinking of something as being right or wrong with someone's thoughts from someone having a choice of right or wrong because I think someone can choose to be thinking of something as being right or wrong with someone having a sense of right or wrong as I think someone can be right or wrong with someone having a sense of right or wrong. I think someone can choose to be thinking of something as being right or wrong with someone having a sense of right or wrong as I think someone can be right or wrong with someone having a sense of right or wrong because I think someone can think of something as being right or wrong with someone having a choice of right or wrong for someone to be right or wrong about what someone thinks of something. If I think someone can choose to be thinking of something as being right or wrong with someone having a sense of right or wrong as I think someone can be right or wrong with someone having a sense of right or wrong, than I think someone can think of something as being right or wrong because I think someone can choose to be thinking of something as being right or wrong with someone's sense of right and wrong as I think someone can choose to be thinking of something as being right or wrong with someone's state of consciousness, and someone's will, and someone's thoughts, and someone's mind that is apart of someone's being, and therefore, I think someone can choose to be thinking of something as being right or wrong with someone's being because I think someone can choose to be thinking of something as being right or wrong with someone's state of consciousness, and someone's will, and someone's thoughts, and someone's mind that is apart of someone's being, even though, I do not think something is right or wrong because I think someone can choose something with someone having a choice of right or wrong for something not to be right or wrong, however, I think someone can choose yes or no with something because I think someone has a choice of right or wrong for someone to be choosing yes or no with something.

If I think someone can choose yes or no with something, than I think someone can think of something as being right or wrong because I think someone's thoughts is of something for someone to be thinking of something as being right or wrong, and therefore, I think someone can think of someone's thoughts as being right or wrong because I think someone's thoughts is of something for someone to be thinking of someone's thoughts as being right or wrong. I think someone's thoughts is of something for someone to be thinking of someone's thoughts as being right or wrong because I think someone's thoughts can be right or wrong. I think someone's thoughts can be right or wrong because I think someone has a choice of right or wrong for someone to be choosing to be thinking of someone's thoughts as being right or wrong. I think someone has a choice of right or wrong for someone to be choosing to be thinking of someone's thoughts as being right or wrong because I think someone can be right or wrong for someone to be thinking of someone's thoughts as being right or wrong. I think someone can be right or wrong for someone to be thinking of someone's thoughts as being right or wrong because I think someone can think of someone's thoughts as being right or wrong for someone thinking of someone's thoughts, and therefore, I think someone can think of someone's thoughts as being right or wrong because I think someone can choose something that is right or wrong with someone's thoughts for someone to be thinking of someone's thoughts as being right or wrong. I think someone can choose something that is right or wrong with someone's thoughts for someone to be thinking of someone's thoughts as being right or wrong because I think someone has a choice of right or wrong for someone to be thinking of someone's thoughts as being right or wrong. I think someone has a choice of right or wrong for someone to be thinking of someone's thoughts as being right or wrong because I think someone can choose to be thinking of something as being right or wrong with someone's thoughts from someone having a choice of right or wrong. I think someone can choose to be thinking of something as being right or wrong with someone's thoughts from someone having a choice of right or wrong because I think someone can choose to be thinking of someone's thoughts as being right or wrong with someone having a sense of right or wrong as I think someone can be right or wrong with someone having a sense of right or wrong. I think someone can choose to be thinking of someone's thoughts as being right or wrong with someone having a sense of right or wrong as I think someone can be right or wrong with someone having a sense of right or wrong because I think someone can think of someone's thoughts of something as being right or wrong with someone having a choice of right or wrong for someone to be right or wrong about what someone thinks of someone's thoughts. If I think someone can choose to be thinking of someone's thoughts as being right or wrong with someone having a sense of right or wrong as I think someone can be right or wrong with someone having a sense of right or wrong, than I think someone can think of someone's thoughts as being right or wrong because I think someone can choose to be thinking of something as being right or wrong with someone's sense of right and wrong as I think someone can choose to be thinking of something as being right or wrong with someone's state of consciousness, and someone's will, and someone's thoughts, and someone's mind that is apart of someone's being, and therefore, I think someone can choose to be thinking of someone's thoughts as being right or wrong with someone's being because I think someone can choose to be thinking of something as being right or wrong with someone's state of consciousness, and someone's will, and someone's thoughts, and someone's mind that is apart of someone's being, even though, I do not think someone's thoughts is right or wrong because I think someone can choose to be thinking of something with someone having a choice of right or wrong for someone's thoughts not to be right or wrong, however, I think someone can choose yes or no with someone's thoughts because I think someone has a choice of right or wrong for someone to be choosing yes or no with someone's thoughts.

If I think someone can choose yes or no with someone's thoughts, than I think someone's thoughts can be right or wrong because I think someone can think of someone's thoughts as being right or wrong for someone's thoughts to be right or wrong, even though, I do not think someone's thoughts is right or wrong because I do not think someone's thoughts has a sense of right or wrong as I think someone has a sense of right or wrong. I do not think someone's thoughts has a sense of right or wrong as I think someone has a sense of right or wrong because I do not think someone's thoughts is able to be choosing something that is right or wrong for someone's thoughts not to be having a sense of right or wrong as I think someone is able to be choosing something that is right or wrong for someone to be having a sense of right or wrong. I do not think someone's thoughts is able to be choosing something that is right or wrong for someone's thoughts not to be having a sense of right or wrong as I think someone is able to be choosing something that is right or wrong for someone to be having a sense of right or wrong because I think someone is able to be choosing something that is right or wrong with someone's thoughts as I think someone's thoughts of something is in someone's mind that is apart of someone's being. I think someone is able to be choosing something that is right or wrong with someone's thoughts as I think someone's thoughts of something is in someone's mind that is apart of someone's being because I think someone has a choice of right or wrong for someone to be able to be choosing something that is right or wrong with someone's thoughts. If I think someone has a choice of right or wrong for someone to be able to be choosing something that is right or wrong with someone's thoughts, than I think someone can think of something as being right or wrong because I think someone is able to be choosing something that is right or wrong with someone's thoughts for someone to be thinking of something as being right or wrong as I think someone has a sense of right or wrong for someone to be thinking of something as being right or wrong, and therefore, I think someone can think of someone's thoughts as being right or wrong because I think someone is able to be choosing something that is right or wrong with someone's thoughts for someone to be thinking of someone's thoughts as being right or wrong, but I do not think someone's thoughts is right or wrong because I think someone is able to be choosing something that is right or wrong with someone's thoughts for someone's thoughts not to be right or wrong. I think someone is able to be choosing something that is right or wrong with someone's thoughts for someone's thoughts not to be right or wrong because I think someone has a choice of right or wrong for someone to be choosing something that is right or wrong with someone's thoughts. I think someone has a choice of right or wrong for someone to be choosing something that is right or wrong with someone's thoughts because I think someone can be right or wrong with someone having a choice of something that is right or wrong with someone's thoughts. I think someone can be right or wrong with someone having a choice of something that is right or wrong with someone's thoughts because I think someone can be right or wrong for someone to be choosing something that is right or wrong with someone's thoughts.

I think someone can be right or wrong for someone to be choosing something that is right or wrong with someone's thoughts because I think someone's thoughts is of something as I think someone can choose something that is right or wrong with someone's thoughts. I think someone's thoughts is of something as I think someone can choose something that is right or wrong with someone's thoughts because I think someone can choose to be thinking of something as being right or wrong with someone's sense of right and wrong for someone to be choosing something that is right or wrong with someone's thoughts as I think someone can choose to be thinking of something as being right or wrong with someone's state of consciousness, and someone's will, and someone's thoughts, and someone's mind that is apart of someone's being for someone to be choosing something that is right or wrong with someone's thoughts. I think someone can choose to be thinking of something as being right or wrong with someone's sense of right and wrong for someone to be choosing something that is right or wrong with someone's thoughts as I think someone can choose to be thinking of something as being right or wrong with someone's state of consciousness, and someone's will, and someone's thoughts, and someone's mind that is apart of someone's being for someone to be choosing something that is right or wrong with someone's thoughts because I think someone can choose something that is right or wrong for someone to be choosing something that is right or wrong with someone's thoughts. I think someone can choose something that is right or wrong for someone to be choosing something that is right or wrong with someone's thoughts because I think someone can choose to be thinking of something as being right or wrong with someone's being for someone to be choosing something that is right or wrong with someone's thoughts as I think someone can choose to be thinking of something as being right or wrong with someone's state of consciousness, and someone's will, and someone's thoughts, and someone's mind that is apart of someone's being for someone to be choosing something that is right or wrong with someone's thoughts. I think someone can choose to be thinking of something as being right or wrong with someone's being for someone to be choosing something that is right or wrong with someone's thoughts as I think someone can choose to be thinking of something as being right or wrong with someone's state of consciousness, and someone's will, and someone's thoughts, and someone's mind that is apart of someone's being for someone to be choosing something that is right or wrong with someone's thoughts because I think someone can choose something that is right or wrong with someone's thoughts. I think someone can choose something that is right or wrong with someone's thoughts because I think someone has a choice of right or wrong for someone to be choosing something that is right or wrong with someone's thoughts. I think someone has a choice of right or wrong for someone to be choosing something that is right or wrong with someone's thoughts because I think someone can be right or wrong for someone to be choosing something that is right or wrong with someone's thoughts. I think someone can be right or wrong for someone to be choosing something that is right or wrong with someone's thoughts because I think someone can choose to be thinking of something that is right or wrong with someone's thoughts, and therefore, I think someone has a choice of yes or no with something because I think someone has a choice of right or wrong for someone to be having a choice of yes or no with something. I think someone has a choice of right or wrong for someone to be having a choice of yes or no with something because I think someone can choose yes or no with something for someone to be having a choice of yes or no with something.

If I think someone has a choice of right or wrong for someone to be having a choice of yes or no with something, than I think someone can be learning a lesson because I think someone can learn from something that is right or wrong for someone to be learning a lesson. I think someone can learn from something that is right or wrong for someone to be learning a lesson because I think someone can learn a lesson from what someone thinks is right or wrong. I think someone can learn a lesson from what someone thinks is right or wrong because I think someone can learn from what someone thinks is right or wrong for someone to be learning a lesson. I think someone can learn from what someone thinks is right or wrong for someone to be learning a lesson because I think someone can think of something that someone thinks is right or wrong for someone to be learning a lesson. I think someone can think of something that someone thinks is right or wrong for someone to be learning a lesson because I think someone can learn a lesson from something that someone thinks is right or wrong. I think someone can learn a lesson from something that someone thinks is right or wrong because I think someone can think of something that someone thinks is right or wrong for someone to be learning a lesson from something that someone thinks is right or wrong. I think someone can think of something that someone thinks is right or wrong for someone to be learning a lesson from something that someone thinks is right or wrong because I think someone's lesson is a lesson in life. I think someone's lesson is a lesson in life because I think someone can learn from something that someone thinks is right or wrong for someone's lesson to be a lesson in life. I think someone can learn from something that someone thinks is right or wrong for someone's lesson to be a lesson in life because I think someone can learn from something that someone thinks is right or wrong for something that someone thinks is right or wrong to be someone's lesson in life. I think someone can learn from something that someone thinks is right or wrong for something that someone thinks is right or wrong to be someone's lesson in life because I think everything is a lesson in life as I think something is a lesson in life. I think everything is a lesson in life as I think something is a lesson in life because I think everything is of something for everything to be a lesson in life. I think everything is of something for everything to be a lesson in life because I think someone can learn from something that someone thinks is right or wrong for everything to be a lesson in life. I think someone can learn from something that someone thinks is right or wrong for everything to be a lesson in life because I think someone can learn from everything that someone thinks is right or wrong for everything to be someone's lesson in life. I think someone can learn from everything that someone thinks is right or wrong for everything to be someone's lesson in life because I think everything is a lesson to be learned in life.

If I think someone can learn from everything that someone thinks is right or wrong for everything to be someone's lesson in life, than I think someone can think of someone as being right or wrong as I think someone can think of something as being right or wrong because I think someone's thoughts is of the thoughts of someone's physical being for someone to be thinking of someone as being right or wrong as I think someone's thoughts is of the thoughts of something's physical being for someone to be thinking of something as being right or wrong, and therefore, I think someone can think of themselves, and someone else as being right or wrong because I think someone is someone, and someone else for someone to be thinking of themselves, and someone else as being right or wrong. If I think someone can think of themselves, and someone else as being right or wrong, than I think someone can think of themselves, and someone else as being right or wrong about something as I think someone can think of themselves, and someone else as being right or wrong because I think someone can choose something that is right or wrong with someone's thoughts for someone to be thinking of themselves, and someone else as being right or wrong about something as I think someone can choose something that is right or wrong with someone's thoughts for someone to be thinking of themselves, and someone else as being right or wrong, and therefore, I think someone can think of themselves, and someone else as being right or wrong about something because I think God created someone to be choosing something that is right or wrong for someone to be thinking of themselves, and someone else as being right or wrong about something. I think God created someone to be choosing something that is right or wrong for someone to be thinking of themselves, and someone else as being right or wrong about something because I think someone has a choice of right or wrong for someone to be thinking of themselves, and someone else as being right or wrong about something. I think someone has a choice of right or wrong for someone to be thinking of themselves, and someone else as being right or wrong about something because I think someone can choose to be thinking of themselves, and someone else as being right or wrong about something with someone's thoughts from someone having a choice of right or wrong.

I think someone can choose to be thinking of themselves, and someone else as being right or wrong about something with someone's thoughts from someone having a choice of right or wrong because I think someone can choose to be thinking of themselves, and someone else as being right or wrong about something with someone having a sense of right or wrong as I think someone can be right or wrong with someone having a sense of right or wrong. I think someone can choose to be thinking of themselves, and someone else as being right or wrong about something with someone having a sense of right or wrong as I think someone can be right or wrong with someone having a sense of right or wrong because I think someone can think of themselves, and someone else as being right or wrong about something with someone having a choice right or wrong for someone to be right or wrong about what someone thinks of themselves, and someone else. If I think someone can choose to be thinking of themselves, and someone else as being right or wrong about something with someone having a sense of right or wrong as I think someone can be right or wrong with someone having a sense of right or wrong, than I think someone can think of themselves, and someone else as being right or wrong about something because I think someone can choose to be thinking of themselves, and someone else as being right or wrong about something with someone's sense of right and wrong as I think someone can choose to be thinking of themselves, and someone else as being right or wrong about something with someone's state of consciousness, and someone's will, and someone's thoughts, and someone's mind that is apart of someone's being, and therefore, I think someone can choose to be thinking of themselves, and someone else as being right or wrong about something with someone's being because I think someone can choose to be thinking of themselves, and someone else as being right or wrong about something with someone's state of consciousness, and someone's will, and someone's thoughts, and someone's mind that is apart of someone's being. If I think someone can choose to be thinking of themselves, and someone else as being right or wrong about something with someone's being, than I think someone can learn something from themselves, and someone else because I think someone can think of themselves, and someone else as being right or wrong about something for someone to be learning something from themselves, and someone else, and therefore, I think someone can choose yes or no with themselves, and someone else about something because I think someone has a choice of right or wrong for someone to be choosing yes or no with themselves, and someone else about something. If I think someone can choose yes or no with themselves, and someone else about something, than I think someone can think of God as being right or wrong about something because I think someone has a choice of right or wrong for someone to be thinking of God as being right or wrong about something, and therefore, I think someone can be right or wrong about what someone thinks of God because I think someone can think of God as being right or wrong about something for someone to be right or wrong about what someone thinks of God, even though, I do not God is right or wrong about something because I think God is always good, and right for God not to be right or wrong about something as I think God is always good, and right for God to always be good, and right about something, however, I think someone can choose yes or no with God about something because I think someone has a choice of right or wrong for someone to be choosing yes or no with God about something.

If I think someone can choose yes or no with God about something, than I think someone has a choice of right or wrong because I think someone has someone's free will for someone to be having a choice of right or wrong. I think someone has someone's free will for someone to be having a choice of right or wrong because I think someone's free will is someone's choice as I think someone's choice is right or wrong. I think someone's free will is someone's choice as I think someone's choice is right or wrong because I think someone's choice is someone's free will. I think someone's choice is someone's free will because I think someone's free will is someone's will as I think someone's choice is someone's will. I think someone's free will is someone's will as I think someone's choice is someone's will because I think someone's will is someone's free will as I think someone's will is someone's choice. I think someone's will is someone's free will as I think someone's will is someone's choice because I think someone has a choice with someone's free will as I think someone has a choice with someone's will. I think someone has a choice with someone's free will as I think someone has a choice with someone's will because I think someone has a choice of right or wrong with someone's free will as I think someone has a choice of right or wrong with someone's will. I think someone has a choice of right or wrong with someone's free will as I think someone has a choice of right or wrong with someone's will because I think someone has a choice of right or wrong. If I think someone has a choice of right or wrong with someone's free will as I think someone has a choice of right or wrong with someone's will, than I think someone having a state of consciousness, and someone having a choice of right or wrong with someone's free will proves that someone is alive because I do not think someone would be alive, without someone having a state of consciousness, and someone having a choice of right or wrong with someone's free will for someone to be alive, and therefore, I think someone is alive because I think someone has a state of consciousness, and I think someone has a choice of right or wrong with someone's free will for someone to be alive. If I think someone is alive, than I think God created someone to be having a state of consciousness, and a choice of right or wrong with someone's free will from the very instance God created someone for someone to be alive because I do not think someone would be alive, without God creating someone to be having a state of consciousness, and a choice of right or wrong with someone's free will for someone to be alive, and therefore, I think someone is alive because I think God created someone to be having a state of consciousness, and a choice of right or wrong with someone's free will from the very instance God created someone for someone to be alive. If I think someone is alive, than I think God created someone to be having state of consciousness, along with someone having a choice of right or wrong with someone's will because I think God created someone to be choosing to be doing something that is right or wrong with themselves, someone else, something, and God with someone having a choice of right or wrong with someone's will for someone to be choosing to be aware of someone choosing to be doing something that is right or wrong with themselves, someone else, something, and God or not, even though, I think someone can choose to be doing something that is right or wrong with themselves, someone else, something, and God for someone to be choosing to be aware of someone doing something that is right or wrong with themselves, someone else, something, and God or not because I think someone has a choice of right or wrong with someone's will for someone to be choosing to be aware of someone choosing to be doing something that is right or wrong with themselves, someone else, something, and God or not, and therefore, I think someone can choose to be having a conscious or not because I think someone can choose to be aware of someone choosing to be doing something that is right or wrong with themselves, someone else, something, and God or not with someone having a choice of right or wrong with someone's will for someone to be choosing to be having a conscious or not.

If I think someone can choose to be having a conscious or not, than I think someone has a choice of right or wrong because I think someone has a choice of right or wrong with someone's free will for someone to be right or wrong. I think someone has a choice of right or wrong with someone's free will for someone to be right or wrong because I think someone's free will is someone's choice as I think someone has a choice of right or wrong for someone to be right or wrong. I think someone's free will is someone's choice as I think someone has a choice of right or wrong for someone to be right or wrong because I think someone is right or wrong with someone having a choice of right or wrong with someone's free will as I think someone is right or wrong with someone having a choice of right or wrong. I think someone is right or wrong with someone having a choice of right or wrong with someone's free will as I think someone is right or wrong with someone having a choice of right or wrong because I think someone has a choice of right or wrong. I think someone has a choice of right or wrong because I think someone has a choice of themselves, someone else, and something that is right or wrong for someone to be having a choice of right or wrong. I think someone has a choice of themselves, someone else, and something that is right or wrong for someone to be having a choice of right or wrong because I think someone has a choice of right or wrong for someone to be choosing themselves, someone else, and something that is right or wrong. I think someone has a choice of right or wrong for someone to be choosing themselves, someone else, and something that is right or wrong because I think someone can choose themselves, someone else, and something with someone having a choice of right or wrong for someone to be choosing themselves, someone else, and something that is right or wrong as I think someone can choose themselves, someone else, and something that is right or wrong for someone to be right or wrong about themselves, someone else, and something, and therefore, I think someone can choose themselves, someone else, and something that is right or wrong for someone to be right or wrong about themselves, someone else, and something because I think someone can be right or wrong with someone having a choice of right or wrong for someone to be right or wrong with someone choosing themselves, someone else, and something that is right or wrong. I think someone can be right or wrong with someone having a choice of right or wrong for someone to be right or wrong with someone choosing themselves, someone else, and something that is right or wrong because I think someone can choose themselves, someone else, and something that is right or wrong with someone having a choice of right or wrong. I think someone can choose themselves, someone else, and something that is right or wrong with someone having a choice of right or wrong because I think someone has a choice of themselves, someone else, and something that is right or wrong with someone's free will as I think someone has a choice of right or wrong with someone's free will. I think someone has a choice of themselves, someone else, and something that is right or wrong with someone's free will as I think someone has a choice of right or wrong with someone's free will because I think someone has a choice of right or wrong with someone's free will for someone to be choosing themselves, someone else, and something that is right or wrong. I think someone has a choice of right or wrong with someone's free will for someone to be choosing themselves, someone else, and something that is right or wrong because I think someone can choose themselves, someone else, and something that is right or wrong with someone's free will for someone to be right or wrong about themselves, someone else, and something. I think someone can choose themselves, someone else, and something that is right or wrong with someone's free will for someone to be right or wrong about themselves, someone else, and something because I think someone can be right or wrong with someone having a choice of right or wrong with someone's free will as I think someone can be right or wrong with someone choosing themselves, someone else, and something that is right or wrong with someone's free will. I think someone can be right or wrong with someone having a choice of right or wrong with someone's free will as I think someone can be right or wrong with someone choosing themselves, someone else, and something that is right or wrong with someone's free will because I think someone can choose themselves, someone else, and something that is right or wrong with someone's free will having a choice of right or wrong. I think someone can choose themselves, someone else, and something that is right or wrong with someone's free will having a choice of right or wrong because I think someone has a choice of right or wrong with someone's free will for someone to be choosing themselves, someone else, and something that is right or wrong with someone's free will, and therefore, I think someone can learn a lot from someone's free will because I think someone can learn a lot from someone choosing themselves, someone else, and something that is right or wrong with someone's free will. I think someone can learn a lot from someone choosing themselves, someone else, and something that is right or wrong with someone's free will because I think someone can choose to be living by someone's example or not. I think someone can choose to be living by someone's example or not because I think someone can be right or wrong with someone choosing themselves, someone else, and something that is right or wrong with someone's free will for someone to be choosing to be living by someone's example or not, and therefore, I think someone can choose themselves, someone else, and something that is right or wrong with someone's free will because I think someone has a choice of themselves, someone else, and something that is right or wrong with someone's free will for someone to be right or wrong about themselves, someone else, and something as I think someone has a choice of themselves, someone else, and something that is right or wrong for someone to be right or wrong. I think someone has a choice of themselves, someone else, and something that is right or wrong with someone's free will for someone to be right or wrong about themselves, someone else, and something as I think someone has a choice of themselves, someone else, and something that is right or wrong for someone to be right or wrong because I think someone can be right or wrong with someone having a choice of right or wrong with someone's free will for someone to be right or wrong about themselves, someone else, and something as I think someone can be right or wrong with someone having a choice of right or wrong for someone to be having a choice of themselves, someone else, and something that is right or wrong.

If I think someone has a choice of themselves, someone else, and something that is right or wrong with someone's free will for someone to be right or wrong about themselves, someone else, and something as I think someone has a choice of themselves, someone else, and something that is right or wrong for someone to be right or wrong, than I think someone can look good on the outside because I think someone can be good looking, and have a lot of money, and have a lot of nice things, but I do not think someone is always good on the inside just because someone looks good on the outside because I think someone can be bad on the inside as I think someone can look good on the outside. I think someone can be bad on the inside as I think someone can look good on the outside because I think someone can be wrong with someone's free will for someone to be bad on the inside as I think someone can look good on the outside. I think someone can be wrong with someone's free will for someone to be bad on the inside as I think someone can look good on the outside because I think someone can have the wrong motive of what someone is doing with someone's free will for someone to be bad on the inside as I think someone can look good on the outside. I think someone can have the wrong motive of what someone is doing with someone's free will for someone to be bad on the inside as I think someone can look good on the outside because I think someone can be bad on the inside as I think someone can look good on the outside, and therefore, I think someone can be good or bad on the inside as I think someone can look good or not look good on the outside because I think someone can have the right or wrong motive of what someone is doing with someone's free will for someone to be good or bad on the inside as I think someone can look good or not look good on the outside. I think someone can have the right or wrong motive of what someone is doing with someone's free will for someone to be good or bad on the inside as I think someone can look good or not look good on the outside because I think someone is right or wrong with someone's free will for someone to be good or bad on the inside as I think someone does or doesn't look that good on the outside.

If I think someone can have the right or wrong motive of what someone is doing with someone's free will for someone to be good or bad on the inside as I think someone can look good or not look good on the outside, than I think someone's free will is like God's free will because I think someone has a choice of right or wrong with someone's free will as I think God has a choice of right or wrong with God's free will, but I do not think someone's free will is alike God's free will because I think someone has a choice of right or wrong with someone's free will for someone to be right or wrong, and I think God has a choice of right or wrong with God's free will for God to be right. I think someone has a choice of right or wrong with someone's free will for someone to be right or wrong, and I think God has a choice of right or wrong with God's free will for God to be right because I think someone is right or wrong with someone having a choice of right or wrong with someone's free will, and I think God is always good, and right with God having a choice of right or wrong with God's free will, and therefore, I do not think someone's free will is like God's free will because I think someone has a choice of right or wrong with someone's free will for someone to be right or wrong, and I think God has a choice of right or wrong with God's free will for God to be right. If I do not think someone's free will is like God's free will, than I think everyone's free will is exactly the same as everyone's free will because I think everyone has a choice of right or wrong for everyone's free will to be exactly the same as everyone's free will, and therefore, I think everyone has everyone's free will wherever everyone is in life because I think everyone has everyone's own choice of right or wrong for everyone to be having everyone's free will wherever everyone is in life. If I think everyone has everyone's free will wherever everyone is in life, than I think someone's free will explains everything someone can be doing because I think someone can do everything someone can be doing with someone's free will, and therefore, I think everything someone can be doing is everything someone can be doing with someone's free will because I think someone can choose something that is right or wrong with someone's free will for someone to be doing everything someone can be doing. I think someone can choose something that is right or wrong with someone's free will for someone to be doing everything someone can be doing because I think someone's free will has a part in every aspect of someone's life, and therefore, I think someone's free will has no age limit because I think someone can right or wrong at any age with someone's free will. If I think someone's free will has no age limit, than I think someone is always free because I think someone has someone's free will for someone to always be free. I think someone has someone's free will for someone to always be free because I think someone always has a choice to be doing something with someone's free will for someone to always be free.

If I think someone has someone's free will for someone to always be free, than I think there are two aspects of someone's free will because I think someone has a positive and negative aspect of someone's free will for someone to be having two aspects of someone's free will. I think someone has a positive and negative aspect of someone's free will for someone to be having two aspects of someone's free will because I think someone has a choice of right and wrong for someone to be having a positive and negative aspect of someone's free will. If I think someone has a positive and negative aspect of someone's free will for someone to be having two aspects of someone's free will, than I think someone's positive aspect of someone's free will can represent anything that is good about someone, and I think someone's negative aspect of someone's free will can represent anything that is bad about someone because I think someone's positive aspect of someone's free will is someone having a right choice for someone to be good about anything that someone can be choosing that is right, and I think someone's negative aspect of someone's free will is someone having a wrong choice for someone to be bad about anything that someone can be choosing that is wrong, and therefore, I think someone has a positive and negative aspect of someone's free will for someone to be having two aspects of someone's free will because I think someone can choose something that is right or wrong for someone to be having a positive and negative aspect of someone's free will. If I think someone has a positive and negative aspect of someone's free will for someone to be having two aspects of someone's free will, than I think there is a battle of free will because I think there is a battle between everyone that has a choice of right or wrong, as to what everyone thinks is right or wrong for there to be a battle of free will, and therefore, I think there is a battle of good and evil because I think there is a battle of free will as I think there is a battle between everyone, as to what everyone thinks is right or wrong for there to be a battle of good and evil, even though, I do not think goodness always triumphs over evil because I do not think everyone that is good is always able to overcome everyone that is evil, however, I think there is a battle of good and evil as I think there is a battle of free will because I think someone has a choice of right or wrong for there to be a battle of good and evil as I think someone has a choice of right or wrong for there to be a battle of free will. If I think there is a battle of good and evil as I think there is a battle of free will, than I think everyone can possibly be living in a state of purgatory in this part of life that everyone is living in life because I think God created everyone to be having a choice of right or wrong with everyone's free will for everyone to be choosing to be good or bad with everyone's free will as I think everyone can choose to be good or bad with everyone's free will for everyone to possibly be living in a state of purgatory in this part of life that everyone is living in life, and therefore, I think God is responsible for creating all of the drama because I think God created someone to be having a choice of right or wrong for God to be responsible for creating all of the drama.

I think God created someone to be having a choice of right or wrong for God to be responsible for creating all of the drama because I think someone has a choice of right or wrong for someone to be right or wrong. I think someone has a choice of right or wrong for someone to be right or wrong because I think someone is right or wrong. I think someone is right or wrong because I think God created someone to be having a choice of right or wrong for someone to be choosing to be doing something that is right or wrong as I think God created someone to be having a choice of right or wrong for someone to be choosing something that is right or wrong. I think God created someone to be having a choice of right or wrong for someone to be choosing to be doing something that is right or wrong as I think God created someone to be having a choice of right or wrong for someone to be choosing something that is right or wrong because I think someone can choose to be doing something that is right or wrong as I think someone can choose something that is right or wrong. I think someone can choose to be doing something that is right or wrong as I think someone can choose something that is right or wrong because I think someone can choose to be doing something that is right or wrong for someone to be choosing something that is right or wrong. I think someone can choose to be doing something that is right or wrong for someone to be choosing something that is right or wrong because I think someone can be right or wrong for someone choosing to be doing something that is right or wrong, and therefore, I think someone can have a path for someone to be having a way because I think someone can choose to be doing something that is right or wrong for someone to be having a way as I think someone can choose to be doing something that is right or wrong for someone to be having a path. If I think someone can have a path for someone to be having a way, than I think someone can choose to be doing something with themselves, someone else, and something for someone to be doing something right or wrong with themselves, someone else, and something because I think someone can choose to be doing something right or wrong with someone having a choice of right or wrong for someone to be choosing to be doing something right or wrong with themselves, someone else, and something. I think someone can choose to be doing something right or wrong with someone having a choice of right or wrong for someone to be choosing to be doing something right or wrong with themselves, someone else, and something because I think God created someone to be having a choice of right or wrong for someone to be choosing to be doing something right or wrong with themselves, someone else, and something. If I think someone can choose to be doing something right or wrong with someone having a choice of right or wrong for someone to be choosing to be doing something right or wrong with themselves, someone else, and something, than I think someone's downfall is God creating someone to be having a wrong choice with God creating someone to be having a choice of right or wrong because I think someone can choose to be doing something that is wrong with someone having a choice wrong for someone's downfall to be God creating someone to be having a choice of wrong with God creating someone to be having a choice of right or wrong, and therefore, I think God is creating someone to be having a wrong choice with God creating someone to be having a choice of right or wrong for someone's downfall to be someone having a wrong choice with someone having a choice of right or wrong because I think God is creating everyone throughout all time to be having a wrong choice with God creating someone to be having a choice of right or wrong for someone's downfall to be someone having a wrong with someone having a choice of right or wrong. If I think God is creating someone to be having a wrong choice with God creating someone to be having a choice of right or wrong for someone's downfall to be someone having a wrong choice with someone having a choice of right or wrong, than I think there is right or wrong because I think someone has a choice of right or wrong for there to be right or wrong, otherwise, I do not think there would be right or wrong because I do not think someone can possibly conceive or think of what right or wrong is in life, without someone having a choice of right or wrong for someone to be conceiving or thinking of what right or wrong is in life, and therefore, I think there is right or wrong because I think someone can choose something that is right or wrong with someone having a choice of right or wrong for someone to be noticing the effects of what is right or wrong with someone having a choice of right or wrong. If I think there is right or wrong, than I think someone can think of someone or something as being more or less right or wrong, than someone or something else that is right or wrong because I think someone can choose something that is right or wrong with someone having a choice of right or wrong for someone to be noticing the effects of someone or something as being more or less right or wrong, than someone or something else that is right or wrong, even though, I think right is right, and wrong is wrong because I think someone can choose to be doing something that is right or wrong for right to be right, and wrong to be wrong.

If I think right is right, and wrong is wrong, than I think someone can choose to be doing something that is right or wrong because I think someone has a choice of right or wrong for someone to be choosing to be doing something that is right or wrong, and therefore, I think someone can do something that is right or wrong because I think someone has a choice of right or wrong for someone to be doing something that is right or wrong. If I think someone can do something that is right or wrong, than I think someone can choose to be doing something that is right or wrong because I think someone has a choice of right or wrong for someone to be choosing to be doing something that is right or wrong with themselves, someone else, something, and God as I think someone can choose to be doing something that is right or wrong with themselves, someone else, something, and God for someone to be choosing to be doing something that is right or wrong, and therefore, I think someone can do something that is right or wrong because I think someone can choose to be doing something that is right or wrong with themselves, someone else, something, and God for someone to be doing something that is right or wrong. If I think someone can do something that is right or wrong, than I think someone can do something that is right or wrong with themselves, someone else, something, and God because I think someone can choose to be doing something that is right or wrong with themselves, someone else, something, and God for someone to be doing something that is right or wrong with themselves, someone else, something, and God, and therefore, I think someone can be right or wrong with everything someone can choose to be doing with themselves, someone else, something, and God because I think someone has a choice of right or wrong for someone to choose to be doing something that is right or wrong with everything someone can choose to be doing with themselves, someone else, something, and God. If I think someone can be right or wrong with everything someone can choose to be doing with themselves, someone else, something, and God, than I think someone can do something that is right or wrong to themselves, someone else, something, and God because I think someone can do something that is right or wrong with themselves, someone else, something, and God for someone to be doing something that is right or wrong to themselves, someone else, something, and God, and therefore, I think someone can do something that is right or wrong because I think someone can do something that is right or wrong to themselves, someone else, something, and God for someone to be doing something that is right or wrong. If I think someone can be doing something that is right or wrong, than I think someone can do something that is right or wrong to God as I think someone can do something that is right or wrong to themselves, someone else because I think someone can do something that.is right or wrong with themselves, and someone else for someone to be doing something that is right or wrong to God as I think someone can do something that is right or wrong with themselves, someone else, and something for someone to be doing something that is right or wrong to themselves, and someone else, and therefore, I think someone can do something that is right or wrong to themselves, and someone else for someone to be doing something that is right or wrong to God because I think someone can do something that is right or wrong to God from someone doing something that is right or wrong to themselves, and someone else. I think someone can do something that is right or wrong to God from someone doing something that is right or wrong to themselves, and someone else because I think someone is of God for someone to be doing something that is right or wrong to God from someone doing something that is right or wrong to themselves, and someone else, however, I think someone's free will is someone having a choice of right or wrong for someone to be choosing to be doing something that is right or wrong with themselves, someone else, something, and God because I think someone has a choice of right or wrong with someone's will for someone to be choosing to be doing something that is right or wrong with themselves, someone else, something, and God, and therefore, I think someone can be right or wrong with someone's free will because I think someone can be right or wrong with someone having a choice of right or wrong for someone to be right or wrong with someone's free will.

If I think someone can be right or wrong with someone's free will, than I think someone can learn from themselves, and someone else doing something that is right or wrong because I think someone is someone, and someone else for someone to be learning from someone doing something that is right or wrong, and therefore, I think someone can learn from someone doing something that is right or wrong because I think someone can learn from someone doing something that is right or wrong with themselves, someone else, something, and God. I think someone can learn from someone doing something that is right or wrong with themselves, someone else, something, and God because I think someone can choose to be doing something that is right or wrong with themselves, someone else, something, and God for the right or wrong reasons. I think someone can choose to be doing something that is right or wrong with themselves, someone else, something, and God for the right or wrong reasons because I think someone has a choice of right or wrong for someone to be choosing to be doing something that is right or wrong with themselves, someone else, something, and God for the right or wrong reasons, and therefore, I think someone can be right or wrong for someone choosing to be doing something that is right or wrong with themselves, someone else, something, and God for the right or wrong reasons because I think someone can choose to be doing something that is right or wrong with themselves, someone else, something, and God for the right or wrong reasons for someone to be right or wrong. I think someone can choose to be doing something that is right or wrong with themselves, someone else, something, and God for the right or wrong reasons for someone to be right or wrong because I think someone can be right with someone doing something that is right or wrong with themselves, someone else, something, and God for the right reasons as I think someone can be wrong with someone doing something that is right or wrong with themselves, someone else, something, and God for the wrong reasons. I think someone can be right with someone doing something that is right or wrong with themselves, someone else, something, and God for the right reasons as I think someone can be wrong with someone doing something that is right or wrong with themselves, someone else, something, and God for the wrong reasons because I think someone is right with someone doing something with themselves, someone else, something, and God for the right reasons as I think someone is wrong with someone doing something with themselves, someone else, something, and God for the wrong reasons, even though, I think someone is wrong with someone doing something wrong with themselves, someone else, something, and God for the right reasons because I think someone is doing something wrong with themselves, someone else, something, and God for someone to be wrong with someone doing something wrong with themselves, someone else, something, and God for the right reasons, and therefore, I think someone can think of having justice because I think someone can think of doing something that is right or wrong with someone else for the right reasons for someone to be having justice. If I think someone can think of having justice, than I think someone can learn what to do or what not to do because I think someone can learn to be doing something or not to be doing something for someone to be learning what to do or what not to do, and therefore, I think someone can learn to be doing something or not to be doing something because I think someone has a choice of right or wrong for someone to be choosing to be doing or not to be doing something for the right or wrong reasons as I think someone can choose to be doing something or not to be doing something for the right or wrong reasons for someone to be learning to be doing something or not to be doing something. If I think someone can learn to be doing something or not to be doing something, than I think someone can have a history because I think someone can choose to be doing something for someone to be having a history, and therefore, I think someone's history can be good, and bad because I think someone can choose to be doing something that is good, and bad with someone having a choice of right or wrong for someone's history to be good, and bad. If I think someone's history can be good, and bad, than I think someone's life is someone's history as I think someone's history is someone's life because I think someone can choose to be doing something that is good, and bad for someone's life to be someone's history as I think someone can choose to be doing something that is good, and bad for someone's history to be someone's life, even though, I think someone choosing to be doing something that is good or bad can be hard or easy for someone because I think someone can choose to be doing something that is good just a much as someone can choose to be doing something that is bad with someone having a choice of right or wrong for someone to be choosing to be doing something that is good or bad to be hard or easy for someone.

If I think someone choosing to be doing something that is good or bad can be hard or easy for someone, than I think someone is created by God for someone to be living, learning, and enjoying themselves within good reason as I think someone is created by God for someone to be living, learning, and enjoying themselves within bad reason because I think God created someone to be living, learning, and enjoying themselves for the right reasons as I think God created someone to be living, learning, and enjoying themselves for the wrong reasons, even though, I think someone is created by God mainly for someone to be living, learning, and enjoying themselves within good reason because I think if someone isn't living, learning, and enjoying themselves within good reason, than I think someone living their lives within excess because I think someone is living, learning, and enjoying themselves for the wrong reasons from someone not living, learning, and enjoying themselves within good reason, and therefore, I think someone is created by God for someone to be living, learning, and enjoying themselves within good reason because I do not think someone would be living their lives within excess from someone living, learning, and enjoying themselves within good reason. If I think someone is created by God for someone to be living, learning, and enjoying themselves within good reason, than I do not think life is all about someone just living because I do not think life is all about someone coasting for life to be all about someone just living. I do not think life is all about someone coasting for life to be all about someone just living because I do not think someone can be learning, and enjoying themselves from someone just living. I do not think someone can be learning, and enjoying themselves from someone just living because I do not think someone can just be living, without someone learning, and enjoying themselves. I do not think someone can just be living, without someone learning, and enjoying themselves because I do not think life is all about someone just living, and therefore, I do not think life is all about someone just living, and enjoying themselves for someone to be thinking life is just one great big party because how can someone learn something with someone thinking life is just one great big party? I do not think life is all about someone just living, and enjoying themselves for someone to be thinking life is just one great big party because I do not think someone can be learning something with someone to be thinking life is just one great big party, and therefore, I think life is all about someone living, learning, and enjoying themselves because I do not think someone can be living, without someone living, learning, and enjoying themselves. I do not think someone can be living, without someone living, learning, and enjoying themselves because I think someone is able to be alive from someone living, learning, and enjoying themselves. I think someone is able to be alive from someone living, learning, and enjoying themselves because I think life is all about someone living, learning, and enjoying themselves within good reason for someone to be alive, even though, I think someone learning is how someone can live because I do not think someone can make fire, without someone learning how to make fire, and therefore, I think someone learning is more important than someone living, and enjoying themselves because I do not think someone can live without someone learning for someone learning to be more important that someone living, and enjoying themselves, even though, I think someone can learn for someone to be living, and enjoying themselves because I think someone learning is how someone can live as I think someone can live with someone learning for someone to be living, and enjoying themselves.

If I think someone can learn for someone to be living, and enjoying themselves, than I think someone can be selfish because I think someone can be doing something that is wrong with themselves for the right reasons for someone to be selfish, and therefore, I think someone can be selfless because I think someone can be doing something that is right or wrong with themselves, and someone else for the right or wrong reasons for someone to be selfless. If I think someone can be selfless, than I think someone is right or wrong as I think someone has a choice of right or wrong because I think someone is right or wrong with someone having a choice of right or wrong. I think someone is right or wrong with someone having a choice of right or wrong because I think someone is right or wrong with someone having a choice of something as I think someone has a choice of right or wrong. I think someone is right or wrong with someone having a choice of something as I think someone has a choice of right or wrong because I think someone is right or wrong with someone having a choice of something that is right or wrong. I think someone is right or wrong with someone having a choice of something that is right or wrong because I think someone can choose of something that is right or wrong. I think someone can choose of something that is right or wrong because I think someone has a choice of right or wrong for someone to be choosing something that is right or wrong. I think someone has a choice of right or wrong for someone to be choosing something that is right or wrong because I think someone can choose something that is right or wrong with someone having a choice of something that is right or wrong. I think someone can choose something that is right or wrong with someone having a choice of something that is right or wrong because I think someone is right or wrong for someone to be choosing something that is right or wrong. I think someone is right or wrong for someone to be choosing something that is right or wrong because I think someone is right or wrong with someone having a choice of something that is right or wrong, and therefore, I think someone can choose to be doing something that is good or bad because I think someone has a choice of right or wrong for someone to be choosing to be doing something that is good or bad. If I think someone has a choice of right or wrong for someone to be doing something that is good or bad, than I think someone can do something that is good or bad because I think someone can choose to be doing something that is good or bad as I think someone has a choice of right or wrong for someone to be doing something that is good or bad, even though, I think someone can be doing good or bad because I think someone can do something that is right or wrong for someone to be doing good or bad, and therefore, I think someone is good or bad because I think someone can be doing good or bad for someone to be good or bad, even though, I do not think someone is perfect because I think someone can be good or bad with someone doing something that is right or wrong, however, I think someone is good because I do not think someone can be good if someone is doing bad. If I think someone is good, than I do not think right is wrong as I do not think wrong is right because I think someone can do something that is right or wrong with someone having a choice of right or wrong for right not to be wrong as I think someone can do something that is right or wrong with someone having a choice of right or wrong for wrong not to be right, and therefore, I do not think good is bad as I do not think bad is good because I think someone can do something that is right or wrong with someone having a choice of right or wrong for good not to be bad as I think someone can do something that is right or wrong with someone having a choice of right or wrong for bad not to be good. If I do not think good is bad as I do not think bad is good, than I think someone can learn how to be good or bad because I think someone can learn how to be doing something that is good or bad for someone to be learning how to be good or bad, and therefore, I think someone can learn how to be good or bad as I think someone can learn how to be doing something that is good or bad because I think someone can choose to be doing something that is right or wrong with someone having a choice of right or wrong for someone to be learning how to be good or bad as I think someone can choose to be doing something that is right or wrong with someone having a choice of right or wrong for someone to be learning how to be doing something that is good or bad, even though, I think someone can think someone isn't able to be learning how to be good because I think someone can think someone isn't able to be doing something that is good, and right for someone to be thinking someone isn't able to be learning how to be good, however, I think anything someone does is someone's choice because I do not think someone can choose to be doing anything, without someone having a choice for someone to be doing anything, and therefore, I think someone always has a choice for someone to be learning how to be good or bad as I think someone always has a choice for someone to be learning how to be doing something that is good or bad because I think someone always has a choice with someone having a choice of right or wrong for someone to be choosing to be good or bad as I think someone always has a choice with someone having a choice of right or wrong for someone to be choosing to be doing something that is good or bad.

If I think someone always has a choice for someone to be learning how to be good or bad as I think someone always has a choice for someone to be learning how to be doing something that is good or bad, than I think someone can have goals because I think someone's choices is someone's goals. I think someone's choices is someone's goals because I think someone's choices is of someone choosing to be doing something that is good or bad as I think someone can choose to be doing something that is good or bad for someone to be having goals. I think someone's choices is of someone choosing to be doing something that is good or bad as I think someone can choose to be doing something that is good or bad for someone to be having goals because I think someone has a choice of right or wrong for someone's choices to be of someone choosing to be doing something that is good or bad as I think someone can choose to be doing something that is good or bad for someone's choices to be someone's goals. I think someone has a choice of right or wrong for someone's choices to be of someone choosing to be doing something that is good or bad as I think someone can choose to be doing something that is good or bad for someone's choices to be someone's goals because I think someone can choose to be doing something that is good or bad for someone to be having goals. I think someone can choose to be doing something that is good or bad for someone to be having goals because I think someone has a choice of right or wrong for someone's goals to be of someone choosing to be doing something that is good or bad as I think someone's goals is of someone choosing to be doing something that is good or bad for someone to be having goals, and therefore, I think someone can have hope because I think someone can have goals for someone to be having hope. I think someone can have goals for someone to be having hope because I think someone's goals gives someone hope. I think someone's goals gives someone hope because I think someone can choose to be doing something that is good or bad for someone's goals to give someone hope. I think someone can choose to be doing something that is good or bad for someone's goals to give someone hope because I think someone's goals is of someone choosing to be doing something that is good or bad for someone's goals to be giving someone hope. I think someone's goals is of someone choosing to be doing something that is good or bad for someone's goals to be giving someone hope because I think someone's goals can be of someone hoping for something good or bad to happen for someone to be having hope. I think someone's goals can be of someone hoping for something good or bad to happen for someone to be having hope because I think someone can hope for something good or bad to happen with someone having a choice of right or wrong for someone to be having hope as I think someone can hope for something good or bad to happen with someone having a choice of right or wrong for someone's goals to be of someone hoping for something good or bad to happen. I think someone can hope for something good or bad to happen with someone having a choice of right or wrong for someone to be having hope as I think someone can hope for something good or bad to happen with someone having a choice of right or wrong for someone's goals to be of someone hoping for something good or bad to happen because I think someone can choose to be doing something that is good or bad with someone having a choice of right or wrong for someone to be having hope as I think someone can choose to be doing something that is good or bad with someone having a choice of right or wrong for someone's goals to be of someone hoping for something good or bad to happen, otherwise, I do not think someone would have any hope, without someone having any goals for someone to be having any hope because I do not think someone can have any goals, without someone having choices for someone to be having any goals, but I think someone has goals for someone to be having any hope because I think someone has choices for someone to be having hope as I think someone has choices for someone to be having any goals, and therefore, I think someone has goals for someone to having any hope because I think someone has hope from someone having someone's goals. If I think someone has goals for someone to having any hope, than I think someone can be right or wrong with someone having hope as I think someone can be right or wrong with someone having goals because I think someone can choose to be doing something that is right or wrong with themselves, someone else, something, and God for someone to be right or wrong with someone having hope as I think someone can choose to be doing something that is right or wrong with themselves, someone else, something, and God for someone to be right or wrong with someone having goals, and therefore, I think someone can choose to be having any hope or not as I think someone can choose to be having any goals or not because I think someone has a choice of right or wrong for someone to be choosing to be having any hope or not as I think someone has a choice of right or wrong for someone to be choosing to be having any goals or not, even though, I do not think someone can live without someone having any hope as I do not think someone can live without someone having any goals, regardless if goals are good or bad for someone to be having any hope because I do not think someone can choose to be doing absolutely nothing for someone not to be having any hope as I do not think someone can choose to be doing absolutely nothing for someone not to be having any goals, however, I think someone can have hope as I think someone can have goals because I think someone can choose to be doing something that is right or wrong with themselves, someone else, something, and God for someone to be having hope as I think someone can choose to be doing something that is right or wrong with themselves, someone else, something, and God for someone to be having goals. If I think someone can have hope as I think someone can have goals, than I think someone can hope to be doing something with themselves, someone else, something, and God because I think someone can choose to be doing something with themselves, someone else, something, and God for someone to be hoping to be doing something with themselves, someone else, something, and God, even though, I think someone can be right or wrong with someone hoping to be doing something with themselves, someone else, something, and God because I think someone can choose to be doing something that is right or wrong with themselves, someone else, something, and God for someone to be right or wrong with someone hoping to be doing something with themselves, someone else, something, and God, and therefore, I think someone can hope to be doing something with themselves, someone else, something, and God or not because I think someone has a choice of right or wrong for someone to be choosing to be doing something with themselves, someone else, something, and God or not as I think someone can choose to be doing something with themselves, someone else, something, and God or not for someone to be hoping to be doing something with themselves, someone else, something, and God or not. If I think someone can hope to be doing something with themselves, someone else, something, and God or not, than I think someone can choose to be having hope in God or not because I think someone can be right or wrong with someone having a choice of right or wrong for someone to be choosing to be having hope in God or not, even though, I think someone can be good, and right with someone choosing to be having hope in God because I think God is always good, and right for someone to be good, and right with someone choosing to be having hope in God.

If I think someone can be good, and right with someone choosing to be having hope in God, than I think someone can have dreams because I think someone can have goals for someone to be having dreams, and therefore, I think someone's dreams is someone's goals because I think someone can choose to be doing something that is right or wrong with themselves, someone else, something, and God for someone's dreams to be someone thinking about doing something that is right or wrong with themselves, someone else, something, and God as I think someone's dreams can be someone thinking about doing something that is right or wrong with themselves, someone else, something, and God for someone's dreams to be someone's goals. If I think someone's dreams can be someone's goals, than I think someone's goals is someone's dreams because I think someone can choose to be doing something that is right or wrong with themselves, someone else, something, and God for someone's goals to be someone thinking about doing something that is right or wrong with themselves, someone else, something, and God as I think someone's goals can be someone thinking about doing something that is right or wrong with themselves, someone else, something, and God for someone's goals to be someone's dreams, and therefore, I think someone's goals is someone having dreams for someone to be having goals because I do not think someone can have goals, without someone having dreams for someone to be having goals, but I think someone has dreams for someone to be having goals because I think someone's goals is someone's dreams for someone to be having goals. If I think someone has dreams for someone to be having goals, than I think someone's purpose is someone's goals because I think what someone's goals are in life is what someone's purpose is in life for someone's purpose to be someone's goals, and therefore, I think someone's goal is someone's purpose for someone to be having a purpose because I do not think someone can have a purpose, without someone having a goal for someone to be having a purpose. If I think someone's goal is someone's purpose for someone to be having a purpose, than I think someone's goal is someone's purpose because I think someone's purpose is what someone's goal is in life of what someone chooses to be doing with themselves, someone else, something, and God for someone's goal to be someone's purpose. I think someone's purpose is what someone's goal is in life of what someone chooses to be doing with themselves, someone else, something, and God for someone's goal to be someone's purpose because I think someone's purpose is what someone's goal is in life of what someone wants to be for someone's goal to be someone's purpose, and therefore, I think someone's goal is someone's purpose because I think someone's purpose is what someone's goal is in life for someone's goal to be someone's purpose.

If I think someone's goal is someone's purpose, than I think someone is better with someone trying to be right, rather than someone trying to be wrong because I do not think someone is right with someone trying to be wrong, and therefore, I think someone is better with someone trying to be right because I think someone is right with someone trying to be right. If I think someone is better with someone trying to be right, than I do not think someone is right with someone thinking of themselves, and someone else as always being right because I do not think someone is always right for someone to always be right, even though, I think someone can think of themselves, and someone else as always being right because I think someone can think someone is right for someone to be thinking of themselves, and someone else as always being right, but I do not think someone is always right for someone to be thinking of themselves, and someone else as always being right because I do not think someone can prove that is someone is always right for someone to be thinking of themselves, and someone else as always being right, and therefore, I think someone is insulting God with someone thinking of themselves, and someone else as always being right because I think God is always right for someone not to always be right. If I think God is always right for someone not to always be right, than I think someone is right or wrong with everything that someone does because I think someone has a choice of right or wrong for someone to be right or wrong with everything that someone does. I think someone has a choice of right or wrong for someone to be right or wrong with everything that someone does because I think someone is right or wrong about everything that someone does. I think someone is right or wrong about everything that someone does because I think someone is right or wrong with someone having a choice of something that is right or wrong.

I think someone is right or wrong with someone having a choice of something that is right or wrong because I think God created someone to be choosing something that is right or wrong. I think God created someone to be choosing something that is right or wrong because I think someone can be right or wrong from someone choosing something that is right or wrong. I think someone can be right or wrong from someone choosing something that is right or wrong because I think someone is constantly able to be choosing something that is right or wrong. I think someone is constantly able to be choosing something that is right or wrong because I think someone is always right or wrong. I think someone is always right or wrong because I do not think someone can always be right as I do not think someone can always be wrong. I do not think someone can always be right as I do not think someone can always be wrong because I do not think someone is always right for someone to always be right as I do not think someone is always wrong for someone to always be wrong. I do not think someone is always right for someone to always be right as I do not think someone is always wrong for someone to always be wrong because I think someone can be right or wrong for someone to always be right or wrong. I think someone can be right or wrong for someone to always be right or wrong because I do not think someone can always be right as I do not think someone can always be wrong. I do not think someone can always be right as I do not think someone can always be wrong because I think someone has a choice of right or wrong for someone to always be right or wrong, and therefore, I think someone can be right or wrong about something, regardless if someone is or isn't consciously aware that someone is right or wrong about something because I think someone has a choice of right or wrong for someone to always be right or wrong about something, regardless if someone is or isn't consciously aware that someone is right or wrong about something. I think someone has a choice of right or wrong for someone to always be right or wrong about something, regardless if someone is or isn't consciously aware that someone is right or wrong about something because I do not think someone is always aware of everything that someone can be right or wrong about in life. I do not think someone is always aware of everything that someone can be right or wrong about in life because I think someone is always right or wrong. I think someone is always right or wrong because I think someone can be right or wrong about something for someone to always be right or wrong.

If I think someone is always right or wrong, than I think someone can be fence sitting because I think someone can choose not to be doing something with themselves, someone else, something, and God for someone to be neutral about someone not doing something with themselves, someone else, something, and God as I think someone can be neutral about someone not doing something with themselves, someone else, something, and God for someone to be fence sitting, however, I think someone can be right or wrong to be fence sitting because I think someone can choose to be doing something that is right or wrong with themselves, someone else, something, and God for someone to be right or wrong with someone choosing not to be doing something with themselves, someone else, something, and God as I think someone can be right or wrong with someone choosing not to be doing something with themselves, someone else, something, and God for someone to be right or wrong to be fence sitting, and therefore, I think someone can choose to be fence sitting or not because I think someone can choose to be doing something with themselves, someone else, something, and God or not for someone to be choosing to be fence sitting or not, even though, I think someone can right or wrong with someone choosing to be fence sitting or not because I think someone can choose to be doing something that is right or wrong with themselves, someone else, something, and God or not with someone having a choice of right or wrong for someone to be right or wrong with someone choosing to be fence sitting or not. If I think someone can right or wrong with someone choosing to be fence sitting or not, than I think someone can choose to be on either side of fence because I think someone can choose to be doing something to be helping, and supporting someone that is on either side of the fence, even though, I think someone can choose not to be admitting which side of the fence someone is on because I do not think someone will always admit that someone is doing something wrong, but I think someone can be doing something wrong, regardless if someone admits that someone is doing something wrong or not because I do not think someone would be doing something wrong, if someone isn't thinking of doing something wrong, and therefore, I think someone's actions speaks louder than someone's words because I think someone can choose to be doing something that is right or wrong with themselves, someone else, something, and God for someone's actions to determine which side of the fence someone is or isn't on as I think someone can choose to be doing something that is right or wrong with themselves, someone else, something, and God, regardless of what someone says for someone's actions to be speaking louder than someone's words. If I think someone's actions speaks louder than someone's words, than I think someone can do something that is right or wrong with themselves, someone else, something, and God for someone to be thinking about doing something that is right or wrong with themselves, someone else, something, and God because I do not think someone can think about something that is right or wrong with themselves, someone else, something, and God, without someone choosing to be doing something that is right or wrong with themselves, someone else, something, and God, and therefore, I think someone's actions can speak louder than someone's thoughts because I do not think someone can think about something that is right or wrong with themselves, someone else, something, and God, without someone choosing to be doing something that is right or wrong with themselves, someone else, something, and God for someone's actions to be speaking louder than someone's thoughts.

If I think someone's actions can speak louder than someone's thoughts, than I do not think someone is always right as I do not think someone is always wrong because I think someone is always right or wrong. I think someone is always right or wrong because I think someone can be right or wrong. I think someone can be right or wrong because I think someone can be right or wrong about something. I think someone can be right or wrong about something because I think someone can be right or wrong about what someone thinks, and therefore, I think someone can right or wrong about what someone thinks is right or wrong because I think someone can be right or wrong about what someone thinks for someone to be right or wrong about what someone thinks is right or wrong. If I think someone can right or wrong about what someone thinks is right or wrong, than I think someone can be right or wrong about what someone thinks because I think someone can be right or wrong about what someone thinks of something. I think someone can be right or wrong about what someone thinks of something because I do not think someone is always right about what someone thinks of something as I do not think someone is always wrong about what someone thinks of something. I do not think someone is always right about what someone thinks of something as I do not think someone is always wrong about what someone thinks of something because

I think someone can think someone is right or wrong about what someone thinks of something. I think someone can think someone is right or wrong about what someone thinks of something because I think someone can be right or wrong about something that someone can think of as being right or wrong. I think someone can be right or wrong about something that someone can think of as being right or wrong because I think someone's thoughts of something is either the same or not the same as someone else's thoughts of something as I think someone's thoughts is either the same or not the same as something that someone can think of for someone to be right or wrong about something that someone can think of as being right or wrong. I think someone's thoughts of something is either the same or not the same as someone else's thoughts of something as I think someone's thoughts is either the same or not the same as something that someone can think of for someone to be right or wrong about something that someone can think of as being right or wrong because I think someone can be right or wrong about what someone thinks of something. I think someone can be right or wrong about what someone thinks of something because I think someone else can think someone is wrong about what someone thinks of something as I think someone can think someone else is wrong about what someone else thinks of something, and therefore, I think someone can be right or wrong about what someone thinks of something because I think someone can be right or wrong about something for someone to be right or wrong about what someone thinks of something.

If I think someone can be right or wrong about what someone thinks of something, than I think someone can be right or wrong because I think someone is constantly right or wrong for someone to be always right or wrong. I think someone is constantly right or wrong for someone to be always right or wrong because I think someone is always right or wrong with someone having a choice of right or wrong. I think someone is always right or wrong with someone having a choice of right or wrong because I think someone's being is somehow always able to right or wrong as I think someone's state of consciousness, and someone's will, and someone's thoughts, and someone's mind is apart of someone's being. I think someone's being is somehow always able to right or wrong as I think someone's state of consciousness, and someone's will, and someone's thoughts, and someone's mind is apart of someone's being because I think someone's being is ultimately what makes someone able to be making any choices that is always right or wrong as I think someone's state of consciousness, and someone's will, and someone's thoughts, and someone's mind is apart of someone's being, and therefore, I think God created someone's will to be apart of someone's being for someone's being to have a sense of right and wrong with someone's will because I do not think someone can be able to be choosing something that is right or wrong, without someone having a will for someone to be able to be choosing something that is right or wrong with someone's will as I think someone's will is apart of someone's being. If I think God created someone's will to be apart of someone's being for someone's being to have a sense of right and wrong with someone's will, than I think God created someone's will to have a sense of right and wrong with someone's will because I think someone is able to be choosing something that is right or wrong with someone's will as I think someone's will is apart of someone's being, and therefore, I think God created someone's sense of consciousness for someone to have a sense of right or wrong because I do not think someone can be consciously aware of someone being right or wrong, without someone having a sense of consciousness for someone to have a sense of right or wrong.

If I think God created someone's sense of consciousness for someone to have a sense of right or wrong, than I think someone's sense of right and wrong comes from someone's being for someone's will to be able to be having a sense of right and wrong with someone's will because I think someone's being is ultimately what makes someone's will able to be making any choices that is always right or wrong with someone's will as I think someone's will is apart of someone's being. I think someone's being is ultimately what makes someone's will able to be making any choices that is always right or wrong with someone's will as I think someone's will is apart of someone's being because I think someone's being is ultimately what makes someone able to be making any choices that is always right or wrong with someone's being as I think someone's will is apart of someone's being, and therefore, I think someone has a sense of right and wrong with someone's will as I think someone has a sense of right and wrong with someone's being because I think someone's sense of right and wrong comes from someone's being for someone's will to be able to be having a sense of right and wrong with someone's will. I think someone's sense of right and wrong comes from someone's being for someone's will to be able to be having a sense of right and wrong with someone's will because I think someone's being is ultimately what makes someone's will able to be making any choices that is always right or wrong with someone's will as I think someone's will is apart of someone's being, and therefore, I think someone has a sense of right or wrong as I think someone has a sense of right and wrong with someone's being because I think someone is someone's being as I think someone has a sense of right or wrong. If I think someone has a sense of right or wrong as I think someone has a sense of right and wrong with someone's being, than I think someone has a sense of right or wrong as I think someone's being has a sense of right or wrong because I think someone is able to be choosing something that is right or wrong for someone to have a sense of right or wrong as I think someone's being is able to be choosing something that is right or wrong for someone's being to have a sense of right or wrong, and therefore, I think someone is constantly able to be choosing something that is right or wrong as I think someone's being is constantly able to be choosing something that is right or wrong because I think someone is constantly right or wrong as I think someone's being is constantly right or wrong. If I think someone is constantly able to be choosing something that is right or wrong as I think someone's being is constantly able to be choosing something that is right or wrong, than I think someone constantly has a sense of right or wrong as I think someone's being constantly has a sense of right or wrong because I think someone is constantly able to be choosing something that is right or wrong as I think someone's being is constantly able to be choosing something that is right or wrong, and therefore, I think someone has a sense of right or wrong as I think someone's being has a sense of right or wrong because I think someone's sense of right or wrong is someone choosing something that is right or wrong as I think someone's sense of right or wrong is someone's being choosing something that is right or wrong. I think someone's sense of right or wrong is someone choosing something that is right or wrong as I think someone's sense of right or wrong is someone's being choosing something that is right or wrong because I think someone is someone's being as I think someone has a sense of right or wrong.

If I think someone's sense of right or wrong is someone choosing something that is right or wrong as I think someone's sense of right or wrong is someone's being choosing something that is right or wrong, than I think someone has a sense of right or wrong because I think someone always has a choice of right or wrong for someone to always have a sense of right or wrong. I think someone always has a choice of right or wrong for someone to always have a sense of right or wrong because I think someone's being has a sense of always being right or wrong as I think someone's being instinctively has a sense of always being right or wrong. I think someone's being has a sense of always being right or wrong as I think someone's being instinctively has a sense of always being right or wrong because I think God created someone's being to have a sense of right or wrong for someone's being to instinctively have a sense of right or wrong, and therefore, I think someone instinctively has a sense of right or wrong as I think someone's being instinctively has a sense of right or wrong because I think someone is someone's being as I think someone instinctively has a sense of right or wrong. If I think someone instinctively has a sense of right or wrong as I think someone's being instinctively has a sense of right or wrong, than I think someone has a sense of right or wrong as I think someone instinctively has a sense of right or wrong because I think someone has a sense of right or wrong for someone to instinctively have a sense of right or wrong. I think someone has a sense of right or wrong for someone to instinctively have a sense of right or wrong because I think someone can choose something that is right or wrong for someone to instinctively be having a sense of right or wrong as I think someone can choose something that is right or wrong for someone to be having a sense of right or wrong. I think someone can choose something that is right or wrong for someone to instinctively be having a sense of right or wrong as I think someone can choose something that is right or wrong for someone to be having a sense of right or wrong because I think someone can choose something that is right or wrong with someone having a choice of right or wrong for someone to be having a sense of right or wrong as I think someone has a choice of right or wrong for someone to instinctively be having a sense of right or wrong. I think someone can choose something that is right or wrong with someone having a choice of right or wrong for someone to be having a sense of right or wrong as I think someone has a choice of right or wrong for someone to instinctively be having a sense of right or wrong because I think someone instinctively having a sense of right or wrong is someone having a sense of right or wrong as I think someone can have a sense of right or wrong with someone having a choice of right or wrong for someone to be choosing something that is right or wrong, and therefore, I think someone can choose something that is right or wrong with someone having a choice of right or wrong as I think someone can choose something that is right or wrong with someone having a sense of right or wrong because I think someone's choice of right or wrong is someone's sense of right or wrong as I think someone has a choice of right or wrong for someone to be right or wrong with someone choosing something that is right or wrong. I think someone's choice of right or wrong is someone's sense of right or wrong as I think someone has a choice of right or wrong for someone to be right or wrong with someone choosing something that is right or wrong because I think someone's choice is right or wrong for someone to be choosing something that is right or wrong. I think someone's choice is right or wrong for someone to be choosing something that is right or wrong because I think someone can be right or wrong for someone to be choosing something that is right or wrong.

If I think someone's choice is right or wrong for someone to be choosing something that is right or wrong, than I think someone's sense of right and wrong comes from God because I think God created someone's being to have a sense of right or wrong. I think God created someone's being to have a sense of right or wrong because I think God created someone's being to be able to be choosing something that is right or wrong. I think God created someone's being to be able to be choosing something that is right or wrong because I think God created someone's being to be right or wrong from someone's being choosing something that is right or wrong. I think God created someone's being to be right or wrong from someone's being choosing something that is right or wrong because I think God created someone's being to be able to be choosing something that is right or wrong. I think God created someone's being to be able to be choosing something that is right or wrong because I think God created someone's being to have a sense of right or wrong from someone's being choosing something that is right or wrong. I think God created someone's being to have a sense of right or wrong from someone's being choosing something that is right or wrong because I think God created someone's being to be able to be choosing something that is right or wrong for someone's being to have a sense of right or wrong, and therefore, I think God created someone's being to have a sense of right or wrong because I think God created someone's being to be able to be choosing something that is right or wrong. If I think God created someone's being to have a sense of right or wrong, than I think God created someone to have a sense of right or wrong as I think God created someone's being to have a sense of right or wrong because I think someone is someone's being as I think God created someone to have a sense of right or wrong, and therefore, I think God created someone to have a sense of right or wrong because I think God created someone to be able to be choosing something that is right or wrong.

If I think God created someone to have a sense of right or wrong, than I think someone has a sense of right or wrong for someone to be choosing themselves, someone else, something, and God because I think someone, something, and God can be someone's choice for someone to be choosing themselves, someone else, something, and God as I think someone can be right or wrong with someone choosing themselves, someone else, something, and God. I think someone, something, and God can be someone's choice for someone to be choosing themselves, someone else, something, and God as I think someone can be right or wrong with someone choosing themselves, someone else, something, and God because I think someone can choose themselves, someone else, something, and God with someone having a choice of right or wrong for someone to be right or wrong with themselves, someone else, something, and God, and therefore, I think someone can choose themselves, someone else, something, and God with someone having a choice of right or wrong as I think someone can choose themselves, someone else, something, and God with someone having a sense of right or wrong because I think someone's choice of right or wrong is someone's sense of right or wrong as I think someone has a choice of right or wrong for someone to be right or wrong with someone choosing themselves, someone else, something, and God. I think someone's choice of right or wrong is someone's sense of right or wrong as I think someone has a choice of right or wrong for someone to be right or wrong with someone choosing themselves, someone else, something, and God because I think someone's choice is right or wrong for someone to be choosing themselves, someone else, something, and God. I think someone's choice is right or wrong for someone to be choosing themselves, someone else, something, and God because I think someone can be right or wrong with someone choosing themselves, someone else, something, and God, and therefore, I think someone can have common sense because I think someone has sense of right or wrong with someone having a choice of right or wrong for someone to sense someone doing something that is right or wrong with themselves, someone else, something, and God as I think someone can sense someone doing something that is right or wrong with themselves, someone else, something, and God for someone to be having common sense, even though, I think someone can choose to be having common sense or not because I think someone can choose to be doing something that is right or wrong with themselves, someone else, something, and God for someone to be choosing to be having common sense or not.

If I think someone can choose to be having common sense or not, than I think someone can choose themselves, someone else, something, and God with someone having a sense of right or wrong because I think someone's thoughts is of the thoughts of someone's, and something's physical being, and God's thoughts for someone to be choosing themselves, someone else, something, and God as I think someone's thoughts is of themselves, someone else, something, and God's thoughts for someone to be choosing to be thinking of themselves, someone else, something, and God as being right or wrong. I think someone's thoughts is of the thoughts of someone's, and something's physical being, and God's thoughts for someone to be choosing themselves, someone else, something, and God as I think someone's thoughts is of themselves, someone else, something, and God's thoughts for someone to be choosing to be thinking of themselves, someone else, something, and God as being right or wrong because I think someone can choose to be thinking of themselves, someone else, something, and God with someone having a sense of right or wrong. I think someone can choose to be thinking of themselves, someone else, something, and God with someone having a sense of right or wrong because I think someone's thoughts is of the thoughts of someone's, and something's physical, and God's thoughts for someone to be choosing to be thinking of themselves, someone else, something, and God as being right or wrong. I think someone's thoughts is of the thoughts of someone's, and something's physical, and God's thoughts for someone to be choosing to be thinking of themselves, someone else, something, and God as being right or wrong because I think someone has a choice of right or wrong for someone to be choosing to be thinking of themselves, someone else, something, and God as being right or wrong, and therefore, I think someone can think of themselves, someone else, something, and God as being right or wrong because I think someone has a sense of right or wrong for someone to be thinking of themselves, someone else, something, and God as being right or wrong. If I think someone can think of themselves, someone else, something, and God as being right or wrong, than I think someone can think of themselves, someone else, something, and God with someone having a choice of right or wrong as I think someone can think of themselves, someone else, something, and God with someone having a sense of right or wrong because I think someone's choice of right or wrong is someone's sense of right or wrong as I think someone has a choice of right or wrong for someone to be thinking of themselves, someone else, something, and God as being right or wrong. I think someone's choice of right or wrong is someone's sense of right or wrong as I think someone has a choice of right or wrong for someone to be thinking of themselves, someone else, something, and God as being right or wrong because I think someone's choice is right or wrong for someone to be thinking of themselves, someone else, something, and God as being right or wrong. I think someone's choice is right or wrong for someone to be thinking of themselves, someone else, something, and God as being right or wrong because I think someone can be right or wrong for someone to be thinking of themselves, someone else, something, and God as being right or wrong.

If I think someone's choice is right or wrong for someone to be thinking of themselves, someone else, something, and God as being right or wrong, than I think someone can choose to be doing something with themselves, someone else, something, and God because I think someone can choosing to be thinking about doing something with themselves, someone else, something, and God for someone to be choosing to be doing something with themselves, someone else, something, and God, and therefore, I think someone has a sense of right or wrong for someone to be choosing to be doing something with themselves, someone else, something, and God because I think someone, something, and God can be someone's choice for someone to be choosing to be doing something with themselves, someone else, something, and God as I think someone can be right or wrong with someone choosing to be doing something with themselves, someone else, something, and God. I think someone, something, and God can be someone's choice for someone to be choosing to be doing something with themselves, someone else, something, and God as I think someone can be right or wrong with someone choosing to be doing something with themselves, someone else, something, and God because I think someone can choose to be doing something with themselves, someone else, something, and God with someone having a choice of right or wrong for someone to be right or wrong with someone choosing to be doing something with themselves, someone else, something, and God, and therefore, I think someone has a sense of right or wrong for someone to be right or wrong with someone choosing to be doing something with themselves, someone else, something, and God because I think someone can choose to be doing something that is right or wrong with themselves, someone else, something, and God with someone having a sense of right or wrong. I think someone can choose to be doing something that is right or wrong with themselves, someone else, something, and God with someone having a sense of right or wrong because I think someone has a sense of right or wrong for someone to be choosing to be doing something that is right or wrong with themselves, someone else, something, and God, and therefore, I think someone can choose to be doing something with themselves, someone else, something, and God with someone having a choice of right or wrong as I think someone can choose to be doing something with themselves, someone else, something, and God with someone having a sense of right or wrong because I think someone's choice of right or wrong is someone's sense of right or wrong as I think someone has a sense of right or wrong for someone to be right or wrong with someone choosing to be doing something with themselves, someone else, something, and God. I think someone's choice of right or wrong is someone's sense of right or wrong as I think someone has a sense of right or wrong for someone to be right or wrong with someone choosing to be doing something with themselves, someone else, something, and God because I think someone's choice is right or wrong for someone to be right or wrong with someone choosing to be doing something with themselves, someone else, something, and God. I think someone's choice is right or wrong for someone to be right or wrong with someone choosing to be doing something with themselves, someone else, something, and God because I think someone can be right or wrong with someone choosing to be doing something themselves, someone else, something, and God.

If I think someone's choice is right or wrong for someone to be right or wrong with someone choosing to be doing something with themselves, someone else, something, and God, than I think someone can be wrong because I think someone can do something to be harming themselves, and someone else for someone to be wrong. I think someone can do something to be harming themselves, and someone else for someone to be wrong because I think someone has a wrong choice with someone having a choice or right or wrong for someone to be doing something to be harming themselves, and someone else as I think someone has a wrong choice with someone having a choice of right or wrong for be wrong, and therefore, I think someone can be right or wrong because I think someone can choose not to be doing something to be harming themselves, and someone else from someone having a right choice with someone having a choice of right or wrong for someone to be right as I think someone can choose to be doing something to be harming themselves, and someone else from someone having a wrong choice with someone having a choice of right or wrong for someone to be wrong. If I think someone can be right or wrong, than I think someone can think of many different words to be describing someone is right or wrong because I think someone can think of many different words to be describing how someone is right or wrong, but I do not think someone needs to be thinking of every possible word to be describing someone is right or wrong as I do not think someone needs to be thinking of every possible word to be describing how someone is right or wrong because I think right is right, and wrong is wrong as I think someone is right or wrong about whatever someone is right or wrong about in life, even though, I think someone can think of any word to be describing someone is right or wrong as I think someone can think of any word to be describing how someone is right or wrong because I think someone has a choice of right or wrong for someone to be thinking of any word to be describing someone is right or wrong as I think someone has a choice of right or wrong for someone to be thinking of any word to be describing how someone is right or wrong. I think someone has a choice of right or wrong for someone to be thinking of any word to be describing someone is right or wrong as I think someone has a choice of right or wrong for someone to be thinking of any word to be describing how someone is right or wrong because I think someone has a choice of right or wrong for someone to be thinking of themselves, and someone else as being right or wrong, even though, I think someone's free will can be a problem for someone because I think someone can cause problems with someone harming themselves, and someone else from someone choosing to be doing something that is wrong to be harming themselves, and someone else with someone having a wrong choice with someone's free will for someone's free will to be a problem for someone, and therefore, I think someone can potentially harm themselves, and someone else with everything someone can do with themselves, and someone else because I think someone can potentially do something wrong with everything someone can do with themselves, and someone else for someone to potentially be harming themselves, and someone else with everything someone can do with themselves, and someone else, and however, I think someone can take care of themselves, and someone else with someone being careful with themselves, and someone else because I think someone try not to be doing something wrong to be harming themselves, and someone else with someone having a choice a right with someone's free will for someone to be taking care of themselves, and someone else with someone being careful with themselves, and someone else.

If I think someone can take care of themselves, and someone else with someone being careful with themselves, and someone else, than I do not think there is such a thing as there being no suffering because I think someone can do something to be harming themselves, and someone else as I think someone has a wrong choice with someone having a choice of right or wrong for there to be no such thing as there being no suffering, and therefore, I think someone's downfall is someone's wrong choice with someone having a choice of right or wrong because I think someone can choose to be doing something that is wrong with themselves, someone else, something, and God with someone having a wrong choice for someone's downfall to be someone's wrong choice with someone having a choice of right or wrong. If I think someone's downfall is someone's wrong choice with someone having a choice of right or wrong, than I do not think someone likes to be suffering because I do not think someone likes to be hurt for someone not to like to be suffering, even though, I think someone can enjoy suffering because I think someone can enjoy getting hurt as I think someone can enjoy hurting someone else for someone to enjoy suffering, however, I do not think suffering is something that is good because I think suffering is someone doing something to be causing harm, and pain onto themselves, and someone else for suffering not to be something that is good, even though, I think there is suffering, regardless of how much suffering is something that isn't good because I think someone can do something to be harming themselves, and someone else from someone having a wrong choice with someone having a choice of right or wrong for there to be suffering, and therefore, I think the only way in how there can possibly be no suffering is if God makes someone not to be having a wrong choice with someone having a choice of right or wrong for there to be no suffering, even though, I do not know if God can make someone not to be having a wrong choice with someone having a choice of right or wrong for there to be no suffering because I think God knows if God can make someone not to be having a wrong choice with someone having a choice of right or wrong for there to be no suffering, however, I think someone can find out from God after someone dies if God can make someone not to be having a wrong choice with someone having a choice of right or wrong for there to be no suffering because I think someone's life is God's choice for God to be choosing to be making someone not to be having a wrong choice with someone having a choice of right or wrong after someone dies. I think someone's life is God's choice for God to be choosing to be making someone not to be having a wrong choice with someone having a choice of right or wrong after someone dies because if I think someone's life is God's choice for someone to be alive, than I think someone's life is God's choice, as to what will happen to someone after someone dies because I do not think someone's life is someone's choice to be alive for someone's life not to be someone's choice, as to what will happen to someone after someone dies, and therefore, I think someone's life is God's choice for God to be choosing to be making someone not to be having a wrong choice with someone having a choice of right or wrong after someone dies because I think someone's life is God's choice, as to what will happen to someone after someone dies, and I think if God can make someone not to be having a wrong choice with someone having a choice of right or wrong after someone dies, than I think someone can always be good, and right like God is always good, and right with someone not having a wrong choice, even though, I do not know if there is such a thing as there being no suffering because I do not know if God can make someone not to be having a wrong choice with someone having a choice of right or wrong after someone dies for there to be no suffering, and therefore, I think there is suffering because I think God created someone to be having a wrong choice with someone having a choice of right or wrong for someone to be suffering as I think God created someone to be suffering for there to be suffering. I think God created someone to be having a wrong choice with someone having a choice of right or wrong for someone to be suffering as I think God created someone to be suffering for there to be suffering because I think God created someone to be having a wrong choice with someone having a choice of right or wrong for someone to be doing something to be harming themselves, and someone else as I think God created someone to be having a wrong choice with someone having a choice of right or wrong for God to be creating someone to be suffering.

If I think God created someone to be having a wrong choice with someone having a choice of right or wrong for someone to be suffering as I think God created someone to be suffering for there to be suffering, than I do not think someone is perfect because I think someone is imperfect for someone not to be perfect, and therefore, I think someone is imperfect because I do not think someone is perfect for someone to be imperfect. If I think someone is imperfect, than I think someone is imperfect as I do not think someone is perfect because I think someone is imperfect with someone having a wrong choice with someone having a choice of right or wrong for someone to be able to be choosing to be doing something that is wrong as I think someone can choose to be doing something that is wrong with someone having a wrong choice with someone having a choice of right or wrong for someone not to be perfect, and therefore, I think someone is imperfect for someone not to be perfect with someone's imperfection because I think someone's imperfection is someone having a wrong choice with someone having a choice of right or wrong for someone to be able to be choosing to be doing something that is wrong as I think someone can choose to be doing something that is wrong with someone having a wrong choice with someone having a choice of right or wrong for someone not to be perfect with someone's imperfection. If I think someone is imperfect for someone not to be perfect with someone's imperfection, than I do not think someone is able to be inheriting someone's imperfection from someone else as I think someone's imperfection is someone having a wrong choice with someone having a choice of right or wrong for someone to be able to be choosing to be doing something that is wrong because I do not think someone can create someone to be having a wrong choice with someone having a choice of right or wrong for someone to be able to be choosing to be doing something that is wrong as I do not think someone can create someone for someone not to be able to be inheriting someone's imperfection from someone else, and therefore, I think God created someone to be imperfect as I think God created someone not to be perfect because I think God created someone to be having a wrong choice with someone having a choice of right or wrong for God to be creating someone to be imperfect as I think God created someone to be having a wrong choice with someone having a choice of right or wrong for God to be creating someone not to be perfect.

If I think God created someone to be imperfect as I think God created someone not to be perfect, than I think someone can think life is hard for someone because I think someone can think someone's life is difficult or not easy for someone to be living someone's life for someone to be thinking life is hard for someone, even though, I do not think life is always hard for someone because I think God created someone to be living, learning, and enjoying themselves for life not to always be hard for someone, however, I think life can be hard for someone because I think someone's life can be difficult or not easy for someone to be living someone's life for life to be hard for someone, and therefore, I think life can be hard for someone as I think someone's life can be hard for someone because I think someone can live a hard life for life to be hard for someone as I think someone can live a hard life for someone's life to be hard for someone. I think someone can live a hard life for life to be hard for someone as I think someone can live a hard life for someone's life to be hard for someone because I think someone can suffer for someone to be living a hard life as I think someone can suffer for someone's life to be hard for someone, and therefore, I think God created someone to be living a hard life as I think God created someone's life to be hard for someone because I think God created someone to be suffering for someone to be living a hard life as I think God created someone to be suffering for someone's life to be hard for someone. I think God created someone to be suffering for someone to be living a hard life as I think God created someone to be suffering for someone's life to be hard for someone because I think someone can suffer for someone to be living a hard life as I think someone can suffer for someone's life to be hard for someone. I think someone can suffer for someone to be living a hard life as I think someone can suffer for someone's life to be hard for someone because I think someone's life can be hard for someone to be living a hard life as I think someone can suffer for life to be hard for someone. If I think someone can suffer for someone to be living a hard life as I think someone can suffer for someone's life to be hard for someone, than I do not think life is easy for someone because I think someone can suffer, regardless of how much someone does or doesn't have for life not to be easy for someone, and therefore, I think life can be hard for someone because I think someone can suffer for life to be hard for someone.

If I think life can be hard for someone, than I think someone has rights because I think someone can be right about something for someone to be having rights. If I think someone has rights, than I think everyone has the right to be free for everyone to be having the right to freedom because I think everyone has the right not to be bound to someone else with someone else not going against someone's will for everyone to be having the right to be free as I think freedom is someone not being bound to someone else with someone else not going against someone's will for someone to be free, and therefore, I think everyone has the right to be free because I think everyone is the same for everyone to be having the right to be free. If I think everyone has the right to be free, than I think someone can be free because I think someone can choose to be doing something that is good, and right for someone to be free, and therefore, I think someone can be free, providing there isn't any consequences to someone's actions for someone to be free because I do not think someone is free with there being any consequences to someone's actions. If I think someone can be free, providing there isn't any consequences to someone's actions for someone to be free, than I think someone can pass judgment onto someone else because I think someone can think of someone else as being right or wrong about something for someone to be passing judgment onto someone else. I think someone can think of someone else as being right or wrong about something for someone to be passing judgment onto someone else because I think someone can be right or wrong about what someone thinks of someone else for someone to be passing true or false judgment onto someone else. I think someone can be right or wrong about what someone thinks of someone else for someone to be passing true or false judgment onto someone else because I think someone can have a true or false judgment of someone else for someone to be passing true or false judgment onto someone else. I think someone can have a true or false judgment of someone else for someone to be passing true or false judgment onto someone else because I think someone has the right to be passing judgment onto someone else. I think someone has the right to be passing judgment onto someone else because I think someone has the ability to be passing judgment onto someone else. I think someone has the ability to be passing judgment onto someone else because I think someone has a choice of right or wrong for someone to be able to be having the ability, and the right to be passing judgment onto someone else, and if that isn't true, than I do not think someone can be judging, and I do not think there would be any judges, but I think someone can pass judgment onto someone else because I think someone can be judging, and I think there are judges, and therefore, I think someone can be their own judge with someone passing their own judgment onto someone else because I think someone has a choice of right or wrong for someone to be able to be ability, and the right to be passing judgment onto someone else. If I think someone can be their own judge with someone passing their own judgment onto someone else, than I do not think someone has the right to be judging someone else, if someone else is doing something wrong, that doesn't necessarily concern or have something to do with what someone is doing for someone to be passing judgment onto someone else about what someone else is doing wrong, and therefore, I do not think someone has the right to be judgmental towards someone else from someone passing false judgment onto someone else because I think someone is wrong for someone passing false judgment onto someone else.

If I think someone is wrong for someone passing false judgment onto someone else, than I think someone can pass judgment onto themselves, someone else, something, and God, without someone passing false judgment onto themselves, someone else, something, and God because I think someone has the right to be passing judgment onto themselves, someone else, something, and God if someone thinks someone needs to be passing judgment onto themselves, someone else, something, and God. I think someone has the right to be passing judgment onto themselves, someone else, something, and God if someone thinks someone needs to be passing judgment onto themselves, someone else, something, and God because I think someone can think of themselves, someone else, something, and God as being good or bad with someone having a choice of right or wrong for someone passing someone's own honest judgment onto themselves, someone else, something, and God. I think someone can think of themselves, someone else, something, and God as being good or bad with someone having a choice of right or wrong for someone passing someone's own honest judgment onto themselves, someone else, something, and God because I think someone can have an honest judgment of themselves, someone else, something, and God, as to whether or not if someone thinks themselves, someone else, something, and God has done something right or wrong for someone to be thinking of themselves, someone else, something, and God as being good or bad. If I think someone can think of themselves, someone else, something, and God as being good or bad with someone having a choice of right or wrong for someone passing someone's own honest judgment onto themselves, someone else, something, and God, than I think someone can have a good or a bad judgment of themselves, someone else, something, and God because I think someone can be right or wrong about what someone thinks of themselves, someone else, something, and God for

Jeffery A. Smith

someone to be having a good or bad judgment of themselves, someone else, something, and God, and therefore, I think someone can have good or bad judgment because I think someone can choose to be good or bad from someone choosing to be good or bad with themselves, someone else, something, and God, even though, I think someone can choose not to be judging someone else because I think someone can accept how someone is in life, regardless if someone is harming themselves, and someone else or not.

If I think someone can choose not to be judging someone else, than I think someone can be good or bad because I think someone can choose to be doing something that is right or wrong for someone to be good or bad, and therefore, I think someone can choose to be good or bad because I think someone has a choice of right or wrong for someone to be choosing to be good or bad. I think someone has a choice of right or wrong for someone to be choosing to be good or bad because I think someone can choose to be good or bad for someone to be good or bad, and therefore, I think someone being good or bad can be hard or easy for someone because I think someone can choose to be good just a much as someone can choose to be bad with someone having a choice of right or wrong for someone being good or bad to be hard or easy for someone. If I think someone being good or bad can be hard or easy for someone, than I think someone can think someone is good to be bad because I think someone can think someone is good to be doing something that is bad for someone to be thinking someone is good to be bad, even though, I do not think someone is good to be bad because I think someone can do something that is bad for someone not to be good to be bad, however, I think someone can think someone is good to be bad because I think someone can think someone can choose to be doing something that is wrong for the right reasons for someone to be a vigilante or hero as I think someone can be a vigilante or hero for someone to be thinking someone is good to be bad, even though, I think someone can be bad with someone being good to be bad because I think someone can be doing something that is bad with someone choosing to be doing something that is wrong for the right reasons for someone to be bad with someone being good to be bad, and therefore, I think someone is good or bad because I think someone can choose to be doing something that is good or bad for someone to be good or bad. If I think someone is good or bad, than I think someone can choose to be doing something that is good or bad because I think someone can choose to be doing something that is right or wrong for someone to be choosing to be doing something that is good or bad, and therefore, I think someone can choose to be good or bad because I think someone can choose to be doing something that is good or bad with someone having a choice of right or wrong for someone to be choosing to be good or bad. If I think someone can choose to be good or bad, than I think someone can be good or bad because I think someone can choose to be doing something that is good or bad for someone to be good or bad, and therefore, I think someone is good or bad because I think someone can choose to be good or bad for someone to be good or bad. If I think someone is good or bad, than I think someone can choose to be good or bad because I think someone can choose to be right or wrong for someone to be choosing to be good or bad, and therefore, I think someone can be good or bad because I think someone can be right or wrong for someone to be good or bad. If I think someone can be good or bad, than I think someone can be right or wrong because I think someone can choose to be doing something that is right or wrong for someone to be right or wrong, and therefore, I think someone can choose to be right or wrong because I think someone has a choice of right or wrong for someone to be choosing to be right or wrong. I think someone has a choice of right or wrong for someone to be choosing to be right or wrong because I think someone can choose to be right or wrong for someone to be right or wrong, and therefore, I think someone is right or wrong because I think someone can choose to be doing something that is right or wrong for someone to be right or wrong. If I think someone is right or wrong, than

I think someone can choose to be right or wrong because I think someone can choose to be doing something that is right or wrong for someone to be choosing to be right or wrong, and therefore, I think someone is right or wrong because I think someone can choose to be right or wrong for someone to be right or wrong. I think someone can choose to be right or wrong for someone to be right or wrong because I think someone can be right or wrong with someone having a choice of right or wrong, and therefore, I think someone has a choice of right or wrong for someone to be right or wrong because I think someone is created from God having a choice of right or wrong for someone to be having a choice of right or wrong. I think someone is created from God having a choice of right or wrong for someone to be having a choice of right or wrong because I think someone has a choice of right or wrong for someone to be having a choice of right or wrong, and therefore, I think someone has a choice of right or wrong because I think someone's choice of right or wrong is of the dimension of someone's will for someone to be having a choice of right or wrong.

Chapter 17

Something not having a choice of right or wrong

I would like to talk about how dimensions are in life in relation to what dimensions are in life by talking about something not having a choice of right and wrong, that can possibly have something to do with how dimensions are in life is in relation to what dimensions are in life because I do not think something has a choice of right and wrong for something not to be having a choice of right or wrong, and therefore, I do not think something has a choice of right or wrong because I do not think God created something to be having a choice of right or wrong for something not to be having a choice of right or wrong. I do not think God created something to be having a choice of right or wrong for something not to be having a choice of right or wrong because I think God created something with God's thoughts that is apart of making up something for something not to be having a choice of right or wrong, and therefore, I do not think something's will has a choice of right or wrong because I do not think something has a choice of right and wrong for something's will not to be having a choice right or wrong. If I do not think something's will has a choice of right or wrong, than I think God created something because I think God created something to have a choice. I think God created something to have a choice because I think God created something to be a choice of itself for something to have a choice, but I do not think God created something to be choosing to be right or wrong for something to be right or wrong because I do not think God created something to be having a choice of right or wrong for something to be right or wrong as I do not think God created something to be having a choice of right or wrong for something to be choosing to be right or wrong, and therefore, I do not think God created the being of something to be having a sense of right or wrong because I do not think God created something to be having a choice of right or wrong for God to be creating the being of something not to be having a sense of right or wrong. If I do not think God created the being of something to be having a sense of right or wrong, than I do not think God created something to be choosing something that is right or wrong because I do not think God created something to be having a choice of right or wrong for something to be choosing something that is right or wrong, and therefore, I do not think God created something to be right or wrong because I do not think God created something to be having a choice of right or wrong for God to be creating something to be right or wrong. I do not think God created something to be having a choice of right or wrong for God to be creating something to be right or wrong because I do not think something is right or wrong. I do not think something is right or wrong because I do not think something has a sense of right or wrong for something to be right or wrong. I do not think something has a sense of right or wrong for something to be right or wrong because I do not think something has a choice of right or wrong for something to be right or wrong as I do not think something has a choice of right or wrong for something not to be having a sense of right or wrong, and therefore, I do not think something can choose something that is right or wrong for something to be right or wrong because I do not think something has a choice of right or wrong for something to be right or wrong as I do not think something has a choice of right or wrong for something not to be choosing something that is right or wrong. If I do not think something can choose something that is right or wrong for something to be right or wrong, than I do not think something is right or wrong because I think something is constantly not right or wrong. I think something is constantly not right or wrong because I think something is always not right or wrong. I think something is always not right or wrong because I think something is neutral from being right or wrong. I think something is neutral from being right or wrong because I do not think something is right or wrong.

If I think something is neutral from being right or wrong, than I do not think something can choose to be doing something that is right or wrong because I do not think something has a choice of right or wrong for something not to be choosing to be doing something that is right or wrong, and therefore, I think God created something not to be choosing to be doing something that is right or wrong because I think God created something not to be having a choice of right or wrong for God to be creating something not to be choosing to be doing something that is right or wrong. If I think God created something not to be choosing to be doing something that is right or wrong, than I think something is always right because I do not think something choose to be doing something that is right or wrong with something not having a choice of right or wrong for something to always be right, and therefore, I think someone can think something is always right, and something never lies, and something is never wrong because I do not think something choose to be doing something that is right or wrong with something not having a choice of right or wrong for something to always be right. If I think someone can think something is always right, and something never lies, and something is never wrong, than I do not think something can choose to be doing something that is right or wrong with itself, something else, someone, and God because I do not think something has a choice of right or wrong for something not to be choosing to be doing something that is right or wrong with itself, something else, someone, and God, and therefore, I think God created something not to be choosing to be doing something that is right or wrong with itself, something else, someone, and God because I think God created something not to be having a choice of right or wrong for God to be creating something not to be choosing to be doing something that is right or wrong with itself, something else, someone, and God. If I think God created something not to be choosing to be doing something that is right or wrong with itself, something else, someone, and God, than I do not think something can choose to be wanting or needing to be doing something as I think someone can choose to be wanting or needing to be doing something because I do not think something has a choice of wanting or needing to be doing something as I think someone has a choice of wanting or needing to be doing something. I do not think something has a choice of wanting or needing to be doing something as I think someone has a choice of wanting or needing to be doing something because I do not think something has a choice of right or wrong for something not to be having a choice of wanting or needing to be doing something as I think someone has a choice of right or wrong for someone to be having a choice of wanting or needing to be doing something, and therefore, I do not think something can choose to be wanting or needing to be doing something as I think someone can choose to be wanting or needing to be doing something because I do not think something has a choice of right or wrong for something not to be choosing to be wanting or needing to be doing something as I think someone has a choice of right or wrong for someone to be choosing to be wanting or needing to be doing something. If I do not think something can choose to be wanting or needing to be doing something as I think someone can choose to be wanting or needing to be doing something, than I do not think something can be right or wrong with something wanting or needing to be doing something as I think someone can be right or wrong with someone wanting or needing to be doing something because I do not think something has a choice of right or wrong for something not to be right or wrong with something wanting or needing to be doing something as I think someone has a choice of right or wrong for someone to be right or wrong with someone wanting or needing to be doing something.

If I do not think something can be right or wrong with something wanting or needing to be doing something as I think someone can be right or wrong with someone wanting or needing to be doing something, than I think God created right and wrong because I think God created something to be opposite to something else for God to be creating right or wrong. I think God created something to be opposite to something else for God to be creating right or wrong because I think something is opposite to something else. I think something is opposite to something else because I think something is opposite of something else. I think something is opposite of something else because I think God created something to be opposite of something else. I think God created something to be opposite of something else because I think God created something to be a duality of something else. I think God created something to be a duality of something else because I think something is a duality of something else as I think something is opposite of something else. I think something is a duality of something else as I think something is opposite of something else because I think something is in opposition of something else, even though, I do not think there is someone or something that can possibly be in opposition of God because I think God is always present, and awaiting to be helping someone, regardless if someone chooses to be accepting God or not, however, I think someone can in opposition to God because I think someone can oppose God with someone having nothing to do with God for someone to be in opposition to God, even though, I do not think someone can be in opposition to God because I think God is beyond everything for someone not to be able to be physically harming God as I do not think someone can physically harm God for someone not to be in opposition to God, and therefore, I do not think someone or something is a duality of God as I do not think someone or something is opposite of God because I do not think God is created for someone or something not to be a duality of God as I do not think God is created for someone or something not to be opposite of God. If I do not think someone or something is a duality of God as I do not think someone or something is opposite of God, than I think God created something to be opposite of something else because I think God created something that is opposite of something else. I think God created something that is opposite of something else because I think something that is opposite of something else are two completely different something of themselves. I think something that is opposite of something else are two completely different something of themselves because I think something is opposite of something else, and therefore, I think something is overlapping, and co-existing along with something else because I think something is opposite of something else for something to be overlapping, and co-existing along with something else.

If I think something is overlapping, and co-existing along with something else, than I think something that is opposite of something else are two completely different something of themselves because I think something that is opposite of something else is of the same something of themselves. I think something that is opposite of something else is of the same something of themselves because I think God created something to be unlike something of itself as I think God created something to be alike something of itself. I think God created something to be unlike something of itself as I think God created something to be alike something of itself because I think God created something to be opposite of itself, such as up and down, or left and right, or in and out, or right and wrong. I think God created something to be opposite of itself because I think God created something to be in balance with itself. I think God created something to be in balance with itself because I think God created something to be opposite of itself for something to be in balance with itself. I think God created something to be opposite of itself for something to be in balance with itself because I think God created something that is opposite of itself, and therefore, I think God created everything to be in balance because I think God created something

302

that is opposite of itself for everything to be in balance. I think God created something that is opposite of itself for everything to be in balance because I think God created something that is apart of making up everything as I think God created something that is opposite of itself, and therefore, I think everything is constantly in balance because I think God created something that is opposite of itself for everything to be in balance. If I think everything is constantly in balance, than I think God created something that is opposite of itself because I do not think something that is opposite of itself is able to be canceling the opposite of itself completely out, without something completely canceling itself out. I do not think something that is opposite of itself is able to be canceling the opposite of itself completely out, without something completely canceling itself out because I think something that is opposite of itself is of the exact same something of itself as I think something is something that is opposite of itself. I think something that is opposite of itself is of the exact same something of itself as I think something is something that is opposite of itself because I think something has a reversible effect of itself with something that is opposite of itself. I think something has a reversible effect of itself with something that is opposite of itself because I think the reversible effect of something is something that is opposite of itself. I think the reversible effect of something is something that is opposite of itself because I think something is opposite of itself.

If I think the reversible effect of something is something that is opposite of itself, than I think something can have a positive and a negative effect because I think something is something that is opposite of itself for something to be positive and negative as I think something is something that is opposite of itself for something to be having a positive and a negative effect, and therefore, I think something has a reversible positive and negative effect because I think something has a positive and negative effect for something to be having a reversible positive and negative effect. I think something has a positive and negative effect for something to be having a reversible positive and negative effect because I think something is something that is opposite of itself for something to be having a reversible positive and negative effect as I think something is something that is opposite of itself for something to be having a positive and a negative effect, and therefore, I think something can be how something is in life because I think something has a reversible positive and negative effect for something to be how something is in life. If I think something has a reversible positive and negative effect for something to be how something is in life, than I think God created something to be how something is in life because I think God created something to be something that is opposite of itself with God's thoughts for God to be creating something to be having a reversible positive and negative effect as I think God created something to be having a reversible positive and negative effect for something to be how something is in life, and therefore, I think God is amazing for God to be creating something to be how something is in life because I think God is amazing for God to be creating something to be having a reversible positive and negative effect.

If I think God is amazing for God to be creating something to be having a reversible positive and negative effect, than I think any dimension that is apart of making up everything can be something that is opposite of itself because I think any dimension that is apart of making up everything is something as I think something is something that is opposite of itself. If I think any dimension that is apart of making up everything can be something that is opposite of itself, than I think an example how I think any dimension that is apart of making up everything can be something that is opposite of itself can be the dimension of sound because I think the dimension of sound is any sound that is of any high or low sound range of sound, and therefore, I think something is overlapping, and co-existing along with the opposite of itself because I think something is something that is opposite of itself for something to be overlapping, and co-existing along with the opposite of itself. If I think something is overlapping, and co-existing along with the opposite of itself, than I think something is something that is opposite of itself because I think something is opposite of itself, and therefore, I think someone can think of something that is opposite of itself as being the dimension of something that is opposite of itself because I think the dimension of something is something that is opposite of itself. I think the dimension of something is something that is opposite of itself because I think something is opposite of itself. If I think the dimension of something is something that is opposite of itself, than I think everything is opposite of itself as I think something is opposite of itself because I think everything is of something that is opposite of itself for everything to be opposite of itself. I think everything is of something that is opposite of itself for everything to be opposite of itself because I think everything is of something as I think something is opposite of itself, and therefore, I think everything is overlapping, and co-existing along with the opposite of itself because I think everything is of something that is opposite of itself for everything to be opposite of itself. If I think everything is overlapping, and co-existing along with the opposite of itself, than I think everything that is opposite of itself is overlapping, and co-existing along with something that is opposite of itself because I think everything is of something as I think something is opposite of itself.

If I think everything that is opposite of itself is overlapping, and co-existing along with something that is opposite of itself, than I think something is opposite of itself because I think God created something to be opposite of itself with God's thoughts for something to be opposite of itself. I think God created something to be opposite of itself with God's thoughts for something to be opposite of itself because I think something is of God's thoughts as I think something is opposite of itself. I think something is of God's thoughts as I think something is opposite of itself because I think something is of God's thoughts for something to be opposite of itself. I think something is of God's thoughts for something to be opposite of itself because I think God's thoughts is apart of making up something for something to be opposite of itself. I think God's thoughts is apart of making up something for something to be opposite of itself because I think God's thoughts is apart of making up something as I think something is opposite of itself, and therefore, I think the dimension of God's thoughts is overlapping, and co-existing along with the dimension of something that is opposite of itself because I think something is of God's thoughts as I think something is opposite of itself. If I think the dimension of God's thoughts is overlapping, and co-existing along with the dimension of something that is opposite of itself, than I think everything is opposite of itself because I think God created everything to be opposite of itself with God's thoughts for everything to be opposite of itself. I think God created everything to be opposite of itself with God's thoughts for everything to be opposite of itself because I think everything is of God's thoughts as I think everything is opposite of itself. I think everything is of God's thoughts as I think everything is opposite of itself because I think everything is of God's thoughts for everything to be opposite of itself. I think everything is of God's thoughts for everything to be opposite of itself because I think God's thoughts is apart of making up everything for everything to be opposite of itself. I think God's thoughts is apart of making up everything for everything to be opposite of itself because I think God's thoughts is apart of making up everything as I think everything is opposite of itself, and therefore, I think the dimension of God's thoughts is overlapping, and co-existing along with everything that is opposite of itself because I think everything is of God's thoughts as I think everything is opposite of itself. I think everything is of God's thoughts as I think everything is opposite of itself because I think everything is something that is of God's thoughts for everything to be opposite of itself. I think everything is something that is of God's thoughts for everything to be opposite of itself because I think everything is of something that is opposite of itself as I think something is of God's thoughts for something to be opposite of itself. I think everything is of something that is opposite of itself as I think something is of God's thoughts for something to be opposite of itself because I think something is of God's thoughts as I think something is opposite of itself.

If I think everything is of something that is opposite of itself as I think something is of God's thoughts for something to be opposite of itself, than I think God created right and wrong with God's thoughts for right and wrong to be something that is opposite of itself because I think right and wrong is of something as I think right and wrong is something that is opposite of itself. I think right and wrong is of something as I think right and wrong is something that is opposite of itself because I think right and wrong is of God for right and wrong to be something that is opposite of itself. I think right and wrong is of God for right and wrong to be something that is opposite of itself because I think God created right or wrong from God always being good, and right for right and wrong to be something that is opposite of itself. I think God created right or wrong from God always being good, and right for right and wrong to be something that is opposite of itself because I think God created right or wrong from God creating something that is opposite of itself for right and wrong to be something that is opposite of itself. I think God created right or wrong from God creating something that is opposite of itself for right and wrong to be something that is opposite of itself because I think God created right or wrong from God creating something that is opposite of itself for God to be having a choice of right or wrong. I think God created right or wrong from God creating something that is opposite of itself for God to be having a choice of right or wrong because I think God's choice of right or wrong is of something that is opposite of itself for God to be having a choice of right or wrong. I think God's choice of right or wrong is of something that is opposite of itself for God to be having a choice of right or wrong because I think God has a choice of right or wrong from God creating something that is opposite of itself for God to be having a choice of right or wrong. I think God has a choice of right or wrong from God creating something that is opposite of itself for God to be having a choice of right or wrong because I think God created right or wrong for God to be having a choice of right or wrong. I think God created right or wrong for God to be having a choice of right or wrong because I think God has a choice of right or wrong for God to be having a sense of right or wrong. I think God has a choice of right or wrong for God to be having a sense of right or wrong because I think God's sense of right or wrong is God having a choice of right or wrong. I think God's sense of right or wrong is God having a choice of right or wrong because I think God has a choice of right or wrong for God to be having a sense of right or wrong as I think God has a choice of right or wrong for God to be having a choice of right or wrong. I think God has a choice of right or wrong for God to be having a sense of right or wrong as I think God has a choice of right or wrong for God to be having a choice of right or wrong because I think God has a choice of right or wrong from God creating something that is opposite of itself for God to be having a choice of right or wrong.

If I think God has a choice of right or wrong for God to be having a sense of right or wrong as I think God has a choice of right or wrong for God to be having a choice of right or wrong, than I think God's sense of right or wrong is something that is opposite of itself as I think God's choice of right or wrong is something that is opposite of itself because I think God's sense of right or wrong is of something for God's sense's of right or wrong to be something that is opposite of itself as I think God's choice of right or wrong is of something for God's choice of right or wrong to be something that is opposite of itself. I think God's sense of right or wrong is of something for God's sense's of right or wrong to be something that is opposite of itself as I think God's choice of right or wrong is of something for God's choice of right or wrong to be something that is opposite of itself because I think God's sense of right or wrong is of God for God's sense's of right or wrong to be something that is opposite of itself as I think God's choice of right or wrong is of God for God's choice of right or wrong to be something that is opposite of itself. I think God's sense of right or wrong is of God for God's sense's of right or wrong to be something that is opposite of itself as I think God's choice of right or wrong is of God for God's choice of right or wrong to be something that is opposite of itself because I think God's sense of right or wrong is God's choice for God's sense's of right or wrong to be something that is opposite of itself as I think God's choice of right or wrong is God's choice for God's choice of right or wrong to be something that is opposite of itself, and therefore, I think God has a choice of right or wrong because I think God's choice is something that has a choice of right or wrong as I think God's choice of right or wrong is of something that is opposite of itself for God to be having a choice of right or wrong, but I do not think something has a choice of right or wrong because I do not think something has a choice of right or wrong for something not to be having a choice of right or wrong as I think God has a choice of right or wrong with God's choice that is something for God to be having a choice of right or wrong. If I do not think something has a choice of right or wrong, than I think God's thoughts can have a choice of right or wrong because I think God created right or wrong with God's thoughts for God to be having a choice of right or wrong with God's thoughts as I think God has a choice of right or wrong with God's thoughts for God's thought to be having a choice of right or wrong, and therefore, I think God's thoughts is overlapping, and co-existing along with God's will because I think God has a choice of right or wrong with God's thoughts for God's thought to be overlapping, and co-existing along with God's will. If I think God's thoughts is overlapping, and co-existing along with God's will, than I think God can have a choice of right or wrong with God's will because I think God's will is of something that is opposite of itself for God's will to be something that is opposite of itself as I think God's will is something that is opposite of itself for God to be having a choice of right or wrong with God's will, and therefore, I think the embodiment of God is apart of God because I think the embodiment of God consists of God having a state of consciousness, a will, something that is opposite of itself for God to be having a choice of right or wrong with God's will, God's thoughts, God's mind, and God's being that is apart of making up the embodiment of God for the embodiment of God to be apart of God.

If I think the embodiment of God is apart of God, than I think God has a choice of right or wrong from God creating something that is opposite of itself for God to be having a choice of right or wrong because I think God has a choice of right or wrong for God to be creating someone to be having a choice of right or wrong. I think God has a choice of right or wrong for God to be creating someone to be having a choice of right or wrong because I think God created right or wrong for someone to be having a choice of right or wrong. I think God created right or wrong for someone to be having a choice of right or wrong because I think God created someone to be having a choice of right or wrong from God having a choice of right or wrong. I think God created someone to be having a choice of right or wrong from God having a choice of right or wrong because I think God has a choice of right or wrong from God creating something that is opposite of itself for God to be creating someone to be having a choice of right or wrong. I think God has a choice of right or wrong from God creating something that is opposite of itself for God to be creating someone to be having a choice of right or wrong because I think someone's choice of right or wrong is of something that is opposite of itself for someone to be having a choice of right or wrong. I think someone's choice of right or wrong is of something that is opposite of itself for someone to be having a choice of right or wrong because I think someone has a choice of right or wrong for someone to be having a sense of right or wrong. I think someone has a choice of right or wrong for someone to be having a sense of right or wrong because I think someone's sense of right or wrong is someone having a choice of right or wrong. I think someone's sense of right or wrong is someone having a choice of right or wrong because I think someone has a choice of right or wrong for someone to be having a sense of right or wrong as I think someone has a choice of right or wrong for someone to be having a choice of right or wrong. I think someone has a choice of right or wrong for someone to be having a sense of right or wrong as I think someone has a choice of right or wrong for someone to be having a choice of right or wrong because I think God has a choice of right or wrong from God creating something that is opposite of itself for God to be creating someone to be having a choice of right or wrong.

If I think someone has a choice of right or wrong for someone to be having a sense of right or wrong as I think someone has a choice of right or wrong for someone to be having a choice of right or wrong, than I think someone's sense of right or wrong is something that is opposite of itself as I think someone's choice of right or wrong is something that is opposite of itself because I think someone's sense of right or wrong is of something for someone's sense's of right or wrong to be something that is opposite of itself as I think someone's choice of right or wrong is of something for someone's choice of right or wrong to be something that is opposite of itself. I think someone's sense of right or wrong is of something for someone's sense's of right or wrong to be something that is opposite of itself as I think someone's choice of right or wrong is of something for someone's choice of right or wrong to be something that is opposite of itself because I think someone's sense of right or wrong is of God for someone's sense's of right or wrong to be something that is opposite of itself as I think someone's choice of right or wrong is of God for someone's choice of right or wrong to be something that is opposite of itself. I think someone's sense of right or wrong is of God for someone's sense's of right or wrong to be something that is opposite of itself as I think someone's choice of right or wrong is of God for someone's choice of right or wrong to be something that is opposite of itself because I think someone's sense of right or wrong is God's choice for someone's sense's of right or wrong to be something that is opposite of itself as I think someone's choice of right or wrong is God's choice for someone's choice of right or wrong to be something that is opposite of itself, and therefore, I think something can have a choice of right or wrong because I think someone's choice is something that has a choice of right or wrong as I think someone's choice of right or wrong is of something that is opposite of itself for someone to be having a choice of right or wrong, but I do not think something has a choice of right or wrong because I do not think something has a choice of right and wrong for something not to be having a choice right or wrong as I think someone has a choice of right or wrong with someone's choice that is something for someone to be having a choice of right or wrong, even though, I think God created something to be right or wrong with God's thoughts because I think God created someone to be having a choice of right or wrong with God's thoughts for God to be creating something to be right or wrong with God's thoughts. If I think God created something to be right or wrong with God's thoughts, than I think God's thoughts can have a choice of right or wrong because I think God created someone with God's thoughts for God to be creating someone to be having a choice of right or wrong with God's thoughts as I think God created someone to be having a choice of right or wrong with God's thoughts for God's thought to be having a choice of right or wrong, and therefore, I think God's thoughts is overlapping, and co-existing along with someone's will because I think God created someone to be having a choice of right or wrong with God's thoughts for God's thought to be overlapping, and co-existing along with someone's will. If I think God's thoughts is overlapping, and co-existing along with someone's will, than I think someone can have a choice of right or wrong with someone's will because I think someone's will is of something that is opposite of itself for someone's will to be something that is opposite of itself as I think someone's will is something that is opposite of itself for someone to be having a choice of right or wrong with someone's will, and therefore, I think embodiment of someone is apart of making up someone because I think the embodiment of someone consists of someone having a state of consciousness, a will, something that is opposite of itself for someone to be having a choice of right or wrong with someone's will, someone's thoughts, someone's mind, and someone's being that is apart of making up the embodiment of someone for the embodiment of someone to be apart of making up someone.

If I think embodiment of someone is apart of making up someone, than I think someone can try to always be right as I think someone can try to always be wrong because I think someone can try to always be doing something right for someone to try to always be right as I think someone can try to always be doing something wrong for someone to try to always be wrong, even though, I do not think someone can always do something right for someone to always be right as I do not think someone can always do something wrong for someone to always be wrong because I think someone can do something wrong for someone not to always be right as I think someone can do something right for someone not to always be wrong, and therefore, I do not think someone can always be right as I do not think someone can always be wrong because I think someone can be right or wrong with someone having a choice of right or wrong for someone not to always be right as I think someone can be right or wrong with someone having a choice of right or wrong for someone not to always be wrong. If I do not think someone can always be right as I do not think someone can always be wrong, than I think someone is in balance with someone having a choice of right or wrong because I think someone can be right or wrong with someone having a choice of right or wrong for someone to be in balance with someone having a choice of right or wrong, and therefore, I think God is in balance with God having a choice of right or wrong because I think God is always good, and right with God having a choice of right or wrong for God to be in balance with God having a choice of right or wrong. If I think God is in balance with God having a choice of right or wrong, than I think something can have a choice of right or wrong because I think God created someone to be having a choice of right or wrong with God's thoughts as I think God's thoughts is something for something to be having a choice of right or wrong, and therefore, I think something is overlapping, and co-existing along with God's thoughts as I think something is overlapping, and co-existing along with someone's will because I think God created someone to be having a choice of right or wrong with God's thoughts for something to be overlapping, and co-existing along with God's thoughts as I think God created someone to be having a choice of right or wrong with God's thoughts for something to be overlapping, and co-existing along with someone's will, even though, I do not think something has a choice of right or wrong because I think God's thoughts is apart of making up something that doesn't have a choice of right or wrong for something not to be having a choice of right or wrong.

Chapter 18

Someone's thoughts

I would like to talk about how dimensions are in life in relation to what dimensions are in life by talking about someone's thoughts, that can possibly have something to do with how dimensions are in life is in relation to what dimensions are in life because I think someone's thoughts is of the dimension of thought for someone to be having thoughts, and therefore, I think someone's thoughts is somehow able to be taking place within someone's mind because I think someone's thoughts is of something for someone's thoughts to somehow be able to be taking place within someone's mind. I think someone's thoughts is of something for someone's thoughts to somehow be able to be taking place within someone's mind because I think someone's thoughts is something as I think someone's thoughts is of something. I think someone's thoughts is something as I think someone's thoughts is of something because I think someone's thoughts is of something for someone's thoughts to be something. I think someone's thoughts is of something for someone's thoughts to be something because I think someone's thoughts is something as I think someone's thoughts is of the thoughts of something. I think someone's thoughts is something as I think someone's thoughts is of the thoughts of something because I think someone's thoughts is of something's thoughts as I think something's thoughts is the thoughts of something. I think someone's thoughts is of something's thoughts as I think something's thoughts is the thoughts of something because I think something is a thought for someone's thoughts to be of something's thoughts. I think something is a thought for someone's thoughts to be of something's thoughts because I think someone's thoughts is of something's thoughts for someone's thoughts to be something. I think someone's thoughts is of something's thoughts for someone's thoughts to be something because I think someone's thoughts is of something for someone's thoughts to be of something's thoughts. I think someone's thoughts is of something for someone's thoughts to be of something's thoughts because I think someone's thoughts is something's thoughts for someone's thoughts to be of something. I think someone's thoughts is of something's thoughts for someone's thoughts to be of something because I think someone's thoughts comes from someone experiencing something for someone's thoughts to be of something. I think someone's thoughts comes from someone experiencing something for someone's thoughts to be of something because I do not think someone would have any thoughts of something, without someone experiencing something for someone's thoughts to be of something, otherwise, I think someone would be thoughtless with someone not having any thoughts of something from someone not experiencing something for someone's thoughts to be of something, but I do not think someone is thoughtless with someone not having any thoughts of something because I think someone has thoughts of something for someone not to be thoughtless with someone not having any thoughts of something, even though, I think someone can be thoughtless because I think someone can be thoughtless of someone or something, from someone choosing not to be thinking of someone or something for someone to be thoughtless, but I do not think someone can be completely thoughtless because I think someone is a thought for someone not to be completely thoughtless, however, I think someone comes into life from someone being created by God for someone to be thoughtless because I think someone starts out not having any thoughts of something for someone to be thoughtless, and therefore, I think someone's thoughts is of something for someone to be having any thoughts of something because I think someone's thoughts is of something's thoughts for someone to be having any thoughts of something. I think someone's thoughts is of something's thoughts for someone to be having any thoughts of something because I think someone's thoughts comes from someone experiencing something for someone to be having any thoughts of something.

I think someone's thoughts comes from someone experiencing something for someone to be having any thoughts of something because I think something is of something's thoughts for someone's thoughts to come from someone experiencing something. I think something is of something's thoughts for someone's thoughts to come from someone experiencing something because I think someone's thoughts is a copy of something's thoughts for someone's thoughts to be coming from someone experiencing something. I think someone's thoughts is a copy of something's thoughts for someone's thoughts to be coming from someone experiencing something because I think someone's thoughts is of something for someone's thoughts to be a copy of something's thoughts as I think someone's thoughts is a copy of something's thoughts for someone's thoughts to be a copy of something, and therefore, how is someone's thoughts a copy of something's thoughts as I think someone's thoughts is of something for someone's thoughts to be a copy of something's thoughts? I think someone's thoughts is of something for someone's thoughts to be a copy of something's thoughts because I think something's thoughts is somehow being recorded in someone's mind for someone's thoughts to be a copy of something's thoughts. I think something's thoughts is somehow being recorded in someone's mind for someone's thoughts to be a copy of something's thoughts because I think someone's thoughts is a copy of something's thoughts for something's thoughts to somehow be recorded in someone's mind. I think someone's thoughts is a copy of something's thoughts for something's thoughts to somehow be recorded in someone's mind because I think someone's thoughts is someone's thoughts of something as I think someone's thoughts of something is in someone's mind.

I think someone's thoughts is someone's thoughts of something as I think someone's thoughts of something is in someone's mind because I think someone's mind is a storage area of someone's thoughts as I think someone's thoughts of something is in someone's mind. I think someone's mind is a storage area of someone's thoughts as I think someone's thoughts of something is in someone's mind because I think someone's mind is a storage area of someone's thoughts for someone's mind to be a storage area of someone's thoughts of something. I think someone's mind is a storage area of someone's thoughts for someone's mind to be a storage area of someone's thoughts of something because I think someone's mind is a storage area of someone's thoughts as I think someone's mind is a storage area of someone's thoughts of something. I think someone's mind is a storage area of someone's thoughts as I think someone's mind is a storage area of someone's thoughts of something because I think someone is a mind as I think someone's thoughts of something is in someone's mind. I think someone is a mind as I think someone's thoughts of something is in someone's mind because I think someone's mind is somehow able to be recording someone's thoughts of something for someone's thoughts of something to be apart of someone's mind. I think someone's mind is somehow able to be recording someone's thoughts of something for someone's thoughts of something to be apart of someone's mind because I think someone's mind is somehow able to be recording something's thoughts for something's thoughts to be apart of someone's mind. I think someone's mind is somehow able to be recording something's thoughts for something's thoughts to be apart of someone's mind because I think someone's mind is somehow able to be recording something's thoughts for someone's thoughts to be of something's thoughts in someone's mind. I think someone's mind is somehow able to be recording something's thoughts for someone's thoughts to be of something's thoughts in someone's mind because I think someone's thoughts is of something's thoughts for someone's thoughts to be of something in someone's mind. I think someone's thoughts is of something's thoughts for someone's thoughts to be of something in someone's mind because I think someone's thoughts is a copy of something's thoughts for someone's thoughts to be of something in someone's mind. I think someone's thoughts is a copy of something's thoughts for someone's thoughts to be of something in someone's mind because I think someone's thoughts is a copy of something's thoughts for someone's thoughts to be something in someone's mind. I think someone's thoughts is a copy of something's thoughts for someone's thoughts to be something in someone's mind because I think someone's thoughts is something as I think someone's thoughts is of something in someone's mind. I think someone's thoughts is something as I think someone's thoughts is of something in someone's mind because I think someone's thoughts is someone's thoughts of something for someone's thoughts to be of something in someone's mind, and therefore, I think someone's thoughts is overlapping, and co-existing along with someone's mind because I think someone's thoughts is a copy of something's thoughts for someone's thoughts to be something in someone's mind.

If I think someone's thoughts is overlapping, and co-existing along with someone's mind, than I think someone's thoughts is something because I think someone's thoughts is of something for someone's thoughts to be something. I think someone's thoughts is of something for someone's thoughts to be something because I think someone's thoughts is a copy of something's thoughts for someone's thoughts to be something, and therefore, I think someone's thoughts is like something because I think someone's thoughts is a copy of something's thoughts for someone's thoughts to be the same as something, but I do not think someone's thoughts is alike something because I think someone's thoughts is a copy of something's thoughts for someone's thoughts to be alike something, and therefore, I think someone's thoughts is overlapping, and co-existing along with something because I think someone's thoughts is a copy of something's thoughts for someone's thoughts to be something. If I think someone's thoughts is overlapping, and co-existing along with something, than I think someone's thoughts is something as I think something is someone's thoughts because I think someone's thoughts is of something for someone's thoughts to be something as I think someone's thoughts is of something for something to be someone's thoughts. I think someone's thoughts is of something for someone's thoughts to be something as I think someone's thoughts is of something for something to be someone's thoughts because I think someone's thoughts is a copy of something's thoughts for someone's thoughts to be something as I think someone's thoughts is a copy of something's thoughts for something to be someone's thoughts. I think someone's thoughts is a copy of something's thoughts for someone's thoughts to be something as I think someone's thoughts is a copy of something's thoughts for something to be someone's thoughts because I think someone's thoughts is a copy of something's thoughts for someone's thoughts to be something in someone's mind. I think someone's thoughts is a copy of something's thoughts for someone's thoughts to be something in someone's mind because I think someone's mind is somehow able to be recording something's thoughts for someone's thoughts to be of something's thoughts in someone's mind, and therefore, I think God created someone's mind to be recording something's thoughts for someone's thoughts to be of something's thoughts in someone's mind because I do not think someone can create someone's mind to be recording something's thoughts for someone's thoughts to be of something's thoughts in someone's mind. I do not think someone can create someone's mind to be recording something's thoughts for someone's thoughts to be of something's thoughts in someone's mind because I do not think someone can create anything for someone to be able to be creating someone's mind to be able to be recording something's thoughts in someone's mind, and therefore, I think God created someone's mind to be recording something's thoughts for someone's thoughts to be of something's thoughts in someone's mind because I think God is somehow able to be responsible for creating everything for God to be able to be creating someone's mind to be able to be recording something's thoughts in someone's mind.

If I think God created someone's mind to be recording something's thoughts for someone's thoughts to be of something's thoughts in someone's mind, than I think God created something to be recording something because I think God created something to be duplicating something for God to be creating something to be recording something. I think God created something to be duplicating something for God to be creating something to be recording something because I think God created something to be copying something for something to be recording something as I think God created something to be copying something for something to be duplicating something, and therefore, I think God created something to be recording something because I think God created something to be duplicating or copying something for something to be a duplicate or copy of something as I think God created something to be duplicating or copying something for something to be recording something, even though, I think something is of something's own original copy because I think something can be copying something for something to be a copy of something as I think something can be copying something for something to be recording something. If I think something is of something's own original copy, than I think something can be of an infinite amount of copy's of something because I think something can copy something for something to infinitely be copying something as I think something can infinitely be copying something for something to be of an infinite amount of copy's of something, even though, I do not know if everything can be recorded because I do not know if something can be a copy of everything for everything to be recorded, however, I think God created something to be recording something because I think God created something to be duplicating or copying something for God to be creating something to be recording something. If I think God created something to be recording something, than I think Good created someone's mind to be recording something because I think God created someone's mind to be duplicating or copying the thoughts of something in someone's mind for God to be creating someone's mind to be recording something, even though, I think someone can think someone's brain can be copying something for someone's thoughts in someone's mind to be a copy of something because I think someone can think someone's thoughts in someone's mind can be coming from someone's brain for someone to be thinking someone's brain can be copying something, however, I do not think someone's brain is copying something for someone's thoughts in someone's mind to be a copy of something because I do not think someone's brain is taking on the shape, and form of something for someone's brain to be copying something, and therefore, I think someone's brain, and someone's sense's is apart of the process of someone's thoughts being recorded in someone's mind as I think a camera is apart of the process of a picture being recorded because I think someone's mind is copying the thoughts or image of something from someone experiencing something with someone's brain, and senses for someone's thoughts in someone's mind to be a copy of something's thoughts or image as I think a picture is copying something from someone taking a picture of something with a camera. If I think someone's brain, and someone's sense's is apart of the process of someone's thoughts being recorded in someone's mind as I think a camera is apart of the process of a picture being recorded, than I think someone's thoughts in someone's mind is copy of something for someone's mind to be copying or recording something because I think someone's thoughts in someone's mind is a copy of something's thoughts or image for someone's mind to be a copying or recording something.

If I think someone's thoughts in someone's mind is copy of something for someone's mind to be copying or recording something, than I think someone's thoughts is God's thoughts as I think someone's thoughts is something because I think something is of God's thoughts for someone's thoughts to be of God's thoughts in someone's mind as I think someone's thoughts is of something's thoughts for someone's thoughts to be of something's thoughts in someone's mind. I think something is of God's thoughts for someone's thoughts to be of God's thoughts in someone's mind as I think someone's thoughts is of something's thoughts for someone's thoughts to be of something's thoughts in someone's mind because I think someone's thoughts is of God's thoughts for someone's thoughts to be of God's thoughts in someone's mind as I think someone's thoughts is of something's thoughts for someone's thoughts to be of something's thoughts in someone's mind. I think someone's thoughts is of God's thoughts for someone's thoughts to be of God's thoughts in someone's mind as I think someone's thoughts is of something's thoughts for someone's thoughts to be of something's thoughts in someone's mind because I think someone's thoughts is God's thoughts as I think someone's thoughts is something. I think someone's thoughts is God's thoughts as I think someone's thoughts is something because I think God's thoughts is something as I think someone's thoughts is of God's thoughts for someone's thoughts to be something. I think God's thoughts is something as I think someone's thoughts is of God's thoughts for someone's thoughts to be something because I think someone's thoughts is God's thoughts as I think God's thoughts is someone's thoughts. I think someone's thoughts is God's thoughts as I think God's thoughts is someone's thoughts because I think someone's thoughts is of God's thoughts for someone's thoughts to be God's thoughts as I think someone's thoughts is of God's thoughts for someone's thoughts to be someone's thoughts. I think someone's thoughts is of God's thoughts for someone's thoughts to be God's thoughts as I think someone's thoughts is of God's thoughts for someone's thoughts to be someone's thoughts because I think someone's thoughts is of God's thoughts for someone's thoughts to be of God's thoughts in someone's mind as I think someone's thoughts is of God's thoughts for someone's thoughts to be of someone's thoughts in someone's mind. I think someone's thoughts is of God's thoughts for someone's thoughts to be of God's thoughts in someone's mind as I think someone's thoughts is of God's thoughts for someone's thoughts to be of someone's thoughts in someone's mind because I think someone's thoughts is a copy of God's thoughts for someone's thoughts to be of God's thoughts in someone's mind as I think someone's thoughts is a copy of God's thoughts for someone's thoughts to be of someone's thoughts in someone's mind, and therefore, I think someone can think of someone's thoughts as being the dimension of someone's thoughts or as being the dimension of God's thoughts because I think someone's thoughts is of God's thoughts for someone's thoughts to be of God's thoughts in someone's mind as I think someone's thoughts is of God's thoughts for someone's thoughts to be of someone's thoughts in someone's mind. If I think someone can think of someone's thoughts as being the dimension of someone's thoughts or as being the dimension of God's thoughts, than I think someone can think of someone's thoughts as being the dimension of thought because I think the dimension of thought is God's thoughts as I think someone's thoughts is of God's thoughts for someone to be thinking of someone's thoughts as being the dimension of thought.

If I think someone can think of someone's thoughts as being the dimension of thought, than I think someone's mind is unlimited in size with someone's thoughts of something because I think someone's thoughts of something is unlimited in someone's mind. I think someone's thoughts of something is unlimited in someone's mind because I think someone's thoughts of something is limitless in someone's mind. I think someone's thoughts of something is limitless in someone's mind because I do not think there is any limit of someone's thoughts of something in someone's mind for someone's thoughts of something to be unlimited in someone's mind. I do not think there is any limit of someone's thoughts of something in someone's mind for someone's thoughts of something to be unlimited in someone's mind because I do not think someone can think enough of something in someone's mind. I do not think someone can think enough of something in someone's mind because I do not think someone can think enough about something in someone's mind for someone not to be thinking enough of something in someone's mind, and therefore, I do not think someone can think enough about something in someone's mind because I think someone's thoughts of something is unlimited in someone's mind. I think someone's thoughts of something is unlimited in someone's mind because I think someone's thoughts of something is infinite in someone's mind for someone's thoughts of something to be unlimited in someone's mind. I think someone's thoughts of something is infinite in someone's mind for someone's thoughts of something to be unlimited in someone's mind because I think someone's thoughts of something is created by God being infinite for someone's thoughts of something to be infinite in someone's mind, and therefore, I think someone's thoughts of something is unlimited in someone's mind because I think someone's thoughts of something is created by God being infinite for someone's thoughts of something to be infinite in someone's mind.

If I think someone's thoughts of something is unlimited in someone's mind, than I think someone can think of themselves, someone else, something, and God as I think someone can think of someone's thoughts because I think someone's thoughts is of God's thoughts for someone to be thinking of themselves, someone else, something, and God, and therefore, I think someone can think of someone's thoughts of God as I think someone can think of someone's thoughts of themselves, someone else, and something because I think someone's thoughts is of God's thoughts for someone to be thinking of someone's thoughts of God in someone's mind with someone's state of consciousness, along with someone's will that is apart of someone's being as I think someone's thoughts is of someone's, and something's physical being for someone to be thinking of someone's thoughts of themselves, someone else, and something in someone's mind with someone's state of consciousness, along with someone's will that is apart of someone's being. If I think someone can think of someone's thoughts of God as I think someone can think of someone's thoughts of themselves, someone else, and something, than I think someone can think of God as I think someone can think of themselves, someone else, and something because I think someone's thoughts is of God's thoughts for someone to be thinking of God in someone's mind with someone's state of consciousness, along with someone's will that is apart of someone's being as I think someone's thoughts is of someone's, and something's physical being for someone to be thinking of themselves, someone else, and something in someone's mind with someone's state of consciousness, along with someone's will that is apart of someone's being, and therefore, I think someone can think of themselves, someone else, something, and God because I think someone is someone's being as I think someone's being can think of themselves, someone else, something, and God in someone's mind with someone's state of consciousness, along with someone's will that is apart of someone's being. If I think someone can think of themselves, someone else, something, and God, than I think someone can choose to be thinking of themselves, someone else, something, and God because I think someone can choosing to be thinking of themselves, someone else, something, and God with someone's state of consciousness, along with someone's will, and someone's thoughts, and someone's mind that is apart of someone's being. If I think someone can choose to be thinking of themselves, someone else, something, and God, than I think someone can think of what someone thinks of themselves, someone else, something, and God because I think someone can think of what someone thinks of themselves, someone else, something, and God in someone's mind with someone's state of consciousness, along with someone's will that is apart of someone's being, and therefore, I think someone can think of themselves, someone else, something, and God in someone's mind because I think someone is mentally able to be thinking of themselves, someone else, something, and God in someone's mind. I think someone is mentally able to be thinking of themselves, someone else, something, and God in someone's mind because I think someone can think of someone's thoughts of themselves, someone else, something, and God in someone's mind as I think someone's mind is apart of someone's being. I think someone can think of someone's thoughts of themselves, someone else, something, and God in someone's mind as I think someone's mind is apart of someone's being because I think someone's being can think of someone's thoughts of themselves, someone else, something, and God in someone's mind as I think someone's mind is apart of someone's being, even though, I think someone can think of someone's thoughts of God as I think someone can think of someone's thoughts of themselves, someone else, and something because I do not think someone would be able to thinking of God in someone's mind, without someone having any experience of everything that someone has experienced in someone's life that is of God's thoughts for someone to be thinking of God in someone's mind as I do not think someone would be able to thinking of themselves, someone else, and something in someone's mind, without someone having any experience of themselves, someone else, and something that someone has experienced in someone's life for someone to be thinking of themselves, someone else, and something in someone's mind, and therefore, I think someone can think of God as I think someone can think of themselves, someone else, and something because I think someone's thoughts is of everything that someone has experienced in someone's life that is of God's thoughts for someone to be thinking of God as I think someone's thoughts is of the thoughts of themselves, someone else, and something that someone has experienced in someone's life for someone to be thinking of themselves, someone else, and something.

If I think someone can think of God as I think someone can think of themselves, someone else, and something, than I think someone can think of themselves, someone else, something, and God with someone's conscious because I think someone can think of someone's thoughts of themselves, someone else, something, and God in someone's mind with someone's state of consciousness, along with someone's will that is apart of someone's being for someone to be thinking of themselves, someone else, something, and God with someone's conscious, even though, I think someone can think of themselves, someone else, something, and God with someone's subconscious because I think someone can randomly choose to be thinking of someone's thoughts of themselves, someone else, something, and God in someone's mind with someone's state of consciousness, along with someone's will that is apart of someone's being for someone to be thinking of themselves, someone else, something, and God with someone's subconscious, and therefore, I think someone has a conscious and subconscious because I think someone's conscious and subconscious is of someone's state of consciousness as I think someone has a state of consciousness for someone to be having a conscious and subconscious. If I think someone has a conscious and subconscious, than I think someone can consciously or subconsciously be right or wrong about what someone thinks of themselves, someone else, something, and God in someone's mind with someone's state of consciousness, along with someone's will that is apart of someone's being as I think someone can be right or wrong about what someone thinks of themselves, someone else, something, and God in someone's mind with someone's state of consciousness, along with someone's will that is apart of someone's being because I think someone has a choice of right or wrong with someone's will that is apart of someone's being for someone to consciously or subconsciously be right or wrong about what someone thinks of themselves, someone else, something, and God in someone's mind with someone's state of consciousness, along with someone's will that is apart of someone's being as I think someone has a choice of right or wrong with someone's will that is apart of someone's being for someone to be right or wrong about what someone thinks of themselves, someone else, something, and God in someone's mind with someone's state of consciousness, along with someone's will that is apart of someone's being, and therefore, I think someone can be right or wrong to consciously or subconsciously be thinking of themselves, someone else, something, and God with someone's state of consciousness, along with someone's will, and someone's thoughts, and someone's mind that is apart of someone's being as I think someone can be right or wrong to be thinking of themselves, someone else, something, and God with someone's state of consciousness, along with someone's will, and someone's thoughts, and someone's mind that is apart of someone's being because I think someone has a choice of right or wrong with someone's will that is apart of someone's being for someone to be right or wrong to consciously or subconsciously be thinking of themselves, someone else, something, and God with someone's state of consciousness, along with someone's will, and someone's thoughts, and someone's mind that is apart of someone's being as I think someone has a choice of right or wrong with someone's will that is apart of someone's being for someone to be right or wrong to be thinking of themselves, someone else, something, and God with someone's state of consciousness, along with someone's will, and someone's thoughts, and someone's mind that is apart of someone's being, even though, I think someone can think of themselves, someone else, something, and God for someone to consciously or subconsciously be thinking of themselves, someone else, something, and God because I think someone can be right or wrong about what someone thinks of themselves, someone else, something, and God in someone's mind with someone's state of consciousness, along with someone's will that is apart of someone's being for someone to consciously or subconsciously be thinking of themselves, someone else, something, and God.

If I think someone can think of themselves, someone else, something, and God for someone to consciously or subconsciously be thinking of themselves, someone else, something, and God, than I think everything can seem as though life is an illusion or a dream or a fantasy to someone, but I do not think everything is an illusion or a dream or a fantasy as I think everything can seem as though life is an illusion or a dream or a fantasy to someone because I think someone can randomly be thinking of something for someone's thoughts to be an illusion or a dream or a fantasy as I think someone can randomly be thinking of something for everything to seem as though life is an illusion or a dream or a fantasy to someone, and therefore, I think someone's thoughts can be someone's illusion or dream or fantasy as I think someone's illusion or dream or fantasy can be someone's thoughts because I think someone can randomly be thinking of something for someone's thoughts to be someone's illusion or dream or fantasy as I think someone's illusion or dream or fantasy is of someone randomly thinking of something. If I think someone's thoughts can be someone's illusion or dream or fantasy as I think someone's illusion or dream or fantasy can be someone's thoughts, than I think someone can be thinking of something that is someone's illusion or dream or fantasy as I think someone can be thinking of something with someone's subconscious because I think someone can randomly be thinking of something with someone's subconscious for someone to be thinking of something that is someone's illusion or dream or fantasy, and therefore, I think someone randomly thinks of something with someone's subconscious because I think someone can randomly be thinking of something as I think someone can randomly be thinking of something with someone's subconscious. If I think someone randomly thinks of something with someone's subconscious, than I think someone can subconsciously be thinking of something when someone is awake or asleep because I think someone can randomly be thinking of something when someone is awake or asleep. I think someone can randomly be thinking of something when someone is awake or asleep because I do not think someone has to be awake or asleep for someone to randomly be thinking of something. I do not think someone has to be awake or asleep for someone to randomly be thinking of something because I think someone can be thinking of something with someone's imagination when someone is awake or asleep. I think someone can be thinking of something with someone's imagination when someone is awake or asleep because I think someone can subconsciously be thinking of something that is of someone's imagination when someone is awake or asleep. I think someone can subconsciously be thinking of something that is of someone's imagination when someone is awake or asleep because I think someone can randomly be thinking of something when someone is awake or asleep, and therefore, I think someone constantly has a subconscious because I do not think someone can think of something, without someone subconsciously thinking of something with someone's subconscious.

If I think someone constantly has a subconscious, than I think someone can think of something with someone's conscious because I think someone can be thinking of something, without someone randomly thinking of something with someone's subconscious for someone to be thinking of something with someone's conscious, and therefore, I think someone can consciously be thinking of something when someone is awake or asleep because I think someone can be thinking of something, without someone randomly thinking of something when someone is awake or asleep. I think someone can be thinking of something, without someone randomly thinking of something when someone is awake or asleep because I do not think someone has to be awake or asleep for someone to be thinking of something, without someone randomly thinking of something when someone is awake or asleep. I do not think someone has to be awake or asleep for someone to be thinking of something, without someone randomly thinking of something when someone is awake or asleep because I think someone can be thinking of something that is true when someone is awake or asleep. I think someone can be thinking of something that is true when someone is awake or asleep because I think someone can consciously be thinking of something that is true when someone is awake or asleep, and therefore, I think someone can consciously be thinking of something because I think someone can be thinking of something that is true when someone is awake or asleep for someone to consciously be thinking of something. I think someone can be thinking of something that is true when someone is awake or asleep for someone to consciously be thinking of something because I think someone can consciously be thinking of something when someone is awake or asleep. I think someone can consciously be thinking of something when someone is awake or asleep because I think someone can be thinking of something, without someone randomly thinking of something when someone is awake or asleep, and therefore, I think someone constantly has a conscious because I do not think someone can think of something, without someone consciously thinking of something with someone's conscious. If I think someone constantly has a conscious, than I think someone constantly has a conscious and subconscious because I think someone constantly has a state of consciousness for someone to constantly be having a conscious and subconscious as I think someone's conscious and subconscious is of someone's state of consciousness for someone to be having conscious and subconscious, even though, I think someone can be unconscious because I think someone can be unawake for someone to be unconscious, however, I do not think someone has no conscious when someone is unconscious because I think someone can consciously or subconsciously be thinking of something when someone's unconscious for someone not to be having no conscious when someone is unconscious.

317

If I do not think someone has no conscious when someone is unconscious, than I do not think someone can fully, and completely be able to be knowing for themselves, as to what someone's conscious and subconscious is in life because I do not think someone can possibly be able to be knowing for themselves, as to how someone is able to be thinking with someone's conscious and subconscious as I think someone's conscious and subconscious is of someone's state of consciousness, but I think someone can try to understand what someone's conscious and subconscious is in life from how someone thinks of something with someone's conscious and subconscious because I think someone can think of something with someone's conscience as I think someone can randomly think of something with someone's subconscious, even though, I think it can be very difficult for someone to be distinguishing the difference, as to when someone is thinking with someone's conscious, and when someone is thinking with someone's subconscious because I think someone can think someone is thinking with someone's conscious, when someone is actually thinking with someone's subconscious as I think someone can think someone is thinking with someone's subconscious, when someone is actually thinking with someone's conscious, and therefore, I think someone might not be able to be distinguishing the difference between someone thinking of something in reality, and when someone thinking of something with someone's imagination because I think someone can be right or wrong to consciously or subconsciously be thinking of something. I think someone can be right or wrong for someone to consciously or subconsciously be thinking of something because I think someone has a choice of right or wrong for someone to consciously and subconsciously think of something as being right or wrong, and therefore, I think someone can consciously and subconsciously think of something as being right or wrong because I think someone can think of something as being right or wrong for someone to consciously and subconsciously be thinking of something as being right or wrong.

If I think someone can consciously and subconsciously think of something as being right or wrong, than I think someone to consciously and subconsciously think of something as being good or bad because I think someone can think of something as being right or wrong for someone to consciously and subconsciously be thinking of something as being good or bad, and therefore, I think someone can consciously and subconsciously think of someone's illusion or dream or fantasy as being good or bad because I think someone can consciously and subconsciously think of something as being good or bad for someone to consciously and subconsciously be thinking of someone's illusion or dream or fantasy as being good or bad. If I think someone can consciously and subconsciously think of someone's illusion or dream or fantasy as being good or bad, than I think someone can consciously and subconsciously think of something as being good or bad as I think someone can think of someone's illusion or dream or fantasy as being good or bad because I think someone has a choice of right or wrong for someone to consciously and subconsciously be thinking of something as being good or bad as I think someone has a choice of right or wrong for someone to think of someone's illusion or dream or fantasy as being good or bad, and therefore, I think someone's illusion or dream or fantasy can be good or bad because I think someone can think of someone's illusion or dream or fantasy as being good or bad for someone's illusion or dream or fantasy to be good or bad. I think someone can think of someone's illusion or dream or fantasy as being good or bad for someone's illusion or dream or fantasy to be good or bad because I think someone's illusion or dream or fantasy is someone thinking of something as being good or bad for someone's illusion or dream or fantasy to be good or bad as I think someone can think of something as being good or bad for someone to be thinking of someone's illusion or dream or fantasy as being good or bad, and therefore, I do not think life is an illusion or dream or fantasy because I think someone's thoughts can be an illusion or dream or fantasy for life not to be an illusion or dream or fantasy. I think someone's thoughts can be an illusion or dream or fantasy for life not to be an illusion or dream or fantasy because I think an illusion or dream or fantasy is someone thinking of something as being good or bad for someone's thoughts to be an illusion or dream or fantasy, and therefore, I do not think life is an illusion or dream or fantasy because I think everything is constantly something for life not to be an illusion or dream or fantasy as I think someone can think of themselves, someone else, something, and God for life not to be an illusion or dream or fantasy. If I do not think life is an illusion or dream or fantasy with, than I think someone's imagination is God's imagination because I think someone's thoughts is of God's thoughts for someone's imagination to be God's imagination, however, I think God created someone to be reasoning because I think God created someone to be having a choice of right or wrong for God to be creating someone to be thinking about what is right or wrong as I think God created someone to be thinking about what is right or wrong for God to be creating someone to be reasoning.

If I think God created someone to be reasoning, than I think someone can think of themselves, someone else, something, and God as being good or bad because I think someone has a choice of right or wrong for someone to be thinking of themselves, someone else, something, and God as being good or bad. I think someone has a choice of right or wrong for someone to be thinking of themselves, someone else, something, and God as being good or bad because I think someone can be right or wrong for someone to be thinking of themselves, someone else, something, and God as being good or bad, and therefore, I think someone can think of themselves, someone else, something, and God as being good or bad because I think someone can be right or wrong about themselves, someone else, something, and God for someone to be thinking of themselves, someone else, something, and God as being good or bad. I think someone can be right or wrong about themselves, someone else, something, and God for someone to be thinking of themselves, someone else, something, and God as being good or bad because I think someone can be right or wrong about what someone thinks of themselves, someone else, something, and God with someone having a choice of right or wrong for someone to be thinking of themselves, someone else, something, and God as being good or bad, and therefore, I think someone can think positive or negative because I think someone has a choice of right or wrong for someone to be thinking positive or negative. I think someone has a choice of right or wrong for someone to be thinking positive or negative because I think someone can be right or wrong for someone to be thinking positive or negative, and therefore, I think someone can think positive or negative because I think someone can be right or wrong about what someone thinks of themselves, someone else, something, and God for someone to be thinking positive or negative. If I think someone can think positive or negative, than I think someone can think someone is right because I think someone can think someone is right about what someone thinks of themselves, someone else, something, and God for someone to be thinking someone is right, even though, I do not think someone is right just because someone thinks someone is right because I do not think someone is perfect for someone not to be right just because someone thinks someone is right, and therefore, I think someone can be right or wrong about what someone thinks of themselves, someone else, something, and God because I do not think someone is perfect for someone to be right or wrong about what someone thinks of themselves, someone else, something, and God.

If I think someone can be right or wrong about what someone thinks of themselves, someone else, something, and God, than I think someone's imagination is someone randomly thinking of themselves, someone else, something, and God as being good or bad because I think someone can randomly be thinking of themselves, someone else, something, and God as being good or bad with someone's thoughts of themselves, someone else, something, and God in someone's mind for someone's imagination to be someone randomly thinking of themselves, someone else, something, and God as being good or bad, and therefore, I think someone's dreams is someone randomly thinking of themselves, someone else, something, and God as being good or bad as I think someone's imagination is someone randomly thinking of themselves, someone else, something, and God as being good or bad because I think someone's dreams is of someone's imagination for someone's dreams to be someone randomly thinking of themselves, someone else, something, and God as being good or bad. If I think someone's dreams is of someone's imagination for someone's dreams to be someone randomly thinking of themselves, someone else, something, and God as being good or bad, than I think someone's fantasy's is someone randomly thinking of themselves, someone else, something, and God as being good or bad as I think someone's imagination is someone randomly thinking of themselves, someone else, something, and God as being good or bad because I think someone's fantasy's is of someone's imagination for someone's fantasy's to be someone randomly thinking of themselves, someone else, something, and God as being good or bad, and therefore, I think someone's dreams, and someone's fantasy's is of someone's imagination because I think someone's imagination is of someone's dreams, and someone's fantasy's for someone's dreams, and someone's fantasy's to be of someone's imagination. I think someone's imagination is of someone's dreams, and someone's fantasy's for someone's dreams, and someone's fantasy's to be of someone's imagination because I think someone's imagination, and someone's dreams, and someone's fantasy's is someone randomly thinking of themselves, someone else, something, and God as being good or bad for someone's dreams, and someone's fantasy's to be of someone's imagination, and therefore, I think someone's imagination, and someone's dreams, and someone's fantasy's can be good or bad because I think someone can think of themselves, someone else, something, and God as being good or bad for someone's imagination, and someone's dreams, and someone's fantasy's to be good or bad, otherwise, I do not think someone would be able to be having an imagination, dreams, and fantasy's, without someone thinking of themselves, someone else, something, and God as being good or bad for someone to be able to be having an imagination, dreams, and fantasy's life, but I think someone is able to be having an imagination, dreams, and fantasy's because I think someone can think of themselves, someone else, something, and God as being good or bad for someone to be able to be having an imagination, dreams, and fantasy's. If I think someone is able to be having an imagination, dreams, and fantasy's, than I think someone can have an imagination, dreams, and fantasy's because I think someone can think of themselves, someone else, something, and God for someone to be having an imagination, dreams, and fantasy's, and therefore, I think someone can have an imagination, dreams, and fantasy's of themselves, someone else, something, and God because I think someone can think of themselves, someone else, something, and God for someone to be having an imagination, dreams, and fantasy's of themselves, someone else, something, and God. If I think someone can have an imagination, dreams, and fantasy's of themselves, someone else, something, and God, than I think someone's imagination, dreams, and fantasy's can be good, and bad because I think someone can think of themselves, someone else, something, and God as being good or bad for someone's imagination, dreams, and fantasy's to be good, and bad, and therefore, I think someone's imagination, dreams, and fantasy's of themselves, someone else, something, and God can be good, and bad because I think someone has a choice of right or wrong for someone to be right or wrong about what someone thinks of themselves, someone else, something, and God as I think someone can think of themselves, someone else, something, and God as being good or bad for someone's imagination, dreams, and fantasy's of themselves, someone else, something, and God to be good, and bad.

If I think someone's imagination, dreams, and fantasy's of themselves, someone else, something, and God can be good, and bad, than I think someone can think of themselves, someone else, something, and God in someone's mind because I think someone's thoughts is of God's thoughts for someone to be thinking of themselves, and someone else, something, and God in someone's mind. If I think someone can think of themselves, someone else, something, and God in someone's mind, than I think someone can think of someone in someone's mind as I think someone can think of something in someone's mind because I think someone is something for someone to be thinking of someone in someone's mind as I think someone's thoughts is of something for someone to be thinking of something in someone's mind, and therefore, I think someone's thoughts is something in someone's mind as I think someone's thoughts is of something in someone's mind because I think someone's thoughts is of something's thoughts for someone's thoughts to be something in someone's mind. I think someone's thoughts is of something's thoughts for someone's thoughts to be something in someone's mind because I think someone's thoughts is something in someone's mind as I think someone's thoughts is in someone's mind. I think someone's thoughts is something in someone's mind as I think someone's thoughts is in someone's mind because I think someone's thoughts is something for someone's thoughts to be in someone's mind. I think someone's thoughts is something for someone's thoughts to be in someone's mind because I think someone's thoughts is something in someone's mind. I think someone's thoughts is something in someone's mind because I think someone's thoughts is in someone's mind for someone's thoughts to be something in someone's mind. I think someone's thoughts is in someone's mind for someone's thoughts to be something in someone's mind because I think someone has thoughts as I think someone's thoughts is in someone's mind. If I think someone's thoughts is in someone's mind for someone's thoughts to be something in someone's mind, than I think someone can think of someone's thoughts of something as being someone's thoughts because I think someone's thoughts is of something for someone to be thinking of someone's thoughts of something as being someone's thoughts, and therefore, I think someone's thoughts proves that a thought is something because I think someone's thoughts is of something's thoughts for someone's thoughts to be something.

If I think someone's thoughts proves that a thought is something, than I think someone's mind is unlimited in size with someone's thoughts because I think someone's thoughts is unlimited in someone's mind. I think someone's thoughts is unlimited in someone's mind because I think someone's thoughts is limitless in someone's mind. I think someone's thoughts is limitless in someone's mind because I do not think there is any limit of someone's thoughts in someone's mind for someone's thoughts to be unlimited in someone's mind. I do not think there is any limit of someone's thoughts in someone's mind for someone's thoughts to be unlimited in someone's mind because I think someone can think of everything in someone's mind that someone can experience in someone's life. I think someone can think of everything in someone's mind that someone can experience in someone's because I think everything is of something for someone to be thinking of everything in someone's mind that someone can experience in someone's life. I think everything is of something for someone to be thinking of everything in someone's mind that someone can experience in someone's because I think someone can think of everything that is something in someone's mind. I think someone can think of everything that is something in someone's mind because I think someone can think of the thoughts of everything in someone's mind that someone has experienced in someone's life. I think someone can think of the thoughts of everything in someone's mind that someone has experienced in someone's because I think someone can think of something's thoughts of everything in someone's mind that someone has experienced in someone's life. I think someone can think of something's thoughts of everything in someone's mind that someone has experienced in someone's life because I think everything is of something for someone to be thinking of something's thoughts of everything in someone's mind that someone has experienced in someone's life. I think everything is of something for someone to be thinking of something's thoughts of everything in someone's mind that someone has experienced in someone's life because I think someone can think of everything that is something in someone's mind. I think someone can think of everything that is something in someone's mind because I do not think someone can think enough of someone's thoughts in someone's mind. I do not think someone can think enough of someone's thoughts in someone's mind because I do not think someone can think enough about someone's thoughts in someone's mind for someone not to be thinking enough of someone's thoughts in someone's mind, and therefore, I do not think someone can think enough about someone's thoughts in someone's mind because I think someone's thoughts is unlimited in someone's mind. I think someone's thoughts is unlimited in someone's mind because I think someone's thoughts is infinite in someone's mind for someone's thoughts to be unlimited in someone's mind. I think someone's thoughts is infinite in someone's mind for someone's thoughts to be unlimited in someone's mind because I think someone's thoughts is created by God being infinite for someone's thoughts to be infinite in someone's mind, and therefore, I think someone's thoughts is unlimited in someone's mind because I think someone's thoughts is created by God being infinite for someone's thoughts to be infinite in someone's mind.

If I think someone's thoughts is unlimited in someone's mind, than I think someone's thoughts is infinite in someone's mind for someone's thoughts to be unlimited in someone's mind because I think someone's thoughts is infinite. I think someone's thoughts is infinite because I think someone's thoughts is of something for someone's thoughts to be infinite as I think everything is of something for everything to be infinite. I think someone's thoughts is of something for someone's thoughts to be infinite as I think everything is of something for everything to be infinite because I think someone's thoughts is of something that is infinite for someone's thoughts to be infinite as I think everything is of something that is infinite for everything to be infinite. I think someone's thoughts is of something that is infinite for someone's thoughts to be infinite as I think everything is of something that is infinite for everything to be infinite because I think someone's thoughts is of something's thoughts for someone's thoughts to be infinite as I think everything is of something's thoughts for everything to be infinite. I think someone's thoughts is of something's thoughts for someone's thoughts to be infinite as I think everything is of something's thoughts for everything to be infinite because I think something's thoughts is apart of making up someone's thoughts for someone's thoughts to be infinite as I think something's thoughts is apart of making up everything for everything to be infinite. I think something's thoughts is apart of making up someone's thoughts for someone's thoughts to be infinite as I think something's thoughts is apart of making up everything for everything to be infinite because I think something's thoughts is apart of making up someone's thoughts that is infinite as I think something's thoughts is apart of making up everything that is infinite. I think something's thoughts is apart of making up someone's thoughts that is infinite as I think something's thoughts is apart of making up everything that is infinite because I think someone's thoughts is of something that is infinite as I think everything is of something that is infinite. I think someone's thoughts is of something that is infinite as I think everything is of something that is infinite because I think someone's thoughts is of something for someone's thoughts to be infinite as I think someone's thoughts is of everything for someone's thoughts to be infinite. I think someone's thoughts is of something for someone's thoughts to be infinite as I think someone's thoughts is of everything for someone's thoughts to be infinite because I think someone's thoughts is of something that is apart of making up everything for someone's thoughts to be infinite. I think someone's thoughts is of something that is apart of making up everything for someone's thoughts to be infinite because I think someone's thoughts is of everything that is something for someone's thoughts to be infinite. I think someone's thoughts is of everything that is something for someone's thoughts to be infinite because I think someone's thoughts is infinite.

I think someone's thoughts is infinite because I think someone's thoughts is constant for someone's thoughts to be infinite. I think someone's thoughts is constant for someone's thoughts to be infinite because I think someone is constantly thinking of something in someone's mind for someone's thoughts to be infinite. I think someone is constantly thinking of something in someone's mind for someone's thoughts to be infinite because I think someone is constantly thinking of someone's thoughts of something in someone's mind for someone's thoughts to be infinite. I think someone is constantly thinking of someone's thoughts of something in someone's mind for someone's thoughts to be infinite because I think someone is constantly thinking of something's thoughts in someone's mind for someone's thoughts to be infinite. I think someone is constantly thinking of something's thoughts in someone's mind for someone's thoughts to be infinite because I think someone's thoughts of something is constantly taking place within someone's mind for someone's thoughts to be infinite. I think someone's thoughts of something is constantly taking place within someone's mind for someone's thoughts to be infinite because I think someone's thoughts is of something as I think someone's thoughts is constantly taking place within someone's mind for someone's thoughts to be infinite. I think someone's thoughts is of something as I think someone's thoughts is constantly taking place within someone's mind for someone's thoughts to be infinite because I think someone is infinitely thinking of someone's thoughts of something in someone's mind for someone's thoughts to be infinite. I think someone is infinitely thinking of someone's thoughts of something in someone's mind for someone's thoughts to be infinite because I think someone's thoughts of something is infinitely taking place within someone's mind for someone's thoughts to be infinite. I think someone's thoughts of something is infinitely taking place within someone's mind for someone's thoughts to be infinite because I think someone's thoughts is of something as I think someone's thoughts is infinitely taking place within someone's mind for someone's thoughts to be infinite. I think someone's thoughts is of something as I think someone's thoughts is infinitely taking place within someone's mind for someone's thoughts to be infinite because I think someone is infinitely thinking of someone's thoughts in someone's mind for someone's thoughts to be infinite. I think someone is infinitely thinking of someone's thoughts in someone's mind for someone's thoughts to be infinite because I think someone's thoughts is infinite.

I think someone's thoughts is infinite because I think someone thinks for someone's thoughts to be infinite. I think someone thinks for someone's thoughts to be infinite because I think someone thinks of someone's thoughts for someone's thoughts to be infinite. I think someone thinks of someone's thoughts for someone's thoughts to be infinite because I think someone's thinks, even though, I think someone can think someone can think too much because I think someone can think someone can be thinking of something too much for someone to be thinking someone can think too much, but I do not think someone can think too much because I think someone is constantly thinking of something, regardless if someone is consciously aware that someone is constantly thinking of something or not, and therefore, I do not think there is such a thing as someone thinking too much because I think someone is constantly thinking of something for someone not to be thinking too much. I think someone is constantly thinking of something for someone not to be thinking too much because I do not think someone can not think of something for someone not to be thinking too much, although, I think someone can think someone thinks too much because I think someone's brain can hurt from someone thinking a lot about something for someone to be thinking someone thinks too much, even though, I think someone's brain can hurt from someone thinking a lot about something because I do not think someone's brain can keep up with how much someone can be thinking about something in someone's mind for someone's brain to be limited in comparison to how much someone can possibly be able to be thinking about something in someone's mind, however, I think someone can think someone thinks too much because I think someone can thinking a lot about something for someone not to be sure about something that someone is thinking about, even though, I do not think someone can think too much because I think someone is always thinking of something for someone to be thinking as I think someone is always thinking of something for someone not to be thinking too much, and therefore, I think someone thinks because I think someone thinks of someone's thoughts for someone to be thinking, even though, I do not think someone can think too much because I think someone can be right or wrong about what someone thinks of themselves, someone else, something, and God for someone not to be thinking too much. If I do not think someone can think too much, than I am, therefore I think because I am for me to think. If I am for me to think, than I think something's thoughts is someone's choice because I think someone's thoughts of something is someone's choice for someone's thoughts to be of something. I think someone's thoughts of something is someone's choice for someone's thoughts to be of something because I think someone's thoughts is of something's thoughts for someone's thoughts to be someone's choice of something. I think someone's thoughts is of something's thoughts for someone's thoughts to be someone's choice of something because I think someone's thoughts of something is someone's choice of something. I think someone's thoughts of something is someone's choice of something because I think someone's thoughts of something in someone's mind is someone's choice of something in someone's mind. I think someone's thoughts of something in someone's mind is someone's choice of something in someone's mind because I think every thought in someone's mind is someone's choice of something in someone's mind. I think every thought in someone's mind is someone's choice of something in someone's mind because I think every thought in someone's mind is someone's choice for every thought in someone's mind to be of something in someone's mind. I think every thought in someone's mind is someone's choice for every thought in someone's mind to be of something in someone's mind because I think everything someone can think of is someone's choice. I think everything someone can think of is someone's choice because I think someone always has a choice for someone to be thinking of something. I think someone always has a choice for someone to be thinking of something because I think something's thoughts is of something for something to be someone's choice.

If I think someone always has a choice for someone to be thinking of something, than I do not think someone can be able to be erasing someone's thoughts in someone's mind because I think someone's thoughts is constantly taking place within someone's mind for someone not to be able to be erasing someone's thoughts in someone's mind. I think someone's thoughts is constantly taking place within someone's mind for someone not to be able to be erasing someone's thoughts in someone's mind because I think someone's mind is recording someone's thoughts of someone, and something for someone's thoughts to constantly be taking place within someone's mind. I think someone's mind is recording someone's thoughts of someone, and something for someone's thoughts to constantly be taking place within someone's mind because I think someone's thoughts of someone, and something is being recorded in someone's mind for someone not to be erasing someone's thoughts in someone's mind. I think someone's thoughts of someone, and something is being recorded in someone's mind for someone not to be erasing someone's thoughts in someone's mind because I do not think someone can erase someone's thoughts in someone's mind for someone's thoughts of someone, and something to be recorded in someone's mind. I do not think someone can erase someone's thoughts in someone's mind for someone's thoughts of someone, and something to be recorded in someone's mind because I do not think someone can forget someone's thoughts of someone, and something in someone's mind for someone not to be able to be erasing someone's thoughts in someone's mind, even though, I think someone can try to forget about thinking of someone, and something in someone's mind because I think someone's thoughts, and feelings about someone, and something can be too painful for someone to be thinking about something bad that happened in someone's life, however, I do not think someone can completely forget about thinking of someone, and something in someone's mind, regardless of how much someone's thoughts, and feelings about someone, and something can be too painful for someone to thinking about something that someone has experienced with themselves, someone else, and something in someone's life because I do not think someone can erase someone's thoughts in someone's mind for someone not to be able to be completely forgetting about someone thinking of something that someone has experienced with themselves, someone else, and something in someone's life.

If I do not think someone can completely forget about thinking of someone, and something in someone's mind, than I think someone can think someone's brain is someone's mind because I think someone can think of something with someone's brain for someone to be thinking someone's brain is someone's mind, but I do not think someone's brain is someone's mind because I think someone can think of something that happened in someone's life, regardless if someone can suffer from having somewhat, to severe brain damage, even though, I think someone's brain is a mind because I think everything is a mind for someone's brain to be a mind, however, I do not think someone's brain is someone's mind because I think if someone's brain is someone's mind, than I think someone's thoughts, and someone's mind can be apart of someone's brain when someone's dies for someone's brain to be someone's mind, even though, I do not think someone's thoughts, and someone's mind is apart of someone's brain when someone's dies for someone's brain not to be someone's mind because I think if someone's thoughts, and someone's mind is apart of someone's brain when someone's dies for someone's brain to be someone's mind, than I think someone would be alive because I think someone's thoughts, and someone's mind can apart of someone's brain when someone's dies for someone to be alive, but I do not think someone's brain is someone's mind because I do not think someone's thoughts, and someone's mind is apart of someone's brain when someone dies for someone not to be alive, and therefore, I do not think someone's brain is someone's mind because I think someone's mind, along with someone's thoughts in someone's mind goes with someone when someone dies. If I do not think someone's brain is someone's mind, than I think someone takes someone's thoughts along with them when someone dies because I do not think someone can erase someone's thoughts in someone's mind for someone not to be taking someone's thoughts with them when someone dies, even though, I think someone's brain can affect someone's mind with someone having something like alzimers with someone's brain because I think someone's thoughts can be of something like alzimers with someone's brain for someone's thoughts of something like alzimers with someone's brain to be affecting someone's mind as I think someone's thoughts can be of something like alzimers with someone's brain for someone's brain to be affecting someone's mind, and therefore, I think someone can choose to be doing something that is right or wrong for someone to be right or wrong with someone affecting someone's brain as I think someone can choose to be doing something that is right or wrong for someone to be right or wrong with someone affecting someone's mind because I think someone's thoughts can be of someone choosing to be doing something that is right or wrong with someone's brain for someone to be right or wrong with someone affecting someone's brain as I think someone's thoughts can be of someone choosing to be doing something that is right or wrong with someone's mind for someone to be right or wrong with someone affecting someone's mind. If I think someone can choose to be doing something that is right or wrong for someone to be right or wrong with someone affecting someone's brain as I think someone can choose to be doing something that is right or wrong for someone to be right or wrong with someone affecting someone's mind, than I think someone's thoughts can affect someone's mind because I think someone's thoughts can be of something that can affect someone's mind for someone's thoughts to be affecting someone's mind, and therefore, I think someone can be right or wrong with someone's thoughts affecting someone's mind because I think someone's thoughts can be of someone choosing to be doing something that is right or wrong for someone to be right or wrong with someone's thoughts affecting someone's mind.

If I think someone can be right or wrong with someone's thoughts affecting someone's mind, than I think someone can think someone's thoughts is right or wrong because I think someone has a choice of right or wrong for someone to be thinking someone's thoughts is right or wrong. I think someone has a choice of right or wrong for someone to be thinking someone's thoughts is right or wrong because I think someone's thoughts can be right or wrong for someone to be thinking of someone's thoughts. I think someone's thoughts can be right or wrong for someone to be thinking of someone's thoughts because I think someone has a choice of right or wrong for someone to be thinking of someone's thoughts as being right or wrong. I think someone has a choice of right or wrong for someone to be thinking of someone's thoughts as being right or wrong because I think someone can think of someone's memories as being right or wrong for someone to be thinking of someone's memories as I think someone can think of someone's thoughts as being right or wrong for someone to be thinking of someone's thoughts. I think someone can think of someone's memories as being right or wrong for someone to be thinking of someone's memories as I think someone can think of someone's thoughts as being right or wrong for someone to be thinking of someone's thoughts because I think someone's thoughts is someone's memories for someone to be thinking of someone's memories as being right or wrong as I think someone's memories is someone's thoughts for someone to be thinking of someone's thoughts as being right or wrong. I think someone's thoughts is someone's memories for someone to be thinking of someone's memories as being right or wrong as I think someone's memories is someone's thoughts for someone to be thinking of someone's thoughts as being right or wrong because I think someone's memories can be right or wrong for someone to be thinking of someone's memories as I think someone's thoughts can be right or wrong for someone to be thinking of someone's thoughts. I think someone's memories can be right or wrong for someone to be thinking of someone's memories as I think someone's thoughts can be right or wrong for someone to be thinking of someone's thoughts because I think someone has a choice of right or wrong for someone to be thinking of someone's memories as being right or wrong as I think someone has a choice of right or wrong for someone to be thinking of someone's thoughts as being right or wrong. I think someone has a choice of right or wrong for someone to be thinking of someone's memories as being right or wrong as I think someone has a choice of right or wrong for someone to be thinking of someone's thoughts as being right or wrong because I think someone can be right or wrong for someone to be thinking of someone's memories as being right or wrong as I think someone can be right or wrong for someone to be thinking of someone's thoughts as being right or wrong.

I think someone can be right or wrong for someone to be thinking of someone's memories as being right or wrong as I think someone can be right or wrong for someone to be thinking of someone's thoughts as being right or wrong because I think someone can think of someone's memories as being good or bad for someone to be thinking of someone's memories as I think someone can think of someone's thought as being good or bad for someone to be thinking of someone's thoughts. I think someone can think of someone's memories as being good or bad for someone to be thinking of someone's memories as I think someone can think of someone's thought as being good or bad for someone to be thinking of someone's thoughts because I think someone has a choice of right or wrong for someone to be thinking of someone's memories as being good or bad as I think someone has a choice of right or wrong for someone to be thinking of someone's thoughts as being good or bad. I think someone has a choice of right or wrong for someone to be thinking of someone's memories as being good or bad as I think someone has a choice of right or wrong for someone to be thinking of someone's thoughts as being good or bad because I think someone can be right or wrong for someone to be thinking of someone's memories as being good or bad as I think someone can be right or wrong for someone to be thinking of someone's thoughts as being good or bad, and therefore, I think someone's thoughts is someone's memories as I think someone can think of someone's memories as being good or too painful for someone to be thinking of someone's memories because I think someone has a choice of right or wrong for someone to be thinking of someone's memories as being good or too painful for someone to be thinking of someone's memories. I think someone has a choice of right or wrong for someone to be thinking of someone's memories as being good or too painful for someone to be thinking of someone's memories because I think someone's thoughts can be good or too painful for someone to be thinking of someone's thoughts of someone's memories. I think someone's thoughts can be good or too painful for someone to be thinking of someone's thoughts of someone's memories because I think someone has a choice of right or wrong for someone to be thinking of someone's thoughts as being good or too painful for someone to be thinking of someone's thoughts of someone's memories. I think someone has a choice of right or wrong for someone to be thinking of someone's thoughts as being good or too painful for someone to be thinking of someone's thoughts of someone's memories because I think someone can think of someone's thoughts of someone's memories with someone's thoughts as I think someone can think of someone's thoughts as being right or wrong for someone to be thinking of someone's thoughts. I think someone can think of someone's thoughts of someone's memories with someone's thoughts as I think someone can think of someone's thoughts as being right or wrong for someone to be thinking of someone's thoughts because I think someone's thoughts is someone's memories for someone to be thinking of someone's thoughts as being right or wrong. I think someone's thoughts is someone's memories for someone to be thinking of someone's thoughts as being right or wrong because I think someone has a choice of right or wrong for someone to be right or wrong about what someone thinks. I think someone has a choice of right or wrong for someone to be right or wrong about what someone thinks because I think someone can be right or wrong about what someone thinks. I think someone can be right or wrong about what someone thinks because I think someone's thoughts is what someone's thinks as I think someone can be right or wrong about someone's thoughts. I think someone's thoughts is what someone's thinks as I think someone can be right or wrong about someone's thoughts because I think someone can think of what someone thinks with someone's thoughts as I think someone can be right or wrong about someone's thoughts. I think someone can think of what someone thinks with someone's thoughts as I think someone can be right or wrong about someone's thoughts because I think someone has a choice of right or wrong for someone to be right or wrong about someone's thoughts.

If I think someone can think of what someone thinks with someone's thoughts as I think someone can be right or wrong about someone's thoughts, than I think someone's thoughts is of something that someone can possibly experience in someone's life as I think someone's thoughts is of everything that someone can possibly experience in someone's life because I think someone's thoughts is of something's thoughts that someone can possibly experience in someone's life as I think someone's thoughts is of everything's thoughts that someone can possibly experience in someone's life. I think someone's thoughts is of something's thoughts that someone can possibly experience in someone's life as I think someone's thoughts is of everything's thoughts that someone can possibly experience in someone's life because I think someone's thoughts is of the thoughts of something that someone can possibly experience in someone's life as I think someone's thoughts is of the thoughts of everything that someone can possibly experience in someone's life. I think someone's thoughts is of the thoughts of something that someone can possibly experience in someone's life as I think someone's thoughts is of the thoughts of everything that someone can possibly experience in someone's life because I think someone's thoughts is of something's thoughts that someone can possibly experience in someone's life for someone's thoughts to be of the thoughts of something that someone can possibly experience in someone's life as I think someone's thoughts is of everything's thoughts that someone can possibly experience in someone's life for someone's thoughts to be of the thoughts of everything's thoughts that someone can possibly experience in someone's life. I think someone's thoughts is of something's thoughts that someone can possibly experience in someone's life for someone's thoughts to be of the thoughts of something that someone can possibly experience in someone's life as I think someone's thoughts is of everything's thoughts that someone can possibly experience in someone's life for someone's thoughts to be of the thoughts of everything's thoughts that someone can possibly experience in someone's life because I think someone's thoughts is of the thoughts of something that someone can possibly experience in someone's life as I think the thoughts of something is apart of making up the thoughts of everything that someone can possibly experience in someone's life. I think someone's thoughts is of the thoughts of something that someone can possibly experience in someone's life as I think the thoughts of something is apart of making up the thoughts of everything that someone can possibly experience in someone's life because I think someone's thoughts is of something's thoughts that someone can possibly experience in someone's life as I think something's thoughts is apart of making up everything's thoughts that someone can possibly experience in someone's life. I think someone's thoughts is of something's thoughts that someone can possibly experience in someone's life as I think something's thoughts is apart of making up everything's thoughts that someone can possibly experience in someone's life because I think someone's thoughts is of something that someone can possibly experience in someone's life as I think something is apart of making up everything that someone can possibly experience in someone's life. I think someone's thoughts is of something that someone can possibly experience in someone's life as I think something is apart of making up everything that someone can possibly experience in someone's life because I think someone's thoughts is of something for someone's thoughts to be of something that someone can possibly experience in someone's life as I think everything is of something for someone's thoughts to be of something that someone can possibly experience in someone's life. I think someone's thoughts is of something for someone's thoughts to be of something that someone can possibly experience in someone's life as I think everything is of something for someone's thoughts to be of something that someone can possibly experience in someone's life because I think someone's thoughts is of something for someone's thoughts to be of everything that someone can possibly experience in someone's life as I think everything is of something for someone's thoughts to be of everything that someone can possibly experience in someone's life. I think someone's thoughts is of something for someone's thoughts to be of everything that someone can possibly experience in someone's life as I think everything is of something for someone's thoughts to be of everything that someone can possibly experience in someone's life because I think someone's thoughts is of everything that someone can possibly experience in someone's life for someone's thoughts to be of everything that someone can possibly experience in someone's life as I think everything is of something for someone's thoughts to be of something that someone can possibly experience in someone's life. I think someone's thoughts is of everything that someone can possibly experience in someone's life for someone's thoughts to be of everything that someone can possibly experience in someone's life as I think everything is of something for someone's thoughts to be of something that someone can possibly experience in someone's life because I think someone's thoughts is of everything that someone is experiencing in someone's life as I think someone's thoughts is of something that someone is experiencing in someone's life. I think someone's thoughts is of everything that someone is experiencing in someone's life as I think someone's thoughts is of something that someone is experiencing in someone's life because I think someone is experiencing everything in someone's life for someone's thoughts to be of everything that someone is experiencing in someone's life as I think someone is experiencing something for someone's thoughts to be of something that someone is experiencing in someone's life. I think someone is experiencing everything in someone's life for someone's thoughts to be of everything that someone is experiencing in someone's life as I think someone is experiencing something for someone's thoughts to be of something that someone is experiencing in someone's life because I think someone is experiencing everything in someone's life as I think someone is experiencing something in someone's life.

I think someone is experiencing everything in someone's life as I think someone is experiencing something in someone's life because I think someone is experiencing something in someone's life for someone to be experiencing everything in someone's life, and therefore, I think someone would have to experience something in someone's life for someone to be experiencing everything in someone's life because I do not think someone can experience everything in someone's life, without someone experiencing something in someone's life for someone to be experiencing everything in someone's life, otherwise, I do not think someone would have any experience in someone's life because I do not think someone can have any experience in someone's life, without someone experiencing something in someone's life for someone to be having any experience in someone's life, even though, I think someone has experience in someone's life because I think someone can experience something in someone's life for someone to be having any experience in someone's life. I think someone cam experience something in someone's life for someone to be having any experience in someone's life because I think someone's experience is of something for someone to be having any experience in someone's life. I think someone's experience is of something for someone to be having any experience in someone's life because I think someone's experience of something is someone's experience of everything in someone's life. I think someone's experience of something is someone's experience of everything in someone's life because I think someone is experiencing something for someone to be experiencing everything in someone's life.

I think someone is experiencing something for someone to be experiencing everything in someone's life because I think everything is of something for someone to be experiencing everything in someone's life as I think everything is of something for someone to be experiencing something. I think everything is of something for someone to be experiencing everything in someone's life as I think everything is of something for someone to be experiencing something because I think someone is experiencing everything that is something for someone to be experiencing everything in someone's life as I think someone is experiencing everything that is something for someone to be experiencing something. I think someone is experiencing everything that is something for someone to be experiencing everything in someone's life as I think someone is experiencing everything that is something for someone to be experiencing something because I think someone's thoughts is of everything that is something for someone to be experiencing everything in someone's life as I think someone's thoughts is of everything that is something for someone to be experiencing something. I think someone's thoughts is of everything that is something for someone to be experiencing everything in someone's life as I think someone's thoughts is of everything that is something for someone to be experiencing something because I think everything is something for someone's thoughts to be of everything that is something as I think someone's thoughts is of everything that is something for someone to be experiencing everything that is something. I think everything is something for someone's thoughts to be of everything that is something as I think someone's thoughts is of everything that is something for someone to be experiencing everything that is something because I think someone's thoughts is of something for someone to be experiencing everything in someone's life as I think someone's thoughts is of something for someone to be experiencing something. I think someone's thoughts is of something for someone to be experiencing everything in someone's life as I think someone's thoughts is of something for someone to be experiencing something because I think someone is experiencing everything in someone's life for someone's thoughts to be of something as I think someone is experiencing something for someone's thoughts to be of something. I think someone is experiencing everything in someone's life for someone's thoughts to be of something as I think someone is experiencing something for someone's thoughts to be of something because I think someone's thoughts is of something for someone's thoughts to be of everything that someone can experience in someone's life. I think someone's thoughts is of something for someone's thoughts to be of everything that someone can experience in someone's life because I think someone is experiencing everything in someone's life for someone's thoughts to be of everything that someone can experience in someone's life. I think someone is experiencing everything in someone's life for someone's thoughts to be of everything that someone can experience in someone's life because I think someone's thoughts is of everything that someone can experience in someone's life for someone's thoughts to be someone's thoughts of everything in someone's life. I think someone's thoughts is of everything that someone can experience in someone's life for someone's thoughts to be someone's thoughts of everything in someone's life because I think someone's thoughts is someone's thoughts of everything in someone's life as I think someone's thoughts of everything in someone's life is all of someone's thoughts. I think someone's thoughts is someone's thoughts of everything in someone's life as I think someone's thoughts of everything in someone's life is all of someone's thoughts because I think someone's thoughts is someone's thoughts of everything in someone's life as I think someone's thoughts is all of someone's thoughts. I think someone's thoughts is someone's thoughts of everything in someone's life as I think someone's thoughts is all of someone's thoughts because I think someone's thoughts of everything in someone's life is someone's thoughts in someone's mind as I think all of someone's thoughts is someone's thoughts in someone's mind. I think someone's thoughts of everything in someone's life is someone's thoughts in someone's mind as I think all of someone's thoughts is someone's thoughts in someone's mind because I think someone's thoughts in someone's mind is someone's thoughts of everything in someone's life as I think someone's thoughts in someone's mind is all of someone's thoughts. I think someone's thoughts in someone's mind is someone's thoughts of everything

330

in someone's life as I think someone's thoughts in someone's mind is all of someone's thoughts because I think someone's thoughts of everything in someone's life is all of someone's thoughts as I think someone's thoughts in someone's mind is something. I think someone's thoughts of everything in someone's life is all of someone's thoughts as I think someone's thoughts in someone's mind is something because I think someone's thoughts in someone's mind is of everything in someone's life as I think someone's thoughts in someone's mind is of something. I think someone's thoughts in someone's mind is of everything in someone's life as I think someone's thoughts in someone's mind is of something because I think everything is of something for someone thoughts in someone's mind to be of everything in someone's life as I think someone's thoughts is of something for someone thoughts in someone's mind to be of something.

I think everything is of something for someone thoughts in someone's mind to be of everything in someone's life as I think someone's thoughts is of something for someone thoughts in someone's mind to be of something because I think someone's mind is somehow able to be recording someone's thoughts of everything in someone's life for someone's thoughts in someone's mind to be of everything in someone's life as I think someone's mind is somehow able to be recording someone's thoughts of something for someone's thoughts in someone's mind to be of something. I think someone's mind is somehow able to be recording someone's thoughts of everything in someone's life for someone's thoughts in someone's mind to be of everything in someone's life as I think someone's mind is somehow able to be recording someone's thoughts of something for someone's thoughts in someone's mind to be of something because I think someone's thoughts in someone's mind is of everything in someone's life for someone's mind to somehow be able to be recording someone's thoughts of everything in someone's life as I think someone's thoughts in someone's mind is of something for someone's mind to be somehow be able to recording someone's thoughts of something. I think someone's thoughts in someone's mind is of everything in someone's life for someone's mind to somehow be able to be recording someone's thoughts of everything in someone's life as I think someone's thoughts in someone's mind is of something for someone's mind to be somehow be able to recording someone's thoughts of something because I think someone's mind is somehow able to be recording the thoughts of everything, that someone can possibly experience in someone's life for someone's thoughts in someone's mind to be of everything in someone's life as I think someone's mind is somehow able to be recording the thoughts of something, that someone can possibly experience in someone's life for someone's thoughts in someone's mind to be of something. I think someone's mind is somehow able to be recording the thoughts of everything, that someone can possibly experience in someone's life for someone's thoughts in someone's mind to be of everything in someone's life as I think someone's mind is somehow able to be recording the thoughts of something, that someone can possibly experience in someone's life for someone's thoughts in someone's mind to be of something because I think someone's thoughts in someone's in mind is of everything in someone's life for someone's mind to somehow be able to be recording the thoughts of everything, that someone can possibly experience in someone's life as I think someone's thoughts in someone's in mind is of something for someone's mind to somehow be able to be recording the thoughts of something, that someone can possibly experience in someone's life.

I think someone's thoughts in someone's in mind is of everything in someone's life for someone's mind to somehow be able to be recording the thoughts of everything, that someone can possibly experience in someone's life as I think someone's thoughts in someone's in mind is of something for someone's mind to somehow be able to be recording the thoughts of something, that someone can possibly experience in someone's life because I think someone's thoughts in someone's mind is of the thoughts of everything in someone's life for someone's thoughts in someone's mind to be of everything in someone's life as I think someone's thoughts in someone's mind is of the thoughts of something for someone's thoughts in someone's mind to be of something. I think someone's thoughts in someone's mind is of the thoughts of everything in someone's life for someone's thoughts in someone's mind to be of everything in someone's life as I think someone's thoughts in someone's mind is of the thoughts of something for someone's thoughts in someone's mind to be of something because I think someone's thoughts in someone's mind is of everything in someone's life for someone's thoughts in someone's mind to be of someone's thoughts of everything in someone's life as I think someone's thoughts in someone's mind is of something for someone's thoughts in someone's mind to be of someone's thoughts of something. I think someone's thoughts in someone's mind is of everything in someone's life for someone's thoughts in someone's mind to be of someone's thoughts of everything in someone's life as I think someone's thoughts in someone's mind is of something for someone's thoughts in someone's mind to be of someone's thoughts of something because I think someone's thoughts in someone's mind is of the thoughts everything in someone's life for someone's thoughts in someone's mind to be of someone's thoughts of everything in someone's mind as I think someone's thoughts in someone's mind is of the thoughts something for someone's thoughts in someone's mind to be of someone's thoughts of something in someone's mind. I think someone's thoughts in someone's mind is of the thoughts everything in someone's life for someone's thoughts in someone's mind to be of someone's thoughts of everything in someone's mind as I think someone's thoughts in someone's mind is of the thoughts something for someone's thoughts in someone's mind to be of someone's thoughts of something in someone's mind because I think someone's thoughts in someone's mind is a copy of the thoughts everything in someone's life for someone's thoughts in someone's mind to be of someone's thoughts of everything in someone's mind as I think someone's thoughts in someone's mind is a copy of the thoughts something for someone's thoughts in someone's mind to be of someone's thoughts of something in someone's mind. I think someone's thoughts in someone's mind is a copy of the thoughts everything in someone's life for someone's thoughts in someone's mind to be of someone's thoughts of everything in someone's mind as I think someone's thoughts in someone's mind is a copy of the thoughts something for someone's thoughts in someone's mind to be of someone's thoughts of something in someone's mind because I think someone's mind is somehow recording the thoughts of everything in someone's life for someone's thoughts in someone's mind to be a copy of the thoughts of everything in someone's life as I think someone's mind is somehow recording the thoughts of something for someone's thoughts in someone's mind to be a copy of the thoughts of something. I think someone's mind is somehow recording the thoughts of everything in someone's life for someone's thoughts in someone's mind to be a copy of the thoughts of everything in someone's life as I think someone's mind is somehow recording the thoughts of something for someone's thoughts in someone's mind to be a copy of the thoughts of something because I do not think someone can erase someone's thoughts in someone's mind as I think someone's thoughts in someone's mind is of everything that someone can possibly experience in someone's life. I do not think someone can erase someone's thoughts in someone's mind as I think someone's thoughts in someone's mind is of everything that someone can possibly experience in someone's life because I do not think someone can create someone's thoughts in someone's mind for someone to be able to be erasing someone's thoughts in someone's mind, and therefore, I think someone's thoughts in someone's mind is of everything that someone can possibly experience in someone's life because I think someone's mind is recording everything that someone can possibly experience in someone's life for someone's thoughts in someone's mind to be of everything that someone can possibly experience in someone's life. I think someone's mind is recording everything that someone can possibly experience in someone's life for someone's thoughts in someone's mind to be of everything that someone can possibly experience in someone's life because I think someone's thoughts in someone's mind is of everything that someone can possibly experience in someone's life for someone's mind to be recording everything that someone can possibly experience in someone's life.

I think someone's thoughts in someone's mind is of everything that someone can possibly experience in someone's life for someone's mind to be recording everything that someone can possibly experience in someone's life because I think God created someone's mind to be recording everything that someone can possibly experience in someone's life. I think God created someone's mind for someone's mind to be recording everything that someone can possibly experience in someone's life because I do not think someone can create someone's mind to be able to be recording everything that someone can possibly experience in someone's life, and therefore, I think God created someone's mind to be recording everything that someone can possibly experience in someone's life because I think God created someone to be having a mind for someone's mind to be recording everything that someone can possibly experience in someone's life. I think God created someone to be having a mind for someone's mind to be recording everything that someone can possibly experience in someone's life because I think God created someone's mind to be recording God's thoughts as I think everything that someone can possibly experience in someone's life is of God's thoughts for someone's mind to be recording everything that someone can possibly experience in someone's life. I think God created someone's mind to be recording God's thoughts as I think everything that someone can possibly experience in someone's life is of God's thoughts for someone's mind to be recording everything that someone can possibly experience in someone's life because I think God created someone's mind to be recording everything that someone can possibly experience in someone's life for someone's mind to be recording someone's history. I think God created someone's mind to be recording everything that someone can possibly experience in someone's life for someone's mind to be recording someone's history because I think God created someone's mind to be recording someone's history as I think everything that someone can possibly experience in someone's life is someone's history. I think God created someone's mind to be recording someone's history as I think everything that someone can possibly experience in someone's life is someone's history because I think God created someone's mind to be recording everything that someone can possibly experience in someone's life for someone's mind to be a record of someone's history. I think God created someone's mind to be recording everything that someone can possibly experience in someone's life for someone's mind to be a record of someone's history because I think someone's thoughts in someone's mind is a record of someone's history as I think someone's mind is of everything that someone can possibly experience in someone's life for someone's mind to be a record of someone's history.

I think someone's thoughts in someone's mind is a record of someone's history as I think someone's mind is of everything that someone can possibly experience in someone's life for someone's mind to be a record of someone's history because I think someone's mind is of someone's thoughts for someone's thoughts to be in someone's mind as I think someone's thoughts in someone's mind is of everything that someone can possibly experience in someone's life for someone's thoughts in someone's mind to be a record of someone's history. I think someone's mind is of someone's thoughts for someone's thoughts to be in someone's mind as I think someone's thoughts in someone's mind is of everything that someone can possibly experience in someone's life for someone's thoughts in someone's mind to be a record of someone's history because I think someone's mind is of someone's thoughts for someone's thoughts in someone's mind to be a record of someone's history as I think someone's thoughts in someone's mind is of everything that someone can possibly experience in someone's life for someone's thoughts to be a record of someone's history. I think someone's mind is of someone's thoughts for someone's thoughts in someone's mind to be a record of someone's history as I think someone's thoughts in someone's mind is of everything that someone can possibly experience in someone's life for someone's thoughts to be a record of someone's history because I think someone's thoughts is a record of someone's history as I think someone's thoughts is of everything that someone can possibly experience in someone's life for someone's thoughts to be a record of someone's history. I think someone's thoughts is a record of someone's history as I think someone's thoughts is of everything that someone can possibly experience in someone's life for someone's thoughts to be a record of someone's history because I think someone's thoughts is a record of someone's history for someone's thoughts to be a history of someone's life. I think someone's thoughts is a record of someone's history for someone's thoughts to be a history of someone's life because I think someone's thoughts is a history of someone's life for someone's thoughts to be a record of someone's life. I think someone's thoughts is a history of someone's life for someone's thoughts to be a record of someone's life because I think someone's thoughts is a record of someone's history for someone's thoughts to be someone's history as I think someone's thoughts is a history of someone's life for someone's thoughts to be someone's history.

I think someone's thoughts is a record of someone's history for someone's thoughts to be someone's history as I think someone's thoughts is a history of someone's life for someone's thoughts to be someone's history because I think someone's thoughts is of everything that someone can possibly experience in someone's life for someone's thoughts to be someone's history. I think someone's thoughts is of everything that someone can possibly experience in someone's life for someone's thoughts to be someone's history because I think someone's thoughts is of everything that someone can possibly experience in someone's life for someone's thoughts in someone's mind to be someone's history. I think someone's thoughts is of everything that someone can possibly experience in someone's for someone's thoughts in someone's mind to be someone's history because I think someone's thoughts in someone's mind is someone's history. I think someone's thoughts in someone's mind is someone's history because I think someone's thoughts in someone's mind is of everything that someone can possibly experience in someone's life for someone's thoughts in someone's mind to be of everything that someone can possibly be able to be remembering in someone's life as I think someone's thoughts in someone's mind is of everything that someone can possibly be able to be remembering in someone's life for someone's thoughts in someone's mind to be someone's history, and therefore, I think someone's thoughts in someone's mind is of everything that someone can possibly be able to remember experiencing in someone's life for someone's thoughts in someone's mind to be someone's history because I think someone's thoughts in someone's mind is someone's history for someone's thoughts in someone's mind to be someone's history of someone's life. I think someone's thoughts in someone's mind is someone's history for someone's thoughts in someone's mind to be someone's history of someone's life because I think someone's thoughts in someone's mind is someone's history of someone's life for someone's thoughts in someone's mind to be someone's history. I think someone's thoughts in someone's mind is someone's history of someone's life for someone's thoughts in someone's mind to be someone's history because I think someone's thoughts in someone's mind is someone's history. I think someone's thoughts in someone's mind is someone's history because I think someone's thoughts is someone's history for someone's thoughts in someone's mind to be someone's history. I think someone's thoughts is someone's history for someone's thoughts in someone's mind to be someone's history because I think someone's thoughts is someone's history. I think someone's thoughts is someone's history because I think someone's thoughts is someone's history for someone's thoughts to be someone's history of someone's life. I think someone's thoughts is someone's history for someone's thoughts to be someone's history of someone's life because I think someone's thoughts is someone's history of someone's life for someone's thoughts to be someone's history. I think someone's thoughts is someone's history of someone's life for someone's thoughts to be someone's history because I think someone's thoughts is someone's history.

I think someone's thoughts is someone's history because I think someone's thoughts is someone's history of someone's life for someone's thoughts to be someone's history throughout someone's life. I think someone's thoughts is someone's history of someone's life for someone's thoughts to be someone's history throughout someone's life because I think someone's thoughts is someone's history of someone's life after someone dies for someone's thoughts to be someone's history throughout someone's life. I think someone's thoughts is someone's history of someone's life after someone dies for someone's thoughts to be someone's history throughout someone's because I think someone can take someone's thoughts with them when someone dies for someone's thoughts to be someone's history of someone's life after someone dies. I think someone can take someone's thoughts with them when someone dies for someone's thoughts to be someone's history of someone's life after someone dies because I think someone's thoughts is of someone choosing to be good or bad for someone's thoughts to be someone's history of someone's life. I think someone's thoughts is of someone choosing to be good or bad for someone's thoughts to be someone's history of someone's life because I think someone can choose to be good or bad for someone's thoughts to be someone's history of someone's life as I think someone can choose to be good or bad for someone's thoughts to be of someone choosing to be good or bad. I think someone can choose to be good or bad for someone's thoughts to be someone's history of someone's life as I think someone can choose to be good or bad for someone's thoughts to be of someone choosing to be good or bad because I think someone's thoughts is of someone choosing to be good or bad for someone's thoughts to be someone's history of someone that is good or bad. I think someone's thoughts is of someone choosing to be good or bad for someone's thoughts to be someone's history of someone that is good or bad because I think someone can choose to be good or bad for someone's thoughts to be someone's history of someone that is good or bad as I think someone can choose to be good or bad for someone's thoughts to be of someone choosing to be good or bad. I think someone can choose to be good or bad for someone's thoughts to be someone's history of someone that is good or bad as I think someone can choose to be good or bad for someone's thoughts to be of someone choosing to be good or bad because I think someone's thoughts is of someone choosing to be good or bad for someone's thoughts to be someone's history of someone choosing to be living a good or a bad kind of life. I think someone's thoughts is of someone choosing to be good or bad for someone's thoughts to be someone's history of someone choosing to be living a good or a bad kind of life because I think someone can choose to be good or bad for someone's thoughts to be someone's history of someone choosing to be living a good or a bad kind of life as I think someone can choose to be good or bad for someone's thoughts to be of someone choosing to be good or bad. I think someone can choose to be good or bad for someone's thoughts to be someone's history of someone choosing to be living a good or a bad kind of life as I think someone can choose to be good or bad for someone's thoughts to be of someone choosing to be good or bad because I think someone's thoughts is someone's history, as to what kind of a life someone can choose to be living. I think someone's thoughts is someone's history, as to what kind of a life someone can choose to be living because I think someone can choose to be good or bad for someone's thoughts to be someone's history of someone choosing to be living a good or a bad kind of life.

I think someone can choose to be good or bad for someone's thoughts to be someone's history of someone choosing to be living a good or a bad kind of life because I think someone can choose to be good or bad for someone to be choosing to be living a good or a bad kind of life. I think someone can choose to be good or bad for someone to be choosing to be living a good or a bad kind of life because I think someone has a choice of right or wrong for someone to be choosing to be good or bad as I think someone has a choice of right or wrong for someone to be choosing to be living a good or bad a kind of life. I think someone has a choice of right or wrong for someone to be choosing to be good or bad as I think someone has a choice of right or wrong for someone to be choosing to be living a good or bad a kind of life because I think someone can choose to be good or bad for someone to be choosing to be living a good or a bad kind of life. I think someone can choose to be good or bad for someone to be choosing to be living a good or a bad kind of life because I think someone's thoughts is of someone choosing to be good or bad for someone's thoughts to be someone's history of someone choosing to be living a good or a bad kind of life as I think someone can choose to be good or bad for someone's thoughts to be someone's history of someone choosing to be living a good or a bad kind of life. I think someone's thoughts is of someone choosing to be good or bad for someone's thoughts to be someone's history of someone choosing to be living a good or a bad kind of life as I think someone can choose to be good or bad for someone's thoughts to be someone's history of someone choosing to be living a good or a bad kind of life because I think has a choice of right or wrong for someone's thoughts to be someone's history of someone choosing to be good or bad as I think someone can choose to be good or bad for someone's thoughts to be someone's history of someone choosing to be living a good or bad kind of life. I think has a choice of right or wrong for someone's thoughts to be someone's history of someone choosing to be good or bad as I think someone can choose to be good or bad for someone's thoughts to be someone's history of someone choosing to be living a good or bad kind of life because I think someone can choose to be good or bad for someone's thoughts to be someone's history of someone choosing to be good or bad as I think someone's thoughts can be someone's history of someone choosing to be good or bad for someone choosing to be living a good or bad kind of life. I think someone can choose to be good or bad for someone's thoughts to be someone's history of someone choosing to be good or bad for someone choosing to be living a good or bad kind of life because I think someone's thoughts is someone's history of someone choosing to be good or bad for someone to be good or bad with someone choosing to be living a good or a bad kind of life, and therefore, I think someone can choose to be good or bad for someone to be choosing to be living a good or a bad kind of life because I think someone's thoughts is someone's history, as to what kind of a life someone can choose to be living as I think someone can choose to be good or bad for someone's thoughts to be someone's history of someone choosing to be living a good or a bad kind of life.

I think someone's thoughts is someone's history, as to what kind of a life someone can choose to be living as I think someone can choose to be good or bad for someone's thoughts to be someone's history of someone choosing to be living a good or a bad kind of life because I think someone's thoughts is someone's history of someone's life for someone to be taking someone's thoughts with them when someone dies. I think someone's thoughts is someone's history of someone's life for someone to be taking someone's thoughts with them when someone dies because I think someone's thoughts is a history of someone's life for someone and God to be aware of someone's history with someone's thoughts, as to what kind of a life someone has chosen to be living as I think someone can be good or bad with someone choosing to be living a good or bad kind of life. I think someone's thoughts is a history of someone's life for someone and God to be aware of someone's history with someone's thoughts, as to what kind of a life someone has chosen to be living as I think someone can be good or bad with someone choosing to be living a good or bad kind of life because I think someone's thoughts is of God's thoughts for someone and God to both be aware of someone's history with someone's thoughts, as to what kind of a life someone has chosen to be living as I think someone can choose to be good or bad for someone to be good or bad with someone choosing to be living a good or a bad kind of life, therefore, I think someone is going to have to answer to God, as to what kind of a life someone has chosen to be living as I think someone can be good or bad for living a good or a bad kind of life because I think someone and God can both be aware of someone's history with someone's thoughts, as to what kind of a life someone has chosen to be living as I think someone can be good or bad with someone choosing to be living a good or a bad kind of life. I think someone and God can both be aware of someone's history with someone's thoughts, as to what kind of a life someone has chosen to be living as I think someone can be good or bad with someone choosing to be living a good or a bad kind of life because I think someone's thoughts is of God's thoughts for someone and God to both be aware of someone's history with someone's thoughts, as to what kind of a life someone has chosen to be living as I think someone can be good or bad for living a good or a bad kind of life. If I think someone and God can both be aware of someone's history with someone's thoughts, as to what kind of a life someone has chosen to be living as I think someone can be good or bad with someone choosing to be living a good or a bad kind of life, than I think someone is going to have to answer to God, as to what kind of a life someone has chosen to be living as I think someone can be good or bad for living a good or a bad kind of life because I think someone and God can both be aware of everything that someone can possibly experience in someone's life for someone to be having to answer to God, as to what kind of a life someone has chosen to be living as I think someone is experiencing everything that someone can possibly experience in someone's life for someone and God to both be aware, as to what kind of a life someone can choose to be living. I think someone and God can both be aware of everything that someone can possibly experience in someone's life for someone to be having to answer to God, as to what kind of a life someone has chosen to be living as I think someone is experiencing everything that someone can possibly experience in someone's life for someone and God to both be aware, as to what kind of a life someone can choose to be living because I think someone is experiencing everything that someone can possibly experience in someone's life for someone to be having to answer to God, as to what kind of a life someone has chosen to be living as I think everything that someone can possibly experience in someone's life is of God's thoughts for someone and God to both be aware, as to what kind of a life someone can choose to be living. I think someone is experiencing everything that someone can possibly experience in someone's life for someone to be having to answer to God, as to what kind of a life someone has chosen to be living as I think everything that someone can possibly experience in someone's life is of God's thoughts for someone and God to both be aware, as to what kind of a life someone can choose to be living because I think someone's thoughts is of someone experiencing everything that someone can possibly experience in someone's life for someone to be having to answer to God, as to what kind of a life someone has chosen to be living as I think someone's thoughts is of God's thoughts for someone and God to both be aware, as to what kind of a life someone can choose to be living. I think someone's thoughts is of someone experiencing everything that someone can possibly experience in someone's life for someone to be having to answer to God, as to what kind of a life someone has chosen to be living as I think someone's thoughts is of God's thoughts for someone and God to both be aware, as to what kind of a life someone can choose to be living because I think someone's thoughts is of God's thoughts for someone to be having to answer to God, as to what kind of a life someone has chosen to be living as I think someone is experiencing everything that someone can possibly experience in someone's life for someone and God to both be aware, as to what kind of a life someone can choose to be living. I think someone's thoughts is of God's thoughts for someone to be having to answer to God, as to what kind of a life someone has chosen to be living as I think someone is experiencing everything that someone can possibly experience in someone's life for someone and God to both be aware, as to what kind of a life someone can choose to be living because I think someone's thoughts is of everything that someone can possibly experience in someone's life for someone to be having to answer to God, as to what kind of a life someone has chosen to be living as I think someone's thoughts is someone's history for someone and God to both be aware, as to what kind of a life someone can choose to be living. I think someone's thoughts is of everything that someone can possibly experience in someone's life for someone to be having to answer to God, as to what kind of a life someone has chosen to be living as I think someone's thoughts is someone's history for someone and God to both be aware, as to what kind of a life someone can choose to be living because I think someone's thoughts is someone's history for someone to be having to answer to God, as to what kind of a life someone has chosen to be living as I think someone's thoughts is someone's history of someone's life, as to what kind of a life someone can choose to be living.

I think someone's thoughts is someone's history for someone to be having to answer to God, as to what kind of a life someone has chosen to be living as I think someone's thoughts is someone's history of someone's life, as to what kind of a life someone can choose to be living because I think someone's thoughts is someone's history of someone's life, as to what kind of a life someone can choose to be living as I think someone can choose to be good or bad for someone's thoughts to be someone's history of someone's life, as to what kind of a life someone can choose to be living. I think someone's thoughts is someone's history of someone's life, as to what kind of a life someone can choose to be living as I think someone can choose to be good or bad for someone's thoughts to be someone's history of someone's life, as to what kind of a life someone can choose to be living because I think someone's thoughts is of everything that someone can possibly experience in someone's life for someone's thoughts to be someone's history of someone's life, as to what kind of a life someone can choose to be living as I think someone can choose to be good or bad with everything that someone can possibly experience in someone's life for someone's thoughts to be someone's history of someone's life, as to what kind of a life someone can choose to be living, and therefore, I think someone's thoughts is someone's history of someone's life, as to what kind of a life someone can choose to be living as I think someone can choose to be good or bad for someone's thoughts to be someone's history of someone's life, as to what kind of a life someone can choose to be living because I think someone's thoughts is of everything that someone can possibly experience in someone's life for someone's thoughts to be someone's history of someone's life, as to what kind of a life someone can choose to be living as I think someone can choose to be good or bad with everything that someone can possibly experience in someone's life for someone's thoughts to be someone's history of someone's life, as to what kind of a life someone can choose to be living. I think someone's thoughts is of everything that someone can possibly experience in someone's life for someone's thoughts to be someone's history of someone's life, as to what kind of a life someone can choose to be living as I think someone can choose to be good or bad with everything that someone can possibly experience in someone's life for someone's thoughts to be someone's history of someone's life, as to what kind of a life someone can choose to be living because I think someone's thoughts is someone's history for someone's thoughts to be someone's history of someone's life as I think someone's thoughts is of someone choosing to be good or bad with everything that someone can possibly experience in someone's life for someone's thoughts to be someone's history of someone choosing to be living a good or a bad kind of life. I think someone's thoughts is someone's history for someone's thoughts to be someone's history of someone's life as I think someone's thoughts is of someone choosing to be good or bad with everything that someone can possibly experience in someone's life for someone's thoughts to be someone's history of someone choosing to be living a good or a bad kind of life because I think someone can choose to be good or bad with everything that someone can possibly experience in someone's life for someone's thoughts to be someone's history of someone choosing to be living a good or a bad kind of life.

I think someone can choose to be good or bad with everything that someone can possibly experience in someone's life for someone's thoughts to be someone's history of someone choosing to be living a good or a bad kind of life because I think someone can choose to be good or bad with everything that someone can possibly experience in someone's life for someone to be good or bad with someone living a good or a bad kind of life. I think someone can choose to be good or bad with everything that someone can possibly experience in someone's life for someone to be good or bad with someone living a good or a bad kind of life because I think someone can choose to be good or bad for someone to be good or bad with everything that someone can possibly experience in someone's life as I think someone can choose to be to be good or bad for someone to be good or bad with someone living a good or a bad kind of life. I think someone can choose to be good or bad for someone to be good or bad with everything that someone can possibly experience in someone's life as I think someone can choose to be to be good or bad for someone to be good or bad with someone living a good or a bad kind of life because I think someone can be good or bad with everything that someone can possibly experience in someone's life as I think someone can be good or bad with someone living a good or a bad kind of life. I think someone can be good or bad with everything that someone can possibly experience in someone's life as I think someone can be good or bad with someone living a good or a bad kind of life because I think someone can be good or bad with everything that someone can possibly experience in someone's life for someone to be good or bad with someone living a good or a bad kind of life.

I think someone can be good or bad with everything that someone can possibly experience in someone's life for someone to be good or bad with someone living a good or a bad kind of life because I think someone can be right or wrong with someone having a choice of right or wrong for someone to be good or bad as I think someone can be right or wrong with everything that someone can possibly experience in someone's life for someone to be right or wrong with someone living a good or a bad kind of life. I think someone can be right or wrong with someone having a choice of right or wrong for someone to be good or bad as I think someone can be right or wrong with everything that someone can possibly experience in someone's life for someone to be right or wrong with someone living a good or a bad kind of life because I think someone can be right or wrong about everything that someone can possibly experience in someone's life for someone to be right or wrong with everything that someone can possibly experience in someone's life as I think someone can be right or wrong about everything that someone can possibly experience in someone's life for someone to be right or wrong with someone living a good or a bad kind of life. I think someone can be right or wrong about everything that someone can possibly experience in someone's life for someone to be right or wrong with everything that someone can possibly experience in someone's life as I think someone can be right or wrong about everything that someone can possibly experience in someone's life for someone to be right or wrong with someone living a good or a bad kind of life because I think someone can be right or wrong about everything that someone can possibly experience in someone's life for someone to be right or wrong about everything that someone can be right or wrong about in someone's life as I think someone can be right or wrong about everything that someone can be right or wrong about in someone's life for someone to be right or wrong with someone living a good or a bad kind of life. I think someone can be right or wrong about everything that someone can possibly experience in someone's life for someone to be right or wrong about everything that someone can be right or wrong about in someone's life as I think someone can be right or wrong about everything that someone can be right or wrong about in someone's life for someone to be right or wrong with someone living a good or a bad kind of life because I think someone's thoughts is someone's history of someone that can be right or wrong about everything that someone can be right or wrong about in someone's life for someone's thoughts to be someone's history of someone that can be right or wrong with someone living a good or a bad kind of life.

If I think someone's thoughts is someone's history of someone that can be right or wrong about everything that someone can be right or wrong about in someone's life for someone's thoughts to be someone's history of someone that can be right or wrong with someone living a good or a bad kind of life, than I think someone and God can both be aware of someone's history with someone's thoughts because I think someone's thoughts is someone's history for someone and God to both be aware of someone's history with someone's thoughts. I think someone's thoughts is someone's history for someone and God to both be aware of someone's history with someone's thoughts because I think someone's thoughts is of God's thoughts for someone and God to both be aware of someone's history with someone's thoughts. I think someone's thoughts is of God's thoughts for someone and God to both be aware of someone's history with someone's thoughts because I think someone's thoughts is of everything that someone can be right or wrong about in someone's life for someone and God to both be aware of someone's history with someone's thoughts. I think someone's thoughts is of everything that someone can be right or wrong about in someone's life for someone and God to both be aware of someone's history with someone's thoughts because I think someone's thoughts is of everything that someone can be right or wrong about in someone's life for someone's thoughts to be someone's history of everything that someone can be right or wrong about in someone's life as I think someone's thoughts is someone's history of everything that someone can be right or wrong about in someone's life for someone and God to both be aware of everything that someone can be right or wrong about in someone's life. I think someone's thoughts is of everything that someone can be right or wrong about in someone's life for someone's thoughts to be someone's history of everything that someone can be right or wrong about in someone's life as I think someone's thoughts is someone's history of everything that someone can be right or wrong about in someone's life for someone and God to both be aware of everything that someone can be right or wrong about in someone's life because I think someone's thoughts is of everything that someone can be right or wrong about in someone's life for someone and God to both be aware of everything that someone can be right or wrong about in someone's life. I think someone's thoughts is of everything that someone can be right or wrong about in someone's life for someone and God to both be aware of everything that someone can be right or wrong about in someone's life because I think someone's thoughts is of God's thoughts for someone and God to both be aware of everything that someone can be right or wrong about in someone's life. I think someone's thoughts is of God's thoughts for someone and God to both be aware of everything that someone can be right or wrong about in someone's life because I think someone's thoughts is of everything that someone can be right or wrong about in someone's life for someone's thoughts to be someone's history of everything that someone can be right or wrong about in someone's life as I think someone's thoughts is of God's thoughts for someone and God to both be aware of someone's history with someone's thoughts.

I think someone's thoughts is of everything that someone can be right or wrong about in someone's life for someone's thoughts to be someone's history of everything that someone can be right or wrong about in someone's life as I think someone's thoughts is of God's thoughts for someone and God to both be aware of someone's history with someone's thoughts because I think someone's thoughts is of everything that someone can be right or wrong about in someone's life for someone's thoughts to be someone's history of someone's life as I think someone's thoughts is someone's history of someone's life for someone and God to both be aware of someone's history of someone's life. I think someone's thoughts is of everything that someone can be right or wrong about in someone's life for someone's thoughts to be someone's history of someone's life as I think someone's thoughts is someone's history of someone's life for someone and God to both be aware of someone's history of someone's life because I think someone's thoughts is of everything that someone can be right or wrong about in someone's life for someone and God to both be aware of someone's history of someone's life, as to whether or not if someone is good or bad. I think someone's thoughts is of everything that someone can be right or wrong about in someone's life for someone and God to both be aware of someone's history of someone's life, as to whether or not if someone is good or bad because I think someone's thoughts is of God's thoughts for someone and God to both be aware of someone's history of someone's life, as to whether or not if someone is good or bad. I think someone's thoughts is of God's thoughts for someone and God to both be aware of someone's history of someone's life, as to whether or not if someone is good or bad because I think someone's history of someone's thoughts is of someone that is good or bad with everything that someone can be right or wrong about in someone's life for someone's history of someone's thoughts to be of someone that is good or bad, and therefore, I think someone's thoughts is undisputable proof or evidence before God and someone, as to whether or not if someone is good or bad because I think someone's thoughts is of someone that is good or bad for someone's thoughts to be undisputable proof or evidence before God and someone, as to whether or not if someone is good or bad. If I think someone's thoughts is undisputable proof or evidence before God and someone, as to whether or not if someone is good or bad, than I think someone that is bad would be a fool to be arguing or disputing about themselves not being bad because I think someone would be arguing or disputing about someone's own thoughts of themselves being bad for someone that is bad to be a fool to be arguing or disputing about themselves not being bad, and therefore, I think someone's thoughts just stands to reason as being reasonably true that someone has to answer to God, as to whether or not if someone is good or bad because I think someone's thoughts is undisputable proof or evidence before God and someone, as to whether or not if someone is good or bad.

If I think someone's thoughts just stands to reason as being reasonably true that someone has to answer to God, as to whether or not if someone is good or bad, than I think someone can be setting a good or a bad example because I think someone can be good or bad for someone to be setting a good or a bad example, and therefore, I think someone can be setting a good or a bad example before someone else for someone to be setting a good or a bad example before God because I think someone is created by God to be good or bad for someone to be setting a good or a bad example before someone else as I think someone can be good or bad for someone to be setting a good or a bad example before God, even though, I think someone can be right or wrong with God because I think someone can be in the right or wrong with God as I think someone can be good or bad for someone to be right or wrong with God. If I think someone can be right or wrong with God, than I think someone's life is God's choice, as to what will happen to someone after someone dies because I do not think someone's life is someone choice, as to what will happen to someone after someone dies. I do not think someone's life is someone choice, as to what will happen to someone after someone dies because if I think someone's life is someone choice, as to what will happen to someone after someone dies, than I think someone would know what will happen to someone after someone dies for someone's life to be someone' choice, as to what will happen to someone after someone dies, even though, I do not think someone's life is someone choice, as to what will happen to someone after someone dies because I do not think someone knows what will happen to someone after someone dies for someone's life to be someone' choice, as to what will happen to someone after someone dies, and therefore, I think someone's life is God's choice, as to what will happen to someone after someone dies because I think someone has to answer to God, as to whether or not if someone is good or bad, otherwise, I do not think there would be any point in someone being good or bad because I do not think there would be any point in God creating someone to be having a choice of right or wrong for someone to be good or bad, but I think there is a point in God creating someone to be having a choice of right or wrong for someone to be good or bad because I think someone has to answer to God, as to whether or not if someone is good or bad, and therefore, I think God can pass judgment onto someone with someone having to be answering to God, as to whether or not if someone is good or bad because I think God is always good, and right with God having a choice of right or wrong for God to be passing judgment onto someone with someone having to be answering to God, as to whether or not if someone is good or bad. I think God is always good, and right with God having a choice of right or wrong for God to be passing judgment onto someone with someone having to be answering to God, as to whether or not if someone is good or bad because I think there can be rewards or consequences with someone having to be answering to God, as to whether or not if someone is good or bad.

I think there can be rewards or consequences with someone having to be answering to God, as to whether or not if someone is good or bad because I think God has a choice of right or wrong with God always being good, and right for God to instinctively be choosing someone that is good or bad as I think God can instinctively choose someone that is good or bad for God to instantly choose to be putting someone in a good or a bad place when someone dies, and therefore, I think someone can refer to that good or bad place as being heaven or hell because I think God can instantly choose to be putting someone in a good or a bad place when someone dies for someone to be referring to that good or bad place as being heaven or hell, even though, I do not know what that good or bad place is in life as I think God can instantly choose to be putting someone in a good or a bad place when someone dies for someone being good or bad, but I think God can instantly choose to be putting someone in a good or a bad kind of place when someone dies for someone being good or bad because I think God can instinctively choose someone that is good or bad for God to instantly choose to be putting someone in a good or a bad place when someone dies. I think God can instinctively choose someone that is good or bad for God to instantly choose to be putting someone in a good or a bad place when someone dies because I think God instinctively has a choice of right or wrong with God always being good, and right for God to instantly choose to be putting someone in a good or a bad kind of place when someone dies. I think God instinctively has a choice of right or wrong with God always being good, and right for God to instantly choose to be putting someone in a good or a bad kind of place when someone dies because I think someone's life is God's choice, as to what will happen to someone after someone dies.

I think someone's life is God's choice, as to what will happen to someone after someone dies because I think someone is created by God for someone's life to be God's choice, as to what will happen to someone after someone dies. I think someone is created by God for someone's life to be God's choice, as to what will happen to someone life when someone dies because I think someone has to answer to God, as to whether or not if someone is good or bad. I think someone has to answer to God, as to whether or not if someone is good or bad because I think someone is created by God for someone to be having to answer to God, as to whether or not if someone is good or bad. I think someone is created by God for someone to be having to answer to God, as to whether or not if someone is good or bad because I think someone is good or bad for someone to be having to answer to God, as to whether or not if someone is good or bad. I think someone is good or bad for someone to be having to answer to God, as to whether or not if someone is good or bad because I think someone is created by God for someone to be good or bad. I think someone is created by God for someone to be good or bad because I think someone is good or bad for someone's life to be God's choice, as to what will happen to someone's life when someone dies. I think someone is good or bad for someone's life to be God's choice, as to what will happen to someone's life when someone dies because I think someone's thoughts is of someone that is good or bad for someone to be having to be answering to God, as to whether or not if someone is good or bad. I think someone's thoughts is of someone that is good or bad for someone to be having to be answering to God, as to whether or not if someone is good or bad because I think someone's thoughts is someone's history of someone's life for someone to be having to be answering to God, as to whether or not if someone is good or bad. I think someone's thoughts is someone's history of someone's life for someone to be having to be answering to God, as to whether or not if someone is good or bad because I think someone is created by God for someone's thoughts to be someone's history of someone's life, as to whether or not if someone is good or bad. I think someone is created by God for someone's thoughts to be someone's history of someone's life, as to whether or not if someone is good or bad because I think someone's thoughts is of someone that is good or bad for someone's thoughts to be someone's history of someone's life, as to whether or not if someone is good or bad, and therefore, I think someone's thoughts is someone's history of someone's life, as to whether or not if someone is good or bad because I think someone's thoughts is of someone that is good or bad with everything that someone can possibly experience in someone's life for someone's thoughts to be someone's history of someone's life, as to whether or not if someone is good or bad. I think someone's thoughts is of someone that is good or bad with everything that someone can possibly experience in someone's life for someone's thoughts to be someone's history of someone's life, as to whether or not if someone is good or bad because I think someone is good or bad with everything that someone can possibly experience in someone's life for someone to be good or bad.

If I think someone is good or bad with everything that someone can possibly experience in someone's life for someone to be good or bad, than I do not think someone has to experience what someone has experienced for someone to think someone is right or wrong about what someone has done because I think someone can think someone is right or wrong about something with someone having a choice of right or wrong for someone to be thinking with deductive reasoning that someone is right or wrong about what someone has done, and therefore, I think there can be consequences with someone having to be answering to someone, as to whether or not if someone is good or bad because I think someone can instantly choose

343

to be putting someone in a bad kind of place or not for someone being good or bad. I think someone can instantly choose to be putting someone in a bad kind of place or not for someone being good or bad because I think someone has a choice of right or wrong for someone to instinctively be choosing someone that is good or bad as I think someone can instinctively choose someone that is good or bad for someone to be choosing to be putting someone in a bad kind of place or not. I think someone has a choice of right or wrong for someone to instinctively be choosing someone that is good or bad as I think someone can instinctively choose someone that is good or bad for someone to be choosing to be putting someone in a bad kind of place or not because I think someone instinctively has a choice of right or wrong with someone always being right or wrong for someone to instinctively be choosing to be putting someone in a bad kind of place or not. I think someone instinctively has a choice of right or wrong with someone always being right or wrong for someone to instinctively be choosing to be putting someone in a bad kind of place or not because I think someone's life can be someone's choice, as to what will happen to someone, and therefore, I think someone can pass judgment onto someone with someone having to be answering to someone, as to whether or not if someone is good or bad because I think someone is always right or wrong with someone having a choice of right or wrong for someone to be passing judgment onto someone with someone having to be answering to someone, as to whether or not if someone is good or bad. I think someone is always right or wrong with someone having a choice of right or wrong for someone to be passing judgment onto someone with someone having to be answering to someone, as to whether or not if someone is good or bad because I think there can be consequences or not with someone having to be answering to someone, as to whether or not if someone is good or bad. I think there can be consequences or not with someone having to be answering to someone, as to whether or not if someone is good or bad because I think someone is good or bad with everything that someone can possibly experience in someone's life for someone to be good or bad.

If I think there can be consequences or with someone having to be answering to someone, as to whether or not if someone is good or bad, than I think someone can think of someone, and something for someone to be thinking of everything that someone can possibly experience in someone's life because I think someone's thoughts is of someone, and something for someone to be thinking of everything that someone can possibly experience in someone's life, even though, I do not think someone can completely forget about thinking of someone or something that someone has experienced in someone's life because I do not someone can erase someone's thoughts in someone's mind for someone not to be able to completely forget about thinking of someone or something that someone has experienced in someone's life, but I think someone can try to forget about thinking of someone or something that someone has experienced in someone's life, from someone trying not to be thinking of someone or something that someone has experienced in someone's life for someone to try to forget about thinking of someone or something that someone has experienced in someone's life because I think someone can think someone doesn't care to be thinking about someone or something that someone has experienced in someone's life for someone to try to forget about thinking of someone or something that someone has experienced in someone's life. I think someone can think someone doesn't care to be thinking about someone or something that someone has experienced in someone's life for someone to try to forget about thinking of someone or something that someone has experienced in someone's life because I think someone or something can be too painful for someone to be thinking about someone or something that someone has experienced in someone's life for someone to be trying to be forgetting about thinking of someone or something that someone has experienced in someone's life, and therefore, I think someone can think of something else for someone not to be thinking about someone or something that doesn't care to be thinking about in someone's life because I think someone can try to forget about thinking of someone or something for someone not to be thinking about someone or something that someone doesn't care to be thinking about in someone's life. If I think someone can think of something else for someone not to be thinking about someone or something that doesn't care to be thinking about in someone's life, than I think something can be hard or difficult for someone to be remember someone or something because I think someone may not have experienced someone or something for awhile in someone's life, or I think someone can think something is too painful to be thinking about someone or something in someone's life, or I think someone could have easily have forgotten someone or something for something to be hard or difficult for someone to be remembering someone or something, even though, I think someone can possibly remember someone or something that can be hard or difficult for someone to be remembering someone or something because I think someone can think of someone or something that can remind someone of someone or something that someone has experienced in someone's life, or I think someone can experience someone, something or someplace that someone has experienced in someone's life for someone to possibly be remembering someone or something that can be hard or difficult for someone to be remembering someone or something, however, I think someone may not want to remember someone or something because I think someone may not want to go down memory lane about something with themselves, and someone else for someone not to be wanting to be remember someone or something, and therefore, I think someone can try to remember or forget someone or something because I think someone can try to think about something or not for someone to be remembering or forgetting someone or something, even though, I think someone can try to remember or forget someone or something because I think someone can ask God to help someone to be remembering or forgetting someone or something as I think someone can ask God to help someone to be thinking about something or to be thinking about something else for someone to be trying to be remembering or forgetting someone or something. I think someone can ask God to help someone to be remembering or forgetting someone or something as I think someone can ask God to help someone to be thinking about something or to be thinking about something else for someone to be trying to be remembering or forgetting someone or something because I think God can help someone to be remembering or forgetting someone or something, from someone asking God to be helping someone to be remembering or forgetting someone or something, and therefore, I think someone can try to remember or forget someone or something because I think God can help someone to be remembering or forgetting someone or something, from someone asking God to be helping someone to be remembering or forgetting someone or something.

If I think someone can try to remember or forget someone or something, than I think someone's memories is of everything that someone can possibly experience in someone's life as I think someone's memories is of something that someone can possibly experience in someone's life because I think someone's memories is someone's thoughts for someone's memories to be of everything that someone can possibly experience in someone's life as I think someone's memories is someone's thoughts for someone's memories to be of something that someone can possibly experience in someone's life. I think someone's memories is someone's thoughts for someone's memories to be of everything that someone can possibly experience in someone's life as I think someone's memories is someone's thoughts for someone's memories to be of something that someone can possibly experience in someone's life because I think someone's memories is someone's thoughts of everything that someone can possibly experience in someone's life for someone's memories to be someone's thoughts as I think someone's memories is someone's thoughts of something that someone can possibly experience in someone's life for someone's memories to be someone's thoughts. I think someone's memories is someone's thoughts of everything that someone can possibly experience in someone's life for someone's memories to be someone's thoughts as I think someone's memories is someone's thoughts of something that someone can possibly experience in someone's life for someone's memories to be someone's thoughts because I think someone's memories is of everything that someone can possibly be able to remember experiencing in someone's life as I think someone's thoughts is of everything that someone can possibly be able to remember experiencing in someone's life. I think someone's memories is of everything that someone can possibly be able to remember experiencing in someone's life as I think someone's thoughts is of everything that someone can possibly be able to remember experiencing in someone's life because I think someone's thoughts is of everything that someone can possibly experience in someone's life for someone's memories to be someone's thoughts. I think someone's thoughts is of everything that someone can possibly experience in someone's life for someone's memories to be someone's thoughts because I think someone's thoughts is of everything that someone can possibly experience in someone's life for someone's thoughts to be what someone's thinks.

If I think someone's thoughts is of everything that someone can possibly experience with themselves for someone's memories to be someone's thoughts, than I do not think God has memories because I think God created everything for God not to be having memories, and therefore, I do not think someone, and something is a memory in God's mind because I do not God has memories for someone, and something not to be a memory in God's mind. If I do not think someone, and something is a memory in God's mind, than I do not think God has to be remembering someone, and something because I do not think God has memories for God not to be remembering someone, and something, and therefore, I do not think God has memories as I do not think God has to be remembering someone, and something because I think God created everything for God not to be having memories as I think God created everything for God not to be having to be remembering someone, and something, even though, I think someone can think God can have memories as I think someone can think God can remember someone, and something because I think God created someone, and something with God's thoughts for someone to be thinking God can have memories as I think God created someone, and something with God's thoughts for someone to be thinking God can remember someone, and something, however, I do not think God has memories as I do not think God has to be remembering someone, and something because I think God is beyond everything for God not to be having memories as I think God is beyond everything for God not to be remembering someone, and something. If I do not think God has memories as I do not think God has to be remembering someone, and something, than I do not think God has to be learning something because I think God created everything for God to be knowing everything that God has created as I think God knows everything that God has created for God not to be learning something, and therefore, I do not think God can learn something because I think God created everything with God having a state of consciousness for God to be aware of everything as I think God is aware of everything for God not to be learning something. If I do not think God can learn something, than I do not think God has memories as I do not think God has to be remembering someone, and something because I think God is aware of everything for God not to be having memories as I think God is aware of everything for God not to be remembering someone, and something, and therefore, I think God is beyond everything for God not to be having memories, and not to be remembering someone, and something, and not to be learning something because I think God created everything for God not to be having memories, and not to be remembering someone, and something, and not to be learning something.

If I think God created everything for God not to be having memories, and not to be remembering someone, and something, and not to be learning something, than I think an idea is someone's idea because I think someone's idea is what someone thinks for an idea to be someone's idea, and therefore, I think an idea is what someone thinks because I think an idea is someone thinking about what someone thinks of themselves, someone else, something, and God as I think someone can think about what someone thinks of themselves, someone else, something, and God for an idea to be what someone thinks. If I think an idea is what someone thinks, than I think someone's thoughts is an idea as I think someone's thoughts is someone's idea because I think someone has thoughts for someone's thoughts to be an idea as I think someone has thoughts for someone's thoughts to be someone's idea, and therefore, I think what someone thinks is what someone's idea is in life because I think someone's thoughts is someone's idea for someone's idea to be what someone's thinks as I think someone's idea is what someone thinks for someone's thoughts to be what someone's idea is in life. If I think what someone thinks is what someone's idea is in life, than I think what someone's thinks is what someone's thoughts are in life because I think someone's thoughts is what someone's thinks for someone's thoughts to be what someone's thoughts are in life. I think someone's thoughts is what someone's thinks for someone's thoughts to be what someone's thoughts are in life because I think someone has thoughts for someone to be thinking what someone is thinking. I think someone has thoughts for someone to be thinking what someone is thinking because I think someone's thoughts is of the dimension of thought for someone to be having thoughts.

Chapter 19

The truth or a lie

I would like to talk about how dimensions are in life in relation to what dimensions are in life by talking about the truth or a lie, that can possibly have something to do with how dimensions are in life is in relation to what dimensions are in life because I think someone has a choice of right or wrong for someone to be choosing the truth or a lie. I think someone has a choice of right or wrong for someone to be choosing the truth or a lie because I think someone can choose the truth or a lie for someone to be right or wrong. I think someone can choose the truth or a lie for someone to be right or wrong because I think someone can be right or wrong for someone to be choosing the truth or a lie, and therefore, I think someone can choose the truth or a lie for the right or wrong reasons because I think someone has a choice of right or wrong for someone to be choosing the truth or a lie for the right or wrong reasons, even though, I think someone can be right or wrong for choosing the truth or a lie, regardless if someone choosing the truth or a lie for the right or wrong reasons because I think the truth or a lie is someone's choice for someone to be right or wrong. I think the truth or a lie is someone's choice for someone to be right or wrong because I think someone has a choice of right or wrong for the truth or a lie to be someone's choice as I think someone has a choice of right or wrong for someone's choice to be of someone that is right or wrong. I think someone has a choice of right or wrong for the truth or a lie to be someone's choice as I think someone has a choice of right or wrong for someone's choice to be of someone that is right or wrong because I think someone's choice is of someone choosing the truth or a lie for the truth or a lie to be someone's choice as I think someone's choice is of someone choosing to be right or wrong for someone's choice to be of someone that is right or wrong. I think someone's choice is of someone choosing the truth or a lie for the truth or a lie to be someone's choice as I think someone's choice is of someone choosing to be right or wrong for someone's choice to be of someone that is right or wrong because I think someone can be right or wrong for someone to be choosing the truth or a lie. If I think someone can be right or wrong for someone to be choosing the truth or a lie, than I think truth or a lie is the same as right or wrong because I think someone can choose the truth or a lie with someone having a choice of right or wrong for the truth or a lie to be the same as right or wrong, and therefore, I think the truth or a lie is something because I think the truth or a lie is someone's choice as I think someone can choose the truth or a lie with someone having a choice of right or wrong for the truth or a lie to be something.

If I think the truth or a lie is something, than I think someone can choose something that is the truth or a lie for someone to be right or wrong because I think someone can choose something that is right or wrong for someone to be choosing something that is the truth or a lie. I think someone can choose something that is right or wrong for someone to be choosing something that is the truth or a lie because I think someone has a choice of right or wrong for someone to be choosing something that is the truth or a lie as I think someone has a choice of right or wrong for someone to be choosing something that is right or wrong. I think someone has a choice of right or wrong for someone to be choosing something that is the truth or a lie as I think someone has a choice of right or wrong for someone to be choosing something that is right or wrong because I think someone can be right or wrong for someone to be choosing something that is the truth or a lie as I think someone can be right or wrong for someone to be choosing something that is right or wrong. I think someone can be right or wrong for someone to be choosing something that is the truth or a lie as I think someone can be right or wrong for someone to be choosing something that is right or wrong because I think someone can choose something that is the truth or a lie for someone to be right or wrong. I think someone can choose something that is the truth or a lie for someone to be right or wrong because I think someone can be right or wrong for someone to be choosing something that is the truth or a lie, and therefore, I think someone can choose something that is the truth or a lie for the right or wrong reasons because I think has a choice of right or wrong for someone to be choosing something that is the truth or a lie for the right or wrong reasons, even though, I think someone can be right or wrong for choosing something that is the truth or a lie, regardless if someone choosing something that is the truth or a lie for the right or wrong reasons because I think someone can be right or wrong about something as I think someone can choose something that is right or wrong for someone to be right or wrong for choosing something that is the truth or a lie.

If I think someone can be right or wrong for choosing something that is the truth or a lie, than I think someone can be right or wrong for someone to be choosing something that is the truth or a lie because I think someone can choose to be thinking of something that is the truth or a lie for someone to be right or wrong. I think someone can choose to be thinking of something that is the truth or a lie for someone to be right or wrong because I think someone can choose to be thinking of something that is right or wrong for someone to choosing to be thinking of something that is the truth or a lie. I think someone can choose to be thinking of something that is right or wrong for someone to choosing to be thinking of something that is the truth or a lie because I think someone has a choice of right or wrong for someone to choose to be thinking of something that is the truth or a lie as I think someone has a choice of right or wrong for someone to choose to be thinking of something that is right or wrong. I think someone has a choice of right or wrong for someone to choose to be thinking of something that is the truth or a lie as I think someone has a choice of right or wrong for someone to choose to be thinking of something that is right or wrong because I think someone can be right or wrong for someone to be choosing to be thinking of something that is the truth or a lie as I think someone can be right or wrong for someone to be choosing to be thinking of something that is right or wrong. I think someone can be right or wrong for someone to be choosing to be thinking of something that is the truth or a lie as I think someone can be right or wrong for someone to be choosing to be thinking of something that is right or wrong because I think someone can choose to be thinking of something that is the truth or a lie for someone to be right or wrong. I think someone can choose to be thinking of something that is the truth or a lie for someone to be right or wrong because I think someone can be right or wrong for someone to be choosing to be thinking of something that is the truth or a lie, and therefore, I think someone can choose to be thinking of something that is the truth or a lie for the right or wrong reasons because I think someone has a choice of right or wrong for someone to be choosing to be thinking of something that is the truth or a lie for the right or wrong reasons, even though, I think someone can be right or wrong for choosing to be thinking of something that is the truth or a lie, regardless if someone choosing to be thinking of something that is the truth or a lie for the right or wrong reasons because I think someone can be right or wrong about what someone thinks of something as I think someone can choose to be thinking of something that is right or wrong for someone to be right or wrong for choosing to be thinking of something that is the truth or a lie.

If I think someone can be right or wrong for choosing to be thinking of something that is the truth or a lie, than I think someone can be right or wrong for someone to be choosing to be thinking of something that is the truth or a lie because I think someone can think of something as being the truth or a lie for someone to be right or wrong. I think someone can think of something as being the truth or a lie for someone to be right or wrong because I think someone can think of something as being right or wrong for someone to be thinking of something as being the truth or a lie. I think someone can think of something as being right or wrong for someone to be thinking of something as being the truth or a lie because I think someone has a choice of right or wrong for someone to be thinking of something as being the truth or a lie as I think someone has a choice of right or wrong for someone to be thinking of something as being right or wrong. I think someone has a choice of right or wrong for someone to be thinking of something as being the truth or a lie as I think someone has a choice of right or wrong for someone to be thinking of something as being right or wrong because I think someone can be right or wrong for someone to be thinking of something as being the truth or a lie as I think someone can be right or wrong for someone to be thinking of something as being right or wrong. I think someone can be right or wrong for someone to be thinking of something as being the truth or a lie as I think someone can be right or wrong for someone to be thinking of something as being right or wrong because I think someone can think of something as being the truth or a lie for someone to be right or wrong as I think someone can think of something as being right or wrong for someone to be right or wrong. I think someone can think of something as being the truth or a lie for someone to be right or wrong as I think someone can think of something as being right or wrong for someone to be right or wrong because I think someone can think of something as being right or wrong for someone to be thinking of something as being the truth or a lie. I think someone can think of something as being right or wrong for someone to be thinking of something as being the truth or a lie because I think someone can be right or wrong for someone to be thinking of something as being the truth or a lie.

If I think someone can think of something as being right or wrong for someone to be thinking of something as being the truth or a lie, than I think someone can think something is possible for someone to be thinking something is true because I think someone can experience something, such as someone traveling and time for someone to be thinking something, such as time travel is possible, even though, I do not think time travel is possible because I do not think everything is interfering with everything for time travel to be possible as I do not think God is interfering with everything for God to be allowing time travel to be possible, and therefore, I do not think something is true just because someone can experience something for someone to be thinking something is true because I do not think something is true just because someone thinks something is true, without something actually being true, however, I think someone can think something is true because I think something can be possible for someone to be thinking something is true. If I think something can be possible for someone to be thinking something is true, than I think someone can think something that seems impossible to be possible as I think someone can think something is possible that is impossible because I think something can be possible that someone can think is impossible as I think something can be impossible that someone can think is possible, and therefore, I think someone can think something is possible or impossible because I think something can be possible or impossible for someone to be thinking something is possible or impossible. If I think someone can think something is possible or impossible, than I think someone can think something is true because I think someone can have proof or evidence to be supporting something is true for someone to be thinking something is true, and therefore, I think someone can have proof or evidence to be supporting something that is true because I do not think someone can think about something that is true, without someone having any proof or evidence to be supporting something that is true for someone to be thinking about something that is true. If I think someone can have proof or evidence to be supporting something that is true, than

I think someone can think something is or isn't true for someone to be right or wrong because I think something can be true or not true for someone to be thinking something is or isn't true, and therefore, I think someone can be right or wrong for someone to be thinking something is or isn't true because I think someone can think of something as being the truth or a lie for someone to be right or wrong. I think someone can think of something as being the truth or a lie for someone to be right or wrong because I think someone can be right or wrong for someone to be thinking of something as being the truth or a lie.

I think someone can be right or wrong for someone to be thinking of something as being the truth or a lie because I think someone can think of something as being the truth or a lie for someone to be right or wrong about something. I think someone can think of something as being the truth or a lie for someone to be right or wrong about something because I think someone can be right or wrong about something for someone to be thinking of something as being the truth or a lie. I think someone can be right or wrong about something for someone to be thinking of something as being the truth or a lie because I think someone can think of something that is the truth or a lie for someone to be right or wrong about something. I think someone can think of something that is the truth or a lie for someone to be right or wrong about something because I think someone can be right or wrong about something for someone to be thinking of something that is the truth or a lie. I think someone can be right or wrong about something for someone to be thinking of something that is the truth or a lie because I think someone has a choice of right or wrong for someone to be right or wrong about something as I think someone has a choice of right or wrong for someone to be thinking of something that is the truth or a lie. I think someone has a choice of right or wrong for someone to be right or wrong about something as I think someone has a choice of right or wrong for someone to be thinking of something that is the truth or a lie because I think someone can be right or wrong for someone to be right or wrong about something as I think someone can be right or wrong for someone to be thinking of something that is the truth or a lie. I think someone can be right or wrong for someone to be right or wrong about something as I think someone can be right or wrong for someone to be thinking of something that is the truth or a lie because I think someone can think of something as being right or wrong for someone to be right or wrong about something as I think someone can think of something as being right or wrong for someone to be thinking of something that is the truth or a lie. I think someone can think of something as being right or wrong for someone to be right or wrong about something as I think someone can think of something as being right or wrong for someone to be thinking of something that is the truth or a lie because I think someone can think of something that is the truth or a lie for someone to be right or wrong about something.

I think someone can think of something that is the truth or a lie for someone to be right or wrong about something because I think someone can think of something that is right or wrong for someone to be thinking of something that is the truth or a lie. I think someone can think of something that is right or wrong for someone to be thinking of something that is the truth or a lie because I think someone has a choice of right or wrong for someone to be thinking of something that is the truth or a lie as I think someone has a choice of right or wrong for someone to be thinking of something that is right or wrong. I think someone has a choice of right or wrong for someone to be thinking of something that is the truth or a lie as I think someone has a choice of right or wrong for someone to be thinking of something that is right or wrong because I think someone can be right or wrong for someone to be thinking of something that is the truth or a lie as I think someone can be right or wrong for someone to be thinking of something that is right or wrong. I think someone can be right or wrong for someone to be thinking of something that is the truth or a lie as I think someone can be right or wrong for someone to be thinking of something that is right or wrong because I think someone can think of something as being right or wrong for someone to be thinking of something that is the truth or a lie as I think someone can think of something as being right or wrong for someone to be thinking of something that is right or wrong. I think someone can think of something as being right or wrong for someone to be thinking of something that is the truth or a lie as I think someone can think of something as being right or wrong for someone to be thinking of something that is right or wrong because I think someone can think of something that is right or wrong for someone to be thinking of something that is the truth or a lie. I think someone can think of something that is right or wrong for someone to be thinking of something that is the truth or a lie because I think someone can think of something that is the truth or a lie for someone to be right or wrong. I think someone can think of something that is the truth or a lie for someone to be right or wrong because I think someone can be right or wrong for someone to be thinking of something that is the truth or a lie.

If I think someone can think of something that is the truth or a lie for someone to be right or wrong, than I think someone can think of the truth or a lie because I think someone can think of something that is the truth or a lie for someone to be thinking of the truth or a lie, and therefore, I think the truth or a lie is something because I think someone can think of something that is the truth or a lie for the truth or a lie to be something. I think someone can think of something that is the truth or a lie for the truth or a lie to be something because I think someone can think of something that is right or wrong for the truth or a lie to be something as I think someone can think of something that is right or wrong for someone to be thinking of something that is the truth or a lie. I think someone can think of something that is right or wrong for the truth or a lie to be something as I think someone can think of something that is right or wrong for someone to be thinking of something that is the truth or a lie because I think someone can be right or wrong for the truth or a lie to be something as I think someone can be right or wrong for someone to be thinking of something that is the truth or a lie. I think someone can be right or wrong for the truth or a lie to be something as I think someone can be right or wrong for someone to be thinking of something that is the truth or a lie because I think someone can think of something that is the truth or a lie for the truth or a lie to be something, and therefore, I think the truth or a lie is something because I think someone can think of something that is the truth or a lie for someone to be right or wrong as I think someone can be right or wrong for the truth or a lie to be something.

If I think the truth or a lie is something, than I think someone can think of something that is the truth or a lie for someone to be right or wrong because I think someone can be right or wrong for someone to be thinking of the truth or a lie. I think someone can be right or wrong for someone to be thinking of the truth or a lie because I think someone has a choice of right or wrong for someone to be thinking of the truth or a lie. I think someone has a choice of right or wrong for someone to be thinking of the truth or a lie because I think someone can think of the truth or a lie for someone to be right or wrong. I think someone can think of the truth or a lie for someone to be right or wrong because I think someone can be right or wrong for someone to be thinking of the truth or a lie. I think someone can be right or wrong for someone to be thinking of the truth or a lie because I think someone can think of the truth or a lie for someone to be right or wrong. I think someone can think of the truth or a lie for someone to be right or wrong because I think someone can be right or wrong about what someone's thinks for someone to be thinking of the truth or a lie. I think someone can be right or wrong about what someone's thinks for someone to be thinking of the truth or a lie because I think someone can of the truth or a lie for someone to be right or wrong about what someone thinks. I think someone can of the truth or a lie for someone to be right or wrong about what someone thinks because I think someone can be right or wrong for someone to be thinking of the truth or a lie about what someone thinks. I think someone can be right or wrong for someone to be thinking of the truth or a lie about what someone thinks because I think someone has a choice of right or wrong for someone to be thinking of the truth or a lie about what someone thinks. I think someone has a choice of right or wrong for someone to be thinking of the truth or a lie about what someone thinks because I think someone can think of the truth or a lie about what someone thinks for someone to be right or wrong. I think someone can think of the truth or a lie about what someone thinks for someone to be right or wrong because I think someone can be right or wrong for someone to be thinking of the truth or a lie about what someone thinks. I think someone can be right or wrong for someone to be thinking of the truth or a lie about what someone thinks because I think someone can think of the truth or a lie for someone to be right or wrong about what someone thinks. I think someone can think of the truth or a lie for someone to be right or wrong about what someone thinks because I think someone can be right or wrong about what someone thinks for someone to be thinking of the truth or a lie.

I think someone can be right or wrong about what someone thinks for someone to be thinking of the truth or a lie because I think someone can be right or wrong about what someone can think of themselves, someone else, something, and God for someone to be thinking of the truth or a lie. I think someone can be right or wrong about what someone can think of themselves, someone else, something, and God for someone to be thinking of the truth or a lie because I think someone can think of the truth or a lie for someone to be right or wrong about themselves, someone else, something, and God. I think someone can think of the truth or a lie for someone to be right or wrong about themselves, someone else, something, and God because I think someone can be right or wrong about what someone thinks of themselves, someone else, something, and God for someone to be thinking of the truth or a lie. I think someone can be right or wrong about what someone thinks of themselves, someone else, something, and God for someone to be thinking of the truth or a lie because I think someone can be right or wrong for someone to be thinking of the truth or a lie about what someone thinks of themselves, someone else, something, and God. I think someone can be right or wrong for someone to be thinking of the truth or a lie about what someone thinks of themselves, someone else, something, and God because I think someone has a choice of right or wrong for someone to be thinking of the truth or a lie about what someone thinks of themselves, someone else, something, and God. I think someone has a choice of right or wrong for someone to be thinking of the truth or a lie about what someone thinks of themselves, someone else, something, and God because I think someone can think of the truth or a lie about what someone thinks of themselves, someone else, something, and God for someone to be right or wrong. I think someone can think of the truth or a lie about what someone thinks of themselves, someone else, something, and God for someone to be right or wrong because I think someone can be right or wrong for someone to be thinking of the truth or a lie about what someone thinks of themselves, someone else, something, and God. I think someone can be right or wrong for someone to be thinking of the truth or a lie about what someone thinks of themselves, someone else, something, and God because I think someone can think of the truth or a lie for someone to be right or wrong about what someone thinks of themselves, someone else, something, and God. I think someone can think of the truth or a lie for someone to be right or wrong about what someone thinks of themselves, someone else, something, and God because I think someone can be right or wrong about what someone thinks of themselves, someone else, something, and God for someone to be thinking of the truth or a lie. I think someone can be right or wrong about what someone thinks of themselves, someone else, something, and God for someone to be thinking of the truth or a lie because I think someone can be right or wrong about what someone thinks for someone to be thinking of the truth or a lie. I think someone can be right or wrong about what someone thinks for someone to be thinking of the truth or a lie because I think someone can be right or wrong for someone to be thinking of the truth or a lie about what someone thinks. If I think someone can be right or wrong about what someone thinks for someone to be thinking of the truth or a lie, than I think someone's mind is very complex because I think someone can be unsure of what someone is thinking is true or false as I think someone can be thinking about what someone thinks is true or false for someone's mind to be very complex, even though, I think God can help someone to be thinking about what is true or false for God to be helping someone to be thinking about the truth because I think God is always good, and right for God to be helping someone to be thinking about the truth as I think God is always good, and right for God to be helping someone to be thinking about what the truth is in life, and therefore, I think God can help someone to be thinking about the truth with themselves, someone else, something, and God because I think God can help someone to be doing something that is good, and right with themselves, someone else, something, and God for God to be helping someone to be thinking about the truth with themselves, someone else, something, and God.

If I think God can help someone to be thinking about the truth with themselves, someone else, something, and God, than I think someone can be right or wrong about what someone thinks for someone to be right or wrong with someone thinking of the truth or a lie because I think someone has a choice of right or wrong for someone to be right or wrong with someone thinking of the truth or a lie as I think someone has a choice of right or wrong for someone to be right or wrong about what someone thinks, and therefore, I think someone can be right or wrong about what someone thinks because I think someone can be right or wrong with someone thinking of the truth or a lie for someone to be right or wrong about what someone thinks. I think someone can be right or wrong with someone thinking of the truth or a lie for someone to be right or wrong about what someone thinks because I think someone can think of telling the truth or a lie for someone to be right or wrong about what someone thinks as I think someone can think of telling the truth or a lie for someone to be right or wrong with someone thinking of the truth or a lie, and therefore, I think someone can think of telling the truth or a lie because I think someone can think of something that is right or wrong for someone to be thinking of telling the truth or a lie. I think someone can think of something that is right or wrong for someone to be telling the truth or a lie because I think someone can be right or wrong about what someone thinks of themselves, someone else, something, and God for someone to be telling the truth or a lie about what someone thinks of themselves, someone else, something, and God. I think someone can be right or wrong about what someone thinks of themselves, someone else, something, and God for someone to be telling the truth or a lie about what someone thinks of themselves, someone else, something, and God because I think someone can be right or wrong for someone to be telling the truth or a lie about what someone thinks of themselves, someone else, something, and God. I think someone can be right or wrong for someone to be telling the truth or a lie about what someone thinks of themselves, someone else, something, and God because I think someone can be telling the truth or a lie about themselves, someone else, something, and God for someone to be right or wrong. I think someone can be telling the truth or a lie about themselves, someone else, something, and God for someone to be right or wrong because I think someone can be right or wrong for someone to be telling the truth or a lie about themselves, someone else, something, and God. I think someone can be right or wrong for someone to be telling the truth or a lie about themselves, someone else, something, and God because I think someone can be telling the truth or a lie for someone to be right or wrong. I think someone can be telling the truth or a lie for someone to be right or wrong because I think someone can be right or wrong for someone to be telling the truth or a lie. I think someone can be right or wrong for someone to be telling the truth or a lie because I think someone can think of telling the truth or a lie for someone to be right or wrong. I think someone can think of telling the truth or a lie for someone to be right or wrong because I think someone can tell the truth or a lie. I think someone can tell the truth or a lie because I think someone can think of the truth or a lie for someone to be telling the truth or a lie. I think someone can think of the truth or a lie for someone to be telling the truth or a lie because I think someone can tell the truth or a lie for someone to be right or wrong. I think someone can tell the truth or a lie for someone to be right or wrong because I think someone can be right or wrong for telling the truth or a lie. I think someone can be right or wrong for telling the truth or a lie because I think someone can think of telling the truth or a lie for someone to be right or wrong. If I think someone can be right or wrong for telling the truth or a lie, than I think someone can think of telling the truth for the right or wrong reasons because I think someone has a choice of right or wrong for someone to be thinking of telling the truth or a lie for the right or wrong reasons, and therefore, I think someone can think there is a grey area for someone to be telling the truth or a lie because I think someone can think someone can be telling the truth or a lie for the right or wrong reasons for someone to be thinking there is a grey area for telling the truth or a lie, even though, I do not think there is a grey area for someone to be telling the truth or a lie because I think someone is either telling the truth or a lie, regardless if someone is telling the truth or a lie for the right or wrong reasons for there not to be a grey area for someone to be telling the truth or a lie.

If I do not think there is a grey area for someone to be telling the truth or a lie, than I do not think the truth or a lie is just someone telling the truth or a lie because I think someone has a choice of right or wrong for someone to be telling the truth or a lie as I think someone has a choice of right or wrong for someone to be honest or dishonest. I think someone has a choice of right or wrong for someone to be telling the truth or a lie as I think someone has a choice of right or wrong for someone to be honest or dishonest because I think someone can be right or wrong for telling the truth or a lie as I think someone can be right or wrong for being honest or dishonest. I think someone can be right or wrong for telling the truth or a lie as I think someone can be right or wrong for being honest or dishonest because I think someone can be telling the truth or a lie for someone to be right or wrong as I think someone can be telling the truth or a lie for someone to be honest or dishonest. I think someone can be telling the truth or a lie for someone to be right or wrong as I think someone can be telling the truth or a lie for someone to be honest or dishonest because I think someone can be right or wrong for someone being honest or dishonest with someone telling the truth or a lie. I think someone can be right or wrong for someone being honest or dishonest with someone telling the truth or a lie because I think someone telling the truth or a lie is someone being honest or dishonest for someone to be right or wrong. I think someone telling the truth or a lie is someone being honest or dishonest for someone to be right or wrong because I think someone can choose the truth or a lie for someone to be right or wrong as I think someone can choose to be honest or dishonest for someone to be right or wrong. I think someone can choose the truth or a lie for someone to be right or wrong as I think someone can choose to be honest or dishonest for someone to be right or wrong because I think someone can be right or wrong for choosing the truth or a lie as I think someone can be right or wrong for choosing to be honest or dishonest. I think someone can be right or wrong for choosing the truth or a lie as I think someone can be right or wrong for choosing to be honest or dishonest because I think the truth or a lie is someone being honest or dishonest for someone to be right or wrong. I think the truth or a lie is someone being honest or dishonest for someone to be right or wrong because I think someone can be right or wrong with the truth or a lie. I think someone can be right or wrong with the truth or a lie because I think someone can be right or wrong about the truth or a lie for someone to be right or wrong with the truth or a lie.

If I think someone can be right or wrong with the truth or a lie, than what is the truth or a lie? I think the truth or a lie is something that is or isn't so, and therefore, I think an example how I think the truth or a lie is something that is or isn't so can be someone asking me, "did you go to the store", and if I say, "no", and someone found out from someone else that I did go to the store, than the truth is I lied because I did go to the store, and therefore, I think the true is something that is so because I did go to the store, and I think a lie is something that isn't so because I did go to the store, even though I lied when I said "no" for a lie to be something that isn't so because I did go to the store. If I lied when I said "no" for a lie to be something that isn't so, than I think the truth can be something that isn't so, and I think a lie can be something that is so because if someone asks me, "did you go to the store", and if I say, "yes", and someone found out from someone else that I didn't go to the store, than the truth is I lied because I didn't go to the store, and therefore, I think the true is something that isn't so because I didn't go to the store, and I think a lie is something that is so because I didn't go to the store, even though I lied when I said "yes", for a lie to be something that is so because I didn't go to the store. If I lied when I said "yes", for a lie to be something that is so, than I think the truth or a lie is something that is or isn't so because I think the truth can be something that is or isn't so for the truth to be something that is or isn't so as I think a lie can be something that is or isn't so for a lie to be something that is or isn't so, and therefore, I think the truth or a lie is something that is or isn't so because I think the truth or a lie is something that is or isn't a fact of life for the truth or a lie to be something that is or isn't so, even though, I think someone can think the truth or a lie is only someone's own truth or lie because I think someone can think the truth or a lie is something that someone thinks is or isn't a fact for someone to be thinking the truth or a lie is only someone's own truth or lie, but I do not think the truth or a lie is only someone's own truth or lie because I think if someone found out from someone else that I did or didn't go to the store, than I do not think the truth or lie is something that is only my truth or lie because I think someone found out from someone else that I did or didn't go to the store for the truth or lie to be someone else's, and my truth or lie that I did or didn't go to the store, and therefore, I do not think the truth or a lie is only someone's own truth or lie because I think the truth or a lie is something that is or isn't a fact of life for the truth or a lie not to be only someone's own truth or lie.

I think the truth or a lie is something that is or isn't a fact of life for the truth or a lie not to be only someone's own truth or lie because I think the truth or a lie is something that is true or false as I think the truth or a lie is something that is or isn't a fact of life. I think the truth or a lie is something that is true or false as I think the truth or a lie is something that is or isn't a fact of life because I think the truth or a lie is something that is or isn't a fact of life for the truth or a lie to be something that is true or false. I think the truth or a lie is something that is or isn't a fact of life for the truth or a lie to be something that is true or false because I think something is or isn't a fact of life for the truth or a lie to be something that is true or false as I think something is true or false for the truth or a lie to be something that is or isn't a fact of life. I think something is or isn't a fact of life for the truth or a lie to be something that is true or false as I think something is true or false for the truth or a lie to be something that is or isn't a fact of life because I think the truth or a lie is something that is true or false as I think the truth or a lie is or isn't a fact of life. I think the truth or a lie is something that is true or false as I think the truth or a lie is or isn't a fact of life because I think the truth or a lie is or isn't a fact of life for the truth or a lie to be something that is true or false. I think the truth or a lie is or isn't a fact of life for the truth or a lie to be something that is true or false because I think the truth or a lie is true or false as I think the truth or a lie is or isn't a fact of life. I think the truth or a lie is true or false as I think the truth or a lie is or isn't a fact of life because I think the truth or a lie is or isn't a fact of life for the truth or a lie to be true or false. I think the truth or a lie is or isn't a fact of life for the truth or a lie to be true or false because I think the truth or a lie is or isn't a fact of life for the truth or a lie to be a fact of life. I think the truth or a lie is or isn't a fact of life for the truth or a lie to be a fact of life because I think the truth or a lie is or isn't a fact in life for the truth or a lie to be a fact of life, and therefore, I think the truth or a lie is or isn't a fact of life because I think the truth or a lie is or isn't a fact in life for the truth or a lie to be a fact of life.

If I think the truth or a lie is or isn't a fact in life for the truth or a lie to be a fact of life, than I think the truth or a lie is a fact of life because I think the truth or a lie is or isn't a fact of life for the truth or a lie to be a fact of life. I think the truth or a lie is or isn't a fact of life for the truth or a lie to be a fact of life because I think the truth is a fact in life for the truth to be a fact of life as I think a lie isn't a fact in life for a lie to be a fact of life. I think the truth is a fact in life for the truth to be a fact of life as I think a lie isn't a fact in life for a lie to be a fact of life because I think the truth or a lie is or isn't something that is a fact in life for the truth or a lie to be a fact of life, and therefore, I think the truth or a lie is a fact of life because I think the truth is something that is a fact of life for the truth to be a fact of life as I think a lie isn't something that is a fact of life for a lie to be a fact of life. I think the truth is something that is a fact of life for the truth to be a fact of life as I think a lie isn't something that is a fact of life for a lie to be a fact of life because I think the truth or a lie is or isn't something that is a fact of life for the truth or a lie to be a fact of life. I think the truth or a lie is or isn't something that is a fact of life for the truth or a lie to be a fact of life because I think the truth or a lie is or isn't something that is a fact in life for the truth or a lie to be a fact of life. I think the truth or a lie is or isn't something that is a fact in life for the truth or a lie to be a fact of life because I think the truth or a lie is or isn't a fact in life for the truth or a lie to be a fact of life, and therefore, I think the truth or a lie is a fact of life because I think the truth or a lie is or isn't a fact in life for the truth or a lie to be a fact of life. If I think the truth or a lie is a fact of life, than I do not think someone can learn something from a lie as I think someone can learn something from the truth because I think a lie is something that isn't a fact in life for someone not to be learning something from a lie as I think the truth is something that is a fact in life for someone to be learning something from the truth, even though, I think someone can learn something from a lie as I think someone can learn something from the truth because I think a lie is something that is a fact of life for someone to be learning something from a lie as I think the truth is something that is a fact of life for someone to be learning something from the truth, and therefore, I think someone can learn from a lie as I think someone can learn from the truth because I think a lie is something that isn't a fact in life for someone to be learning from a lie as I think the truth is something that is a fact in life for someone to be learning from the truth. If I think someone can learn from a lie as I think someone can learn from the truth, than I think someone can learn from a lie as I think someone can learn from the truth because I think someone can learn a lie is a lie for someone to be learning from a lie as I think someone can learn a lie is a lie for someone to be learning from the truth, and therefore, I think someone can the truth because I think someone can learn a lie is a lie for someone to be learning a lie as I think someone can learn a lie for someone to be learning the truth, otherwise, I do not think someone can learn something from a lie as I think someone can learn something from the truth because I think a lie is something that isn't a fact in life for someone not to be learning something from a lie as I think the truth is something that is a fact in life for someone to be learning something from the truth. I think a lie is something that isn't a fact in life for someone not to be learning something from a lie as I think the truth is something that is a fact in life for someone to be learning something from the truth because I think the truth or a lie is or isn't a fact in life for the truth or a lie to be a fact of life.

I think the truth or a lie is or isn't a fact in life for the truth or a lie to be a fact of life because I think the truth or a lie is a fact of life for someone to be asking what the truth or a lie is in life, and therefore, I think someone can ask what the truth or a lie is in life because I think someone think of what the truth or a lie is in life for someone to be asking what the truth or a lie is in life. I think someone think of what the truth or a lie is in life for someone to be asking what the truth or a lie is in life because I think the truth is something that is a fact in life for someone to be thinking of what the truth is in life as I think a lie is something that isn't a fact in life for someone to be thinking of what a lie is in life, and therefore, I think someone can ask what the truth or a lie is in life for someone to be thinking of what the truth or a lie is in life because I think the truth or a lie something that is or isn't a fact in life for someone to be asking what the truth or lie is in life. I think the truth or a lie something that is or isn't a fact in life for someone to be asking what the truth or lie is in life because I think the truth or a lie something that is or isn't a fact of life for someone to be thinking of what the truth or lie is in life. I think the truth or a lie something that is or isn't a fact of life for someone to be thinking of what the truth or lie is in life because I think the truth or a lie is something that is a fact of life for someone to be asking what the truth or lie is in life, and therefore, I think someone can ask what the truth or a lie is in life for someone to be thinking of what the truth or a lie is in life because I think the truth or a lie is a fact of life for someone to be asking what the truth or a lie is in life. I think the truth or a lie is a fact of life for someone to be asking what the truth or a lie is in life because I think someone can think of what the truth or a lie is in life for the truth or a lie to be a fact of life. I think someone can think of what the truth or a lie is in life for the truth or a lie to be a fact of life because I think the truth or a lie is someone thinking of what the truth or a lie is in life for the truth or a lie to be a fact of life, and therefore, I think someone can ask what the truth or a lie is in life for someone to be thinking of what the truth or a lie is in life because I think the truth or a lie is someone thinking of what the truth or a lie is in life for someone to be asking what the truth or a lie is in life. I think the truth or a lie is someone thinking of what the truth or a lie is in life for someone to be asking what the truth or a lie in life because I think someone has a choice of right or wrong for someone to be thinking of what the truth or a lie is in life as I think someone has a choice of right or wrong for someone to be asking what the truth or a lie is in life, and therefore, I think the truth or a lie is someone thinking of what the truth or a lie is in life for someone to be asking what the truth or a lie is in life because I think someone can ask what the truth or a lie is in life for someone to be thinking of what the truth or a lie is in life. I think someone can ask what the truth or a lie is in life for someone to be thinking of what the truth or a lie is in life because I think someone can think of what the truth or a lie is in life from someone asking what the truth or a lie is in life. I think someone can think of what the truth or a lie is in life from someone asking what the truth or a lie is in life because I think the truth or a lie something that is or isn't a fact in life for someone to be asking what the truth or a lie is in life as I think the truth or a lie something that is or isn't a fact in life for someone to be thinking of what the truth or a lie is in life, and therefore, I think someone can think of what the truth or a lie is in life from someone asking what the truth or a lie is in life because I think someone can ask what the truth or a lie is in life for someone to be thinking of what the truth or a lie is in life. I think someone can ask what the truth or a lie is in life for someone to be thinking of what the truth or a lie is in life because I think someone can ask something for someone to be thinking of what the truth or a lie is in life. I think someone can ask something for someone to be thinking of what the truth or a lie is in life because I think someone can think of what the truth or a lie is from someone asking something. I think someone can think of what the truth or a lie is in life from someone asking something because I think the truth or a lie something that is or isn't a fact in life for someone to be asking something as I think the truth or a lie something that is or isn't a fact in life for someone to be thinking of what the truth or a lie is in life, and therefore, I think someone can think of what the truth or a lie is in life from someone asking something because I think someone can ask something for someone to be thinking of what the truth or a lie is in life. If I think someone can think of what the truth or a lie is in life from someone asking something, than I think someone can be thinking for themselves about what the truth is in life because I do not think someone is always going to be told from someone else what the truth is in life for someone to be thinking for themselves about what the truth is in life, and therefore, I think someone can ask themselves what the truth is in life because I think someone can think for themselves about what the truth is in life from someone asking themselves what the truth is in life.

If I think someone can ask themselves what the truth is in life, than I think someone can question something as I think someone can ask something because I think someone can be asking something for someone to be questioning something as I think someone can be questioning something for someone to be asking something. I think someone can be asking something for someone to be questioning something as I think someone can be questioning something for someone to be asking something because I think someone questioning something is someone asking something as I think someone asking something is someone questioning something, and therefore, I think someone can be questioning something as I think someone can be asking about something because I think someone can be asking about something for someone to be questioning something as I think someone can be questioning something for someone to be asking about something. I think someone can be asking about something for someone to be questioning something as I think someone can be questioning something for someone to be asking about something because I think someone can think of questioning something for someone to be thinking of asking about something as I think someone can think of asking about something for someone to be thinking of questioning something. I think someone can think of questioning something for someone to be thinking of asking about something as I think someone can think of asking about something for someone to be thinking of questioning something because I think someone can think of asking any question about something for someone to be thinking of asking about something as I think someone can think of asking something for someone to be thinking of asking any question about something. I think someone can think of asking any question about something for someone to be thinking of asking about something as I think someone can think of asking something for someone to be thinking of asking any question about something because I think someone can think of something for someone to be thinking of asking about something as I think someone can think of something for someone to be thinking of asking any question about something. I think someone can think of something for someone to be thinking of asking about something as I think someone can think of something for someone to be thinking of asking any question about something because I think someone can think of questioning something for someone to be thinking of asking something as I think someone can think of asking something for someone to be thinking of questioning something. I think someone can think of questioning something for someone to be thinking of asking something as I think someone can think of asking something for someone to be thinking of questioning something because I think someone can think of asking any question for someone to be thinking of asking something as I think someone can think of asking something for someone to think of asking any question. I think someone can think of asking any question for someone to be thinking of asking something as I think someone can think of asking something for someone to think of asking any question because I think someone can think of something for someone to be thinking of asking something as I think someone can think of something for someone to think of asking any question. I think someone can think of something for someone to be thinking of asking something as I think someone can think of something for someone to think of asking any question because I think someone can think of something for someone to questioning something. I think someone can think of something for someone to questioning something because I think someone can think of questioning something as I think someone can think of asking something. I think someone can think of questioning something as I think someone can think of asking something because I think someone can think of asking something for someone to be questioning something.

I think someone can think of asking something for someone to be questioning something because I think someone can ask what someone thinks of something for someone to be thinking of what someone thinks is the truth or a lie as I think someone can ask what someone thinks of something for someone to be thinking of what someone thinks is right or wrong. I think someone can ask what someone thinks of something for someone to be thinking of what someone thinks is the truth or a lie as I think someone can ask what someone thinks of something for someone to be thinking of what someone thinks is right or wrong because I think what someone thinks is right or wrong is what someone thinks is the truth or a lie as I think someone can think of what someone thinks is right or wrong for someone to be asking what someone thinks of something, and therefore, I think someone can think of what someone thinks is right or wrong for someone to be asking what someone thinks of something because I think someone can ask what someone thinks is right or wrong for someone to be thinking of what is right or wrong. I think someone can ask what someone thinks is right or wrong for someone to be thinking of what is right or wrong because I think someone has a choice of right or wrong for someone to be thinking of what is right or wrong as I think someone has a choice of right or wrong for someone to be asking what someone thinks is right or wrong, and therefore, I think someone can ask what someone thinks is right or wrong for someone to be thinking of what is right or wrong because I think someone can think of what is right or wrong for someone to be asking what someone thinks is right or wrong. I think someone can think of what is right or wrong for someone to be asking what someone thinks is right or wrong because I think someone can ask what is right or wrong for someone to be thinking of what is right or wrong. I think someone can ask what is right or wrong for someone to be thinking of what is right or wrong because I think someone can ask something for someone to be thinking of what is right or wrong. I think someone can ask something for someone to be thinking of what is right or wrong because I think someone can think of what is right or wrong for someone to be asking something. I think someone can think of what is right or wrong for someone to be asking something because I think someone can think of something that is right or wrong for someone to be asking something.

I think someone can think of something that is right or wrong for someone to be asking something because I think someone can ask what someone thinks of something for someone to be thinking of something that is right or wrong. I think someone can ask what someone thinks of something for someone to be thinking of something that is right or wrong because I think someone can think of something that is right or wrong from someone asking what someone thinks of something. I think someone can think of something that is right or wrong from someone asking what someone thinks of something because I think someone can ask what someone thinks of something for someone to be asking what someone thinks is right or wrong. I think someone can ask what someone thinks of something for someone to be asking what someone thinks is right or wrong because I think someone can ask what someone thinks is right or wrong from someone asking what someone thinks of something. I think someone can ask what someone thinks is right or wrong from someone asking what someone thinks of something because I think someone can think of what someone thinks is right or wrong from someone asking what someone thinks of something. I think someone can think of what someone thinks is right or wrong from someone asking what someone thinks of something because I think someone can think of what the answer is to what someone's question is in life. I think someone can think of what the answer is to what someone's question is in life because I think the answer to someone's question can be right or wrong. I think the answer to someone's question can be right or wrong because I think someone can be right or wrong with someone answering someone's question for the answer to someone's question to be right or wrong. I think someone can be right or wrong with someone answering someone's question for the answer to someone's question to be right or wrong because I think someone can answer someone's question with someone having a choice of right or wrong for the answer to someone's question to be right or wrong as I think has a choice of right or wrong for someone to be right or wrong with someone answering someone's question, and therefore, I think the answer to someone's question can be right or wrong because I think someone can be right or wrong with someone answering someone's question for the answer to someone's question to be right or wrong.

I think someone can be right or wrong with someone answering someone's question for the answer to someone's question to be right or wrong because I think the question is the answer as I think someone can ask any question for someone to be right or wrong with someone answering someone's question, and therefore, I think the question is the answer as I think the answer is the question because I think the question is the answer for someone to be asking any question. I think the question is the answer for someone to be asking any question because I think someone asking any question is an answer for the question to be the answer, and therefore, I think the question is the answer as I think the answer is the question because I think someone can ask any question for the question to be the answer. I think someone can ask any question for the question to be the answer because I think the question is the answer for someone to be asking any question. I think the question is the answer for someone to be asking any question because I think someone can ask any question for someone to be right or wrong with someone answering any question as I think someone can be right or wrong with someone answering any question for the question to be the answer, even though, I do not think the answer to any question is right or wrong for the question to be the answer as I think someone can be right or wrong with someone answering any question for the question to be the answer because I think the answer to every question is always true, correct, and right for every question to always have an answer that is always true, correct, and right, and therefore, I think the question is the answer as I think the answer is the question because I think there is always a true, correct, and right answer to every question for the question to be the answer. If I think the question is the answer as I think the answer is the question, than I think an example of how I think there is always a true, correct, and right answer to every question for the question to be the answer can be 1+1=2 because I think 2 is always the true, correct, and right answer with 1+1 being in question for 1+1 to always be equaling 2, and therefore, I think there is always a true, correct, and right answer to every question for the question to be the answer because I think 2 is always the true, correct, and right answer with 1+1 being in question for there is always a true, correct, and right answer to every question as I think 1+1=2 for the question to be the answer.

If I think there is always a true, correct, and right answer to every question for the question to be the answer, than I think someone can think there are dumb or wrong questions that someone can asking because I think someone can think someone can be asking a dumb or wrong question for someone to be thinking there are dumb or wrong questions that someone can asking, but I do not think there is any dumb or wrong questions that someone can be asking because I do not think there is a wrong question that someone can be asking for there to be any dumb or wrong questions that someone can asking, even though, I think someone can think someone can be asking a dumb or wrong question for someone to be thinking there are dumb or wrong questions that someone can be asking because I think someone has a choice of right or wrong for someone to be thinking there are dumb or wrong questions that someone can be asking as I think someone has a choice of right or wrong for someone to be thinking someone can be asking a dumb or wrong question, however, I do not think there is a wrong question for there to be any dumb or wrong questions that someone can be asking because I think there is always a true, correct, and right answer to every question for there not to be any dumb or wrong questions that someone can be asking, and therefore, I do not think there are any wrong questions because I think there is always a true, correct, and right answer to every question for there not to be any wrong questions. If I do not think there are any wrong questions, than I think someone can learn something from someone questioning something because I think the answer to every question is something that is always true, correct, and right for someone to be learning something from someone questioning something. I think answer to every question is something that is always true, correct, and right for someone to be learning something from someone questioning something because I think answer to every question is of something that is always true, correct, and right for someone to be learning something from someone questioning something, and therefore, I think someone can learn something from someone questioning something because I think there is always a true, correct, and right answer to every question for someone to be learning something from someone questioning something.

If I think someone can learn something from someone questioning something, than I think someone can ask questions because I think someone is created by God for someone to be asking questions. I think someone is created by God for someone to be asking questions because I think God created someone to be questioning something for someone to be asking questions, and therefore, I think someone is created by God for someone to be questioning something because I think God created someone to be thinking of any word or sound to be describing someone thinking of something for someone to be questioning something. I think God created someone to be thinking of any word or sound to be describing someone thinking of something for someone to be questioning something because I think God created someone to be thinking of something for someone to be questioning something, and therefore, I think someone can question something because I think someone is created by God for someone to be questioning something. I think someone is created by God for someone to be questioning something because I think God created someone to be asking questions from someone questioning something, and therefore, I think God created someone for someone to be asking questions because I think God created someone to be questioning something for someone to be asking questions. I think God created someone to be questioning something for someone to be asking questions because I think God created someone to be answering questions from someone questioning something as I think God created someone to be answering questions from someone asking questions, and therefore, I think someone is created by God for someone to be asking, and answering questions because I think God created someone to be questioning something for someone to be asking, and answering questions. If I think someone is created by God for someone to be asking, and answering questions, than I think God created someone to be curious because I think God created someone to be asking, and answering questions for God to be creating someone to be curious, and therefore, I think someone is curious because I think someone can be asking, and answering questions for someone to be curious. If I think someone is curious, than I think God created someone to be surviving from someone asking, and answering questions because I do not think someone can survive, without someone asking, and answering questions, and therefore, I think God created someone to be asking, and answering questions for someone to be surviving because I do not think someone can live without someone asking, and answering questions for someone to be surviving. If I think God created someone to be asking, and answering any questions for someone to be surviving, than I think God created someone to be surviving because I think God created someone to be asking, and answering questions with themselves, someone else, something, and God for God to be creating someone to be surviving, and therefore, I think God created someone to be a student, and a teacher because I think God created someone to be asking, and answering questions with themselves, someone else, something, and God for God to be creating someone to be a student, and a teacher.

If I think God created someone to be a student, and a teacher, than I think God created someone to be asking, and answering questions because I think God created someone to be asking, and answering questions for someone to be asking, and answering questions, and therefore, I think someone can be asking, and answering questions because I think someone can think of something about themselves, someone else, something, and God for someone to be asking, and answering questions. I think someone can think of something about themselves, someone else, something, and God for someone to be asking, and answering questions because I think someone can be asking, and answering questions about themselves, someone else, something, and God for someone to be asking, and answering questions about themselves, someone else, something, and God as I think someone can ask, and answer questions about themselves, someone else, something, and God for someone to be asking, and answering questions, and therefore, I think someone can be asking, and answering questions because I think someone can choose to be communicating in any possible way for someone to be asking, and answering questions with themselves, someone else, something, and God. If I think someone can be asking, and answering questions, than I think God created someone for someone to be learning because I think God created someone to be learning something for someone to be learning, and therefore, I think God created someone to be learning something because I think God created something for someone to be learning something from something as I think God created everything with something for someone to be learning something from everything. If I think God created someone to be learning something, than I think God created someone to be learning because I think God created someone to be asking, and answering questions with themselves, someone else, something, and God for God to be creating someone to be learning, and therefore, I think someone can learn because I think someone can be asking, and answering questions with themselves, someone else, something, and God for someone to be learning. If I think someone can learn, than I think God created someone to be learning something because I think God created someone to be asking, and answering questions about themselves, someone else, something, and God for God to be creating someone to be learning something, and therefore, I think someone can learn something because I think someone can be asking, and answering questions about themselves, someone else, something, and God for someone to be learning something.

If I think someone can learn something, than I do not think someone can learn something from a lie because I think there is always a true, correct, and right answer to every question for someone not to be learning something from a lie, otherwise, I think someone can learn something from a lie because I think there would be a false, incorrect, and wrong answer to every question for someone to be learning something from a lie, but I do not think someone can learn something from a lie because I do not think there is any false, incorrect, and wrong answer to every question for someone to be learning something from a lie, and therefore, I think someone can learn something from the truth because I think there is always a true, correct, and right answer to every question for someone to be learning something from the truth. I think there is always a true, correct, and right answer to every question for someone to be learning something from the truth because I think the truth is something that is always true, correct, and right for there to always be a true, correct, and right answer to every question. I think the truth is something that is always true, correct, and right for there to always be a true, correct, and right answer to every question because I think there is always a true, correct, and right answer to every question for the question to be the answer, and therefore, I think the question is the answer because I think everything is an answer to every question for the question to be the answer. I think everything is an answer to every question for the question to be the answer because I think every answer to every question is of everything for everything to be an answer to every question. I think every answer to every question is of everything for everything to be an answer to every question because I think every question is of everything that is an answer to every question, even though, I do not think every question, and every answer is strictly someone's questions, and answers as I think every question, and every answer can be someone's questions, and answers because I think every question is of everything that is an answer to every question for every question, and every answer not to be strictly someone's questions, and answers, and therefore, where did every question, and every answer come from as every question is of everything that is an answer to every question? I think every question, and every answer came from God because I think everything is of God's creation for everything to be an answer to every question as I think everything is of God's creation for every question, and every answer to come from God, and therefore, I think there is an infinite amount of questions, and answers because I think every question, and answer came from God being infinite for there to be an infinite amount of questions, and answers. If I think there is an infinite amount of questions, and answers, than I think every question, and answer is first, and foremost God's questions, and answers because I think God created everything for every question to be of everything that is an answer to every question, and therefore, I think there is always a true, correct, and right answer to every question because I think God created everything with God always being good, and right for there to always be a true, correct, and right answer to every question. If I think there is always a true, correct, and right answer to every question, than I think every question is of everything that is an answer to every question because I think everything is an answer, and therefore, I think everything is happening for a reason because I think everything is an answer for everything to be happening for a reason. I think everything is an answer for everything to be happening for a reason because I think everything is happening for a reason with everything being an answer for everything to be happening for a reason, and therefore, I think everything is an answer because I think there is a reason for everything for everything to be an answer. If I think everything is an answer, than I think everything is happening for a reason because I think there is a reason for everything for everything to be happening for a reason, and therefore, I do not think everything is happening by chance or coincidence because I think there is a reason for everything as I think everything is happening for a reason for everything not to be happening by chance or coincidence. If I do not think everything is happening by chance or coincidence, than I think everything is an answer for everything to be happening for a reason because I think there is an answer for everything for everything to be happening for a reason, and therefore, I think the meaning of life is everything is happening for a reason because I think there is an answer for everything as I think everything is an answer for everything to be happening for a reason.

If I think the meaning of life is everything is happening for a reason, than I think someone can think of what the truth is in life with how everything is happening for a reason because I think the truth is everything is happening for a reason for someone to be thinking of what the truth is in life with how everything is happening for a reason, and therefore, I think everything is happening for a reason because I think there is always a true, correct, and right answer with everything for everything to be happening for a reason. I think there is always a true, correct, and right answer with everything for everything to be happening for a reason because I think there is always a true, correct, and right answer to every question as I think every question is of everything that is an answer to every question for everything to be happening for a reason, even though, I think there can be more than one true, correct, and right answer to every question because I think there is always a true, correct, and right answer with everything for there to be more than one true, correct, and right answer to every question, however, I think there is always a true, correct, and right answer to every question because I think everything is happening for a reason for there to always be a true, correct, and right answer to every question, and therefore, I think there is a lot of mysteries because I do not think someone has all of the answers to everything for there to be a lot of mysteries, even though, I think the greatest lessens someone can be learning is someone learning something from the truth and God because I think the truth and God is always good, and right for the greatest lessens someone can be learning to be someone learning something from the truth and God. If I think the greatest lessens someone can be learning is someone learning something from the truth and God, than I think the truth is a fact of life because I think the truth is God's fact of life for the truth to be a fact of life, and therefore, I think the truth is God's truth because I think the truth is a fact of life for the truth to be God's truth as I think the truth is God's fact of life for the truth to be God's truth. I think the truth is a fact of life for the truth to be God's truth as I think the truth is God's fact of life for the truth to be God's truth because I think truth is always good, and right for the truth to be God's fact of life as I think God is always good, and right for the truth to be God's fact of life, and therefore, I think the truth is God's truth because I think God is always good, and right as I think the truth is always good, and right for the truth to be God's truth.

If I think the truth is God's truth, than I think someone can argue with someone else about something because I think someone can disagree with someone else about something for someone to be arguing with someone else about something, even though, I think someone can be right or wrong to be disagreeing with someone else about something for someone to be right or wrong to be arguing with someone else about something because I think someone has a choice of right or wrong for someone to be right or wrong to be arguing with someone else about something as I think someone has a choice of right or wrong for someone to be right or wrong to be disagreeing with someone else about something, however, I think someone can disagree with someone else about something for someone to be arguing with someone else about something because I think someone can disagree with someone else about something that someone thinks is true for someone to be arguing with someone else about something. I think someone can disagree with someone else about something that someone thinks is true for someone to be arguing with someone else about something because I think someone can be arguing with someone else about what someone thinks is true for someone to be arguing with someone else about something. I think someone can be arguing with someone else about what someone thinks is true for someone to be arguing with someone else about something because I think someone can be arguing with someone else about the truth for someone to be arguing with someone else about what someone thinks is true, even though, I think someone has a choice of right or wrong for someone to be right or wrong to be arguing with someone else about the truth because I think someone may or may not be able to prove that something is true for someone to be right or wrong to be arguing with someone else about the truth, and therefore, I think someone can be wrong to be arguing with someone else about something that someone can not prove is true because I think someone can be arguing just for argument sakes with someone else about something that someone can not prove is true. I think someone can be arguing just for argument sakes with someone else about something that someone can not prove is true because I think someone can be argumentative with someone else about something that someone can not prove is true, even though, I think someone may not be able to be prove something is true for someone to be suspecting someone has done something wrong because I think someone may not be able to be prove someone has done something for someone to be suspecting that someone has done something wrong, however, I think someone can be wrong for someone doing something wrong, regardless if someone is not be able to be prove someone has done something wrong because I think someone could have done something wrong without someone being able to prove that someone has done something wrong, and therefore, I think someone will have to answer to God for someone doing something wrong, regardless if someone is not be able to be prove someone has done something wrong because I think God is aware of everything for God to be aware of everything that is true as I think God is aware of everything that is true for someone to be having to answer to God for someone doing something wrong, otherwise, I think someone can be right to be arguing with someone else about the truth because I think someone can be arguing with someone else about the truth within good reason for someone to be right to be arguing with someone else about the truth. I think someone can be arguing with someone else about the truth within good reason for someone to be right to be arguing with someone else about the truth because I think someone can be right to be arguing with someone else about the truth within good reason for someone to be right to be arguing with someone else about the truth. I think someone can be right to be arguing with someone else about the truth within good reason for someone to be right to be arguing with someone else about the truth because I think someone can be right about the truth for someone to be arguing with someone else about the truth within good reason. I think someone can be right about the truth for someone to be arguing with someone else about the truth within good reason because I think someone can be right to be arguing with someone else about the truth within good reason. I think someone can be right to be arguing with someone else about the truth within good reason because I think someone can disagree with someone else about something for someone to be right to be arguing with someone else about the truth within good reason. I think someone can disagree with someone else about something for someone to be right to be arguing with someone else about the truth within good reason because I think someone can be right about something that is true for someone to be right to be arguing with someone else about the truth within good reason. I think someone can be right about something that is true for someone to be right to be arguing with someone else about the truth within good reason because I think someone can prove something is true for someone to be right to be arguing with someone else about the truth within good reason.

If I think someone can be right about something that is true for someone to be right to be arguing with someone else about the truth within good reason, than I think someone can be right to be arguing with someone else about the truth within good reason because I think someone can be learning more about what someone thinks is true, from someone disagreeing with someone else about something for someone to be right to be arguing with someone else about the truth within good reason, even though, I think someone arguing about the truth with someone else is someone's preference, as to whether or not if someone chooses to be arguing about the truth with someone else because I think someone else may not be willing to listen to what someone thinks is true, from someone arguing with someone else about the truth within good reason, but I think someone can be right to be arguing with someone else about the truth within good reason because I think someone can be arguing about what someone thinks is true with someone else, without someone getting mad or upset with someone else for someone to be arguing with someone else about the truth within good reason. I think someone can be arguing about what someone thinks is true with someone else, without someone getting mad or upset with someone else for someone to be arguing with someone else about the truth within good reason because I think someone can explain, and prove what someone thinks is true for someone to be arguing with someone else about the truth within good reason, and therefore, I think someone can be right to be arguing with someone else about the truth within good reason because I think someone can be debating with someone else, as to what someone thinks is true, from someone arguing with someone else about the truth within good reason. I think someone can be debating with someone else, as to what someone thinks is true, from someone arguing with someone else about the truth within good reason because I think someone has a choice of right or wrong for someone to be right or wrong about what someone thinks is true, otherwise, I think someone can agree to disagree with someone else for arguments sakes because I think someone else may not agree with what someone thinks is true, even though, I think someone can argue with someone else about the truth within good reason because I think someone can be learning more about something that is true, from someone disagreeing with someone else about something that isn't true, and therefore, I think someone can be arguing about the truth because I think someone can be in favor of something that is true for someone to be arguing about the truth. If I think someone can be arguing about the truth, than I think someone may not care to be arguing with someone else about something because I think someone may not want to be explaining themselves over, and over again about something with someone else, and therefore, I think someone can choose to be arguing with someone else about something or not because I think someone arguing is someone's choice for someone to be choosing to be arguing with someone else about something or not, even though, I think someone can learn someone is right or wrong about something from someone arguing or debating with someone else about something because I think someone else can explain, and prove something is or isn't true for someone to be learning someone is right or wrong about something that someone thinks is or isn't true. If I think someone can learn someone is right or wrong about something from someone arguing or debating with someone else about something, than I think someone can play head games with someone else because I think someone can choose to be lying about something with someone else for someone to be playing head games with someone else, even though, I do not think has someone has to be playing head games with someone else because I think someone can choose to be honest about something with someone else for someone not to be playing heads games with someone else, and therefore, I think someone playing head games with someone else is someone's choice because I think someone can choose to be honest or dishonest about something with someone else for someone playing head games with someone else to be someone's choice. If I think someone playing head games with someone else is someone's choice, than I do not think someone can always be honest or dishonest about something because I think someone has a choice of right or wrong for someone not to always be honest or dishonest about something, however, I think God is always honest because I think God is always good, and right for God to always be honest, and therefore, I do not think God can be dishonest and lie because I think God is always good, and right for God not to be dishonest and lying.

If I do not think God can be dishonest and lie, than I think someone can be closed-minded because I think someone can be closed-minded about something for someone to be closed-minded. I think someone can be closed-minded about something for someone to be closed-minded because I think someone may not be willing to learn or think about something for someone to be closed-minded about something, and therefore, I think closed-mindedness is someone being closed-minded because I think closed-mindedness is someone not being willing to learn or think about something for someone to be closed-minded. If I think closed-mindedness is someone being closed-minded, than I think someone can be closed because I think someone can be closed-minded for someone to be closed, and therefore, I think someone can be closed-minded as I think someone can be closed because I think someone may not be willing to be sharing something with someone else for someone to be closed-minded as I think someone may not be willing to be sharing something with someone else for someone to be closed. If I think someone can be closed-minded as I think someone can be closed, than I think someone may not be willing to be sharing something with someone else because I think someone may not be willing to be giving something to someone else, or I think someone may not be willing to be saying something to someone else for someone not to be willing to be sharing something with someone else, and therefore, I think someone may not share what someone thinks with someone else because I think someone may not say something to someone else as I think someone else can try not to listen, and understand something that someone is saying to someone else for someone not to be sharing what someone thinks with someone else. If I think someone may not share what someone thinks with someone else, than I think someone else may not share what someone else thinks with someone for someone to be closed-minded about what someone else thinks because I think someone may not be willing to learn or think about what someone else thinks of something for someone to be closed-minded about what someone else thinks, and therefore, I think someone can be right or wrong with someone being closed-minded because I think someone has a choice of right or wrong for someone to be right or wrong with someone being closed-minded. I think someone has a choice of right or wrong for someone to be right or wrong with someone being closed-minded because I think someone can be right or wrong about something that someone is closed-minded about for someone to be right or wrong with someone being closed-minded, even though, I think someone can have a mental block because I think someone can be close-minded about something for someone to be having a mental block as I think someone may not be unable to learn or think about something for someone to be having a mental block about something, however, I think the best way in how someone can be relieved with someone having a mental block is someone asking God for someone to be thinking about something because I think God can open someone's mind with someone being able to be thinking more about something for someone to be overcoming someone's mental block with God.

If I think the best way in how someone can be relieved with someone having a mental block is someone asking God for someone to be thinking about something, than I think someone can be strong minded because I think someone can be firm about what someone thinks of something with themselves, and someone else for someone to be strong minded, and therefore, I think someone can be right or wrong with someone being strong minded because I think someone can be right or wrong about what someone firmly thinks of something with themselves, and someone else with someone having a choice of right or wrong for someone to be right or wrong with someone being strong minded. If I think someone can be right or wrong with someone being strong minded, than I think someone can have a peace of mind because I think someone can think of something that is good, and right for someone to be having a peace of mind, and therefore, I think there can be peace because I think someone can choose to be doing something that is good, and right to be getting along with someone else for there to be peace. If I think there can be peace, than I think someone can choose to be peaceful because I think someone can choose to be doing something that is good, and right for someone to be choosing to be peaceful, and therefore, I think someone can be peaceful because I think someone can choose to be peaceful as I think someone can be at peace with themselves for someone to be peaceful, however, I do not think someone is always peaceful because I think someone has a wrong choice with someone having a choice of right or wrong for someone not to always be peaceful, and therefore, I think someone can choose to be peaceful as I think someone choose not to be peaceful because I think someone can choose to be doing something right for someone to be peaceful as I think someone can choose to be doing something wrong for someone not to be peaceful. If I think someone can choose to be peaceful as I think someone choose not to be peaceful, than I think someone can think about the truth because I think someone can think about what is true for someone to be thinking about the truth. I think someone can think about what is true for someone to be thinking about the truth because I think someone can think about what is true for someone to be thinking about what the truth is in life as I think someone can think about what the truth is in life for someone to be thinking about the truth, and therefore, I think someone can have a peace of mind because I think someone thinking about the truth for someone to be having a peace of mind. I think someone thinking about the truth for someone to be having a peace of mind because I think someone can think about what the truth is in life for someone to be having a peace of mind. If I think someone thinking about the truth for someone to be having a peace of mind, than I think someone can be confusing about what someone thinks is true because I think someone can argue about what someone thinks is true, without someone actually thinking about what is true for someone to be confusing about what someone thinks is true, and therefore, I think someone can get caught up thinking about a lie for someone to be believing in a lie because I think someone can argue about what someone thinks is true, without someone actually thinking about what is true for someone to be believing in a lie as I think someone can argue about what someone thinks is true, without someone actually thinking about what is true for someone to be getting caught up thinking about a lie, even though, I do not think someone knows everything that is true because I do not think someone can prove everything that is true for someone not to be knowing everything that is true, however, I think someone can believe in the truth because I think someone can try to prove something is true for someone to be believing in the truth, otherwise, I think someone can be confused in getting caught up thinking about a lie as much as someone likes because I think a lie is someone's choice for someone can be confused in getting caught up thinking about a lie as much as someone likes, even though, I do not think someone can have a peace of mind with someone thinking about a lie as I think someone can have a peace of mind with someone thinking about the truth because I think a lie is something that is wrong, and not correct for someone not to be having a peace of mind with someone thinking about a lie as I think the truth is something that is always true, correct, and right for someone to be having a peace of mind with someone thinking about the truth.

If I do not think someone can have a peace of mind with someone thinking about a lie as I think someone can have a peace of mind with someone thinking about the truth, than I think someone can be open-minded because I think someone can be open-minded about something for someone to be open-minded. I think someone can be open-minded about something for someone to be open-minded because I think someone can be willing to learn or think about something for someone to be open-minded about something, and therefore, I think open-mindedness is someone being open-minded because I think open-mindedness is someone being willing to learn or think about something for someone to be open-minded. If I think open-mindedness is someone being open-minded, than I think someone can be open because I think someone can be open-minded for someone to be open, and therefore, I think someone can be open-minded as I think someone can be open because I think someone can be willing to be sharing something with someone else for someone to be open-minded as I think someone can be willing to be sharing something with someone else for someone to be open. If I think someone can be open-minded as I think someone can be open, than I think someone can be willing to be sharing something with someone else because I think someone can be willing to be giving something to someone else, or someone can be willing to be saying something to someone else for someone to be willing to be sharing something with someone else, and therefore, I think someone can share what someone thinks with someone else because I think someone can say something to someone else as I think someone else can try to listen, and understand something that someone is saying to someone else for someone to be sharing what someone else thinks with someone else. If I think someone can share what someone thinks with someone else, than I think someone can share what someone thinks with someone else for someone else to be open-minded about what someone thinks because I think someone else can be willing to learn or think about what someone thinks of something for someone else to be open-minded about what someone thinks, even though, I think someone can be right or wrong with someone being open-minded because I think someone can be right or wrong about something for someone to be right or wrong with someone being open-minded, however, I think God can help someone to be open-minded because I think God can help someone to be doing something that is good, and right with themselves, someone else, something, and God for God to be helping someone to be open-minded, and therefore, I think someone can be open-minded because I think God can help someone to be open-minded for someone to be open-minded. If I think someone can be open-minded, than I think God can help someone to be open-minded because I think God can help someone to be thinking about the truth with themselves, someone else, something, and God for God to be helping someone to be open-minded, and therefore, I think someone can be open-minded because I think God can help someone to be thinking about the truth with themselves, someone else, something, and God for someone to be open-minded. If I think someone can be open-minded, than I think God can help someone to be open-minded about something because I think God can help someone to be doing something that is good, and right with themselves, someone else, something, and God for God to be helping someone to be open-minded about something, and therefore, I think someone can be open-minded about something because I think God can help someone to be open-minded about something for someone to be open-minded about something.

If I think someone can be open-minded about something, than I think someone can change someone's mind because I think someone can change what someone thinks of themselves, someone else, something, and God in someone's mind for someone to be changing what someone thinks of themselves, someone else, something, and God as I think someone can change what someone thinks of themselves, someone else, something, and God for someone to be changing someone's mind, and therefore, I think someone can be right or wrong to be changing someone's mind because I think someone can be right or wrong to be changing what someone thinks of themselves, someone else, something, and God for someone to be right or wrong to be changing someone's mind. I think someone can be right or wrong to be changing what someone thinks of themselves, someone else, something, and God for someone to be right or wrong to be changing someone's mind because I think someone can be right or wrong to be changing someone's mind about what someone thinks of themselves, someone else, something, and God for someone to be right or wrong to be changing someone's mind, and therefore, I think someone can be right or wrong to be changing someone's mind about themselves, someone else, something, and God because I think someone can be right or wrong about what someone thinks of themselves, someone else, something, and God for someone to be right and wrong to be changing someone's mind about themselves, someone else, something, and God. I think someone can be right or wrong about what someone thinks of themselves, someone else, something, and God for someone to be right and wrong to be changing someone's mind about themselves, someone else, something, and God because I think someone can be right or wrong about themselves, someone else, something, and God for someone to be right or wrong to be changing someone's mind about themselves, someone else, something, and God as I think someone can be right or wrong about themselves, someone else, something, and God for someone to be right or wrong about what someone thinks of themselves, someone else, something, and God, and therefore, I think someone can be right or wrong to be changing someone's mind because I think someone can be right or wrong to be changing someone's mind about themselves, someone else, something, and God for someone to be right or wrong to be changing someone's mind. If I think someone can be right or wrong to be changing someone's mind, than I think someone can try to fix or change someone else because I think someone can make someone else to be doing something for someone to be trying to be fixing or changing someone else, even though, I do not think someone can fix or change someone else because I do not think someone is someone else for someone to be fixing or changing someone else as I think someone can do more harm than good with themselves, and someone else with someone trying to fix or change someone else, and therefore, I think someone can fix or change themselves because I think someone can choose to be doing something that is good, and right with themselves for someone not to be harming themselves as I think someone can choose to be doing something that is good, and right with themselves for someone to be fixing or changing themselves, even though, I think someone can try to change someone with someone trying to change someone else's mind because I think someone can try to persuade or talk someone into thinking about, and doing something for someone to be trying to change someone with someone trying to change someone else's mind, however, I think someone may not be able to change someone with someone trying to change someone else's mind because I think someone may not change what someone thinks of something in someone's mind for someone not to be able to change someone with someone trying to change someone else's mind. If I think someone may not be able to change someone with someone trying to change someone else's mind, than I think something can turn out to be not that important to someone because I think someone can realize or think someone can be wrong about what someone thought was important to someone, or I think someone can think something isn't as important as someone thought something was important to someone for something to be turning out to be not that important to someone, and therefore, I think someone can change someone's mind because I think something can turn out to be not that important to someone for someone to be changing someone's mind. If I think someone can change someone's mind, than I think someone can think something is import to someone because I think someone can choose to be doing something with themselves, someone else, something, and God for someone to be thinking something is important to someone, even though, I think someone can be right or wrong with someone thinking something is important to someone because I think someone can choose to be doing something that is right or wrong with themselves, someone else, something, and God for someone to be right or wrong with someone thinking something is important to someone, however, I think something can be important to someone because I think someone can choose to be doing something that is right with themselves, someone else, something, and God for someone to be thinking about doing something that is good, and right with themselves, someone else, something, and God as I think someone can think about doing something that is good, and right with themselves, someone else, something, and God for something to be important to someone. If I think something can be important to someone, than I think someone can have priorities because I think someone can think about how important someone can be doing something with themselves, someone else, something, and God, before someone can be doing something else with themselves, someone else, something, and God as I think someone can think about how much more important someone or something is compared to someone or something else for someone to be having priorities, and therefore, I think someone can take steps because I think someone can think about doing something that is good, and right with themselves, someone else, something, and God for someone thinking about how important someone can be doing something with themselves, someone else, something, and God as I think someone can think about how important someone can be doing something with themselves, someone else, something, and God for someone to be taking steps.

If I think someone can take steps, than I think someone can have patience because I think someone can be patient with themselves, someone else, and something for someone to be having patience. I think someone can be patient with themselves, someone else, and something for someone to be having patience because I think someone can be patient with themselves, someone else, and something for someone to be having patience with themselves, someone else, and something, and therefore, I think someone can be patient because I think someone can choose to be doing something with themselves, someone else, and something, without someone being irritated doing something with themselves, someone else, and something for someone to be patient. If I think someone can be patient, than I think someone can be impatient as I think someone can be patient because I think someone can have no patience doing something with themselves, someone else, and something for someone to be impatient as I think someone can have patience doing something with themselves, someone else, and something for someone to be patient, even though, I think impatient is someone's choice for someone to be impatient as I think patient is someone's choice for someone to be patient because I think someone can choose to be irritated doing something with themselves, someone else, and something for someone to be impatient as I think someone can choose not to be irritated doing something with themselves, someone else, and something for someone to be patient, and therefore, I think someone can be right or wrong with someone being patient or impatient because I think someone has a choice of right or wrong for someone to be right or wrong with someone being patient or impatient. I think someone has a choice of right or wrong for someone to be right or wrong with someone being patient or impatient because I think someone can be right or wrong with someone being patient or impatient. I think someone can be right or wrong with someone being patient or impatient because I think someone can be patient or impatient with someone choosing to be doing something that is right or wrong with themselves, someone else, and something for someone to be right or wrong with someone being patient or impatient.

If I think someone can be right or wrong with someone being patient or impatient, than I think someone can have tolerance because I think someone can be tolerating someone or something for someone to be having tolerance. I think someone can be tolerating someone or something for someone to be having tolerance because I think someone can be tolerating someone or something for someone to be tolerant, and therefore, I think someone can be tolerant because I think someone can accept how someone or something is in life that someone doesn't like for someone to be tolerant. If I think someone can be tolerant, than I think someone can be intolerant as I think someone can be tolerant because I think someone can choose not to accept how someone or something is in life that someone doesn't like for someone to be intolerant as I think someone can choose to accept how someone or something is in life that someone doesn't like for someone to be tolerant, even though, I think intolerance is someone's choice for someone to be intolerant as I think tolerance is someone's choice for someone to be tolerant because I think someone can choose not to be accepting how someone or something is in life that someone doesn't like for someone to be intolerant as I think someone can choose to be accepting how someone or something is in life that someone doesn't like for someone to be tolerant, and therefore, I think someone can be right or wrong with someone being tolerant or intolerant because I think someone has a choice of right or wrong for someone to be right or wrong with someone being tolerant or intolerant. I think someone has a choice of right or wrong for someone to be right or wrong with someone being tolerant or intolerant because I think someone can be right or wrong with someone being tolerant or intolerant. I think someone can be right or wrong with someone being tolerant or intolerant because I think someone can be right or wrong with someone accepting or not accepting how someone or something is in life that someone doesn't like for someone to be right or wrong with someone being tolerant or intolerant.

If I think someone can be right or wrong with someone being tolerant or intolerant, than I think someone can have patience for someone to be having tolerance because I think someone can be patient with someone or something for someone to be tolerating someone or something. I think someone can be patient with someone or something for someone to be tolerating someone or something because I do not think someone can tolerate someone or something, without someone being patient with someone or something for someone to be tolerating someone or something, even though, I think someone can be patient with someone or something, without someone tolerating someone or something because I think someone can choose to be accepting how someone or something is in life, without someone being irritated with how someone or something is in life for someone to be patient with someone or something, without someone tolerating someone or something, and therefore, I think someone can be patient with someone or something for someone to be tolerating someone or something because I think someone can accept how someone or something is in life, without someone being irritated with someone or something for someone to be tolerating how someone or something is in life, that someone doesn't like. I think someone can accept how someone or something is in life, without someone being irritated with someone or something for someone to be tolerating how someone or something is in life, that someone doesn't like because I think someone can tolerate how someone or something is in life, that someone doesn't like from someone accepting how someone or something is in life, without someone being irritated with how someone or something is in life. I think someone can tolerate how someone or something is in life, that someone doesn't like from someone accepting how someone or something is in life, without someone being irritated with how someone or something is in life because I think someone can have patience for someone to be having tolerance. If I think someone can have patience for someone to be having tolerance, than I think God can have patience and tolerance because I think God is always good, and right for God to be having patience and tolerance, and therefore, I think God has patience and tolerance because I think God created everything for God be accepting how everything is in life as I think God created everything for God to be having patience and tolerance with how everything is in life. If I think God has patience and tolerance, than I think God has the greatest patience and tolerance because I do not think God is interfering with how everything is in life for God to be accepting how everything is in life as I think God is accepting how everything is in life for God to be having the greatest patience and tolerance.

If I think God has the greatest patience and tolerance, than I think someone can be nice because I think someone can be good or bad with someone being nice. I think someone can be good or bad with someone being nice because I think someone can be right or wrong with someone being nice as I think someone can be good or bad with someone being nice. I think someone can be right or wrong with someone being nice as I think someone can be good or bad with someone being nice because I do not think someone is always right with someone being nice as I do not think someone is always good with someone being nice. I do not think someone is always right with someone being nice as I do not think someone is always good with someone being nice because I think someone has a choice of right or wrong for someone to be right or wrong with someone being nice as I think someone has a choice of right or wrong for someone to be good or bad with someone being nice. I think someone has a choice of right or wrong for someone to be right or wrong with someone being nice as I think someone has a choice of right or wrong for someone to be good or bad with someone being nice because I think someone can be right or wrong with someone being nice as I think someone can be good or bad with someone being nice. I think someone can be right or wrong with someone being nice as I think someone can be good or bad with someone being nice because I think someone can be right or wrong with someone being good or bad as I think someone can be right or wrong with someone being nice. I think someone can be right or wrong with someone being good or bad as I think someone can be right or wrong with someone being nice because I think someone can be honest or dishonest with someone being nice. I think someone can be honest or dishonest with someone being nice because I think someone has a choice of right or wrong for someone to be honest or dishonest with someone being nice. I think someone has a choice of right or wrong for someone to be honest or dishonest with someone being nice because I think someone can be right or wrong with someone being honest or dishonest as I think someone can be right or wrong with someone being nice. I think someone can be right or wrong with someone being honest or dishonest as I think someone can be right or wrong with someone being nice because I think someone can be good or bad with someone being honest or dishonest as I think someone can be good or bad with someone being nice, and therefore, I think someone can be good or bad with someone being honest or dishonest as I think someone can be right or wrong with someone being nice because I think someone can be honest and good about something with someone else for someone to be right with someone being nice as I think someone can be dishonest and bad about something with someone else for someone to be wrong with someone being nice. I think someone can be honest and good about something with someone else for someone to be right with someone being nice as I think someone can be dishonest and bad about something with someone else for someone to be wrong with someone being nice because I think someone can be honest and good with someone being nice as I think someone can be dishonest and bad with someone being nice, and therefore, I do not think someone can always trust someone being nice because I think someone can be dishonest and bad with someone being nice for someone not to be always trusting someone being nice, but I think someone can trust someone being nice because I think someone can be honest and good with someone being nice for someone to be trusting someone being nice.

If I think someone can trust someone being nice, than I think someone can earn someone's trust because I think someone can do something that is good, and right for someone for someone to be earning someone's trust, even though, I think someone can trust someone or not because I think someone can choose to be doing something that is right or wrong with themselves, and someone else for someone to be trusting someone or not, and therefore, I think someone can think someone can't trust anyone because I think someone can trust themselves for someone not to be trusting anyone, but how can someone be trusted if someone can't trust anyone? I do not think someone can be trusted if someone can't trust anyone because I do not think someone can trust themselves for someone to be trusting anyone as I do not think someone can be trusted for anyone to be trusting someone. I do not think someone can trust themselves for someone to be trusting anyone as I do not think someone can be trusted for anyone to be trusting someone because I do not think someone can trust anyone, without someone trusting themselves to be trusting anyone as I do not think someone can be trusted, without anyone trusting someone, and therefore, I do not think someone can be trusted as I do not think anyone can be trusted because I do not think someone can trust anyone for someone not to be trusted as I do not think someone can trust anyone for anyone not to be trusted. I do not think someone can trust anyone for someone not to be trusted as I do not think someone can trust anyone for anyone not to be trusted because I do not think someone can trust anyone for someone not to be trusting themselves as I do not think someone can trust anyone for anyone not to be trusting someone. I do not think someone can trust anyone for someone not to be trusting themselves as I do not think someone can trust anyone for anyone not to be trusting someone because I do not think someone can be trusted. I do not think someone can be trusted because I do not think someone can trust anyone for someone not to be trusting themselves as I do not think someone can trust anyone for someone not to be trusted, and therefore, I do not think someone can be trusted from someone not trusting anyone because I think someone can be doing something bad to anyone that someone doesn't trust, such as lying, cheating, and stealing for someone not to be trusted from someone not trusting anyone. If I do not think someone can be trusted from someone not trusting anyone, than I do not think someone can be trusting themselves from someone not trusting anyone as I do not think someone can be trusted from someone not trusting anyone because I do not think someone can trust themselves, without someone trusting anyone as I do not think someone can be trusted, without anyone trusting someone, however, I think someone can trust themselves for someone to be trusting anyone as I think someone can be trusted for anyone to be trusting someone because I think someone can earn anyone's trust for someone to be trusting themselves, and anyone as I think someone can earn anyone's trust for anyone to be trusting someone. I think someone can earn anyone's trust for someone to be trusting themselves, and anyone as I think someone can earn anyone's trust for anyone to be trusting someone because I do not think trust is something that is an automatic given for someone as I think trust is something that has to be given for someone to be having any trust, and therefore, I think trust is something that is a give and take for someone to be earning someone's trust because I think someone can do something that is good, and right for themselves, and someone else for someone to be earning someone's trust. If I think trust is something that is a give and take for someone to be earning someone's trust, than I think God is always nice for someone to be trusting God because I think God is always good, and right for someone to be trusting God as I think God is always good, and right for God to be always be nice, and therefore, I think God is always trustworthy for someone to always be trusting God because I think God is always good, and right for someone to always be trusting God as I think God is always good, and right for God to always be trustworthy.

If I think God is always trustworthy for someone to always be trusting God, than I think someone can be kind because I think someone can do something that is nice, and good for someone to be kind, and therefore, I think kindness is someone being kind because I think someone can do something that is nice, and good for someone else for kindness to be someone being kind. If I think kindness is someone being kind, than I think someone can be kind as I think someone can be kind for someone else because I think someone can do something that is nice, and good for someone to be kind as I think someone can do something that is nice, and good for someone else for someone to be kind for someone else, and therefore, I think kindness is someone's choice for someone to be kind because I think someone can choose to be kind or not for kindness to be someone's choice. I think someone can choose to be kind or not for kindness to be someone's choice because I think someone can be right or wrong with someone choosing to be kind or not, and therefore, I think someone has a choice of right or wrong for someone to be right or wrong with someone choosing to be kind or not because I think someone can be right or wrong with someone choosing to be kind or not. I think someone can be right or wrong with someone choosing to be kind or not because I think someone can be right or wrong with someone choosing to be doing something that is nice, and good for someone else or not for someone to be right or wrong with someone choosing to be kind or not, even though, I think someone can be good with someone being kind with someone else because I think someone can good with someone choosing to be doing something that is nice, and good for someone else for someone to be good with someone being kind with someone else. If I think someone can be good with someone being kind with someone else, than I think God can be kind because I think God is always good, and right for God to be kind, even though, I think God can choose to be kind or not because I think God can choose to be doing something that is nice, and good for someone or not for God to be choosing to be kind or not, however, I think God can be kind because I think God can choose to be doing something that is nice, and good for someone with God always being good, and right for God to be kind, and therefore, I think someone can be kind with God because I think someone can choose to be doing something that is nice, and good for God for someone to be kind with God.

If I think someone can be kind with God, than I think someone can be charitable because I think someone can good and nice to be helping someone else with someone choosing to be giving someone else something that someone else needs for someone to be charitable, and therefore, I think someone can give someone else someone's charity because I think someone choosing to be doing something that is nice and good for someone else for someone to be giving someone else someone's charity. If I think someone can give someone else someone's charity, than I do not think someone's charity is necessarily someone donating or giving someone else money because I think someone's charity is someone choosing to be doing something nice and good for someone else for someone's charity not to necessarily be someone donating or giving someone else money, and therefore, I think someone can be right or wrong with someone giving someone else someone's charity because I think someone can be right or wrong with someone choosing to be doing something nice and good for someone else for someone to be right or wrong with someone giving someone else someone's charity. If I think someone can be right or wrong with someone giving someone else someone's charity, than I think someone can choose to giving someone else someone's charity or not because I think someone has a choice of right or wrong for someone to be right or wrong with someone choosing to be giving someone else someone's charity or not, even though, I think someone's charity is an act of kindness for someone because I think someone can choose to be doing something nice and good for someone else for someone's charity to be an act of kindness for someone, and therefore, I think someone's charity is someone's act of kindness because I think someone can choose to be doing something nice and good for someone else for someone's charity to be someone's act of kindness. If I think someone's charity is someone's act of kindness, than I think someone can be virtuous because I think someone can think choose to be doing something that is good, and right with themselves, someone else, something, and God for someone to be virtuous, and therefore, I think someone can have virtues because I think someone can think choose to be doing something that is good, and right with themselves, someone else, something, and God for someone to be having virtues, even though, I think someone can be right or wrong with someone having virtues because I think someone can choose to be doing something that is right or wrong with themselves, someone else, something, and God for someone to be right or wrong with someone having virtues, however, I think someone can have good virtues because I think someone can think choose to be doing something that is good, and right with themselves, someone else, something, and God for someone to be having good virtues.

If I think someone can have good virtues, than I think someone can choose to be doing nothing about someone or something because I think someone has a choice of right or wrong for someone to be doing nothing about someone or something. I think someone has a choice of right or wrong for someone to be doing nothing about someone or something because I think someone is right or wrong for someone to be doing nothing about someone or something, and therefore, I think someone can be right or wrong with someone doing nothing about someone or something because I think someone may or may not be responsible for doing something with someone or something for someone to be right or wrong with someone doing nothing about someone or something. If I think someone can be right or wrong with someone doing nothing about someone or something, than I think someone can be apathetic because I think apathy is someone choosing not to be doing something with someone or something for someone to be apathetic. I think apathy is someone choosing not to be doing something with someone or something for someone to be apathetic because I think someone can choose not to be doing something with someone or something for someone to be choosing to be nothing with someone or something as I think someone can choose to be doing nothing with someone or something for someone to be apathetic, and therefore, I think apathy is someone's choice for someone to be apathetic because I think someone can choose to be apathetic or not for apathy to be someone's choice. I think someone can choose to be apathetic or not for apathy to be someone's choice because I think someone can be right or wrong with someone choosing to be apathetic or not, and therefore, I think someone has a choice of right or wrong for someone to be right or wrong with someone choosing to be apathetic or not because I think someone can be right or wrong with someone choosing to be apathetic or not. I think someone can be right or wrong with someone choosing to be apathetic or not because I think someone can be right or wrong with someone choosing to be doing nothing with someone, and something or not for someone to be right or wrong with someone choosing to be apathetic or not, even though, I think someone can be bad with someone being apathetic because I think someone can be wrong with someone choosing not doing something that is good, and right for someone to be bad with someone being apathetic.

If I think someone can be bad with someone being apathetic, than I think someone can be empathetic because I think empathy is someone choosing to relate to someone else about something for someone to be empathetic, and therefore, I think empathy is someone's choice for someone to be empathetic because I think someone can choose to be empathetic or not for empathy to be someone's choice. I think someone can choose to be empathetic or not for empathy to be someone's choice because I think someone can be right or wrong with someone choosing to be empathetic or not, and therefore, I think someone has a choice of right or wrong for someone to be right or wrong with someone choosing to be empathetic or not because I think someone can be right or wrong with someone choosing to be empathetic or not. I think someone can be right or wrong with someone choosing to be empathetic or not because I think someone can be right or wrong with someone choosing to be relating to someone else about something or not for someone to be right or wrong with someone choosing to be empathetic or not, even though, I think someone can be good with someone being empathetic for someone else because I think someone can good with someone relating to someone else about something for someone to be good with someone being empathetic for someone else. If I think someone can be good with someone being empathetic for someone else, than I think God can always be empathetic with someone because I think God is always aware of everything for God to always be empathetic with someone, even though, I think God can choose to be empathetic with someone or not because I think someone can choose to be relating to God about something or not for God to be choosing to be empathetic with someone or not. I think someone can choose to be relating to God about something or not for God to be choosing to be empathizing with someone or not because I think God is aware of everything for God to be relating to someone about something as I think God is aware of everything for someone to be choosing to be relating to God about something or not, however, I do not think someone can empathize with God because I do not think someone is aware of everything as I think God is aware of everything for someone not to be empathizing with God.

If I do not think someone can empathize with God, than I think someone can be sympathetic because I think sympathy is someone choosing to understand something about someone else for someone to be sympathetic, and therefore, I think sympathy is someone's choice for someone to be sympathetic because I think someone can choose to be sympathetic or not for sympathy to be someone's choice. I think someone can choose to be sympathetic or not for sympathy to be someone's choice because I think someone can be right or wrong with someone choosing to be sympathetic or not, and therefore, I think someone has a choice of right or wrong for someone to be right or wrong with someone choosing to be sympathetic or not because I think someone can be right or wrong with someone choosing to be sympathetic or not. I think someone can be right or wrong with someone choosing to be sympathetic or not because I think someone can be right or wrong with someone choosing to be understanding something about someone else or not for someone to be right or wrong with someone choosing to be sympathetic or not, even though, I think someone can be good with someone being sympathetic for someone else because I think someone can good with someone trying to understand something about someone else for someone to be good with someone being sympathetic for someone else.

If I think someone can be good with someone being sympathetic for someone else, than I think someone can have compassion because I think someone can have compassion for someone else for someone to be having compassion, and therefore, I think someone can have compassion for someone else because I think someone can choose to be sympathetic for someone else with someone trying to understand something about someone else for someone to be having compassion for someone else. If I think someone can have compassion for someone else, than I think someone can have compassion for someone else or not because I think someone can choose to be sympathetic for someone else or not for someone for someone to be having compassion for someone else or not, and therefore, I think someone has a choice of right or wrong for someone to be right or wrong with someone choosing to be having compassion for someone else or not because I think someone can be right or wrong with someone choosing to be having compassion for someone else or not. I think someone can be right or wrong with someone choosing to be having compassion for someone else or not because I think someone can be right or wrong with someone choosing to be sympathizing with someone else about something or not for someone to be right or wrong with someone choosing to be having compassion for someone else or not, even though, I think someone can be good with someone having compassion for someone else because I think someone can good with someone trying to understand something about someone else for someone to be good with someone having compassion for someone else. If I think someone can be good with someone having compassion for someone else, than I think God can always have sympathy, and compassion for someone because I think God is always aware of everything for God to always have sympathy, and compassion for someone, even though, I think God can choose to be sympathetic, and compassionate with someone or not because I think someone can choose to be relating to God about something or not for God to be choosing to be sympathetic, and compassionate with someone or not. I think someone can choose to be relating to God about something or not for God to be choosing to be sympathetic, and compassionate with someone or not because I think God is aware of everything for God to be understanding something about someone as I think God is aware of everything for someone to be choosing to be relating to God about something or not, however, I do not think someone can have sympathy, and compassion for God because I do not think someone is aware of everything as God is aware of everything for someone not to be having sympathy, and compassion for God.

If I do not think someone can have sympathy, and compassion for God, than I think someone can be right because I think someone can be right about something that someone thinks is true for someone to be right, however, I think someone can be self-righteous because I think someone can act as though someone is better than someone else for someone to be self-righteous, even though, I do not think someone is right for being self-righteous because I do not think someone is good, and right with someone acting as though someone is better than someone else, even if someone is right about something that someone thinks is true, and therefore, I think self-righteousness is someone's choice for someone to be self-righteous because I think someone can choose to be self-righteous or not for self-righteousness to be someone's choice. I think someone can choose to be self-righteous or not for self-righteousness to be someone's choice because I think someone has a choice of right or wrong for someone to be choosing to be self-righteous or not. I think someone has a choice of right or wrong for someone to be choosing to be self-righteous or not because I think someone can choose to be self-righteous or not for someone to be self-righteous or not, and therefore, I think someone can be self-righteous or not because I think someone can choose to acting as though someone is better than someone else for someone to be self-righteous as I think someone can choose not to be acting as though someone is better than someone else for someone not to be self-righteous, even though, I think someone can be good with someone not being self-righteous because I think someone can good with someone trying not to act as though someone is better than someone else for someone to be good with someone not being self-righteous.

If I think someone can be good with someone not being self-righteous, than I think someone can be righteous because I think someone can be good, and right, without someone acting as though someone is better than someone else for someone to be righteous, however, I think someone can have humility because I think someone can be humble for someone to be having humility, and therefore, I think someone can be humble because I think someone can be righteous for someone to be humble. I think someone can be righteous for someone to be humble because I think someone can act as though someone isn't better than someone else for someone to be humble, and therefore, I think humility is someone's choice for someone to be humble because I think someone can choose to be humble or not for humility to be someone's choice. I think someone can choose to be humble or not for humility to be someone's choice because I think someone has a choice of right or wrong for someone to be choosing to be humble or not. I think someone has a choice of right or wrong for someone to be choosing to be humble or not because I think someone can choose to be humble or not for someone to be humble or not, and therefore, I think someone can be humble or not because I think someone can choose not to be acting as though someone is better than someone else for someone to be humble as I think someone can choose to be acting as though someone is better than someone else for someone not to be humble, even though, I think someone can be good with someone being humble because I think someone can good with someone trying not to act as though someone is better than someone else for someone to be good with someone being humble. If I think someone can be good with someone being humble, than I think someone can be humble as I think someone can be righteous because I think someone can be good, and right for someone to be humble as I think someone can be good, and right for someone to be righteous. I think someone can be good, and right for someone to be humble as I think someone can be good, and right for someone to be righteous because I think someone can be righteous for someone to be humble, and therefore, I think God is always humble as I think God is always righteous because I think God is always good, and right for God to be humble as I think God is always good, and right for God to always be righteous. I think God is always good, and right for God to be humble as I think God is always good, and right for God to always be righteous because I think God is always righteous for God to be humble.

If I think God is always good, and right for God to be humble as I think God is always good, and right for God to always be righteous, than I think someone can be in denial because I think someone can be wrong about something that someone thinks is true for someone to be in denial, even though, I think someone can think someone isn't in denial because I think someone can think someone isn't wrong about something that someone thinks is true for someone to be thinking someone isn't in denial, and therefore, I think someone can be in denial or not because I think someone can be wrong about something that someone thinks is true for someone to be in denial as I think someone can prove that someone is right about something that someone thinks is true for someone not to be in denial, even though, I think someone can be in denial because I do not think someone can disprove that someone is wrong about something that someone thinks is true for someone to be in denial. If I think someone can be in denial, than I think someone that is in denial can be rationalizing and justifying for someone to thinking someone is not in denial, even though, I think someone that is rationalizing and justifying is in denial because I think someone that is rationalizing and justifying is someone that is making themselves out to be right about something for someone to be thinking someone is right with someone rationalizing and justifying, but I do not think someone is right just because someone thinks someone is right because I think someone can be wrong about something that someone thinks is true for someone not to be right just because someone thinks someone is right, and therefore, I think someone can be in denial, regardless of how much someone thinks someone is right with someone rationalizing and justifying because I think someone can be wrong about something that someone thinks is true for someone to be in denial. If I think someone can be in denial, than I think someone can be a right or wrong with someone being in denial because I think someone has a choice of right or wrong for someone to be right or wrong with someone being in denial, and therefore, I think someone can be a right or wrong to be in denial because I think someone can be in denial for the right or wrong reasons with someone having a choice of right or wrong for someone to be right or wrong to be in denial, even though, I think someone can be wrong to be in denial, regardless if someone is in denial for the right or wrong reasons because I think someone can be wrong about something that someone thinks is true for someone to be wrong to be in denial. If I think someone can be wrong to be in denial, than I think someone being in denial is a choice because I think someone being in denial is someone's choice to be in denial or not for someone being in denial to be a choice, and therefore, I think someone being in denial is someone's choice to be in denial or not for someone being in denial to be a choice because I think someone has a choice of right or wrong for someone to be in denial or not. I think someone has a choice of right or wrong for someone to be in denial or not because I think someone can choose to be in denial or not for someone to be in denial or not, and therefore, I think someone can be in denial or not because I think someone can be wrong about something that someone thinks is true for someone to be in denial as I think someone can be right about something that someone thinks is true for someone not to be in denial. If I think someone can be in denial or not, than I think someone can be in denial of the truth with what someone thinks is true because I think there can be inconsistencies with what someone thinks is true for someone to be in denial of the truth with what someone thinks is true, and therefore, I think the truth is someone's choice for someone to be accepting the truth or not because I think someone can be in denial of the truth for the truth to be someone's choice for someone to be accepting the truth or not. If I think the truth is someone's choice for someone to be accepting the truth or not, than I think denial can be a powerful state of mind for someone because I think someone can deny the truth for denial to be a powerful state of mind for someone, even though, I think someone can always be in denial because I think someone can always be wrong about something for someone to always be in denial, otherwise, I think someone would be perfect for someone to be never be in denial because I think someone would never be wrong about something for someone to never be in denial, however, I do not think someone is perfect for someone to be never be in denial because I think someone can be wrong about something for someone to be in denial, and therefore, I think someone can always be in denial because I think someone can always be wrong about something for someone to always be in denial. If I think someone can always be in denial, than I think denial can be a powerful state of mind for someone because I think someone can always be in denial for denial to be a powerful state of mind for someone, even though, I do not think someone has to be in denial for denial not to be a powerful state of mind for someone because I think someone can always try to do something that is good, and right for someone not to be in denial of something that someone can be wrong about with themselves, and therefore, I think someone can try not to be in denial because I think someone can always try to be better for someone to try not to be in denial.

If I think someone can try not to be in denial, than I think someone can make good or bad choices as I think someone can make right or wrong choices because I think someone can choose to be doing something that is right or wrong for someone to be making good or bad choices as I think someone can choose to be doing something that is right or wrong for someone to be making right or wrong choices, and therefore, I think someone can make good or bad decisions because I think someone can make good or bad choices for someone to be making good or bad decisions as I think someone can make right or wrong choices for someone to be making good or bad decisions. If I think someone can make good or bad decisions, than I do not think someone is capable of being insane because I think someone is consciously aware of any choices that someone is able to be thinking of making with someone's state of consciousness, regardless if someone is making any right or wrong choices, even though, I think someone can think someone can be insane because I think someone can think insanity is someone doing the same thing over and over again, and expecting different results, but I do not think someone doing the same thing over and over again, and expecting different results is insanity because I think someone doing the same thing over and over again, and expecting different results is someone being in denial. I think someone doing the same thing over and over again, and expecting different results is someone being in denial because I think someone is in denial of what someone is doing with someone doing the same thing over and over again, and expecting different results, otherwise, I think the only way in how someone can be insane is if someone can eliminate someone's state of consciousness because I do not think someone would be aware of anything with someone not having a state of consciousness for someone to be insane, even though, I do not think someone would be insane from someone eliminating someone's state of consciousness because I do not think everything that doesn't have a state of consciousness is insane, and therefore, I think there is no such thing as insanity because I do not think someone is capable of being insane for there to be such a thing as insanity. If I think there is no such thing as insanity, than I do not think someone is always consciously aware of someone making any right or wrong choices as I think someone is consciously aware of any choices someone can be thinking of making because I do not think someone is always interested, as to whether or not if someone is making any right or wrong choices as I think someone is consciously aware of any choices someone can be thinking of making, and therefore, I do not think someone is always consciously aware of someone doing something that is right or wrong as I think someone can choose to be consciously aware of someone doing something that is right or wrong because I think someone has a choice of right or wrong for someone to be choosing not to always consciously aware of someone doing something that is right or wrong as I think someone has a choice of right or wrong for someone to be choosing to be consciously aware of someone doing something that is right or wrong. I think someone has a choice of right or wrong for someone to be choosing not to always consciously aware of someone doing something that is right or wrong as I think someone has a choice of right or wrong for someone to be choosing to be consciously aware of someone doing something that is right or wrong because I think someone can choose to be doing something that is right or wrong for someone to be right or wrong, and therefore, I think someone has a state of consciousness for someone not to be insane because I do not think someone has to always be consciously aware of someone doing something that is right or wrong for someone not to be insane as I think someone can choose to be consciously aware of someone doing something that is right or wrong for someone not to be insane. If I think someone has a state of consciousness for someone not to be insane, than I think someone can be crazy because I think someone can do something wrong for someone to be crazy, and therefore, I think someone can think of someone crazy as someone being insane because I think someone can do something wrong for someone to be thinking of someone crazy as someone being insane, even though, I do not think someone can be insane because I think someone has a state of consciousness for someone not to be insane.

If I do not think someone can be insane, than I do not think addiction is something for someone to be addicted to something because I do not think something is right or wrong for someone to be addicted to something, and therefore, I think addiction is someone's choice for someone to be addicted to something because I think someone's addiction to something is something someone wants, but I do not think someone's addiction to something is something someone needs because I think someone's addiction to something is someone not wanting to let go of something someone wants, even though, I think there are consequences for someone's addiction because I do not think someone's addiction to something is something someone needs, however, I think someone can be addicted to something someone wants because I think someone can want something for someone to need, and become dependant on something someone wants, but I do not think someone's addiction to something is something someone needs because I think someone's addiction to something is something someone wants more than someone's addiction to something is something someone needs. I think someone's addiction to something is something someone wants more than someone's addiction to something is something someone needs because I think what someone needs is something someone can not live without, and I think what someone wants is something someone can live without, even though, I think someone can think addiction isn't someone's choice for someone to be addicted to something because I think someone can think someone is sick or ill to be doing something over, and over again to be harming themselves, and someone else for someone to think addiction isn't someone's choice, and I think someone can be addicted to something because I think someone is sick or ill to be doing something over, and over again to be harming themselves, and someone else for someone to be addicted to something, but I do not think something is right or wrong for someone to be addicted to something or not because I think someone can be right or wrong for someone to be addicted to something or not. I think someone can be right or wrong for someone to be addicted to something or not because I think someone has a choice of right or wrong for someone to be addicted to something or not, and therefore, I think addiction is someone's choice for someone to be addicted to be doing something as I think addiction is someone's choice for someone to be addicted to something because I think someone can choose to be doing something that is wrong with someone having a choice of right or wrong for someone to be addicted to be doing something as I think someone can choose something that is wrong with someone having a choice of right or wrong for someone to be addicted to something, even though, I think addiction is someone's choice for someone to be choosing to be addicted to be doing something or not as I think addiction is someone's choice for someone to be choosing to be addicted to something or not because I think someone can choose to be doing something that is right or wrong with someone having a choice of right or wrong for someone to be choosing to be addicted to be doing something or not as I think someone can choose something that is right or wrong with someone having a choice of right or wrong for someone to be choosing to be addicted to something or not, however, I think God can help someone to be overcoming someone's addiction because I think someone can ask God to help someone not to be acting out in someone's addiction for God to be helping someone to be overcoming someone's addiction. If I think God can help someone to be overcoming someone's addiction, than I think someone can choose to be healthy or sick because I think someone can choose to be doing something that is right or wrong with themselves, someone else, something, and God for someone to be choosing to be healthy or sick, even though, I think someone may not have a choice for someone to be choosing to be healthy or sick because I think someone may not be able to be doing something about something that can be wrong with someone for someone not to be having a choice for someone to be choosing to be healthy or sick, however, I think God can help someone to be healthy because I think God can help someone to be doing something is good, and right with themselves, someone else, something, and God for God to be helping someone to be healthy, and therefore, I think someone can choose to be healthy because I think God can help someone to be doing something is good, and right with themselves, someone else, something, and God for someone to be choosing to be doing something is good, and right with themselves, someone else, something, and God as I think someone can choose to be doing something is good, and right with themselves, someone else, something, and God for someone to be choosing to be healthy.

If I think someone can choose to be healthy, than can someone be addicted to everything? I think someone can be addicted to everything physically in life, but I do not think someone can be addicted to everything because I do not think someone can be addicted to the truth. I do not think someone can be addicted to the truth because I do not think someone can be wrong with someone thinking of the truth about something. I do not think someone can be wrong with someone thinking of the truth about something because I think the truth is always good, and right for someone to be thinking of the truth about something. I think the truth is always good, and right for someone to be thinking of the truth about something because I think the truth is something that is a fact of life for someone to be thinking of the truth about something as I think the truth is something that is a fact of life for the truth to always be good, and right, even though, I think the truth can be about something that someone doesn't want to be thinking about in life because I think the truth can be about something that isn't necessarily good for someone to be thinking about in life, but I think someone can think about the truth because I think the truth is always good, and right for someone to be thinking about the truth, and therefore, I do not think someone can be addicted to the truth because I do not think someone can be wrong with someone thinking about the truth for someone not to be addicted to the truth. If I do not think someone can be addicted to the truth, than I think someone can think someone can be addicted to the truth because I think someone can think someone can be wrong about what someone's thinks is the truth for someone to be addicted to the truth, even though, I think someone can be wrong about what someone's thinks is the truth for someone not to be addicted to the truth because I think the truth is always good, and right for someone not to be addicted to the truth, and therefore, I do not think someone can be addicted to the truth because I do not think there would be any hope what so ever at all for someone if someone is addicted to the truth, and I think someone would always be suffering, and I think there would only be chaos from there not being any hope what so ever at all for someone, but I think there is hope for someone because I do not think someone can be addicted to the truth for someone to be having hope, and therefore, I think there is hope because I think someone can think of something that is the truth for someone to be having hope. I think someone can think of something that is the truth for someone to be having hope because I think someone can think of something that is true for someone to be having hope, and therefore, I think the truth is a preventative to someone's addiction because I think the truth can prevent someone acting out in someone's addiction. I think the truth can prevent someone acting out in someone's addiction because I think someone can think of something that is true for someone to be having hope in someone not to be acting out in someone's addiction, and therefore, I do not think someone can be addicted to the truth because I think the truth is a preventative to someone's addiction. I think the truth is a preventative to someone's addiction because I think someone can think of the truth for someone not to be acting out in someone's addiction.

If I think the truth is a preventative to someone's addiction, than I do not think someone can be addicted to God because I think God ultimately represents what the truth is in life, and I do not think someone can be wrong with someone thinking of God as I do not think someone can be wrong with someone thinking of the truth, and therefore, I think God is one with the truth because I think God ultimately represents what the truth is in life for God to be one with the truth. If I think God is one with the truth, than I do not think someone can be addicted to the truth as I do not think someone can be addicted to God because I do not think someone is wrong for someone to be thinking of truth about what someone thinks of God. I do not think someone is wrong for someone to be thinking of truth about what someone thinks of God because I think God is always good, and right for someone to be thinking of God as I think the truth is always good, and right for someone to be thinking of the truth about something, and therefore, I think God is the truth as I think the truth is God because I think God is always good, and right for God to be the truth as I think the truth is always good, and right for the truth to be God. If I think God is the truth as I think the truth is God, than I think someone can think someone can be addicted to God because I think someone can think someone can be wrong about what someone's thinks of God for someone to be addicted to God, even though, I think someone can be wrong about what someone's thinks of God for someone not to be addicted to God because I think God is always good, and right for someone not to be addicted to God, and therefore, I do not think someone can be addicted to God because I do not think there would be any hope what so ever at all for someone if someone is addicted to God, but I think there is hope for someone because I do not think someone can be addicted to God for someone to be having hope, and therefore, I think there is hope because I think someone can think of God for someone to be having hope. If I think there is hope, than I think God is a preventative to someone's addiction because I think God can prevent someone acting out in someone's addiction. I think God can prevent someone acting out in someone's addiction because I think someone can think of God for someone to be having hope in someone not to be acting out in someone's addiction, and therefore, I do not think someone can be addicted to God because I think God is a preventative to someone's addiction. I think God is a preventative to someone's addiction because I think someone can think of God for someone not to be acting out in someone's addiction, and therefore, I think someone's addiction is someone's choice for someone to be addict to something or not because I think someone has a choice of right or wrong for someone to be addicted to something or not. I think someone has a choice of right or wrong for someone to be addicted to something or not because I think someone can choose to be addicted to something or not. I think someone can choose to be addicted to something or not because I think addiction is someone's choice for someone to be choosing to be addicted to something or not.

If I think someone can choose to be addicted to something or not, than I think someone can talk about God to someone else because I think someone can talk to someone else about what someone thinks of God. I think someone can talk to someone else about what someone thinks of God because I think someone can talk to someone else about what God is in life. I think someone can talk to someone else about what God is in life because I think someone can talk to someone else about how God is in relation to everything for someone to be talking to someone else about what God is in life, and therefore, I think someone can talk to someone else about how God is somehow able to be responsible for creating everything because I think someone can talk to someone else about how God is in relation to everything for someone to be able to be talking to someone else about how God is somehow able to be responsible for creating everything. If I think someone can talk to someone else about how God is somehow able to be responsible for creating everything, than I think someone can talk to someone else about whether or not if someone thinks God exists or not because I think someone can talk to someone else about how God is or isn't somehow able to be responsible everything for someone to be talking to someone else about whether or not if someone thinks God exists or not, and therefore, I think someone can talk to someone else about whether or not if someone thinks God is right or wrong because I think someone can talk to someone else about whether or not if someone thinks God is right or wrong about something with how God is somehow able to be responsible for creating everything. If I think someone can talk to someone else about whether or not if someone thinks God is right or wrong, than I think someone can talk to someone else about God because I think someone can speak for God as I think someone can talk about God to someone else. I think someone can speak for God as I think someone can talk about God to someone else because I think someone can talk to someone else about what God thinks is right or wrong. I think someone can talk to someone else about what God thinks is right or wrong because I think someone can think of what is right or wrong for someone to be talking to someone else about what God thinks is right or wrong. I think someone can think of what is right or wrong for someone to be talking to someone else about what God thinks is right or wrong because I think someone can think of what God thinks is right or wrong from what someone thinks is right or wrong. I think someone can think of what God thinks is right or wrong from what someone thinks is right or wrong because I think someone can think of what someone thinks is right or wrong for someone to be thinking of what God thinks is right or wrong, and therefore, I think someone can talk to someone else about what God thinks is right or wrong because I think someone can speak for God about what God thinks is right or wrong.

I think someone can speak for God about what God thinks is right or wrong because I think someone can think of what someone thinks is right or wrong for someone to be speaking for God about what God thinks is right or wrong, and therefore, I think someone can speak for God as I think someone can speak for someone else because I think someone has a choice of right or wrong for someone to be speaking for God as I think someone has a choice of right or wrong for someone to be speaking for someone else. I think someone has a choice of right or wrong for someone to be speaking for God as I think someone has a choice of right or wrong for someone to be speaking for someone else because I think someone can be right or wrong for someone to be speaking for God as I think someone can be right or wrong for someone to be speaking for someone else. I think someone can be right or wrong for someone to be speaking for God as I think someone can be right or wrong for someone to be speaking for someone else because I think someone can be right or wrong about what God thinks for someone to be right or wrong for someone to be speaking for God as I think someone can be right or wrong about what someone else thinks for someone to be right or wrong for someone to be speaking for someone else. I think someone can be right or wrong about what God thinks for someone to be right or wrong for someone to be speaking for God as I think someone can be right or wrong about what someone else thinks for someone to be right or wrong for someone to be speaking for someone else because I think someone can be right or wrong about what someone thinks of God for someone to be right or wrong about what God thinks as I think someone can be right or wrong about what someone thinks of someone else for someone to be right or wrong about what someone else thinks, even though, I think someone can speak for God as I think someone can speak for someone else because I think someone can think of what someone thinks is right or wrong for someone to be speaking for God about what God thinks is right or wrong as I think someone can think of what someone thinks is right or wrong for someone to be speaking for someone else about what someone else thinks is right or wrong. I think someone can think of what someone thinks is right or wrong for someone to be speaking for God about what God thinks is right or wrong as I think someone can think of what someone thinks is right or wrong for someone to be speaking for someone else about what someone else thinks is right or wrong because I think someone can think of what God thinks is right or wrong for someone to be speaking for God as I think someone can think of what someone else thinks is right or wrong for someone to be speaking for someone else, and therefore, I think someone can speak for God because I think someone can think of what God thinks is right or wrong for someone to be speaking for God. I think someone can think of what God thinks is right or wrong for someone to be speaking for God because I think someone can think of what someone thinks is right or wrong for someone to be speaking for God as I think someone can think of what someone thinks is right or wrong for someone to be thinking of what God thinks is right or wrong, even though, I do not think someone can speak as though someone is God because I do not think someone is God for someone to be speaking as though someone is God, however, I think someone can speak for God because I think God can speak through someone for someone to be speaking for God.

I think God can speak through someone for someone to be speaking for God because I think God can speak through someone for someone to be representing God as I think someone can speak for God for someone to be representing God. I think God can speak through someone for someone to be representing God as I think someone can speak for God for someone to be representing God because I think someone can represent God for someone to be a representative of God, and therefore, I think someone can be messenger of God as I think someone can be representative of God because I think someone can be a representative of God for someone to be a messenger of God, even though, I think someone can be a messenger of God because I think someone can speak for God for someone to be a messenger of God as I think God can speak through someone for someone to be a messenger of God. If I think someone can be a messenger of God, than I think someone can think of what God's thoughts are in life for someone to be a messenger of God because I think someone's thoughts is of God's thoughts for someone to be a messenger of God as I think someone's thoughts is of God's thoughts for someone to be thinking of what God's thoughts are in life, and therefore, I think someone can think of what God's thoughts are in life for someone to be a messenger of God because I think someone can think of what someone's thoughts are in life for someone to be a messenger of God as I think someone can think of what someone's thoughts are in life for someone to be thinking of what God's thoughts are in life, even though, I do not think someone knows what God's thinks because I do not think someone is God for someone to be knowing what God thinks, however, I think someone can be a messenger of God because I think someone can think of what God's thoughts are in life for someone to be a messenger of God. I think someone can think of what God's thoughts are in life for someone to be a messenger of God because I think someone can think of what God thinks is right or wrong for someone to be a messenger of God. I think someone can think of what God thinks is right or wrong for someone to be a messenger of God because I think someone can think of what someone thinks is right or wrong for someone to be thinking of what God thinks is right or wrong as I think someone can think of what someone thinks is right or wrong for someone to be a messenger of God, and therefore, I think someone can be a messenger of God because I think someone can think of what God's thoughts are in life for someone to be thinking of what God thinks as I think someone can think of what God thinks for someone to be a messenger of God. If I think someone can be a messenger of God, than I think everyone can be a messenger of God because I think everyone can think of what God's thoughts are in life for everyone to be a messenger of God. I think everyone can think of what God's thoughts are in life for everyone to be a messenger of God because I think everyone can think of what God thinks is right or wrong for everyone to be a messenger of God. I think everyone can think of what God thinks is right or wrong for everyone to be a messenger of God because I think everyone can think of what everyone thinks is right or wrong for everyone to be thinking of what God thinks is right or wrong as I think everyone can think of what everyone thinks is right or wrong for everyone to be a messenger of God, and therefore, I think everyone can be a messenger of God because I think everyone can think of what God's thoughts are in life for everyone to be thinking of what God thinks as I think everyone can think of what God thinks for everyone to be a messenger of God. If I think everyone can be a messenger of God, than I think someone can be a messenger of God because I think God can speak through someone about what the truth or a lie is in life as I think God can speak through someone about what is right or wrong. I think God can speak through someone about what the truth or a lie is in life as I think God can speak through someone about what is right or wrong because I think someone can think of what the truth or a lie is in life for God to be speaking through someone about what the truth or a lie is in life as I think someone can think of what is right or wrong for God to be speaking through someone about what is right or wrong, and therefore, I think someone can think of what is right or wrong for someone to be thinking of what the truth or a lie is in life because I think someone has a choice of right or wrong for someone to be thinking of what the truth or a lie is in life. I think someone has a choice of right or wrong for someone to be thinking of what the truth or a lie is in life is in life because I think someone can choose to be thinking of what the truth or a lie is in life for someone to be right or wrong. I think someone can choose to be thinking of what the truth or a lie is in life for someone to be right or wrong because I think someone can be right or wrong for someone to be thinking of what the truth or a lie is in life, and therefore, I think someone can choose the truth or a lie for someone to be right or wrong because I think someone can be right or wrong for someone to be choosing the truth or a lie.

Chapter 20

Someone's beliefs

I would like to talk about how dimensions are in life in relation to what dimensions are in life by talking about someone's beliefs, that can possibly have something to do with how dimensions are in life is in relation to what dimensions are in life because I think someone's beliefs is of the dimension of someone's thoughts for someone to be having any beliefs. I think someone's beliefs is of the dimension of someone's thoughts for someone to be having any beliefs because I think the dimension of someone's thoughts is what someone thinks for someone to be having any beliefs, and therefore, I think someone's thoughts is someone's beliefs as I think someone's beliefs is someone's thoughts because I think someone's thoughts is what someone thinks as I think someone's beliefs is what someone thinks. I think someone's thoughts is what someone thinks as I think someone's beliefs is what someone thinks because I think what someone thinks is what someone's thoughts are in life as I think what someone thinks is what someone's beliefs are in life. I think what someone thinks is what someone's thoughts are in life as I think what someone thinks is what someone's beliefs are in life because I think what someone's beliefs are in life is what someone's thoughts are in life as I think what someone's thoughts are in life is what someone's beliefs are in life. I think what someone's beliefs are in life is what someone's thoughts are in life as I think what someone's thoughts are in life is what someone's beliefs are in life because I think someone thinks of what someone's thoughts are in life as I think someone thinks of what someone's beliefs are in life, and therefore, I think someone thinks of what someone's thoughts are in life for someone to be thinking of what someone's beliefs are life because I think someone thinks of what someone's beliefs are in life as I think someone thinks of what someone's thoughts are in life. I think someone thinks of what someone's beliefs are in life as I think someone thinks of what thoughts are in life because I think someone's thoughts is what someone's beliefs are in life as I think what someone's beliefs are in life is someone's thoughts.

If I think someone thinks of what someone's beliefs are in life as I think someone thinks of what thoughts are in life, than I think someone's beliefs is what someone believes as I think what someone believes is someone's beliefs because I think what someone's beliefs are in life is what someone's believes as I think what someone believes is what someone's beliefs are in life. I think what someone's beliefs are in life is what someone's believes as I think what someone believes is what someone's beliefs are in life because I think someone believes in what someone's beliefs are life as I think someone believes in what someone believes. I think someone believes in what someone's beliefs are life as I think someone believes in what someone believes because I think someone's beliefs is what someone believes as I think what someone believes is someone's beliefs. If I think someone believes in what someone's beliefs are life as I think someone believes in what someone believes, than I think someone's thoughts is what someone believes as I think what someone believes is someone's thoughts because I think what someone thinks is someone's thoughts as I think what someone thinks is what someone believes. I think what someone thinks is someone's thoughts as I think what someone thinks is what someone believes because I think what someone thinks is what someone's thoughts are in life as I think what someone thinks is what someone believes. I think what someone thinks is what someone's thoughts are in life as I think what someone thinks is what someone believes because I think what someone believes is what someone's thoughts are in life as I think what someone's thoughts are in life is what someone believes. I think what someone believes is what someone's thoughts are in life as I think what someone's thoughts are in life is what someone believes because I think someone thinks of what someone's thoughts are in life as I think someone thinks of what someone believes, and therefore, I think someone thinks of what someone's thoughts are in life for someone to be thinking of what someone believes because I think someone thinks of what someone believes as I think someone believes in what someone's thinks. I think someone thinks of what someone believes as I think someone believes in what someone's thinks because I think someone's thoughts is what someone believes as I think what someone believes is someone's thoughts.

If I think someone's thoughts is what someone believes as I think what someone believes is someone's thoughts, than I think someone's thoughts is someone's beliefs as I think someone's thoughts is what someone believes because I think someone's beliefs is of someone's thoughts as I think what someone believes is of someone's thoughts. I think someone's beliefs is of someone's thoughts as I think what someone believes is of someone's thoughts because I think someone thinks of what someone's beliefs are in life as I think someone thinks of what someone believes. I think someone thinks of what someone's beliefs are in life as I think someone thinks of what someone believes because I think what someone thinks is what someone's beliefs are in life as I think what someone thinks is what someone believes. I think what someone thinks is what someone's beliefs are in life as I think what someone thinks is what someone believes because I think someone's thoughts is someone's beliefs as I think someone's thoughts is what someone believes, and therefore, I think someone's beliefs is something as I think someone's thoughts is something because I think someone's beliefs is someone's thoughts as I think someone's thoughts is something. I think someone's beliefs is someone's thoughts as I think someone's thoughts is something because I think someone's beliefs is of someone's thoughts as I think someone's thoughts is of something. I think someone's beliefs is of someone's thoughts as I think someone's thoughts is of something because I think someone thinks of what someone's beliefs are life as I think someone thinks of something. I think someone thinks of what someone's beliefs are life as I think someone thinks of something because I think someone's beliefs is of something as I think someone's thoughts is of something. I think someone's beliefs is of something as I think someone's thoughts is of something because I think someone's beliefs is of someone thinking of something as I think someone's thoughts is of someone thinking of something, and therefore, I think someone's beliefs can be right or wrong as I think someone's thoughts can be right or wrong because I think someone's beliefs is of someone thinking of something that is right or wrong for someone's beliefs to be right or wrong as I think someone's thoughts is of someone thinking of something that is right or wrong for someone's thoughts to be right or wrong. I think someone's beliefs is of someone thinking of something that is right or wrong for someone's beliefs to be right or wrong as I think someone's thoughts is of someone thinking of something that is right or wrong for someone's thoughts to be right or wrong because I think someone's beliefs is of someone thinking of something as I think someone can be thinking of something that is right or wrong, and therefore, I think someone can choose someone's beliefs in something that is right or wrong as I think someone can choose to think of something that is right or wrong because I think what someone thinks is what someone's beliefs are in life as I think someone can think of something that is right or wrong. If I think what someone thinks is what someone's beliefs are in life as I think someone can think of something that is right or wrong, than I think someone's thoughts is someone's beliefs as I think what someone's thoughts are in life is what someone's beliefs are in life because I think someone would have to think of something for someone to be thinking of what someone's beliefs are in life as I think what someone's beliefs are in life is of someone thinking of something.

If I think someone's thoughts is someone's beliefs as I think what someone's thoughts are in life is what someone's beliefs are in life, than I think what someone believes is something as I think someone's thoughts is something because I think what someone believes is someone's thoughts as I think someone's thoughts is something. I think what someone believes is someone's thoughts as I think someone's thoughts is something because I think what someone believes is of someone's thoughts as I think someone's thoughts is of something. I think what someone believes is of someone's thoughts as I think someone's thoughts is of something because I think someone thinks of what someone believes as I think someone thinks of something. I think someone thinks of what someone believes as I think someone thinks of something because I think what someone believes is of something as I think someone's thoughts is of something. I think what someone believes is of something as I think someone's thoughts is of something because I think what someone believes is of someone thinking of something as I think someone's thoughts is of someone thinking of something, and therefore, I think what someone believes can be right or wrong as I think someone's thoughts can be right or wrong because I think what someone believes is of someone thinking of something that is right or wrong for what someone believes to be right or wrong as I think someone's thoughts is of someone thinking of something that is right or wrong for someone's thoughts to be right or wrong. I think what someone believes is of someone thinking of something that is right or wrong for what someone believes to be right or wrong as I think someone's thoughts is of someone thinking of something that is right or wrong for someone's thoughts to be right or wrong because I think what someone believes is of someone thinking of something as I think someone can be thinking of something that is right or wrong, and therefore, I think someone can choose to believe in something that is right or wrong as I think someone can choose to think of something that is right or wrong because I think what someone thinks is what someone believes as I think someone can think of something that is right or wrong, even though, I think someone can think what someone thinks is something that is completely separate from what someone believes because I think someone can think what someone thinks is different than what someone believes, but I do not think what someone thinks is something that is completely separate from what someone believes because I do not think someone can think of what someone believes, without someone actually thinking of something for someone to be thinking of what someone believes, and therefore, I think someone's thoughts is what someone believes as I think what someone's thinks is what someone believes because I think someone would have to think of something for someone to be thinking of what someone believes as I think what someone believes is of someone thinking of something.

If I think someone's thoughts is what someone believes as I think what someone's thinks is what someone believes, than I think someone's beliefs is of someone believing in something that is good or bad because I think someone has a choice of right or wrong for someone's beliefs to be of someone believing in something that is good or bad, and therefore, I think someone can believe in something that is good or bad because I think someone can think of something that is good or bad for someone to be believing in something that is good or bad. If I think someone can think of something that is good or bad for someone to be believing in something that is good or bad, than I think someone can believe in something that is good or bad for someone to be good or bad because I think someone can be good or bad from someone to be believing in something that is good or bad. I think someone can be good or bad from someone to be believing in something that is good or bad because I think someone can think of something that is good or bad for someone to be believing in something that is good or bad as I think someone can think of something that is good or bad for someone to be good or bad, and therefore, I think someone can believe in something that is good or bad for someone to be good or bad because I think someone can be good or bad from someone thinking of something that is good or bad. If I think someone can believe in something that is good or bad for someone to be good or bad, than I think someone can think of something, without someone believing in something because I think someone can think something isn't true for someone not to be believing in something, and therefore, I think someone can believe in something that is or isn't true because I think someone can believe in something that is true or false for someone to believe in something that is or isn't true. I think someone can believe in something that is true or false for someone to believe in something that is or isn't true because I think someone can think of something that is true or false for someone to believe in something that is or isn't true, and therefore, I think someone can believe in the truth or a lie because I think someone can believe in something that is the truth or a lie for someone to believe in the truth or a lie. I think someone can believe in something that is the truth or a lie for someone to believe in the truth or a lie because I think someone can think of something that is the truth or a lie for someone to believe in the truth or a lie, and therefore, I think someone can believe in the truth or a lie because I think someone can believe in something that is true or false for someone to believe in the truth or a lie. If I think someone can believe in the truth or a lie, than I think someone's theories is what someone possibly thinks is true because I think someone's theories isn't always true for someone's theories to be what someone possibly thinks is true, and therefore, I think someone can believe in someone's theories because I think someone can believe in what someone possibly thinks is true for someone to be believing in someone's theories.

If I think someone can believe in someone's theories, than I think someone can believe in symbolism because I think someone can symbolically believe in something for someone to believe in symbolism, and therefore, I think someone can believe in symbols as I think someone can believe in symbolism because I think someone can believe that something represents something else for someone to believe in symbols as I think someone can believe that something represents something else for someone to believe in symbolism, even though, I do not think something is something else for something to be representing something else as I think someone can believe that something represents something else for someone to believe in symbols because I do not think something is the same as something else for something to be representing something else as I think someone can think something represents something else for someone to believe in symbols, and therefore, I think someone can believe in symbols or not because I do not think something is something else for someone to be believing in symbols or not. If I think someone can believe in symbols or not, than I think an example of how I do not think something is something else for someone to be believing in symbols or not can be the color red because I think someone can think the color red represents death for someone to be thinking of the color red as being a symbol of death, even though, I do not think the color red is death as I think someone can think the color red is death from someone thinking of the color red as being a symbol of death because I do not think the color red is death for someone to be believing that the color red is or isn't a symbol of death, and therefore, I do not think something is something else for someone to be believing in symbols or not because I think something is someone's choice for someone to be thinking of something as being a symbol of something else or not. I think something is someone's choice for someone to be thinking of something as being a symbol of something else or not because I think someone can believe in something as being a symbol or not as I think someone can believe in symbols or not, and therefore, I think symbols is someone's preference for someone to be believing in symbols or not because I think symbols is neither right or wrong for someone to be believing in symbols or not, even though, I think someone can live with symbols to be representing what someone thinks something is in life because I think any language can consist of numbers, letters, and symbols that can be apart of making up any word, in which someone can possibly be able to be speaking, reading, and writing that can represent what someone thinks something is in life for someone to be living with symbols to be representing what someone thinks something is in life.

If I think someone can live with symbols to be representing what someone thinks something is in life, than I think someone's morals and values can be someone's beliefs because I think someone's morals and values is what someone believes for someone's morals and values to be someone's beliefs. I think someone's morals and values is what someone believes for someone's morals and values to be someone's beliefs because I think someone's morals and values is what someone believes is right or wrong as I think someone's beliefs is what someone believes is right or wrong, and therefore, I think someone's morals and values can be right or wrong as I think someone's beliefs can be right or wrong because I think someone can believe in something that is right or wrong for someone's morals and values to be right or wrong as I think someone can believe in something that is right or wrong for someone's beliefs to be right or wrong. I think someone can believe in something that is right or wrong for someone's morals and values to be right or wrong as I think someone can believe in something that is right or wrong for someone's beliefs to be right or wrong because I think someone can think of something that is right or wrong for someone's morals and values to be right or wrong as I think someone can think of something that is right or wrong for someone's beliefs to be right or wrong, and therefore, I think someone's morals and values can be right or wrong as I think someone's beliefs can be right or wrong because I think someone can believe something is right or wrong for someone's morals and values to be right or wrong as I think someone can believe something is right or wrong for someone's beliefs to be right or wrong. I think someone can believe something is right or wrong for someone's morals and values to be right or wrong as I think someone can believe something is right or wrong for someone's beliefs to be right or wrong because I think someone can think something is right or wrong for someone's morals and values to be right or wrong as I think someone can think something is right or wrong for someone's beliefs to be right or wrong, and therefore, I think someone's morals and values is someone's beliefs because I think someone's morals and values is what someone thinks is right or wrong for someone's morals and values to be someone's beliefs. If I think someone's morals and values can be someone's beliefs, than I think someone can have good or bad morals and values because I think someone can think something is right or wrong for someone to be having good or bad morals and values, and therefore, I think someone can good or bad with someone's morals and values because I think someone can be right or wrong about what someone thinks of something for someone to be good or bad with someone's morals and values. If I think someone can good or bad with someone's morals and values, than I think someone can good or bad with someone's beliefs as I think someone can good or bad with someone's morals and values because I think someone can be right or wrong about what someone thinks of something for someone to be good or bad with someone's beliefs as I think someone can be right or wrong about what someone thinks of something for someone to be good or bad with someone's morals and values, and therefore, I think someone can good or bad with what someone believes as I think someone can good or bad with someone's beliefs because I think someone can be right or wrong about what someone thinks of something for someone to be good or bad with what someone's believes as I think someone can be right or wrong about what someone thinks of something for someone to be good or bad with someone's beliefs.

If I think someone can good or bad with what someone believes as I think someone can good or bad with someone's beliefs, than I think philosophy can be someone's beliefs because I think philosophy is what someone believes for someone's philosophy to be someone's beliefs. I think someone's philosophy is what someone believes for someone's philosophy to be someone's beliefs because I think someone's philosophy is what someone believes is right or wrong as I think someone's beliefs is what someone believes is right or wrong, and therefore, I think someone's philosophy can be right or wrong as I think someone's beliefs can be right or wrong because I think someone can believe in something that is right or wrong for someone's philosophy to be right or wrong as I think someone can believe in something that is right or wrong for someone's beliefs to be right or wrong. I think someone can believe in something that is right or wrong for someone's philosophy to be right or wrong as I think someone can believe in something that is right or wrong for someone's beliefs to be right or wrong because I think someone can think of something that is right or wrong for someone's philosophy to be right or wrong as I think someone can think of something that is right or wrong for someone's beliefs to be right or wrong, and therefore, I think someone's philosophy can be right or wrong as I think someone's beliefs can be right or wrong because I think someone can believe something is right or wrong for someone's philosophy to be right or wrong as I think someone can believe something is right or wrong for someone's beliefs to be right or wrong. I think someone can believe something is right or wrong for someone's philosophy to be right or wrong as I think someone can believe something is right or wrong for someone's beliefs to be right or wrong because I think someone can think something is right or wrong for someone's philosophy to be right or wrong as I think someone can think something is right or wrong for someone's beliefs to be right or wrong, and therefore, I think someone's philosophy is someone's beliefs because I think someone's philosophy is what someone thinks is right or wrong for someone's philosophy to be someone's beliefs. If I think someone's philosophy is someone's beliefs, than I think someone can have a good or bad philosophy because I think someone can think something is right or wrong for someone to be having a good or bad philosophy, and therefore, I think someone can good or bad with someone's philosophy because I think someone can be right or wrong about what someone thinks of something for someone to be good or bad with someone's philosophy. I think someone can be right or wrong about what someone thinks of something for someone to be good or bad with someone's philosophy because I think someone can be right or wrong about what someone thinks of something for someone to be good or bad with someone's beliefs as I think someone can be right or wrong about what someone thinks of something for someone to be good or bad with someone's philosophy, and therefore, I think someone's philosophy is someone's beliefs because I think someone's philosophy is what someone believes for someone's philosophy to be someone's beliefs. If I think someone's philosophy is someone's beliefs, than I think the greatest philosophical question that someone can ask is where did everything come from in life?, and therefore, I do not think someone can think of philosophy, without someone thinking of God because I think everything is created by God for someone to be philosophizing about everything.

If I do not think someone can think of philosophy, without someone thinking of God, than I think someone can meditate because I think someone can close their eyes, and deeply think of nothing for someone to be meditating, and therefore, I think someone can meditate about nothing for someone to be meditating because I think someone can think of nothing for someone to be meditating, even though, I do not think someone has to think of nothing for someone to be meditating because I think someone is thinking of something when someone is thinking of nothing for someone to be meditating about something. I think someone is thinking of something when someone is thinking of nothing for someone to be meditating about something because I think nothing is something for someone to be meditating about something, and therefore, I think someone is always meditating because I think someone is always thinking of something for someone to always be meditating. I think someone is always thinking of something for someone to always be meditating because I think someone meditating is someone is thinking of something for someone to always be meditating, and therefore, I think someone can meditate about something because I think someone can think about something for someone to be meditating about something. If I think someone can meditate about something, than I do not think there has to be any set conditions for someone to be meditating, and I do not think someone has to close their eyes, and deeply think of something for someone to be meditating because I think someone is meditating when someone is thinking about something. and therefore, I think someone can meditate about something that is right or wrong because I think someone can think about something that is right or wrong for someone to be mediating about something that is right or wrong, even though, I think someone can be right or wrong about what someone is meditating about in life because I think someone can be right or wrong about what someone is thinking about in life with someone having a choice of right or wrong for someone to be right or wrong about what someone is meditating about in life. If I think someone can be right or wrong about what someone is meditating about in life, than I think someone can think about doing something that is right or wrong with themselves, someone else, something, and God because I think someone can choose to be doing something that is right or wrong with themselves, someone else, something, and God for someone's thoughts in someone's mind to be of someone choosing to be doing something that is right or wrong with themselves, someone else, something, and God as I think someone's thoughts in someone's mind is of someone choosing to be doing something that is right or wrong with themselves, someone else, something, and God for someone to be thinking about doing something that is right or wrong with themselves, someone else, something, and God, and therefore, I think someone's thoughts in someone's mind is a copy of someone choosing to be doing something that is right or wrong with themselves, someone else, something, and God because I think someone's thoughts in someone's mind is of someone choosing to be doing something that is right or wrong with themselves, someone else, something, and God for someone's thoughts in someone's mind to be a copy of someone choosing to be doing something that is right or wrong with themselves, someone else, something, and God. If I think someone's thoughts in someone's mind is a copy of someone choosing to be doing something that is right or wrong with themselves, someone else, something, and God, than I think someone can think about doing something that is good or bad with themselves, someone else, something, and God because I think someone can think about doing something that is right or wrong with themselves, someone else, something, and God for someone to be thinking about doing something that is good or bad with themselves, someone else, something, and God, and therefore, I think someone's thought or idea is something that can be good or bad because I think someone can choose to be doing something that is good or bad about what someone thinks as I think someone can think about doing something that is good or bad with themselves, someone else, something, and God for someone's thought or idea to be something that can be good or bad. If I think someone's thought or idea is something that can be good or bad, than I think someone can meditate about doing something that is right or wrong with themselves, someone else, something, and God because I think someone can think about doing something that is right or wrong with themselves, someone else, something, and God for someone to be mediating about doing something that is right or wrong with themselves, someone else, something, and God, and therefore, I think someone can meditate in doing something that is right or wrong with themselves, someone else, something, and God because I think someone plan to be doing something that is right or wrong from someone thinking about doing something that is right or wrong with themselves, someone else, something, and God for someone to be meditating in doing something that is right or wrong with themselves, someone else, something, and God, even though, I think someone can be right or wrong about what someone is meditating about in life because I think someone can be right or wrong about what someone is thinking about in life for someone to be right or wrong about what someone is meditating about in life. If I think someone can be right or wrong about what someone is meditating about in life, than I think meditation is what someone thinks because I think someone can think about what someone thinks of themselves, someone else, something, and God for meditation to be what someone thinks, and therefore, I think someone is always meditating because I think someone can think about what someone thinks of themselves, someone else, something, and God for someone to always be thinking about something as I think someone is always thinking about something for someone to be always be meditating.

I think someone can think about what someone thinks of themselves, someone else, something, and God for someone to always be thinking about something as I think someone is always thinking about something for someone to be always be meditating because I think meditation is someone thinking about what someone thinks of themselves, someone else, something, and God for meditation to be someone thinking about something as I think mediation is someone thinking about something for someone to be meditating, and therefore, I think someone can believe in mediation because I think meditation is someone thinking about something for someone to be believing in meditation. I think meditation is someone thinking about something for someone to be believing in meditation because I think someone is always thinking about something for someone to be believing in meditating, and therefore, I think meditation can be someone's beliefs because I think someone can believe in what someone is thinking about in life for meditation to be someone's beliefs, and therefore, I think someone can believe in meditation because I think meditation is what someone is thinking about in life as I think someone can believe in what someone is thinking about in life for someone to be believing in meditation. If I think someone can believe in meditation, than I think someone can believe in what someone is meditating about in life because I think someone can believe in what someone is thinking about in life for someone to be believing in what someone is meditating about in life, and therefore, I think someone can believe in meditation because I think someone can believe in what someone is meditating about in life for someone to be believing in meditation. If I think someone can believe in meditation, than I think someone can believe in someone's meditation as I think someone can believe in meditation because I think someone can believe in meditation for someone to believe in someone's meditation, and therefore, I think someone's meditation can be someone's beliefs because I think someone can believe in what someone is thinking about in life for someone's meditation to be someone's beliefs. If I think someone's meditation can be someone's beliefs, than I think someone can believe in someone's meditation because I think someone can believe in what someone is meditating about in life for someone to be believing in someone's meditation as I think someone can believe in what someone is thinking about in life for someone to be believing in someone's meditation. I think someone can believe in what someone is meditating about in life for someone to be believing in someone's meditation as I think someone can believe in what someone is thinking about in life for someone to be believing in someone's meditation because I think someone can think about what someone is thinking about in life for someone to be believing in someone's meditation, and therefore, I think someone can believe in someone's meditation because I think someone's meditation is what someone thinks for someone to be believing in someone' meditation as I think someone's meditation is what someone is thinking about in life for someone to be believing in someone' meditation. I think someone's meditation is what someone thinks for someone to be believing in someone' meditation as I think someone's meditation is what someone is thinking about in life for someone to be believing in someone' meditation because I think someone is always thinking about something for someone to be believing in meditation as I think someone is always thinking about something for someone to be believing in someone's meditation. I think someone is always thinking about something for someone to be believing in meditation as I think someone is always thinking about something for someone to be believing in someone's meditation because I think someone can believe in meditation for someone to believe in someone's meditation.

If I think someone is always thinking about something for someone to be believing in meditation as I think someone is always thinking about something for someone to be believing in someone's meditation, than I think someone's meditation can be someone's beliefs because I think someone's meditation is what someone believes for someone's meditation to be someone's beliefs. I think someone's meditation is what someone believes for someone's meditation to be someone's beliefs because I think someone's meditation is what someone believes is right or wrong as I think someone's beliefs is what someone believes is right or wrong, and therefore, I think someone's meditation can be right or wrong as I think someone's beliefs can be right or wrong because I think someone can believe in something that is right or wrong for someone's meditation to be right or wrong as I think someone can believe in something that is right or wrong for someone's beliefs to be right or wrong. I think someone can believe in something that is right or wrong for someone's meditation to be right or wrong as I think someone can believe in something that is right or wrong for someone's beliefs to be right or wrong because I think someone can think of something that is right or wrong for someone's meditation to be right or wrong as I think someone can think of something that is right or wrong for someone's beliefs to be right or wrong, and therefore, I think someone's meditation can be right or wrong as I think someone's beliefs can be right or wrong because I think someone can believe something is right or wrong for someone's meditation to be right or wrong as I think someone can believe something is right or wrong for someone's beliefs to be right or wrong. I think someone can believe something is right or wrong for someone's meditation to be right or wrong as I think someone can believe something is right or wrong for someone's beliefs to be right or wrong because I think someone can think something is right or wrong for someone's meditation to be right or wrong as I think someone can think something is right or wrong for someone's beliefs to be right or wrong, and therefore, I think someone's meditation is someone's beliefs because I think someone's meditation is what someone thinks is right or wrong for someone's meditation to be someone's beliefs. If I think someone's meditation is someone's beliefs, than I think someone's meditation can be good or bad because I think someone can think something is right or wrong for someone's meditation to be good or bad, and therefore, I think someone can good or bad with someone's meditation because I think someone can be right or wrong about what someone thinks of something for someone to be good or bad with someone's meditation. I think someone can be right or wrong about what someone thinks of something for someone to be good or bad with someone's meditation because I think someone can be right or wrong about what someone thinks of something for someone to be good or bad with someone's beliefs as I think someone can be right or wrong about what someone thinks of something for someone to be good or bad with someone's meditation, and therefore, I think someone's meditation is someone's beliefs because I think someone's meditation is what someone believes for someone's meditation to be someone's beliefs.

If I think someone's meditation is someone's beliefs, than I think someone can be good from someone meditating about the truth because I think the truth is something that is always good, correct, and right for someone to be good from someone meditating about the truth. I think the truth is something that is always good, correct, and right for someone to be good from someone meditating about the truth because I think someone can think about the truth for someone to be good, and right, and therefore, I think the truth is always good, and right for someone to be meditating about the truth because I think someone can think about the truth for someone to be good, and right. If I think the truth is always good, and right for someone to be meditating about the truth, than I think God is the greatest meditation that someone can be meditating about in life because I think someone can be good from someone to be meditating about God. I think someone can be good from someone to be meditating about God because I think God is always good, and right for someone to be meditating about God. I think God is always good, and right for someone to be meditating about God because I think someone can think about God for someone to be good, and right, and therefore, I think God is the greatest meditation that someone can be meditating about in life because I think God is always good, and right for someone to be meditating about God.

If I think God is the greatest meditation that someone can be meditating about in life, than I think someone can be enlightened because I think enlightenment is someone realizing that something is right or wrong, from someone thinking about something that is right or wrong for someone to be enlightened, and therefore, I think someone can be enlightened from someone meditating because I think someone can be enlightened from someone thinking about something that is right or wrong for someone to be enlightened from someone meditating. I think someone can be enlightened from someone thinking about something that is right or wrong for someone to be enlightened from someone meditating because I think someone can think about something that is right or wrong for someone to be meditating as I think someone can think about something that is right or wrong for someone to be enlightened from someone meditating, and therefore, I think someone can believe in enlightenment as I think someone can believe in meditation because I think someone can think of something that is right or wrong for someone to be believing in enlightenment as I think someone can think of something that is right or wrong for someone to be believing in meditation. I think someone can think of something that is right or wrong for someone to be believing in enlightenment as I think someone can think of something that is right or wrong for someone to be believing in meditation because I think someone can realize that something is right or wrong, from someone thinking about something that is right or wrong for someone to be believing in enlightenment as I think someone can realize that something is right or wrong, from someone thinking about something that is right or wrong for someone to be believing in meditation, and therefore, I think someone can be enlightened as I think someone can meditate because I think enlightenment is someone thinking about something that is right or wrong for someone to be enlightened as I think meditation is someone thinking about something that is right or wrong for someone to be meditating. If I think someone can be enlightened as I think someone can meditate, than I think enlightenment can be someone's beliefs as I think meditation can be someone's beliefs because I think someone can believe in enlightenment for enlightenment to be someone's beliefs as I think someone can believe in meditation for meditation to be someone's beliefs. If I think enlightenment can be someone's beliefs as I think meditation can be someone's beliefs, than I think God is the greatest realization for someone to be enlightened because I think someone realizing that God exists is the greatest realization for God to be the greatest realization for someone to be enlightened, and therefore, I think someone can be enlightened for someone to be at peace with themselves because I think someone can be enlightened with someone thinking of something that is good, and right, such as someone thinking about how God can help someone in someone's life for someone to be at peace with themselves.

If I think someone can be enlightened for someone to be at peace with themselves, than I think fate can be someone's beliefs because I think someone can believe in fate for fate to be someone's beliefs, and therefore, I think someone can believe in fate because I think someone can believe in predestination for someone to be believing in fate. I think someone can believe in predestination for someone to be believing in fate because I think someone can believe that something can happen, before something happens for someone to be believing in fate, even though, I do not think something can always happen, before something happens because I think everything is randomly happening for a reason for something not to always happen, before something happens, however, I think someone can believe in fate as I think someone can believe in predestination because I think someone can believe that everything is planned to happen, before everything happens for someone to believing in fate, even though, I do not think everything is planned to happen, before everything happens because I think everything is randomly happening for a reason for everything not to be planned to happen, before everything happens, and therefore, I think fate is someone's choice for someone to be believing in fate or not because I think someone can choose to believe that everything is planned to happen, before everything happens or not for someone to be believing in fate or not. If I think fate is someone's choice for someone to be believing in fate or not, than I think someone can believe in pre-destiny as I think someone can believe in fate because I think someone can think something is predestined to happen for someone to be believing in pre-destiny as I think someone can think something is predestined to happen for someone to be believing in fate, even though, I do not think something is predestined to happen because I do not think everything is planned to happen, before everything happens as I think everything is randomly happening for a reason for something not to be predestined to happen, however, I think someone can believe in fate as I think someone can believe in someone's or something's fate because I think someone can think something good or bad can happen to someone or something before, and after something good or bad can happen to someone or something for be believing in fate as I think someone can think something good or bad can happen to someone or something before, and after something good or bad can happen to someone or something for be believing in someone's or something's fate, and therefore, I think someone can believe in fate because I think someone can think something good or bad that can happen to someone or something is predestined to happen to someone or something for someone to be believing in fate, even though, I do not think something good or bad that can happen to someone or something is predestined to happen to someone or something because I think something good or bad that can happen to someone or something would have to be planned to happen, before something happens for something good or bad that can happen to someone or something to be predestined to happen to someone or something, and therefore, I do not think something good or bad that can happen to someone or something is planned to happen, before something happens for something good or bad that can happen to someone or something not to be predestined to happen to someone or something because I think everything is randomly happening for a reason for everything not to be planned to happen, before everything happens as I do not think everything is planned to happen, before everything happens for something good or bad that can happen to someone or something not to be predestined to happen to someone or something. If I do not think everything is planned to happen, before everything happens for something good or bad that can happen to someone or something not to be predestined to happen to someone or something, than I do not think something is predestined to happen for everything to be predestined to happen because I think everything is randomly happening for a reason for everything not to be predestined to happen, however, I think someone can believe in destiny as I think someone can believe in fate because I think someone can think something is inevitable, and meant to happen for someone to be believing in destiny as I think someone can think something is inevitable, and meant to happen for someone to be believing in fate, and therefore, I think someone can choose to be believing in destiny or not as I think someone can choose to be believing in destiny or not because I think someone can think something is inevitable, and meant to happen or not for someone to be choosing to be believing in destiny or not as I think someone can think something is inevitable, and meant to happen or not for someone to be choosing to be believing in fate or not, even though, I do not think something is necessarily always inevitable, and meant to happen because I think someone can choose to be doing something for something not to necessarily always be inevitable, and meant to happen as I think someone can choose to be doing something for something not to necessarily be someone's destiny to happen to someone.

If I do not think something is necessarily always inevitable, and meant to happen, than I think something that someone likes or dislikes to be doing can be someone's beliefs because I think someone can believe in something that someone likes or dislikes to be doing for something that someone likes or dislikes to be doing to be someone's beliefs. I think someone can believe in something that someone likes or dislikes to be doing for something that someone likes or dislikes to be doing to be someone's beliefs because I think someone can enjoy something that someone likes or dislikes to be doing for someone to be believing in something that someone likes or dislikes to be doing. I think someone can enjoy something that someone likes or dislikes to be doing for someone to be believing in something that someone likes or dislikes to be doing because I do not think someone can believe in something that someone likes or dislikes to be doing, without someone enjoying something that someone likes or dislikes to be doing, and therefore, I think someone can believe in something that someone likes or dislikes to be doing because I think someone can enjoy something that someone likes or dislikes to be doing for someone to be believing in something that someone likes or dislikes to be doing. I think someone can enjoy something that someone likes or dislikes to be doing for someone to be believing in something that someone likes or dislikes to be doing because I think someone can think of something as being good or bad for someone to be believing in something that someone likes or dislikes to be doing as I think someone can think of something as being good or bad for someone to be enjoying something that someone likes or dislikes to be doing, even though, I think someone can be right or wrong for someone to be believing in something that someone likes or dislikes to be doing as I think someone can be right or wrong for someone to be enjoying something that someone likes or dislikes to be doing because I think something can be good or bad for someone to be believing in something that someone likes or dislikes to be doing as I think something can be good or bad for someone to be enjoying something that someone likes or dislikes to be doing, and therefore, I think something that someone likes or dislikes to be doing can be someone's beliefs because I think someone can enjoy something that someone likes or dislikes to be doing for something that someone likes or dislikes to be doing to be someone's beliefs.

If I think something that someone likes or dislikes to be doing can be someone's beliefs, than I think someone's faith can be someone's beliefs because I think someone can have faith in what someone believes for someone's faith to be someone's beliefs. I think someone can have faith in what someone believes for someone's faith to be someone's beliefs because I think someone can believe in what someone believes for someone to have faith in what someone believes. I think someone can believe in what someone believes for someone to have faith in what someone believes because I think someone can believe in themselves, someone else, something, and God for someone to be having faith in themselves, someone else, something, and God. I think someone can believe in themselves, someone else, something, and God for someone to be having faith in themselves, someone else, something, and God because I think someone can have faith in themselves, someone else, something, and God as I think someone can believe in themselves, someone else, something, and God, and therefore, I think someone can be right or wrong with someone having faith in themselves, someone else, something, and God as I think someone can be right or wrong with someone believing in themselves, someone else, something, and God because I think someone can be right or wrong about what someone thinks of themselves, someone else, something, and God for someone to be right or wrong with someone having faith in themselves, someone else, something, and God as I think someone can be right or wrong about what someone thinks of themselves, someone else, something, and God for someone to be right or wrong with someone believing in themselves, someone else, something, and God. If I think someone can be right or wrong with someone having faith in themselves, someone else, something, and God as I think someone can be right or wrong with someone believing in themselves, someone else, something, and God, than I think someone can choose to have faith in themselves, someone else, something, and God or not as I think someone can choose to believe in themselves, someone else, something, and God or not because I think someone can be right or wrong about what someone thinks of themselves, someone else, something, and God for someone to be choosing to be having faith in themselves, someone else, something, and God or not as I think someone can be right or wrong about what someone thinks of themselves, someone else, something, and God for someone to be choosing to be believing in themselves, someone else, something, and God or not, and therefore, I think someone can have faith in themselves, someone else, something, and God or not as I think someone can believe in themselves, someone else, something, and God or not because I think someone can believe in themselves, someone else, something, and God or not for someone to be having faith in themselves, someone else, something, and God or not, even though, I think someone can have faith in themselves, someone else, something, and God as I think someone can believe in themselves, someone else, something, and God because I think someone can believe in themselves, someone else, something, and God for someone to be having faith in themselves, someone else, something, and God.

If I think someone can believe in themselves, someone else, something, and God for someone to be having faith in themselves, someone else, something, and God, than I think someone can believe in themselves, someone else, something, and God for someone to be having faith in themselves, someone else, something, and God because I think someone's faith is what someone thinks is right or wrong as I think someone's beliefs is what someone thinks is right or wrong. I think someone's faith is what someone thinks is right or wrong as I think someone's beliefs is what someone thinks is right or wrong because I think someone can have faith in what someone thinks is right or wrong for someone's faith to be what someone thinks is right or wrong as I think someone can believe in what someone thinks is right or wrong for someone's beliefs to be what someone thinks is right or wrong, and therefore, I think someone's morals and values, and someone's philosophy, and someone's meditation, and someone's beliefs, and someone's faith, and someone's thoughts is relatively the same because I think someone's morals and values, and someone's philosophy, and someone's meditation, and someone's beliefs, and someone's faith is what someone thinks is right or wrong as I think someone can be right or wrong about what someone thinks for someone's morals, and values, and someone's philosophy, and someone's meditation, and someone's beliefs, and someone's faith, and someone's thoughts to relatively be the same, even though, I think someone's faith is what someone thinks as I think someone's beliefs is what someone thinks because I think someone can have faith in what someone thinks for someone's faith to be what someone thinks as I think someone can believe in what someone thinks for someone's beliefs to be what someone thinks. If I think someone's faith is what someone thinks as I think someone's beliefs is what someone thinks, than I think what someone thinks is what someone's faith is in life as I think what someone thinks is what someone's beliefs are in life because I think what someone thinks is what someone believes for someone to be having faith in what someone's beliefs are in life, and therefore, I think someone can think of what someone's beliefs are in life for someone to be having faith in what someone believes because I think someone can think of what someone believes for someone to be having faith in someone's beliefs. If I think someone can think of what someone's beliefs are in life for someone to be having faith in what someone believes, than I think someone can have faith in someone's beliefs for someone's faith to be what someone believes because I think someone can believe in what someone believes for someone to be having faith in someone's beliefs, and therefore, I think someone's faith is someone's beliefs because I think what someone's believes is what someone's faith is in life for someone's faith to be someone's beliefs. If I think someone's faith is someone's beliefs, than I think someone has faith as I think someone has beliefs because I think someone can believe in what someone believes for someone to be having faith as I think someone can believe in what someone believes for someone to be having beliefs.

If I think someone has faith as I think someone has beliefs, than I think someone can accept themselves, someone else, something, and God or not for acceptance to be someone's choice because I think acceptance is someone's choice for someone to be accepting themselves, someone else, something, and God or not as I think acceptance is someone's choice for someone to be choosing themselves, someone else, something, and God or not, and therefore, I think someone can accept themselves, someone else, something, and God because I think someone can accept themselves, someone else, something, and God or not for someone to be accepting themselves, someone else, something, and God. If I think someone can accept themselves, someone else, something, and God, than I think acceptance is someone's acceptance because I think someone's acceptance is someone's acceptance of themselves, someone else, something, and God for acceptance to be someone's acceptance, and therefore, I think someone's acceptance is someone's acceptance of themselves, someone else, something, and God because I think someone accepting themselves, someone else, something, and God or not is someone's acceptance of themselves, someone else, something, and God for someone's acceptance to be someone's acceptance of themselves, someone else, something, and God. I think someone accepting themselves, someone else, something, and God or not is someone's acceptance of themselves, someone else, something, and God for someone's acceptance to be someone's acceptance of themselves, someone else, something, and God because I think someone can accept themselves, someone else, something, and God or not for someone to be accepting themselves, someone else, something, and God, and therefore, I think someone can accept themselves, someone else, something, and God or not because I think someone can think someone, something, and God has done something that is acceptable or unacceptable for someone to be thinking of themselves, someone else, something, and God as being acceptable or unacceptable as I think someone can think of themselves, someone else, something, and God as being acceptable or unacceptable for someone to be accepting themselves, someone else, something, and God or not. If I think someone can accept themselves, someone else, something, and God or not, than I think someone can be right or wrong for someone to be accepting themselves, someone else, something, and God or not because I think someone has a choice of right or wrong for someone to be accepting themselves, someone else, something, and God or not, and therefore, I think someone can accept themselves, someone else, something, and God or not because I think someone can be right or wrong about themselves, someone else, something, and God for someone to be accepting themselves, someone else, something, and God or not. If I think someone can accept themselves, someone else, something, and God or not, than I think someone can have faith and believe in themselves, someone else, something, and God or not as I think someone can accept themselves, someone else, something, and God or not because I think someone can have faith and believe in themselves, someone else, something, and God or not from someone can accepting themselves, someone else, something, and God or not. I think someone can have faith and believe in themselves, someone else, something, and God or not from someone can accepting themselves, someone else, something, and God or not because I think someone can accept themselves, someone else, something, and God or not for someone to be having faith and to be believing in themselves, someone else, something, and God or not. I think someone can accept themselves, someone else, something, and God or not for someone to be having faith and to be believing in themselves, someone else, something, and God or not because I think someone having faith and believing in themselves, someone else, something, and God or not is someone accepting themselves, someone else, something, and God or not, and therefore, I think someone can have faith and believe in themselves, someone else, something, and God or not as I think someone can accept themselves, someone else, something, and God or not because I think someone can accept themselves, someone else, something, and God or not for someone to be having faith and to be believing in themselves, someone else, something, and God or not.

If I think someone can have faith and believe in themselves, someone else, something, and God or not as I think someone can accept themselves, someone else, something, and God or not, than I think someone can ask themselves what someone believes because I think someone can believe in themselves, someone else, something, and God for someone to be asking themselves what someone believes, and therefore, I think someone can ask themselves who someone believes because I think someone can believe in someone for someone to be asking themselves who someone believes. If I think someone can ask themselves who someone believes, than I think someone can ask themselves if someone believes in God or not because I think someone either believes in God or not for someone to be asking themselves if someone believes in God or not. I think someone either believes in God or not for someone to be asking themselves if someone believes in God or not because I think someone can believe in God or not, even though, I think someone can think of God because I think someone is of God for someone to be thinking of God as I think someone's thoughts is of God's thoughts for someone to be thinking of God, and therefore, I think someone can believing in God or not because I think someone is of God for someone to be believing in God or not as I think someone's thoughts is of God's thoughts for someone to be believing in God or not, even though, I think someone can believe and have faith in God because I do not think there is any proof that everything is a creation of itself for someone not to be believing and having faith in God, and therefore, I think everything is proof that someone can believe and have faith in God because I think everything is of God's creation for someone to be believing and having faith in God, even though, I think someone can believe and have faith in themselves, someone else, and something as I think someone can believe and have faith in God because I think someone, and something is of God's creation for someone to be believing and having faith in themselves, someone else, and something as I think someone, and something is of God's creation for someone to be believing and having faith in God. If I think someone can believe and have faith in themselves, someone else, and something as I think someone can believe and have faith in God, than I think someone can believe and have faith in someone's thoughts because I think someone can believe and have faith in someone's thoughts of anything for someone to be believing and having faith in someone's thoughts, and therefore, I think someone can believe and have faith in anything because I think someone's thoughts can be of anything that is something for someone to be believing and having faith in anything. If I think someone can believe and have faith in anything, than I think someone can believe and have faith in everything because I think everything is created by God for someone to be believing and having faith in everything, even though, I do not think someone can believe and have faith in everything because I do not think someone can possibly experience everything for someone to be believing and having faith in everything as I think someone can choose to believe and have faith in themselves, someone else, something, and God or not for someone not to be believing and having faith in everything, however, I think someone can believe and have faith in everything as I think someone can believe and have faith in God because I think someone can believe that God created everything for someone to be believing and having faith in everything as I think someone can believe that God created everything for someone to be believing and having faith in God, and therefore, I think someone's beliefs is infinite as I think everything is infinite because I think someone can believe and have faith that God created everything to be infinite with God being infinite for someone to believe and have faith in everything that is infinite as I think someone can believe and have faith in everything that is infinite for someone's beliefs to be infinite.

If I think someone's beliefs is infinite as I think everything is infinite, than I think someone can deny God as much as someone wants to deny God because I think God is someone's choice for someone to be denying God as much as someone wants to deny God, but I do not think someone would be alive, regardless of how much someone wants to be denying God because I do not think there is such a thing as nothingness for someone not to be created from nothingness as I do not think someone is created from nothingness for someone to be alive, and therefore, I think someone is created by God for someone to be alive because I think someone's life is God's choice for someone to be alive as I think everything is God's choice for everything to be created. If I think someone is created by God for someone to be alive, than I think someone can choose to be accepting God or not because I think someone can choose to be accepting that God exists or not for someone to be choosing to be accepting God or not, even though, I think strongly think God does exist because I do not think God is going anywhere, regardless of how much someone chooses not to be accepting that God exists, and therefore, I think someone can choose to be accepting that God exists or not because I do not think everything is a creation of itself for God not to exist. If I do not think everything is a creation of itself for God not to exist, than I think God does exist because I think everything is a creation of God for God to exist, and therefore, I think someone can choose to be accepting God or not because I think God does exist for someone to be choosing to be accepting God or not. If I think someone can choose to be accepting God or not, than I think God is waiting for someone to be accepting, believing, and having faith in God because I do not think God is going anywhere for God to be waiting for someone to be accepting, believing, and having faith in God, and therefore, I think someone can be like God from someone accepting God because I think someone good, and right like God is good, and right from someone accepting God, even though, I do not think someone can be God from someone accepting God because I do not think someone is God for someone to be God from someone accepting God.

If I do not think someone can be God from someone accepting God, than I think someone can believe and have faith in God because I think everything is created by God for everything to be proof that God exists as I think everything is created by God for someone to be believing and having faith in God, and therefore, I think someone can be loving and caring about God because I think someone can believe and have faith in God for someone to be loving and caring about God, otherwise, I think someone can choose not to be loving and caring about God because I think someone can choose not to be believing and having faith in God for someone to be choosing not to be loving and caring about God, even though, I do not think everything is created by God for someone not to be believing and having faith in God because I think God created everything for someone to be believing and having faith in God, and therefore, I think everything is created by God for someone to be believing and having faith in God because I think someone can believe and have faith in God for someone to be loving and caring about God. I think someone can believe and have faith in God for someone to be loving and caring about God because I think someone loving and caring about God is someone believing and having faith in God, and therefore, I think someone can believe and have faith in God because I think someone can believe in God for someone to be having faith in God. If I think someone can believe and have faith in God, than I think someone can believe in what someone believes for someone to be having faith in what someone believes because I think what someone thinks is what someone believes for someone to be having faith in someone's beliefs. I think what someone thinks is what someone believes for someone to be having faith in someone's beliefs because I think someone's beliefs is what someone thinks for someone to be believing in what someone thinks. I think someone's beliefs is what someone thinks for someone to be believing in what someone thinks because I think someone's beliefs is of the dimension of someone's thoughts for someone to be having any beliefs as I think the dimension of someone's thoughts is what someone thinks for someone to be believing in what someone thinks.

If I think someone's beliefs is what someone thinks for someone to be believing in what someone thinks, than I think someone's beliefs is of the dimension of God's thoughts because I think someone's beliefs is of God's thoughts for someone's beliefs to be of the dimension of God's thoughts, and therefore, I think someone's beliefs is of the dimension of someone's thoughts as I think the dimension of someone's thoughts is of the dimension of God's thoughts because I think what someone thinks is what someone's believes for someone's beliefs to be of the dimension of someone's thoughts as I think what someone thinks is of God's thoughts for the dimension of someone's thoughts to be of the dimension of God's thoughts. I think what someone thinks is what someone's believes for someone's beliefs to be of the dimension of someone's thoughts as I think what someone thinks is of God's thoughts for the dimension of someone's thoughts to be of the dimension of God's thoughts because I think someone's beliefs is what someone thinks for someone to be believing in what someone thinks as I think what someone thinks is of God's thoughts for someone to be believing in what someone thinks, even though, I do not know if God has any beliefs because I think God is perfect for me not to be knowing if God has any beliefs, however, I think God could have beliefs because I think God created everything with God's thoughts for God to be having beliefs, and therefore, I think God has beliefs because I think God is always good, and right for God to be believing in everything that is good, and right as I think God can believe in everything that is good, and right for God to be having beliefs. If I think God has beliefs, than I think God's beliefs is what God thinks for God to be believing in what God thinks because I think God's beliefs is of the dimension of God's thoughts for God to be having any beliefs as I think the dimension of God's thoughts is what God thinks for God to be believing in what God thinks, and therefore, I think God has beliefs as I think someone has beliefs because I think God's beliefs is of the dimension of God's thoughts for God to be having any beliefs as I think someone's beliefs is of the dimension of someone's thoughts for someone to be having any beliefs.

Chapter 21

Someone's feelings

I would like to talk about how dimensions are in life in relation to what dimensions are in life by talking about someone's feelings, that can possibly have something to do with how dimensions are in life is in relation to what dimensions are in life because I think someone's feelings is of the dimension of thought for someone to be having feelings, and therefore, I think someone's sense of awareness, and I think someone's sense of right and wrong goes beyond someone's five senses that someone can feel because I do not think someone can sense someone's five senses that someone can feel, without someone having a sense of awareness, and someone having a sense of right or wrong for someone to be able to be sensing what someone's five senses are in life that someone can feel. If I think someone's sense of awareness, and I think someone's sense of right and wrong goes beyond someone's five senses that someone can feel, than I think someone's sense of awareness, and someone's sense of right and wrong goes beyond someone's feelings because I do not think someone can feel someone's feelings, without someone having a sense of awareness, and someone having a sense of right or wrong for someone to be able to be feeling what someone's feelings are in life, and therefore, I think someone can feel what someone's feelings are in life with someone's sense of awareness, along with someone's sense of right and wrong because I think someone can sense what someone is feeling with someone's sense of awareness, along with someone's sense of right or wrong for someone to be feeling what someone's feelings are in life. I think someone can sense what someone is feeling with someone's sense of awareness, along with someone's sense of right or wrong for someone to be feeling what someone's feelings are in life because I think someone can sense what someone is feeling with someone's state of consciousness, along with someone's will for someone to be feeling what someone's feelings are in life, and therefore, I think someone can choose to be thinking about what someone's feelings are in life with someone's state of consciousness, along with someone's will as I think someone can choose to be thinking about what someone's feelings are in life with someone's sense of awareness, along with someone's sense of right or wrong because I think someone can sense what someone's feelings are in life with someone's state of consciousness, along with someone's will for someone to be choosing to be thinking about what someone's feelings are in life as I think someone can sense what someone's feelings are in life with someone's sense of awareness, along with someone's sense of right or wrong for someone to be choosing to be thinking about what someone's feelings are in life.

If I think someone can choose to be thinking about what someone's feelings are in life with someone's state of consciousness, along with someone's will as I think someone can choose to be thinking about what someone's feelings are in life with someone's sense of awareness, along with someone's sense of right or wrong, than I think someone's feelings is something as I think something is someone's feelings because I think someone's feelings is of something as I think something is apart of making up someone's feelings. I think someone's feelings is of something as I think something is apart of making up someone's feelings because I think someone's feelings is something as I think someone's feelings is a thought. I think someone's feelings is something as I think someone's feelings is a thought because I think someone's feelings is of a thought as I think a thought is apart of making up someone's feelings, and therefore, I think someone's feelings is something as I think someone's feelings is any thought because I think someone's feelings is of any thought as I think any thought is apart of making up someone's feelings. I think someone's feelings is of any thought as I think any thought is apart of making up someone's feelings because I think someone's feelings is a thought as I think someone's feelings is something. I think someone's feelings is a thought as I think someone's feelings is something because I think someone's thoughts is someone's feelings as I think someone's thoughts is something. I think someone's thoughts is someone's feelings as I think someone's thoughts is something because I think someone's feelings is someone's thoughts as I think someone's thoughts is someone's feelings. I think someone's feelings is someone's thoughts as I think someone's thoughts is someone's feelings because I think someone's thoughts is of someone's feelings as I think someone's feelings is apart of making up someone's thoughts. I think someone's thoughts is of someone's feelings as I think someone's feelings is apart of making up someone's thoughts because I think God's thoughts is someone's feelings as I think someone's thoughts is someone's feelings. I think God's thoughts is someone's feelings as I think someone's thoughts is someone's feelings because I think someone's feelings is God's thoughts as I think someone's feelings is any thought. I think someone's feelings is God's thoughts as I think someone's feelings is any thought because I think any thought is God's thoughts as I think someone's feelings is of God's thoughts. I think any thought is God's thoughts as I think someone's feelings is of God's thoughts because I think someone's feelings is of God's thoughts as I think God's thoughts is apart of making up someone's feelings. I think someone's feelings is of God's thoughts as I think God's thoughts is apart of making up someone's feelings because I think God's thoughts is someone's feelings as I think someone's feelings is God's thoughts, and therefore, I think God's thoughts is someone's feelings as I think someone's feelings is someone's thoughts because I think someone's feelings is of God's thoughts as I think someone's thoughts is of someone's feelings.

If I think God's thoughts is someone's feelings as I think someone's feelings is someone's thoughts, than I think someone's feelings is something as I think someone's thoughts is something because I think someone's feelings is of something for someone's feelings to be something as I think someone's thoughts is of something for someone's thoughts to be something. I think someone's feelings is of something for someone's feelings to be something as I think someone's thoughts is of something for someone's thoughts to be something because I think someone's feelings is a thought for someone's feelings to be of something as I think someone's thoughts is a thought for someone's thoughts to be of something. I think someone's feelings is a thought for someone's feelings to be of something as I think someone's thoughts is a thought for someone's thoughts to be of something because I think someone's feelings is of a thought for someone's feelings to be a thought as I think someone's thoughts is of a thought for someone's thoughts to be a thought. I think someone's feelings is of a thought for someone's feelings to be a thought as I think someone's thoughts is of a thought for someone's thoughts to be a thought because I think someone's feelings is any thought for someone's feelings to be of a thought as I think someone's thoughts is any thought for someone's thoughts to be of a thought. I think someone's feelings is any thought for someone's feelings to be of a thought as I think someone's thoughts is any thought for someone's thoughts to be of a thought because I think someone's feelings is of any thought for someone's feelings to be any thought as I think someone's thoughts is of any thought for someone's thoughts to be any thought. I think someone's feelings is of any thought for someone's feelings to be any thought as I think someone's thoughts is of any thought for someone's thoughts to be any thought because I think someone's feelings is God's thoughts for someone's feelings to be of any thought as I think someone's thoughts is God's thoughts for someone's thoughts to be of any thought. I think someone's feelings is God's thoughts for someone's feelings to be of any thought as I think someone's thoughts is God's thoughts for someone's thoughts to be of any thought because I think any thought is of God's thoughts for someone's feelings to be God's thoughts as I think any thought is of God's thoughts for someone's thoughts to be God's thoughts, and therefore, I think someone's feelings is God's thoughts as I think someone's thoughts is God's thoughts because I think someone's feelings is of God's thoughts for someone's feelings to be God's thoughts as I think someone's thoughts is of God's thoughts for someone's thoughts to be God's thoughts. I think someone's feelings is of God's thoughts for someone's feelings to be God's thoughts as I think someone's thoughts is of God's thoughts for someone's thoughts to be God's thoughts because I think God's thoughts is someone's feelings for someone's feelings to be of God's thoughts as I think God's thoughts is someone's thoughts for someone's thoughts to be of God's thoughts.

If I think someone's feelings is of God's thoughts for someone's feelings to be God's thoughts as I think someone's thoughts is of God's thoughts for someone's thoughts to be God's thoughts, than I think someone's feelings is God's thoughts as I think someone's thoughts is God's thoughts because I think God's thoughts is someone's feelings as I think someone's feelings is someone's thoughts. I think God's thoughts is someone's feelings as I think someone's feelings is someone's thoughts because I think God has feelings as I think someone has feelings. I think God has feelings as I think someone has feelings because I think someone's feelings is God's feelings as I think someone's feelings is someone's feelings. I think someone's feelings is God's feelings as I think someone's feelings is someone's feelings because I think someone's feelings is God's thoughts as I think someone's thoughts is someone's feelings. I think someone's feelings is God's thoughts as I think someone's thoughts is someone's feelings because I think someone's feelings is of God's thoughts as I think someone's thoughts is of someone's feelings. I think someone's feelings is of God's thoughts as I think someone's thoughts is of someone's feelings because I think God's thoughts is apart of making up someone's feelings as I think someone's feelings is apart of making up someone's thoughts. I think God's thoughts is apart of making up someone's feelings as I think someone's feelings is apart of making up someone's thoughts because I think someone's feelings is God's thoughts as I think someone's thoughts is someone's feelings. I think someone's feelings is God's thoughts as I think someone's thoughts is someone's feelings because I think God has feelings as I think someone has feelings. I think God has feelings as I think someone has feelings because I think God's feelings is someone's feelings as I think someone's feelings is someone's feelings.

If I think God has feelings as I think someone has feelings, than I think someone's feelings is God's feelings as I think God's feelings is someone's feelings because I think someone's feelings is God's thoughts as I think God's thoughts is someone's feelings. I think God's feelings is someone's feelings as I think someone's feelings is God's feelings because I think someone's feelings is God's thoughts as I think God's thoughts is God's feelings. I think someone's feelings is God's thoughts as I think God's thoughts is God's feelings because I think someone's feelings is God's feelings as I think someone's feelings is God's thoughts. I think someone's feelings is God's feelings as I think someone's feelings is God's thoughts because I think God's feelings is someone's feelings as I think God's thoughts is someone's feelings, and therefore, I think God's thoughts is God's feelings as I think God's feelings is God's thoughts because I think God's feelings is of God's thoughts as I think God's thoughts is apart of making up God's feelings. I think God's feelings is of God's thoughts as I think God's thoughts is apart of making up God's feelings because I think God's feelings is someone's feelings as I think someone's feelings is God's thoughts. I think God's feelings is someone's feelings as I think someone's feelings is God's thoughts because I think someone's feelings is of God's thoughts as I think God's thoughts is apart of making up someone's feelings. I think someone's feelings is of God's thoughts as I think God's thoughts is apart of making up someone's feelings because I think someone's feelings is of God's thoughts for someone's feelings to be God's feelings, and therefore, I think someone's thoughts is God's feelings as I think someone's feelings is God's feelings because I think someone's thoughts is someone's feelings as I think someone's thoughts is God's feelings. If I think someone's thoughts is someone's feelings as I think someone's thoughts is God's feelings, than I think someone's thoughts is God's feelings as I think God's feelings is someone's thoughts because I think someone's thoughts is God's thoughts as I think God's thoughts is someone's thoughts, and therefore, I think God's feelings is someone's thoughts as I think someone's thoughts is God's feelings because I think someone's thoughts is God's thoughts as I think God's thoughts is God's feelings. If I think God's feelings is someone's thoughts as I think someone's thoughts is God's feelings, than I think someone's thoughts is God's feelings as I think someone's thoughts is God's thoughts because I think God's feelings is someone's thoughts as I think God's thoughts is someone's thoughts. I think God's feelings is someone's thoughts as I think God's thoughts is someone's thoughts because I think God's thoughts is God's feelings as I think someone's thoughts is someone's feelings.

If I think God's feelings is someone's thoughts as I think God's thoughts is someone's thoughts, than I think God has thoughts as I think God's being has thoughts because I think God is God's being as I think God's thoughts is apart of God's being for God to be having thoughts, but I do not think God's thoughts is God's being because I think God's thoughts is taking place within God's mind that is apart of God's being for God's thoughts not to be God's being, and therefore, I think God has feelings as I think God has thoughts because I think God's feelings is apart of God's being as I think God's thoughts is apart of God's being, but I do not think God's feelings is God's being as I do not think God's thoughts is God's being because I think God's feelings is God's thoughts as I think God's thoughts is taking place within God's mind that is apart of God's being for God's thoughts and feelings not to be God's being. If I do not think God's feelings is God's being as I do not think God's thoughts is God's being, than I think God has feelings as I think God's being has feelings because I think God is God's being as I think God's feelings is apart of God's being for God to be having feelings, and therefore, I think God's feelings is God's thoughts as I think God's thoughts is taking place within God's mind that is apart of God's being because I think God's feelings is of God's thoughts as I think God's thoughts is taking place within God's mind that is apart of God's being. I think God's feelings is of God's thoughts as I think God's thoughts is taking place within God's mind that is apart of God's being because I think God's feelings is apart of God's being as I think God's thoughts apart of God's being. I think God's feelings is apart of God's being as I think God's thoughts is apart of God's being because I think God's feelings is God's thoughts for God's thoughts and feelings to be apart of God's being, and therefore, I think God's thoughts is God's feelings for God's thoughts and feelings to be taking place within God's mind that is apart of God's being because I think God's feelings is God's thoughts as I think God's thoughts is God's feelings. I think God's feelings is God's thoughts as I think God's thoughts is God's feelings because I think God's feelings is someone's feelings as I think someone's feelings is of God's thoughts.

If I think God's feelings is God's thoughts as I think God's thoughts is God's feelings, than I think someone can choose to be thinking about what someone's feelings are in life because I think someone's thoughts is of someone's feelings for someone to be choosing be thinking about what someone's feelings are in life, however, I do not think someone's feelings is of someone's being because

I think there are two kinds of feelings that someone can feel, and that is I think someone can physically feel something, and I think someone can mentally feel something. I think someone can physically feel something because I think someone can physically feel something from any part of someone's body for someone to physically be feeling something, and I think someone can mentally feel something because I think someone can mentally be feeling something from a reaction of chemicals that is taking place within someone's brain for someone to mentally be feeling something, and therefore, I think someone's feelings is any thought as I think any thought is someone's feelings because I think someone's feelings is of any thought that is apart of making up someone's feelings. I think someone's feelings is of any thought that is apart of making up someone's feelings because I think someone's feelings physically is of any thought that is apart of making up any part of someone's body for someone to physically be able to be feeling what someone is feeling, and I think someone's feelings mentally is of any thought that is apart of making any of the chemicals that is able to be reacting in someone's brain for someone to mentally be able to be feeling what someone is feeling, and therefore, I think someone's feelings mentally is someone's feelings emotionally because I think someone can experience someone's feelings mentally with someone's brain for someone's feelings mentally to be someone's feelings emotionally.

If I think someone's feelings mentally is someone's feelings emotionally, than I think someone's feelings is someone's emotions because I think someone's feelings is someone's feelings emotionally, and therefore, I think someone's thoughts can be someone's feelings because I think someone's thoughts can be of the thoughts of someone's feelings for someone's thoughts to be someone's feelings, but I do not think someone's feelings can be someone's thoughts because I do not think someone's feelings can be of someone's thoughts. I do not think someone's feelings can be of someone's thoughts because I think someone's feelings is of any thought that is apart of making someone's feelings for someone's feelings not to be of someone's thoughts, and therefore, I think someone's feelings is someone's thoughts as I think someone's thoughts is someone's feelings because I think someone's thoughts is of someone's feelings as I think someone's thoughts is of the thoughts of someone's feelings. I think someone's thoughts is of someone's feelings as I think someone's thoughts is of the thoughts of someone's feelings because I think someone's thoughts is of the thoughts of someone's feelings for someone's thoughts to be of someone's feelings. I think someone's thoughts is of the thoughts of someone's feelings for someone's thoughts to be of someone's feelings because I think someone's thoughts is the thoughts of someone's feelings for someone's thoughts to be someone's feelings, and therefore, I think someone's feelings is someone's thoughts as I think someone's thoughts is someone's feelings because I think someone's thoughts is the thoughts of someone's feelings for someone's thoughts to be someone's feelings. I think someone's thoughts is the thoughts of someone's feelings for someone's thoughts to be someone's feelings because I think someone's thoughts is of the thoughts of someone's feelings as I think the thoughts of someone's feelings is of any thought that is apart of making up someone's feelings, and therefore, I think someone's thoughts is of the thoughts of someone's feelings because I think the thoughts of someone's feelings is apart of making up someone's thoughts for someone's thoughts to be of the thoughts of someone's feelings, but I do not think the thoughts of someone's feelings is apart of making up all of someone's thoughts because I think all of someone's thoughts is of the thoughts of everything that someone can possibly experience in someone's life. I think all of someone's thoughts is of the thoughts of everything that someone can possibly experience in someone's life because I think the thoughts of everything that someone can possibly experience in someone's life is apart of making up all of someone's thoughts.

If I think all of someone's thoughts is of the thoughts of everything that someone can possibly experience in someone's life, than I think someone's thoughts is someone's feelings as I think someone's feelings is someone's thoughts because I think someone's thoughts is a copy of the thoughts of someone's feelings. I think someone's thoughts is a copy of the thoughts of someone's feelings because I think someone's thoughts is of the thoughts of someone's feelings, and therefore, I think someone's thoughts is someone's feelings as I think someone's thoughts is God's thoughts because I think someone's thoughts is a copy of the thoughts of someone's feelings as I think someone's thoughts is a copy of God's thoughts. I think someone's thoughts is a copy of the thoughts of someone's feelings as I think someone's thoughts is a copy of God's thoughts because I think someone's thoughts is of the thoughts of someone's feelings for someone's thoughts to be a copy of the thoughts of someone's feelings as I think someone's thoughts is of God's thoughts for someone's thoughts to be a copy of God's thoughts, and therefore, I think someone's feelings is God's thoughts as I think God's thoughts is someone's feelings because I think someone's feelings is a copy of God's thoughts. I think someone's feelings is a copy of God's thoughts because I think someone's feelings is of God's thoughts for someone's feelings to be a copy of God's thoughts.

If I think someone's feelings is a copy of God's thoughts, than I think someone can think of someone's thoughts as I think someone can think of someone's feelings because I think someone's thoughts is of someone's feelings for someone to be thinking of someone's thoughts of someone's feelings in someone's mind with someone's state of consciousness, along with someone's will that is apart of someone's being. I think someone's thoughts is of someone's feelings for someone to be thinking of someone's thoughts of someone's feelings in someone's mind with someone's state of consciousness, along with someone's will that is apart of someone's being because I think someone's thoughts is of someone's feelings for someone to be thinking of someone's feelings in someone's mind with someone's state of consciousness, along with someone's will that is apart of someone's being, and therefore, I think someone can think of someone's feelings because I think someone is someone's being as I think someone's being can think of someone's feelings in someone's mind with someone's state of consciousness, along with someone's will that is apart of someone's being. If I think someone can think of someone's feelings, than I think someone can think about what someone's feelings are in life because I think someone's thoughts is of someone's feelings for someone to be thinking about what someone's feelings are in life. I think someone's thoughts is of someone's feelings for someone to be thinking about what someone's feelings are in life because I do not think someone can think about what someone's feelings are in life, without someone's thoughts being of someone's feelings for someone to be thinking about what someone's feelings are in life, and therefore, I think someone can think about what someone feels about themselves, someone else, something, and God because I think someone's thoughts is of someone's feelings for someone to be thinking about what someone feels about themselves, someone else, something, and God, even though, I think someone can feel what someone's feelings are in life because I think someone's thoughts is of someone's feelings as I think someone's feelings is of any thought that is apart of making up someone's feelings for someone to be able to be feeling what someone's feelings are in life. If I think someone can feel what someone's feelings are in life, than I think someone can feel what someone's feelings are in life as I think someone's being can feel what someone's feelings are in life because I think someone is someone's being as I think someone can feel what someone's feelings are in life with someone's state of consciousness, along with someone's will, and someone's thoughts, and someone's mind that is apart of someone's being, and therefore, I think someone can feel what someone's feelings are in life with someone's state of consciousness, along with someone's will, and someone's thoughts, and someone's mind that is apart of someone's being because I think someone's thoughts is of someone's feelings for someone to be feeling what someone's feelings are in life with someone's state of consciousness, along with someone's will, and someone's thoughts, and someone's mind that is apart of someone's being, even though, I think someone can think about what someone's feelings are in life because I think someone's thoughts is of someone's feelings for someone to be thinking about what someone's feelings are in life with someone's state of consciousness, along with someone's will, and someone's thoughts, and someone's mind that is apart of someone's being.

If I think someone can think about what someone's feelings are in life, than I think someone can choose to be thinking about what someone's feelings are in life because I think someone's thoughts is of someone's feelings for someone to be choosing to be thinking about what someone's feelings are in life with someone's state of consciousness, along with someone's will, and someone's thoughts, and someone's mind that is apart of someone's being, even though, I think God can think about what someone's feelings are in life as I think someone can think about what someone's feelings are in life because I think someone's feelings is of God's thoughts for God to be thinking about what someone's feelings are in life as I think someone's thoughts is of someone's feelings for someone to be thinking about what someone's feelings are in life, and therefore, I think God can think about what someone is feeling as I think someone can think about what someone is feeling because I think someone's thoughts of someone's feelings is of God's thoughts in God's mind for God to be thinking what someone is feeling with God's state of consciousness, along with God's will, and God's thoughts in God's mind that is apart of God's being as I think someone's thoughts is a copy of the thoughts of someone's feelings in someone's mind for someone to be thinking about what someone is feeling with someone's state of consciousness, along with someone's will, and someone's thoughts in someone's mind that is apart of someone's being. If I think God can think about what someone is feeling as I think someone can think about what someone is feeling, than I think God can feel what someone is feeling for God to be feeling someone's feelings because I think someone's feelings is of God's thoughts for God to be feeling someone's feelings as I think God's thoughts is of God for God to be feeling what someone is feeling.

If I think God can feel what someone is feeling for God to be feeling someone's feelings, than I think both kinds of feelings that someone can physically, and mentally be feeling are both physical feelings because I think both kinds of feelings that someone can physically, and mentally be feeling physically comes from parts of someone's body for someone to be able to be feeling both kinds of feelings, and therefore, I think both kinds of feelings that someone can be physically, and mentally be feeling are both someone's mental feelings because I think both kinds of feelings that someone can physically, and mentally be feeling is of any thought that is apart of making up both kinds of feelings that someone is able to be feeling. I think both kinds of feelings that someone can physically, and mentally be feeling is of any thought that is apart of making up both kinds of feelings that someone is able to be feeling because I think someone's thoughts is of the thoughts of both kinds of feelings that someone can physically, and mentally be feeling. I think someone's thoughts is of the thoughts of both kinds of feelings that someone can physically, and mentally be feeling because I think someone's thoughts is of the thoughts of someone's feelings for someone to be feeling what someone is physically, and mentally feeling. I think someone's thoughts is of the thoughts of someone's feelings for someone to be feeling what someone is physically, and mentally feeling because I think someone's feelings is someone's thoughts. I think someone's feelings is someone's thoughts because

I think someone's feelings is someone's feelings mentally. I think someone's feelings is someone's feelings mentally because I think someone's feelings physically is someone's feelings mentally as I think someone's feelings mentally and emotionally is someone's feelings mentally. I think someone's feelings physically is someone's feelings mentally as I think someone's feelings mentally and emotionally is someone's feelings mentally because I think someone's thoughts is of the thoughts of someone's feelings for someone's feelings to be someone's thoughts as I think someone's thoughts is taking place within someone's mind that is apart of someone's being for someone's thoughts of someone's feelings to be apart of someone's being.

If I think someone's feelings physically is someone's feelings mentally as I think someone's feelings mentally and emotionally is someone's feelings mentally, than I think someone has thoughts as I think someone's being has thoughts because I think someone is someone's being as I think someone's thoughts is apart of someone's being for someone to be having thoughts, but I do not think someone's thoughts is someone's being because I think someone's thoughts is taking place within someone's mind that is apart of someone's being for someone's thoughts not to be someone's being, and therefore, I think someone has feelings as I think someone has thoughts because I think someone's feelings is apart of someone's being as I think someone's thoughts is apart of someone's being, but I do not think someone's feelings is someone's being as I do not think someone's thoughts is someone's being because I think someone's feelings is someone's thoughts as I think someone's thoughts is taking place within someone's mind that is apart of someone's being for someone's thoughts and feelings not to be someone's being. If I do not think someone's feelings is someone's being as I do not think someone's thoughts is someone's being, than I think someone has feelings as I think someone's being has feelings because I think someone is someone's being as I think someone's feelings is apart of someone's being for someone to be having feelings, and therefore, I think someone's feelings is someone's thoughts as I think someone's thoughts is taking place within someone's mind that is apart of someone's being because I think someone's thoughts is of someone's feeling as I think someone's thoughts is taking place within someone's mind that is apart of someone's being. I think someone's thoughts is of someone's feeling as I think someone's thoughts is taking place within someone's mind that is apart of someone's being because I think someone's feelings is apart of someone's being as I think someone's thoughts apart of someone's being. I think someone's feelings is apart of someone's being as I think someone's thoughts apart of someone's being because I think someone's feelings is someone's thoughts for someone's thoughts and feelings to be apart of someone's being, and therefore, I think someone's thoughts is someone's feelings for someone's thoughts and feelings to be taking place within someone's mind that is apart of someone's being because I think someone's feelings is someone's thoughts as I think someone's thoughts is someone's feelings. I think someone's feelings is someone's thoughts as I think someone's thoughts is someone's feelings because I think someone's thoughts is someone's feelings as I think someone's thoughts is of the thoughts of someone's feelings.

If I think someone's feelings is someone's thoughts as I think someone's thoughts is someone's feelings, than I think someone's heart is a misconception of someone's feelings because I do not think someone feels someone's feelings emotionally with someone's heart as much as someone would like to think someone can feel someone's feelings emotionally with someone's heart. I do not think someone feels someone's feelings emotionally with someone's heart as much as someone would like to think someone can feel someone's feelings emotionally with someone's heart because I do not think someone feels someone's feelings emotionally in someone's heart. I do not think someone feels someone's

413

feelings emotionally in someone's heart because I think someone's heart is an organ that pumps blood in someone's body to help someone's body to stay alive, even though, I think someone can feel something with someone's heart because I think someone's heart can be physically injured for someone to be feeling something with someone's heart, however, I do not think someone feels someone's feelings emotionally with someone's heart as much as someone would like to think someone can feel someone's feelings emotionally with someone's heart because I do not think someone feels someone's feelings emotionally in someone's heart, and therefore, I think someone feels someone's feelings emotionally as I think someone feels someone's feelings mentally because I think someone's feelings emotionally is someone's feelings mentally. I think someone's feelings emotionally is someone's feelings mentally because I think someone can feel someone's feelings emotionally in someone's brain as I think someone can feel someone's feelings mentally in someone's brain. I think someone can feel someone's feelings emotionally in someone's brain as I think someone can feel someone's feelings mentally in someone's brain because I think someone can feel someone's feelings emotionally with someone's brain as I think someone can feel someone's feelings mentally with someone's brain. I think someone can feel someone's feelings emotionally with someone's brain as I think someone can feel someone's feelings mentally with someone's brain because I think someone's feelings mentally and emotionally is of any thought that is apart of making any of the chemicals that is able to be reacting in someone's brain for someone to mentally and emotionally be able to be feeling what someone is feeling, even though, I think someone can think what someone is feeling in someone's brain is what someone is feeling is someone's heart because I think someone can sense something is good or bad with someone having a sense of right or wrong for someone to be thinking someone can feel something is good or bad in someone's heart, however, I think someone is feeling what someone thinks someone is feeling in someone's heart is someone feeling what someone is feeling in someone's brain because I think someone's feelings is a reaction of chemicals that is taking place in someone's brain for someone to be feeling what someone's feelings are in life.

If I think someone is feeling what someone thinks someone is feeling in someone's heart is someone feeling what someone is feeling in someone's brain, than I think someone can think someone's feelings is good, and right for someone to be feeling someone's feelings because I think someone can feel good with what someone is feeling with someone's feelings for someone to be thinking someone's feelings is good, and right for someone to be feeling someone's feelings, however, I think someone can be addicted to someone's feelings because I think someone can get high on the chemicals of someone's feelings that is being released in someone's brain for someone to be addicted to someone's feelings, even though, I do not think someone can live without someone's feelings for someone to never be addicted to someone's feelings because I think someone has to live with someone's feelings for someone to be feeling what someone is feeling, and therefore, I think someone's feeling is neither right or wrong because I think someone's feelings is something that is neither right or wrong as I think something is neither right or wrong. If I think someone's feeling is neither right or wrong, than I do not think someone's feelings is right or wrong for someone's feelings to be right or wrong because I do not think someone's feelings has a sense of right or wrong with someone's feelings not having a choice of right or wrong for someone's feelings not to be right or wrong, and therefore, I think someone can think about what someone is feeling because I think someone can feel what someone is feeling for someone to be thinking about what someone is feeling. I think someone can feel what someone is feeling for someone to be thinking about what someone is feeling because I think someone's thoughts is of what someone is feeling for someone to be thinking about what someone is feeling, and therefore, I think someone can think about what someone is feeling because I think someone can feel what someone is feeling for someone to be thinking about what someone's feelings are in life. If I think someone can think about what someone is feeling, than I think someone can think about what someone's feelings are in life because I think someone can think about what someone is feeling for someone to be thinking about what someone's feelings are in life.

If I think someone can think about what someone's feelings are in life, than I think someone can think of someone's feelings as being good or bad for someone to be thinking about what someone's are feeling in life because I think someone's thoughts is of someone's feelings for someone to be thinking of someone's feelings as being good or bad, and therefore, I think someone's feelings can be good or bad because I think someone can think of someone's feelings as being good or bad for someone's feelings to be good or bad. I think someone can think of someone's feelings as being good or bad for someone's feelings to be good or bad because I think someone has a choice of right or wrong for someone to be thinking of someone's feelings as being good or bad, and therefore, I think someone's feelings can be right or wrong as I think someone's thoughts can be right or wrong because I think someone has a choice of right or wrong for someone to be thinking of someone's feelings as being right or wrong as I think someone has a choice of right or wrong for someone to be thinking of someone's thoughts as being right or wrong. If I think someone's feelings can be right or wrong as I think someone's thoughts can be right or wrong, than I think someone can feel good or bad about something because I think someone can think of something as being right or wrong for someone to be feeling good or bad about something. I think someone can think of something as being right or wrong for someone to be feeling good or bad about something because I think someone can be right or wrong about something for someone to be feeling good or bad about something, and therefore, I think someone can be right or wrong for someone to be feeling good or bad about something because I think someone has a choice of right or wrong for someone to be feeling good or bad about something as I think someone can be right or wrong about something for someone to be feeling good or bad about something. If I think someone can be right or wrong for someone to be feeling good or bad about something, than I think someone's feelings can be an indication that something is right or wrong with someone because I think someone's feelings can be an indication that someone is thinking of something that is right or wrong. I think someone's feelings can be an indication that someone is thinking of something that is right or wrong because I think someone can think of something that is right or wrong for someone to be feeling good or bad about something that is right or wrong. I think someone can think of something that is right or wrong for someone to be feeling good or bad about something that is right or wrong because I think someone has choice of right or wrong for someone to be feeling good or bad about something that is right or wrong as I think someone has a choice of right or wrong for someone to be thinking of something that is right or wrong, and therefore, I think someone's feelings can be good or bad as I think someone's thoughts can be good or bad because I think someone's thoughts is someone's feelings for someone to be thinking of someone's thoughts and feelings as being good or bad.

If I think someone's feelings can be good or bad as I think someone's thoughts can be good or bad, than I think there can be lots of different words that someone can think of for someone to be describing what someone's thoughts and feelings are in life because I think someone can think of lots of different words to be describing what someone thinks of what someone's thoughts and feelings are in life, even though, I think there are two different kinds of feelings that someone can mentally and emotionally be experiencing in someone's life because I think someone's feelings can be good or bad for someone to be feeling good or bad as I think someone can feel good or bad for there to be two different kinds of feelings that someone can mentally and emotionally be experiencing in someone's life, and therefore, I think there can be many different words that someone can think of for someone to be describing how someone is feeling good or bad because I think someone can think of lots of different words to be describing how someone is feeling good or bad. I think someone can think of lots of different words to be describing how someone is feeling good or bad because I think someone's thoughts is someone's feelings for someone to be thinking of lots of different words to be describing how someone is feeling good or bad, and therefore, I think there can be lots of different words to be describing what someone's thoughts and feelings are in life because I think someone's thoughts is someone's feelings for someone to be thinking of lots of different words to be describing what someone is thinking and feeling. If I think there can be lots of different words to be describing what someone's thoughts and feelings are in life, than I think someone's thoughts and feelings can be good or bad because I think someone has a choice of right or wrong for someone to be thinking of someone's thoughts and feelings as being good or bad, even though, I think someone's feelings can be right or wrong as I think someone's thoughts can be right or wrong because I think someone can feel good or bad about something for the right or wrong reasons with someone having a choice of right or wrong for someone's feelings to be right or wrong as I think someone can think of something that is good or bad for the right or wrong reasons with someone having a choice of right or wrong for someone's thoughts to be right or wrong, and therefore, I think someone can be right or wrong for feeling good or bad about something as I think someone can be right or wrong for thinking of something that is good or bad because I think someone can feel good or bad about something for the right or wrong reasons for someone to be right or wrong for feeling good or bad about something as I think someone can think of something that is good or bad for the right or wrong reasons for someone to be right or wrong for thinking of something that is good or bad.

If I think someone can be right or wrong for feeling good or bad about something as I think someone can be right or wrong for thinking of something that is good or bad, than I think someone can feel good or bad about doing something that is right or wrong because I think someone can do something that is right or wrong for someone to be feeling good or bad about doing something that is right or wrong. I think someone can do something that is right or wrong for someone to be feeling good or bad about doing something that is right or wrong because I think someone can think about doing something that is right or wrong for someone to be feeling good or bad about doing something that is right or wrong. I think someone can think about doing something that is right or wrong for someone to be feeling good or bad about doing something that is right or wrong because I think someone has choice of right or wrong for someone to be feeling good or bad about doing something that is right or wrong as I think someone has a choice of right or wrong for someone to be thinking about doing something is right or wrong. If I think someone can think about doing something that is right or wrong for someone to be feeling good or bad about doing something that is right or wrong, than I think someone can think about doing something that is good or bad because I think someone can think about doing something that is right or wrong for someone to be thinking about doing something that is good or bad, even though, I think someone's feelings can be right or wrong as I think someone's thoughts can be right or wrong because I think someone can feel good or bad about doing something for the right or wrong reasons with someone having a choice of right or wrong for someone's feelings to be right or wrong as I think someone can think about doing something that is good or bad for the right or wrong reasons with someone having a choice of right or wrong for someone's thoughts to be right or wrong, and therefore, I think someone can be right or wrong for someone to be feeling good or bad about doing something that is good or bad as I think someone can be right or wrong for someone to be thinking about doing something that is good or bad because I think someone can feel good or bad about doing something for the right or wrong reasons for someone to be right or wrong for someone to be feeling good or bad about doing something that is good or bad as I think someone can think about doing something that is good or bad for the right or wrong reasons for someone to be right or wrong for someone to be thinking about doing something that is good or bad.

If I think someone can be right or wrong for someone to be feeling good or bad about doing something that is good or bad as I think someone can be right or wrong for someone to be thinking about doing something that is good or bad, than I think someone can be addicted to something as I think someone can feel good about something because I think someone can be addicted to something that someone can feel good about something as I think someone can feel good about something that someone can be addicted to something, and therefore, I think someone can be addicted to something that someone can feel good about something because I think someone can feel good about doing something that is wrong for someone to be addicted to something that someone can feel good about something, even though, I think someone can feel bad for feeling good about doing something that is wrong because I think someone can realize, and think someone is wrong about doing something for someone to be feeling bad for feeling good about doing something that is wrong, and therefore, I think someone's happiness comes within someone, and not from someone else or something or someplace beyond someone because I think someone's happiness comes from someone naturally feeling good, and happy, and not from someone doing something to artificially making themselves feel good, and happy. If I think someone's happiness comes within someone, and not from someone else or something or someplace beyond someone, than I think someone can feel sorry for someone because I think someone can feel sorry for someone else for someone to be feeling sorry for someone, and therefore, I think someone can feel sorry for someone else because I think someone can feel bad for someone else for someone to be feeling sorry for someone else. I think someone can feel bad for someone else for someone to be feeling sorry for someone else because I think someone can think someone is wrong about something for someone to be feeling sorry for someone else as I think someone can think someone is wrong about something for someone to be feeling bad for someone else, even though, I do not think someone can feel sorry for someone else that is causing trouble or problems for someone because I think someone would have to be dealing with someone else that is causing trouble or problems for someone for someone not to be feeling sorry for someone else, however, I think someone can feel sorry for someone else because I think something can be wrong with someone else for someone to be feeling sorry for someone else, otherwise, I think someone can feel sorry for someone because I think someone can feel sorry for themselves for someone to be feeling sorry for someone, even though, I think someone can be wrong with someone feeling sorry for themselves because I think someone can do something wrong with themselves, and someone else for someone to be wrong with someone feeling sorry for themselves, and therefore, I think someone can be right or wrong with someone feeling sorry for themselves, and someone else because I think someone can choose to be doing something that is right or wrong with themselves, and someone else for someone to be right or wrong with someone feeling sorry for themselves, and someone else. If I think someone can be right or wrong with someone feeling sorry for themselves, and someone else, than I think someone can feel sorry for someone because I think someone can to be feeling empathy or compassion for someone for someone to be feeling sorry for someone, and therefore,

I think someone can feel empathy or compassion for someone because I think someone can feel bad for someone for someone to be feeling empathy or compassion for someone. I think someone can feel bad for someone for someone to be feeling empathy or compassion for someone because I think someone can think something is wrong with someone for someone to be feeling empathy or compassion for someone as I think someone can think something is wrong with someone for someone to be feeling bad for someone.

If I think someone can feel bad for someone for someone to be feeling empathy or compassion for someone, than I think someone's feelings is someone's choice for someone to be feeling what someone is feeling because I think someone can choose to be feeling what someone is feeling for someone's feelings to be someone's choice for someone to be feeling what someone is feeling, and therefore, I think someone's feelings is someone's choice because I think someone can choose to be feeling someone's feelings or not for someone's feelings to be someone's choice. I think someone can choose to be feeling someone's feelings or not for someone's feelings to be someone's choice because I think someone's feelings is someone's choice for someone to be feeling someone's feelings or not. I think someone's feelings is someone's choice for someone to be feeling someone's feelings or not because I think someone can choose to be feeling someone's feelings or not for someone to be dealing with someone's feelings or not. I think someone can choose to be feeling someone's feelings or not for someone to be dealing with someone's feelings or not because I think someone's feelings is someone's choice for someone to be dealing with someone's feelings or not as I think someone's feelings is someone's choice for someone to be feeling someone's feelings or not, and therefore, I think someone's feelings is someone's choice because I think someone can choose to be feeling someone's feelings or not for someone to be dealing with someone's feelings or not. I think someone can choose to be feeling someone's feelings or not for someone to be dealing with someone's feelings or not because I think someone can choose to be feeling good or bad about something or not for someone to be feeling someone's feelings or not as I think someone can choose to be feeling good or bad about something or not for someone to be dealing with someone's feelings or not. I think someone can choose to be feeling good or bad about something or not for someone to be feeling someone's feelings or not as I think someone can choose to be feeling good or bad about something or not for someone to be dealing with someone's feelings or not because I think someone can choose to be feeling good or bad about doing something or not for someone to be feeling someone's feelings or not as I think someone can choose to be feeling good or bad about doing something or not for someone to be dealing with someone's feelings or not, and therefore, I think someone can choose to be feeling someone's feelings or not for someone to be dealing with someone's feelings or not because I think someone choosing to be feeling someone's feelings or not is someone choosing to be dealing with someone's feelings or not. I think someone choosing to be feeling someone's feelings or not is someone choosing to be dealing with someone's feelings or not because I think someone's feelings is someone's choice for someone to be dealing with someone's feelings or not as I think someone's feelings is someone's choice for someone to be feeling someone's feelings or not, and therefore, I think someone's feelings is someone's choice because I think someone can choose to be feeling good or bad about doing something or not for someone's feelings to be someone's choice. I think someone can choose to be feeling good or bad about something or not for someone's feelings to be someone's choice because I think someone's feelings is someone's choice for someone to be feeling good or bad about something or not. I think someone's feelings is someone's choice for someone to be feeling good or bad about something or not because I think someone can choose to be feeling good or bad about doing something or not for someone's feelings to be someone's choice. I think someone can choose to be feeling good or bad about doing something or not for someone's feelings to be someone's choice because I think someone's feelings is someone's choice for someone to be feeling good or bad about doing something or not, and therefore, I think someone's feelings is someone's choice because I think someone can choose to be dealing with someone's feelings or not for someone's feelings to be someone's choice. I think someone can choose to be dealing with someone's feelings or not for someone's feelings to be someone's choice because I think someone's feelings is someone's choice for someone to be dealing with someone's feelings or not.

I think someone's feelings is someone's choice for someone to be dealing with someone's feelings or not because I think someone's feelings is someone's choice to be right or wrong for someone to be dealing with someone's feelings or not. I think someone's feelings is someone's choice to be right or wrong for someone to be dealing with someone's feelings or not because I think someone can be right or wrong for someone to be dealing with someone's feelings or not. I think someone can be right or wrong for someone to be dealing with someone's feelings or not because I think someone can be right for someone to be dealing with someone's feelings as I think someone can be wrong for someone not to be dealing with someone's feelings. I think someone can be right for someone to be dealing with someone's feelings as I think someone can be wrong for someone not to be dealing with someone's feelings because I think someone can feel good or bad about doing something that is right or wrong for someone to be right to be dealing with someone's feelings as I think someone can feel good about doing something that is wrong for someone to be wrong not to be dealing with someone's feelings. I think someone can feel good or bad about doing something that is right or wrong for someone to be right to be dealing with someone's feelings as I think someone can feel good about doing something that is wrong for someone to be wrong not to be dealing with someone's feelings because I think someone can be right or wrong about doing something that someone can feel good or bad about with themselves for someone to be right to be dealing with someone's feelings as I think someone can be wrong about doing something that someone can feel good about with themselves for someone to be wrong not to be dealing with someone's feelings, and therefore, I think someone can be right to be dealing with someone's feelings because I think someone can be right with how someone can be dealing with someone's feelings for someone to be right to be dealing with someone's feelings. I think someone can be right with how someone can be dealing with someone's feelings because I think someone can feel bad about doing something that is wrong, and then I think someone can ask themselves, and think about what someone has done wrong for someone to be feeling bad about doing that is wrong, and then I think someone can think about doing something that is good, and right about what someone has done wrong for someone to overcome, and let go of someone to be feeling bad about doing that is wrong, and then I think someone can feel good about themselves with someone doing something that is good, and right about what someone has done wrong for someone to be right with how someone can be dealing with someone's feelings, and therefore, I think someone can be right with how someone can be dealing with someone's feelings because I think someone can be right to be dealing with someone's feelings for someone to be right with how someone can be dealing with someone's feelings, otherwise, I think someone can be wrong not to be dealing with someone's feelings because I think someone can act out someone's bad feelings, without there being any resolution or answer to someone's bad feelings for someone to be wrong not to be dealing with someone's feelings, even though, I think someone can be good, and right to be dealing with someone's feelings because I think someone can feel good about themselves with someone doing something that is good, and right about what someone has done wrong for someone to be overcoming, and letting go of someone's bad feelings as I think someone can feel good about themselves with someone doing something that is good, and right about what someone has done wrong for someone to be dealing with someone's feelings. If I think someone can be good, and right to be dealing with someone's feelings, than I think someone can choose to be dealing with someone's feelings as I think someone can choose not to be dealing with someone's feelings because I think someone can choose not to be doing something that is wrong for someone to be choosing to be dealing with someone's feelings as I think someone can choose to be doing something that is wrong for someone to be choosing not to be dealing with someone's feelings, and therefore, I think someone can be right or wrong to be dealing with someone's feelings or not because I think someone can choose to be doing something that is right or wrong for someone to be right or wrong to be dealing with someone's feelings or not. If I think someone can be right or wrong to be dealing with someone's feelings or not, than I think someone can choose to be dealing with someone's feelings or not because I think someone has a choice of right or wrong for someone to be choosing to be dealing with someone's feelings or not, and therefore, I think someone can be right or wrong to be dealing with someone's feelings because I think someone can be right or wrong about how someone can be dealing with someone's feelings for someone to be right or wrong to be dealing with someone's feelings, even though, I think someone can be right to be dealing with someone's feelings because I think something good can happen to someone for someone to be right to be dealing with someone's feelings, otherwise, I think someone can be wrong not to be dealing with someone's feelings because I think something bad can happen to someone for someone to be wrong not to be dealing with someone's feelings, however, I think someone can be right to be dealing with someone's feelings because I think someone can choose to be doing something that is right for someone to be right to be dealing with someone's feelings.

If I think someone can be right to be dealing with someone's feelings, than I think someone can deal with someone's feelings because I think if someone doesn't deal with someone's feelings, than I think someone's feelings will deal with someone because I think someone can choose to be doing something that is wrong for someone to be doing something that someone can end up regret doing, and therefore, I think someone can have regrets because I think someone can wish that someone did or didn't do something for someone to be having regrets, even though, I think someone having any regrets is someone's preference, as to whether or not if someone has any regrets because I think someone can wish that someone did or didn't do something, however, I do not think someone having any regrets can change anything for someone because I do not think someone would be where someone is, regardless if someone has any regrets or not, and therefore, I think someone can be grateful for where someone is coming from because I do not think someone can change where someone is coming from, and I do not think someone can be where someone is, and where someone is going without someone coming from where someone is coming from. If I think someone can be grateful for where someone is coming from, than I do not think someone can control someone's feelings because I think someone can feel good or bad about something for someone not to be able to be controlling someone's feelings, and therefore, I do not think someone can do something if someone isn't happy to be doing something because I do not think someone can control someone's feelings for someone not to be making themselves happy to be doing something as I do not think someone can make themselves happy to be doing something for someone not to be doing something that someone isn't happy to be doing. If I do not think someone can do something if someone isn't happy to be doing something, than I do not think someone's feelings is always someone's choice for someone to be feeling what someone is feeling because I do not think someone can control someone's feelings for someone to be feeling what someone is feeling, and therefore, I do not think someone's feelings is always someone's choice for someone to be feeling someone's feeling or not because I do not think someone can control someone's feelings for someone to be choosing to be feeling someone's feelings or not, even though, I think someone can deal with someone's feelings because I think someone can feel what someone is feeling for someone to be dealing with someone's feelings.

If I think someone can deal with someone's feelings, than I think someone can deal with themselves, someone else, something, and God for someone to be dealing with someone's feelings because I think someone can deal with someone's feelings about themselves, someone else, something, and God for someone to be dealing with someone's feelings as I think someone can deal with someone's feelings about themselves, someone else, something, and God for someone to be dealing with themselves, someone else, something, and God, and therefore, I think someone can deal with themselves, someone else, something, and God for someone to be dealing with someone's feelings about themselves, someone else, something, and God because I think someone can think of themselves, someone else, something, and God as being right or wrong with someone having a choice of right or wrong for someone to be feeling good or bad about themselves, someone else, something, and God as I think someone can feel good or bad about themselves, someone else, something, and God for someone to be dealing with someone's feelings about themselves, someone else, something, and God. If I think someone can deal with themselves, someone else, something, and God for someone to be dealing with someone's feelings about themselves, someone else, something, and God, than I think someone's feelings is someone's choice for someone to be dealing with someone's feelings about themselves, someone else, something, and God or not as I think someone's feelings is someone's choice for someone to be dealing with someone's feelings or not because I think someone can be right or wrong to be dealing with someone's feelings about themselves, someone else, something, and God or not as I think someone can be right or wrong to be dealing with someone's feelings or not. I think someone can be right or wrong to be dealing with someone's feelings about themselves, someone else, something, and God or not as I think someone can be right or wrong to be dealing with someone's feelings or not because I think someone can choose to be doing something that is right or wrong for someone to be right or wrong to be dealing with someone's feelings about themselves, someone else, something, and God or not as I think someone can choose to be doing something that is right or wrong for someone to be right or wrong to be dealing with someone's feelings or not.

If I think someone can be right or wrong to be dealing with someone's feelings about themselves, someone else, something, and God or not as I think someone can be right or wrong to be dealing with someone's feelings or not, than I think someone can deal with themselves, someone else, something, and God because I think someone can think of themselves, someone else, something, and God as being right or wrong for someone to be dealing with themselves, someone else, something, and God, and therefore, I think someone, something, and God is someone's choice for someone to be dealing with themselves, someone else, something, and God or not because I think someone can be right or wrong to be dealing with themselves, someone else, something, and God or not. I think someone can be right or wrong to be dealing with themselves, someone else, something, and God or not because I think someone can choose to be doing something that is right or wrong for someone to be right or wrong to be dealing themselves, someone else, something, and God or not. If I think someone can be right or wrong to be dealing with themselves, someone else, something, and God or not, than I think someone can choose to be dealing with themselves, someone else, something, and God or not because I think someone has a choice of right or wrong for someone to be

421

choosing to be dealing with themselves, someone else, something, and God or not, and therefore, I think someone can be right or wrong to be dealing with themselves, someone else, something, and God because I think someone can be right or wrong about how someone can be dealing with themselves, someone else, something, and God for someone to be right or wrong to be dealing with themselves, someone else, something, and God, even though, I think someone can be right to be dealing with themselves, someone else, something, and God because I think something good can happen to someone for someone to be right to be dealing with themselves, someone else, something, and God, otherwise, I think someone can be wrong not to be dealing with themselves, someone else, something, and God because I think something bad can happen to someone for someone to be wrong not to be dealing with themselves, someone else, something, and God, and therefore, I think someone can be right or wrong to be dealing with themselves, someone else, something, and God because I think someone can choose to be doing something that right or wrong for someone to be right or wrong to be dealing with themselves, someone else, something, and God. If I think someone can be right or wrong to be dealing with themselves, someone else, something, and God, than I think someone can deal with themselves, someone else, something, and God because I think someone can deal with something about themselves, someone else, something, and God for someone to be dealing with themselves, someone else, something, and God, and therefore, I think someone can be right or wrong to be dealing with themselves, someone else, something, and God because I think someone can be right or wrong about something with themselves, someone else, something, and God with someone having a choice of right or wrong as I think someone can be right or wrong to be dealing with something about themselves, someone else, something, and God with someone having a choice of right or wrong for someone to be right or wrong to be dealing with themselves, someone else, something, and God, however, I think someone can right to be dealing with something about themselves, someone else, something, and God because I think someone can be right about what someone thinks of themselves, someone else, something, and God for someone to be right to be dealing with something about themselves, someone else, something, and God, even though, I do not think can always choose to be dealing with something about themselves, someone else, something, and God because I do not think someone can make time or is willing to be making time to be dealing with something about themselves, someone else, something, and God, however, I think someone can deal with something about themselves, someone else, something, and God because I think someone can be right or wrong about something with themselves, someone else, something, and God for someone to be dealing with something about themselves, someone else, something, and God.

If I think someone can deal with something about themselves, someone else, something, and God, than I think someone can deal with God because I think someone can be good, and right to be dealing with God. I think someone can be good, and right to be dealing with God because I think someone can be good, and right as God is good, and right for someone to be good, and right to be dealing with God, and therefore, I think someone can deal with God for someone to be good, and right to be dealing with God because I think God is always good, and right for someone good, and right to be dealing with God. If I think someone can deal with God for someone to be good, and right to be dealing with God, than I think someone can be good, and right to be dealing with God because I think God is always good, and right for God to always be good, and right about everything as I think God is always good, and right about everything for someone to be good, and right to be dealing with God. I think God is always good, and right for God to always be good, and right about everything as I think God is always good, and right about everything for someone to be good, and right to be dealing with God because I think God is good, and right about everything for someone to be good, and right about something with themselves, someone else, something, and God as I think God is good, and right about everything for someone to be good, and right to be dealing with God about something with themselves, someone else, something, and God. I think God is good, and right about everything for someone to be good, and right about something with themselves, someone else, something, and God as I think God is good, and right about everything for someone to be good, and right to be dealing with God about something with themselves, someone else, something, and God because I think someone can choose to be dealing with God about something with themselves, someone else, something, and God for someone to be good, and right to be dealing with God, even though, I do not think someone can always choose to be dealing with God about everything in someone's life because I do not think someone can always make time to be dealing with God about everything in someone's life, however, I think someone can think about God when someone isn't making time to be dealing with God because I think someone can try to be good, and right as God is good, and right when someone isn't making time to be dealing with God, however, I think someone can be good, and right to be dealing with God because I think someone can choose to be dealing with God about something with themselves, someone else, something, and God for someone to be good, and right to be dealing with God.

If I think someone can be good, and right to be dealing with God, than I think someone, and God can deal with someone about something with themselves, someone else, something, and God because I think someone can choose to be dealing with someone, and God about something with themselves, someone else, something, and God for someone, and God to be dealing with someone about something with themselves, someone else, something, and God, and therefore, I think someone, and God can choose to be dealing with someone or not because I think someone can choose to be dealing with someone, and God or not for someone, and God to be choosing to be dealing with someone or not, even though, I think someone can be right or wrong to be dealing with someone, and God or not because I think someone has a choice of right or wrong for someone to be right or wrong to be dealing with someone, and God or not, however, I think someone, and God can deal with someone as I think someone can choose to be dealing with someone, and God or not because I think someone can choose to be dealing with someone, and God about something with themselves, someone else, something, and God for someone, and God to be dealing with someone as I think someone can be right or wrong about something with themselves, someone else, something, and God for someone to be choosing to be dealing with someone, and God or not. If I think someone, and God can deal with someone as I think someone can choose to be dealing with someone, and God or not, than I think God can deal with someone about something because I think God can deal with someone about someone's feelings. I think God can deal with someone about someone's feelings because I think someone can choose to be dealing with God about someone's feelings for God to be dealing with someone about someone's, and therefore, I think someone can deal with God for someone to be dealing with someone's feelings because I think someone can be good, and right as God is good, and right for someone to be good, and right to be dealing with someone's feelings.

If I think someone can deal with God for someone to be dealing with someone's feelings, than I think someone can have no conscience because I think someone can choose not to be consciously aware of what someone is doing that is wrong for someone to have no conscience, but I do not think someone has no consciousness for someone to be having no conscience of what someone is doing that is right or wrong because I think someone has thoughts and feelings, and a state of consciousness, and a choice of right or wrong with someone's free will for someone to be having a conscience of what someone is doing that is right or wrong, otherwise, I think someone would be an object for someone to be having no conscience of what someone is doing that is right or wrong because I do not think objects has feelings, and a state of consciousness, and a choice of right or wrong like someone for objects not to be having a conscience of what any object is doing that is right or wrong, and therefore, I think someone has a conscience because I do not think someone would be aware of anything for someone not to be having a conscience, but I think someone is aware of anything for someone to be having a conscience because I think someone has a state of consciousness for someone aware of anything, and therefore, I think someone has a conscience because I think someone has a state of consciousness for someone to be having a conscience. If I think someone has a conscience, than I think someone having no conscience is someone's choice for someone to be having no conscience because I think someone can choose to be consciously aware of what someone is doing that is right or wrong, or I think someone can choose not to be consciously aware of what someone is doing that is right or wrong for someone having no conscience to be someone's choice, and therefore, I think someone can choose to be having no conscience about what someone is doing that is wrong because I think someone can like to be doing what someone is doing that is wrong, and I think someone doesn't want to get caught doing something that is wrong, and I do not think someone wants to be admitting that someone is wrong for someone to be choosing to be having no conscience about what someone is doing that is wrong, otherwise, I think someone can choose to be having a conscience because I think someone can choose to be consciously aware of what someone is doing that is right or wrong for someone to be having a conscience, and therefore, I think someone can choose to be having a guilty conscience about something or not because I think someone can choose to be feeling bad about something or not for someone to be choosing to be feeling guilty about something or not as I think someone can choose to be feeling guilty about something or not for someone to be choosing to be having a guilty conscience about something or not, even though, I think someone can choose to be having a guilty conscience about something or not because I think someone has a choice of right or wrong for someone to be choosing to be having a guilty conscience about something or not, and therefore, I think someone having a guilty conscience is someone's choice because I think someone can choose to be feeling guilty about something or not for someone having a guilty conscience to be someone's choice.

If I think someone having a guilty conscience is someone's choice, than I do not think someone's feelings is right or wrong for someone's feelings to be right or wrong about what someone thinks is right or wrong because I do not think someone's feelings has a choice of right or wrong for someone's feelings to be right or wrong about what someone thinks is right or wrong, and therefore, I think the truth is greater than someone's feelings because I think someone can think about what the truth is in life for the truth to be greater than someone's feelings. I think someone can think about what the truth is in life for the truth to be greater than someone's feelings because I think someone can think of the truth for someone to be overcoming, and letting go of someone's bad feelings as I think someone can think of the truth for someone to be dealing with someone's feelings, however, I think someone can feel good about the truth because I think the truth is always good, and right for someone to be feeling good about the truth. If I think someone can feel good about the truth, than I think someone can be alone without feeling alone because I think someone can be comfortable with someone being alone for someone not to be feeling alone, even though, I think someone can feel alone because I think someone can think someone is alone for someone to be feeling alone, and therefore, I think someone's feeling of loneliness proves, and supports that someone needs to be loving, and caring about someone else for someone not to be feeling alone because I think someone will feel alone from someone not loving, and caring about someone else, even though, I do not think someone likes to feel alone because I think everyone wants to be loved, and cared about with someone else for someone not liking to be feeling alone. If I do not think someone likes to feel alone, than I think someone can feel love because I think someone can feel good for someone to be feeling love, and therefore, I think someone can love someone or something because I think someone can feel good about someone or something for someone to be loving someone or something. If I think someone can love someone or something, than I think someone can think someone loves someone or something because I think someone's thoughts can be of someone feeling good about someone or something for someone to be thinking someone loves someone or something, and therefore, I think someone can love someone or something because I think someone can think of someone or something as being good as I think someone's thoughts can be of someone feeling good about someone or something for someone to be loving someone or something.

If I think someone can love someone or something, than I think someone can feel good or bad for someone else, such as someone feeling happy or sad for someone else because I think someone can feel good or bad for someone to be feeling good or bad for someone else. If I think someone can feel good or bad for someone to be feeling good or bad for someone else, than I think someone can be happy because I think someone can feel happy for someone to be happy, and therefore, I think someone can feel happy because I think someone can feel good for someone to be feeling happy. If I think someone can feel happy, than I think someone can feel happy about someone or something because I think someone can feel good about someone or something for someone to be feeling happy about someone or something, and therefore, I think someone can feel happy because I think someone can like, and enjoy doing something with someone or something as I think someone can say or do something that someone thinks is funny with themselves, and someone else for someone to be feeling happy. If I think someone can feel happy, than I think someone can have a sense of humor for someone to be feeling happy because I think someone can say or do something that someone thinks is funny with themselves, and someone else for someone to be feeling happy with themselves, and someone else as I think someone can say or do something that someone thinks is funny with themselves, and someone else for someone to be having a sense of humor, even though, I think someone can think someone's sense of humor is right or wrong because I think someone may or may not like someone's sense of humor for someone to be thinking someone's sense of humor is right or wrong, but I do not think someone's sense of humor is right or wrong because I think what someone thinks is funny someone else can think is not funny, and therefore, I think someone's sense of humor is someone's preference, as to whether or not if someone else likes someone's sense of humor or not because I think someone else can like, and enjoy what someone thinks is funny as I think someone else can dislike, and not enjoy what someone thinks is funny. If I think someone's sense of humor is someone's preference, as to whether or not if someone else likes someone's sense of humor or not, than I think someone can think of what someone thinks is funny because I think someone can think of something that someone thinks is funny for someone to be thinking of what someone thinks is funny, and therefore, I think someone can think something is funny because I think someone can think of something that someone thinks is funny for someone to be thinking something is funny. If I think someone can think something is funny, than I think someone can think of something that someone thinks is funny because I think someone can say or do something that someone thinks is funny with themselves, and someone else for someone to be thinking of something that someone thinks is funny, and therefore, I think someone can have a sense of humor with themselves, and someone else because I think someone having a sense of humor with themselves, and someone else is someone saying or doing something that someone thinks is funny with themselves, and someone else for someone to be laughing, and enjoying themselves about something that someone thinks is funny with themselves, and someone else.

If I think someone can have a sense of humor with themselves, and someone else, than I think someone can think someone's sense of humor is right or wrong because I think someone else can think someone is laughing with them or at them for someone to be thinking someone's sense of humor is right or wrong. I think someone else can think someone is laughing with them or at them for someone to be thinking someone's sense of humor is right or wrong because I think someone else can think someone is laughing about something with someone else for someone else to be thinking someone is laughing with them as I think someone else can think someone is laughing at something about themselves for someone else to be thinking someone is laughing at them, even though, I think someone can be laughing at someone else for someone to be laughing with someone else as I think someone can be laughing at themselves for someone to be laughing with themselves because I think someone can be laughing at something about someone else for someone to be laughing with someone else about something that someone thinks is funny about someone else as I think someone can be laughing at something about themselves for someone to be laughing with themselves about something that someone thinks is funny about themselves, and therefore, I think someone can be wrong to be thinking someone's sense of humor is right or wrong because I think someone can think someone is right to be laughing at something about themselves, while someone can think someone else is wrong to be laughing at something about themselves for someone to be wrong to be thinking someone's sense of humor is right or wrong. If I think someone can be wrong to be thinking someone's sense of humor is right or wrong, than I do not think someone's sense of humor is right or wrong as I think someone else can think someone is laughing with them or at them for someone to be thinking someone's sense of humor is right or wrong because I think someone can be laughing with someone else about something that someone thinks is funny about someone else for someone's sense of humor not to be right or wrong as I think someone can be laughing at something about someone else for someone's sense of humor not to be right or wrong, however, I think someone else can think someone is insulting them with someone's sense of humor because I think someone else can think someone is putting them down, and laughing at them from someone making fun of them with someone's sense of humor for someone else to be thinking someone is insulting them with someone's sense of humor, even though, I do not think someone having a sense of humor is the same as someone insulting someone else because I think someone having a sense of humor is someone saying or doing something that someone thinks is funny with themselves, and someone else for someone to be laughing, and enjoying themselves about something that someone thinks is funny with themselves, and someone else, and I think someone insulting someone else is someone saying or doing something that is bad, and wrong to someone else for someone to be offending someone else, otherwise, I think someone would always be wrong to be having a sense of humor because I think someone would always be wrong to be laughing, and enjoying themselves about something that someone thinks is funny for someone to always be wrong to be having a sense of humor, but I do not think someone is always wrong to be having a sense of humor because I do not think someone is always wrong to be laughing, and enjoying themselves about something that someone thinks is funny for someone not to always be wrong to be having a sense of humor, however, I think there is a time and place for someone to be having a sense of humor because I think there can be a time and place where someone's sense of humor isn't appropriate with what is happening at that time and place, even though, I think someone having a sense of humor is something that is good, and important for someone because I think someone can feel good about someone to be having a sense of humor with themselves, and someone else as I think someone can feel good about someone saying or doing something that someone thinks is funny with themselves, and someone else. If I think someone having a sense of humor is something that is good, and important for someone, than I think God created someone to be having a sense of humor because I think God created someone to be enjoying themselves for God to be creating someone to be having a sense of humor, even though, I think all humor is God's sense of humor because I think God created everything for God to be creating all humor as I think God created all humor for all humor to be God's sense of humor, and therefore, I think all humor is God's medicine because I think all humor is created by God for someone to be happy, and feeling good about themselves as I think all humor is God's humor for all humor to be God's medicine.

If I think all humor is God's medicine, than I think God created someone to have feelings because I think God created someone to be feeling good or bad for someone to be feeling good or bad with someone's feelings. I think God created someone to be feeling good or bad for someone to be feeling good or bad with someone's feelings because I think God created someone to be feeling good or bad for themselves, someone else, something, and God. I think God created someone to be feeling good or bad for themselves, someone else, something, and God because I think God created someone to be feeling good or bad about themselves, someone else, something, and God. I think God created someone to be feeling good or bad about themselves, someone else, something, and God because I think God created someone to be feeling any good or bad feelings about themselves, someone else, something, and God, and therefore, I think God created someone to be loving, and caring about themselves, someone else, something, and God or not because I think God created someone to be feeling good or bad about themselves, someone else, something, and God for God to be creating someone to be loving, and caring about themselves, someone else, something, and God or not, even though, I think someone can choose to be loving, and caring about themselves, someone else, something, and God or not because I think someone can choose to be accepting themselves, someone else, something, and God or not for someone to be choosing loving, and caring about themselves, someone else, something, and God or not.

If I think someone can choose to be loving, and caring about themselves, someone else, something, and God or not, than I think someone can be right or wrong with someone to be loving, and caring about themselves, someone else, something, and God because I think someone has a choice of right or wrong for someone to be right or wrong with someone loving, and caring about themselves, someone else, something, and God, and therefore, I think someone can be right or wrong for someone to be loving, and caring about themselves, someone else, something, and God because I think someone can love, and care about themselves, someone else, something, and God for the right or wrong reasons for someone to be right or wrong for someone to be loving, and caring about themselves, someone else, something, and God. I think someone can love, and care about themselves, someone else, something, and God for the right or wrong reasons for someone to be right or wrong for someone to be loving, and caring about themselves, someone else, something, and God because I think someone can be right or wrong for someone to be loving, and caring about themselves, someone else, something, and God for the right or wrong reasons, even though, I think someone can think something is more important than someone for someone to be loving, and caring about something more than someone because I think someone can choose something before someone, and I think someone can use someone for something for someone to be loving, and caring about something

427

more than someone, however, I do not think something is more important than someone for someone to be loving, and caring about something more than someone because I do not think something is a living being for something not to be more important than someone as I think someone is a living being for someone to be more important than something, and therefore, I think someone is more important than something for someone to be loving, and caring about someone more than something because I think someone is a living being for someone to be loving, and caring about someone more than something as I think someone is a living being for someone to be more important than something, however, I do not think someone always chooses to be thinking of someone as being more important than something for someone to be loving, and caring about someone more than something because I think someone can choose to be thinking of something as being more important than someone for someone to be loving, and caring about something more than someone, even though, I do not think someone is always good, and right with someone thinking of something as being more important than someone for someone to be loving, and caring about something more than someone because I think someone's life is more important than something for someone to be loving, and caring about someone more than something. If I think someone's life is more important than something for someone to be loving, and caring about someone more than something, than I think someone can be right or wrong to be loving themselves, someone else, something, and God because I think someone can feel good about someone doing something that is right or wrong with themselves, someone else, something, and God with someone having a choice of right or wrong for someone to be right or wrong to be loving themselves, someone else, something, and God, even though, I think love is something that is good because I think someone can feel good about someone doing something that is right with themselves, someone else, something, and God for love to be something that is good, and therefore, I do not think love hurts because I think love is something that is good for love not to hurt.

If I do not think love hurts, than I think someone can choose to be dealing with someone's feelings or not because I think someone's feelings is someone's choice for someone to be feeling good or bad about themselves, someone else, something, and God as I think someone can feel good or bad about themselves, someone else, something, and God for someone to be choosing to be dealing with someone's feelings or not, and therefore, I think someone can choose to be dealing with someone's feelings with themselves, someone else, something, and God or not because I think someone has a choice of right or wrong for someone can choose to be dealing with someone's feelings with themselves, someone else, something, and God or not as I think someone can feel good or bad about themselves, someone else, something, and God for someone can choose to be dealing with someone's feelings with themselves, someone else, something, and God or not. If I think someone can choose to be dealing with someone's feelings with themselves, someone else, something, and God or not, than I think someone can be right or wrong to be dealing with someone's feelings with themselves, someone else, something, and God or not because I think someone can feel good or bad about themselves, someone else, something, and God for someone to be right or wrong to be dealing with someone's feelings with themselves, someone else, something, and God or not, even though, I think someone is right to be dealing with someone's feelings with themselves, someone else, something, and God because I think someone can feel good about themselves, someone else, something, and God for someone can choose to be dealing with someone's feelings with themselves, someone else, something, and God, and therefore, I think someone can be right or wrong to be dealing with someone's feelings with themselves, someone else, something, and God or not because I think someone can choose to be doing something that is right or wrong with themselves, someone else, something, and God for someone to be right or wrong to be dealing with someone's feelings with themselves, someone else, something, and God or not. If I think someone can be right or wrong to be dealing with someone's feelings with themselves, someone else, something, and God or not, than I think someone can choose to be dealing with someone's feelings with themselves, someone else, something, and God or not because I think someone can choose to be doing something that is right or wrong with themselves, someone else, something, and God for someone to be choosing to be dealing with someone's feelings with themselves, someone else, something, and God or not.

If I think someone can choose to be dealing with someone's feelings with themselves, someone else, something, and God or not, than I think God can feel someone's feelings because I think someone's feelings is God's feelings for God to be feeling someone's feelings, and therefore, I think someone's feelings is God's feelings because I think someone's feelings is of God's thoughts for someone's feelings to be God's feelings as I think God's thoughts is apart of making up someone's feelings for someone's feelings to be God's feelings. If I think someone's feelings is God's feelings, than I think God can feel someone's feelings as I think someone can feel someone's feelings because I think someone's feelings is of God's thoughts for God to be feelings someone's feelings as I think someone's feelings is of God's thoughts for someone to be feelings someone's feelings, and therefore, I think someone's feelings is God's feelings as I think someone's feelings is someone's feelings because I think someone's feelings is of God's thoughts for someone's feelings to be God's feelings as I think someone's feelings is of God's thoughts for someone's feelings to be someone's feelings. I think someone's feelings is of God's thoughts for someone's feelings to be God's feelings as I think someone's feelings is of God's thoughts for someone's feelings to be someone's feelings because I think God's thoughts is God's feelings for God to be feeling God's feelings as I think God's thoughts is someone's feelings for someone to be feeling someone's feelings, and therefore, I think God's thoughts is God's feelings as I think God's thoughts is someone's feelings because I think God's feelings is of God's thoughts for God's thoughts to be God's feelings as I think someone's feelings is of God's thoughts for God's thoughts to be someone's feelings. If I think God's thoughts is God's feelings as I think God's thoughts is someone's feelings, than I think God can feel God's feelings as I think someone can feel someone's feelings because I think God's thoughts is God's feelings for God to be feeling God's feelings as I think God's thoughts is someone's feelings for someone to be feeling someone's feelings, and therefore, I think God has feelings as I think someone has feelings because I think God's feelings is of God's thoughts for God to be having feelings as I think someone's feelings is of God's thoughts for someone to be having feelings.

If I think God has feelings as I think someone has feelings, than I think God can feel good or bad as I think someone can feel good or bad because I think God's feelings is of God's thoughts for God to be feeling good or bad as I think someone's feelings is of God's thoughts for someone to be feeling good or bad. I think God's feelings is of God's thoughts for God to be feeling good or bad as I think someone's feelings is of God's thoughts for someone to be feeling good or bad because I think God's thoughts is God's feelings for God to be feeling good or bad as I think God's thoughts is someone's feelings for someone to be feeling good or bad, and therefore, I think God can feel good or bad about someone or something as I think someone can feel good or bad about someone or something because I think God's feelings is of God's thoughts for God to be feeling good or bad about someone or something as I think someone's feelings is of God's thoughts for someone to be good or bad about someone or something. If I think God can feel good or bad about someone or something as I think someone can feel good or bad about someone or something, than I think God can feel love as I think someone can feel love because I think God's feelings is of God's thoughts for God to be feeling love as I think someone's feelings is of God's thoughts for someone to be feeling love. I think God's feelings is of God's thoughts for God to be feeling love as I think someone's feelings is of God's thoughts for someone to be feeling love because I think God's thoughts is God's feelings for God to be feeling love as I think God's thoughts is someone's feelings for someone to be feeling love, and therefore, I think God can feel love as I think someone can feel love because I think love is of God's thoughts for God to be feeling love as I think love is of God's thoughts for someone to be feeling love. If I think God can feel love as I think someone can feel love, than I think God can love, and care about someone as I think someone can love, and care about God because I think God's feelings is of God's thoughts for God to be loving, and caring about someone as I think someone's feelings is of God's thoughts for someone to be loving, and caring about God, even though, I think someone can be close to God as I think someone can be close to someone because I think someone can love and care about God for someone to be close to God as I think someone can love and care about someone for someone to be close to someone, and therefore, I think God can think someone deserves to be one with God's love after someone dies for someone to be one with God because I think God can think someone is good from someone trying to be good before someone dies for God to be thinking someone deserves to be one with God's love after someone dies.

If I think God can think someone deserves to be one with God's love after someone dies for someone to be one with God, than I think God is love as I think love is God because I think love is good for God to be love as I think God is good for love to be God, and therefore, I think God is love because I think everything is created by God for God to be love, even though, I do not think God is literally love because I do not think God is created for God to literally be love, however, I think God is love because I think God created everything for God to be creating love as I think God created love for God to be love. If I think God is love, than I think God can love, and care about someone because I think someone can love, and care about God for God to be loving, and caring about someone. I think someone can love, and care about God for God to be loving, and caring about someone because I think someone can be choose to be loving, and caring about God for God to be loving, and caring about someone. I think someone can be choose to be loving, and caring about God for God to be loving, and caring about someone because I think God can help someone to be doing what is best for someone for someone to be loving, and caring about God, and therefore, I think God can help someone to be doing what is best for someone because I think God is always good, and right for God to be helping someone to be doing something that is good, and right as I think God can help someone to be doing something that is good, and right for God to be helping someone to be doing what is best for someone. If I think God can help someone to be doing what is best for someone, than I think God can help someone to be doing what is best for someone for someone to be loving, and caring about God because I think God can help someone to be doing something that is good, and right for someone to be loving, and caring about God as I think God can help someone to be doing something that is good, and right for God to be helping someone to be doing what is best for someone, and therefore, I think someone can love, and care about God because I think God can help someone to be doing something that is good, and right for God to be helping someone to be doing what is best for someone as I think God can help someone to be doing what is best for someone for someone to be loving, and caring about God. If I think someone can love, and care about God, than I think God can love, and care about someone because I think God can help someone to be doing what is best for someone for God to be loving, and caring about someone. I think God can help someone to be doing what is best for someone for God to be loving, and caring about someone because I think God can help someone to be doing something that is good, and right for God to be loving, and caring about someone as I think God can help someone to be doing something that is good, and right for God to be helping someone to be doing what is best for someone, and therefore, I think God loves, and cares about someone because I think God can help someone to be doing something that is good, and right for God to be helping someone to be doing what is best for someone as I think God can help someone to be doing what is best for someone for God to be loving, and caring about someone.

If I think God loves, and cares about someone, than I think someone can help someone to be doing what is best for someone because I think someone can help themselves, and someone else to be doing what is best for themselves, and someone else for someone to be helping someone to be doing what is best for someone, even though, I think someone can be right or wrong with someone helping themselves, and someone else to be doing what is best for themselves, and someone else because I think someone has a choice of right or wrong for someone to be helping themselves, and someone else to be doing something that is right or wrong as I think someone can help themselves, and someone else to be doing something that is right or wrong for someone to be right or wrong with someone helping themselves, and someone else to be doing what is best for themselves, and someone else, however, I think someone can help themselves, and someone else to be doing what is best for themselves, and someone else as I think God can help someone to be doing what is best for someone because I think someone can help themselves, and someone else to be doing something that is good, and right for someone to be helping themselves, and someone else to be doing what is best for themselves, and someone else as I think God can help someone to be doing something that is good, and right for God to be helping someone to be doing what is best for someone, and therefore, I think someone can love, and care about themselves, and someone else as I think God can be love, and care about someone because I think someone can help themselves, and someone else to be doing what is best for themselves, and someone else for someone to be loving, and caring about themselves, and someone else as I think God can help someone to be doing what is best for someone for God to be loving, and caring about someone. If I think someone can love, and care about themselves, and someone else as I think God can be love, and care about someone, than I think someone can love, and care about themselves, someone else, and God because I think someone can be choose to be loving, and caring about themselves, someone else, and God. I think someone can be choose to be loving, and caring about themselves, someone else, and God because I think someone can help themselves, and someone else to be doing what is best for themselves, and someone else for someone to be loving, and caring about themselves, someone else, and God. I think someone can help themselves, and someone else to be doing what is best for themselves, and someone else for someone to be loving, and caring about themselves, someone else, and God because I think someone can help themselves, and someone else to be doing something that is good, and right for someone to be loving, and caring about themselves, someone else, and God as I think someone can help themselves, and someone else to be doing something that is good, and right for someone to be helping themselves, and someone else to be doing what is best for themselves, and someone else, and therefore, I think someone can love, and care about themselves, someone else, and God because I think someone can help themselves, and someone else to be doing something that is good, and right for someone to be helping themselves, and someone else to be doing what is best for themselves, and someone else as I think someone can help themselves, and someone else to be doing what is best for themselves, and someone else for someone to be loving, and caring about themselves, someone else, and God. If I think someone can love, and care about themselves, someone else, and God, than I think someone can do something for themselves, and someone else to the best of someone's ability because I think someone can help themselves, and someone else to be doing what is best for themselves, and someone else for someone to be doing something for themselves, and someone else to the best of someone's ability, and therefore, I think someone can love, and care about themselves, someone else, and God because I think someone can do something for themselves, and someone else to the best of someone's ability for someone to be loving, and caring about themselves, someone else, and God. If I think someone can love, and care about themselves, someone else, and God, than I think someone can do what is right because I think someone can do something that is good, and right for someone to be doing what is right, even though, I think someone can be right or wrong with someone helping themselves, and someone else to be doing what is best for themselves, and someone else because I think someone can choose to be doing something that is right or wrong with themselves, and someone else with someone having a choice of right or wrong for someone to be right or wrong with someone helping themselves, and someone else to be doing what is best for themselves, and someone else, however, I think God can help someone to be doing something that is good, and right for God to be helping someone to be doing what is best for themselves, and someone else because I think God is always good, and right for God to be helping someone to be doing what is best for themselves, and someone else as I think God is always good, and right for God to be helping someone to be doing something that is good, and right.

If I think God can help someone to be doing something that is good, and right for God to be helping someone to be doing what is best for themselves, and someone else, than I think God can help someone to be doing what is best for someone for God to be loving, and caring about someone because I think God can help someone to be loving, and caring about themselves, someone else, something, and God with God helping someone to be doing what is best for someone for God to be loving, and caring about someone, and therefore, I think God loves, and cares about someone because I think God is showing someone how to be loving, and caring about themselves, someone else, something, and God with God helping someone to be doing what is best for someone for God to be loving, and caring about someone, even though, I think God can choose to be loving, and caring about someone or not as I think someone can choose to be loving, and caring about themselves, someone else, something, and God or not because I think someone can choose to be accepting God or not for God to be choosing to be loving, and caring about someone or not as I think someone can choose to be accepting themselves, someone else, something, and God or not for someone to be choosing to be loving, and caring about themselves, someone else, something, and God or not. If I think God can choose to be loving, and caring about someone or not as I think someone can choose to be loving, and caring about themselves, someone else, something, and God or not, than I think someone can accept themselves, someone else, something, and God for how themselves, someone else, something, and God is in life, and not how someone wants themselves, someone else, something, and God to be in life for someone to be loving, and caring about themselves, someone else, something, and God because I think someone loving, and caring about themselves, someone else, something, and God is someone accepting themselves, someone else, something, and God for how themselves, someone else, something, and God is in life, and not how someone wants themselves, someone else, something, and God to be in life for someone to be loving, and caring about themselves, someone else, something, and God, however, I think someone might not be willing to accept themselves, someone else, something, and God for how themselves, someone else, something, and God is in life for someone not to be loving, and caring about themselves, someone else, something, and God because I think someone might not like themselves, someone else, something, and God for how themselves, someone else, something, and God is in life for someone not to be loving, and caring about themselves, someone else, something, and God, therefore, I think someone can love, and care about themselves, someone else, something, and God from someone liking, and accepting themselves, someone else, something, and God for how themselves, someone else, something, and God is in life because I do not think someone can love, and care about themselves, someone else, something, and God, without someone liking, and accepting themselves, someone else, something, and God for how themselves, someone else, something, and God is in life, however, I think someone can love, and care about themselves, someone else, something, and God because I think someone can like, and accept themselves, someone else, something, and God for how themselves, someone else, something, and God is in life for someone to be loving, and caring about themselves, someone else, something, and God. If I think someone can love, and care about themselves, someone else, something, and God, than I think someone can love, and care about someone else for the right or wrong reasons because I think someone can be right with someone having a right choice for someone to be helping someone else to be doing something that is right, such as someone helping someone else not to be doing drugs for someone to be loving, and caring about someone for the right reasons, or I think someone can be wrong with someone having a wrong choice for someone to be helping someone else to be doing something that is wrong, such as someone helping someone else to be doing drugs for someone to be loving, and caring about someone for the wrong reasons, even though, I think God always loves, and cares about someone for the right reasons because I think God is always good, and right for God to always be helping someone to be doing something that is right, such as God helping someone not to be doing drugs for God to always be loving, and caring about someone for the right reasons.

If I think God always loves, and cares about someone for the right reasons, than I do not think someone's life is about how much pain, and suffering someone is in because I think someone's life is about how much someone loves, and cares about someone for someone's life not to be about much pain, and suffering someone is in, and therefore, I think someone's life is about how much someone loves, and cares about someone, and God for the right reasons as I think God loves, and cares about someone for the right reasons because I think someone can be good, and right for someone to be loving, and caring about someone, and God for the right reasons as I think God is always good, and right for God to be loving, and caring about someone for the right reasons. If I think someone's life is about how much someone loves, and cares about someone, and God for the right reasons as I think God loves, and cares about someone for the right reasons, than I think love is the answer because I think someone can be good, and right with someone loving, and caring about someone, and God for the right reasons for love to be the answer as I think God is always good, and right with God loving, and caring about someone for the right reasons for love to be the answer. If I think love is the answer, than I think someone can feel love because I think someone can like themselves, someone else, something, and God for someone to be feeling love as I think someone can like to be doing something with themselves, someone else, something, and God for someone to be feeling love, and therefore, I think someone can feel love for themselves, someone else, something, and God because I think someone can like themselves, someone else, something, and God for someone to be feeling love for themselves, someone else, something, and God as I think someone can like to be doing something with themselves, someone else, something, and God for someone to be feeling love for themselves, someone else, something, and God. If I think someone can feel love for themselves, someone else, something, and God, than I think someone can love someone because I think there is always someone for someone to love as I think there is always someone to love for someone to be loving someone, and therefore, I do not think someone can love someone enough as I do not think someone can be loved enough because I think there is always someone that can be loved by someone for someone not to be loving someone enough as I think there is always someone that can be loved for someone not to be loved enough, otherwise, I do not think someone can live without someone's love's because I think someone can feel lost, and alone without someone's love for someone not to be living without someone's love, however, I think someone can always love someone as I think someone can always be loved because I think there is always someone that can be loved by someone for someone to always be loving someone as I think there is always someone that can be loved by someone for someone to always be loved.

       If I think someone can always love someone as I think someone can always be loved, than I think love is the greatest feeling that someone can feel, and I think loneliness is the worst feeling that someone can feel because I think someone's feeling of loneliness is extremely opposite of someone's feeling of love as I think someone's feeling of loneliness is the absence of someone feeling love for loneliness to be the absence of love, and therefore, I do not think someone can live with someone's feeling of loneliness because I think someone can be self-destructive with someone's feeling of loneliness as I think someone can think nobody loves someone with someone feeling lonely for loneliness to be the cause of someone feeling depressed, and not wanting to live, however, I think someone can live with someone's feeling of love because I think someone can choose to be doing something with themselves, someone else, something, and God for someone to be having hope with someone feeling love as I think someone can feel love with someone choosing to be doing something with themselves, someone else, something, and God for someone to be living with someone loving themselves, someone else, something, and God. If I think someone can live with someone's feeling of love, than I think God created someone for someone to be loving someone because I do not think God created someone for someone to completely on their own without someone loving someone as I think someone is created by God being someone for someone to be loving themselves, someone else, and God. I do not think God created someone for someone to completely on their own without someone loving someone as I think someone is created by God being someone for someone to be loving themselves, someone else, and God because I do not think God created someone for someone to be always be feeling alone with someone always being alone as I think God created someone for someone to be feeling love with someone being with themselves, someone else, and God, and therefore, I think love is important because I think someone can feel lonely without love for love to be better than loneliness.

       If I think love is important, than I do not think someone's love is any more or any less greater than someone else's love because I think someone's love is the same as someone else's love for someone to be feeling love just like someone else can feel love as I think someone can feel love just like someone else can feel love with someone's love being a chemical reaction of chemicals in someone's brain for someone to be feeling what someone thinks is love, and therefore, I do not think someone can love someone any more or less than someone else for someone to be thinking someone loves someone more than someone loves else because I think love is love for everyone's love to be one in the same as everyone's love. If I think love is love for everyone's love to be one in the same as everyone's love, than I do not think someone can measure someone's love for themselves, someone else, something, and God because I think someone either loves, and cares about themselves, someone else, something, and God or not for someone not to be measuring someone's love for themselves, someone else, something, and God, and therefore, I do not think someone's love can measured because I think love is love for someone's love not to be measured. If I do not think someone's love can measured, than I do not think someone's love has an age limit because I think someone can feel love just like someone else can feel love for someone's love to be the same as someone else's love, regardless of how old someone is, and how long someone has been with someone else, and therefore, I think someone can feel love just like someone else can feel love because I think someone's love is the same as someone else's love for someone to be feeling love just like someone else can feel love. If I think someone can feel love just like someone else can feel love, than I think someone can have conditional or unconditional love because I think someone can expect something in return from someone or not for someone to be having conditional or unconditional love, and therefore, I think God love's someone unconditionally because I think God can help someone to be doing what is best for someone, without God expecting something in return from someone for God to be loving someone unconditionally. If I think God love's someone unconditionally, than I think someone can love God unconditionally because I think God can help someone to be doing what is best for someone, without someone expecting something from God as I think God can help someone to be doing what is best for someone, without God expecting something in return from someone for someone to be loving God unconditionally.

If I think someone can love God unconditionally, than I think someone's feelings is someone's choice for someone to be feeling someone's feelings because I think someone's feelings is someone's choice to be feeling what someone is feeling for someone's feelings to be someone's choice for someone to be feeling someone's feelings. If I think someone's feelings is someone's choice for someone to be feeling someone's feelings, than I do not necessarily think someone has to be acting out on someone's feelings because I think someone's feelings can be set off or triggered from someone's thoughts for someone not to necessarily having to be acting out on someone's feelings, even though, I think someone's thoughts can be set off or triggered from someone's feelings because I think someone's thoughts can be of someone's feelings for someone to be thinking of someone's feelings as I think someone can think of someone's feelings for someone's thoughts to be set off or triggered from someone's feelings, and therefore, I think someone's feelings can be set off or triggered from someone's thoughts because I think someone's thoughts can be of someone's feelings for someone to be thinking of someone's feelings as I think someone can think of someone's feelings for someone's feelings to be set off or triggered from someone's thoughts. If I think someone's feelings can be set off or triggered from someone's thoughts, than I think someone's thoughts can be set off or triggered from something because I think someone's thoughts can be of something for someone to be thinking of something as I think someone can think of something for someone's thoughts to be set off or triggered from something, and therefore, I think someone's feelings can be set off or triggered from something because I think someone's thoughts can be of something for someone to be thinking of something as I think someone can think of something for someone's feelings to be set off or triggered from something. If I think someone's feelings can be set off or triggered from something, than I think someone's thoughts can be set off or triggered from themselves, someone else, and God because I think someone's thoughts can be of themselves, someone else, and God for someone to be thinking of themselves, someone else, and God as I think someone can think of themselves, someone else, and God for someone's thoughts to be set off or triggered from themselves, someone else, and God, and therefore, I think someone's feeling can be set off or triggered from themselves, someone else, and God because I think someone's thoughts can be of themselves, someone else, and God for someone to be thinking of themselves, someone else, and God as I think someone can think of themselves, someone else, and God for someone's feelings to be set off or triggered from themselves, someone else, and God. If I think someone's feeling can be set off or triggered from themselves, someone else, and God, than I think someone's feelings can be set off or triggered because I think someone's thoughts of someone's feelings, and someone's thoughts of something, and someone's thoughts of themselves, someone else, and God can set off or trigger someone's feelings for someone's feelings to be set off or triggered, even though, I do not think someone's feelings has to be set off or triggered because I think someone's feelings is someone's choice for someone to be feeling someone's feelings, and therefore, I think someone's feelings is someone's choice for someone to be feeling what someone is feeling because I think someone has feelings for someone to be feeling what someone is feeling. I think someone has feelings for someone to be feeling what someone is feeling because I think someone's feelings is of the dimension of thought for someone to be having feelings.

Conclusion

I would like to continue from where I left off in the next book because the next book is a continuation of this book.

Printed in the United States
By Bookmasters